Cultural Anthropology

Nancy Bonvillain

Simon's Rock College of Bard

PEARSON

Prentice
Hall

Upper Saddle River, New Jersey 07458

Editorial Director: Leah Jewell
AVP/Publisher: Nancy Roberts
Editorial Assistant: Lee Peterson
Editor in Chief, Editorial Development: Rochelle Diogenes
Development Editor: Mary Ellen Lepionka
Director of Manufacturing and Production: Barbara Kittle
Production Manager: Joan Stone
Senior Marketing Manager: Marissa Feliberty
Marketing Assistant: Anthony DeCosta
Prepress and Manufacturing Manager: Nick Sklitsis
Manufacturing Buyer: Ben Smith
Creative Design Director: Leslie Osher
Art Director: Nancy Wells

Interior and Cover Design: Carmen DiBartolomeo and Kathy Mrozek
Director, Image Resource Center: Melinda Reo
Manager, Rights and Permissions: Zina Arabia
Manager, Visual Research: Beth Brenzel
Image Permission Coordinator: Nancy Seise
Photo Researcher: Francelle Carapetyan
Electronic Art Coordinator: Maria Piper
Composition: Interactive Composition Corporation
Printer/Binder: Von Hoffman Press, Inc.
Cover Printer: Phoenix Color Corp.
Typeface: 10/11.5 New Baskerville
Cover Art: Danny Lehman/Corbis/Bettmann

Acknowledgments for photographs from other sources and reproduced, with permission, in the textbook appear on page 496.

10 9 8 7 6 5 4 3 2 1

Brief Contents

Contents

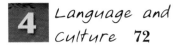

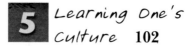
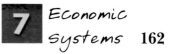

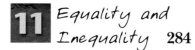

15 *The Arts*   394

16 *Colonialism and Cultural Transformations*   418

17 *Living in a Global World*   446
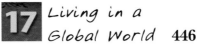

Special Features

Culture Change

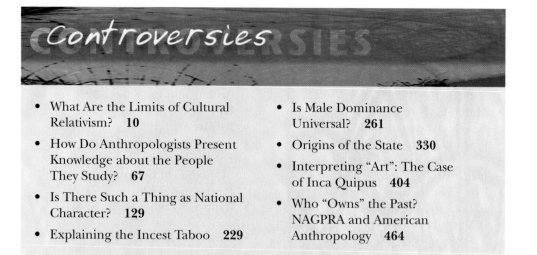

Controversies

In Their Own Voices

Anthropology Applied

Preface

Cultural Anthropology is intended to introduce students to the concepts and methodologies that anthropologists bring to the study of cross-cultural diversity. Its focus is on understanding how cultural practices and beliefs develop, how they are integrated, and how they change. The goal of the book is consistent with one of the goals of anthropology teachers: to spark excitement in students about the world in which we all live. While there is much in peoples' behaviors and attitudes that differs throughout the world, there is also much that unites us. This book, therefore, provides a global view of humanity's many facets. It takes a traditional approach in chapter organization, focusing on various aspects of societal organization and expression. But it also makes central the role of culture change, processes of adaptation and transformation that are integral to all societies. In addition to teaching about other peoples, anthropology both as a discipline and as a framework of analysis has the potential to help students appreciate the cultural patterns underlying their own behaviors, beliefs, and attitudes. The book also attempts to present the voices of the peoples who anthropologists study. Through these voices, and through analyses of indigenous and marginalized peoples today, students may come to understand the global processes that affect us all.

Culture Change

USES OF ETHNOHISTORY IN AUSTRALIA

A field more concerned with causal relationships in culture change than with comparisons is **ethnohistory,** the reconstruction and interpretation of the history of indigenous peoples from their point of view as well as the points of view of outside observers. A survey of ethnohistory usually is part of the preparation for conducting fieldwork. Thus, some anthropological work takes place in libraries and archives containing historical records that help researchers learn about past conditions and events relevant to understanding the present lives of the people they are studying.

Ethnohistorians analyze the processes stemming from historical events and their consequences for changes in indigenous culture. A common focus is the impact of colonialism and conquest on the cultures of colonized peoples. Australian ethnohistorians, for example, piece together the processes of transformation in the lives of Aborigines before and after the arrival of Europeans on the conti-

An important feature distinguishing this text is its thorough focus on culture change, derived both from internal processes of adaptation and innovation as well as from external forces through contact with other peoples. The context of contact is, of course, critical. In some cases, contact is friendly and benign, each group exchanging ideas, practices, and material goods as equals. In other cases, contact occurs between groups that are unequal in their power and ability to control their own lives and exert control over others. In focusing on change, this text highlights the notion that the societies and the cultures that people develop are dynamic systems, adapted to new situations and invigorated by new ideas.

The focus on culture change is carried into the discussions of global trends, whether these are the processes of past colonial expansion or of modern globalization. These two kinds of processes are interrelated because modern globalization has resulted from the legacies of colonial expansion. These issues are discussed throughout the book, with emphasis in the final two chapters.

FORMAT OF THE BOOK

Cultural Anthropology consists of seventeen chapters covering the breadth of the discipline of cultural anthropology. The first three chapters lay the groundwork for the study of human culture. Chapter 1 ("What Is Anthropology?") presents the basic outline of the field of anthropology, describing its development, exemplifying its various subdisciplines, and introducing some of its basic theoretical questions. Chapter 2 ("The Nature of Culture") discusses some universal characteristics of culture and describes how human societies are organized to meet people's needs. It also introduces a key focus of this text: understanding that cultures are dynamic systems of behavior and belief, ever changing and adjusting to internal and external forces. Chapter 3 ("Studying Culture") takes a closer look at the specific methodologies that anthropologists have developed to analyze cultural behavior and formulate theories to explain both similarities and differences found throughout the world. It offers an array of theoretical perspectives used to analyze culture. And it takes the reader into the experience of fieldwork, a hallmark of anthropological research.

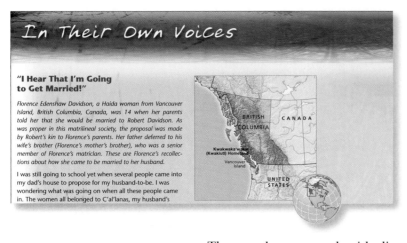

In Their Own Voices

"I Hear That I'm Going to Get Married!"

Florence Edenshaw Davidson, a Haida woman from Vancouver Island, British Columbia, Canada, was 14 when her parents told her that she would be married to Robert Davidson. As was proper in this matrilineal society, the proposal was made by Robert's kin to Florence's parents. Her father deferred to his wife's brother (Florence's mother's brother), who was a senior member of Florence's matriclan. These are Florence's recollections about how she came to be married to her husband.

I was still going to school yet when several people came into my dad's house to propose for my husband-to-be. I was wondering what was going on when all these people came in. The women all belonged to C'al'lanas, my husband's

The next two chapters describe the systems of language and socialization basic to all human societies. Chapter 4 ("Language and Culture") introduces topics in the structure of language but concentrates on the complex relationships between language and other aspects of culture. And Chapter 5 ("Learning One's Culture") discusses the various perspectives taken in different societies about the ways that parents and families raise their children and teach them the norms and values of their communities.

The text then proceeds with discussions of specific topics within cultural anthropology. Chapters 6 ("Making a Living") and 7 ("Economic Systems") focus on subsistence practices, ways of making a living, and patterns of production and exchange. Chapters 8 ("Kinship and Descent") and 9 ("Marriage and Family") describe the various systems of kinship found throughout the world, detailing different ways of reckoning descent and forming marriages and families. In Chapter 10 ("Gender"), we look closely at issues of gender, attempting to understand the conditions under which egalitarian gender relationships and attitudes are sustained, as well as the conditions under which inequality between men and women becomes established. Chapter 11 ("Equality and Inequality") also considers issues of inequality in the realm of social stratification, analyzing social segmentation on the basis of caste, class, race, and ethnicity. Chapter 12 ("Political Systems") furthers this discussion in the analysis of political systems, including ways of establishing leadership, arriving at group decisions, and settling disputes both within a community and between communities. This last topic is continued in Chapter 13 ("Conflict and Conflict Resolution"), a unique chapter that takes a detailed look at the rea-

Case Study

Ethnic Identity in Sudan

In a study of Sudanese agricultural production, Jay O'Brien (1986) details the ways that ethnic identities were formed as different groups of people were incorporated into the work force. Their particular roles in production became linked to their ethnic identity. In the early 1900s, farmers and pastoralists began to work, at least seasonally, on plantations that produced cotton for export. These plantations were located in what came to be known as the Gezira Scheme, a large area of irrigated fields. As elsewhere in the British colonial empire, indigenous people had to pay taxes in cash, but their sources of obtaining money were limited because there were few markets for their subsistence crops, and home craft production was undermined by the importation of manufactured goods sold cheaply.

Sudanese farmers and pastoralists continued to maintain their traditional productive strategies but were available for seasonal work on the plantations when needed during the peak season. They received wages but remained marginal actors in the new economy. Then, as the plantation system expanded, workers from other countries were recruited, especially from Muslim Hausa communities in West Africa. These immigrants were landless and, therefore, readily available to serve as a pool of cheap wage labor. In addition, other groups of West African Muslims settled nearby and provided seasonal labor. They came from several dif-

sons for conflict and the methods of conflict resolution in different types of societies.

Chapters 14 ("Religion") and 15 ("The Arts") focus on various aspects of expressive and symbolic culture. Chapter 14 is concerned with the ways that people express religious beliefs and organize religious practice. It relates these beliefs and practices to other aspects of social, economic, and political life. And Chapter 15 is concerned with aesthetic values and their embodiment in artistic production.

Finally, Chapters 16 ("Colonialism and Cultural Transformations") and 17 ("Living in a Global World") are directly concerned with themes of culture change that permeate the text and are given attention in every chapter. Chapter 16 focuses on the processes of cultural transformation emanating from European colonization beginning in the sixteenth century, although the dynamics of colonial and imperial control both predate and follow European dominance. And in the final chapter of the book, we look at recent global trends influencing the lives of indigenous peoples in the twenty-first century and discover how these trends have their local manifestations.

SPECIAL FEATURES

In addition to the focus on change, the text is tied together by a number of recurring features. Each chapter begins with a narrative, usually a sacred or secular story, that dramatizes important themes discussed in the chapter. Several of the opening narratives are also selected from historical documents or contemporary interviews and accounts relating to the content of the chapter.

Each chapter also contains a feature, "In Their Own Voices," that presents points of view that highlight and exemplify the chapter's theme or content. Most of these "Voices" are of indigenous peoples whose lives are discussed in the text. Some are from memoirs or novels, and others are excerpted from speeches or conferences.

In addition, the text includes numerous case studies that present extended discussions of the processes described in the chapters. These case studies enable students to understand the complex relationships among various aspects of cultural behavior and attitudes. Many of the case studies focus on aspects of culture change, investigating the intricate consequences of innovation and transformation.

Most chapters include "Culture Change" items that focus specifically on the ways that features of culture are transformed. They stress the interconnections among material change, behavioral practices, and ideology, demonstrating the complex interactions that result from change. Each chapter contains a feature on "Anthropology Applied." These features highlight the roles that anthropologists play in applying theory and knowledge to practical concerns. Also, some chapters contain "Controversies" features that present differing opinions about key theoretical or research topics.

The maps in this text were specifically created by Dorling Kindersley, the leading publisher of atlases for educational use and for general consumers. The maps and descriptions illustrate the profound significance of geography as a relevant, essential component to the study of cultural anthropology. They appear throughout the text to help students understand the location of the example or people under discussion.

In addition, there are marginal "global icons" throughout the book. These features contribute to and strengthen the emphasis on culture change and put cultural transformations in their global context.

Finally, the book's pedagogical features include a marginal glossary and marginal questions, preview and summary questions, critical thinking questions, and both sectional reviews and chapter summaries. These features help students focus on significant ideas and concepts presented in the chapters.

Anthropology Applied

Advocacy for Women

Anthropologists work in organizations that champion women's rights, economic independence, and quality of life. For example, anthropologists conduct and report research on the impacts of economic development on women as well as on their households and communities. It has been found that women play an important role in the economies of developing countries as both producers and consumers, even in strongly patriarchal societies that tend to ignore women's contributions outside the home.

International organizations involved in advocacy for women include, for example, the Women's Environment and Development Organization (WEDO), the International Center for Research on Women, and the Women's Rights Project of EarthRights International. Through the efforts of organizations such as Earth-Rights International, rural Burmese women had an opportunity to address the United Nations about human

Female delegates from the Karenni ethnic minority look on during the opening of the Myanmar Constitutional Convention.

Controversies

How Do Anthropologists Present Knowledge about the People They Study?

Since the 1960s, anthropologists have questioned their role as agents of change, as they intentionally or unwittingly facilitate worldwide economic and political processes (Gough, 1968). In addition, some anthropologists side with the people they study against oppressive government policies that destroy the people's land and resources or pressure the people to abandon their way of life.

Anthropologists interested in the impacts of American and European ideologies on other peoples look at the ways groups represent themselves and others and structure people's ideas about these groups. As persons involved in the processes of "writing culture," Western anthropologists

(reported by the husbands) for their spouse's death! Not a very harmonious picture, even on the surface. More recently, the writings of Napoleon Chagnon (1997) among the Yanomami of Brazil and Venezuela downplay the significance of the severe violence inflicted on women by their husbands. And many anthropologists discussing economic systems overemphasize the male role of hunting in comparison to the significant female role of gathering. Today, anthropologists pay more attention to looking past their own subjectivity to more fully represent others.

Because of these problems with the ethnographer's voice, some anthropologists are producing "polyphonous" ethnographies with a multitude of voices. Rather than relying on a single, dominant perspective, they give multiple interpretations of activities and opinions from the points of view of people with different types of roles in the

GLOBALIZATION

With the spread of English and other languages of business, globalization has endangered native languages as well as the ways of life those languages express.

> **REVIEW**
>
> Culture includes cultural knowledge (people's ideas, attitudes, beliefs, and values) and cultural skills (people's activities and behaviors for living and organizing their lives). People's thoughts and behaviors are mutually reinforcing. Some aspects of culture deal with concrete knowledge, such as what food to eat, how to build a shelter, and what clothes to wear. Other aspects of culture deal with abstract ideas, such as how people are expected to behave, what attitudes are appropriate in a given situation, and value systems. Concrete and abstract components of culture and their behavioral analogs are present in all human societies. At the same time that each culture is unique, there is also a global culture.

SUPPLEMENTAL RESOURCES

The ancillary materials that accompany *Cultural Anthropology* are part of a complete teaching and learning package and have been carefully created to enhance the topics discussed in the text.

Print Supplements

Instructor's Resource Manual with Tests.   For each chapter in the text, this valuable resource provides a detailed outline, list of objectives, discussion questions, and classroom activities. In addition, test questions in multiple-choice and short-answer formats are available for each chapter; the answers to all questions are page-referenced to the text.

TestGEN-EQ.   This computerized software allows instructors to create their own personalized exams, to edit any or all of the existing test questions, and to add new questions. Other special features of this program include random generation of test questions, creation of alternate versions of the same test, scrambling question sequence, and test preview before printing.

Prentice Hall Color Transparencies: Anthropology.   Full-color illustrations, charts, and other visual materials from the text as well as from outside sources make up this useful in-class tool. See your Prentice Hall sales representative for more details.

Videos.   A selection of high-quality, award-winning videos from Films for the Humanities and Sciences—chosen specifically because of their relevance to cultural anthropology—is available to qualified adopters upon adoption. Please contact your local sales representative for more information.

Study Guide.   This complete guide helps students review and reflect on the material presented in *Cultural Anthropology*. Each of the seventeen chapters in the Study Guide provides an overview of the corresponding chapter in the student text, summarizes its major topics and concepts, offers review exercises, and features end-of-chapter tests with solutions.

Media Supplements

OneKey.   A one-stop shop for both professors and students, this innovative, premium Website will help professors more effectively prepare lectures and help students more efficiently review the course material. For professors, it will include PowerPoint™ presentations, all of the instructor supplements, and testing software. For students, it will include an electronic version of the text, flashcards, quizzes, and concept tips. Professor access to OneKey can be gained by contacting your Prentice Hall representative or by visiting http://www.prenhall.com/onekey for registration. Students can access OneKey when professors order a special package of *Cultural Anthropology* with a free OneKey access code wrapped with the text. OneKey can be used with WebCT, BlackBoard, or Course Compass™.

Instructor Resource CD-ROM.   Pulling together all of the print and media assets available to instructors, this interactive CD allows instructors to have all of the ancillaries in one place. In addition, they can insert media—PowerPoint® slides, graphs, charts, maps—into their interactive classroom presentations.

Companion Website™.   This online study guide provides unique support to help students with their studies in cultural anthropology. Featuring a variety of interactive learning tools, including online quizzes with immediate feedback, this site is a comprehensive resource organized according to the chapters in *Cultural Anthropology*. It can be found at www.prenhall.com/bonvillain.

The Prentice Hall Guide to Research Navigator™.   This guide focuses on using Research Navigator™—Prentice Hall's own gateway to databases—including *The New York Times* Search-by-Subject Archive, *ContentSelect*™ Academic Journal Database powered by EBSCO, *The Financial Times*, and the *Best of the Web* Link Library. It also includes extensive appendices on documenting online sources and on avoiding plagiarism. This guide, along with the Research Navigator™ access code, is free to students when packaged with *Cultural Anthropology*.

The New York Times
ON THE WEB

The *New York Times*/Prentice Hall *eThemes of the Times*.   The *New York Times* and Prentice Hall are sponsoring *eThemes of the Times*, a program designed to enhance student access to current information relevant to the classroom. Through this program, the core subject matter in the text is supplemented by a collection of timely articles downloaded from one of the world's most distinguished newspapers, the *New York Times*. These articles demonstrate the vital, ongoing connection between what is learned in the classroom and what is happening in the world around us. Access to The *New York Times*/Prentice Hall *eThemes of the Times* is available on the *Cultural Anthropology* Companion Website™.

ACKNOWLEDGMENTS

I wish to thank the many people who contributed ideas, time, and support to this project. The encouragement and advice of Nancy Roberts, Publisher of Anthropology at Prentice Hall, is especially appreciated and acknowledged. Both Ms. Roberts and Sharon Chambliss, managing editor for part of the project, contributed valuable ideas in the formulation of the book. I also wish to thank development editors David Chodoff and Mary Ellen Lepionka, whose advice and constructive criticism were instrumental in shaping the text. The final stages of production were ably managed by Joan Stone, aided by the skillful photo research of Francelle Carapetyan.

In addition, I gratefully thank Cathy Dargi for her patience and skill in typing and transcribing drafts of the manuscript. In this regard, I wish to acknowledge, with thanks, a faculty development grant from Simon's Rock College of Bard that helped defray some of the typing and transcribing expenses. They also provided for a number of student research assistants (Amer Delic, Heather Frost, Sarah Mills-Dirlam, and Emma Rood) who helped identify and collect sources. I thank them for the support and the assistants for their perserverance.

Finally, I would like to thank the reviewers whose careful reading and valuable suggestions aided me in refining early drafts.

Diane Baxter, *University of Oregon*
John Beatty, *Brooklyn College*
Ann Louise Bragdon, *Northwest College–Houston Community College System*
Vaughn M. Bryant, *Texas A&M University*
Andrew Buckser, *Purdue University*
Ratimaya Bush, *Wright State University*
Gregory R. Campbell, *University of Montana*
Erve Chambers, *University of Maryland*
Wanda Clark, *South Plains College*
Samuel Gerald Collins, *Towson University*
Karla L. Davis-Salazar, *University of South Florida*
William W. Donner, *Kutztown University*
Charles O. Ellenbaum, *College of DuPage*
Blenda Femenias, *Brown University*
Carol Hayman, *Austin Community College*
Dorothy Hodgson, *Rutgers—The State University*
David E. Jones, *University of Central Florida*
Barry D. Kass, *State University of New York–Orange*
Theresa Kintz, *Wilkes University*
Joshua S. Levin, *Community College of Southern Nevada, Henderson*
Susan R. Martin, *Michigan Technological University*
Geoffrey G. Pope, *William Patterson University*
Kevin Rafferty, *Community College of Southern Nevada*
Frank A. Salamone, *Iona College*
Josh Schendel, *University of Tennessee–Knoxville*
Wesley Shumar, *Drexel University*
Susan R. Trencher, *George Mason University*

Responsibility for the final version is, of course, my own.

Nancy Bonvillain

Cultural Anthropology

What Is Anthropology?

CHAPTER 1

Preview

1. **What is anthropology? What are the core concepts of anthropology?**
2. **How does anthropology overlap with other fields?**
3. **What are the two perspectives that anthropologists use to study cultures?**
4. **How is globalization defined? How can the concepts of culture contact and culture change help us to understand globalization?**
5. **What are the four subfields of anthropology? How is the study of culture integrated into each subfield?**
6. **What is cultural relativism, and how is it different from ethical relativism?**
7. **What is applied anthropology? What contributions can applied anthropologists offer other fields?**

*T*here were villagers at the Middle Place and a girl had her home there at Wind Place where she kept a flock of turkeys.

At the Middle Place they were having a Yaaya Dance.

They were having a Yaaya Dance, and during the first day this girl wasn't drawn to the dance.

She stayed with her turkeys taking care of them.

That's the way she lived: it seems she didn't go to the dance on the first day, that day she fed her turkeys . . . and so the dance went on and she could hear the drum.

When she spoke to her turkeys about this, they said, "If you went it wouldn't turn out well: who would take care of us?" That's what her turkeys told her.

She listened to them and they slept through the night.

Then it was the second day of the dance and night came.

That night with the Yaaya Dance half over she spoke to her big tom turkey:

"My father-child, if they're going to do it again tomorrow why can't I go?" she said. "Well if you went, it wouldn't turn out well." That's what he told her. "Well then I mustn't go." That's what the girl said, and they slept through the night.

. . . The next day was a nice warm day, and again she heard the drum over there.

Then she went around feeding her turkeys, and when it was the middle of the day, she asked again, right at noon. "If you went, it wouldn't turn out well. There's no point in going: let the dance be, you don't need to go,

and our lives depend on your thoughtfulness," that's what the turkeys told her.

"Well then, that's the way it will be," she said, and she listened to them.

But around sunset the drum could be heard, and she was getting more anxious to go.

She went up on her roof and she could see the crowd of people. It was the third day of the dance.

That night she asked the same one she asked before and he told her, "Well, if you must go, then you must dress well. . . .

"You must think of us, for if you stay all afternoon, until sunset, then it won't turn out well for you," he told her. . . .

The next day the sun was shining, and she went among her turkeys and spread their feed. When she had fed them she said, "My fathers, my children, I'm going to the Middle Place. I'm going to the dance," she said. "Be on your way, but think of us. . . ." That's what her children told her.

And she left. . . .

She went to where the place was, and when she entered the plaza, the dance directors noticed her.

Then they asked her to dance, she went down and danced, and she didn't think about her children.

Finally it was mid-day, and when mid-day came she was just dancing away until it was late, the time when the shadows are very long.

The turkeys said, "Our mother, our child doesn't know what's right."

"Well then, I must go and I'll just warn her and come right back and whether she hears me or not, we'll leave before she gets here," that's what the turkey said, and he flew away.

He flew along until he came to where they were dancing, and there he glided down to the place and perched on the top crotch piece of the ladder, and then he sang,

"Kyana tok tok Kyana tok tok."
The one who was dancing heard him.

He flew back to the place where they were penned, and the girl ran all the way back. When she got to the place where they were penned, they sang again, they sang and flew away. . . .

When she came near they all went away and she couldn't catch up to them.

Long ago, this was lived. . . .

From *Finding the Center: Narrative Poetry of the Zuni Indians.* 2nd edition translated by Denis Tedlock by permission of The University of Nebraska Press. © 1999 by Denis Tedlock.

This narrative, "The Girl Who Took Care of the Turkeys," is told by the Zuni, a Native American people who live in what is now New Mexico. The Zuni traditionally supported themselves by farming. Their main crops were corn, beans, and squash. They also kept domesticated turkeys, whose feathers they used to make ceremonial gear. In the story, the young girl uses kin terms when addressing the turkeys in order to indicate her close bonds with them. The Zuni used these forms of address when talking to members of their community as a sign of respect and affection.

Many readers may have noticed similarities between the Zuni story and the European story of Cinderella. In both, the central character is a young woman who wants to go to a dance but is at first dissuaded or, in Cinderella's case, prevented from doing so. Eventually, she does attend, but is warned that she must be sure to return home early. In both stories, the girl stays past the appointed time because she is enjoying herself. Beyond a general outline, however, the Zuni and European stories differ in both outcomes and details.

A comparison of the European Cinderella story with its Zuni counterpart reveals many differences between Europeans and Zuni. These differences fit into a constellation of features—the languages they speak, how they feed and shelter themselves, what they wear, the material goods they value, how they make those goods and distribute them among themselves, how they form families, households, and alliances, how they worship the deities they believe in—that define Zuni and European culture. This concept—culture—is central to the discipline of anthropology in general and to cultural anthropology, the subject of this book, in particular.

THE STUDY OF HUMANITY

anthropology
The study of humanity, from its evolutionary origins millions of years ago to its current worldwide diversity.

societies
Populations of people living in organized groups with social institutions and expectations of behavior.

Anthropology, broadly defined, is the study of humanity, from its evolutionary origins millions of years ago to its present great numbers and worldwide diversity. Many other disciplines, of course, share with anthropology a focus on one aspect or another of humanity. Like sociology, economics, political science, psychology, and other behavioral and social sciences, anthropology is concerned with the way people organize their lives and relate to one another in interacting, interconnected groups—**societies**—that share basic beliefs and practices. Like economists, anthropologists are interested in society's material foundations—how people produce and distribute food and other valued goods. Like sociologists, anthropologists are interested in the way people structure their relations in society—in families, at work, in institutions. Like political scientists, anthropologists are interested in power and authority: who has them and how they are allocated. And, like psychologists, anthropologists are interested in individual development and the interaction between society and individual people.

Also, anthropologists share with those in the biological sciences an interest in human evolution and human anatomy. They share with historians an interest in humanity's past as well as an interest in the past of particular peoples and communities. As the discussion of the story that opens this chapter suggests, they share with students of literature, art, and music an interest in human expressiveness. And they are interested in the diversity of human philosophical systems, ethical systems, and religious beliefs.

Culture Change

SELECTIVE BORROWING AMONG THE ZUNI

The similarities and differences between the Zuni story of "The Girl Who Took Care of the Turkeys" and the European story of Cinderella are no coincidence. The Zuni first learned the Cinderella story from Americans in the 1880s and transformed the tale to make it consistent with their circumstances, values, and way of life. This is an example of selective borrowing that takes place when members of different cultures meet, share experiences, and learn from each other. Global influences have been instrumental in accelerating processes of borrowing over the last five centuries. Instead of a nameless European kingdom, the Zuni situate the tale in their own territory with references to specific villages, such as Wind Place and Middle Place. The aristocratic ball that Cinderella yearns to attend becomes the Yaaya Dance, an important Zuni festival. Consistent with the prominence of the number 3 in European tradition, Cinderella's ball takes place over three days, but the Yaaya festival, consistent with the Zuni belief that 4 is a sacred number, takes place over four days.

The Zuni also reverse the ethical standing of the story's characters. Cinderella is virtuous and long-suffering, her family wicked. Her stepmother and stepsisters oppress her, forcing her to serve them and depriving her of her deserved place at the ball. The girl in the Zuni story likewise serves as caretaker for her family, the flock of turkeys (whom she significantly addresses as "father" and "child"), but she is not a figure of virtue. On the contrary, to go to the dance she has to neglect her duties, threatening the turkeys' well-being.

And what happens? Cinderella emerges triumphant. She marries the handsome prince and lives happily ever after. No such good fortune befalls the Zuni girl. The disaster that ends her story occurs because she thinks of her own pleasure before her responsibility to those under her care. The European story of individual virtue and fortitude rewarded has become a Zuni story of moral failing and the consequences of irresponsibility to one's relatives and dependents. As the turkey tells the girl, "You must think of us."

How did the Zuni change the Cinderella story to fit their cultural folkways?

Although anthropology shares many interests with other disciplines, several key features distinguish it as a separate area of study:

- A focus on the concept of culture
- A comparative perspective
- A holistic perspective

These features are the source of anthropology's important insights into both our common humanity and the great diversity in which that humanity finds expression.

The Concept of Culture

Anthropology is unique in its focus on the role of **culture** in shaping human behavior. We examine this important concept in detail in Chapter 2. For now, we briefly define culture as the learned values, beliefs, and rules of conduct, shared to some extent by the

culture
The learned values, beliefs, and rules of conduct shared to some extent by the members of a society that govern their behavior with one another.

A cultural anthropologist seeks to explain people's thoughts and behaviors in terms of their culture, or way of life. Culture is viewed as a complex whole made up of interdependent parts, so that a change in one element of culture affects other elements. Cultural anthropologists compare elements of culture at different times within a society and also among different societies at one time.

symbolic culture
The ideas people have about themselves, others, and the world, and the ways that people express these ideas.

material culture
The tools people make and use, the clothing and ornaments they wear, the buildings they live in, and the household utensils they use.

comparative perspective
An approach in anthropology that uses data about the behaviors and beliefs in many societies to document both cultural universals and cultural diversity.

culture change
Changes in peoples' ways of life over time through both internal and external forces.

globalization
The rapid transformation of local cultures around the world in response to the economic and other influences of a dominant culture.

holistic perspective
A perspective in anthropology that views culture as an integrated whole no part of which can be completely understood without considering the whole.

members of a society, that govern their behavior with one another and their thinking about themselves and the world. Culture can be broadly divided into **symbolic culture**—people's ideas and means of communicating those ideas—and **material culture**—all the tools, utensils, clothing, housing, and other objects that people make or use.

A Comparative Perspective

The juxtaposition of the Cinderella story and the Zuni narrative of "The Girl Who Took Care of the Turkeys" provides a small example of anthropology's comparative perspective at work. A comparison of the two stories opens a window onto the contrasting values of Zuni and European cultures and increases our understanding of each.

Anthropology is fundamentally comparative, basing its findings on cultural data drawn from societies throughout the world and from throughout human history. Anthropologists collect data about behavior and beliefs in many societies in order to document the diversity of human culture and to understand common patterns in the ways in which people adapt to their environments, adjust to their neighbors, and develop unique cultural institutions. This **comparative perspective** can challenge commonly held assumptions about human nature based solely on European or North American culture. For example, as you will learn in Chapter 9, marriage and family take many different forms worldwide. Only through systematic comparison can we hope to determine what aspects of marriage and family—or any other aspect of culture, for that matter, might be universal (found in all human societies) and which aspects vary from society to society. For example, marriage is a universal human social institution, but particular marriage rules, such as those calling for various forms of monogamy or polygamy, vary from society to society.

The Comparative Perspective and Culture Change. The comparative, or "cross-cultural," perspective also helps people to reexamine their own culture. Cultures are not static. They change over time in response to internal and external pressures. Anthropology's comparative perspective provides a powerful tool for understanding the processes of **culture change.** Because of the importance of this concept, each chapter of this textbook contains a special feature on culture change, such as the one on page 5 about selective borrowing in the Zuni folktale.

The Comparative Perspective and Globalization.   The comparative perspective also allows anthropologists to evaluate the impact of globalization, a powerful process of economic forces with other cultural consequences at work in the world today, as in the past. **Globalization** is the spread of economic influences throughout a very large geographic area or a great number of different societies. Through globalization, many countries and local communities are enmeshed in economic networks. Today, the centers of gravity of these networks tend to be concentrated in the United States and Western Europe. Along with the export of products and technologies, rapid communications systems also spread attitudes and values derived from Euro-American cultures to other parts of the world.

Globalization as a process has occurred among different peoples in the past when states and empires expanded their influence far beyond their borders. Today's globalization is seen in the rapid transformation of local cultures as participants in a worldwide system of interconnected economies. These influences also have an effect on changing other aspects of culture, including political systems and family structures. In addition, globalization includes the spread of dominant American and European cultural practices, consumerism, cultural icons, and media and entertainment.

Processes of cultural transformation, their causes and consequences, are explored further in Chapter 2 and considered in depth in Chapters 16 and 17.

A Holistic Perspective

Unlike other behavioral and social sciences, anthropology views cultures from a **holistic perspective.** In other words, anthropologists view culture as an integrated whole, no part of which can be completely understood in isolation. The arrangement of rooms in homes people live in, for example, is related to their marriage and family patterns, which in turn are related to the way they earn a living. Thus, the single-family home with individual bedrooms that became the norm in America's suburbs in the twentieth century reflects the value Americans place on individualism and the nuclear family—husband and wife and their children. These values, in turn, are consistent with an economy in which families are dependent on wage earners acting individually and competitively to find employment. Thus, the kinds of homes people live in can be understood meaningfully through a holistic perspective.

Anthropologists, then, attempt to understand all aspects of human culture, past and present. They are interested in people's economic life and in learning about the kinds of food people eat, how they obtain their food, and how they organize their work. They also study people's political life to know how they organize their communities, how they select their leaders, and how they make group decisions. And they investigate people's social life to understand how they organize their families—whom they live with, to whom they consider themselves related, and whom they may marry. Anthropologists also study people's religious life to learn about the kinds of deities they worship, their beliefs about the spirit world, and the kinds of ceremonies that they perform.

In their investigation of all aspects of culture, anthropologists understand that cultural norms and values guide but do not dictate people's behavior. And they also know that people often conceptualize their own practices in ideal terms, projecting beliefs

GLOBALIZATION

Culture contact and culture change, such as occurred between the Europeans and Zuni, underlie the phenomenon of globalization. Globalization is a major theme of this textbook. The symbol that appears here and elsewhere throughout this textbook calls your attention to globalization-related issues.

? What signs of globalization do you see in your immediate surroundings—for example, in your clothes, cars, and information or communications technologies?

American and European societies are also influenced by their contact with other peoples and they absorb cultural features from elsewhere. For example, the spread of "world music," the popularity of cuisines from Thailand and India, as well as the ubiquity of electronics equipment developed in Japan and Korea, are all examples of global exchange.

about what they do even though their actual behavior may differ. For example, when workers are asked about their job responsibilities, they may talk about official procedures and regulations despite the fact that their daily activities are more flexible and unpredictable.

> ## REVIEW
>
> Anthropology focuses on the study of humans and all aspects of being human. The field has many concepts and subjects in common with other disciplines in the behavioral and social sciences, as well as biological sciences. Core concepts include culture, culture change, and globalization. Three characteristics differentiate anthropology from other fields: the concept of culture, the comparative perspective, and the holistic perspective.

THE FOUR SUBFIELDS OF ANTHROPOLOGY

Almost since it emerged as an academic discipline in the late nineteenth century, North American anthropology has encompassed four subfields, each with its own focus, methodologies, and theories. These subfields are cultural anthropology, linguistic anthropology, archaeology, and biological (or physical) anthropology. Each subfield has branches or interest areas as well (see Figure 1.1). Table 1.1 identifies some of the many kinds of work that anthropologists perform.

Cultural Anthropology

Cultural anthropology is, as the term implies, the study of culture—any cultural behavior and especially people's ways of life. Cultural anthropologists are involved in the comparative study of living and recent cultures. Their work centers on **ethnology,** building theories to explain cultural processes based on the comparative study of societies throughout the world. The method of gathering these data is called **ethnography,** a holistic, intensive study of groups through observation, interview, and participation.

cultural anthropology
The study of cultural behavior, especially the comparative study of living and recent human cultures.

ethnology
Aspect of cultural anthropology involved with building theories about cultural behaviors and forms.

ethnography
Aspect of cultural anthropology involved with observing and documenting peoples' ways of life.

Figure 1.1
Subfields of Anthropology

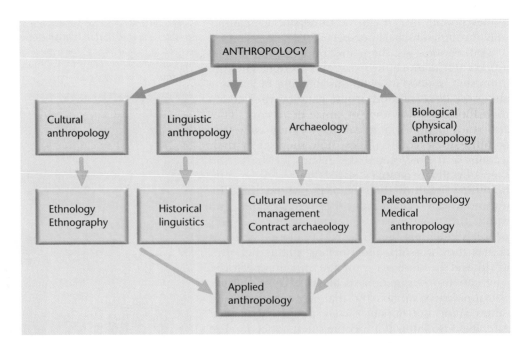

Table 1.1 CAREER OPPORTUNITIES IN THE FOUR SUBFIELDS OF ANTHROPOLOGY

Field	Definition	Examples
Cultural Anthropology	The study of human culture.	Ethnographer Ethnologist Museum curator University or college professor International business consultant Cross-cultural researcher
Linguistic Anthropology	The study of language.	International business consultant Diplomatic communications worker Administrator Ethnographer Domestic communications worker University or college professor
Archaeology	The study of past cultures.	Cultural resource management worker Museum curator University or college professor State archaeologist Historical archaeologist Zoo archaeologist Environmental consultant
Biological (Physical) Anthropology	The study of human origins and biological diversity.	Primatologist Geneticist University or college professor Medical researcher Genetic counselor Forensic specialist Government investigator Human rights investigator Biomedical anthropologist

To conduct ethnographic research, anthropologists live among the people they are studying to compile a full record of their activities. They learn about people's behaviors, beliefs, and attitudes. They study the ways in which they make their living, obtain their food, and supply themselves with tools, equipment, and other products necessary for their well-being. They study the way families and communities are organized, how people form clubs or associations, how they discuss matters of common interest, and how they resolve disputes. And they investigate the relationship of the people to the larger social institutions—the nations they are part of and their place in the local, regional, and global economies.

Collecting ethnographic information is a significant part of the preservation of indigenous cultures. And it contributes to the fund of comparative data cultural anthropologists use to address questions about human cultural diversity. These questions—such as how people acquire culture, for example, or how culture affects personality, or how family structures and gender roles vary, or the role of art and religion, or the impact of global economic forces on local cultures—are the subjects of the chapters of this textbook.

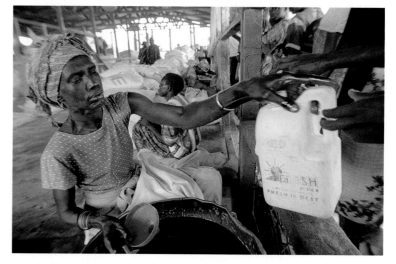

In 2003, these Somali Bantu refugees in Kenya were awaiting relocation to the United States. Their refugee status stems from their former lives as slaves in war-torn Sudan. The U.S. government transported 12,000 Somali Bantus to cities in Arizona, Texas, and other states. Their adaptations to American life, as well as the adaptations of American communities to the refugees, are topics of interest to cultural anthropologists.

Controversies

What Are the Limits of Cultural Relativism?

A controversial practice prevalent in twenty-eight countries in Africa and found in other regions as well illustrates the uneasy relationship between cultural relativism and concern for individual human rights. Female genital mutilation (FMG), or female circumcision, is an example. The practice consists of the removal of part or all of the genitals of prepubescent girls. The specific procedure varies but usually entails the removal of the clitoris. In some areas, particularly in southern Egypt, the Sudan, Somalia, Ethiopia, and Mali, it also includes the removal of all external genitalia and *infibulation*—the stitching closed—of the vaginal opening, leaving only a tiny opening for the passage of urine and menstrual blood. An estimated 80 million women living today have undergone some form of the procedure (Armstrong, 1991:42). Although it is now sometimes performed in hospitals, FMG is usually done by local midwives working with crude tools and without anesthesia on girls who are typically between 5 and 11 years old.

The two most common names by which the practice is known—female genital mutilation and female circumcision—reflect opposing attitudes toward it. Calling the practice *female circumcision* equates it with the widespread practice of male circumcision, which is also debated but more widely accepted. The term *female genital mutilation,* on the other hand, was introduced by the United Nations Inter-African Committee (IAC) on Traditional Practices Affecting the Health of Women and Children, a group established to help end the practice. This term reflects "the cruel and radical operation so many young girls

are forced to undergo" involving "the removal of healthy organs" (Armstrong, 1991:42).

FGM has a long history. Although its exact origin is unknown, it is believed to have arisen in North Africa, possibly in ancient Egypt or along the shores of the Red Sea many centuries B.C. (Sanderson and Sanderson, 1981:26–27). It is, in other words, a well-entrenched feature of the cultures in which it is found. It predates both Christianity and Islam and occurs among peoples of both faiths as well as among followers of traditional African religions. The procedure is most common, however, in predominantly Islamic regions of Africa. The most severe forms of FGM are found in Egypt, Sudan, Ethiopia, and Somalia. Some forms of excision occur in the Arabian Peninsula, and less severe procedures have been reported in Indonesia and Malaysia (Sanderson and Sanderson, 1981:32). Whatever its relationship to religion, FGM is certainly associated with strongly patriarchal cultures—that is, cultures that stress the subordination of women to male authority.

Because the practice is often shrouded in secrecy, little systematic data have been collected about the medical consequences of FGM. Risks for girls undergoing the procedure reportedly include pain, shock, loss of bladder and bowel control, and potentially fatal infections and hemorrhaging (Gruenbaum, 1993). Infibulation in particular can have serious, painful, long-term consequences. Defenders of the procedure, however, claim that there is no reliable evidence of its increasing a girl's risk of death or of excessive rates of medical complication. Opponents claim that FGM reduces a woman's capacity for sexual pleasure and that infibulation makes sexual intercourse and childbirth painful.

FGM is defended among the people who practice it— women as well as men—on cultural grounds. Some

---

indigenous societies
Peoples who are now minority groups in state societies but who were formerly independent and have occupied their territories for a long time.

ethnocentrism
The widespread human tendency to perceive the ways of doing things in one's own culture as normal and natural and that of others as strange, inferior, and possibly even unnatural or inhuman.

In anthropology's early years, cultural anthropologists primarily studied non-Western societies, particularly traditional, **indigenous societies**—peoples who were once independent and have occupied their territories for a long time but are now usually minority groups in large, state societies. These early researchers favored societies in regions of the world that seemed to be relatively unaffected by the West's expanding influence or, like the native societies of southern Africa or North and South America, those overwhelmed and transformed by conquest. The idea was that a small, comparatively homogeneous society could serve as a kind of laboratory for understanding humanity. Over the years, cultural anthropologists have challenged this view, however, and forces of globalization have all but ended cultural isolation. Today, cultural anthropologists are likely to do an ethnographic study of, say, a small town in the American Midwest, Somali refugees adapting to life in Minnesota, Americans participating in a hospice program, the changing political systems in Afghanistan, or life in a prison.

Two important concepts—ethnocentrism and cultural relativism—have a bearing on the anthropological approach to ethnography and cross-cultural research. **Ethnocentrism**

justifications involve beliefs about the dangers of female sexuality and the need to ensure virginity as a condition of marriage. Infibulation is said to help ensure a woman's premarital chastity and her sexual fidelity to her husband while also increasing his sexual pleasure. Some prominent African women, such as Fuambai Ahmadu, an anthropologist from Sierra Leone, defend the practice. On the basis of her research, Ahmadu views it as an emotionally positive validation of womanhood (2000:304–305). In Ahmadu's interviews with circumcised African women, the women reported that the practice did not diminish their sexual drive, inhibit sexual activity, or prevent sexual satisfaction, and that it did not adversely affect their health or birthing. The women supported the practice and looked forward to carrying on the tradition in initiating their younger female relatives into the pride of womanhood. Other native observers, such as Olayinka Koso-Thomas (1992), a physician and also from Sierra Leone, oppose the practice for its brutality, its dangerous consequences, and its role in perpetuating the subordination of women.

Some anthropologists, citing cultural relativism and the ideal of objectivity, refuse to support outside organizations that exert pressure on African, Middle Eastern, and Indonesian governments to abolish FGM. While not condoning the procedure, they prefer to hope for change from within. Other anthropologists point out that while cultural relativism may help us understand a culture on its own terms, it can also help us understand how cultural beliefs reinforce inequalities by convincing people to accept as natural practices that may be harmful and demeaning. Consider, for example, that in U.S. history some slaves strongly defended slavery prior to Emancipation. It may appear that women approve of genital mutilation because they say they do, and it is women as midwives who perform FGM and women as mothers who arrange it for their daughters. But if genital mutilation is a prerequisite for marriage, as it apparently is in some places, women may say they accept the practice because they believe they must.

Many anthropologists, together with health workers, women's rights advocates, and human rights organizations, oppose FGM and are actively working to end it. They have had some success. In 1995, a United Nations–sponsored Conference on the Status of Women declared FGM to be a violation of human rights. In 1996, the U.S. Board of Immigration Appeals granted political asylum to Fauziya Kassindja, a young woman from Togo who feared returning to her native country because she would be forced to undergo the procedure as a prelude to her arranged marriage. The board ruled that female genital mutilation is a form of persecution (Dugger:A1, B2).

In response to campaigns against female genital mutilation by the World Health Organization (WHO) and UNICEF (United Nations Children's Fund), a few African governments have outlawed FGM, and others have taken steps to limit its severity and improve the conditions under which it is performed (Armstrong, 1991:45–46). These initiatives, inadequately funded and only half-heartedly enforced, have done little so far to eradicate what many see as a dangerous and degrading practice. However, recent reports indicate that some women who specialize in the procedure have decided not to continue their work. For example, a grass-roots organization called Womankind Kenya has persuaded some influential practitioners to join their cause. Among the arguments they use are teachings from the Koran that some imams interpret as opposing FGM (Lacey, 2004). When women with status and influence in their communities begin to oppose the practice, their opinions carry weight. Other organizations are training women in other work, such as selling or making soap, because they understand that it is difficult for poor women to give up a steady source of income.

CRITICAL THINKING QUESTIONS

What do you think? Are there universal human rights? Who defines those rights? What might be some benefits and risks of intervening in other people's ways of life?

refers to the widespread human tendency for people to see themselves as being at the center of the universe. They perceive the way of doing things in their own culture (making a living, raising children, governing, worshiping) as normal and natural and that of others as strange and inferior and possibly even unnatural or inhuman. Westerners, for example, often ethnocentrically justify their economic and military dominance over other peoples in terms of ideas about the natural superiority of their culture. The ancient Romans, Chinese, Aztecs, Incas, and others similarly held themselves superior to the people they conquered.

In the nineteenth and early twentieth centuries, many Europeans assumed they represented the highest form of civilization, and ranked other societies beneath them according to the degree to which they approached middle-class European appearance, practices, and values. Early anthropologists, hardly immune to this pervasive ethnocentrism, developed evolutionary schemes that ranked people on a scale of progress from "savagery" to "civilization," with middle- and upper-class Europeans at the top.

GLOBALIZATION

Globalization has included the spread of Western beliefs and values codified as laws on human rights.

? *How might you view genocide from the perspective of cultural relativism? Does this mean you would condone genocide? How might someone view genocide from the perspective of ethical relativism?*

cultural relativism
An approach in anthropology that stresses the importance of analyzing cultures in their own terms rather than in terms of the culture of the anthropologist. This does not mean, however, that all cultural behavior must be condoned.

ethical relativism
The belief that all rights and wrongs are relative to time, place, and culture, such that no moral judgments of behavior can be made.

linguistic anthropology
The study of language and communication and the relationship between language and other aspects of culture and society.

To counter the influence of ethnocentrism, cultural anthropologists try to approach cultures from the viewpoint of **cultural relativism.** That is, they try to analyze a culture in that culture's own terms, rather than in terms of their own culture. This principle is central to the concerns of the field of cultural anthropology in its founding as a discipline. For example, in the nineteenth century, Native peoples of the Pacific Northwest of North America engaged in rituals, called potlatches, which included feasting and giveaways of large amounts of food as well as personal and ceremonial property. Missionaries and government officials in the United States and Canada thought that these activities were harmful, wasteful, and illogical because they contradicted Euro-American values that stress the importance of accumulating and saving wealth. Looking at these practices from the point of view of the Native peoples, however, anthropologists came to understand the economic and social significance of potlatches. The meaning of potlatches is considered in greater detail in Chapter 7, but for now note that they functioned effectively to redistribute food and other goods to all members of a community. These feasts also raised the social standing of the hosts through their display of generosity.

Although cultural anthropologists usually take for granted the need to embrace cultural relativism in their work, there is debate within the field about the extent to which it is possible to apply the principle in practice. Anthropologists, like everyone else, are products of their own society. No matter how objective they try to be, the way they interpret the behavior of people in other cultures is inevitably colored by their own cultural experience. Anthropologists need to acknowledge the potential effect of their own attitudes and values in influencing the kinds of research problems they formulate and the ways that they interpret other people's behavior.

Although cultural relativism requires anthropologists to try to understand other cultures on their own terms, it does not require them to abandon their own ethical standards or to condone oppressive practices. Cultural relativism, in other words, is not the same as **ethical relativism,** the acceptance of all ethical systems as equivalent. Nevertheless, anthropologists differ in their views on the applicability of cultural and ethical relativism, as the Controversies feature on pp. 10–11 illustrates.

Linguistic Anthropology

Linguistics, the study of language, is a separate academic discipline independent of anthropology. But language is a key concern of anthropology. Not only is it a defining feature of all cultures, language is also the primary means by which we express culture and transmit culture from one generation to the next.

Linguistic anthropology, discussed in more detail in Chapter 4, shares with linguistics an interest in the nature of language itself, but with an added focus on the interconnections among language, culture, and society. Linguistic anthropologists might investigate the ways people use language in different social contexts, for example, to gain insight into the social categories that are important to them. Do people use a formal style

In 2004, Mrs. Marie Smith Jones was one of fifty people of Eyak descent and the only living speaker of Eyak, a Na-Dene language of Alaska. Linguistic anthropologists estimate that many of the 6,000 languages alive today will become extinct as their last speakers die.

In Their Own Voices

Extinction in a Nutshell

In September 1992, Dune Lankard and Marie Smith Jones of Alaska were interviewed in connection with their involvement in an unsuccessful lawsuit against the Eyak Corporation to stop the corporation from clear-cutting on lands sacred to the Eyak people. Dune Lankard is part-Eyak and has served on the board of the Eyak Corporation. Marie Smith Jones is the chief of the traditional elders council, established to protect the remaining heritage of the Eyaks. She is the last full-blooded Eyak Indian.

In answer to the question, What factors have led to the extinction of the Eyak people? *Dune Lankard said:*

From 1889 to about 1915, a couple of events took place that were very destructive to our way of life and our people. In the late 1890s, five canneries were built in the Copper River Delta area. The Eyaks' livelihood and subsistence lifestyle was drastically changed because the cannery workers placed nets five miles off-shore, funneled the fish into the canneries and blocked off the traditional salmon runs. So the Eyaks became dependent on the canneries for survival. And at the same time that they were taking the entire run, they were dynamiting streams. They basically wiped out our way of life.

When whites moved into the area and built the canneries, they brought alcohol. The canneries brought in a cheap Chinese labor force and the Chinese brought in opium. Just think about the destruction, about what can happen when the alcohol is mixed with the drugs: there is rape, there is violence, there is the abuse of Indian women.

Shortly after that, the railroad was built, right over the top of the last Eyak village site in Cordova. Then the government schools came in, the public schools that allowed only white children. Some of the Eyak children were shipped away to boarding schools in Oregon, some never to return.

The population of our people prior to the canneries being built was over 300; we were diminished to 50 by about 1920. The final event that wiped out many of our people was the 1918 flu.

Now, Marie is the last full-blooded Eyak Indian on the face of the earth. If Marie were white, this would not be happening. It would be a whole different ballgame then. People would be really concerned that a race of people is being destroyed. But we are just another Indian clan to a lot of people, so they are not taking this seriously. I believe that when Marie does pass on, there will probably be books written about her, maybe even a movie, like "The Last of the Mohicans"—"The Last of the Eyaks." By then it will already be a done deal. And it is so sad.

We were the last "founded," or rediscovered, tribe in North America and we are the first language and race of Alaskan Indians that will be wiped off the face of the earth when Marie dies. We were recognized as a tribe by anthropologists in 1933 and now, 60 years later, we are facing extinction. So more than anything, we want people to learn from this sad story and grasp its meaning so it never happens again.

From Dune Lankard, "Stewards to Shareholders: Eyaks Face Extinction," *Multinational Monitor.* Reprinted by permission.

CRITICAL THINKING QUESTION

How does Dune Lankard's story illustrate the value of the perspectives that cultural anthropology can bring to the study of people and their ways of life?

---

of speech in one situation and an informal style in another? Do they vary the words, pronunciation, and grammar they use in different social contexts? Do they speak differently to relatives and nonrelatives, friends and strangers, males and females, children and adults?

Some linguistic anthropologists study the languages of indigenous peoples to document their grammars and vocabularies. This is critical work, especially now in the face of increasing globalization. With globalization, the advancement of English and other languages of business has been a prime factor in the extinction of native languages. Native peoples are losing their traditions and languages in their attempts to keep pace with the new world order.

? *Do you use words among friends that you would never use in a job interview, in class, or with children? What does your use of language reveal about your relationships to the people you address?*

Many indigenous peoples are under pressure to abandon their own languages and adopt the official languages of the countries in which they find themselves. For example, in the United States and Canada, many indigenous languages have only a few speakers because of the intense pressures brought upon native peoples to learn English or French and abandon their own languages. There are now dozens of programs run by indigenous Americans and Canadians, assisted by linguists, aimed at documenting and teaching indigenous languages.

Linguistic anthropologists also document the way language changes over time within a single culture. And they are witnesses to how the expanding influence of a few globally spoken languages has reduced the number of indigenous languages spoken in the world. Endangered languages include Western languages as well, such as Irish, Catalan (spoken in Spain), and Yiddish.

Other linguistic anthropologists specialize in **historical linguistics.** Their work is based on the premise that people speaking related languages are culturally and historically related, descended from a common ancestral people. By looking at the relationships among languages in a large area, historical linguists can help determine how people have migrated over time to arrive in the territories they now occupy. For example, the Apaches in New Mexico, the Navajos in Arizona, and the Hupas of northern California all speak related languages, and these languages are, in turn, related to a family of languages known as Athabascan. Most of the people who speak Athabascan languages occupy a large area of western Canada and Alaska. These linguistic ties suggest that the Hupas, Navajos, and Apaches are all descended from one or more Athabascan groups that migrated south from the Athabascan homeland in Canada.

By studying how people have borrowed words and grammatical patterns from other languages, historical linguists can also gain insight into how groups have interacted over time. Combined with archaeological evidence, these kinds of analyses can produce a rich picture of the historical relationship among peoples who otherwise left no written records, contributing to our understanding of the processes of culture change.

Archaeology

Archaeology is the study of material culture. Its methods apply to both historic cultures, those with written records, and prehistoric cultures, those that predate the invention of writing. Archaeologists have also applied their methods to living societies, a subfield called ethnoarchaeology, with sometimes surprising results.

Unlike cultural anthropologists, who can observe and talk to living people, archaeologists rely mostly on evidence from material culture and the sites where people lived. Such evidence includes, among many other things, the tools that people made and used, the clothing and ornaments they wore, the buildings they lived and worked in, the remains of the plants and animals they relied on, and the way they buried their dead.

This kind of evidence can reveal how people lived in the past. The remains of small, temporary encampments, for example, might indicate that the people who used them lived by foraging for their food. If the encampment had a concentration of stone debris, it was likely used as a workshop for making stone tools. A settlement with permanent dwellings near farmable land and irrigation canals would have been a village of agriculturalists.

Judging from the density of settlements and household refuse like fragments of pots, archaeologists can estimate the population of a region at a particular time. The size and distribution of dwellings in a settlement or region can reveal aspects of a society's social structure. If a few of the houses in a settlement are much larger than the majority, if they contain many more objects, and especially if they contain luxury items that are absent from other dwellings, we can conclude that some people were wealthier than others. In contrast, if all of the houses are more or less the same size and contain similar types and amounts of possessions, we can infer that all of the people lived in more or less the same fashion and were probably of equal status.

Skeletal remains can provide similar clues to social structure. Archaeologists working at a site in Peru called Chavín de Huántar, which flourished from around 800 B.C.

to 200 B.C., found evidence from skeletons that the people living close to the site's center ate better than those who lived on its margins. This evidence, combined with similar findings from other sites, suggests that society in the region was becoming more stratified—that is, divided into classes—during the Chavín period (Burger, 1992a, 1992b).

Archaeologists can also tell us about people's relationships with members of other communities. In much of the world, indigenous trading networks supplied people with goods and products not found in their own territories. Archaeologists can reconstruct these trading networks by studying the distribution of trade goods in relation to their place of origin. Similar evidence also can be used to trace migrations, warfare, and the conquest of one people by another.

Written historical records add enormously to our understanding of the past, but they do not replace the need for archaeology. Archaeology provides a richer understanding of how people lived and worked than do documents alone. People write about and keep records on what is important to them. Because it is usually the elite members of a society who are literate, the historical record is more likely to reflect their interests and point of view than that of poor and marginal people. Archaeology can help correct those biases. Excavations at Skunk Hollow, in northern New Jersey, for example, re-

These 3.6-million-year-old tracks of hominids walking through an ash fall from a distant volcanic eruption in Tanzania are the first evidence of fully bipedal locomotion in ancient humans.

vealed the existence there during the nineteenth century of an African American community that did not appear on any maps of the time (Geismar, 1982).

Archaeological methods applied to living societies can help address important issues of public concern. In the 1970s, the archaeologist William Rathje founded the Arizona Garbage Project to study what Americans throw away and what happens to this refuse. Rathje defined archaeology as the discipline that learns from garbage (Rathje and Murphy, 1992). Among the surprising findings of the project: Contrary to popular opinion and the estimates of experts, fast-food packaging actually makes up less than 1 percent of the volume of American landfills. Compacted paper takes up the most space.

Archaeology's great chronological depth—from humanity's origins millions of years ago to twenty-first-century landfills—makes it particularly suited to the study of culture change. Not surprisingly, then, theories of culture change are one of the discipline's main concerns. As one example, many archaeologists are interested in the processes that led to the appearance of the first cities thousands of years ago, and with them the appearance of the first state—societies with centralized governments, administrative bureaucracies, and inequalities of wealth and power.

? *What might an analysis of refuse reveal about life in a dormitory?*

Biological Anthropology

Biological, or **physical, anthropology** is the study of human origins and contemporary biological diversity. In the popular imagination, the study of human origins, or **paleoanthropology,** is probably the most visible face of biological anthropology. Paleoanthropologists seek to decipher the fossil record—the usually fragmentary remains of human forebears and related animals—to understand the process of human evolution. Paleoanthropologists have also turned to the science of genetics and the study of DNA for clues to human origins.

Humans are primates; we belong, in other words, to the same order of animals that includes monkeys and apes. Evidence from DNA indicates that we share a common ancestor with gorillas and chimpanzees—our closest living relatives—and

biological, or **physical, anthropology**
The study of human origins and biological diversity.

paleoanthropology
The study of the fossil record, especially skeletal remains, to understand the process and products of human evolution.

medical anthropology
A discipline that bridges cultural and biological anthropology, focusing on health and disease in human populations.

GLOBALIZATION

The global spread of humans was made possible by the evolution of the capacity for culture and the development and spread of the first tool traditions.

that our evolutionary line separated from theirs in Africa between 5 million and 8 million years ago. Working from fossil evidence, paleoanthropologists are reconstructing the complex course of human evolution. They study changes in the environment in which our ancestors emerged millions of years ago to understand the adaptive benefits of the physical changes they underwent. They study the size and structure of teeth to learn about the diet of our ancestors. And they study the distribution of fossils worldwide to learn how and when our ancestors migrated out of Africa and populated almost all the lands of Earth.

With culture, humans no longer depended exclusively on their physical characteristics for survival. They could create clothes, shelters, and tools appropriate for many environments, from the Arctic to the tropics. With language and more complex social organization they could enhance group survival. Thus, paleoanthropologists are particularly interested in clues to the emergence of human culture. Here their interests and methods overlap with those of archaeologists as they excavate sites looking for evidence of early toolmaking in association with fossils.

Some physical anthropologists study nonhuman primates to gain insight into the nature of our own species. Jane Goodall, for example, spent years observing the behavior of chimpanzees in the wild, and her discoveries about their social behavior have a bearing on the origins of our own social behavior. Goodall also found that chimpanzees were capable of making and using rudimentary tools.

In addition to human origins and primate social behavior, physical anthropologists also study the interaction of biology, culture, and environment to understand humanity's current biological diversity. For example, the Inuit, an indigenous people of Arctic Canada, have developed ways to clothe and shelter themselves to survive in their harsh environment, but they also appear to have a greater rate of blood flow to the extremities in response to cold than other people do (Itoh, 1980; McElroy and Townsend, 1989:26–29). Indigenous inhabitants of the Andes in South America have a greater than average lung capacity, which is an adaptation to the low oxygen of their high-altitude environment. And people from regions with high production and consumption of dairy products are genetically adapted to digest milk easily, whereas people from regions where milk is not a traditional part of the diet are not. These lactase-deficient people get sick when they drink milk. It is well known that skin color also is in part an adaptation to climatic conditions and exposure to sun, since darker skin has a higher content of melanin, a substance that protects against overabsorption of the sun's harmful ultraviolet rays (Rensberger, 2001:83). The social significance and interpretation of skin color are discussed further in Chapter 12.

Paleoanthropologists analyze fossil skeletal material or otherwise preserved human remains to learn about ancient populations and their ways of life.

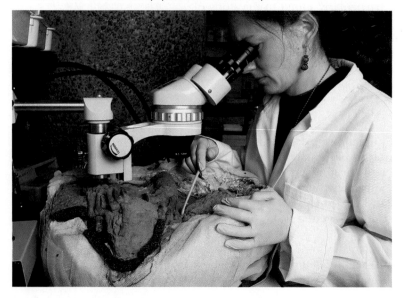

The subfield of **medical anthropology** bridges the disciplines of cultural anthropology and biological anthropology in its focus on health and disease in human populations. Medical anthropologists investigate the susceptibilities or resistances of certain populations to specific diseases. They also trace the spread of diseases within a population and from one population to another. Before the arrival of the first Europeans and Africans in North and South America in the sixteenth century, for example, smallpox, measles, and other infectious diseases were unknown. As a result, Native Americans, unlike the newcomers, had no natural immunity to the diseases. The results were catastrophic: Once exposed to the diseases, millions of Native Americans died.

In contrast to the vulnerabilities of indigenous peoples of the Americas, some populations have advantageous resistances to diseases endemic in their area, as the following Case Study investigates.

Case study

Environment, Adaptation, and Disease: Malaria and Sickle-Cell Anemia in Africa and the United States

Study of the incidence of two diseases, malaria and sickle-cell anemia, demonstrates how the processes of biological adaptation and culture change can interact in complex ways to affect human health.

Sickle-cell anemia is a genetic disease that causes red blood cells to have a sickle shape rather than their normal disc shape. Sickled cells are incapable of holding and transporting oxygen normally. The disease can be fatal in those who have inherited the recessive gene from both parents. Because the disease is often fatal, one might expect that the sickle-cell trait would naturally die out in a population. However, individuals who are heterozygous for the trait—that is, people who carry one dominant and one recessive copy of the gene—survive, and also happen to have immunity from another disease—malaria. Malaria is an infectious disease spread by the *Anopheles* mosquito. Both diseases are extremely debilitating and potentially fatal. And both are endemic to West Africa, the ancestral homeland of most African Americans.

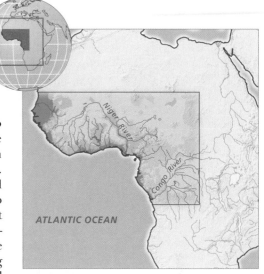

The genetic trait that causes sickle-cell anemia probably evolved in human populations in West Africa about 2,400 years ago (Edelstein, 1986). At the time, much of West Africa was covered with dense forests. The region's inhabitants had lived for millennia by hunting and collecting wild plants. The *Anopheles* mosquito was present, but because it breeds in unshaded pools of standing water, the mostly shady conditions of the forest kept its numbers in check.

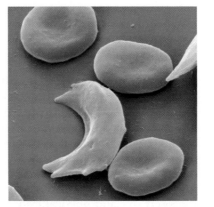

Around 2,000 years ago, however, farming peoples from East Africa began to filter into West Africa, displacing the indigenous population. As they established themselves, the farmers began clearing forestlands for their fields. In the process, they were unwittingly creating the open areas with standing pools of water in which the *Anopheles* mosquito thrives (Foster and Anderson, 1978). As a result, malaria spread as farming spread. And as the human population increased along with their cattle herds, so too did the mosquito population.

It turns out, however, that the sickle-cell gene, although it can be fatal to those who inherit it from both parents, confers some resistance to malaria on those who inherit the gene from one parent. It does not confer complete immunity, but it does lessen the severity of the infection. As a result, the sickle-cell gene has spread in malaria-stricken areas. It is most prevalent among West African farmers, an estimated 30 percent of whom carry the gene. The lowest incidence of the gene is among those who live in still-forested peripheral areas of West Africa, where the *Anopheles* mosquito and malaria are also less prevalent.

The adaptive advantage of the sickle-cell trait, then, is high in populations with endemic malaria but is less in areas without the disease. In the United States, where malaria is rare, people of West African descent have higher rates of the sickle-cell gene than do non-Africans but their rates are much lower than among West Africans today.

By not transporting oxygen properly and clogging organs, sickled red blood cells cause lifelong, potentially life-threatening health problems for people with this genetic disorder.

? *What does this analysis of sickle-cell anemia and malaria suggest about the relationships between biological and cultural factors in human health?*

If a cultural practice—farming—contributed to the spread of malaria in West Africa, others—specifically, dietary practices—may contribute to the adaptive advantage of the sickle-cell gene. Common crops grown in Africa and the West Indies, including cassava (manioc), yams, sorghum, millet, sugarcane, and lima beans, reduce the severity of the symptoms of sickle-cell anemia because they contain chemical compounds that interfere with the sickling of the red blood cells. This feature may explain why a lower percentage of Africans suffer from sickle-cell anemia than do African Americans, even though their prevalence rates are higher. A study of Jamaicans revealed that people with sickle-cell anemia had relatively mild symptoms when they lived in Jamaica and ate a Jamaican diet, but when they migrated to the United States or Great Britain and changed their eating habits, they developed more severe symptoms (Frisancho, 1981).

> **REVIEW**
>
> Anthropology has four subfields: cultural anthropology (also known as ethnology), linguistic anthropology, archaeology, and biological (or physical) anthropology. Because we all are prone to be ethnocentric, cultural anthropologists adopt the method of ethnography and the perspective of cultural relativism to avoid being judgmental of other cultures. The work of linguistic anthropologists and archaeologists sheds light on culture change, while subdisciplines such as medical anthropology combine biological and cultural anthropology in their studies.

APPLIED ANTHROPOLOGY

applied anthropology
An area of anthropology that applies the techniques and theories of the field to problem solving outside of traditional academic settings.

forensic anthropologists
Biological anthropologists who analyze human remains in the service of criminal justice and families of disaster victims.

cultural resource management
The application of archaeology to preserve and protect historic structures and prehistoric sites.

contract archaeology
The application of archaeology to assess the potential impact of construction on archaeological sites and to salvage archaeological evidence.

Applied anthropology is an area of anthropology that intersects with and draws from the four major subfields. Indeed, many anthropologists regard applied anthropology as a fifth subfield of anthropology. Applied anthropologists employ anthropological understandings and perspectives to work outside traditional academic settings. For example, some biological anthropologists work as **forensic anthropologists,** applying their knowledge of human anatomy to help solve crimes. Working for police departments, the Federal Bureau of Investigation, and other law enforcement agencies, forensic anthropologists can help determine the cause of death by examining the victim's remains and physical evidence found at a crime scene. Also, their knowledge of skeletal anatomy, blood types, and biochemical markers in the blood help identify the victim and the cause of death as well as provide leads to possible suspects. Forensic anthropologists have been called upon to study human remains for evidence of human rights abuses in the wake of wars and civil conflicts.

The U.S. government employs forensic anthropologists in many agencies, such as the FBI's behavioral science unit VICAP (Violent Criminal Apprehension Program). Forensic anthropologists and archaeologists also work for the Central Identification Laboratory—Hawaii (CILHI). Members of CILHI traveled to Vietnam and, more recently, to Korea to find the remains of downed airplanes in attempts to identify MIAs from the war in Vietnam and the Korean War. Forensic anthropologists helped to identify remains of victims of the terrorist attacks on the World Trade Center in New York City.

Applied archaeology has grown as a result of federal and state laws protecting archaeological resources, which has led to the field of **cultural resource management (CRM).** In addition, laws now require that archaeological surveys be conducted in advance of many highway and other construction projects to assess their impact on archaeological sites. The need for site impact assessments has led to the rise of **contract archaeology,** in which archaeologists, working privately, contract themselves out for this kind of research.

In addition, archaeologists' findings about the past can sometimes be used to solve present-day problems. Archaeologists working in the region of Lake Titicaca in the

Anthropology Applied

Cultural Survival

Cultural anthropologists sometimes work for communities of indigenous people to help them improve their economic conditions, adapt to change, and preserve their traditions. They help communities find ways to use their resources productively while at the same time protecting their environment and cultural heritage. Some anthropologists have worked in the legal domain helping to promote and protect indigenous political rights.

Cultural Survival is an organization founded by anthropologists that promotes the rights, voices, and visions of indigenous peoples all over the world. They deal with conflict and migration, cultural preservation, improvement of health care, indigenous economic enterprises, law and self-determination, and the preservation of natural resources. Their initiatives include publications to publicize issues and share news, indigenous curricula, fair trade stores and exchanges such as the Coffee Alliance, legal defense, and an indigenous action network.

Not all applied anthropology is necessarily in the interests of native peoples and their cultural survival, however. Some cultural anthropologists advise government agencies and private companies on how to overcome resistance from indigenous and rural communities to policies and projects that benefit national governments and private concerns but that threaten indigenous rights and resources.

CRITICAL THINKING QUESTION

What might be some issues or concerns in the application of anthropological research to public policy, private enterprise, and advocacy of indigenous peoples?

The primary goal of the Cultural Survival organization is to champion the rights and well-being of indigenous peoples and cultural minorities throughout the world.

Andes of South America, for example, discovered an ancient and productive method of cultivation that had fallen into disuse. They helped reintroduce the method to local farmers, who found that it substantially increased their yields.

Some linguistic anthropologists apply their skills to the preservation of indigenous languages. They may work with Native speakers to prepare dictionaries, teaching grammars, and other instructional aids for use in community language classes and schools. Their work helps indigenous communities counter the rapid decline in the number of people who speak local languages. Collecting data from speakers of endangered languages is a fieldwork priority for linguistic anthropologists.

Cultural anthropologists doing applied anthropology work in nonacademic settings, such as government agencies, nongovernment organizations, charitable foundations, and private companies. Some help shape the policies of city, state, and federal agencies that deliver services to local communities, advising, for example, on the best ways to contact different populations in a community to deliver services. These may be health care services, such as vaccinations, legal aid services, or preschool and other

? *What is so important about language that people feel the need to preserve it?*

GLOBALIZATION

Anthropology-based advocacy centers on protecting and preserving the native cultures of small-scale societies that share these goals from the impacts of globalization.

? *How might Western pharmaceutical companies employ the services of anthropologists?*

educational opportunities for children. Cultural anthropologists work in research firms and think tanks to solve social problems. They also help communities, companies, and organizations in dispute management and conflict resolution. They help resolve labor and workplace issues and also work for courts developing and implementing programs of alternative sentencing for some offenders.

Anthropologists may work to support native claims to land or other benefits or rights, acting as advocates and testifying in court, as well as helping indigenous people to develop materials that present their history and culture from a native perspective. An example of anthropology-based advocacy is Cultural Survival, an organization of anthropologists that helps Amerindians in Ecuador, Peru, and Brazil, as well as indigenous peoples in other parts of the world, to protect their interests in the face of globalization. (See the Anthropology Applied feature on p. 19.)

Medical anthropologists may contribute to the preservation of traditional medical practices and pharmaceuticals and encourage practitioners of both traditional and Western medicine to understand the physical and psychological benefits of both medical models. Specialists in medical anthropology develop treatment procedures that combine indigenous medical beliefs and practices with those of standard Western medicine.

Anthropologists who work for industries and corporations analyze workplace interactions to suggest ways of improving the working environment and worker productivity. American businesspeople planning to travel overseas and meet with their foreign counterparts may receive sensitivity training from anthropologists. Anthropologists even study consumer habits to aid companies in increasing sales or developing new products and services. For example, Canon employed a team of anthropologists to go into people's homes to study the kinds of pictures and notes that families create and affix to their walls and refrigerators. Based on the findings, the company increased printer sales through the development of Canon Creative software, which allows families to make their own greeting cards, posters, and T-shirts (Hafner, 1999).

REVIEW

Applied anthropology is the practical use of anthropology outside the realms of academia and is part of all four subfields of anthropology. Workers in applied anthropology include forensic anthropologists, workers in cultural resource management, and contract archaeologists, as well as linguistic and cultural anthropologists. All applied anthropologists implement knowledge gained through their training in other fields of anthropology.

Chapter Summary

The Study of Humanity

- Anthropology is the study of humanity, from its evolutionary origins millions of years ago to today's worldwide diversity of peoples and cultures.

- Anthropology is distinguished from other social sciences by three prominent features: a focus on the concept of culture, a comparative perspective, and a holistic perspective.

- Culture is the constellation of learned values, beliefs, and rules of conduct shared by members of a society. Culture change and globalization are two features of cultures that are important subjects of anthropological research.

- Anthropology's comparative perspective is based on cultural data drawn from societies throughout the

world and from throughout human history, documenting the diversity of human culture in an attempt to understand common patterns in peoples' adaptation to their environment and their unique cultural institutions.

- Anthropology's holistic perspective focuses on culture as an integrated whole the various features and patterns of which can only be understood in relation to one another.

The Four Subfields of Anthropology

- The academic discipline of anthropology encompasses four subfields, each with its own focus, methodologies, and theories.

- Cultural anthropology is the comparative study of living and recent cultures. Cultural anthropologists use ethnographic fieldwork and the perspective of cultural relativism.
- Linguistic anthropology is the study of language in its cultural and historical context. It includes the study of languages of indigenous peoples, language change, and the relationships between language and other aspects of culture, thought, and belief.
- Archaeology is the study of past cultures. Archaeologists study historic cultures with written records and prehistoric cultures whose lives can be inferred from the collection of material artifacts, settlement patterns, and remains of foods and tools.
- Biological anthropology is the study of human origins, basing theories on the fossil record in order to understand the process of human evolution. Some biological anthropologists study present-day biological diversity of human populations.

Applied Anthropology

- Applied anthropology is an area of anthropology that intersects with and draws from all of the major subdisciplines. Some physical anthropologists work in forensics, applying their knowledge of human anatomy to help solve crimes. Some archaeologists survey and document archaeological resources prior to new construction. Some linguistic anthropologists apply their skills to the preservation of indigenous languages, helping to create dictionaries, grammars, and other instructional aids. And many cultural anthropologists work in nonacademic settings in public and government agencies, foundations, and private companies.
- Applied anthropologists can provide advice that helps shape government policies for delivering services to local communities. Others work with indigenous peoples to help them improve their economic conditions and secure their political rights.

Key Terms

anthropology 4	globalization 6	ethical relativism 12	medical anthropology 16
societies 4	holistic perspective 6	linguistic	applied anthropology 18
culture 5	cultural anthropology 8	anthropology 12	forensic
symbolic culture 6	ethnology 8	historical linguistics 14	anthropologists 18
material culture 6	ethnography 8	archaeology 14	cultural resource
comparative	indigenous societies 10	biological, or physical,	management
perspective 6	ethnocentrism 10	anthropology 15	(CRM) 18
culture change 6	cultural relativism 12	paleoanthropology 15	contract archaeology 18

Review Questions

1. What features distinguish anthropology from other social and behavioral sciences? What roles do the concepts of culture and culture change play in the field of anthropology?
2. Why is globalization a major concern in anthropology today? How does culture change relate to globalization?
3. What are the rationales for using the comparative and holistic perspectives in anthropology?
4. How does each of the four subfields of anthropology seek to fulfill anthropology's mission?
5. How do cultural anthropologists conduct research, and to what end?
6. Why is cultural relativism important in studying other cultures? How does cultural relativism differ from ethical relativism?
7. What can linguistic anthropologists and archaeologists learn about symbolic and material culture?
8. How do diseases like sickle-cell anemia and malaria highlight the relationship between biology and culture?
9. How can research in each of the subfields of anthropology be applied to problem solving and policymaking in the world today?

The Nature of Culture

CHAPTER 2

Preview

1. **What is culture? With what basic definition of culture do anthropologists tend to agree?**
2. **What elements of culture are regarded as universal, and why?**
3. **In what sense can culture be both shared and not shared by members of a society?**
4. **How is culture learned and transmitted?**
5. **In what sense can culture be both adaptive and maladaptive?**
6. **What are some forces of cultural integration?**
7. **In what ways is culture based on symbols?**
8. **How do cultures change from within?**
9. **How do cultures change through contact?**
10. **What are the dynamics of global culture change today?**

*A*t the beginning there was on the earth only a single man; he had neither house nor tent, for at that time the winter was not cold, and the summer was not hot; the wind did not blow so violently, and there fell neither snow nor rain; the tea grew of itself on the mountains, and the flocks had nothing to fear from beasts of prey. This man had three children, who lived a long time with him, nourishing themselves on milk and fruits. After having attained to a great age, this man died. The three children deliberated what they should do with the body of their father, and they could not agree about it; one wished to put him in a coffin, the other wanted to burn him, the third thought it would be best to expose the body on the summit of a mountain. They resolved then to divide it into three parts. The eldest had the body and arms; he was the ancestor of the great Chinese family, and that is why his descendants have become celebrated in arts and industry, and are remarkable for their tricks and stratagems. The second son had the breast; he was the father of the Tibetan family, and they are full of heart and courage, and do not fear death. From the third, who had inferior parts of the body, are descended the Tartars, or simple and timid, without head or heart, and who know nothing but how to keep themselves firm in their saddles.

From *A Cultural History of Tibet;* David L. Snellgrove and Hugh Richardson; Bangkok 2003, © Orchid Press, by permission of the publisher.

This Tibetan narrative, describing the origin of the Tibetan people and two ethnic groups who live nearby, tells us much about Tibetan attitudes toward themselves and toward other peoples. These attitudes are part of the core of Tibetan culture: that is, Tibetans' understanding of the world they live in, its origins, and the people who inhabit it. In the beginning, the world is depicted as an idyllic, peaceful place, without harsh weather and hardship. The story also theorizes about the original unity of the Tibetans with their neighbors, all derived from the same original founder. And it tells us about how the Tibetans see themselves as a people with qualities that differentiate them from others. Their attitude toward the Chinese mixes praise for their arts and accomplishments as well as disapproval for their trickery. Their attitude toward the Tartars seems disparaging and condescending. And they think of themselves as people of courage and kindness.

This story also gives us some information about burial practices. Each brother advocated a method of burial that is practiced in different societies around the world: interment in the ground, cremation, and exposure to

The cultural knowledge of these Sami includes everything there is to know about reindeer, living in the Arctic, and coping with citizenship in the modern state society of Norway.

the elements. These practices are aspects of culture: the ways that people organize their lives. The Tibetan story thus provides us with insight into different features of Tibetan culture. We learn about how the people view themselves, how they view their neighbors, and how they think about their relationships with other groups. And we learn something of the particular practices that they engage in. In this chapter, we will explore issues of culture—what culture is and how cultural practices and attitudes change.

WHAT IS CULTURE?

Chapter 1 proposed a beginning definition of culture: the behaviors, values, and attitudes shared by a group of people. This chapter expands on this definition. Although defining what culture is may sound like a simple task, anthropologists have struggled to define and specify culture since the late nineteenth century, when anthropology was established as a discipline. The British social anthropologist Edward Tylor was the first to attempt a formal definition. Writing in *Primitive Culture* in 1871, he stated, "Culture is that complex whole which includes knowledge, belief, art, morals, law, custom, and any other capabilities and habits acquired by man as a member of society."

Tylor's classic statement captures several significant features that have been preserved in most definitions of culture today. It focuses on the holistic quality of culture ("that complex whole") and embraces all the activities, attitudes, and beliefs of human beings. Significantly, these are traits "acquired" by people. That is, people's attitudes, beliefs, and ways of acting are learned rather than inherited, instinctual, or automatic. Finally, Tylor stressed that people acquire culture "as a member of society." People live and interact with other people, learning skills and attitudes from them and in turn transmitting their knowledge and beliefs to others.

Since Tylor, anthropologists have expanded on and refined the definition of culture innumerable times. By the 1950s, Alfred Kroeber and Clyde Kluckhohn had collected more than one hundred definitions, and all differ according to their focus and the theoretical orientation that underlies them (Kroeber and Kluckhohn, 1952). Nevertheless, all definitions include statements about human behavior and activities in the context of families, groups, and communities. They also include statements about people's selectively shared knowledge, attitudes, values, and beliefs.

Cultural knowledge refers to the information people have that enables them to function in their social and physical environments. Some of this information is practical—how to make a living, what kinds of clothes to wear and shelters to build, and so on. Other cultural knowledge is less obvious. For example, people also share knowledge about the world, why people do the things they do, what a person can expect from others, and so on. This kind of cultural knowledge is expressed in people's attitudes, values, and beliefs, including ethical values about what is right and wrong and what is proper and improper behavior. Cultural knowledge thus includes religious and scientific beliefs about the past, life, the world, people and their origins, and people's relationships to plants, animals, and the natural world.

In addition to cultural knowledge, social and cultural skills are included in the definition of culture, such as the activities and practices that people engage in to obtain their food, provide themselves with clothing and shelter, and make or procure goods needed in their households. Cultural behaviors include the ways that people organize themselves to provide leadership, make decisions, and carry out communal activities. In all societies, people need to develop modes of subsistence and economic exchange, methods of social control and conflict resolution, and principles of leadership and governance. And they need to organize families and provide for child care and socialization. Other aspects of culture, such as religion and artistic expression, are also part of the human experience. People share similar basic societal needs with members of other societies, but the strategies and institutions they develop to satisfy or cope with those needs vary.

? *To what extent is culture shared? For example, what could you say about "American" attitudes toward self and others and "American" ways of organizing life?*

cultural knowledge
Information that enables people to function in their society and contributes to the survival of the society as a whole.

Thus, people in all societies have their own specific thoughts (cultural knowledge) and behaviors (cultural skills) that vary from group to group. But although each culture is unique, any culture also shares similarities with others. What, then, is meant by a global culture? What is the content of this global culture?

GLOBALIZATION

What is global culture? This question is widely debated among social scientists. What thoughts, behaviors, tools, and skills do you identify as making up today's global culture?

REVIEW

Culture includes cultural knowledge (people's ideas, attitudes, beliefs, and values) and cultural skills (people's activities and behaviors for living and organizing their lives). People's thoughts and behaviors are mutually reinforcing. Some aspects of culture deal with concrete knowledge, such as what food to eat, how to build a shelter, and what clothes to wear. Other aspects of culture deal with abstract ideas, such as how people are expected to behave, what attitudes are appropriate in a given situation, and value systems. Concrete and abstract components of culture and their behavioral analogs are present in all human societies. At the same time that each culture is unique, there is also a global culture.

CHARACTERISTICS OF CULTURE

Although each culture is unique, a number of characteristics in their organization and functioning are universal. To begin with, any culture is a product of a group of people who share and transmit some basic attitudes and assumptions about the world. In addition, aspects of culture tend to interrelate and function together with some consistency to form a coherent system of behaviors and beliefs. Through their cultures people adapt to their life situations and to changes in their social and physical environments. What do we mean when we say that culture is shared, learned, adaptive, and integrated?

Culture Is Shared

Humans are by nature social creatures; that is, we do not live as individuals alone. Rather, we live with other people in families, households, and communities of various sizes and relationships. The way we behave, our attitudes about right and wrong, our ideas about the world we live in—all are formed through our interactions with others. We do not act alone and we do not have ideas all to ourselves. We, together with these other people, are societies. As defined in Chapter 1, a society is a group of people who live within an acknowledged territory, who could potentially interact with each other, and who share certain practices and values. Societies are held together through social structures that organize family life, means of making a living, and ways of arriving at decisions and establishing methods of leadership.

To say that culture is shared is not to say that all members of a particular society have exactly the same attitudes and do exactly the same things in the same way. Rather, the general principles of culture are shared. For example, not all "Americans" vote or believe that voting is efficacious, but most would staunchly defend everyone's right to vote. Thus, voting is included in the broad cultural conception of legitimate governance in the United States.

Societies can function as groups to minimize conflicts, because their members agree about the basic parameters of living. If this were not so, people would not be able to coordinate their activities or agree on what to do next. And even though they might speak the same language, they would not be able to accurately interpret each other's meanings and intentions if they did not share basic cultural assumptions about the world. These shared assumptions, or **cultural models,** form a background ideology in terms of which behavior becomes relatively coherent and consistent.

Despite cultural models, there are disagreements and conflicts within any community. In all communities, some people are more fully committed to general societal norms than others. Societal **norms** are sets of commonly held expectations and attitudes that people have about appropriate behavior. And although these norms

cultural models
Shared assumptions that people have about the world and about the ideal culture.

norms
Sets of expectations and attitudes that people have about appropriate behavior.

This young woman in Western dress was photographed with her aunt in traditional Burkino Faso garb. The attitudes and values that lead young people to deviate in this way might be sources of conflict in other ways in their families and community.

are generally held to be valid within each culture, not everyone acts in accordance with them.

Deviance from expected and appropriate behavior occurs in every community. Some types of deviance are tolerated while others are not. And, in fact, behavior that may be considered deviant within a community as a whole may be a marker of identity for a particular group. For example, body piercings or tattooing might violate adult conceptions of beauty, but teenagers may engage in these physical alterations in order to conform to youthful standards. Violent behavior such as assault and murder are deviant acts that are not tolerated in most societies. Other kinds of violence, though, that occur within the family, such as spousal abuse, may be tolerated, even if not condoned.

People occupying different social roles and statuses may hold opposing views about the existing social order and prevailing cultural norms. For example, age may be a factor in the way people organize their lives and in the kinds of attitudes that they hold. Younger and older people have different experiences and different frames of reference. Opposing activities and norms for older and younger people may be relatively stable, though; that is, as younger people age, they adopt the lifestyles and norms of their elders. Differences between the young and the old may also signal ongoing social and culture change, if young people introduce new ways of living as they replace their elders through the normal aging process.

Gender differences are another common source of distinctions in people's activities and attitudes. In most societies, women and men usually have certain specific tasks that they fulfill in their homes and communities. The relationships between men and women in the family and in the public sphere influence the ways they experience their lives. For example, depending on who are the dominant decision makers and authorities in their households, men and women are likely to have different ideas about their rights and responsibilities. Women who have the major share of the household and child-rearing responsibilities and tasks to perform may feel burdened and restricted, or they may feel challenged and fulfilled. In societies that sanction violence against women and permit men to abuse their wives, women's experience of household life certainly contrasts sharply with men's.

Like differences in age and gender, other status differences in society result in incomplete sharing of culture. Such differences also may be a source of social tension and cultural disagreement. Members of elite groups may reap greater economic and social benefits from the way in which society is structured, for example, than do members of marginalized or oppressed groups. Such differences are more likely to exist in complex heterogeneous societies than in small-scale, relatively homogeneous ones. Societies may be segmented by class, race, or ethnicity, creating group cultural distinctions in how people organize their lives. In addition, people adhering to different religions may apply different philosophical orientations and moral principles to their daily lives.

Thus, members of different groups in stratified societies may have different attitudes and values. For example, when economists and politicians in the United States tell us that the economy is booming, not everyone in the country shares this experience or optimism. Wealthy people and people who own shares on the stock market experience an economic boom very differently from people who worked in factories that have been relocated abroad, or from people who receive welfare benefits. Thus, a culture is not fully shared in a diverse society.

In addition to differences derived from distinct social roles and statuses, some societies contain groups that participate in

In the diverse society of Bolivia, this peasant woman of the Andes does not fully share the same culture as her counterpart in La Paz, the capital.

identifiable subcultures. A **subculture** is a group of people who think of themselves, and are thought of by others, as different in some significant way from the majority of people living in the society. Members of subcultures interact more frequently among themselves than with "outsiders" and share attitudes and practices that distinguish them from other groups.

In diverse societies, including our own, ethnic groups may comprise subcultures, especially if members have allegiance to their native country, use their native language, and observe ethnic food preferences and family relations. Some occupational groups may also function as subcultures. For example, police officers may work together, socialize together, have special shared vocabulary, and share expectations of life patterns, cooperation, and mutual aid.

All of these sources of difference modify our understanding of culture as a constellation of shared behaviors and beliefs. Still, when people interact within the same society, they must share some basic premises about social order and social values. If they did not, community cohesion would disintegrate and the groups within the society would separate.

Hasidic families are one American urban subculture among many in New York City. Their subculture is distinguished through ethnic background and religious beliefs and practices. Hasidim (also spelled Chassidim) are members of a Jewish ultraorthodox sect founded in Eastern Europe in the eighteenth century.

Culture Is Learned

Culture is transmitted from generation to generation and is learned mainly in childhood and during maturation. We learn not only our behavior but also our attitudes and values. The ability to acquire culture in this way makes humans highly adaptable to different cultural environments. Humans are born with a potential to learn whatever knowledge and skills are practiced in their communities. They do this through the process of **enculturation**—learning one's culture through informal observation and formal instruction, beginning in earliest childhood. Children learn the culture that they are exposed to, as the Case Study illustrates. We all can acquire any culture if we are raised in it, just as any normal person can learn any language. It is through these processes of exposure and learning that people acquire their culture and transmit it to others. Chapter 5 further explores the topic of enculturation.

While most human cultural behavior is the result of learning, this behavior also is influenced by inherited drives as well as acquired needs. People must fulfill important physical and survival needs, just like all living creatures. People need to eat, drink, sleep, eliminate body wastes, and engage in sexual activity. And, like other primates, people also need to interact with one another for food getting and protection. Culture intervenes and influences the ways in which people satisfy these needs.

For example, each culture has attitudes about what kinds of foods are edible and suitable for human consumption. People do not eat everything that is edible in their environment; they select some foods and reject others, expressing these choices as preferences and prohibitions, or **taboos.** In North America, most people consider eating insects distasteful, but many peoples of Australia, Asia, and Africa think of insects as a delicacy. Maasai drink the blood of their cattle. Koreans farm puppies for meat. Religion-based food taboos of Muslims, Hindus, and Jews further illustrate the mediation of survival needs through culture. Further, people also have norms about how many meals to have, when to eat them, and which foods to eat at each meal.

Although all people need to sleep, they normally do so at a culturally prescribed time and place. No matter how tired you are at work, it probably would be inappropriate to lie down on the floor or desk and go to sleep. People follow culturally prescribed rules about where and when to eliminate body wastes. Most people are taught not to urinate or defecate in public in any circumstances, for example. In fact, doing so may be a criminal offense. All cultures also have norms about when and how to satisfy sexual

subculture
a group whose members and others think of their way of life as in some significant way different from that of other people in the larger society.

enculturation
Process of learning one's culture through informal observation and formal instruction.

taboos
Norms specifying behaviors that are prohibited in a culture.

? How many meals do you eat in a day, and at what times? What kinds of foods do you eat at each meal? If you ate eggs at different mealtimes, how might you prepare them differently for each meal, and why? What do your answers to these questions reveal about your cultural norms and values?

Case study

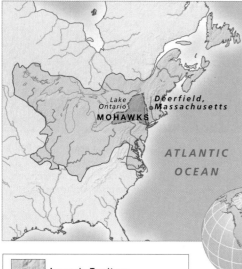

Iroquois Territory

Present-Day New York State

? *Based on this case study, what effect would children's ability to acquire culture rapidly have on immigrant families?*

Growing Up Mohawk

An interesting historical example of enculturation is the case of the abduction of a child in colonial New England. In 1703, Eunice Williams was an English girl of 7 years living in Deerfield, Massachusetts, the daughter of a Protestant minister, John Williams. John, his five children, and dozens of other people of the town were abducted during a raid carried out by a combined force of French soldiers and native warriors. Some of the captives were released, including Eunice's father, others escaped, and the rest were eventually taken to villages in the territory of the Mohawks, an indigenous people whose territory encompassed a large region in what is now eastern New York State and western Vermont and Massachusetts. Eunice was among those taken to a place called Kahnawake, a mission village established by French Jesuit priests and inhabited by Mohawks who had converted to Catholicism. When she was 15, Eunice married a Mohawk man and settled into her life there. Despite her father's efforts to persuade her to leave, she remained with the Mohawks and adopted their culture. She learned their language, converted to Catholicism, and raised her own daughter according to Mohawk tradition. In 1743, Eunice agreed to meet with her father and brother, but refused to leave the people whose culture and language she had taken as her own (Demos, 1994; Namias, 1995). She died at Kahnawake at the age of 89, never returning to colonial Massachusetts and never again speaking the English language.

The story of Eunice Williams demonstrates the power of a basic premise of anthropology, that *culture is learned* through social interaction in social contexts, and that in childhood this learning is especially powerful.

urges appropriately. These norms include strong taboos that prohibit sexual relations between parents and their children and between siblings.

Societies enculturate children in culturally specific ways. In many small-scale societies children are expected to learn skills informally by observation and imitation. That is, they watch and observe their parents or other elders and learn by trying to do the same thing. Adults may offer guidance, but for the most part the child learns by doing and is an active participant in the process. This type of learning takes place in all communities in some contexts, but in large-scale societies, training and education also take place in formal settings such as schools.

Casual observation of others as they interact informally also plays a role in enculturation. Through observation, children learn attitudes: They hear what people have to say about themselves and others, and what they think of other people's behavior. And they listen to people express their beliefs about the world. Through these conversations and interactions, children learn what is valued and what is criticized by members of the community. In these contexts, they gain a sense of personal identity as well as a sense of the world and their place in it.

Culture Is Adaptive

When anthropologists say that culture is adaptive, they are usually referring to behaviors and beliefs that respond to environmental constraints and opportunities that ensure a community's survival. People must adapt to their environment, and culture is their chief mechanism of adaptation. Because of their capacity for adaptation, humans can survive in nearly any environment. Further, people can modify their environments and create artificial ones to enhance survival. Cultural adaptations often involve technological innovation and the elaboration of material culture. For example, people living in island or coastal environments construct rafts, canoes, and boats to cross rivers, bays, and oceans, and people everywhere make a vast array of tools and equipment to help them obtain food and perform other kinds of subsistence tasks. The tools and practices that enable people to satisfy their survival and adaptation needs make up what is called a **cultural core.**

While adaptation through culture is a fundamental and universal process, not all cultural practices are adaptive. Some practices may be maladaptive or have unintended negative consequences as circumstances change. Sometimes, solving one problem may lead to new, unforeseen problems.

The archaeological record gives us some clues about the decline of several large and prosperous ancient cultures in both the Eastern and Western Hemispheres because of agricultural techniques that turned out to have unforeseen negative consequences. The ancient Mesopotamian society of Sumer, located in what is now southern Iraq, developed into large-scale city-states by 3000 B.C. Sumerian economy was based on intensive farming, made possible by extensive irrigation systems that brought water from the Euphrates and other rivers to fields under cultivation. Sumerian farmers produced a greater yield of crops than has been achieved since in the region (Sasson, 1995).

One reason for the decline in yields and the eventual fall of the Sumerian Empire was that intensive irrigation led to rapid evaporation of water from the soil, causing an increase in salinization, or salt content, of the land. As the land deteriorated and crop yields declined, Sumer was no longer able to support large populations without a decline in living standards. Other contributing factors were indirect consequences of the agricultural productivity achieved by Sumerian farmers. Families that controlled the land began to compete for political and economic supremacy and encouraged overproduction. Political instability was another important factor in Sumer's decline (Peregrine, 2003).

As another example, the unintended negative consequences of the Industrial Revolution for people and their environments are well known. The ability to supply many millions of people with an ever-increasing amount and variety of products has led to problems of pollution, contamination, and overexploitation of natural resources and nonrenewable energy resources. Many techniques and technologies commonly used in agriculture are maladaptive in the long run, although they may provide short-term benefits of increased productivity.

Thus, the idea that culture is adaptive needs to be considered in context. That is, a particular practice may be adaptive in one situation but not in another. For instance, farming techniques used in temperate climates to increase crop yields may be counterproductive in the Amazon rain forest because of the thinness and relative infertility of the topsoil, actually destroying the land. This is exactly what is happening in parts of the Amazon today, where environmentally inappropriate farming techniques are harming the long-term viability of agriculture (Schmink and Hood, 1992).

Anyone can acquire any culture if he or she is raised in it, just as any normal person can learn any language.

cultural core
Practices by which people organize their work and produce food and other goods necessary for their survival.

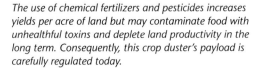

The use of chemical fertilizers and pesticides increases yields per acre of land but may contaminate food with unhealthful toxins and deplete land productivity in the long term. Consequently, this crop duster's payload is carefully regulated today.

Culture Change

South Fore People

MALADAPTIVE ADAPTATIONS: KURU AND MAD COW

By 1910, a new disease appeared among the South Fore (pronounced For´ray), a farming people of New Guinea. The disease, called *kuru* (meaning "trembling" or "fear" in the Fore language), affects the central nervous system. It is a progressive disease that slowly leads to complete physical incapacitation and death. During the course of the illness, victims gradually become unable to control muscular movements. They cannot sit or walk unaided, focus their eyes, speak clearly, or even swallow. Death usually occurs in six to twelve months of the onset of symptoms, although some people may survive as long as two years.

Investigation of the spread of kuru during the 1950s led to suspicion that it correlated with particular ritual practices engaged in by Fore women. In Fore society, as elsewhere in New Guinea, women are the primary farmers, growing sweet potatoes, yams, and other vegetables. They also care for the domesticated pigs kept by each household. Men clear the fields but then do little of the farm labor. Their work includes hunting for small mammals, reptiles, and birds. Men and women live separately most of the time. Men reside communally in a "men's house," eating and sleeping away from their families. Fore culture emphasizes concepts of pollution and danger, against which rituals serve as antidotes. This includes the belief that women pose a threat to male strength and vitality. Women live in separate small huts with their children and pigs. Men and women participate in different social and ceremonial activities as well.

In the early 1900s, South Fore women began practicing cannibalism as part of their mourning ceremonies when a female relative died. This ritual involved eating the brains and body parts of the deceased kin. According to anthropologist Shirley Lindenbaum (1979), this practice had some adaptive value in the context of protein scarcity, particularly for women. As populations increased and more land came under cultivation, sources of animal protein declined. In addition, men had access to more high-quality protein because they claimed greater rights to the pigs. They believed that other sources of protein, such as insects, frogs, and small mammals, were not only unfit for men but might threaten a man's health and vigor. In this context, according to Lindenbaum, women may have turned to cannibalism as a way of securing more protein.

When a South Fore woman died, her body was dismembered and eaten by her female relatives. Some of the meat was given to children of either sex, but it was rarely eaten by adult men because of the belief that contact with women (and, logically, eating their flesh) was dangerous and polluting. The Fore did not associate cannibalism with kuru, but they were alarmed by the high incidence of the disease, particularly among women. The people attributed kuru to sorcery, a common cause of illness and death in their medical belief system. When someone died of kuru, kinspeople tried to identify the evildoer, usually accusing someone who might have had reason to wish the victim harm.

According to Lindenbaum, between 1957 and 1968, when the disease was at its height, there were about 1,000 deaths in the South Fore population of 8,000. The fact that nearly all the deaths were of adult women added to the social and economic burden, because women produced the crops, tended the pigs, and gave birth. In some villages, nearly half of the adult female deaths and nearly all of the deaths of children between 5 and 16 years of age were due to kuru (Foster and Anderson, 1978).

The riddle of kuru was not solved until the late 1960s. Following on the work of anthropologists Robert Glasse and Shirley Lindenbaum, the anthropologist-virologist Carlton Gajdusek discovered the mode of transmission of the disease. Gajdusek (who was awarded the Nobel Prize for his discovery in 1976) identified the disease agent as a prion, the same kind of agent responsible for mad cow disease (or bovine spongiform encephalopathy). Prions remain dormant for many years after they are ingested, but eventually cause progressive damage to the brain. Thus, when South Fore women and children ate the brains of their female relatives, they unknowingly ingested the cause of their own deaths.

The incidence of kuru began to decline after the Australian colonial administration sent patrols into the Fore region of New Guinea and persuaded the people to discontinue ritual cannibalism and associated warfare. Kuru continued long after cannibalism stopped, however, because of the disease's long incubation period.

The Fore had adopted a maladaptive practice. Similarly, the spread of mad cow disease in Great Britain in the 1980s and 1990s resulted from a procedure that seemed financially beneficial in the short term but ultimately proved disastrous. Companies that produced feed for cattle began to use bonemeal derived from sheep brains as a cheap source of protein filler. However, some of the bonemeal was infected with a disease called *scrapie,* caused by agents of the family of prions similar to the agents that caused kuru. When living cattle ate the infected bonemeal, they became sick with symptoms similar to those manifested by the Fore. The agents are slow-acting proteins that attack and destroy brain tissue. Humans who ate the diseased cattle also became ill.

Once the disease became known and its source identified, more than 140,000 cows in Great Britain had to be slaughtered to prevent the disease from spreading (*Columbia Encyclopedia,* 2003). Therefore, the procedure of using cheap sheep brains to fatten cattle for market ended up costing millions of dollars and many lives.

In 1996, some people in Great Britain who died of a prion-caused disease called Creutzfeldt-Jakob disease were thought to have gotten sick after eating beef infected with mad cow disease. As a consequence, more British cattle were slaughtered to stem a potential epidemic. The European Union banned the export of British beef from 1996 to 1999, and nearly half of the country's 11 million cattle were destroyed (*Seattle Times,* 1996). Some British cattle imported into Canada and the United States also were destroyed.

In response to mad cow disease and its possible transmission to humans in the form of Creutzfeldt-Jakob disease, the U.S. Department of Agriculture bars importation of cattle and many cattle by-products from Great Britain and from most other European nations as well. The federal Food and Drug Administration has banned the use of beef proteins or hormonal extracts from cattle organs in medicines, dietary supplements, and cosmetics (*San Francisco Chronicle,* 1996). The economic loss to the European cattle industry has been disastrous. Japan restricts U.S. beef imports as well. In 2005 the Centers for Disease Control warned of infected cattle in Canada (Centers for Disease Control, http://www.cdc.gov/mcidod/diseases/cjd/cjd.htm).

Mad cow disease, like kuru among the Fore, demonstrates that people sometimes engage in practices that seem to make sense when first introduced but in the long term have consequences that are maladaptive and even life-threatening. These two syndromes are vastly different in their cultural causes, one stemming from religious beliefs and the other driven by the economic motive to cut costs. But they share a similar process, namely, the fact that people's behavior, seemingly sensible at the time, often has unforeseen and dangerous consequences.

? *What are some other examples of "maladaptive" adaptations in today's world?*

cultural integration
Tendency for people's practices and beliefs to form a relatively coherent and consistent system.

symbol
A word, image, or object that stands for cultural ideas or sentiments.

Culture Is Integrated

Cultural integration refers to the observation that people's practices and beliefs form a relatively coherent and consistent system. Cultures are not simply random collections of activities but instead are patterned and interrelated in systematic ways. For example, behaviors that take place in one domain, such as political organization, tend to be compatible with and support behaviors taking place in other domains, such as family organization. Anthropologists recognize that terms such as "economy," "social organization," "family organization," and "government" are not discrete, separable units of activity but are closely intertwined. For example, economic activities usually are integrated with, affect, and are affected by other kinds of activities. The work of obtaining food and other goods and services is often performed by people who occupy particular social roles and statuses. Gender roles may assign men and women different kinds of work in contributing to their household economies. Also, social norms or, in complex societies, laws enacted by legislators and policies formulated by political agencies tend to be consistent with particular economic consequences and to reinforce particular economic goals.

The shared ways that people organize their lives are major integrating factors. In many traditional societies, religious beliefs permeate and guide all aspects of daily life. Religion then becomes an overarching, integrative system of beliefs and practices. People in a small-scale society integrated by religion might perform daily rituals to bless and safeguard themselves and their families; they may recite prayers when hunting or planting crops to ensure success; and they may ask for spirit protection when engaging in any dangerous activity. People in these societies believe that the human and spiritual realms are not separable but that spiritual forces are omnipresent and continually affect their lives.

Naturally, not all aspects of cultural behavior and belief are internally consistent or integrated with all others. Humans and their experiences are not so neat and tidy. Nevertheless, cultural systems as wholes tend toward consistency. A consequence of this consistency and integration is that change in one societal domain causes change in others (see the Case Study on women and work in the United States, for example).

Culture Is Based on Symbols

People's behaviors and understandings of the world are based on meanings expressed through symbols. A **symbol** is a sound or object that represents or stands for an idea, event, meaning, or sentiment. Language is a pervasive and powerful symbol system. Words in any language are just sequences of sounds, but each sequence is a symbol of something other than the sounds themselves. The collection of sounds in each word in this sentence, for instance, stands for some arbitrarily assigned meaning.

Symbols permeate human culture in ways other than language. Objects, art, and artistic performances may represent powerful cultural ideas and attitudes. The colors and designs of national flags, for instance, come to be associated with complex levels of meaning. People can understand those meanings by examining the contexts of flag use, the way people talk about their national colors, and the way people react to them. Flags are used to symbolically represent a country, a territorial and cultural unit differentiated from all other similarly organized territorial and cultural units. Flags take on additional associations, demonstrated by the emotional reactions they can trigger in observers. Also, people may use their country's flag in ways that show their attitudes and political beliefs.

? *What emotional reactions can be stirred by images of national flags? How has the American flag been used to display both positive and negative feelings about the U.S. government or its policies?*

Religion, too, is a domain filled with symbolic meanings. Believers invest tremendous importance to objects considered to have religious significance. Ordinary objects and substances used in rituals take on sacred properties. Books, cups, images, pieces of cloth or wood, or foodstuffs can be symbols of beliefs and can evoke powerful emotions and dramatize sacred actions. Symbolic culture thus includes both sacred and secular meanings and all the ways in which those meanings are communicated.

Culture often is expressed in symbolic interaction between individuals using verbal and nonverbal language. Thus, language can also be used to challenge basic assumptions

Case study

Consequences of Cultural Integration: Women and Work in the United States

In the United States, changes in women's participation in paid employment have affected their roles in other spheres of life, as well as prevailing attitudes about men and women (Fox and Hesse-Biber, 1984). Women's rates of employment began to rise significantly during World War II as a consequence of the nation's military and economic policies. As millions of men entered the armed forces, millions of jobs necessary to support the economy and the war effort were left vacant. Public policy encouraged women to do their patriotic duty by working in factories and offices, where they had previously met resistance and discrimination. The banner of women's rights, which had won American women the right to vote after World War I, was raised again.

After the war, many women returned to exclusively domestic roles, but many others remained in the work force, partly for personal reasons and partly because of their families' desire to purchase an expanding array of consumer goods and to improve their standard of living.

Also, through work outside the home, women gained some degree of financial equality with their husbands. Women's economic gains contributed to rising rates of divorce both because wives could leave unhappy situations if they felt that they could live independently and husbands could leave if they felt that their wives could be at least partially self-supporting (Costello et al., 1998). In intact families, greater financial equality as well as the greater amount of time that women spent outside the home contributed to shifting the roles of husbands toward some household and child-care responsibilities.

By the late twentieth century, the percentage of marriages that ended in divorce had risen, and attitudes toward divorce had changed as well. The social stigma commonly associated with divorce in the 1950s had all but disappeared in most sectors of society. Also, women's paid employment and opportunities to make prominent contributions in public arenas had expanded. More legislators, governors, and heads of government agencies are women. Women's leadership roles in religion also have broadened, such that many Protestant and Jewish denominations allow for the ordination of women as ministers and rabbis. Women also have more higher education and greater acceptance in formerly male-dominated occupations and professions, such as law and law enforcement, military service, and the building trades.

Changes in the roles and status of women in American society have affected men's lives as well as the society as a whole.

Changes in women's roles also affected the way that men thought about themselves and about their work. Husbands were now able to expect that their wives would contribute to household incomes. And work roles for men became somewhat more flexible. A father could opt to be a "stay-at-home Dad" if his wife's work brought in more money than his or simply if he preferred that role. And societal norms moved to a greater acceptance of men working in certain jobs traditionally associated with women, such as nursing and elementary school teaching.

Thus, within a mere fifty years, the United States witnessed a cultural transformation in which changes in one societal sphere led to changes in other spheres as well as to lasting changes in people's thoughts and behaviors. These multiple and interrelating effects illustrate the concept of cultural integration.

naturalized concepts
Ideas and behaviors so deeply embedded in a culture that they are regarded as universally normal or natural.

? *What would you learn about cultural communication from studying in your workplace or dorm?*

GLOBALIZATION

Afro-Lingua is a language that was created to challenge symbolically the basic assumptions encoded in the ordinary speech of European colonizers of the Caribbean.

encoded in ordinary speech. For example, a dialect of Caribbean immigrants and their descendants in Great Britain, called Afro-Lingua, focuses on the ways that standard English transmits common cultural assumptions about race in the uses and meanings that associate *white* with "good" and *black* with "bad." For example, in common English expressions, "a black day" means a day when things go drastically wrong, and "a black sheep" means an outcast family member (Bones, 1986:46). Afro-Lingua speakers might refer to "a white day" and "a white sheep" in equivalent contexts. In addition, Afro-Lingua changes syllables in some English words to highlight cultural and political meanings: the word *politics* is transformed into "politricks," and *oppression* becomes "downpression" (Wong, 1986:119).

Humor is another form of symbolic cultural communication. For example, western Apache communities in New Mexico have a repertoire of joke routines that ridicule Anglos by imitating and exaggerating their intrusive, domineering communicative styles (Basso, 1979). Apaches find these Anglo communication styles insensitive at best or offensive. Scorned behaviors include making direct eye contact with or staring at interlocutors, touching another person while talking to him or her, calling casual acquaintances "friend," and asking intrusive, personal questions. Through their informal comic routines, Apaches share the opposite norms and values.

Culture Organizes the Way People Think about the World

Through exposure to cultural symbols and through enculturation and the acquisition of shared cultural concepts, people develop ways of thinking about themselves, their lives, other people, and the world. These underlying shared concepts become so ingrained that they are taken for granted, assumed to be true. People understand them as "natural" and "common sense." These are **naturalized concepts,** ideas thought to be essential and to exist in nature.

All societies have a core of naturalized ideas, based on societal norms. For example, in most capitalist societies, it is taken for granted that people want to own property and obtain wealth. It is assumed that people are naturally competitive and want to continually acquire more property, own larger and more expensive houses, and have unlimited access to possessions. Yet people in these societies generally may not understand that their attitudes and values about property and wealth stem from the kind of economic system they live in. Those who lack an anthropological perspective think that their attitudes and values are natural and universal rather than products of their culture. Thus, naturalized concepts orient people's thinking about themselves and the world. They form a background ideology that organizes and gives meaning to people's

In these photographs, Chinese and American children are forming group identities through symbolic culture. What aspects of symbolic culture are evident in the pictures? What is being communicated to the children through these symbols? What is the role of children's exposure to symbols in these settings in the process of their enculturation?

behaviors and attitudes. And to the extent that they shape the way we view other cultures, they are also a source of ethnocentrism.

Although all cultures have fundamental organizing concepts, these principles may be challenged from within the society. In all societies there are alternative and conflicting values held by members of different subcultures or subgroups. Alternative views may be discussed and debated in the context of mutual respect or they may erupt in more contentious challenges, in what some observers refer to as **culture wars.** Expressions of antipathy between conservatives and liberals over many social policy issues in the United States are an example of a so-called culture war.

On the other hand, individuals and groups engaging in practices with underlying meanings that conflict with prevailing assumptions and norms may be participants in a **counterculture**—an alternative culture model. Members of a counterculture view themselves as in active opposition to dominant cultural themes. For example, the hippies of the 1960s openly rejected prevailing puritanical attitudes toward sex and the authoritarian, militaristic policies of the government.

Challenges to widely recognized assumptions often come from members of groups that are marginalized or oppressed, who hold different **worldviews** than those of the dominant groups or elites. For example, apartheid, South Africa's dominant racist cultural ideology, came from a powerful white minority who had inherited power through colonial rule. That rule was challenged by the majority of black South Africans, who eventually rebelled against the government that oppressed them. Black South Africans asserted not only their political rights but also their right to replace the cultural model of white supremacy with one of racial equality. Thus, many political movements seek more than a reordering of social and political forces. They also seek the institutionalization of new cultural models as organizing principles in the society.

Similarly, through symbolic culture, some segment of a society might resist the official culture or offer an alternative cultural model. In the Middle East and North Africa, women's challenges to the ideology of male dominance often take the form of poetry and song, a low-risk context for expressing discontent. Bedouin women, for example, recite poetry and compose songs expressing their longings for love and respect. Song lyrics express passion and joy in attentions they receive from clandestine lovers (Abu-Lughod, 1986, 1990). Artistic genres thus permit women to verbalize private feelings that run contrary to accepted norms of female deference and modesty.

Table 2.1 summarizes the characteristics of culture as it is defined in this chapter. This section then closes with a story, In Their Own Voices, about an anthropologist's field experience that highlights the challenges of understanding cultures as unique collections of symbols and meanings.

? *What are some examples of culture wars in U.S. society today? What are some examples of countercultures in U.S. history?*

REVIEW

Characteristics of culture include the fact that it is shared. Individuals who belong to a culture share assumptions about the world and develop cultural models and societal norms and taboos that define how one should and should not behave. Members of different subcultures in a society share culture differently. Culture also is learned through enculturation. We are enculturated both formally and informally through social interactions with other members of society. Culture is adaptive in that people change their culture when needed or when influenced to change. The knowledge, skills, and tools people use to survive and adapt are referred to as the cultural core. Culture is integrated—that is, all aspects of culture are interconnected and mutually reinforcing. Thus, cultural integration means that change in one aspect of culture leads to changes in other aspects. The existence of culture wars and countercultures within a society illustrates, however, how cultures are not fully integrated. Culture is based on symbols, and language is the most important symbol system people use. Symbolic objects and symbolic communication are used in diverse contexts, such as religion and humor. Culture influences the way people organize their experience and their worldview. They use naturalized concepts to apply their cultural assumptions to other people's ways of life.

culture wars
Internal disagreements in a society about cultural models or about how society or the world should be organized.

counterculture
An alternative cultural model within a society that expresses different views about the way that society should be organized.

worldview
Culture-based, often ethnocentric, way that people see the world and other peoples.

Culture contact, a major force in the process of globalization, leads to several strategies and consequences of culture change, including acculturation, assimilation, and reactive adaptation.

Table 2.1 CHARACTERISTICS OF CULTURE

Culture Is Shared	Behavior, attitudes, and ideas are formed through interaction with others.
	Norms: Sets of expectations and attitudes that people have about appropriate behavior. **Subculture:** A group whose members interact more frequently among themselves and share attitudes and practices that are distinct from others.
Culture Is Learned	Culture is acquired rather than inherited.
	Enculturation: The learning of one's cultural behaviors, attitudes, and values.
Culture Is Adaptive	Aspects of behavior and belief are responses to environmental constraints and the need to ensure a community's survival.
	Cultural core: Basic practices that function to satisfy people's adaptive needs.
Culture Is Integrated	Practices and beliefs that form a relatively coherent and consistent system.
	Cultural model: Comprehensive shared ideas about the ideal culture.
Culture Is Based on Symbols	People's behavior and understanding of the world are based on meanings expressed through language, art, and symbolic objects.
	Symbols: Words, images, or objects that stand for cultural ideas or sentiments.
Culture Organizes the Way People Think about the World	**Naturalized concepts:** Ideas and behaviors so deeply embedded in a culture that they are regarded as universally normal or natural.
	Worldview: The culture-based, often ethnocentric, way that people see the world and other peoples. **Counterculture:** Alternative cultural model within a society that expresses opposition to dominant social and political views.

CULTURE CHANGE

Cultures are dynamic systems that respond to societal and historical changes from numerous sources. Some sources of culture change are internal, emerging from new practices and attitudes, technological innovations, or adaptations to the consequences of earlier practices. Other sources of culture change are external, emerging as people borrow ideas or artifacts from their neighbors or from people with whom they interact through migration, trade, or other contacts. Some borrowings take place in friendly interactions during **culture contact,** but others are forced on people, as in conquest or foreign intervention.

Changes stimulated by external culture change then typically undergo further change through internal processes. For example, as you read in Chapter 1, people usually adapt outside cultural borrowings to their own cultures. They may borrow only parts of a cultural item, whether a story or a way of organizing economic activity, and combine those parts with items that already exist in their cultural repertoire. For example, in the realm of religion, people often combine elements of their traditional beliefs with those that they learn from external sources as a consequence of culture contact. This process, called **syncretism,** is seen in religions such as Santeria, which

culture contact
Direct interaction between peoples of different cultures through migration, trade, invasion, or conquest.

syncretism
Process by which a cultural product is created when people adapt a cultural item selectively borrowed from another culture to fit their existing culture.

*Aboriginal star singer Archie Roach, here with Ruby Hunter, was a member of Australia's "Stolen Generation."
In the 1950s as many as one-tenth of Aboriginal babies were removed from their natural parents and taken
into foster care by white families. Postcolonial authorities believed that this forced removal and assimilation
would be in the best interests of all Australians. Roach was taken from Framingham Mission in Victoria,
Australia, by a policeman and the Aborigines Protection Board at the age of 3 and put into a Salvation Army
Home with his two sisters. Separated from his sisters, he was fostered out to three different white families
ending with Scottish migrants who falsely believed his Aboriginal family had been killed in a house fire.*

combines traditional Afro-Caribbean beliefs in magic and witchcraft with Roman
Catholicism. Spanish colonizers derisively called this religion of the Yorubas—and
other Bantu slaves from Nigeria, Senegal, and the Guinea Coast—Santeria, "Way of the
Saints," but other, more proper names include *Regla de Ocha,* "Rule of the Orisha."

Anthropologists have other terms to describe the kinds of internal change that take
place following culture contact, depending on the power relations between peoples
and the extent of change. For example, **assimilation** occurs when a less numerous and
less powerful group changes its ways to blend in with the dominant culture. In assimilating, people abandon their prior beliefs and practices and adopt the cultural repertoire of the dominant population. For example, immigrants may voluntarily change
their national and cultural identities by assimilating the language and culture of their
new country. But assimilation is sometimes forced on a people by a dominant culture,
especially in the context of conquest and colonization.

A group's adjusting to living within another, more dominant, culture while at the
same time maintaining its original cultural identity is called **acculturation.** For
example, many Native Americans in the United States and Canada adopt many
features of dominant American culture such as the economic and political systems
but maintain their own languages, family systems, and religious beliefs. The term
cultural pluralism describes a stratified society that contains many diverse cultural
groups who ideally live together equally and harmoniously. Other complex changes
that occur through combinations of external and internal processes include economic transformations, such as **modernization,** based on industrialism and a market economy.

Internal Culture Change

Early anthropologists, such as Edward B. Tylor, believed that cultures evolve through
various stages, from a simpler and more primitive state to a complex and more culturally advanced state. To Tylor and his contemporaries, middle-class Euro-American culture represented the pinnacle of this **cultural evolution,** which other cultures could
naturally and eventually achieve. Others treated the concept of cultural evolution as
analogous to biological evolution, claiming that some cultures were naturally superior

assimilation
Process by which a less
numerous and less powerful
cultural group changes its
ways and cultural identity to
blend in with the dominant
culture.

acculturation
Process by which a group
adjusts to living within a
dominant culture while at
the same time maintaining
its original cultural identity.

cultural pluralism
Condition in a stratified
society in which many
diverse cultural groups
ideally live together equally
and harmoniously without
losing their cultural
identities and diversity.

modernization
Complex culture change,
both internal and external,
based on industrialism and a
transnational market
economy.

cultural evolution
Belief of early
anthropologists that
cultures evolve through
various stages from a
simpler and more primitive
state to a complex and
more culturally advanced
state.

In Their Own Voices

Hamlet and the Tiv

An anthropologist's effort to explain Shakespeare's Hamlet *to Tiv villagers in Nigeria illustrates how, for both the anthropologist and the Tiv, culture shapes the way they think about the world. When Laura Bohannan lived among the Tiv, they were a farming people living in small villages in central Nigeria. Village life centered on groups of families related through men, with fathers, sons, and brothers forming the core of households. After marriage, women moved from their families to live with their husband's relatives. Men prepared fields for planting, but women did most of the farmwork. They planted the seeds, weeded the plants, and harvested crops. In addition to their families, men depended on their age-mates—other men of the same age group—to come to their aid in times of trouble.*

Bohannan was prompted to tell the story of Hamlet because she thought it had a single universal meaning that people everywhere would understand in the same way. The Tiv elders also thought the story had universal meaning—but a different one. To both the anthropologist and the elders, their particular understanding seemed obvious, showing how powerful our cultural assumptions can be. If you need to refresh your memory on what Hamlet is about, read the summary at http://shakespeare.palomar.edu/lambtales/LTHAMLET.HTM. To read the rest of Laura Bohannan's amusing and insightful article, go to http://fieldworking.com/library/bohannan.html.

The following excerpt expresses the views of both Bohannan and Tiv villagers on the meaning of the play.

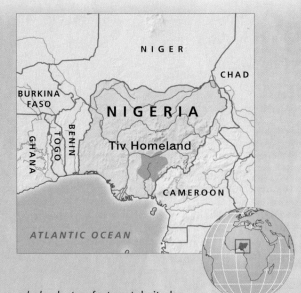

I began in the proper style, "Not yesterday, not yesterday, but long ago, a thing occurred. One night three men were keeping watch outside the homestead of the great chief, when suddenly they saw the former chief approach them."

"Why was he no longer their chief?"

"He was dead," I explained. "That is why they were troubled and afraid when they saw him."

"Impossible," began one of the elders. "Of course it wasn't the dead chief. It was an omen sent by a witch. Go on."

Slightly shaken, I continued. "One of these three was a man who knew things"—the closest translation for scholar, but unfortunately it also meant *witch*. "So he spoke to the dead chief saying, "Tell us what we must do so you may rest in your grave," but the dead chief did not answer. . . .

There was a general shaking of heads round the circle. "Had the dead chief no living brothers? Or was this son the chief?". . .

"He had one living brother who became the chief when the elder brother died. In our country the son is next to the father. The dead chief's younger brother had become the great chief. He had also married his elder brother's widow only about a month after the funeral.". . .

"He did well," the old man beamed and announced to the others, "I told you that if we knew more about Europeans, we could find they really were very like us. In our country also," he added to me, "the younger brother marries the elder brother's widow and becomes the father of his children. Now, if your uncle, who married your widowed mother, is your father's full brother, then he will be a real father to you. Did Hamlet's father and uncle have one mother?"

His question barely penetrated my mind; I was too upset and thrown too far off balance by having one of the most important elements of Hamlet knocked straight out of the picture. Rather uncertainly I said that I thought they had the same mother, but I wasn't sure—the story didn't say. The old man told me severely that these genealogical details made all the difference and that when I got home I must ask the elders about it. . . .

Determined to save what I could of the mother motif, I took a deep breath and began again. "The son Hamlet was very sad because his mother had married again so quickly. There was no need for her to do so, and it is our custom for a widow not to go to her next husband until she has mourned for two years."

"Two years is too long," objected the elder's wife. "Who will hoe your farms for you while you have no husband?"

I gave up. . . .

"That night Hamlet kept watch with the three who had seen his dead father. The dead chief again appeared, and although the others were afraid, Hamlet followed his dead father off to one side. When they were alone, Hamlet's dead father spoke."

"Omens can't talk!" The old man was emphatic. . . .

"It was Hamlet's dead father. It was a thing we call a *ghost*." I had to use the English word, for unlike many of the neighboring tribes, these people didn't believe in the survival after death of any individuating part of the personality. . . .

"Dead men can't walk," protested my audience as one man.

I was quite willing to compromise. "A ghost is the dead man's shadow."

But again they objected. "Dead men cast no shadows."

"They do in my country," I snapped. . . .

"Anyhow," I resumed, "Hamlet's dead father said that his own brother, the one who became chief, had poisoned him. He wanted Hamlet to avenge him. Hamlet believed this in his heart, for he did not like his father's brother.". . .

"Now Hamlet's age mates," I continued, "had brought with them a famous storyteller. Hamlet decided to have this man tell the chief and all his homestead a story about a man who had poisoned his brother because he desired his brother's wife and wished to be chief himself. Hamlet was sure the great chief could not hear the story without making a sign if he was indeed guilty, and then he would discover whether his dead father had told him the truth. . . . It was true, for when the storyteller was telling his tale

before all the homestead, the great chief rose in fear. Afraid that Hamlet knew his secret he planned to have him killed.". . .

This time I had shocked my audience seriously. "For a man to raise his hand against his father's brother and the one who has become his father—that is a terrible thing. The elders ought to let such a man be bewitched. . . .

I then pointed out that after all the man had killed Hamlet's father.

"No," pronounced the old man, speaking less to me than to the young men sitting behind the elders. "If your father's brother has killed your father, you must appeal to your father's age mates; they may avenge him. No man may use violence against his senior relatives." Another thought struck him. "But if his father's brother had indeed been wicked enough to bewitch Hamlet and make him mad that would be a good story indeed, for it would be his fault that Hamlet, being mad, no longer had any sense and thus was ready to kill his father's brother."

There was a murmur of applause. Hamlet was again a good story to them, but it no longer seemed quite the same story to me. . . .

The old man made soothing noises. "You tell the story well, and we are listening. But it is clear that the elders of your country have never told you what the story really means. No, don't interrupt! We believe you when you say your marriage customs are different, or your clothes and weapons. But people are the same everywhere; therefore, there are always witches and it is we, the elders, who know how witches work. We told you it was the great chief who wished to kill Hamlet, and now your own words have proved us right. . . .

"Sometime," concluded the old man, "you must tell us some more stories of your country. We, who are elders, will instruct you in their true meaning, so that when you return to your own land your elders will see that you have not been sitting in the bush, but among those who know things and who have taught you wisdom."

From Laura Bohannan, "Shakespeare in the Bush," *Natural History* (August/September 1966).

CRITICAL THINKING QUESTION

What Tiv cultural assumptions and values caused them to interpret the story of Hamlet differently?

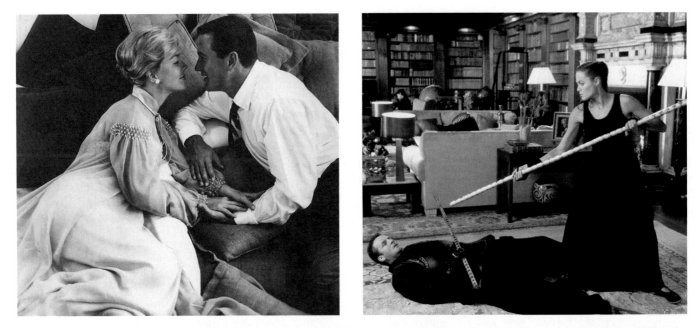

How could you use comparisons of movie posters like these to interpret cultures and culture change? What do these particular examples from popular culture suggest about changes in American social and cultural norms over the past sixty years? How do those changes reflect changes in attitudes and values? What factors do you think have contributed to changes in Americans' attitudes toward gender stereotypes, violence, and sex?

? *What are some problems with applying principles of biological evolution to explanations of culture change?*

social Darwinism
Early belief that cultures compete for survival of the fittest, as in the process of natural selection in biological evolution.

culture history
Ongoing culture change in which people respond and adapt to their environment.

ethnogenesis
Ongoing process in which people develop, define, and direct their own cultural and ethnic identities.

to others, modeled on the concepts of competition and the survival of the fittest way of life. This faulty reasoning, known as **social Darwinism,** claimed that the wealth and power of Western societies were due to their natural and cultural superiority rather than to the consequences of historical processes.

Today, however, evolutionary biologists study the adaptive value of social behavior, cognitive skills, and the capacity for both material and symbolic culture, all of which have contributed to the evolutionary success of the primates, and which all living human groups possess equally. Thus, **culture history** may be a more apt term than cultural evolution for ongoing culture change in which people respond and adapt to their environment and experiences. In adapting, people make themselves. That is, people develop, define, and direct their own cultural and ethnic identities, a process called **ethnogenesis** (Hill, 1992).

Some changes in societies are not intentional, like ethnogenesis, but result from gradual shifting of public norms and private sentiments. For example, in art and public performance certain behaviors and language use that were unacceptable in the past have become standard, although not without arousing conflict among some sectors of the population.

Since the 1960s, the content of American films has changed considerably. In previous periods, violence generally was shown only from a distance, and its effects on the human body were not made explicit. Today the depiction of explicit violence and its effects is commonplace. Nudity and sexual activity also have become routine in American films and videos, and language is not censored as it was in the past. These changes reflect changes in attitudes and values rather than in technology. And these changes are embedded in the wider social and political contexts of the times. The Motion Picture Production Code of the 1930s, which imposed strict limits on language, subject matter, and sexual representation, has been replaced by a rating system identifying film content. Publicized ratings warn potential viewers who do not want themselves or their children exposed to particular content. Thus, what has changed is the public's willingness to tolerate the display and discussion of previously forbidden subjects.

Another source of internal culture change is the adaptations that people make by inventing new technologies and skills to better adjust to existing conditions or to deal with new problems. **Inventions** usually are based on previous tools, knowledge, and skills in a process called **innovation.** New environmental challenges and opportunities stimulate innovation and the invention of new adaptive strategies. Some technology-based cultural transformations are so sweeping that they are referred to as revolutions. **Revolution,** in which people try to overturn the social order and replace it with a new, ideal society and culture, is another widespread form of internal culture change that has been a part of the history of many state societies.

External Culture Change

Culture change also occurs through culture contact as people migrate, trade, invade, intermarry, or interact in other ways. People learn ideas and skills and borrow tools, foods, clothing, and luxury items from other people with whom they have direct or indirect contact. This process, called **diffusion,** is responsible for the spread of material objects and cultural practices from one place to another.

Diffusion may be local, such as the spread of the invention of blow darts and use of poisons among South American Indians. Diffusion also can be widespread, even global within geographic constraints, such as the invention of agriculture, which spread east and west along certain latitudes over thousands of years, based on the cultivation of diverse kinds of grain. In addition to diffusion, independent invention may account for the appearance of similar cultural traits in different parts of the world. An example is the invention of writing systems, which likely occurred more than once in prehistory among different peoples in the ancient Middle East, Mexico, and China.

Invasion and conquest also are common causes of external culture change. Most early state societies probably developed partly through the process of expanding into neighboring territories and incorporating the peoples (Carniero, 1970). Colonization or conquest not only forced indigenous peoples to accept foreign goods and practices but also compelled them to alter many of their cultural practices to conform to their conquerors' ways. The attitudes and values of subject peoples eventually transformed as well to be more consistent with the changes in their behavior. However, subjects of colonial or conquered states are not passive pawns in national and global policies and processes. Rather, indigenous peoples make choices and engage in actions that in their view best achieve their goals of maintaining their communities while adapting to their changing conditions. The situations of colonial peoples and their strategies for survival are further explored in Chapters 16 and 17.

The imposition of British colonial rule on the Luo of Kenya in the nineteenth century, for example, led to many interrelated changes in the economic, social, and political systems of that tribal society. The Luo (speakers of the Luo language, today known mainly as the Karivongo) settled in Kenya and Tanzania in the fifteenth or sixteenth century, migrating south from the Sudan. In the Sudan, their economy had been centered on cattle herding but shifted gradually to farming after they arrived in Kenya. This change affected gender relations, because men had been primarily responsible for herding the cattle and women were the farmers. Following Luo custom, land was owned communally by groups of relatives headed by men, but women actually controlled the production and distribution of crops resulting from their labor. In the colonial and postcolonial periods, however, women's rights to the land and their economic independence were undermined by British land reforms.

In 1899, the British colonial government imposed policies aimed at consolidating individual holdings that were intentionally scattered in different locations. Traditional Luo patterns of landholding gave individuals use rights in scattered parcels so that they could obtain food resources in different ecological zones. People thus could plant a variety of crops suited to each zone. British authorities did not understand this custom, however; in their view the traditional system was inefficient. In keeping with European ideals, the British combined landholdings into single parcels, which were registered in the names of male heads of households.

In addition, British colonial authorities imposed hut taxes that had to be paid in cash. To obtain cash for taxes, Luo men as heads of households often had to find wage work away from their local communities. At the same time that taxation was a

GLOBALIZATION

Today as in the past, diffusion is a major force in the process of globalization, as concepts, technologies, languages, and symbols spread from one culture to another, aided in part by past conquests and the history of colonization.

inventions
New technologies and systems of knowledge.

innovation
Process by which new technologies and systems of knowledge are based on or built from previous tools, knowledge, and skills.

revolution
Process by which people try to change their culture or overturn the social order and replace it with a new, ideal society and culture.

diffusion
Spread of ideas, material objects, and cultural practices from one society to another through direct and indirect culture contact.

Case study

The Great Plains

Paiute Territories

The Ghost Dance Movement of the Plains Indians

The **Ghost Dance movement** of nineteenth-century North American Plains Indians was a nativistic revitalization movement that arose at a time when all of the native peoples had been forcibly confined to reservations after brutal military campaigns. The vast majority of their land had been taken from them and their traditional economic systems were obliterated, as the buffalo on which they had depended were slaughtered by the millions. Epidemic diseases such as measles and smallpox decimated the populations, wiping out whole families and in some cases nearly whole communities. Reduced to poverty and dependence on rations meagerly handed out by the government, and withheld from people who were known resisters to the imposition of American authority, a spiritual reawakening took place.

Although the movement advocated a message of peace and a return to traditional values and ways of living, it was completely misunderstood and distorted by agents of the U.S. government, with tragic results (Mooney, 1965). Begun in 1889 by a northern Paiute prophet named Wovoka, the Ghost Dance movement predicted an imminent end to the world during a cataclysmic earthquake, to be followed by the reappearance of Indians who had died, the return of the buffalo, and the disappearance of white people.

Although Wovoka taught the necessity of establishing peace, harmony, and good moral principles, his message was distorted by frightened settlers and government officials who feared an armed uprising of impoverished and beleaguered native people who were forced to give up their lands, their economies, and their ways of living. Performances of the Ghost Dance were banned, and participants were threatened with imprisonment.

Finally, in 1890, after outlawing the dances and harassing followers, government superintendents in charge of the Lakota reservations in South Dakota had the influential leader Sitting Bull arrested and murdered and continued to harass Ghost Dance participants. Army units were sent to arrest other Ghost Dance adherents, leading to the entrapment of more than 300 Lakotas and their massacre at Wounded Knee Creek on December 29, 1890. This final tragedy put an end to Ghost Dance performances.

Since then, the message of the Ghost Dance has changed from foretelling the end of American control to focusing on personal improvement and spirituality (Kehoe, 1989). Nevertheless, Wounded Knee continues as a potent symbol to Native Americans of government policies that crushed native peoples and their indigenous cultures.

Ghost Dance movement
Nineteenth-century revitalization movement of the Plains Indians of North America.

Arapaho Ghost Dancers, 1890. Specific elements of the Ghost Dance varied from group to group, but the main message was that Native Americans would achieve deliverance from white domination by supernatural means. The ritual dance with spirit possession would restore the balance of nature, and the whites would disappear. In some groups, all the dead Indians would return to life, along with their horses and the buffalo. Whole again, the people would rebuild their societies and live as they had before contact.

financial burden, men benefited from colonial policies. Participating in the cash economy gave them access to valuable manufactured goods, and their official status as individual landowners gave them greater power and authority. To raise more cash, Luo men turned land production over from home use to cash crops for export, making families more dependent on more expensive imported food to sustain themselves. The Kenyan government continued these land policies after independence in 1960.

Colonized or conquered peoples have responded to external sources of culture change in diverse ways, including assimilation and acculturation, discussed earlier here. Another kind of outcome is **reactive adaptation,** in which people react against loss, deprivation, and oppression through passive resistance or violence. Traditional religious leaders and beliefs may play a role in social movements aimed at restoring or revitalizing the traditional culture. A classic example of a **revitalization movement** is the Ghost Dance movement of the North American Plains Indians, discussed in the Case Study (Wallace, 1956; Mooney, 1965).

REVIEW

Culture change can result from either internal or external forces, which usually are mutually reinforcing. Internal culture changes can come about from technological inventions or innovation within a society or introduced through culture contact and spread through borrowing, or diffusion. In syncretism, people modify and adapt borrowed items of religious belief and practice to fit their own culture. Culture history and ethnogenesis describe change processes within a society that are self-defining as well as adaptive to both internal and external stimuli. Although the capacity for culture is an important adaptation in human evolution, culture change does not involve cultural evolution, an outdated idea based on beliefs in human progress, racial superiority, and social Darwinism. Outcomes of culture contact include, among others, assimilation and acculturation. Cultural pluralism describes culturally diverse societies in which groups have equal status under the law. Reactive adaptation is an outcome based on unrelieved stresses, often expressed through either violence or spiritual revitalization movements. Sweeping social and culture changes involving both internal and external factors stem from economic and political changes, such as the processes of modernization and revolution.

GLOBAL CULTURE

It is commonplace to hear people say that cultures throughout the world are becoming more similar, that a kind of **global culture** is spreading to all corners of the earth. Global culture "clubs" are springing up on the Internet for people who want to participate actively in this ongoing trend. Today's globalization stems from economic and political processes that have expanded from their original centers in Europe and the United States to many other countries. These processes have affected national governments, urban centers, and the cultures of traditional and indigenous peoples everywhere. Some observers claim that globalization is creating a homogenized world culture dominated by similar values and practices, while others see the development of ever greater variety and vitality through new cross-cultural combinations of cultural elements. These views emphasize contrasting themes in global change. The first stresses the influence of Euro-American economic and political forces, associated with cultural values and norms, while the second focuses on the worldwide exchange from all regions of products, peoples, and arts.

The historical origin of contemporary globalization can be traced to European mercantile and colonial expansion of the fifteenth and sixteenth centuries. For hundreds of years, it was centered in Europe, especially in Great Britain, France, Portugal, and Spain. In the late nineteenth century, the United States began to influence other regions, particularly Latin America and the Pacific, competing with the European powers. In the mid-twentieth century, after World War II, the centers of world power were concentrated in the United States and the Soviet Union, seen

reactive adaptation
Coping response of captive, conquered, or oppressed peoples to loss and deprivation.

revitalization movement
Type of nonviolent reactive adaptation in which people try to resurrect their culture heroes and restore their traditional way of life.

global culture
A constellation of technologies, practices, attitudes, values, and symbols that spread internationally from one broad cultural origin, most recently from the Anglo-European-American cultural complex.

GLOBALIZATION

Today's globalization stems from economic and political processes that have expanded from their original centers in Europe and the United States, mainly through consumerism and the mass media. How should we evaluate the consequences of this globalization?

? *Do you think the assumptions used to justify globalization are warranted? Why, or why not?*

as representing opposing views of economic, political, and cultural orders. Since the early 1990s and the dismantlement of the Soviet Union, world power has been centered in the United States, although several countries in Asia, especially Japan and South Korea, also exert substantial economic influence. Due in part to the speed of transportation and communication, the influence of economic and political interests originating in the United States has intensified and accelerated throughout the world. Cultural influences also flow from non-Western countries as Asian and African music, comics, video games, and other items of popular culture are adopted worldwide.

Principal agents of globalization are multinational corporations, which control much of the world's industry and commerce, and the mass media. A global network of finance, manufacture, export, and import has developed, incorporating every nation and many local communities. The prices that farmers receive for their crops are affected by worldwide economic forces through linkages from local to regional to national and to international networks. Wages received in the manufacturing sector are also connected to worldwide patterns of labor and job availability. National and multinational consumer outlets sell their products in nearly every country. Companies such as McDonald's, Coca-Cola, Sony, and Nintendo are icons of global consumerism. Companies and their advertisers create demand for consumer goods through mass communication systems, such as radio, television, the cinema, and the Internet.

Chapters 16 and 17 further explore the long-term effects of colonialism and the efforts of small-scale societies to participate in a globalized modern economy without sacrificing their cultural traditions, natural resources, economic interests, and social welfare (see also the Anthropology Applied feature). Participation remains a challenge, however. Euro-American societies tend to sanction world domination

As governments, corporations, and the media spread their economic, political, and cultural influences, the traditional ways of life of the world's indigenous peoples are increasingly threatened. In addition, according to one estimate about half of the world's 6,000 languages will no longer be spoken by the end of the twenty-first century (Krauss, 1992). Urban settlers, displaced farmers, prospectors, miners, timber and other industrialists, and a host of national and international interests put pressure on indigenous peoples, such as this Tarahumara woman's group and its territory. They, like other indigenous peoples today, are mobilizing to protect and preserve their environments, languages, and cultures.

Anthropology Applied

Development Anthropology

Development anthropology is a comparatively new branch of cultural anthropology in which the knowledge and skills of anthropologists are put to the task of helping developing countries to maneuver through the processes of culture change. Many developing countries want and need help, for example, to balance their economic growth and industrialization with the maintenance of a sustainable environment. Countries also may need help in dealing with the impacts of economic growth and industrialization on their traditional social institutions and systems of social relationships.

The goals of development anthropologists are reflected in the mission statement of the Institute for Development Anthropology (IDA). The IDA is "an independent, nonpartisan, non-profit, nongovernmental organization with a mission to promote environmentally sustainable development through poverty elimination, equitable economic growth, respect for human rights, gender equity, and cultural pluralism." This is done by applying the comparative and holistic theories and methods of anthropology to "empowering low-income majorities in developing countries." The IDA seeks to enhance the rights of low-income populations to land, natural resources, food, shelter, health, education, income, employment, and participation in democratic and transparent polities. Its activities relate directly to policies involving management and access to productive resources (land, water, forests), credit, employment and enterprise generation, marketing, rural cooperatives, extension programs, resettlement, river-basin development, social forestry, health delivery systems, and education (http://www.developmentanthropology.org/).

As an example of the work that organizations like the IDA do, consider Senegal's decision to permit flooding of the Senegal River valley to sustain traditional riverine economies rather than rely exclusively on damming and irrigation, which would have prevented water from reaching valley crops and pastures in small landholdings. The researchers were able to show that traditional flooding actually made the land more productive than did irrigation. The floodplain could support five to ten times more livestock than irrigated rangeland, and also would sustain the Senegal Valley's yield of fish, an important subsistence resource for the people living there.

In 2002, the IDA was awarded a five-year Women-in-Development research contract, which encompasses projects in women's legal rights; antitrafficking of women and children and antidomestic violence activities; studies on the gender dimensions of population, health, and nutrition; and studies on the gender dimensions of democracy, governance, and the environment. Included under this grant are studies of rural women in central Bolivia; the interplay of ethnicity, gender, class, and caste in Pakistan; the gender dimensions of desertification (the spread of deserts) among pastoralists; and the gender dimensions of water use and water management in central Tunisia.

CRITICAL THINKING QUESTION

Based on these examples, how might you define the role of development anthropologists in relation to the forces of globalization at work in the world today?

through globalization on the assumptions that Western technology, industrialism, capitalism, environmental exploitation, and democracy are naturally necessary and superior and that global progress toward those goals is good. The loss or destruction of other ways of life is seen as sometimes unfortunate but nevertheless inevitable and unavoidable.

REVIEW

Present-day globalization started in the fifteenth and sixteenth centuries with European state expansion affecting African, North and South American, and Asian peoples and nations. The center of globalization later shifted to the United States and the global economy instituted by multinational corporations. Economic and political forces and a global culture disseminated by the mass media threaten the loss of traditional ways of life of small-scale societies and cultural diversity among the world's peoples.

Chapter Summary

What Is Culture?

- Anthropologists use the term *culture* to refer to all of the customs, attitudes, values, and beliefs of members of a society. People acquire these elements of culture in the context of their interactions with others. As members of families, social groups, and communities, people learn the kinds of behaviors considered appropriate and encouraged. They also learn what kinds of behavior are inappropriate and therefore disvalued and avoided.

Characteristics of Culture

- Several characteristics of culture are fundamental to the way all societies function. Culture consists of behaviors and beliefs that are "shared" by members of the group. If this were not the case, people would not be able to act in unity to achieve common goals. However, there are sometimes disagreements and conflicts among members, often as a result from contrasting views and opinions held by people occupying different social statuses within the community. Age and gender differentiate members of a society, leading to distinctions in people's activities and attitudes. In addition, societies may be segmented on the basis of class, race, and ethnicity. These distinctions may create differences in the ways in which people's lives are organized and in the attitudes and values held by members.

- Another characteristic of culture is that it is "learned." That is, people's behavior is the result of learning, and not instinct. Even when human beings must fulfill critical physical and survival needs, their cultures intervene and influence the ways that their needs are satisfied. The fact that many of our attitudes and actions seem "natural" is testimony to the strength and the effectiveness of our enculturation.

- In addition, culture is "adaptive." That is, people adapt to their environments through cultural means. Human beings can survive in nearly any climate and environment because of the inventions and cultural practices that they develop, keeping them sheltered, clothed, and fed. However, some practices that start out as adaptive may become maladaptive over time. Solving one problem may lead to the creation of new and unforeseen problems. Furthermore, a particular cultural practice may be adaptive in one context but not in another.

- Culture is "integrated," forming a relatively coherent and consistent system. Cultures are not random collections of activities but instead are patterned and systematic. Change in one aspect of culture usually affects and leads to changes in other aspects as well. And when cultural traits are borrowed from other peoples, they usually are altered and adapted to fit more closely with the borrower's norms and expectations.

- Another characteristic of culture is that it is "symbolic." People's behavior and understandings of the world are based on meanings expressed through symbols. Language is the most obvious and powerful of our symbolic systems, but human beings also use objects and rituals to represent deeply held cultural ideas and attitudes. Religion, for example, is a cultural domain built with symbolic meanings, objects, and actions.

- Culture organizes the way people think about the world. Through learning and interacting with others, members of a society absorb an array of underlying, taken-for-granted assumptions about the world that help to integrate their activities and beliefs. These concepts become naturalized, so they feel innate and commonsensical rather than acquired. Not everyone, however, accepts the dominant cultural models of his or her society. In fact, these underlying assumptions can be the source of struggle and contention, which may, in turn, be sources of change.

Culture Change

- Cultures are dynamic systems that respond to change from internal and external sources. Internal development in particular practices and attitudes may take place over time through invention and innovation, leading to new adaptive strategies, new customs, new technologies, and new ideas about the world. Culture history describes the selective record of change in a society, but cultures do not evolve in the same way as species. Peoples define themselves through a process of ethnogenesis. Broad culture changes, such as modernization or revolution, are internal changes that usually are strongly influenced by external forces.

- Culture change also occurs through culture contact. People may borrow traits (both material and ideological) from other groups whom they meet in trade, travel, or social activities. In the process of syncretism, items borrowed through diffusion are modified to fit the existing culture. Culture changes also may be imposed on members of one society by members of another through invasion and conquest. Colonized people are forced to adopt practices and beliefs consistent with those of their rulers.

- When a cultural group is in close contact with a dominant culture, the people may become assimilated or acculturated. Cultural pluralism describes a society with diverse cultural groups who retain their distinctiveness but live side by side on more or less equal terms. In contrast, conquered and oppressed peoples may undergo reactive adaptation in an effort to cope with deprivation and loss. Revitalization movements are examples of nonviolent reactive adaptation.

Global Culture

- A global culture, originating in Europe and the United States, is spreading to all parts of the world. This global culture is characterized by consumer spending and is fueled by advertising on behalf of multinational corporations. While globalization has helped to unify many different peoples in a global economy, it may also lead to a loss of cultural and linguistic diversity and independence.

 ## Key Terms

cultural knowledge 24	naturalized concepts 34	modernization 37	Ghost Dance
cultural models 25	culture wars 35	culture evolution 37	movement 42
norms 25	counterculture 35	social Darwinism 40	reactive adaptation 43
subculture 27	worldview 35	culture history 40	revitalization
enculturation 27	culture contact 36	ethnogenesis 40	movement 43
taboos 27	syncretism 36	inventions 41	global culture 43
cultural core 29	assimilation 37	innovation 41	
cultural integration 32	acculturation 37	revolution 41	
symbol 32	cultural pluralism 37	diffusion 41	

Review Questions

1. In what sense is culture shared? How is it not shared?

2. How does the story of Eunice Williams illustrate that culture is learned?

3. How did the Tiv react to Bohannan's rendition of Shakespeare's *Hamlet*? Why was the idea of Hamlet's mother marrying his uncle not surprising to the Tiv?

4. Why is culture referred to as a functionally integrated system? How does the history of women in the United States illustrate the concept of cultural integration?

5. What are internal and external culture changes? What are some examples of internal and external changes in your culture?

6. Why do you think the loss of a language is of concern to anthropologists? In what other ways is culture symbolic?

7. In what ways can culture be both adaptive and maladaptive? What is an example of reactive adaptation to culture change?

8. What are the characteristics and implications of a global culture?

Studying Culture

CHAPTER 3

Preview

1. **How did anthropology begin as a discipline? What important figures shaped the development of anthropology?**

2. **What theoretical perspectives do anthropologists bring to their study of cultures?**

3. **What is ethnographic fieldwork? How is it done, and why is it important in anthropology?**

4. **How do anthropologists use ethnohistories and cross-cultural comparisons in their work?**

5. **What are some controversies about the impacts anthropologists have on the people they study?**

Long ago, when the animal people walked the earth, a giant beaver monster lived in Lake Cle Elum, high in the Cascade Mountains. His name was Wishpoosh. [Even though the Lake was full of fish, the monster refused to give any to the other animal people. They appealed to Coyote to save them. With the help of his sisters, Coyote devised a plan. He went to the Lake with a huge spear, and when Wishpoosh tried to stop him from fishing, he drove the spear into the monster's side. In their struggle, Coyote and the monster fell to the bottom of the Lake.]

They fought so hard that they shook the mountains around the Lake and made a great hole in them. The waters of the Lake rushed through this hole, plunged down the mountainside, and soon made a larger lake below, in the Kittitas Valley.

Wishpoosh, still roaring, was carried along with the waters. He tried to drown Coyote, but Coyote hung on. As they tore their way out of the second big Lake, they cut a channel for the Yakima River. As the two fighters plunged down the Yakima River, the waters followed them and made a big lake in the Yakima country. The monster tore through the next ridge and made Union Gap. He plunged eastward across the valley, continuing to dig a channel for the Yakima River as he went. The waters overflowed the new channel and made a big lake in the Walla Walla country.

Then the monster turned sharply toward the west, dragging Coyote after him and cutting the channel of Big River [the Columbia River] as he went. Coyote tried to stop his journey by clutching at the trees and rocks along the shore. But the trees broke off or came up by the roots. The rocks crumbled away, and the channel which the monster tore out was made wider by Coyote's struggle. Wishpoosh dragged him on and on. The waters of the lakes followed. The monster tore through the high mountains and made the gorge of Big River. Coyote pulled rocks from the shores and made many little waterfalls.

At last they came to the mouth of Big River, where it flows into the ocean. By this time, Coyote was so tired he almost drowned in the waves. Muskrat laughed at him. [The story continues describing the plan that Coyote uses to kill the beaver monster. Eventually, he succeeds and cuts up the monster's body, creating a different group of people from each part. As Coyote creates the groups, he disperses the people of each group to a different area of the Pacific Northwest, some along the coast and some inland.]

From Ella Clark, *Indian Legends of the Pacific Northwest*, pp. 172–175. Copyright © 1965 The Regents of the University of California; © renewed 1981 Ella E. Clark. Reprinted by permission.

This narrative can be interpreted on many levels. For instance, on one level the story expresses the way in which the Salish and Kootenai peoples symbolize and explain the origins of the different tribal groups living in their region. Coyote created each group from a different part of the body of the beaver monster whom he destroyed. The story takes note of cultural and linguistic differences among neighboring peoples and gives meaning to an understanding of those differences. Another reading of this narrative may relate to climatic and ecological upheavals that occurred in the Pacific Northwest many thousands of years ago. In this interpretation, the narrative gives an account of geological events and an explanation of the formation of geographic features in the region. The story accounts for the creation of lakes and rivers resulting from a catastrophic flood that geologists now believe occurred in the Northwest about 12,000 years ago, when an ice dam that had created a huge lake (Lake Missoula) gave way (Deloria, 1995). Scientists suggest that when the lake broke through its natural dam during the last ice age, the water flowed "at a rate 10 times all the rivers on the planet" toward the Pacific Ocean, draining "like a giant bathtub, in as little as 48 hours" (Robbins, 2004). According to geologist Dr. Eugene Kiver, the "floods may have happened when people were around. Native Americans have myths about floods" (Robbins, 2004).

Stories that seem to parallel actual occurrences suggest the accuracy of people's memories of their past, even though events may be embellished, in the rich, poetic language of tradition. **Narratives** may dramatize real events in symbolic form consistent with cultural practices of storytelling. Thus, they may preserve and transmit across generations the memories of people who witnessed events that changed their geographic landscape. We will never know whether this Coyote story encapsulates such memories or whether it imagines an explanation for the landscape that existed when the people developed the narrative. Whatever the particular facts, narratives have the power to create and to transmit a people's worldview.

Without a writing system, indigenous peoples use storytelling to preserve their history. Collecting and interpreting these stories is one of the methods of cultural anthropology. Anthropologists analyze narratives to identify aspects of cultural identity, social values, moral themes, people's practices and attitudes, and artistic principles and motifs.

Traditional narratives also may be dramatic renditions of historical events. The accuracy of chronologies and events may be uncertain, but **oral traditions** like the story of Coyote and Wishpoosh have validity as artifacts of culture and experience. In 1997, for example, the Supreme Court of Canada ruled in a land claims case brought by the Gitksan, an indigenous people of British Columbia, that oral traditions have validity as legal testimony and as records of the past. This chapter further explores the theories and methods involved in the anthropological interpretation of culture.

ANTHROPOLOGY AND THE EXPLANATION OF CULTURAL DIVERSITY

Although the field of anthropology as an academic discipline is only slightly more than a century old, its intellectual roots in Europe go back much farther. Although people everywhere may note cultural differences between themselves and others, anthropology has its roots in the exploration and colonial expansions that originated in Europe in the fifteenth and sixteenth centuries. Explorers, traders, and missionaries, bent on their far-flung journeys of discovery and conquest, often wrote about and commented on the differences they observed in the ways of life of the peoples they encountered.

Europeans wrote many journals, diaries, letters, and memoirs during the first centuries of colonization in North and South America, Africa, Asia, and the Pacific. Although many writers were biased and ethnocentric, they nevertheless often left detailed observations of cultures at the time of contact. For example, Jesuit missionaries wrote detailed accounts about working in North America in the seventeenth century. These men were better educated than most of the explorers and adventurers who preceded and followed them. They were familiar with the scholarly literary and philosophical works of their age. Although critical of many of the practices they described, the Jesuits often were astute observers and recorders. They sometimes judged native customs and attitudes to be superior to the French, for example, such as the people's rules for hospitality and generosity and their relatively harmonious, noncompetitive

? *What are some oral traditions from your cultural group (such as your family) that you could analyze from an anthropological perspective?*

narratives
Stories and myths that dramatize actual memories or events in symbolic form consistent with cultural practices of storytelling.

oral traditions
Cultural narratives that have validity as artifacts of culture and experience.

community life. In some ways, these missionaries were like anthropologists, both observers and participants in others' lifeways.

The goal of anthropology as a discipline is to record and account for the great diversity in human cultures. But today there is diversity in anthropology as well, as anthropologists choose different conceptual frameworks to achieve their goals. This section explores a number of perspectives that have been proposed to account for similarities and differences in human societies. These perspectives differ in their focus and in the kinds of theories that they offer to explain human behavior and cultural diversity. A cultural theory is one that attempts to formulate explanations that help us understand why particular practices originate and how they are developed and maintained in particular populations. From an understanding of cultural diversity, some anthropologists also propose theories that can help explain universal trends and processes.

Another early colonial observer in the Western Hemisphere was the Dominican missionary Bartolemé de las Casas, a sixteenth-century scholar, historian, and human rights advocate who observed Native Americans living in traditional and colonial conditions. His history of the Spanish conquest of Mexico and descriptions of the effects of colonial life on Native Americans led to humanitarian social reforms.

Some approaches in anthropology that were developed in the nineteenth and early twentieth centuries, such as evolutionism, have been discarded as inadequate or incomplete, either because they were unscientific and based on fragmentary and poorly understood data or because they were based on social attitudes and prejudices that were then prevalent. Nevertheless, the works of some early anthropologists continue to inform aspects of modern inquiry.

Evolutionism

Eighteenth-century European social philosophers relied on the writings of sixteenth- and seventeenth-century observers in their thinking about human cultural diversity. Some social philosophers took a comparative evolutionary perspective, and understood cultural diversity from the point of view of human "progress." During the Enlightenment, scholars focused on finding rational, reasoned, and scientific explanations for human differences. They understood that people adapt to their social environments and historical conditions as well as to their physical surroundings. The goal of this adaptation was seen as progress and the possibility of betterment, both in a person's life and in a society as a whole. Enlightenment philosophers began to look for what they considered evolutionary trends in the development of human societies. Thus, in **evolutionism,** human differences could be accounted for by different rates of progress, leading to different levels of achievement. Various hypotheses were put forward, demonstrating a progression from stages of primitive culture to civilization. Although these schemes were ethnocentric, using middle-class European culture as a measure of progress, they laid the foundation for nineteenth-century anthropological thinking about sociocultural evolution.

Throughout the nineteenth century, European and American scholars concentrated on developing and refining comparative evolutionary approaches toward understanding the similarities and differences among cultures. The Englishmen Herbert Spencer (1877) and Edward Tylor (1871) and the American Lewis Henry Morgan (1877) proposed models outlining stages of cultural development from the earliest human societies to late nineteenth-century European culture. Both Morgan and Spencer focused on understanding how cultures are integrated and systematized and how the various features of one culture indicate an evolutionary status in comparison with other cultures. For example, Morgan proposed three stages of cultural evolution: savagery, in which people subsist on wild plants and animals; barbarism, in which people start to use agriculture; and civilization, which begins with the invention of writing. Spencer, a social Darwinist, believed that European influence or domination over other peoples was the natural result of evolutionary progress toward human perfection.

evolutionism
View held by early social philosophers that human differences can be accounted for by different rates of progress, leading to different levels of cultural achievement.

The adventures and misadventures of anthropologists living alone in "primitive" conditions with "uncivilized" peoples gave the new discipline romantic overtones that persist to this day. The public was astonished by Margaret Mead's reports about growing up in Samoa and living among the Manus of New Guinea. Other students of Franz Boas—Alfred Kroeber among the Zuni, Julian Steward among the Shoshoni, Robert Lowie among the Crow, and others—told the stories of the native peoples of California and the Great Plains.

Using eighteenth- and nineteenth-century ideas and data, sources that varied widely in their reliability and accuracy, early anthropologists nevertheless advanced the study of human societies by proposing a more thorough analysis of cultural features and their significance for the development of social forms. For example, Morgan first explained the kinship systems of tribes making up the Iroquois Confederacy and the links between a kinship system and the economic system, family organization, and social structure.

Empiricism

Anthropology began to take modern form as a discipline in the late nineteenth and early twentieth centuries with the work of the German-born American Franz Boas (1896), the Polish-born British Bronislaw Malinowski (1922), and several others. In this period, fieldwork, rather than "armchair philosophy," became central to the pursuit of knowledge about human cultures. That is, anthropology came to be seen as a scientific inquiry into facts that can be observed directly.

Boas began his career in Germany as a geographer, but on a trip to the Arctic in 1883 to investigate Arctic waters, he became interested in the indigenous peoples and their cultures. He spent a year living with the Inuit, deepening his appreciation of cultural traits and his conviction that only by living with other people can one truly understand cultural differences. In 1886, Boas traveled to British Columbia to learn about Bella Coola (Nuxalk) culture, and two years later he immigrated to the United States. While studying the Kwakiutl of the Pacific Northwest and their ceremonial life, he became the major figure and driving force in the development of American anthropology. At Columbia University, his students included Ruth Benedict and Margaret Mead, who later developed a focus on culture and personality development. Boas trained many of the most prominent anthropologists of his and the next generation, sending them into the field to collect and archive meticulous data about many different cultures.

Boas consistently stressed the need for **empiricism,** the practice of conducting studies based on direct observation and objective description. He also introduced the concept of cultural relativism, and believed that each way of life is a unique adaptation to particular historical conditions, a view that critics referred to as "historical particularism." Boas refuted the earlier stages of cultural evolution theory, criticizing the concept as being essentially ethnocentric and racist. According to Boas, cultures should be understood and evaluated in their own terms, not in terms of the cultural practices, beliefs, and values of the observer. In his own work and that of his students, Boas stressed the importance of learning the native languages in order to understand the people's attitudes and beliefs literally in their own terms.

Boas also stressed that similarities and differences should be understood as outcomes of the functions and meanings of cultural traits within a society. He pointed out that the same traits can have different meanings in different cultures. Polygamy, or plural marriage, for example, may occur for different reasons in different societies depending on the cultural context. Marriage rules allowing men to take more than one wife, for instance, may function to signal a man's comparative wealth, power, and prestige; to relieve women of household burdens by providing additional labor; or, in societies where women outnumber men, to ensure that all women can have husbands.

Functionalism

Functionalism, or the study of the social functions of cultural traits, was a hallmark of the research of Bronislaw Malinowski, whose work especially influenced British social

empiricism
The practice of conducting studies through direct observation and objective description.

functionalism
View that cultural traits have social functions that contribute to the smooth operation of the whole society.

anthropology. Malinowski believed that the social, economic, and political structures of societies were organized to satisfy human needs and that people's diverse institutions and practices have specific functions that address those needs. According to Malinowski, men and women living together in a community develop an "invisible network of social bonds" made up of shared values, attitudes, and practices that "integrate the group into a whole" (1922). All cultural behaviors and artifacts can be explained by understanding their role in maintaining this whole.

Like Boas, Malinowski was dedicated to fieldwork. Malinowski lived with the Trobriand Islanders of the western Pacific in Melanesia, immersing himself in Trobriand culture and language. He stressed the importance of anthropologists learning the native language of the people they study, because people express their values and attitudes through their language. Malinowski used functionalism to explain his observations of Trobriand life. Students of Malinowski, such as A. R. Radcliffe-Brown and others, applied functionalist interpretations to field data collected among other Pacific Islanders, Africans, and Australian Aborigines. These interpretations are now sometimes criticized for overemphasizing functional stability rather than acknowledging societal change as an ongoing, continuous process.

? *If you were a functionalist how would you argue that even negative practices, such as antisocial behavior, can have positive functions for society as a whole?*

Modern Theoretical Perspectives: An Overview

Of the current emphases in anthropological theory, one approach is to study culture from a materialist perspective, which places technological and economic adaptations at the center of cultural diversity. Another perspective analyzes cultures from a structuralist perspective, emphasizing the role of social structures in fulfilling human needs and integrating social systems. A variation of the structuralist perspective stresses the role of ideas and habits of mind as the sources of diversity. A third perspective places status and power relations at the center of diversity, focusing on how it operates within societies and between societies in a worldwide system of dominance and subordination, power, and influence. And a fourth perspective is interpretive, with an emphasis on the meanings that people communicate through symbols. Table 3.1 summarizes some of the modern perspectives in anthropological theory.

Table 3.1 EXPLAINING CULTURAL DIVERSITY

Materialist Perspectives Marvin Harris	Emphasizes the centrality of environmental adaptation, technology, and methods of acquiring or producing food in the development of culture.
Cultural Ecology	Cultural traits related to the satisfaction of basic human needs form a cultural core that is directly influenced by the physical environment.
Cultural Materialism	All aspects of a society's culture are derived from its economic foundation.
Structuralist Perspectives Claude Lévi-Strauss	Cultural diversity stems from differences in the forms by which people express universal meanings. These forms define and structure their lives and experiences and may serve universal social functions.
Interpretive Perspectives Clifford Geertz	Culture is a unique system of symbols with multiple layers of meaning. Through their behavior, people act out those meanings and communicate them to one another.
Conflict Perspectives	Culture is an expression of power relations within a society and between societies. Distributions of power are linked to distributions of wealth and status and affect gender relations as well as processes such as colonialism.

materialist perspectives
Explanations of cultural differences that emphasize environmental adaptation, technologies, and methods of acquiring or producing food.

cultural ecology
Field that studies cultures as dynamic wholes based on the satisfaction of human needs through cultural behaviors.

cultural materialism
Explanations of cultural differences as the results of cultural adaptations through economic production.

emic
Subjective, based on insiders' views, as in explanations people have for their own cultural behavior.

etic
Objective, based on outsiders' views, as in explanations of people's behavior by anthropologists or other observers.

Materialist Perspectives

Materialist perspectives emphasize environmental adaptation, technologies, and methods of acquiring or producing food in the development of culture. Humans, and possibly other higher primates, adapt to their environments to some extent through culture. Humans address the scarcity of resources by developing methods of extracting, exploiting, storing, and processing whatever foods are available. As you read in Chapter 1, these behaviors, and the satisfaction of other human needs, form a cultural core from which other aspects of society develop and are integrated into a cultural whole. This analytic and explanatory focus in anthropology is called **cultural ecology,** a term introduced by anthropologist Julian Steward in the 1930s. In societies that depend directly on their environment, ecological factors, such as resources, climate, and topography, have more pervasive effects on cultural development than in societies where people can control and modify their immediate environment.

Another materialist perspective centering on cultural adaptations through economic production is referred to as **cultural materialism,** developed by anthropologist Marvin Harris (1979). This approach, influenced by the economic views of Karl Marx, gives greatest importance to economic systems and economic relations in the development of culture. In this view, cultural traits can be explained as a response to some economic necessity or benefit. Similarly, people need to organize work in order to produce and exchange foods, other goods, and services. From this basic organization, other features of culture follow. For example, to ensure adequate supplies of resources, people must regulate the size of their communities, increasing or decreasing population growth depending on resource availability. People also must develop methods of arriving at group decisions and controlling behavior to conform to those decisions. Basic economic behaviors and relationships influence how these traits are developed. In other words, what people do ultimately shapes what they believe, rather than the other way around.

Cultural materialism makes a distinction between *subjective* explanations for cultural behavior that are offered by the people engaged in that behavior (**emic** views) and *objective* explanations for cultural behavior that are given by anthropologists or other observers (**etic** views). Cultural materialists claim that people usually are not aware of the underlying adaptive reasons for their actions. Thus, researchers look for explanations based on observations of people's behavior and other objective criteria developed from an understanding of broad cultural and historical processes.

In his popular book *Cows, Pigs, Wars and Witches: The Riddles of Culture* (1974), Harris contrasted emic and etic explanations of why Hindus in India do not eat or even kill cows. According to an emic analysis, Hindus do not kill cows because cows are sacred animals, symbolic of "everything that is alive." This is an explanation that a Hindu believer might give. In an etic analysis, however, the meaning of the sacredness of cows has to be analyzed in the context of the economic needs of farmers in India. Harris concluded that cattle are "sacred" in order to protect them from slaughter, because they are vital to the continuation of Indian farming practices. Thus, to understand the origin and continuation of a practice, it must be analyzed in the structural and historical context of its occurrence in a particular society.

From the perspective of cultural materialism, cattle are not slaughtered for food in India because they are too important for agriculture. Cattle are used as draft animals to pull plows in an unmechanized farming system. In addition, their dung is used for fuel in cooking and heating houses. Dung mixed with water makes a paste used in house floors. Cattle are, therefore, more valuable to Indian farmers alive than dead.

Structuralist Perspectives

Taking a different turn in the analysis of culture, some anthropologists emphasize the centrality of forms and structure in the expression of culture, called

structuralism. For example, the French scholar Claude Lévi-Strauss used theories from structural linguistics (Saussure, 1916) to analyze symbolic expressions of culture in terms of their structures or patterns in addition to their meanings. His goal was to identify the underlying pattern that all the expressions have in common or the underlying code on which all the expressions are based. Cultures could then be understood in terms of pattern variance.

Lévi-Strauss was interested in explaining why myths from different cultures around the world seem so similar. Treating mythology as a form of language or symbolic communication, he proposed a "principle of opposition" that all myths share, much like all novels have a protagonist who engages in some kind of struggle that is somehow resolved. In mythology, heroic struggles involve a contest between opposites, especially between various forms of good and evil, with or without third-party mediation. Myths can be told and retold with elaborations, but the basic structure always stays the same. In this case, understanding cultural diversity would involve identifying the particular hero, type of struggle, type of mediation, if any, and type of outcome in each case.

Lévi-Strauss thus essentially developed a theory of mind, based on structural analysis, to explain cultural differences as variations in basic themes of universal human thinking. He also applied this method to the study of kinship (1949). He was interested in the fact that kinship structures are limited in the number of basic types and are strongly supported by myths and taboos. He looked for a basic unit of kinship that could explain all the variations. For any society requiring a man to marry outside his own hereditary line, for example, Lévi-Strauss identified a cluster of four roles—brother, sister, father, son. These roles structure the exchanges that maintain the circulation of women in the society and establish cooperative relationships or alliances among kin groups. He proposed that marriage is the means through which people, and men in particular, form alliances that promote social cohesion and stability. Marriages forge alliances through a reciprocal exchange between one group that gives women as wives to another group, receiving gifts in return. This sets up patterned relationships between wife givers and wife receivers that over time establish enduring bonds between the groups. Chapters 8 and 9 further explore these topics. Understanding cultural diversity in this case would involve identifying the different marriage rules, kin roles, forms of exchanges, and forms of alliances. Although Lévi-Strauss is criticized for his focus on men as the primary social actors in these relationships, the perspective of structuralism remains useful today.

Interpretive Anthropology

In contrast to structural–functional analyses, some anthropologists focus on culture as meanings rather than as forms and functions. American anthropologist Clifford Geertz (1973), for example, focuses on mental and cognitive processes in the development and transmission of culture. This kind of analysis, sometimes called **interpretive anthropology,** stresses the multilayered symbolic meanings of people's actions. From this perspective, cultural behavior is the acting out of those meanings.

Geertz developed his theory while working among the Javanese. According to Geertz, "Man is an animal suspended in webs of significance he himself has spun; I take culture to be those webs, and the analysis of it to be therefore not an experimental science in search of law but an interpretative one in search of meaning" (1973:4–5). Geertz has called culture an "acted document" that is essentially public and therefore observable and analyzable. Doing ethnography, then, is like trying to read or construct a reading from a manuscript. To understand culture, interpretive anthropologists pay close attention to people's expressions of values, attitudes, meanings, intentions, and the felt importance of their actions (1973:9–10). As the collective property of a group, these meanings define cultural differences among groups.

Conflict Perspectives and the Analysis of Culture and Power

Conflict perspectives focus on social problems or social issues in societies, especially those that arise as a result of the distribution of power among groups or social categories.

structuralism
View that cultural differences can be explained by differences in forms or conceptual categories rather than in meanings.

interpretive anthropology
View that cultural differences can be understood as complex webs of meaning rather than through forms.

conflict perspectives
Understanding cultural differences as a consequence of conflict in the interests and goals of various groups within a society and focusing on issues of power and resistance.

Anthropologist Eleanor Leacock's (1981) pioneering work on the Montagnais and Naskapi in eastern Québec and Labrador pointed to the role of colonial government agents in undermining indigenous culture. These agents exerted both direct and indirect pressure on native peoples to change their practices and attitudes, including gender roles and patterns of leadership.

Much of this analysis focuses on the relationship between culture and various forms of social, economic, and political power. Its adherents often use a Marxist framework to analyze how capitalist institutions penetrate and transform indigenous cultures to suit their own needs.

One important concern in the analysis of power is the issue of gender, which also plays a role in the field of anthropology. Many anthropological writings (by both male and female anthropologists) have a conceptual male bias. This bias often results in the assumption that male dominance exists (and has existed) in all societies. Reconstructions of indigenous social life prior to European contact tell a different story, however, about the roles of men and women. Evidence indicates that in many societies, especially in small communities relying on a hunting and gathering economy, gender relations were often essentially equal, certainly more equal than after European conquest or colonization led to conformity to a European cultural model. This conformity also led to patterns of leadership and decision-making procedures in small-scale societies that were confronted by and overwhelmed by European powers. Attitudes about communal and family control of land were undermined and altered as notions of private property and individual control of resources became the norm, in keeping with European economic systems. Students of power and colonial control often use conflict perspectives, feminist perspectives, or Marxist frameworks to analyze how indigenous cultures have been transformed.

REVIEW

Anthropology is a relatively new discipline; however, some missionaries, explorers, and colonists observing other cultures made accurate accounts. Observers also have recorded narratives and oral traditions of other peoples. Evolutionism influenced nineteenth-century works by Herbert Spencer, Edward Tylor, and Lewis Henry Morgan. Two important figures in early twentieth-century anthropology are Franz Boas, who called for an anthropology based on cultural relativism and empiricism, and Bronislaw Malinowski, who explained cultural traits from the perspective of functionalism. Anthropologists use several other perspectives to describe and explain cultural differences, depending on their intellectual preferences. They may use a materialist perspective (either cultural ecology or cultural materialism), structuralist perspectives and symbolic analyses, or conflict perspectives involving the analysis of culture and power. Interpretive anthropology focuses on the interconnectivity, subjectivity, and multiplicity of cultural meanings.

ETHNOGRAPHY AND FIELDWORK

Since the pioneering work of anthropologists in the early twentieth century, **fieldwork**—living with the group under study—remains a hallmark of modern anthropological methods. In the past, most anthropologists worked in societies different than their own, but today many work in their own countries and some even in their own communities. In addition, now as in the past, some anthropologists focus on secondary analyses of existing data rather than gathering primary data. Two types of studies based on secondary sources are comparisons using databases and ethnologies based on historical documents.

Cross-Cultural Comparisons

In 1949, anthropologists at Yale University founded the Human Relations Area Files (HRAF) to gather in one database and codify all the known cultural facts and details about the world's peoples for purposes of comparison and contrast. Recall from Chapter 1 that anthropologists use the comparative method in understanding similarities and differences among human cultures. HRAF data consist of facts extracted from

fieldwork
In anthropology, living and interacting with the people or group under study.

Culture Change

USES OF ETHNOHISTORY IN AUSTRALIA

A field more concerned with causal relationships in culture change than with comparisons is **ethnohistory,** the reconstruction and interpretation of the history of indigenous peoples from their point of view as well as the points of view of outside observers. A survey of ethnohistory usually is part of the preparation for conducting fieldwork. Thus, some anthropological work takes place in libraries and archives containing historical records that help researchers learn about past conditions and events relevant to understanding the present lives of the people they are studying.

Ethnohistorians analyze the processes stemming from historical events and their consequences for changes in indigenous culture. A common focus is the impact of colonialism and conquest on the cultures of colonized peoples. Australian ethnohistorians, for example, piece together the processes of transformation in the lives of Aborigines before and after the arrival of Europeans on the continent. They base their studies on documents describing Europeans' experiences and the policies carried out by agents of change, such as explorers, missionaries, traders, settlers, and government officials. Maps, photographs, biographies, and oral traditions are other sources of data for ethnohistorians in understanding change.

Ethnohistorians also document how societies invent and reinvent themselves and their cultures in response to internal and external forces. For example, the Aboriginal Family History Project of the South Australia Museum researches Aboriginal genealogies and associated community histories. They use archival source material collected by museum anthropologists, ethnographers, and historians over the past century, but in particular the records of Norman Tindale and Joseph Birdsell, early twentieth-century anthropologists who collected data on Australian Aborigines. The museum's collection includes thousands of photos taken at Aboriginal sites around Australia.

Among many other Australian ethnohistory databases is the record of European

Australian Aborigines are reinventing themselves today. You can find Internet communities run by and for confederated Aboriginal groups intent on preserving sacred lands, and you can read a formal government apology for past colonial atrocities against the native peoples of Australia.

contacts with the Awaba Aborigines of the Lake Macquarie region of Australia, housed at the University of Newcastle. Records include hundreds of documents about the Awabakal people and language, prepared by various local scholars, writers, and community leaders. Included is a translation of The Gospel of St. Mark in Awabakal, from a manuscript prepared in 1837 by the Lake Macquarie missionary L. E. Threlkeld. Other documents describe the genocide of Aborigines by Europeans and the forced assimilation of survivors, along with the struggles of present-day Australians as they try to gain recognition of their claims to land, to improve their economic conditions, and to preserve elements of their traditional culture.

ethnohistory
Field of study for reconstructing and interpreting the history of indigenous peoples from their point of view as well as the points of view of ethnohistorians.

cross-cultural comparisons
Means of understanding cultural differences and similarities through data analysis rather than direct observation.

ethnographies written by anthropologists doing fieldwork in all parts of the world. The collection is divided into five world areas: Africa, Asia, North America, South America, and Oceania. Hundreds of cultural features and practices are coded and cross-referenced for making **cross-cultural comparisons.** Researchers use the HRAF data to find statistical correlations among certain cultural features or to test hypotheses about what cultural facts or forms are likely to be found in association with other facts or forms.

For example, a study by Melvin Ember and Carol Ember (1996) used HRAF data to propose hypotheses about the cultural settings in which couples choose to live near the family of the husband after marriage in contrast to when couples choose to live near the wife's family. Another HRAF-based study by the Embers (1996) showed a strong correlation among different kinds of violence in societies. Societies that frequently engage in warfare also are more likely to tolerate high levels of violence in other social contexts, such as murder, rape, assault, and domestic abuse.

Although large-scale comparative studies like the Embers' can uncover associations among cultural traits, it is difficult to compare data that have been collected from numerous ethnographies and articles written by different researchers. That is, the data may not be comparable. In addition, when gleaned from ethnographies, practices and traits are taken out of their full cultural and historical contexts, which also may make them difficult to compare. Another danger in comparative studies is imputing causality. That is, although certain traits may appear in association, it may not be clear whether they are causally related or whether one trait causes or is an effect of another.

Ethnographic Fieldwork

Much of the work of anthropology consists of collecting and analyzing information about culture—that is, people's activities, beliefs, and attitudes. As you read in Chapter 1, the reports that result from doing cultural anthropology are called *ethnography* (from the Greek word *ethnos*, meaning "people" or "a division of people"). The methods used in ethnographic work obviously depend on the kind of data required. Since cultural anthropology is concerned with the complex study of living cultures, anthropologists need to obtain many different kinds of information in many

GLOBALIZATION

Imagine that your e-mails or blogs are among the records on which an ethnohistory of Internet culture is based. What kinds of information would your records provide? How could your records be interpreted to explain changes in Internet culture? How could your records help to document the changes we call globalization?

Today, much anthropological fieldwork takes place in large-scale societies, often focused on a village or subcultural group within the larger nation. Today anthropologists realize that the older view, which saw small, indigenous communities as isolated and timeless, was a distortion and failed to appreciate the complexity of people's lives and their ties to other peoples. Here Elisha Renne (right) confers with University of Ibadan (Nigeria) professors Dr. Babatunde Agbaje-Williams and Dr. Aderonke Adesanya.

different kinds of settings. Fieldwork is usually a part of an anthropologist's training, a rite of passage that most graduate students go through as they complete their training and establish themselves in the discipline. Anthropologists' initial fieldwork experiences often set the framework in which their research interests develop and continue throughout their careers. Anthropologists traditionally chose research problems and sites in foreign countries. This is still a common approach, but today many anthropologists work in their own countries, even in their own communities.

Doing Fieldwork

Fieldwork involves a complex process of observing and participating in another culture. As you read in Chapter 1, participant observation is at the core of the fieldwork experience. Anthropologists both observe the activities taking place in the community and participate in them as much as possible and as appropriate. Anthropologists usually live in the community that they are studying, sometimes renting a house or a room in someone else's dwelling. Fieldwork, then, is an ongoing, multifaceted research experience.

Choosing a Problem and Site.   Anthropologists begin by choosing a research problem and then where to conduct their study. Most anthropologists do their first research project when they are graduate students. Their interest in a particular subject may develop from an especially exciting course or from an especially stimulating teacher. Some anthropologists have long-standing interests in a particular country or community. Others choose a research site that best suits their theoretical or topical interests.

Obtaining Funding.   Fieldwork is often costly, especially if it involves travel to another country and residence far from home for an extended period of time. Most graduate students embarking on their first field trip are advised to plan to be on site for about one year. This allows observations during a full annual cycle of economic, social, and ritual activities. Longer field stays are always beneficial but may not be possible for lack of funding. Public and private agencies and research institutions are potential grantors of funds for field studies.

Doing Preliminary Research.   Before embarking on the fieldwork trip, researchers gather as much information about their subject of study as they can in order to situate their own project within the discipline. They read what other anthropologists have written about the topic, attempting to understand the data and the theoretical approaches that others have used in analyzing the problem. They also gather information about their chosen place of study. To prepare themselves for entering a foreign country or community, they will want to know as much as they can about the culture, the history, the conditions, and significant current events of that region, as well as the rules for entering and residing in the country. Anthropologists also study the language of the country so that they can communicate directly with the residents. Before setting out for the site, anthropologists often make contact with local people to make sure that their presence in the community will be acceptable.

Arrival and Culture Shock.   After arriving at the field site, anthropologists often experience **culture shock**—the feeling of being out of place in unfamiliar surroundings, like losing one's cultural bearings. In the field, researchers must immediately learn new customs, new faces, new foods and ways of living, and a new language and ways of communicating. This learning is intense, because, unlike tourists, anthropologists are immersing themselves in a new way of life in which they will participate. Often, it is the unstated rules of decorum and etiquette that are most easily, and unknowingly, violated. An anthropologist needs to be keenly observant, not only of other people's activities but also paying attention to the way other people react. By being sensitive to people's reactions, anthropologists can learn much about attitudes, values, and norms. Their experiences also afford them new insights into their own culture, their own behavior, and their own beliefs. Nevertheless, doing fieldwork has emotional ups and downs. At the beginning an anthropologist may have feelings of uncertainty or fear and loneliness as he or she seeks acceptance and cooperation.

culture shock
Feeling an anthropologist may have at the start of fieldwork of being out of place in unfamiliar surroundings.

? *Have you ever experienced culture shock? What was the situation? How did you respond to it?*

In Their Own Voices

Notes from the Field in Morocco

In this excerpt, a member of the "tribe" of anthropologists re-flects on his work in the field and his understanding that from the people's point of view, he is the "Other." In his book, Reflections on Fieldwork in Morocco, *Paul Rabinow writes about his gradual immersion into the village of Sidi Lahcen, his acceptance by the people in the community, and his under-standing of the process of cultural encounters fundamental to the fieldwork experience.*

After the first several months, my work in Sidi Lahcen was more painstakingly fragmentary and less immediately gratifying. During long, uneventful stretches I struggled with the increasingly imperative need to begin synthesizing my material, formulating specific questions, and searching for ways to answer them.

In the months which followed, I spent a great many hours merely wandering around the village and its fields, engaging in casual talk while sitting around the stores, setting up interviews, waiting for informants, and just being bored. My Arabic was considerably better by this time. I tried to maintain a regular work schedule with Malik [one of Rabinow's key consultants] and several other villagers, but this proved difficult. One particularly trying afternoon when I was cajoling Malik into discussing the local political activity against the French, he became exasperated with my persistent questions and said I was squeezing him like an olive press: if you squeeze too hard, you get the pulp but not the best oil.

After months of consistently self-absorbing activity, I knew I had passed a threshold of acceptance. Slowly and sporadically, I was moving toward the kind of understanding I was seeking. Thus the further along

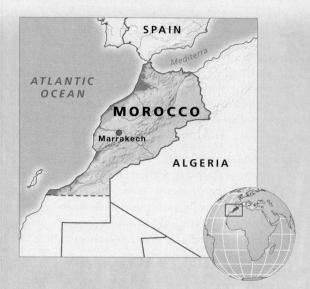

I was, the more I questioned myself as to the state of the data. Particularly toward the end of the stay, I might have to search for weeks for someone who had the knowledge of a specific subject and the willingness to discuss it with me. If I failed to find such a person and convince him to work with me, I was out of luck. There would be a gap and there was no way to fill it back in Chicago. I awoke each morning with the sense that the material was there if only I could figure out a way to get at it. But as Malik put it, there was only one door open to me—patience, only patience. . . .

Driss ben Mohammed, a jovial, portly, and even-tempered young man, had consistently refused to work as an informant. Over the course of my stay we had come to know each other casually, as time permitted, almost accidentally. Gradually, a certain trust had flowered between

Choosing a Place to Live. Once on site, an anthropologist obtains a place of resi-dence, arranging to live in or near a household or renting a dwelling. Living in a household has the advantage of proximity to people through family networks and rou-tine participation in household and community events. Of course, the anthropologist needs to find someone willing to be a host, sometimes a difficult task. A disadvantage to staying with a family, however, is that members of a household may try to ally them-selves with the anthropologist against the interests of others in the community or may try to involve the anthropologist on their side in local social and political networks. In many field locations, anthropologists may have high status among the people they study. In poor and marginalized communities, they may be perceived as rich and powerful. A challenge of fieldwork, then, is to establish good relations without allow-ing people to use a relationship to gain benefits or advantages over others in the community. Thus, while friendships may develop between an anthropologist and the us. At its root, I think, was an awareness of our differences and a mutual respect.

Ben Mohammed was not afraid of me (as many other villagers were), nor did he have hesitations about associating with Europeans (although he had had almost no personal contact with them), nor did he seek to profit from my presence (he refused most gifts). Simply, he was my host and treated me with the respect which is supposed to be reserved for a guest, even one who stayed as long as I did.

As time wore on and my friendship with ben Mohammed deepened, I was learning more and more from him. During the last months of fieldwork, when he was home from school and we could spend many of the hot hours together, the field experience, now nearing its completion, reached a new emotional and intellectual depth. Casually, without plan or schedule, just walking around the fields, ripe with grain or muddy from the irrigation water in the truck gardens, we had a meandering series of conversations. Ben Mohammed's initial refusal of informant status set up the possibility of another type of communication. But clearly our communication would not have been possible without those more regularized and disciplined relationships I had had with others. Partly in reaction to the professional situation, we had slipped into a more unguarded and relaxed course over the months. . . .

From Paul Rabinow, *Reflections on Fieldwork in Morocco.* Copyright © 1977 The Regents of the University of California. Reprinted by permission.

CRITICAL THINKING QUESTIONS

What parts of this account reveal an anthropologist reporting observations? What parts reveal an individual responding to personal experience? Why are both parts necessary in ethnographic fieldwork?

"Culture is interpretation. The 'facts' of anthropology, the material which the anthropologist has gone to the field to find, are already themselves interpretations. . . . The fact that all cultural facts are interpretations, and multivocal ones at that, is true both for the anthropologist and for his informant, the Other with whom he works. His informant (and the word is accurate) must interpret his own culture and that of the anthropologist. The same holds for the anthropologist. Both live in rich, partially integrated, ongoing life worlds. They are, however, not the same. Nor is there any mechanical and easy means of translation from one set of experiences to the other. That problem and the process of translation, therefore, become one of the central arts and crucial tasks of fieldwork. . . . That the communication was often painstaking and partial is a central theme. That it was not totally opaque is an equally important theme. It is the dialectic between these poles, ever repeated, never quite the same, which constitutes fieldwork."

(From Paul Rabinow, Reflections on Fieldwork in Morocco, *pp. 150–151, 155.)*

people in the community, the researcher needs to remain nonpartisan in village conflicts, disputes, and controversies.

Working in an Unfamiliar Language.   As fieldwork begins, the anthropologist usually hires an interpreter unless he or she is fluent in the local language. Learning the field language is clearly desirable, and even necessary, if the anthropologist truly wants to learn what kinds of meanings people ascribe to their own behavior. Working through translation is very different from speaking directly to the people. Many nuances of meaning and attitudes that are conveyed in language are lost in translation regardless of the interpreter's skill.

Gathering Data.   Once they are established, anthropologists often survey their village or community or other field site. They may draw a map, situating the site within its local environment and the houses, other structures, farm fields, open spaces, or other areas where people congregate and socialize. A social survey may include information about the composition of households and the relationships between members of nearby houses. From these data, the anthropologist learns about family ties and neighborhood networks. Anthropologists sometimes hire assistants to help with these tasks. If the assistant comes from the village, she or he can provide a personal connection to other people and help broaden the anthropologist's social network.

Gathering data includes interviewing members of the community. Traditional anthropological methodology includes collecting data concerning kinship, that is, how people trace relationships and descent from generation to generation and among members of the same generation. Combining genealogical information with residence histories that record how long people have resided in which houses allows the anthropologist to learn about systems of relationships, people's geographic mobility, and intercommunity relations. It is also traditional to gather data about the ways that people obtain their food, earn a living, and provide themselves and others with goods and services. Economic and social networks may link groups and societies through trade, intermarriage, and friendships.

The researcher also gathers data through formal interviews and by attending meetings, informal gatherings, religious activities, and other community events. Anthropologists try to participate as much as possible to the extent that their presence is acceptable to members of the community. Anthropologists need to be sensitive to villagers' attitudes about an outsider's participation in community life. Outsiders may be welcome in some settings but not in others, particularly in sacred or secret activities or in meetings where controversial issues are discussed. Women anthropologists might find their access to certain men's activities limited, and men anthropologists might likewise find their access to certain women's activities restricted. Anthropologists usually want to interview community political officials, religious functionaries, teachers, and doctors for certain kinds of information. It is important, however, not to become over-reliant on local authorities, in order to avoid interpretation of village life from the perspective of the local elite. Despite increasing involvement with villagers, researchers usually remain outsiders, except sometimes for those who are themselves indigenous or native to the group they are studying. Some of the best ethnographic accounts are written by native anthropologists.

After living in the field for an extended period of time and becoming comfortable in a different culture, anthropologists often go through a period of culture shock after they leave the field, not unlike the culture shock they felt when they first entered the site. When they return to their own neighborhoods, they may see the behavior of their friends and relatives in a new light, with new eyes. For awhile they are the outside observers, now observing their own culture, once so familiar and taken for granted. Of course, in a short time, they are readily integrated into their own daily lives. But the experience of living with other people in another society has profound and lasting meaning. And for many, it gives them new insights into their own behavior and their own beliefs.

Interpreting and Reporting Data. During and after fieldwork, anthropologists reflect on their interactions and the data they have collected. New research questions may arise, new opportunities for observation and participation may present themselves, and new understandings of what has happened may be revealed. Field notes are rewritten as ethnographic accounts and papers, which are published as books and journal articles and presented at professional meetings. Sharing the results of research is important in a community of scholars and often leads to new research questions to answer. Anthropological reports are framed within the analytic and theoretical perspectives of the researcher. Other anthropologists may undertake reanalyses of data, focusing on additional questions and employing different theoretical frameworks. And although fieldwork is a fundamental experience and research method in anthropology, some anthropologists choose instead to focus on archival and historical materials. All of these various works combine to enrich the discipline.

GLOBALIZATION

The communities in which anthropologists conduct fieldwork are linked to other communities, the nation, and other nations through local, regional, national, and transnational systems of exchange and the global market economy. A farm family in India, for example, might sell produce and handicrafts in regional markets that link ultimately to international export and import markets. Anthropologists must trace these kinds of connections and understand their impacts on people's daily lives.

? *How could you apply each of the steps described in this section in a fieldwork situation close to home?*

Anthropological Research in Large-Scale Societies

When anthropologists conduct research in large-scale societies, they use many of the same data-collection techniques that they use in small-scale societies. Rarely, however, do they study a whole community. Instead, they investigate a specific topic within a defined subculture or group. For example, some researchers specialize in **urban anthropology,** a field that focuses on studying the lives of people living in cities or urban neighborhoods. Urban anthropologists may analyze a neighborhood association, a particular occupational group, a school setting, a religious network, a health care delivery system, or a senior citizen center. The people in these groups may or may not reside near each other, but they interact frequently in particular areas of their lives.

In conducting this kind of research, anthropologists use data-gathering techniques similar to those used by sociologists and other researchers, including survey research. **Survey research** involves the use of formal questionnaires, administered to a random sample of subjects, to elicit social data such as occupation, income, level of education, marital status, participation in clubs and associations, political and religious affiliations, size of household, number of computers in the home, and so on. Questionnaires also elicit information about people's attitudes, values, and practices, which are then analyzed in terms of the social data. Survey data provide information about conditions and trends in the community under study, including socioeconomic conditions, social participation, social norms, people's attitudes and opinions, and cultural practices. In these studies data analysis can emphasize statistical correlations to answer a particular research question or narrative descriptions to understand the life of the group or community as a whole.

Anthropologists also use participant observation in urban settings. Consider, for example, the work of urban anthropologist Judith Freidenberg (2000), who studied elderly Puerto Ricans in New York City's El Barrio (a predominantly Hispanic neighborhood on the Upper East Side of Manhattan). Freidenberg consulted archival and historical records on immigration from Puerto Rico, neighborhood residency, and age and gender distribution of the Puerto Rican community in New York in order to situate her field community within its larger geographic, social, and historical contexts. She gathered statistics on income, occupation, and education to obtain a social and economic profile of the community. Then, before entering the field, she made a survey of neighborhood associations, church groups, after-school programs, and clinics and hospitals to understand the extent of Puerto Rican involvement in community services and networks.

After obtaining enough background information, Freidenberg began attending community functions and visiting senior centers and health care clinics so that she could get to know the people who used these services and they could get to know her. She then talked with individuals whom she thought would be interested in working with her and began conducting in-depth interviews with them. She also accompanied her consultants in their daily activities, such as shopping, attending church, going to the doctor, and visiting with friends.

Over a long time, Freidenberg gained firsthand knowledge about the people's activities, attitudes, and opinions on a wide range of subjects. By collecting extended life histories, she got a fairly complete picture of people's experiences through the life course. She was able to understand their perspective on what it means to grow older as immigrants in a large city and to need health care and social services. As months and years passed, Freidenberg became part of their lives and they part of hers. She used the knowledge she gained to make policy recommendations about the delivery of medical and social services to the elderly in New York City.

In addition to focusing on particular groups and neighborhoods, urban anthropologists may also analyze the cultural and structural linkages among diverse populations within a city. And they may focus on structural linkages between communities, larger urban contexts, and national social and political entities. This focus guided the research of Jagna Sharff (1998), who led a team of three urban anthropologists in a long-term (fifteen years) research project in a poor, predominantly Hispanic neighborhood on the Lower East Side of New York City.

urban anthropology
Field that focuses on studying the lives of people living in cities or urban neighborhoods.

survey research
Use of formal questionnaires, administered to a random sample of subjects, eliciting social data that can be analyzed statistically.

Case study

Life in Riverfront: A Middle-Western Town Seen through Japanese Eyes

In their book, *Life in Riverfront: A Middle-Western Town Seen through Japanese Eyes* (2001), two Japanese anthropologists, Mariko Fujita Sano and Toshiyuki Sano, write about the process of doing ethnography of a foreign culture in a complex, heterogeneous society. They tell about their initial expectations prior to embarking on fieldwork and about their gradual immersion as both observers and participants in community life. The town, located in central Wisconsin, has a population of about 22,000 residents, nearly all of European American ancestry, principally Anglo-Saxon, Irish, Scandinavian, German, and Polish. Both anthropologists were born and raised in Japan and received Ph.D.'s in anthropology from Stanford University in California. They had absorbed stereotypes about "Middle America" that they feared might affect their observations, and they also were concerned that they might not be readily accepted or trusted in Riverfront, which had few Asian residents.

There were other concerns as well. The couple worried about finding a place to live, especially after the owner of the first apartment they looked at asked, "Which church do you go to?" They were afraid that people might be hostile to them because Japan had attacked Pearl Harbor. Mariko Sano was concerned that "conservative Middle Americans" would think of her as a housewife accompanying her husband rather than as a well-educated professional woman. They were worried that they would be treated as "foreigners" and that "everything we would do would stand out." Despite all this, the Sanos were gradually able to establish themselves in the community and were taken seriously by its residents.

Another preconception that the Sanos brought to Riverfront was that the town would be ethnically uniform because of the residents' European ancestry. As they stated in their book, "Although we had known that American society is ethnically diverse, we tended to associate ethnicity with racial minorities such as African-Americans, Hispanics, and Asians and tended to see European-American people as a uniform ethnicity" (2001:1). Yet Europeans proved equally diverse.

The Sanos imagined Riverfront as a rural community in the midst of farms and open country. They thought that life would be simpler than in a large city, although they really hadn't thought about what "simpler" might mean. They decided to drive from California to Wisconsin rather than fly, because they wanted a gradual transition to their fieldwork site and to place Riverfront in its geographic context. They found, of course, that "Middle America" is much more complex than they had anticipated based on their preconceived notions and stereotypes. They found that Riverfront is embedded not only in a geographic context but also in an economic and political context of competing interests and identities.

Mariko and Toshiyuki combined several research methodologies. To understand contemporary Riverfront and its residents, they delved into archival material to trace the town's development since its incorporation in 1856. They traced the geographic spread and economic growth of the town, its industrial and manufacturing development, and its relationship to a campus in the University of Wisconsin system. They also collected life histories from older residents, and through these personal narratives, they were able to "sketch a picture" of life in Riverfront as early as the 1920s and 1930s. They were careful to obtain life histories representative of the different ethnic groups there to ascertain similarities and differences in the immigrant experience. In addition, the Sanos analyzed statistical data from official census lists dating back to the mid-nineteenth century, detailing population, ethnic and national origin, and residential mobility within the town. The Sanos also participated as volunteers at a senior citizen center, helping to serve meals as part of an aid program for elderly townspeople. This activity gave the Sanos a way to meet people, establish friendly relations, and become contributing and involved members of the community.

About a year after their arrival in town, life changed for the Sanos and their relations with people in Riverfront when Mariko gave birth to their first child. As they point out in their book, "Anthropologists in the field often reach a turning point at which the nature of the relationship with their interviewees changes dramatically. For us, the turning point was the birth of our son." Even before the baby was born, people began to give them advice about how to take care of the child, in effect beginning the process of integrating the child into the culture of Riverfront. Attitudes toward the Sanos, especially on the part of regulars at the senior citizens center, transformed them from outsiders and strangers into friends and community members. People commented that the child, because of its birth in Riverfront, would be an American. One person even observed that "your baby will be half-Polish."

Mariko and Toshiyuki Sano left Riverfront after nearly two years of fieldwork. They returned some twelve years later to see many economic changes as old industries disappeared and new shopping malls were constructed. Immigrants continued to arrive in town, some from Europe and others from urban and rural American communities. The Sanos realized that these immigrants were much like themselves, arriving in a new place and adapting to its culture. As they conclude, "We have carried on cultural dialogues between 'them' and 'us' and among 'ourselves.'" And they note that these are the same "cultural-dialogical experiences" that all newcomers have, whatever their origins and whatever their purposes.

? Have you ever been a newcomer? What preconceptions did you bring with you?

As an urban anthropologist, how might you go about studying this Puerto Rican community in New York City? What aspects of the culture of this community would you want to try to understand through your study?

The Sharff team collected economic data on income and employment, information on household composition and residence, and social indicators such as health, education, and friendship networks. They opened an office in the neighborhood as headquarters and space for their team to meet together and with community residents. The researchers interacted with people daily, but they framed their research and interpretation of data in terms of a larger picture: the city's economy and national policies affecting poor people. The researchers were untangling the web of economic and political relationships that had an impact on the daily lives of low-income Hispanics. That web included deindustrialization, leading to loss of employment, and interrelated problems stemming from lack of educational opportunity, cuts in social service spending, neighborhood deterioration, and increased crime and drug use. According to Sharff and her colleagues, the violence in the community resulted from the "violence of poverty" inflicted on poor people by national and local forces beyond their control.

As you can imagine, doing fieldwork in one's own society poses special problems of objectivity. Many anthropologists believe that it is impossible to be completely objective when studying any culture, because all observers bring with them their own learned values, attitudes, and expectations. At the same time, anthropologists need to "know" something about the subjects of study. The challenge, then, is to "learn" about them in a different way, taking account of what they think they already know but looking afresh from an anthropological perspective.

> **REVIEW**
>
> Boas, Malinowski, and other early twentieth-century anthropologists emphasized the importance of fieldwork. Ethnohistory and cross-cultural comparisons using databases such as the Human Relations Area Files are examples of anthropological approaches based on records and data rather than on direct observations. When anthropologists do fieldwork, they often write descriptive accounts called ethnographies. Conducting fieldwork involves many steps before even entering the field, at which time most first-time anthropologists experience some degree of culture shock. Fieldwork can focus on entire small-scale societies or on subcultures or subgroups within a large-scale society. Anthropologists also study groups, communities, and institutions within their own societies. Using methods such as interviews and survey research as well as participant observation, researchers in urban anthropology focus on segments of larger societies and their connections with other societies and the world.

THE ANTHROPOLOGY OF ANTHROPOLOGY

The study of anthropology by anthropologists is called **reflexive anthropology.** It has been developed and championed by anthropologists in the tradition of postmodernism. The goal of such studies is to understand cultural impacts on the observations and writings of anthropologists, which must be taken into account in understanding other cultures (Clifford and Marcus, 1986).

Labeling Issues in Anthropology

Early anthropologists saw their study populations as "primitive." As a result of colonialism and imperialism, societies were created that often appeared to later European and American anthropologists as static, timeless, and "traditional," when they were not. Other labels include the terms *non-Western, native,* and *indigenous.*

Today, rather than viewing societies as isolates and ideal types with unique sets of cultural traits, anthropologists investigate how the cultural practices and attitudes of a society relate to processes of globalization, such as modernization and economic development. Many anthropologists look for ways to apply their knowledge and theories to address these contemporary problems. In addition, anthropologists recognize that many voices cooperate and compete in the production of meaning, creating **polyphony**—or the many sounds and voices of people in all segments or groups in a society. In this context, some anthropologists question the choice of voice in the texts that they produce and their own role in the process of presentation (see the Controversies feature).

reflexive anthropology
The anthropology of anthropology, which focuses on the labels that anthropologists use, the impacts of anthropologists on the people they study, and professional ethics.

polyphony
The many voices of people from all the different segments and groups that make up a society; a quality of ethnographic writing today that presents multiple views of a culture.

How Do Anthropologists Present Knowledge about the People They Study?

Since the 1960s, anthropologists have questioned their role as agents of change, as they intentionally or unwittingly facilitate worldwide economic and political processes (Gough, 1968). In addition, some anthropologists side with the people they study against oppressive government policies that destroy the people's land and resources or pressure the people to abandon their way of life.

Anthropologists interested in the impacts of American and European ideologies on other peoples look at the ways groups represent themselves and others and structure people's ideas about these groups. As persons involved in the processes of "writing culture," Western anthropologists influence the representation of non-Western peoples. How do anthropologists write about and present another culture? Often through the construction of the "other" as alien, unusual, different, and exotic. To counteract this tendency, some anthropologists present their findings as a dialogue between themselves and members of the society among whom they have lived. The production of any text, including an ethnography, can be seen as a "dialogic" process with multiple voices and multiple meanings (Bakhtin, 1981). In the past, ethnographies tended to present a unified voice in their description of a people's lifeways rather than polyphony. Very likely they contributed to cultural stereotypes and depicted greater conformity, uniformity of opinion, and idealized behavior than actually existed in the society. Deeply contested issues were often glossed over. Because ethnographies focused on a view of culture from the perspective of people with greater prestige and privilege, the voices of marginalized members of communities were muted or unheard.

In addition, because in the past most anthropologists were male, and because they worked primarily with male consultants, ethnographies tended to be told from a male perspective. Women's concerns, women's lives, and women's voices were relatively unknown and unheard. Examples of gender bias in ethnological interpretation are common in the writings of some anthropologists. Writing about the Nuer of southern Sudan, for example, the British social anthropologist E. E. Evans-Pritchard concluded that Nuer family life was "remarkably harmonious on the surface" (1955:133). Yet his research, based entirely on the testimony of men, disclosed culturally sanctioned wife abuse and the wishes of both husbands and wives

(reported by the husbands) for their spouse's death! Not a very harmonious picture, even on the surface. More recently, the writings of Napoleon Chagnon (1997) among the Yanomami of Brazil and Venezuela downplay the significance of the severe violence inflicted on women by their husbands. And many anthropologists discussing economic systems overemphasize the male role of hunting in comparison to the significant female role of gathering. Today, anthropologists pay more attention to looking past their own subjectivity to more fully represent others.

Because of these problems with the ethnographer's voice, some anthropologists are producing "polyphonous" ethnographies with a multitude of voices. Rather than relying on a single, dominant perspective, they give multiple interpretations of activities and opinions from the points of view of people with different types of roles in the community. The voices of men and women, of the elites and the marginal contribute to a diversity of representations. By focusing on dialogue and polyphony, anthropologists locate culture not only in behavior but also in conversation about behavior, ideas, attitudes, and emotions. Ethnographers also focus on their own issues of power, their relations with communities in their own societies, and their relations with people in the communities they study.

Controversies within the discipline about the role of the anthropologist and the focus of ethnography do not weaken the field but, rather, invigorate it with debate, bringing out important issues for thought and dialogue. Anthropology plays a vital role in today's world. The discipline has the tools with which to understand and analyze complex issues of power that structure and confront our world. The theories and methods that anthropologists use provide the knowledge and techniques for understanding people's behavior and the ways in which they organize, transmit, evaluate, and express their experiences. Anthropologists can contribute meaningfully not only to the collection of knowledge as an academic pursuit but also to debates about public policy in national and international arenas. They can help inform people about the value of all cultures.

CRITICAL THINKING QUESTIONS

How do you think your roles and status as a member of your society might affect your observations of other people? How might they color what you say to an anthropologist interviewing you about your people's way of life?

If you were writing an ethnography of your community, whose voices might you want to represent or include? Why?

Anthropology Applied

Anthropology on Trial in the Amazon

In the first years of the twenty-first century, scandal erupted concerning the conduct of anthropologists, other scientists, and journalists working among foragers and horticulturalists in the Amazon River Basin in South America during the 1960s. In charges that have not been substantiated to the satisfaction of the academic community, a cultural anthropologist and ethnographic filmmaker was accused of staging events for the camera, interfering with local politics, and inciting Indians to warfare, partly to support his claim that they were naturally violent (Grossman, 2000).

Another problem was the use of weapons—machetes and axes—as trade goods to win the acceptance and confidence of the study population. The use of trade goods to ease contact between peoples is an ancient custom. However, in the hands of people with traditions of intertribal warfare and Stone Age weapons, modern steel tools led to significant increases in injury and death among the Indians. The claim also was made that scientists were responsible for introducing measles to remote communities in the region, killing an unknown number of native people, and that they may have done so intentionally to test genetic theories (Grossman, 2000).

These claims may not be true. According to an investigative report by the American Anthropological Association, "These misrepresentations fail to live up to the ethics of responsible journalism even as they pretend to question the ethical conduct of anthropology" (2001). Nevertheless, during the 1970s, attitudes about fieldwork changed as anthropologists became more concerned about native people's rights. A new code of ethics emerged for all social scientists working with human subjects, including the principle of informed consent. Today, the ethics of informed consent require that social scientists explain to their informants how the information they collect will be used—especially how that information could be used against them and what the consequences could be. Thus informed, some groups might reasonably decline to become subjects of study.

In addition, although anthropologists are dependent on the people they research for both information and assistance, they are trained to avoid acting in ways that may upset the established order in people's social relations, social norms, decision-making processes, and economic exchanges. Thus, family relations, village politics, and intertribal relations are areas in which anthropologists should not be fully participant observers. Also, observers must be aware that new, casually introduced technologies can have disastrous unintended consequences. Taken together, the new ethical standards for social science research reflect the concern expressed in the prime directive of medical ethics: "First, do no harm."

CRITICAL THINKING QUESTIONS

Should these ethics apply to native anthropologists studying their own people? Should these ethics apply to workers involved in advocacy and activism for indigenous rights?

Ethical Issues in Anthropology

Other issues concerning anthropology relate to the ethics of conducting research involving human subjects. Cultural anthropologists make their living and build their careers by studying other people. They live among them, learn from them, and write about them. As a result, the most important ethical issues they face involve their relationships with and obligations to those people.

The American Anthropological Association, the professional association to which most anthropologists belong, formulated a Code of Ethics, setting out a number of principles that it recommends to its members (American Anthropological Association, 1998). The code mandates intellectual honesty, forbidding any falsification or intentional biasing of data. Stage-directing ethnographic film footage would be regarded as unethical, for example. The code also advises that an anthropologist's ethical obligations to the people they study are more important than the pursuit of knowledge or the completion of research projects. Ethical obligations include avoiding harm to or exploitation of the people, and fully disclosing the goals and uses of the research. Anthropologists also must consider the social and political implications of the material that they produce. Finally, the code notes that although some anthropologists use their research to advocate for the people they study, this is not an ethical responsibility but rather an individual choice. Anthropologists are also guided by federal legal requirements safeguarding the rights of human subjects in any type of research project. These rights include full disclosure of research goals, research methods, types of analyses, and reporting procedures.

Anthropologists do not agree on their proper roles in relation to the people they study. Perhaps their basic obligation can be phrased as "First, do no harm." For some anthropologists, research is an end in itself. People in the community extend their hospitality voluntarily. And while anthropologists should certainly avoid doing anything that they feel may be harmful (in the short or long term) to the community, some believe that they have no continuing obligation to the people. Other anthropologists believe that they have ongoing responsibilities to the community and lend their help. Anthropologists may be able to collect and analyze documents or testify in court proceedings regarding native territories and indigenous land claims cases. Others can use their training and knowledge to represent native interests in dealings with local and national governments. At the least, anthropologists can present information about the needs of indigenous communities to the public in their writings and in classes. As experts, they can talk to the media, countering negative stereotypes about poor and marginalized peoples. As discussed in Chapter 1, applied anthropologists focus on this goal.

REVIEW

Reflexive anthropology focuses on anthropology itself, the language it uses to describe people, and its impacts on both knowledge and people. Today many ethnographies are written to reflect polyphony—the many voices of people from all the different segments and groups that make up a society. Concern with the impacts of anthropologists on study populations has led to the establishment of a professional Code of Ethics for the conduct of anthropology.

Chapter Summary

Anthropology and the Explanation of Cultural Diversity

- Although the field of anthropology as an academic discipline is only slightly more than a century old, its intellectual roots in Europe go back much farther. It has its origins in the colonial expansion of Europe that began in the fifteenth and sixteenth centuries. Explorers, traders, and missionaries visited and commented on the peoples and cultures they encountered in their worldwide search for land, wealth, and religious converts. During the eighteenth century, European social philosophers consulted the journals and writings of earlier observers. Their evolutionism—proposals about the progress of humankind from one cultural stage to the next—established a basis for later anthropological theories.

- The anthropology that emerged in the late nineteenth and early twentieth centuries in the United States and Europe focused on classifying and comparing peoples and cultures throughout the world, attempting to determine their evolutionary relationships to one another. Two important figures were Franz Boas, who championed attention to historical details, empiricism, and cultural relativism, and Bronislaw Malinowski, who contributed the perspective of functionalism. Their work, emphasizing the importance of fieldwork and direct interactions with and observations of other cultures, form the central core of anthropology.

- Anthropologists have developed a number of conceptual frameworks to explain human cultures. Materialist perspectives (cultural ecology and cultural materialism) emphasize the centrality of environmental adaptation, technology, and methods of acquiring or producing food in the development of culture. Cultural ecology focuses on how the physical environment directly influences the satisfaction of basic human needs and how people's adaptive behaviors interact with other aspects of culture. Cultural materialists often distinguish between emic explanations of behavior, based on the reasons people themselves offer to account for what they do, and etic explanations, based on the analysts' observations of people's behavior and other objective criteria.

• Taking a different approach, some anthropologists emphasize the centrality of concepts and structures rather than meanings in organizing culture. Structuralist approaches look at the role of concepts in structuring experiences and relationships, for example, myths and kinship systems. Interpretive anthropologists focus on relationships among meanings in the development and transmission of culture. Conflict perspectives focus on social and cultural inequalities and power relations.

• Some anthropologists analyze issues of culture and power, with emphasis on the shaping of culture through forms of social, economic, and political power. Some of their attention is directed toward anthropology itself, uncovering unstated biases in the field and in the analysis of culture. Today anthropologists are rethinking commonly accepted notions about "traditional" society and focusing more on the complex ways in which traditional societies substantially reshaped themselves (and were reshaped by) the impacts of European expansion and colonial control. Worldwide processes of modernization and globalization also raise issues about the ways in which people are enmeshed in economic institutions and political forces beyond their control.

Ethnography and Fieldwork

• The central tool of anthropological research is fieldwork, especially participant observation. Anthropologists live among the people they are studying for an extended period of time to gain an understanding of their culture from the people's point of view. As participant observers, anthropologists observe and record the communities' activities and participate in them as much as possible and appropriate. Earlier anthropologists focused on foreign cultures, usually small, seemingly isolated indigenous societies. But today many anthropologists work in large-scale societies, including their own, focusing on specific subcultures or communities. Fieldwork involves multiple tasks, including choosing a research problem and a site for study, finding a place to live, working in and learning an unfamiliar language, and overcoming culture shock.

• In addition to fieldwork, some anthropologists use the techniques of ethnohistory, researching in libraries and archives to learn about past conditions and events relevant to understanding the present lives of the people they are studying. Anthropologists also employ the comparative method in understanding cross-cultural similarities and differences in human cultures.

The Anthropology of Anthropology

• Cultural anthropologists are concerned with ethical issues involving their relationships with the people they study. They think about what kinds of obligations they may have in return for the opportunity and privilege of living with, learning from, and writing about other people. Some anthropologists feel that they have legitimate roles as advocates for the communities that they have studied, while others see their obligations as scholars to disseminate information that counters negative stereotypes about poor and marginalized peoples.

 *Key Terms*

Review Questions

1. How did anthropology become an academic discipline? What were the principal goals of early anthropologists?

2. What influences did Boas and Malinowski have on the development of anthropology?

3. What main theoretical perspectives do anthropologists use to describe and explain cultural differences and changes?

4. What are the differences between an emic and etic perspective?

5. How might a cultural event be analyzed differently by a conflict theorist and an interpretivist?

6. What steps do anthropologists take to prepare for fieldwork? What are the key benchmarks in conducting fieldwork?

7. What are some pitfalls of living and participating in family and community life while doing fieldwork?

8. What is the anthropology of anthropology? What are some issues concerning the roles of anthropologists and the writing of ethnographies?

Language and Culture

Brueghel, Jan the Elder. Tower of Babel. Pinacoteca Nazionale, Sienna, Italy. Copyright Scala/Art Resource, NY.

CHAPTER 4

Preview

1. **What three features distinguish human language from animal communication?**

2. **How are languages described? What are the differences between phonemes and morphemes?**

3. **Why is it important to include nonverbal behavior in the study of language and culture?**

4. **What were Edward Sapir's and Benjamin Whorf's contributions to linguistic anthropology?**

5. **What is a dialect? A jargon? How does language relate to gender, class, and race?**

6. **What might be included in an ethnosemantic study of communication?**

7. **What are some internal and external processes of language change?**

8. **How can the study of languages help reconstruct their histories and the history of human migrations and contacts?**

N*ow the whole earth had one language and the same words. And as they migrated from the east, they came upon* a plain in the land of Shinar and settled there. And they said to one another, "Come, let us make bricks, and burn them thoroughly." Then they said, "Come, let us build ourselves a city, and a tower with its top in the heavens, and let us make a name for ourselves; otherwise we shall be scattered abroad upon the face of the whole earth." The Lord came down to see the city and the tower, which mortals had built. And the Lord said, "Look, they are one people, and they have all one language; and this is only the beginning of what they will do; nothing that they propose to do will now be impossible for them. Come, let us go down, and confuse their language there, so that they will not understand one another's speech." So the Lord scattered them abroad from there over the face of all the earth, and they left off building the city. Therefore it was called Babel, because there the Lord confused the language of all the earth; and from there the Lord scattered them abroad over the face of all the earth.

A biblical narrative accounting for the diversity of languages (Genesis 11:9).

C*reator and Changer first made the world in the East. Then he slowly came westward, creating as he came. With him* he brought many languages, and he gave a different one to each group of people he made.

When he reached Puget Sound, he liked it so well that he decided to go no further. But he had many languages left, so he scattered them all around Puget Sound and to the north. That's why there are so many different Indian languages spoken there.

These people could not talk together, but it happened that none of them were pleased with the way the Creator had made the world. The sky was so low that the tall people bumped their heads against it. Finally the wise men of all the different tribes had a meeting to see what they could do about lifting the sky. They agreed that the people should get together and try to push it up higher. "We can do it," a wise man said, "if we all push at the same time. We will need all the people and all the animals and all the birds when we push." "How will we know when to push?" asked another. "Some of us live in this part of the world, some in another. We don't all talk the same language. How can we get everyone to push at the same time?"

At last one of them suggested that they use a signal. "When the time comes for us to push, when we have everything ready, let someone shout "Ya-hoh" that means "Lift together!" in all our languages." The day for the sky lifting came. All the people raised their poles and touched the sky with them. Then the wise men shouted

"Ya-hoh." Every body pushed, and the sky moved up a little. They kept on shouting "Ya-hoh" and pushing until the sky was in the place where it is now. Since then, no one has bumped his head against it.

A Snohomish narrative accounting for the diversity of languages.

The Snohomish are an indigenous people of the state of Washington. Their story explains the extraordinary diversity of languages spoken in the Pacific Northwest of North America. It also tells how, despite their differences, the people of the region found a way to cooperate to make the world more to their liking. Like the Snohomish story, the biblical story of the tower of Babel also explains the origin of linguistic diversity, but it has a very different outcome. In the biblical story, the creation of different languages stops people from working together, confusing and separating them. In contrast, the Snohomish story depicts a world in which people join together to achieve common goals despite their linguistic (and cultural) differences.

Today, about 6,200 languages are spoken in the world, some by millions of people and some by only several hundred. While 6,200 is a steep decline from the number of languages spoken several centuries ago, it still reflects a rich array of linguistic and cultural diversity. Languages are repositories of cultural knowledge and history, and as such, they are integral to personal and group identity.

Language is a fundamental part of human behavior. It is our primary medium for interacting with one another. We use it to convey our thoughts, feelings, intentions, and desires to others. We learn about people through what they say and how they say it; we learn about ourselves through the ways other people react to what we say; and we learn about our relationships with others through the give-and-take of conversation. In this chapter, you will learn something about the structure of human languages as well as the ways in which anthropologists study the relationship between language and culture.

WHAT IS LANGUAGE?

All animals communicate in some manner, but **language,** it seems, is unique (or almost so) to humans. Language has four key features that together distinguish it from other forms of animal communication (Table 4.1). First, language is symbolic. That is, it is based on symbols—the arbitrary association of sounds with meanings. For instance, the sounds in the word *cat* have no particular association with the animal the word represents. It is just that, in English, this sound has come to "mean" a particular animal. Even words that speakers think imitate noises (such as the words for the noises animals make) are only stylized approximations. Cats don't really say *meow;* dogs don't really say *bowwow.*

Another feature of language is **displacement,** the ability to communicate about something that is not happening at the moment. Indeed, we use language far more to

language
Any form of communication that involves symbols, displacement, and productivity.

displacement
Ability to communicate about something that is not happening at the moment.

Table 4.1 FOUR KEY FEATURES OF LANGUAGE

Symbolism	Based on the arbitrary association of sounds with meanings.
Displacement	The ability to communicate about something that is not happening at the moment.
Productivity	The ability to join words in infinite meaningful combinations.
Duality of Patterning	The use of a relatively small number of units of sound to combine and thereby create and transmit meaning in words.

communicate about things that have already happened in the past or will happen in the future than about what is happening right now. It is displacement, also, that permits us to talk about imagined events, or in other words, to tell stories, as well as to deceive or lie.

The third and fourth features of language are productivity and duality of patterning. **Duality of patterning** refers to the fact that an arbitrary and relatively small number of sounds with no intrinsic meaning can combine in specific orders to create and transmit meaning in words. Sounds represented by letters of the alphabet, for example, do not have meaning in themselves, but they can be combined in many ways to produce an infinite number of words. Words also can be combined to form larger, or compound, words—for example, stair + case = staircase; book + case = bookcase; shore + line = shoreline. **Productivity** refers to the fact that words, in turn, can be combined in an infinite number of phrases and sentences. Every language contains many thousands of words that can be combined and recombined to form an infinite number of sentences. In a sense, nearly every sentence spoken or written is a new sentence, because it is a new combination of words.

Many nonhuman animals communicate with **call systems** (or **signal systems**). Unlike human language, these systems consist of a relatively small number of sounds or vocalizations that express moods and sensations, like fear, delight, contentment, anger, or pain. They can be used as warnings, threats, alarms, or requests for attention and affection. Also, research suggests that the calls of some nonhuman primates indicate the direction and location of food sources (Jolly, 1985). If so, this ability demonstrates a limited kind of displacement because the animals are signaling information that is not present at the time. But as far as we know, even such impressively intelligent animals as chimpanzees and gorillas, our closest primate relatives, do not, in the wild at least, talk about their plans for the future or reminisce about the past.

For decades, researchers have been trying to determine whether or not chimpanzees and gorillas can learn language. The earliest studies involved trying to teach chimpanzees to pronounce English words. These efforts were doomed to failure because, it turns out, chimpanzees and gorillas are physically incapable of articulating words. They are, however, capable of intricate hand gestures and can certainly manipulate physical objects. A fascinating series of later studies sought to take advantage of these abilities. In some, chimpanzees and gorillas raised in homelike settings were taught American Sign Language (ASL), the gestural language of the deaf. In other studies, animals were taught to press keys on computers or to manipulate cutout symbols on boards. Many of the animals learned to recognize and use hundreds of words for objects, actions, and feelings. Some even appeared to make up new words by combining words into compounds.

The difference between the natural call systems of nonhuman primates and their abilities in the laboratory may provide some insights into the fascinating but difficult question of the origin of human language. Chimpanzees and gorillas apparently have a rudimentary capacity for understanding and manipulating symbols but seem not to use it in the wild. Presumably, our prehuman ancestors had the same capacity long before they began using language. If this is so, we can look for the origin of human language in conditions that would have made the complex communication it permits advantageous for survival. Displacement, one of the features of language that distinguishes it from call systems, makes it possible to communicate about the past and future. Perhaps language emerged because of our ancestors' need to apply memories of past experiences to present and future plans in order to coordinate group activities—to relocate their camps, for example, or to plan food-gathering expeditions. Language is also a primary vehicle for the transmission of individual and cultural knowledge. Although we

duality of patterning
Principle that sounds are arbitrarily associated with meaning.

productivity
Ability to join sounds and words in theoretically infinite meaningful combinations.

call systems (signal systems)
Animal communication systems that consist of a relatively small number of sounds to express moods and sensations, like fear, delight, contentment, anger, or pain.

? *How is human communication different from the call and signal systems of nonhuman primates?*

Since the late 1970s, researchers have taught chimpanzees and gorillas American Sign Language in order to study their ability to communicate. Most primate studies reveal, however, that apes do not understand the importance of putting words in order, patterns called syntax.

phonology
Study of sound systems in language, including phonetics and phonemics.

phonetics
Study of the articulation and production of human speech sounds.

phonemics
Analysis of the use of sounds to differentiate the meanings of words.

learn from observing other people, we gain most of our knowledge and skills through language, through hearing other people's advice and instruction based on their stored-up memories and experiences.

Nonhuman primates, as already noted, are physically incapable of speech. The emergence of spoken language thus required changes in the physical structure of the mouth and throat. We cannot know exactly when these changes began to occur or when our ancestors first started to use spoken language. Some researchers suggest it may have been about 100,000 to 150,000 years ago. Almost all agree that the people who, some 40,000 years ago, created the earliest known examples of another characteristically human form of symbolic communication—art—were also speaking to one another.

REVIEW

Four principles that characterize human language are arbitrary symbols (association of sounds to specific meanings, with the sounds symbolizing the item being described); displacement (the ability of people to talk about events, people, and objects that are not present); productivity (the ability to put together sounds and words to form larger words and sentences); and duality of patterning (use of an arbitrary and relatively small inventory of sounds to combine and recombine to create an infinite number of words and sentences). To understand the relationship between human language and animal call systems or signal systems, researchers began to teach chimpanzees and gorillas American Sign Language and other methods of communicating.

THE COMPONENTS OF LANGUAGE

Languages consist of sounds, structures, and meanings. When we use language, we produce and understand these elements together as a whole. However, we can learn much about how language works by studying each element separately.

Phonology: The System of Sounds

Phonology is the study of sound systems in language. It includes **phonetics,** the study of human speech sounds, and **phonemics,** the analysis of the use of those sounds to differentiate words. The vocal apparatus with which we produce the sounds, or "phones," of language consists of lungs, pharynx, larynx, glottis, vocal cords, nose, mouth, tongue, teeth, and lips (Figure 4.1). As sound is produced, air passes from the lungs through the throat, into the mouth, and then is expelled either through the mouth or nose.

We produce specific sounds by manipulating various parts of the vocal apparatus—for example, by positioning our tongue on our teeth or palate; by closing, opening, or rounding our lips; or by constricting or opening our throats. In addition, sounds are either oral or nasal, voiced or voiceless. Oral sounds are produced when air is expelled only through the mouth; nasal sounds are produced when air passes through the nose. The consonants /m/ and /n/, for example, are nasal. (Linguists use slashes to set off specific sounds.)

Sounds are voiced if they are produced with the vocal cords close together and vibrating; otherwise, sounds are voiceless. The only difference between the English consonants /p/, as in "pit," and /b/, as in "bit," for example, is that /p/ is voiceless and /b/ is voiced. Try making the sounds in Table 4.2, which gives some examples of voiceless and voiced consonant pairs.

No language uses the full range of sounds that the human vocal system can produce, but every language organizes the sounds it does use—its phonetic inventory—into a system of

Figure 4.1
The Vocal Apparatus (adapted from Wardhaugh, 1977:33)

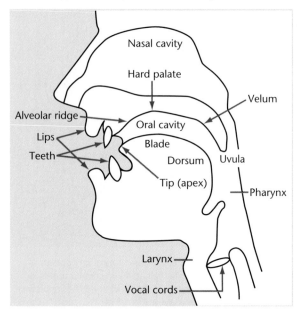

- Nasal cavity
- Hard palate
- Velum
- Alveolar ridge
- Oral cavity
- Lips
- Blade
- Teeth
- Dorsum
- Uvula
- Tip (apex)
- Pharynx
- Larynx
- Vocal cords

Table 4.2 SOME EXAMPLES OF VOICELESS AND VOICED CONSONANT PAIRS

Voiceless	Voiced
p: pit	b: bit
tap	tab
t: ten	d: den
bit	bid
f: fan	v: van
grief	grieve
s: sap	z: zap
hiss	his

phoneme
A minimal unit of sound that differentiates meaning in a particular language.

stress
Phonemic use of accented sounds or syllables.

pitch
Phonemic use of rising and falling speech cadences.

phonemes. A **phoneme** is a minimal unit of sound that has no meaning by itself but functions to distinguish one word from another. The contrast between the sounds /p/ and /b/, for example, distinguishes the English word "pit" from the word "bit." In English, then, /p/ and /b/ are separate phonemes.

You learn to apply the rules for differentiating phonemes unconsciously as you acquire your native language in childhood. These rules are not universal but, instead, operate within each language according to its own patterns. People who speak a second language with a foreign accent are simply applying the pronunciation rules of their native language to the new one.

In addition to consonants and vowels, several other features of vocal sound can distinguish one word from another. These include stress, pitch, and length. **Stress** refers to the degree of emphasis placed on the accented syllables of words. In some languages, the placement of stress is unvarying. In Czech, Finnish, and Hungarian, every word is accented on the first syllable; in French and Mayan, every word is accented on the last syllable; and in Polish, Swahili, and Samoan, the next to last syllable is always stressed. In other languages, the placement of stress varies and can carry meaning (see Table 4.3).

Many languages also use the vocal **pitch** at which syllables are spoken to distinguish words from one another. Pitch is important in Asian languages such as Chinese and Thai; African languages such as Yoruba, Zulu, and Luganda; Native American languages such as Navajo and Sarcee; and the European language Latvian. For example, in Chinese, the sequence /ma/ can be pronounced with four different pitches or tones, giving each word a completely different meaning:

high level pitch	mā	mother
high rising pitch	má	hemp
low falling/rising	mǎ	horse
falling	mà	scold

Pitch is also a feature of sentences. In English, for example, the pitch patterns of statements and questions contrast, with level or falling pitch at the ends of statements and rising pitch at the ends of questions.

Table 4.3 EXAMPLES OF THE EFFECT OF STRESS ON MEANING IN ENGLISH

Noun	Verb
present	present
object	object
construct	construct
implant	implant

? *What are some examples in English of exaggerating the meaning of a word by lengthening or stretching out its vowel sound?*

The **length,** or duration, of a syllable also can differentiate meaning. In Mohawk, the length of a vowel changes the meaning of words. For example, a word with a short "i" sound means "there" (íse) but the same word with a long "i" sound means "you" (í:se). In some languages, changes in the duration of sounds mark emphasis or exaggeration, but the basic meaning of the word remains the same (he is so b-i-i-i-g!) (Lakoff and Johnson, 1980).

Morphology: The Structure of Words

Morphology is the analysis of word structure. Words are composed of units of sound and meaning called **morphemes.** Morphemes may be words or sounds that are not words but carry special meanings when attached to words. In English, for example "-s" is a morpheme that attaches to the end of nouns to indicate plural, as in "cats." Thus, a word may contain combinations of morphemes. "Inactivity," for example, consists of the units of meaning, "in-" (meaning "not"), "act" (a verb meaning "to do"), "-ive" (making the verb into an adjective), and "-ity" (making the adjective into a noun).

Like phonemes, morphemes can have two or more sounds, depending on context. The English morpheme for plural, for example, is pronounced /-s/ after voiceless consonants, as in "cats"; /-z/ after voiced consonants, as in "dogs"; and /-iz/ after certain consonants called *sibilants* (/s/, /z/, /sh/), as in "classes" or "dishes."

Syntax: The Structure of Sentences

Most talk consists of multiword units—phrases and sentences—not single words spoken in isolation. Every language has rules of **syntax** that govern the ordering of words in phrases and sentences to show their relationship. In English, for example, the subject of a sentence precedes the verb and the direct object follows it. All the words in the English sentences "The dog chased the cat" and "The cat chased the dog" are the same, but the meanings are different because of the difference in word order.

Each of the world's languages has its own rules of syntax, and these rules vary greatly. Yet all languages share certain features. In all, for example, sentences are composed of subject, object, and verb, and in most languages the subject comes before the object. What varies is the position of the verb. Thus, in English, a basic sentence is ordered Subject + Verb + Object (SVO); in other languages, the basic order is Verb + Subject + Object (VSO) or Subject + Object + Verb (SOV). In only a few languages does the basic word order place objects before subjects.

Since subjects precede objects in the vast majority of languages, this pattern probably reflects human cognition. People perceive subjects as more important than objects because subjects are more active and in control. That is, subjects initiate, control, direct, or affect actions and events. Objects, on the other hand, are not "doers" but "receivers" of actions and, therefore, are less cognitively significant or salient. Cognitive salience thus is reflected in linguistic structure.

According to the linguist Noam Chomsky, there are a number of abstract rules of word order and sentence construction that appear to underlie all languages. These common structural features of language reflect a **universal grammar,** part of an innate capacity for language in the human brain. According to this view, the actual syntax of any particular language derives from the basic generic structures of universal grammar. The existence of an innate structure may account for the ease with which children quickly learn to understand and speak their native language (Chomsky, 1968).

Semantics: The Study of Meaning

The function of language is to express meaning. We hear language linearly, one word at a time, but we grasp meaning as a unified whole. **Semantics,** or the study of meaning, is complicated because a host of factors contribute to that whole. To begin with, words often carry culturally symbolic freight beyond their specific meaning. To an American, for example, "apple pie" may be more than the name of a particular dessert. It may also conjure up images of home and childhood and a mix of associated values and beliefs.

length
Phonemic characteristic in which the duration of a syllable has meaning.

morphology
The study of the internal structure of words and the combination of meaningful units within the words.

morpheme
A unit of sound and meaning, either a separate word or a meaningful part of a word.

syntax
The rules that generate the combination of words to form phrases and sentences.

universal grammar
Abstract rules that underlie the structure of phrases and sentences in all languages, generally thought to be an innate capacity of human thought.

semantics
Study of systems of meaning in language.

Semantics also is the study of how meaning varies with social context. At a formal dinner, for example, the expression "Please pass the salt" would seem unremarkable, whereas "Gimme the salt" would be startlingly rude. In an informal context, however, "Please pass the salt" might seem inappropriately stuffy.

Words or phrases and sentences also convey interactional meaning that varies with the relationship people have with one another as well as the context in which they are speaking. A husband and wife might call each other "sweetheart" at home, but as doctors in the same hospital, they are likely to address each other as "Doctor" at work. Finally, utterances can have affective meaning, indicating attitudes of speakers. For example, "John told me about his accomplishments" is a neutral statement of fact, whereas "John boasted about his accomplishments" is implicitly critical of John. The meanings of words and their use in context are powerful signals of people's intentions and reflect social relationships and cultural norms.

Despite these complexities, linguists have tried to develop tools for identifying some basic rules of semantics. One approach is to analyze words in terms of overlapping and contrasting units of meaning. Linguists have abstracted some units of meaning that they claim are universal, developing a kind of universal semantics on the model of the universal grammar of Chomsky and others. Among these meaning units relevant to nouns are "animate" (contrasted with "inanimate"), "human" (contrasted with "nonhuman"), and "countable" (contrasted with "mass"). Others include the opposition between "male/female" and "adult/nonadult." So, for example, the meaning units that apply to the word "woman" include "animate," "female," "human," "adult," and "countable." Changing one unit—"female"—to "male" defines the closely related word "man." Similarly, replacing "adult" with "nonadult" gives us "girl" or "boy."

Having specified the meaning components of words, linguists can determine how they can go together in a sentence. Some verbs, for example, require particular kinds of subjects. Thus only animate subjects—human or animal—can breathe, sleep, walk, or remember. Similarly, only human subjects can talk or lie. These restrictions account for the problems with sentences like Noam Chomsky's often quoted "Colorless green ideas sleep furiously" and other semantically unacceptable statements that have proper syntax but do not make sense. The problem is that "ideas" do not "sleep" because they are not alive; "ideas" are not "green" because they are not objects; and something that is "green" cannot be "colorless" because these meanings are contradictory. In poetic and playful uses of language, however, words can be combined in novel ways to convey new meanings.

nonverbal communication
Communication through gestures, facial expressions, body posture, use of space, and touch.

emblems
Nonverbal actions with specific meanings that substitute for spoken words.

body language
The meanings people communicate through their posture, stance, movements, expressions, gestures, and proximity to other communicants.

REVIEW

Humans are genetically predisposed to learn language. Phonology is the study of sound systems in language. Different sounds are made through manipulation of the vocal apparatus, whether the sound is oral or nasal and whether the sound is voiced or voiceless. Phonology includes phonetics, the study of human speech sounds, and phonemics, the analysis of the use of those sounds to differentiate words. Phonemes are minimal units of sounds that differentiate meanings in words. Stress, pitch, and length cause differences in meaning. Morphemes are units of sound and meaning that make up words. Syntax is the rules for word order in phrases and sentences. Universal grammar consists of abstract rules of word order and sentence construction that appear to underlie all languages. Semantics is the study of meaning.

NONVERBAL COMMUNICATION

Human communication is hardly limited to language. We also convey information nonverbally, through gestures, facial expressions, body posture, use of space, and touch. Some forms of **nonverbal communication** may be universal in that they mean the same thing to everybody, regardless of culture. Some research suggests that we share with other primates certain innate or biologically based signals of enjoyment, distress, threat, and submissiveness, as the photograph on this page suggests (Jolly, 1985).

In general, the meanings of gestures, expressions, and body postures do not flow from the actions themselves any more than the meanings of words flow from the particular sounds with which they are made. The same gesture may mean one thing in one culture and something entirely different in another. In every culture, some nonverbal actions have the status of **emblems**—gestures often substituted for spoken words that are understood to have a specific meaning. Emblems in European and North American cultures include nodding the head, to signal assent, or shrugging the shoulders, to convey uncertainty.

Cultural differences in the interpretation of nonverbal behaviors, including **body language,** can lead to cross-cultural misunderstandings. A person from one culture simply may not recognize an emblem or signal used by someone from another culture, in which case no meaning is conveyed. More serious problems can arise when a particular behavior is meaningful to both parties in an encounter, but the meaning is different for each. Confronted with an act you understand one way but the other person intends to mean something else, you may respond inappropriately. For example, hand gestures that Americans routinely make to convey positive support can be offensive in other countries. The familiar "thumbs up," meaning "good job" or "good luck" or "I'm okay," is interpreted in Bangladesh, Australia, and many Islamic countries as the equivalent of the raised middle finger. The "A-O.K." sign, made with the thumb and index finger joined in a circle, means "zero" or "worthless" in France.

In all primates, certain facial muscles are involved in the expression of fear or anxiety. Recently, however, anthropologists studying nonverbal communication have questioned the universality of even basic kinds of expressions and gestures. Culture, they argue, colors our understanding of any gesture or expression, whatever its origins (Farnell, 1995).

Some gestures have achieved nearly universal meaning through the process of globalization, as different peoples incorporate foreign gestures into their cultural repertoires. One example of this is the peace sign, which is made by extending the index and middle fingers, palm-out, to form a "V." The sign originated in wartime Europe as a sign for "Victory!" which implied a coming time of peace. The original meaning has been extended to mean nonviolence, to signal any hard-won success, and to make a gestural "bunny ears" joke at a peer's expense, commonly seen in snapshots. Many cultures around the world have adopted the peace sign along with one or more of its meanings.

A study conducted in Israel suggests how common misunderstandings are in nonverbal as well as verbal **intercultural communication.** A group of students from fourteen different cultural backgrounds viewed videotaped gestures made by recent immigrants to Israel from Ethiopia. The students recognized 85 percent of the gestures as meaningful. However, of the gestures they recognized, they interpreted only 23 percent correctly to mean what the people who made them intended. They were approximately correct about another 7 percent, and misinterpreted entirely the remaining 70 percent of the gestures (Schneller, 1988:158).

In any society, nonverbal behaviors can signal differences in status, just as nonverbal behaviors reveal dominance and subordination among other primate groups. In human societies, who has higher status and who has lower status depends on cultural attitudes. Dominant individuals tend to use broad gestures; look or even stare at others; maintain serious, unsmiling faces; and take up large areas of personal space. In encounters between nonequals, subordinates tend to use restricted, small gestures; avert their eyes when looked at; smile frequently; and allow the higher-status person to encroach on their personal space and even to touch them. High-status individuals try to make themselves appear large; low-status individuals try to make themselves small by lowering their heads and keeping their limbs close to their bodies.

Gender inequalities in the United States, for example, are reflected in submissive and dominant nonverbal behaviors that women and men learn as members of their culture. Studies have shown that men are more likely than women to assume a dominant posture, and women are more likely than men to assume a deferential posture. Women typically smile, avert their eyes when looked at, condense their bodies and gestures, avoid encroaching on others' space, and allow intrusions into their own space (Henley, 1977; Hall, 1984). In studies of mixed-sex interactions, men touched women twice as often as women touched men, men initiated eye contact twice as often with women as women did with men, and women returned smiles of men nearly all the time whereas men returned only two-thirds of the smiles of women (Henley, 1977:115, 164, 176).

What roles will gestures and other body language play in the intercultural communication suggested in this photograph? What meanings will the participants' emblematic behaviors express?

GLOBALIZATION

Some gestures, such as the peace sign, have achieved nearly universal meaning through the process of globalization.

REVIEW

Nonverbal communication includes distance between speakers, facial expressions, body postures (body language), gestures, and touching. Nonverbal communication has a basis in primate evolution, but in human cultures few actions have universal meaning. Every culture has a repertoire of nonverbal communication, called emblems. Cultural differences in nonverbal (and verbal) communication can lead to misunderstandings in intercultural communication. Common gestures, for example, can have completely different, and sometimes impolite or insulting, meanings in another culture. In human societies, culturally defined status differences, such as gender inequality, can be inferred from nonverbal communication that expresses dominance and subordination.

intercultural communication
The communication of meanings between people of different languages and cultures.

How would you describe the nonverbal interaction between these individuals?

LINGUISTIC ANTHROPOLOGY

Linguistic anthropology investigates connections between language, culture, and worldview. Researchers study the vocabulary and grammar of particular languages to determine how language reflects and is reflected in culture. Linguistic anthropologists are interested in drawing connections between a people's language and their worldview, defined in Chapter 2 as people's perceptions of their environment, their relations with other people and other creatures, and their concepts of time and space. Linguistic anthropology also is concerned with understanding the social dimensions of language use, investigating the ways that social categories such as gender, class, and race influence the use and interpretation of distinctive speech styles. These concerns overlap with the field of **sociolinguistics,** the study of the interplay of social variables such as class, gender, and race on language use.

The Sapir-Whorf Hypothesis

The two most influential figures in the early development of linguistic anthropology were Edward Sapir (1884–1939) and his student Benjamin Whorf (1897–1941). Both men studied the languages and cultures of several Native American peoples. And both are associated with the concept—known as the **Sapir-Whorf hypothesis**—that the language people speak influences the way they think.

According to Sapir, language affects all human experience to some extent. Vocabulary, in particular, both reflects what is culturally important to a people and at the same time influences what they pay attention to. Speakers give names (words) to important entities and events in their physical and social worlds, and, once named, those entities and events become culturally and individually noticed and experienced. In other words, the relationship between vocabulary and cultural value is bidirectional. Over time, this interdependent process creates and reinforces a unique mental model for each culture. As Sapir noted, "The worlds in which different societies live are distinct worlds, not merely the same world with different labels attached" (1949:162).

As evidence for this conclusion, Sapir examined the vocabulary of the Paiute people living in semidesert areas of Arizona, Utah, and Nevada. The Paiute, he noted, distinguish fine details of their environment with separate words. Among them are words for (as translated by Sapir) "divide, ledge, sand flat, semicircular valley, circular valley

sociolinguistics
Study of the impacts of socioeconomic and cultural factors, such as gender and class, on language and communication within a society.

Sapir-Whorf hypothesis
The assertion that the form and content of language influence speakers' behaviors, thought processes, and worldview.

or hollow, spot of level ground in mountains surrounded by ridges, plain valley surrounded by mountains, plain, desert, knoll, plateau, canyon without water, canyon with creek, wash or gutter, gulch, slope of mountain or canyon wall receiving sunlight, shaded slope of mountain or canyon wall, rolling country intersected by several small hill-ridges" (1949:91).

As Sapir's translation indicates, English can be used to describe each of these features. The Paiute language, however, labels each feature with a separate word and thereby gives it distinctive value. This classification suggests how culturally important these kinds of environmental features are to Paiute speakers but not to English speakers. This contrast is consistent with the differences in the two peoples' ways of living. The Paiute depended on hunting and gathering to obtain their food. Therefore, detailed knowledge of and sensitivity to their natural environment were crucial to their survival. Similar studies of specialized vocabularies in different languages can provide insights into the cultural attitudes and priorities of the people who speak them.

Like Sapir, Benjamin Whorf was interested in the influence of vocabulary on culture, thought, and behavior. For example, while working for a fire insurance company, he noticed that fires often resulted from confusion over the meaning of words. In some cases, workmen had thrown matches and cigarette stubs into "empty" gasoline drums, even though the drums contained combustible vapors and invisible traces of gasoline. Whorf concluded that the men acted inappropriately because they interpreted "empty" according to its usual meaning of "null and void, negative, inert" (1956:135).

Whorf also went beyond vocabulary to consider the influence a language's grammatical structures might have on speakers' thoughts and behaviors. Comparing English to the language of the Hopi of Arizona, Whorf noted that whereas English tenses divide time into three distinct units—past, present, and future—Hopi verbs do not indicate the time of an event. Rather, they focus on the manner or duration of an event. He concluded that because of these differences, Hopi speakers have different concepts of time, number, and duration than English speakers do (1956). In turn, because of

American vocabulary for different kinds and qualities of automobiles is highly differentiated. In what sense does this vocabulary express American values? How does this vocabulary affect the way we think about cars and value them?

these differences, Hopi speakers and English speakers perceive the world in fundamentally different ways. As Whorf put it, "Concepts of 'time' and 'matter' are not given in substantially the same form by experience to all [people] but depend upon the nature of the language or languages through the use of which they have been developed" (p. 158).

The concepts underlying the Sapir-Whorf hypothesis focus on differences in the ways that language expresses and influences speakers' knowledge and attitudes. However, these differences do not imply that any language is superior to any other, only that people adapt their language to fit their environment and culture. That is, a language with a more elaborate set of words in any one category expressing certain concepts is not superior overall to any other language. And, although language may have a role in affecting the way people view the world, it is not strongly deterministic but, rather, consists of indirect links. That is, the words and structures of a language may set guideposts but do not ultimately constrain people's thoughts. Finally, since languages and cultures change all the time, there is no neat fit between a particular element of language and a particular element of culture.

Language, Culture, and Society

Most linguistic anthropologists today understand that language influences thought, and at the same time, thought influences language. The idea that language is

In Their Own Voices

Honoring Native Languages

The Spring 2000 issue of Tribal College Journal *focused on efforts by Native American educators and elders to maintain and increase knowledge of indigenous languages by members of their communities. Contributors to the journal not only voiced their opinions about the types of language revival and mainte-nance programs suited to their localities but also made explicit connections between language and cultural heritage.*

Knowing diverse languages is important to the country, to the tribes, and to the individuals. Without the language, ceremonies cannot continue; children cannot communicate with their grandparents; and adults cannot voice their prayers. Some attribute their tribes' social disintegration to the loss of their language and culture. "Our moral imperatives are in the language," said Alan Caldwell, director of the College of the Menominee Nation Culture Institute in Wisconsin. On the Blackfeet Reservation in Montana, teachers at the Head Start have noticed that children with behavioral problems have been transformed by their experiences in [language] immersion school. By connecting them with their language, the Head Start instructors link the children with their traditional values. The Winnebago Tribal Diabetes Project Director

believes that language classes help improve physical and mental health.

Native languages differ from English not just in the words used but also in the concepts conveyed. The common Navajo greeting, *Ya'at'eeh,* is much more than "Hello, how are you?" To the Dine people, it means, "Everything is good between us," according to Frank Morgan of Dine College. Many common expressions have spiritual connotations, according to Blackfeet Community College language instructor Marvin Weatherwax. In groundbreaking research, Blackfoot language scholars at Red Crow Community College in Alberta are using words and phrases to reconstruct their culture. In the process, they are healing themselves, according to Duane Mistaken Chief. For example, by studying the word *Ainna'kowa* (to show respect), they learned *Ainna'kohsit*—to respect themselves.

The Learning Lodge Institute [a project developed by seven tribal colleges in Montana] has the goal of "using education for the teaching of language and culture," said project director Lanny Real Bird. This dual mission is key. All this helps tribal communities reach a larger goal, said Real Bird. It is part of each college's mission to "empower the cultures so they can empower themselves," he said. This means directing "their own education, their own health,

an intimate part of culture and shapes people's worldview has influenced efforts to maintain or revive indigenous languages in Hawaii, New Zealand, Australia, North America, and other places. In regions where most native peoples no longer speak the language of their ancestors, community members have developed projects aimed at preventing language loss. Many of these projects are based on the importance of the role of language as an integral part of cultural identity and cultural vitality. In New Zealand, the Maoris have been working to preserve their language, te reo Maori. Revitalization efforts of the next two decades included *kohanga reo,* literally "language nests," for preschoolers and radio stations broadcasting in Maori. Nevertheless, by 1995, there were fewer than 10,000 Maori speakers, and of them, only about 14 per-cent held daily conversations in Maori in their homes. Factors in the continuing endangerment of this language include television, industrialization, intercultural marriages, and the low social status of the language in the eyes of its speakers as well as other New Zealanders.

The Study of Language Speakers

Linguistic anthropologists also study the demographics of specific languages—that is, the frequency, distribution, and range of languages and their variants within a nation, region, or geographic area. This, too, is a concern that overlaps the work of their own government. To utilize their own resources." Language instruction is therefore not an exercise in sentimentality but part of a strategy for self-determination.

A Culture Leadership Program is giving a select group of students a more intensive, culturally based approach to language instruction. In this innovative program, a small group of tribal members spend a year working with Salish elder Johnny Arlee. Language instruction is only one part of the program. Students also learn the traditional activities of the Salish people throughout the four seasons, learning about hunting, preparing game, gathering roots and other wild foods. Arlee also presents the songs and spiritual aspects of seasonal activities. As a result, language is learned informally, but also more naturally, crossing an artificial boundary between language and culture.

Learning Lodge participants believe language is essential for the survival of tribal cultures. Lanny Real Bird summarized it this way: "Without a language to speak, there is no culture because there are words and expressions unique to particular tribes. They are holy and supernatural. To be translated and used in the context of interpretation of another language would not be possible." Marvin Weatherwax gave an example from everyday experience. "I can tell somebody something in English, and it will sound so plain. Maybe I would say, "Would you give me a glass of water?" But in Blackfeet the same request translates this way: "Would you please take me to the water?" "It has such a different feeling when you say it this way. Each word and phrase has spiritual connotations." So the loss of language is more than the loss of words. Instead, "it would be the loss of culture as it is. I cannot teach you culture. Culture is something you have to live. Through the language we can give a part of the culture that can be lived."

Elders involved in the Anishnabe or Ojibwe language program at the Bay Mills Community College in Michigan said that those who cannot speak their own language are only people whose ancestors were Anishnabe; they are no longer Anishnabe themselves. "It's harsh, but I kind of agree with that view" said Tom Peters, who graduated from the Institute this year. Peters views the Anishnabe language as a sacred gift. "Language is the first step to recovering culture. It's authentic culture because the Native perspective is not taken out of it." His fellow graduate, Sidney Martin, agrees. "The language means everything. It is the powwow, the culture, the basket making, the values," she said. "It is everything." And according to Doris Boissoneau, a language curriculum developer, "If we are going to call ourselves a Nation with sovereignty rights and inherited rights, we need a language and a culture. The fires have never gone out amongst the Anishnabeg. They have dimmed. The adults and Elders are rekindling the fires, and they will burn even brighter and rekindle the hopes of all Anishnabe."

From "Honoring Native Languages, Defeating the Shame," *Tribal College Journal* (Spring 2000). Essays by Marjane Ambler, Paul Boyer, and Jennifer Dale. Reprinted with permission from Tribal College Journal of American Indian Higher Education, www.tribalcollegejournal.org. Copyright © 2000.

sociolinguists. In pluralistic societies such as the United States, for example, language diversity is common. As the Case Study describes, the United States is a multilingual nation inhabited by millions of people who speak more than one language. Although English is the country's dominant language, it is not the first language of many native-born citizens. And numerous immigrants continue to use their original language on a daily basis in most social interactions. The demographics of language speakers often reveals the history of migration and regional occupation.

Language and Dialects

In all language communities, there are variations in the ways that various groups of people, or people in different regions, speak. People in one group may pronounce sounds differently than those in another, or use different words for objects or actions, or structure sentences in a distinctive way. Taken together, these differences are called **dialects.** Even in small-scale societies, there might be variations in dialect from village to village. In modern nations with large territories and diverse populations, regional distinctions abound, especially in pronunciation, or *accent.*

Among English speakers in North America, a Canadian accent differs from a U.S. accent, with regional accents prevalent within each country. Similarly, accents differ among English speakers around the world, from Britain to Australia and India.

dialect
A variety of a language spoken by a particular group of people, based on regional differences or social differences such as gender, class, race, or ethnicity.

Case Study

The Status of English in the United States

In the United States, no federal legislation specifically grants official status to English, but most political leaders support and promote its exclusive use in public domains. This was not always the case, however. From the late eighteenth through the mid-nineteenth centuries, many of the country's leading figures saw no reason to discourage the use of other languages, although they thought all Americans should be encouraged to learn English. They understood that different languages express different thoughts and cultural orientations and believed that linguistic diversity strengthened the development and exchange of ideas (Heath, 1977). During that period, some states promoted multilingualism by publishing laws in other languages as well as English. Pennsylvania, with its large German-speaking population, published laws in German, and Louisiana, with its large French-speaking population, published laws in French. Some laws affecting Native Americans were printed in Native American languages.

Official attitudes toward multilingualism changed in the late nineteenth century, and policies promoting or protecting other languages were retracted. This change was prompted by the large influx of immigrants coming into the United States from southern and eastern Europe at the time and the prejudice against them. Educators and public figures promoted the teaching of "correct" Standard English. Many states enacted laws designating English as the only language to be used in schools, and mandated fines for teachers who spoke other languages in the classroom. Children often were punished for speaking their native languages in school. The English-only trend accelerated in the twentieth century, particularly during World Wars I and II, when speaking German or Japanese could provoke suspicions of treason. Although the U.S. Supreme Court in 1923 upheld the right of private schools to provide instruction in languages other than English, the ruling did not apply to public schools, which most students attended (Grosjean, 1982).

Today, state and local governments determine whether to permit or bar the use of languages other than English as primary modes of communication in schools. A number of organizations actively promote English-only policies with the goal of eliminating bilingual education programs in public schools. Some English-only advocates also want to ban the use of public money to disseminate information in other languages to residents, including voter registration information, motor vehicle forms, and health care pamphlets. The "English-only" states are Arizona, Arkansas, California, Colorado, Florida, Georgia, Illinois, Indiana, Kentucky, Mississippi, Nebraska, North Carolina, North Dakota, South Carolina, Tennessee, and Virginia (American Civil Liberties Union, 2005). English-only state legislation efforts coincide with rising rates of immigration from Mexico and Spanish-speaking countries in Central and South America and from the Caribbean.

Despite these pressures, however, and the de facto official status of English, the United States continues to be a country of great linguistic diversity. According to the U.S. Census Bureau, nearly one in five people, or 47 million U.S. residents age 5 and older, spoke a language other than English at home in 2000 (Public Information Office, October 8, 2003). That was an increase of 15 million people since 1990. About 380 different languages are spoken in the United States, including 155 Native American languages. The following table lists the most prominent of these.

According to a government report entitled "Language Use and English-Speaking Ability: 2000," about 55 percent of the people who spoke a language other than English at home reported they spoke English "very well." Combined with those who spoke only English at home, 92 percent of the population age 5 and over had no difficulty speaking English. Among those who spoke a language other than English at home were almost 11 million Spanish speakers. According to the report, Spanish speakers increased

Language	Number of speakers in 2000
Spanish	28,100,000
Asian and Pacific Island	4,900,000
Chinese	2,000,000
French	1,600,000
German	1,380,000
Italian	1,000,000
Native American	364,000

from 17.3 million in 1990 to 28.1 million in 2000, a 62 percent rise. Just over half the Spanish speakers reported speaking English "very well."

The concentration of people with a native language other than English varies nationwide. Only six states have 2 million or more: California (12 million), Texas (6 million), New York (5 million), Florida (3.4 million), Illinois (2.2 million), and New Jersey (2 million). The states with the highest *proportion* of people whose native language is not English are California (39.5 percent), New Mexico (36.5 percent), and Texas (31.2 percent). The distribution of specific languages also varies. Spanish has by far the most speakers, but French is the most frequently spoken non-English language in Louisiana, Maine, New Hampshire, and Vermont; German is the most frequently spoken in Montana, Minnesota, and North and South Dakota; and Portuguese is first in Rhode Island. The Native American language Yupik dominates in Alaska, and Japanese is the most frequently spoken in Hawaii.

Surveys of Native American languages indicate that Navajo has the most speakers, with 178,000 who speak it at home, according to 2000 census figures. (A "home language" is one regularly spoken in the home. There may be other people who know a language other than English but do not use it as their regular mode of communication.) Other languages with more than 10,000 speakers (1990 data) include Dakota/ Lakhota, Yupik, Apache, Cherokee, and Pima and Papago. Those with between 5,000 and 10,000 speakers are Choctaw and Chickasaw, Keres, Zuni, Muskogee/Creek, Hopi, and Ojibwa (Broadwell, 1995:146–147). In addition, some 17,000 people reported their home language as "Indian" or "American Indian" without mentioning a specific language. Approximately 10,000 people claimed a Native American language as their only language.

Linguistic diversity is a natural feature of multiethnic societies such as the United States, made up largely of people who are either themselves immigrants or are descendants of immigrants. However, most descendants of immigrants in the United States stop speaking their ancestral languages by the third generation (Fishman, 1981). First-generation Americans usually can speak their parents' language because it is used in the home on a regular basis. Second-generation Americans often are able to understand their ancestral language and may be able to converse in a rudimentary way. But by the third generation, any ability to understand or use the language generally disappears. Several factors contribute to this trend. Intermarriage is a powerful force that dissipates an ethnic and linguistic focus on the country of origin. If the husband and wife come from different ethnic groups, English is their only language in common. Their children, therefore, will rarely be exposed to the ancestral language of either parent, except perhaps in larger family gatherings. In addition, immigrants and their descendants usually want to assimilate into their new country, abandoning former customs and languages.

Finally, while maintaining linguistic diversity is an important goal for many people because of the unique identity that it carries, it is obviously beneficial that residents of a country speak a common language. People need to be able to communicate and they need to be able to access information from public sources that are disseminated in a language common to everyone in the society.

Figure 4.2
Dialect Map of American English
(Delaney, 2000)

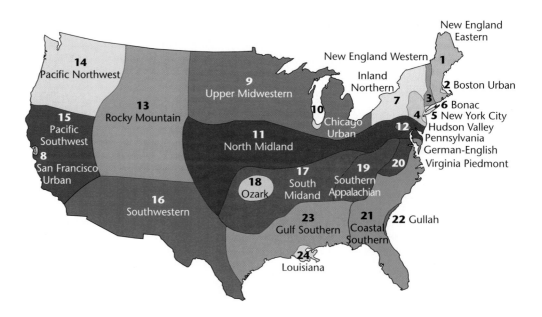

You immediately notice a speaker's accent and can often guess where he or she comes from based on it. Similarly, regions may have their own distinctive vocabulary. For example, the word *cabinet* is used in parts of Rhode Island to refer to what other North Americans would call a *milkshake*. Some Americans put items in a *bag*, others in a *sack*. Some call a carbonated sweet drink *pop*, others *soda*, and still others *tonic*. And in parts of Pennsylvania, some people say *snicklefritz* when they're talking about a rowdy child. The dialect map in Figure 4.2 shows local dialect variations in one region of the United States.

Language and Gender, Class, and Race

In addition to region, languages also may vary based on social categories, such as gender, class, and race or ethnicity. The study of such differences is central to the field of sociolinguistics and forms an important part of inquiry in linguistic anthropology. Sociolinguists tend to focus on the social dimensions of language use in large urban societies, whereas linguistic anthropologists investigate these issues among peoples and languages of indigenous communities.

Since gender is a powerful feature of personal and social identity, it is often reflected in language use. Women and men may differ in the frequency with which they use certain pronunciations or words. In both the United States and England, for example, women and girls are more likely to pronounce words ending in "ing"—*running, talking*—according to standard usage, whereas men and boys are more likely to employ colloquial usage, clipping the "ng" sound, as in *runnin'* and *talkin'* (Trudgill, 1972). Men also are more likely than women to use profanity and obscenity. Gender differences can be great. In some societies women speak an entirely different language dialect among themselves than that used by men.

Accent and usage differ with class as well. Middle-class speakers studied in the United States, England, France, and Belgium, for example, tend to use longer sentences and more complex grammatical constructions than working-class speakers (Labov, 1972b; Trudgill, 1974; Lindenfeld, 1969; van de Broeck, 1977). Differences in pronunciation, word choice, and grammar often become part of what defines ethnic and racial identities.

In most contemporary countries, one dialect is selected as "standard." There is nothing inherently "better" about this dialect than any others. Rather, its dominance is the result of social, economic, and political factors. Usually, the dialect of a society's elite—the educated, the prosperous, and those in power—becomes the standard. In England, for example, the dialect of English spoken within the geographic triangle linking the cities of London, Cambridge, and Oxford emerged as standard sometime

GLOBALIZATION

The spread of English throughout the world has led to the development of new "Englishes" (Platt, Weber, and Ho, 1984). These English languages are more than dialects because they involve vocabulary, syntax, grammar, and semantics, as well as pronunciations. Other than in the United States, Canada, and the United Kingdom, English is spoken as an official language in Australia, New Zealand, South Africa, India, parts of the Caribbean, the Philippines, and China (Hong Kong).

? *What are some examples of Briticisms in American English? What are the characteristics of your dialect, and what does that say about who you are?*

in the fourteenth century. This area was and continues to be Britain's economic and political center. In the United States, upper-class pronunciations often retain the sounds of standard British English, which, in turn, is based on the dialect of upper-class British.

In every society, once a dialect is recognized as the standard, others become stigmatized and marginalized the more they deviate from it. Standard pronunciation and usage are considered "correct" and other versions are considered "wrong" or "debased." Speakers of the standard dialect gain prestige and respect, whereas speakers of nonstandard dialects are looked down upon. Speakers of nonstandard dialects may look down on themselves as well, thinking that their speech reflects their educational and even moral shortcomings (Bourdieu, 1991). These attitudes are transmitted in many settings, especially the schools, the media, and public institutions.

African-American English

In the United States and elsewhere, language use may identify people by race and ethnicity, concepts defined more completely in Chapter 11. Many, but by no means all, African Americans in the United States speak a dialect known as African-American English, or **African-American Vernacular English (AAVE).** Some speakers use this dialect all the time, whereas others use it only within certain contexts—with family and friends, for example—and speak **Standard English** in other situations—as in school or at work. Individuals also switch from one dialect to the other, depending on the topic under discussion and the attitude and identity of the people they are speaking with.

AAVE has patterned rules of phonology, syntax, and semantics equivalent to those of any other language or dialect. Most AAVE rules are identical to those of Standard English, except for a few regularly occurring exceptions. The current consensus among linguists is that some features of AAVE derive from the speech of rural white southerners—itself derived from the Scots-Irish dialect of the region's early white settlers—and that other features, particularly several grammatical rules in the verb system, have their origins in African languages.

Among the most distinctive features of AAVE is the omission of the verb "to be" in the present tense. For instance, "she's smart" becomes "she smart." Other examples are "He fast in everything he do," "We on tape," and "He always coming over to my house to eat" (Labov, 1972a:67–68). Another prominent feature of AAVE is the use of the verb "to be" to describe an event that occurs over a period of time or one that occurs and is expected to reoccur. Here are some examples (from Labov, 1972a, and Baugh, 1984):

1. The office be closed on weekends.

2. She say, "Why you be runnin in the street so much?"

3. But the teachers don't be knowing the problems like the parents do.

Also, in AAVE, "done" is used to mark an action that is completed. For example

1. The teacher done lost her keys.

2. We done told him bout these pipes already.

Finally, AAVE is characterized by a proliferation of negation to mark emphasis and stylistic effect:

1. They didn't never do nothing to nobody.

2. He ain't not never gon say it to his face.

3. They can't do nothing if they don't never try.

4. Didn't nobody see it, didn't nobody hear it!

These children probably do not know the West African linguistic origins of some of the words they or their parents may use as speakers of African-American Vernacular English (AAVE). Some of those words take both their form and meaning from West African languages, such as bogus, *"fake/fraudulent," which comes from the Hausa* boko, *or* boko-boko, *meaning "deceit, fraud"; or* hep, hip, *"well informed, up-to-date," from the Wolof* hepi, hipi, *"to open one's eyes, be aware of what is going on"; and* dig, *"to understand, appreciate, pay attention," from the Wolog* deg, dega, *"to understand, appreciate."*

Case study

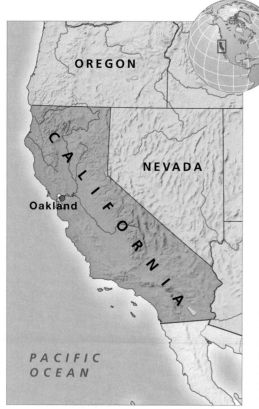

Ebonics, Language, and Politics

In December 1996, the school board of Oakland, California, prompted by the poor performance of African American children on tests of reading and language arts skills, passed a resolution to implement a new approach to the teaching of those skills. The goal of the new approach was to bridge the gap between the vernacular language that many African American children used at home and in the community and the Standard English demanded in the school setting. Teachers were to be trained to appreciate AAVE as a legitimate variant of English, and children were to be instructed in both AAVE and Standard English. The assumption was that children would master basic concepts better if they learned them in their own vernacular dialect:

> The Superintendent shall devise and implement the best possible academic program for imparting instruction to African-American students in their primary language for the combined purposes of maintaining the legitimacy and richness of such language . . . and to facilitate their acquisition and mastery of English language skills. (quoted in *The Black Scholar*, 1997:4)

Some research supports the effectiveness of this approach (Rickford, 1997; McWhorter, 1997). In one study, AAVE-speaking children in kindergarten and first and second grades took a standard test in reading that had been translated into AAVE. They scored significantly higher than children who took an untranslated version (Williams, 1997:212). Another study involved an AAVE-based reading program, called "Bridge," which had been developed in the 1970s. This program began with reading material written only in the vernacular, then presented texts that were written 50 percent in AAVE and 50 percent in Standard English, and finally switched completely to the standard.

Students were introduced to the new program with a motivational talk recorded by a young black man:

> What's happenin', brothers and sisters? I want to tell you about this here program called "Bridge," a cross-cultural reading program. Now I know what you thinkin'. This is just another one of them jive reading programs, and that I won't be needin' no readin' program. But dig it. This here reading program is really kinda different. It was done by a brother and two sisters, soul folk, you know. (quoted in Rickford, 1997:179)

To evaluate the effectiveness of the Bridge approach, children in grades 7 through 12 were tested after 4 months and compared to a group who had not been exposed to the program. Reading scores of the Bridge children increased by a measure of 6.2 months, meaning that they improved more than would be expected for the time period (4 months). In contrast, children in the standard school programs increased only by 1.6 months, less than the increase expected for the 4-month period. The Bridge children not only surpassed children in standard programs but also did better than the norm (4 months' gain for 4 months of instruction) (Rickford, 1997:179). Unfortunately, despite their effectiveness, the publisher discontinued the Bridge readers because of criticism by educators and the media.

The Oakland school board's proposal succumbed to a storm of protest and ridicule. Unfortunately, the board undermined itself by claiming that AAVE, which it called **Ebonics,** was derived from "Niger-Congo African languages" and was "not a dialect of English." However, no linguistic evidence supports the claim that AAVE is a separate language rather than a dialect of English. And although AAVE certainly shares features with some African languages, it has complex origins that involve more than a simple affiliation to one particular language family.

Ebonics
Another name for African-American Vernacular English.

These errors gave critics ammunition to oppose the development of special educational programs to serve the needs of African American children. Opponents inaccurately claimed that Ebonics called for children to be instructed exclusively in AAVE, and not to learn Standard English. Even influential African Americans, such as Jesse Jackson and Maya Angelou, voiced opposition to the school board's resolution. Hoping to counter the barrage of criticism, the Linguistics Society of America voted unanimously in favor of the board, but its support was not widely reported nationally. In the end, Oakland failed to get bilingual education funding and abandoned the program.

What is to be done to teach reading and language skills to children whose home language differs from the standard? Some argue that the dual-language approach is the best answer, while others believe that immersion in Standard English is preferable. Black scholars and public figures writing in special issues of *The Black Scholar* (1997) and the *Journal of Black Psychology* (1997) devoted to the Ebonics controversy argued both points of view.

To gain perspective on this controversy, consider the social context in which AAVE-speaking children may resist learning Standard English. When people elevate a particular language or dialect over another, they convey a message of superiority. Children in countries such as Switzerland, Germany, and Scotland, who grow up speaking a regional dialect, easily learn a standard dialect of their language when they enter school (McWhorter, 1997:12–13). Unlike these European children, however, African American children may confront a legacy of racial and regional prejudice and social attitudes demeaning to them as well as to the way they speak. As one commentary concludes:

> Many of our students resort to not learning as a means of resistance. . . . We need to help them move beyond the resistance that keeps them stifled and saddled in the same place. We are advocating that educators provide Black youths with the history of Black and Standard English and encourage them to critically examine these two linguistic forms and the social and political situations that created them. Merging this knowledge with the pride and confidence that comes from a healthy sense of self and peoplehood, Black youths can move forward knowing the differences between languages and the value of language and culture, never having to surrender one language (Black English) for another (Standard English). (Smitherman and Cunningham, 1997:230–231)

The Bridge program has since been tested in other school systems, with greater success. According to William Labov (2004), it has proven to be one of the most useful approaches to improving reading scores for African American children. Its particular strength is that it combines a linguistic and a cultural approach to reading. It employs words and grammatical constructions that are familiar to the children. And it contextualizes language in a cultural background in which the children feel comfortable. Finding techniques that will improve reading scores is especially critical at this time when test scores and linguistic observations point to increasing divergence between AAVE and Standard English.

? *What do you think is the best approach to the education of AAVE-speaking children, and why?*

Serious controversies have arisen in relation to AAVE and the education of African American children. Children who speak AAVE face a host of educational roadblocks. Many teachers regard any nonstandard speech negatively, a bias that colors their judgment of AAVE speakers. Children who have difficulty with Standard English or refuse to use it are sometimes perceived to be hostile, and may even be labeled as learning-disabled or mentally handicapped. Because of AAVE's grammatical differences from Standard English, teachers also may have trouble understanding AAVE speakers and misinterpret what they are saying. The children themselves often feel conflict between their desire to succeed in school, which requires them to speak Standard English, and their desire to be accepted by their peers. Other children may ridicule and reject students who speak Standard English and perform well in school. The desire for peer acceptance, combined with the perception that they will never get teachers' approval, may lead children to reject the norms of Standard English.

Some of these issues were raised in a case brought to a federal court in Michigan in 1977. The case arose because of parents' concerns about their children's poor school performance and their feeling that it did not reflect the children's ability but rather a lack of cultural and linguistic understanding between teachers and students. The plaintiffs argued that the local school in Ann Arbor had not taken any remedial action

ethnosemantics
Study of culture through people's use of language to categorize and classify people, objects, activities, and experiences.

jargons
Specialized or technical words and expressions spoken by people who share a particular occupation or interest.

componential analysis
A technique of analyzing the similarities and contrasts among words in a particular category, such as kinship terms or animal names.

? *What jargons do you use? How do you use them?*

to address their children's educational problems. In 1979, after hearing testimony from many linguists about the origins and structure of African-American English, the judge in the case handed down a historic decision. Finding for the plaintiffs, he ordered the Ann Arbor school board to institute procedures to correct teachers' misconceptions about African-American English and to help students better learn the standard language. The judge found that "the language barrier that did exist was in the form of unconscious negative attitudes formed by teachers towards children who spoke African-American English, and the reactions of children to those attitudes" (cited in Labov, 1982:193). The school board began instructing teachers about the characteristics of AAVE and developing methods to help children learn the standard language. Despite the findings of the Michigan court, however, attempts to address the use of AAVE in public schools continue to spark controversy (see the Case Study on ebonics, language, and politics on page 90).

> **REVIEW**
>
> The field of linguistic anthropology examines the interrelationships between language and culture, for example how language both influences and reflects a culture's worldview. The Sapir-Whorf hypothesis argues that language predisposes people to selectively perceive and think about things in certain ways and that those ways affect their behavior and attitudes. Dialects, regional and group distinctions of a language, can include differences in pronunciation and vocabulary. They can vary by sex, gender, race, ethnicity, and social class or socioeconomic background. Sociolinguistics is the study of the impacts of socioeconomic and cultural factors on language and communication within a society. Standard dialects, such as Standard English, usually are derived from the versions spoken by social elites. African-American Vernacular English (AAVE) is a well-known dialect in the United States. Also called Ebonics, AAVE is derived from English spoken by rural white southerners and African languages; it has some African loanwords and several distinctive grammatical rules for verbs.

ETHNOSEMANTICS

Building on the pioneering foundations of the first half of the twentieth century, linguistic anthropologists have broadened their exploration of the relationship between language and culture. Some continue to study what vocabulary can reveal about the structure of human thought. Others investigate how cultural values and symbols are encoded in words or expressions and are then used by speakers to transmit emotional, attitudinal, and symbolic meanings. Researchers also examine the systems or ways of categorizing words that people use to name people, objects, or forces in their physical and social environments, a field called **ethnosemantics.**

Studies of vocabulary usually focus on the comparative analysis of categories of words or systems of classification, such as words for animals, kinship terms, words for parts of the body, words for colors, or words for phenomena such as weather. Linguistic anthropologists also study occupational **jargons,** the specialized vocabularies used by people who share specific communication needs relating to their work or some other activity. Philosophy professors, baseball announcers, Web hosts, and thieves are examples of groups that use jargons to communicate.

Componential Analysis

By analyzing similarities and contrasts among the words in a category, you can learn something about what is culturally important to the speakers of a language and how they experience their world. This comparative approach, called **componential analysis,** involves isolating components of meaning within the words in a category. The goal is to understand the ethnosemantics, or indigenous systems of meaning, of a culture or group and its members.

Take, for example, words for animals in English. For some animals, English has many more words than it does for others, and these differences reflect differences in cultural interest. For horses, English has separate words that specify female and male adults (*mare* and *stallion*), babies (*foal*), female and male juveniles (*filly* and *colt*), and neutered adult males (*gelding*). English has a similarly extensive vocabulary to differentiate age and sex among cattle and other domestic food and draft animals, which historically have played a crucial role in the subsistence and economy of English-speaking peoples. In addition, there are many words for different breeds of these animals. In contrast, other species—chipmunk, otter, and moose, for example—are treated in a more generalized way, with only one term for all members of the class of animals.

Cultural Presuppositions

When people speak, they understand one another because of an array of shared knowledge and assumptions, or **cultural presuppositions,** that mean far more than what words alone convey. Smooth conversation depends on these unstated presuppositions. Without them, people cannot accurately assess how their words are being understood. Americans talking to one another about the World Series, for example, assume they share knowledge that the term refers to professional baseball, that professional baseball teams are organized into leagues, that the teams in a league compete throughout a season to determine the league champions, and that the World Series is the culminating competition between the league champions.

Other cultural presuppositions are more complex and more subtly embedded within language. For example, the language of the Navajo of New Mexico and Arizona reflects different presuppositions about individual self-assertion (Young, 1987). English has many verbs that express types of coercion: *cause, force, oblige, make, compel, order, command, constrain, must, have to, ought to.* In contrast, the Navajo language lacks such verbs. Rather than saying, "I must go there," a Navajo speaker says the equivalent of "It is only good that I shall go there." Similarly, whereas English readily expresses the idea that people have a right to impose their will on other creatures, the Navajo language does not. Where an English speaker might say, "I make the horse run," a Navajo speaker would say, "The horse is running for me."

Cultural norms of communicative behavior—the pragmatics of communication—also involve presuppositions. Two casually acquainted North Americans might use a greeting such as "Hi! How are you?" Both parties know that this greeting is a routine social ritual, not a true request for information. The expected response is "Fine, how are you?"—not a detailed account of one's personal problems.

In all cultures, people use language to influence hearers: to convey information, ask questions, persuade, or issue commands. Few words are neutral in their connotations. They have associations that presuppose culturally shared symbolic meanings. Cultural symbols are transmitted through language and obtain their strength because speakers and hearers unconsciously accept the assumptions on which they are based. For example, to promote products, advertisers manipulate the presuppositions associated with such words as *new, bigger,* and *improved.* The word *free* is charged with cultural presuppositions. Repetitive exposure to such use of language reinforces overt and covert cultural messages implied and presupposed by the words.

Ethnography of Communication

Linguistic anthropologists analyze speech behavior and nonverbal communication in their widest cultural and social contexts. Dell Hymes (1974) introduced the term **ethnography of communication** to describe the study of all explicit and implicit norms for communication—verbal and nonverbal—in a particular setting. Included in such a study would be a description of the setting in which the communication occurred, the participants involved, the language they used, the way they communicated (speaking, writing, nonverbal signals), the genre or form of the communication (conversation, folktale, chant, debate), the topic or subject of the communication, and the attitudes and goals of the participants (p. 10).

An ethnographic description of communication in an American courtroom, for example, might run like this: The setting, a courtroom, is structured to provide separate

? *What cultural presuppositions do you and your classmates share about your participation in the course?*

cultural presuppositions Shared knowledge and unspoken assumptions that people have as members of their culture.

ethnography of communication Study of communication as it occurs within a particular cultural context, considering such features as settings, participants, and participants' attitudes and goals.

As a cultural anthropologist, what might you say about the ethnography of communication in a setting like the one in this photograph? Who are the participants, what language do they use, how do they communicate and in what forms, what are the topics of communication, and what are the participants' attitudes and goals?

seating areas for various categories of participants and to regulate contact between participants. Among the participants are judges, lawyers, defendants, plaintiffs, witnesses, jurors, spectators, and court officials. Participants behave according to their role in the proceedings. The judge, seated on a raised platform at the front of the room and distinguished by special attire, physically dominates the room. From this dominant position, the judge controls the communication of the other participants, each of whom has certain obligations to speak or not to speak. Failure to obey the judge may be considered "contempt of court," a legally punishable offense. Only judges, lawyers, and witnesses may speak publicly. Other participants (jurors, spectators, officers) must remain silent. Each type of participant communicates in expected ways. Lawyers may make introductory and concluding statements or ask questions. Witnesses answer questions. Judges make statements, ask questions, and issue commands and rulings.

Topics of discussion in a courtroom are rigidly defined. A trial is intended to resolve a specific issue, and all communication must be relevant to that issue. The goals of participants vary according to their roles in the proceedings. Speakers choose their words, tone of voice, facial expressions, and gestures to accomplish their goals. The judge seeks to appear impartial, lawyers speak and act persuasively or aggressively, defendants may portray themselves as innocent, witnesses appear honest and reliable, and jurors remain silent but convey interest in the speech and behavior of others.

REVIEW

Ethnosemantics, or indigenous systems of meaning, can lead to a better understanding of what is important in a culture. Systems of meaning include jargons, which are specific to certain occupations or activities. Examples of word comparisons using componential analysis include kin terms and terms for animals. The shared knowledge and assumptions that speakers use are cultural presuppositions. The ethnography of communication involves examining all aspects of communication (setting, participants, topics, and goals) to understand language as cultural expression.

PROCESSES OF LANGUAGE CHANGE

Languages change over time. Change sometimes results from processes internal to a language. For instance, a language may gradually eliminate grammatical distinctions, meanings of words may be altered, or the order of words within sentences may change. Evidence of such patterns can be found in the history of English. Old English (the language spoken in the British Isles until about 1066, the year of the Norman invasion from France), had noun endings that indicated whether the noun was a subject or object in a sentence. Modern English nouns lack these markers. However, English retains distinctions between subject and object for pronouns: "I, he, she, we, they" are subjects, whereas "me, him, her, us, them" are objects. "You" can be either subject or object. Modern English is currently undergoing a further loss of the subject-object distinction in the relative pronouns "who" and "whom." While the object form "whom" is still used in writing and formal speech, most speakers no longer use it in colloquial and informal contexts. We are, therefore, witnesses to ongoing language change.

Changes in the meanings of words also are commonplace. When modern English speakers read the works of William Shakespeare, for example, they often have difficulty understanding them because some words that Shakespeare used have different meanings today, and others have gone out of the language entirely. Many nations try to "freeze" their official national language in time. In the service of linguistic nationalism, France, for example, has a committee in charge of eliminating foreign words from the French language. As you might expect, English is the main influence, with new words and phrases in French such as "le hamburger" and "le blue jeans."

Language change is constant and natural as new words and expressions are invented and others discarded and as vocabularies are elaborated to reflect cultural priorities. Thus, people who are concerned about the "purity" of their language are chasing a phantom. Also, as Edward Sapir pointed out about the relationship between vocabulary and cultural priorities, cultures often change more rapidly than languages. As a result of this "linguistic lag," a specialized vocabulary may not reflect a society's current cultural interests. In time, as linguistic change catches up with culture change, the specialized words are likely to change meaning or to disappear.

? *In your experience, what are some examples of new vocabularies that reflect changing cultural priorities?*

Creoles, Pidgins, and Lingua Francas

In addition to internal adjustments, languages also change in response to the influence of other languages, as evidenced in the Culture Change feature. This kind of change is universal because no language is completely isolated from others. External change occurs when peoples with different languages and cultures come into contact, with three possible general results: The languages will remain distinct; one language will become dominant; or the languages will meld into a new language.

One process of language change that results in a new language is creolization, or the creation of creole languages. **Creoles** are languages that combine sounds, grammatical forms, and vocabularies from several different linguistic sources. They arise in situations of close contact and interaction among people who speak different languages. The United States is home to three creole languages, for example, that came into existence in the past several hundred years. The three American creoles are Gullah, Louisiana Creole, and Hawaiian Creole. Gullah (spoken mostly on the Sea Islands off the coast of South Carolina) is derived from various African languages and English. Louisiana Creole is derived from various African languages and French. Hawaiian Creole is a complex mixture of English, Native Hawaiian, and several Asian and Pacific languages.

Creoles often develop from pidgin languages. **Pidgins** are forms of communication made by combining words and constructions from several languages, but they differ from creoles because they are not full languages but, rather, have small vocabularies and simple constructions. They are used for special purposes, especially for trade.

Lingua francas are full languages that are used among numerous peoples who come into contact regularly but who speak distinct languages. Some of these lingua

creoles
Languages that have historic roots as an amalgamation of vocabulary and grammar derived from two or more independent languages.

pidgins
Rudimentary languages that have a simplified grammar and a limited vocabulary.

lingua francas
Languages used in particular areas by speakers of many different languages in order to communicate with each other.

GLOBALIZATION

Through today's dynamics of globalization, English is now spoken by more than a billion people throughout the world, rivaled only by Chinese. English has become global in three ways: countries such as Australia and South Africa are dominated by English-speaking inhabitants; countries with few native English speakers nevertheless have English as an official language; and many other countries give priority to English in foreign-language learning.

Of the many different languages spoken in India, Hindustani remains the lingua franca of the western and northern regions. It is also often used as the language of choice in popular culture. The Indian film industry produces movies in Hindustani. This industry is called Bollywood, a conflation of Bombay (a city today called Mumbai) and the American Hollywood.

francas are pidgins, such as those that arose to serve the Arab and European slave trades, some are creoles such as Rasta, spoken in Jamaica and other West Indian islands, and others are the regular language of one group that came to be widely used by many other people, such as Swahili, spoken in eastern Africa. More recently, English and French have become international lingua francas.

Historical Linguistics

Among groups of people who speak variants of a language, differences between dialects can accumulate to the extent that people no longer understand one another. Thus, mutual intelligibility is a definition of language as shared by its speakers. When people no longer understand one another, new, separate languages emerge. Tracing changes in languages over time and relationships between languages in the past is the goal of historical linguistics.

Over time, from centuries to millennia, as the descendants of people who spoke a single language separated from one another and migrated into different regions, their speech changed into distinct dialects and, ultimately, when speakers could no longer understand one another, into separate languages. Mutual intelligibility is often taken as a test of whether two forms of speech are dialects of the same language or two different languages. By comparing the sounds, vocabularies, and syntax of today's languages, historical linguists can reconstruct the processes that led to change, grouping languages into families descended from a common ancestral form. A **language family,** then, is a group of languages spoken by people who are historically related.

One method for determining the relationships among languages, estimating when they separated, and even reconstructing features of the parent language is to study a core vocabulary of up to 500 words. This core vocabulary consists of words for objects or ideas that every language can be expected to have words for, including pronouns, some numerals, some colors, words for body parts, and common adjectives (such as large, small) and verbs (such as to eat, to sleep). Words with related meanings that are found to share a common heritage are referred to as **cognates.** The English *to pay* and the French *payer* are cognates, for example. English and French are related historically,

language family
A group of languages that are historically related, descendants of a common ancestral form.

cognates
Words in different languages that are derived from the same word in their parent language.

Culture Change

LOANWORDS

All languages borrow words from other languages. These **loanwords** are often incorporated into a language when the speakers borrow a new cultural item from another group. The words often name new foods, articles of clothing, tools and other equipment, occupations, or new ideas. The following list contains a small number of the many thousands of words borrowed into English from a variety of origins (Pyles and Algeo, 1982:297–316).

loanwords
Words borrowed from one language into another.

Source	Loanwords
Greek	agnostic, chlorine, idiosyncrasy, telephone
Irish-Gaelic	brogue, leprechaun, shamrock
Scots-Gaelic	clan, plaid, slogan, whiskey
Scandinavian	muggy, rug, ski
Spanish	bonanza, canyon, patio, ranch
Portuguese	albino, flamingo, molasses
Italian	balcony, bandit, studio, umbrella
Dutch	boss, cookie, pit (of fruit), sleigh
German	hamster, pretzel, semester
Yiddish	kibitzer, nebbish, phooey, schlep
Russian	czar, mammoth, tundra, vodka
Turkish	fez, tulip, turban
Arabic	candy, mattress, orange, sugar
Hebrew	cherub, hallelujah, jubilee, kosher
Persian	caravan, bazaar, shawl
Sanskrit	karma, yoga
Hindi	bungalow, dungaree, jungle, pajamas
Chinese	tea, kowtow, tycoon
Japanese	hara-kiri, samurai, soya
Pacific languages	bamboo, kangaroo, launch, tattoo
African languages	gorilla, jazz, tote, yam
Native North American languages	bayou, moccasin, moose, pecan
Native Central American languages	chocolate, maize, tomato, potato

In some cases when people borrow foreign words with meanings similar to words that already exist in the language, they give the words special usage. For example, after the Norman invasion of England in 1066, English incorporated the French names of common farm animals to refer to the animals' meat, and the English names were kept for referring to the animals.

Animal	Meat	French source
steer	beef	boeuf
pig	pork	porc
calf	veal	veau
sheep	mutton	mouton

Similarly, foreign words sometimes have a different connotation than their native equivalents. In English, for example, some words of French origin are considered more formal or polite than their Old English counterparts:

Old English source	French source
smell	odor
sweat	perspiration
eat	dine
dead	deceased
want	desire
look at	regard
go away	depart
come back	return

Just as English has borrowed thousands of words from foreign sources, other languages have borrowed words from English. And just as English has modified foreign words to fit English sound patterns, so other languages have altered sounds of English words to fit their systems.

English Word	Borrowing Language	Loanword
roof	Spanish (Puerto Rico)	rufo
police	Swahili (Africa)	polisi
car	Swahili (Africa)	kaa
ruler	Ganda (Africa)	luula
railway	Ganda (Africa)	leerwe
thumbtacks	Mohawk (North America)	tamtaks
number	Navajo (North America)	noomba
Christmas	Navajo (North America)	kesmis
elevator	Japanese	erebeta
baseball	Japanese	beisuboru
casual	Tagalog (Philippines)	kazwal

Sources: Puerto Rican Spanish: Zentella, 1985:45; Costa Rican Spanish: Appel and Muysken, 1987:169; Ganda: Halle and Clements, 1983:51; Mohawk: Bonvillain, 1978:37; Navajo: Young and Morgan, 1987:7; Swahili, Japanese: Berlitz, 1982:299–300; Tagalog: Molony, 1977:141–142.

? *Relationships between languages are determined by finding regularities in sound shifts between cognates. What regular sound shifts can you identify in the following Indo-European cognates for "father"?*

Examples of Indo-European Cognates

father (Modern English)
fader (Middle English)
faeder (Old English)
fader (Swedish, Norwegian, Danish)
vader (Dutch)
vater (German)
pater (Latin)
padre (Spanish, Italian)
père (French)
pai (Portuguese)
patēr (Greek)
pitar (Sanskrit)
pitā (Hindi)

and both are members of the much larger language family called Indo-European, which also includes languages as diverse as Sanskrit, Hindi, Polish, German, and Norwegian. These languages very likely all started out as one language in central Eurasia an estimated 8,000 to 10,000 years ago.

Language families provide insight into the historical relationships between neighboring and even distant peoples. For instance, if neighboring groups speak unrelated languages, they probably did not always live near one another. They may both have

Anthropology Applied

Languages Lost and Found

Closely associated with globalization is the loss of native languages to new languages or to replacement by languages that are used in business and international politics. The six official languages of the United Nations are Arabic, Chinese, Russian, Spanish, English, and French. The UN conducts most of its business in English and French. Many Native Americans and minorities in other pluralistic societies are not taught their native languages, but instead focus is on English in order to succeed in the larger society.

Globalization thus can lead to language loss, which leads to the loss of cultural content, including people's genealogies, folktales, culture histories, and cultural identities. An estimated 6,800 languages are spoken today. In the last 500 years, 4,000 to 9,000 languages became extinct due to wars, genocide, incorporation of ethnic minorities into majority populations, and bans of languages by colonial governments. By the end of the twenty-first century, it is estimated that more than half of the remaining languages will become extinct (Krauss, 1992). The 357 languages with fewer than 50 speakers include Saami (Sweden), Birale (Ethiopia), and Menomini (United States). Examples of recently extinct languages are Ubykh (Turkey), Eyak (Alaska), Dalmatian (Albania), and Ainu (Japan).

Linguistic anthropologists, concerned that language loss leads to the loss of culture, have helped Native American groups document their languages and their stories and also implement programs to teach younger generations their native tongue. With the help of anthropologists, Tsalagi (Cherokee) people and others, for example, can learn to speak Tsalagi with language-learning software and games, free MP3 downloads, and other online resources, such as study groups, discussion lists, dictionaries, and texts. The survival of Tsalagi in some form is guaranteed because it is a written language. Languages that are only spoken die when their last speaker dies. For some researchers, recording these languages and cultures has become a life's work. After the collapse of the Soviet Union, for example, many multinational teams of linguists and anthropologists raced to Siberia to record rare and disappearing languages such as Itel'men of Kamchatka.

CRITICAL THINKING QUESTIONS

What languages were spoken by your forebears? Can you understand, speak, or read those languages? What might you be missing?

---

migrated to their current locations from elsewhere, or perhaps one had long residence in the region and the other was a more recent immigrant. And if the language spoken by one group of people is related to a language spoken hundreds or even thousands of miles away, both groups have a common ancestor that spoke their one ancestral language.

Plotting the distribution of related languages helps to trace the history of migrations, contacts, and conquests among the world's peoples. Although no one knows when or how the first language was spoken, or who spoke it, some historical-comparative linguists believe that they might one day be able to reconstruct "proto-human," the first language spoken by the first modern humans.

REVIEW

All languages change through time. Sounds shift, words change meanings, words are borrowed (loanwords), new words are invented, and languages become extinct. Language change can be both internal and external. Processes of language change that result from culture contact include the creation of pidgins and creoles. Historical linguistics is the comparative study of changes in languages over time and relationships between languages and language families in the past. Divergence of languages is measured by comparing changes in core vocabularies to find cognates, words from different languages with shared sound shifts and similar meanings. Historical linguistics can provide insights into the history of human migration and contact and relationships between contemporary cultures.

Chapter Summary

What Is Language?

- All languages are based on arbitrary symbols for relationships between the sounds of a word and the object, activity, quality, or idea that the word is used to name. Languages are characterized by displacement—that is, the ability to talk about events of the past and the future, not just events that are ongoing at the moment of speech. And languages are productive, in that sounds, words, and sentence constructions can be joined in infinite novel combinations.

The Components of Language

- Linguists have developed numerous descriptive and explanatory tools to analyze the structure of language. Talk is achieved through the interdependent components of sounds, words, sentences, and meanings. Although every language is unique, there are some universals, including the human range of phonetic inventories, recurring types of morphological and syntactic constructions, and underlying semantic relationships.

Nonverbal Communication

- Nonverbal communication also consists of both unique and common behaviors. Although some actions may occur in many societies, they are always given culturally specific interpretations.

Linguistic Anthropology

- Linguistic anthropologists investigate associations between language and cultural meaning. Some study the degrees of specialization and principles of classification within semantic domains that indicate cultural interest. And others examine the "presuppositions" inherent in words and expressions that transmit and reinforce complex social and cultural messages.
- African-American Vernacular English is a variety of speech employed by some (but not all) people of African ancestry in the United States that diverges from Standard English. It has some unique features, although it shares most linguistic rules with the standard variety. Attitudes toward vernacular speech are complex, both on the part of the speakers themselves and in the rest of society. Controversies focus primarily on proposals to incorporate vernacular speech in schools.
- The United States is a complex, multilingual nation with millions of speakers of languages other than English. These include languages of indigenous peoples as well as languages spoken by immigrants from every corner of the globe. Spanish is the most widely spoken of these immigrant languages.

Ethnosemantics

- An "ethnography of communication" attempts to uncover all of the rules that connect language to social behavior. Components of any speech interaction include the participants, the code used, the physical and social settings, the topic of conversation, and the goals of the speakers.

Processes of Language Change

- All languages are in constant processes of change. Some change derives from internal linguistic processes while others derive from contact with other languages. New sounds may be introduced and/or grammatical constructions may be altered. In addition, all languages borrow words from foreign sources to name introduced items, activities, or ideas.
- When varieties of the same language diverge to the point where people speaking different dialects can no longer understand each other, new languages come into being. A language family consists of languages that are related historically and are the common descendants of an ancestral code. Using methods of historical and comparative linguistics, researchers establish relationships among languages by discovering regular correspondences between their sound systems.

Key Terms

language 74	length 78	sociolinguistics 82	cultural
displacement 74	morphology 78	Sapir-Whorf	presuppositions 93
duality of patterning 75	morpheme 78	hypothesis 82	ethnography of
productivity 75	syntax 78	dialect 85	communication 93
call systems (signal	universal grammar 78	African-American	creoles 95
systems) 75	semantics 78	Vernacular English	pidgin 95
phonology 76	nonverbal	(AAVE) 89	lingua francas 95
phonetics 76	communication 80	Standard English 89	language family 96
phonemics 76	emblems 80	Ebonics 90	cognates 96
phoneme 77	body language 80	ethnosemantics 92	loanwords 97
stress 77	intercultural	jargons 92	
pitch 77	communication 81	componential analysis 92	

Review Questions

1. What are the connections between language and culture?

2. Why are chimpanzees and other apes unable to communicate verbally? How do they communicate symbolically? What are some differences in primate communication under laboratory conditions and natural settings?

3. What characteristics distinguish phonemes? What is the difference between a phoneme and a morpheme?

4. What are some applications of the Sapir-Whorf hypothesis? How are language and thought connected?

5. Why is nonverbal communication important in understanding culture and intercultural communication?

6. What are some internal processes of language change that occur in all languages?

7. What are some processes of language change that occur as a result of cultural contact and forces of globalization?

8. What are the goals and methods of historical-comparative linguistics? How are all human languages ultimately related in space and time?

Learning One's Culture

CHAPTER 5

Preview

1. **What is enculturation?**
2. **How do people incorporate children into their society?**
3. **What are the social, cultural, and psychological effects of rites of passage?**
4. **What are some formal and informal means by which individuals learn their culture?**
5. **What social and cultural factors influence an individual's age- and gender-related behavior?**
6. **How do culture, personality, and human psychology intersect?**
7. **In what ways is mental illness both culture-specific and universal?**

There once lived a widow, Ballingokan, and her son, Agkon. Every morning the rooster would wake up Agkon by crowing: "Kook-ko-ko-oook! Agkon, come and trap me." Agkon would answer, "Wait, I'll first look for some fibers to make up my snare." The next day, the rooster again jumped on Agkon's window and crowed: "Oo-oo-oo-o! Agkon, come and snare me." And Agkon said, "Wait, I'll get some strings for my snare." On the third day, the rooster flap his wings loudly and cried out: "O-oo-ook! Agkon, when will you come?"

Agkon ran out, laid his snare with care, and after a few moments it caught a wild fat rooster, which he proudly showed to his mother. "What a nice fat rooster. Now we shall have some nice food," his mother said happily when she saw the rooster.

Agkon burned the feathers of the rooster, cut it into pieces, and began to cook it. When it was almost cooked he dropped the ladle. "Mother," Agkon cried, "I dropped the ladle." "Never mind," his mother said as she quickly went out of the house, "I'll pick it up."

As soon as his mother was down, Agkon quickly drew up the ladder. Then he asked for the ladle and after telling his mother that he would eat first and call her later, he proceeded to do so. After a while the mother said, "Agkon, please leave the wings for me." "But the wings are delicious, mother," Agkon said and started to eat them. "Leave me the claws, my son," the mother pleaded. "They are just what I want, mother," he said. "Surely, you will leave me the neck, Agkon." "It is just what I am eating, mother," Agkon said.

Only the head was now left. "Agkon, my son, will you not give the head to your mother?" "But, mother," Agkon answered, "you know very well that I need to eat the brains."

When nothing was left of the rooster, Agkon put back the ladder and the mother wearily went up the steps. She looked at the pot and found a little soup left, which she took, and mashing some rice in it, ate in tears. She decided to revenge herself on her son.

The mother went upstream and after walking for a long time she heard loud weeping and found a family mourning over a man who had been dead [for a long time]. Ballingokan offered to buy the dead man, but the relatives were already happy to have someone take care of the dead so they gladly gave it to her free. She told the Ladag [Dead Man], "I will carry you on my back." The dead man climbed on her back and she brought him to her granary where she covered him with rice. Then going to the house she called her son and said, "there are some ripe bananas in the granary."

Agkon went down and peeped inside the granary where the Ladag caught him and proceeded to eat him. He shouted to his mother, "Mother," he cried, "the Ladag is eating my feet." "That is for the claws of the chicken that you would not share with your mother," the mother answered. "Mother, the Ladag is eating my arms." "But you did not give me the wings either, my child," his mother said. "Now he is eating my breast, mother." "Neither did you share the breast of the rooster with me, my son." "He's beginning to feed on my neck, mother." "Well, you ate the neck of the rooster, Agkon." "Go ahead, Ladag," said the mother, "eat his head."

That night, Balligokan felt lonely; there was no one to talk with. The following day, there was no one to carry fuel, no one to help her. Her loneliness was worse, and feeling sad, she went to the granary to look for any remains of her son. She found a little blood on the floor, which she took, and going to the river began to perform some ritual. She took some water and began to bathe the blood and said, "May I bathe Agkon! May I bathe his hands!" At once his hands were formed.

And as she said, "legs, feet, arms," all were formed into a man.

Then the mother and son were reconciled and both resolved to love each other truly. And Agkon said, "Mother, from now on, we shall always eat together!"

Excerpts from *Folktales Told around the World*, by Richard Dorson. pp. 257–259. Copyright 1975. Reprinted by permission of The University of Chicago Press.

This tale relates in vivid images the consequences of wrong behavior. Agkon violates cultural rules of how one ought to treat other people, especially relatives and especially one's own mother. As punishment, he is eaten by the Ladag, as his mother wished. But in the end, she relents and brings him back to life because she recognizes that she needs him too. The narrative, therefore, teaches children proper behavior and highlights the economic and social reciprocity that characterizes relationships among kin.

Like language, which is an element of culture, culture as a whole is a symbolic system. As with language, all humans have the capacity to learn any culture, but the specific culture they learn is the one they are born into and raised in. The process by which children acquire their culture is called enculturation, and it is similar to the process of learning social norms, called **socialization.** This chapter examines how enculturation works, then looks at a related issue, the relationship between culture and individual personality.

THE PROCESS OF ENCULTURATION

Humans are born helpless, too weak and uncoordinated to move on their own. Without speech, they are unable to communicate their thoughts, needs, and wants to others. Infants, as a result, are completely dependent on adults to be carried, cared for, and fed. Even after they can walk and talk, human children remain dependent on adults. Indeed, humans have the longest period of juvenile dependency of any animal species. Human young don't reach sexual maturity until around the age of 13 or 14, and not full adult maturity until a few years after that.

Many evolutionary pressures account for these characteristics. Infant helplessness probably resulted from a combination of the increasingly large brains of our ancestors and their shift to an upright, or bipedal, posture. Structural changes in the skeleton that made bipedalism possible also favored immature births, before infant head size grew very large. The lengthy period of childhood dependency reflects the human characteristic that a large brain made possible—culture. Where other animals depend mostly on their physical adaptations for survival, humans rely on culture. But culture is learned, and learning it—enculturation—takes a long time.

All societies have beliefs and practices surrounding childbirth and maternal and infant care. Ju/'hoansi mothers in Namibia and Botswana are attended by healers when they are in difficult labor. The healers go into a trance (called *kia*) in order to confront the spirits causing harm to mother and child (Katz, 1982). The healer lays his or her hands on the mother's abdomen, transferring healing energy and substance (called *num*) in the hopes of protecting the mother and baby.

After the birth, mother and child often remain in their separate dwelling or room for a prescribed length of time. During that period, the mother may follow similar food, activity, and contact restrictions as she had before the birth. After a set number of days, weeks, or even months, the woman and her child are reincorporated into family and community life. That final transition and re-incorporation may be marked by ritualized blessings on both mother and child.

In all societies, the process of enculturation begins as soon as a baby is born and continues into maturity. Infants may be helpless, but they are immediately responsive to the world around them. Gradually, they learn how to communicate through gesture and sound, and they learn how to understand the myriad messages sent their way. Children not only learn to control their muscles, make purposeful actions, and acquire the

socialization
A similar process to enculturation that emphasizes social rather than cultural factors in learning one's culture.

language and communication practices of their society but also, most crucially, they learn to behave in ways that their culture deems appropriate.

Enculturation is so extraordinarily effective because it takes place primarily through informal, nonexplicit means. Because we learn most of our cultural rules unconsciously, we come to feel that our behavior is natural, a result of our nature rather than our culture. And since we feel that our behavior, attitudes, and values come from our nature, we generally don't question their appropriateness. Instead, we "naturalize" our culture, taking these behaviors and attitudes as part of our nature rather than recognizing their cultural origins. Naturalization of attitudes and behaviors results in unquestioning acceptance of cultural norms. The practices that we engage in and the values that we hold become so much a part of our thoughts and feelings that we do not see them as distinct from ourselves. Rather, we see them as forming our very essence as people. We seem to absorb cultural messages without conscious effort, beginning with the great dependency of infancy and continuing through childhood's protracted period of physical and psychological maturation.

While enculturation is a process begun in earliest childhood, learning one's culture does not end upon adulthood. Rather, people learn throughout their lives, continually acquiring new skills but also continually reshaping and reinforcing attitudes and values. Life's experiences teach new lessons that may encourage people to question old ways of interpreting behavior, or they may strengthen their convictions. Just as maintaining traditions reinforces cultural stability, discoveries and innovations enrich individuals and societies.

Becoming a Human Being

When does human life begin? This question may be familiar because of the heated debate over abortion, but there is more cultural variability in the answer than the two positions heard frequently in that debate: conception or birth. In many cultures, newborns are not considered human until a few days or even weeks after birth. They are thought instead to occupy some liminal (in-between), transitional, and not fully human state. Not until the end of this period are infants thought of and treated as members of their family and community. This transition to personhood, or **social birth,** is often marked by ritual.

Among the Lohorung Rai, of eastern Nepal, babies are introduced to the ancestors when they are 5 (girls) or 6 (boys) days old (Hardman, 2000). Until the rite is performed, infants (and their mothers) are thought to be both in danger and dangerous. As yet unprotected by the ancestors, they are vulnerable to harm from evil spirits. This vulnerability and lack of protection make them dangerous to other people, who avoid contact with them. The rite raises the child's ancestral soul and introduces it to the house ancestors, placing it firmly within its family and wider kinship group. Failure to perform the ceremony or to perform it well jeopardizes the child's future health and chances for success.

The Zuni of the American Southwest consider newborns to be unripe or soft "as are germinating seeds or unfinished clay vessels" (Cushing, 1979:205). For eight days after birth, babies and their mothers are isolated indoors, away from the sun, until they are sufficiently hardened for safe exposure to "the world of sunlight." At the end of the period of seclusion, the baby's umbilical cord is buried nearby, and the burial site becomes the child's "midmost shrine," connecting it to Earth Mother and the underworld from which the ancestors emerged in primordial times. At sunrise on the eighth day after birth, the baby's paternal grandmother washes the baby's head, puts it in its cradle, places cornmeal in its hands, and takes it out into the dawn air, facing east toward the rising sun. While other female relatives of both parents sprinkle offerings of cornmeal to Sun in the east, the paternal grandmother recites a blessing prayer (Bunzel, 1932).

Practices of delayed social birth are generally found in societies that have (or had) high rates of infant mortality. High rates of infant mortality may discourage parental emotional attachment to their child. An infant is most vulnerable right after birth, and the belief that it is not yet fully human can temper parents' grief should it die during this period. For similar reasons, in many cultures, deaths of infants or young children are not marked ritually in any significant way. The body is instead disposed of quickly and without ceremony. In contrast, in societies with comparatively low infant mortality

social birth
Social recognition of the transition to personhood.

rates, social birth may even precede actual birth—for example, in customs such as sending fetal sonograms and holding baby showers.

Beliefs about the humanity of infants also reflect a psychological accommodation to the political and economic circumstances that foster high infant mortality. According to a belief prevalent among impoverished communities in northeastern Brazil, for example, infants who are sickly, weak, and passive are thought to be uninterested in living (Scheper-Hughes, 1989, 1992). In other words, in contrast to robust, emotionally engaged infants, sickly infants are thought to *want* to die. They are consequently often ignored, inadequately fed, and little cared for. Those who die are not mourned. A mother's tears are thought to weigh down the infant's angel wings and hinder its ascent to heaven. These beliefs may provide comfort to the child's mother, but they also divert attention from the crushing poverty responsible for the region's high infant mortality rate. Rather than a victim of its circumstances, the child becomes an agent in its own demise.

? *How were you named, and why? Does your name have any special meaning or carry any special expectations?*

Naming.   An important process linked to the recognition of a baby as a social person is naming. In North American societies, a child is usually named at birth or before. Children may be named after a relative or friend of the parents, or they may be given a name from a large stock of familiar names or one that is made up. Some people name their son after the father or, more rarely, a daughter after the mother. Others, such as members of the Jewish faith, never name a child for someone who is living but prefer to name a child after a deceased relative.

In some Native American societies, people often receive new names at various times in their lives, sometimes in hopes of obtaining spiritual powers or protection. For instance, a nineteenth-century Hidatsa woman from North Dakota recounted the reasons for her name change from "Good Way" to "Buffalo-Bird Woman":

> I was a rather sickly child and my father wished after a time to give me a new name. We Indians thought that sickness was from the gods. A child's name was given as a kind of prayer. A new name often moved the gods to help a sick or weakly child. So my father gave me another name, Waheenee-wea, or Buffalo-Bird Woman. My father's gods were birds; and these, we thought, had much holy power. Perhaps the buffalo-birds had spoken to him in a dream. I am still called by the name my father gave me; and, as I have lived to be a very old woman, I think it has brought me good luck from the gods. (Wilson, 1981:8)

Baptism for Christians marks a kind of social birth and functions as an introduction to a social and religious community. In most denominations, baptism ideally takes place as soon as possible after birth, because of the belief that if a baptized baby were to die, it would go to heaven. Other theological explanations for infant baptism also exist. Among Baptists and some other groups, however, people are not baptized until they are old enough to understand the significance of the ritual and to make the decision for themselves.

In many societies the choice of a name is never casual and always carries cultural implications. For example, the Ju/'hoansi of the Kalahari Desert in Botswana and Namibia have an extremely complex naming system. The Ju/'hoansi, who until recently were hunting-and-gathering nomads, have only sixty-seven names, thirty-five for males

Among the Ju/'hoansi of the Kalahari Desert, children are named for specific relatives according to strict rules. People with the same name are considered to be related regardless of their actual biological connection. People who share a name treat each other as relatives. Being treated like a relative means having rights to live near and share resources with one another. It sets up a network of reciprocal obligations, rights, and responsibilities. The effect of this system is to create a web of relationships throughout Ju/'hoansi society that individuals can call on for access to the Kalahari's scarce resources.

and thirty-two for females (Lee, 2003). A name is assigned systematically to each new-born: a first son is named after his father's father, a second son after his mother's father; a first daughter is named after her father's mother, a second daughter after her mother's mother. Subsequent children are named after their father's and mother's siblings. In contrast to European and North American practice, children can never be named after their own parents, nor can they marry someone with the same name as a parent or sibling.

Child Rearing

In the process of enculturation, once children are named and thought likely to survive, cultural practices begin to teach them the kinds of behaviors and mold personalities deemed appropriate. Child-rearing practices vary greatly across cultures and across times. There is enormous cultural diversity in attitudes toward infants and children and in beliefs about what they are capable of. There are also cultural differences in practices aimed at teaching children and molding them into the kinds of people acceptable in their society.

Attitudes toward children and child-rearing practices are generally consistent with core values prevalent in a society. In societies where competition for economic resources and for social prestige and power is the norm, children are taught to be competitive and to develop a sense of individuality and uniqueness. In societies where adults need to cooperate economically and to feel part of a network of reciprocal rights and obligations, children are taught to play and work communally. Of course, no society has only one set of values and needs. No matter how competitive an economic and political system may be, people also have to cooperate with others in some endeavors. And no matter how cooperative work and social networks may be, people sometimes compete with each other. However, while children in all cultures need to learn both cooperative and competitive strategies, one type is more dominant than another. And although there is variation within a society about child-rearing attitudes, most parents accept the norms prevalent in their communities because these norms are consistent with environmental constraints or social goals.

Child rearing includes both implicit and explicit messages. Children learn by observing other people, seeing the ways in which they interact and listening to what people have to say about other people's behavior. Children are also directly instructed about their own behavior. They may be given explicit directions about how to behave in particular circumstances. They may be praised and rewarded for some actions and criticized, punished, or ignored for others. And in all cultures, children are taught lessons about behavior and values through storytelling. Sacred narratives and folktales impart fundamental cultural attitudes that children absorb by listening to stories told and retold by respected relatives and elders.

Child-rearing practices are culturally defined techniques for dealing with universal problems relating to the dependency of children. All children need to be fed, carried, and otherwise cared for in order to satisfy their survival needs to eat, eliminate body wastes, and sleep. These strategies both reflect and transmit cultural values and environmental constraints.

Feeding and Weaning.   In many traditional societies, infants are nursed by their mothers for several years, sometimes for as long as three or four years or until another child is born. They are fed on demand—allowed to nurse whenever they want. In other societies, even young infants are put on feeding schedules that conform more to the mother's needs than to the child's. In a classic study, according to data reported for fifty-one cultures around the world and analyzed by John Whiting and Irvin Child (1953), about half of the sample was clustered high on a constructed scale of nursing indulgence. Only a few societies had marked restrictions on infant feeding. The lowest rating was given to inhabitants of the Marquesas, an island group in the South Pacific.

The Marquesans believe that frequent nursing makes a child difficult to raise, too willful and disobedient. No other groups were as restrictive as the Marquesans, but an American middle-class sample received a rating of only two points higher than the

child-rearing practices
Methods used to take care of infants and young children, including ways of feeding, playing with, carrying, and sleeping arrangements.

Marquesans. Whiting and Child point out that some of the worldwide variation can be explained on the basis of allocation of mothers' time. That is, in societies where mothers can rely on other family members to perform household tasks, more time can be spent providing for and catering to a baby's needs. In societies where mothers have numerous other duties, either within their own households or outside the domestic sphere, they, by necessity, have to restrict their child's access to them.

Both the age at which children are weaned and the weaning process itself vary cross-culturally. In general, in societies where a child can nurse on demand, weaning tends to take place late and gradually, whereas in societies where nursing or feeding is scheduled, weaning tends to take place early and abruptly. Weaning also takes place later in rural or poor communities as mother's milk normally is a reliably available source of food. The interrelationships among these practices form an integrated cultural pattern varying from indulgence to restrictions that is consistent with mothers' overall economic duties.

? Did you sleep in the same bed or room with your parents or other family members as a child? Why, or why not? At what age were you expected to sleep alone? To drink from a cup? To feed yourself?

Sleeping.   Cultural differences are found in sleeping arrangements for infants, young children, and adults. A review of research by psychologists investigating relationships between sleeping arrangements and children's independence reported that only about one-third of American infants slept in the same room as their parents (co-sleeping) and very few slept in their parents' bed (Morelli et al., 1992). Some studies indicate that more than half of infants as young as 2 months of age sleep in rooms separate from their parents, and by 6 months of age, 98 percent of American infants sleep alone. This pattern contrasts sharply with that of "most communities around the world," where infants usually sleep in the same bed with their mothers or, if not in her bed, at least in her room.

Data from the United States indicate variation in different cultural and regional groups. African American parents are more likely to allow their children to sleep in their bed or room than are Caucasian parents. And all families in rural communities are more likely to sleep in the same room. American middle-class sleeping arrangements are consistent with child-rearing goals that emphasize independence. In contrast, co-sleeping may help develop interpersonal relationships. Attitudes expressed by people in cultures that routinely practice co-sleeping are especially revealing in their criticism of typical American patterns (see the Case Study). For example, according to studies by T. B. Brazelton, Japanese parents consider American culture to be "rather merciless in pushing small children toward such independence at night" (1990:7).

Physical and Social Stimulation.   The ways children are held and the degree of contact that they have with caregivers and with other children significantly influence their physical and emotional development. In many cultures, children are in nearly constant contact and involvement with other people, either older siblings or adult caregivers. In many societies, babies and young children are carried in slings on the backs or hips of their caregivers. Because of this constant body contact, they move about just as their caregivers do. The physicality of movement, of walking, bending, straightening, and turning, is a constant part of their daily stimuli. In contrast, in some native cultures of North America, babies were placed in cradleboards and carried around on the mother's back. If the caregiver were indoors or working or resting outside, she might prop up the cradleboard against a wall or tree, giving the baby a front-facing perspective and enabling the child to be part of the family group and always in visual contact with others. Other societies require babies to spend a good deal of their waking and sleeping hours separated from other people. In cribs, highchairs, and playpens, children may be essentially isolated from the rest of the family group for significant amounts of time.

Research carried out among the Efe, a hunting and gathering society of Zaire, increases our understanding of the interrelationships between child-rearing strategies and personality values (Tronick et al., 1992). Observation of Efe children's activities revealed a high degree of interactions with parents, older siblings, community members, and peers. From the very beginning of life, Efe infants (from birth to 4 months of age)

Sleeping Arrangements in Two Cultures

Sleeping arrangements of American middle-class urban families have been contrasted with those of Maya Indians in rural Guatemala (Morelli et al., 1992). While all fourteen Maya mothers in the study slept in the same bed with their infants well into the child's second year of life, none of the eighteen American mothers slept in the same bed with their infants regularly, although fifteen had newborns sleeping in a crib near the parents. As early as 3 months of age, more than half the American babies were sleeping in a separate room, and by the sixth month 80 percent were sleeping alone. The remaining three American families never shared rooms with their newborns. American parents' comments about their practices revealed their concerns with dependency: "I think that he would be more dependent . . . if he was constantly with us like that" and "It was time to give him his own space, his own territory" (p. 607). These attitudes reveal a focus on individuality and self-reliance.

The researchers also found consistencies between sleeping arrangements and nighttime feedings of infants. Maya mothers allow their babies to nurse on demand during the night as well as during the day. Most of the mothers reported that they did not have to wake up to feed their babies but merely had to turn toward the child to make the breast accessible. American mothers, in contrast, reported staying awake during nighttime feedings even when they nursed their child. Few of them nursed the babies in the parental bed but sat in a chair in their own or the infant's room. These contrasting patterns are consistent with differences in attitudes toward on-demand and scheduled feeding. That is, since American mothers do not sleep in the same bed as their child, they need to interrupt their own sleep to feed their infants and thus strive to keep the baby on a regular schedule. Maya mothers are not disturbed when sleeping, so they are willing to allow the baby to nurse on demand.

Finally, Morelli and coworkers drew a connection between sleeping arrangements and bedtime routines. They noted the elaborate bedtime activities such as dressing for bed and storytelling typical of American families and the need to "coax the baby to sleep," in contrast with Maya patterns, where the transition to sleeping was made easily and without formality. The researchers suggest that American families often experience bedtime struggles because of the stress that infants may have about going to sleep without assistance or companionship. This stress results in the child's fear of falling asleep and being alone.

The contrasts between American and Maya practices reflect differences in each society's attitudes and values. While American parents stress the value of a child's independence and avoid encouraging dependent relationships, Maya parents stress the importance of interdependence between their children and themselves. Maya mothers believe that their children learn social rules more quickly, obey their elders' admonitions, and can be trusted not to touch dangerous objects because of the strong bond between mother and child. One Maya mother commented: "In our community the babies are always with the mother, but with North Americans, you keep the babies apart. Maybe that's why the children here understand their mothers more; they feel close. Maybe U.S. children feel the distance more. . . . If children do not feel close, it will be harder for them to learn and understand the ways of the people around them" (Morelli et al., 1992:610). In the United States, parents are concerned with fostering independence and self-reliance, in keeping with the society's dominant notions of the importance of individuality. Practices of American parents are also consistent with attitudes about privacy, stressing each person's needs for and rights to his or her own private space and own private concerns.

Efe infants and toddlers are always around adults, whom they see and hear performing numerous activities, learning through observation and interaction. They are almost never alone. Through nearly constant interaction with others, Efe children learn how to relate to male and female adults and children. This training leads to a high degree of sensitivity toward others and a "broad array of social skills" (Tronick et al., 1992:575). Given an economy of hunting and gathering, which necessitates initiative and risk, Efe child-rearing practices can be understood as adaptive strategies for survival.

GLOBALIZATION

While fully industrialized nations have tended to make child labor illegal, globalization has contributed to the exploitation of child labor in developing countries. Many organizations are working to help countries solve the problems of poverty and child labor in the face of forces of globalization. Education and improvements in living conditions are critical parts of the solution.

spent more than half their time with people other than their mothers, interacting with five or more different people per hour. And although they were frequently nursed by their mothers, other women nursed them as well. By the age of 3, they were having social contact with people not their mothers for about 70 percent of the day. Tronick and coworkers believe that Efe child-rearing practices are enmeshed in economic and social systems that require adults' attention to multiple activities throughout the day. But they also reflect the people's value of "sharing and cooperation" and help to enculturate Efe children in this "intensely social society" (1992:569).

Like every other aspect of culture, child-rearing practices and attitudes toward children are not static but change over time. They may change when people introduce and develop new technologies and new ways of living. The possibility of children's contribution to household economies may influence attitudes toward them. In hunting and gathering and in farming societies, children's dependence on adults may be of much shorter duration than in modern industrial societies. This difference is because, in the former, children can begin to work gathering or producing food when they are fairly young. In contrast, children in modern industrial nations are in schools and in training for their future roles until well into their teens. If they go on to post–high school education, their financial dependence on their parents may be lengthened.

REVIEW

Enculturation is the process all humans go through to learn their culture. Enculturation begins with social birth and naming. In all societies, child-rearing practices meet children's dependency needs and include feeding, weaning, sleeping arrangements, toilet training, and physical and social stimulation. Attitudes and values about children and child rearing are adaptive and, therefore, vary culturally as well as with changing contexts throughout the history of a society.

INFORMAL AND FORMAL LEARNING

Children acquire their culture through both formal and informal means. They learn their future economic and social roles by observing older siblings and the adults in their family. Typically, children play with toys that represent or imitate these roles. In societies with economies based on hunting and gathering, boys play with bows and arrows or other hunting gear, while girls play with digging sticks, carrying devices, and dolls. Among herding peoples, children may begin to accompany adults to take animals to pasture. They observe adults working with animals and assist with minor tasks. In some herding societies, such as the Diné (or Navajo) of the American Southwest, boys and girls accompany adult herders as early as the age of 5 or 6, preparing for the herding roles of both men and women. In other cultures, herding activities are restricted to men. For example, among African cattle herders such as the Nuer of southern Sudan, only men and boys who have been initiated are permitted to tend and herd cattle, although women and children usually milk the animals. Therefore, part of a boy's training consists of observing the work of older boys and adult men in anticipation of maturing and assuming adult roles.

In farming economies, children start work at a young age. Such tasks as scattering seeds, weeding, and manual harvesting can easily be done by children. Children as young as 5 or 6 can participate productively in farm labor and are taught to do so by accompanying adults and observing them at work. The Bangladeshi children in this photograph live in an industrializing nation. How do you think attitudes toward child labor will change as Bangladesh industrializes?

In industrial societies, child labor can be efficient in certain settings, but laws regarding children's work vary from country to country. Children are physically capable of doing hand manufacture and working with light and simple machinery before the age of 10. However, many countries outlaw such practices because of ethical stances held by a majority of citizens or by the world community. In countries where child labor is permitted (whether overtly or covertly), children may be apprenticed to their future employers, acquiring manufacturing skills in home and work settings. In postindustrial societies such as the United States, children would be in competition with their parents for jobs, a factor that delays the legal age of paid employment.

Learning Skills and Values

In much of the world, children are trained for their future roles in schools, where they learn to read and write, a prerequisite for most of the jobs that they will attain as adults. Education in formal settings so familiar to North Americans also instills competition and conformity even though these two values may seem contradictory. Children learn to compete with each other for the attention of the teacher when they raise their hands to answer questions. They compare their grades on tests and in classes with other pupils. They learn the value of individual achievement, feeling pride in their success or shame in their failure. But children also learn to conform to the rigors of obedience to authority, following explicit rules without questioning them as they are taught to respect the culture of institutions.

Cultural values are powerful influences on people's thinking and behavior. Values include norms of behavior, attitudes, and ethics. We manifest our values in how we act toward other people, in what we think about our own and other people's behavior, and in our notions of right and wrong. These values are taught to children in numerous ways. Children observe how people act, and they hear what people say in the course of daily activities. They may listen to discussions of other people's behavior, absorbing the attitudes expressed when someone is either praised or criticized.

Values are also transmitted in more formal settings. Children may be given direct instruction, told what to do and what not to do. They may be told why certain behavior is acceptable and why other behavior is unacceptable. Some actions or thoughts

? *What are some traditional sayings in your culture that teach moral lessons of industriousness, courage in the face of adversity, and other valued personality traits?*

may even be seen as evil, loading negative attributes about people who commit them. Because children (like adults) want to be perceived as appropriate members of their culture, they learn to act in ways viewed positively and avoid negatively viewed behavior.

In some societies, proverbs have a significant role in both private and public discourse. Among the Yoruba of Nigeria, for example, proverbs are used in child rearing, in ordinary conversations between adults, and in public and ceremonial settings. Yoruba proverbs teach proper behavior and transmit cultural wisdom. Examples include "Children are the clothes of men" (that is, a man's most valuable possessions); "A hungry man does not hear sermons"; "Words are like eggs, when they drop, they scatter"; and "You are making love to your thigh" (that is, you are deceiving yourself) (Lindfors and Owomoyela, 1973).

Sacred and secular traditional narratives, or **folklore,** convey important lessons about a people's philosophical and ethical principles. The power of the stories comes partly from frequent repetition and social validation. Their power also lies in the artistic and aesthetic appeal of dramatic episodes and heroic characters. The lives of ordinary people can be told and retold, making them larger than life and giving extraordinary meaning to ordinary events. The Philippine narrative that opened this chapter, for example, teaches lessons about the negative consequences of greediness.

Narratives also can be used to criticize someone's behavior by repeating stories whose moral lessons are known by everyone in the community. For example, Western Apaches use the telling of "historical tales" about former events that had negative consequences to "alarm and criticize social delinquents . . . , thereby impressing such individuals with the undesirability of improper behavior and alerting them to the punitive consequences of further misconduct" (Basso, 1990:115). The tales are aimed at particular hearers in the group who come to understand that the message in the story is directed at them. They are thus encouraged to think about their behavior and hopefully to profit from the lesson by changing their ways.

folklore
Texts that relate traditional stories, the exploits of cultural heroes and characters handed down from generation to generation.

Learning Behavioral Expectations

In addition to training for their social acceptance and future occupations, children need to learn how to behave when interacting with other people. Children acquire appropriate social expectations and behavior by observing their elders in the household and community. Because language is a key feature of human interactions, children need to know when to speak and when not to speak, and what to speak about. They learn rules of authority and deference. They see how decisions are made, whose voices are heard and whose are silenced, who may exert authority over whom, and who must defer to whom. Children learn the ways in which differences of age, gender, and social standing influence the behavior of others and mold their actions and speech. Through trial and error, they understand what behaviors are appropriate because they are corrected, reprimanded, or punished for transgressing social rules. Children also learn important lessons about social privilege, because they see that certain people are occasionally permitted to violate social norms while others are not. These are powerful lessons children learn informally through which they construct themselves as social individuals with specific social identities (see the Case Study).

Rules of politeness, deference, and status are often inculcated in children through language, through the ways in which people speak to them and the ways in which they are encouraged to speak. Children are encouraged to be cooperative or competitive through language interactions. In some societies, children learn to express their own opinions and judgments directly and forcefully, believing that speech is an aspect of one's individuality. In other societies, children learn to express themselves indirectly, to defer to others rather than to assert themselves. They become attuned to other people's needs and wishes. But since other people also express themselves indirectly, children learn to develop the skills of observation and inference.

Case study

Language and Interaction in Japan

A study of child-rearing and language-socialization practices in Japan reveals how children learn culturally appropriate patterns of interaction. Research concerned with Japanese social ideals uncovers the importance of *omoiyari*, or empathy with others (Clancy, 1986). People are socialized to be sensitive to each other's feelings, attitudes, and needs. They learn to express their own opinions indirectly and ambiguously so as to avoid conflict and to interpret other people's intentions and opinions from surface clues.

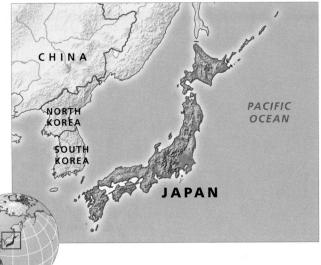

Japanese caregivers teach communication skills to children by example and direct admonition to instill the virtues of politeness and attentiveness toward others. Adults often use explicit classifications of behaviors as acceptable or deviant. They correct children's behavior by emphasizing the wishes of other people, especially elders, relatives, or people of higher social status.

In the following exchange, documented in Patricia Clancy's study (1986) of Japanese families, a mother chastises her child for not responding to another adult's questions:

[Child, age 2 years 1 month, is pretending to eat food from a toy dish]

ADULT: "Are you eating something? What is in there?"

CHILD: [No response]

MOTHER: "I wonder what could be in there. Older sister is asking: 'What is in there?'"

CHILD: "Pudding."

Repeating the question, the mother names a third participant, the researcher Patricia Clancy, whom the mother refers to as "older sister" to emphasize the child's kin-like obligation to answer the question. Aware of her place in a network of social responsibilities, the child responds.

Since Japanese culture highly values the expression of accommodation and agreement and the avoidance of overt conflict, children are taught to comply with the wishes of others regardless of their personal inclinations. One mother responded to her child's (age 2 years) refusal to lend a toy to a younger child by admonishing him:

"Do you say 'No!'"? You must lend one to Hirochan, saying, 'Help yourself.' The baby is cute/lovable, isn't he?"

Not only is the mother teaching her child to give in to the wishes of another, but she is instructing him to make an outright offer of the desired object. Whatever her child's inner feelings, she asks him to agree with her praise of the baby. In this way the mother teaches her child that complying with another person's wishes is more important than expressing one's own feelings.

As in all cultures, certain behaviors are considered appropriate while deviations from them trigger negative reactions. Japanese mothers often give exaggerated responses to a child's nonconformity:

[Child, 2 years 1 month, was playing hostess and suddenly began pretending to eat one of the toy dishes]

MOTHER: "Isn't it strange to do that kind of thing, if you eat a plate? No one eats plates, do they? Who eats plates?"

CHILD: "Maho [child's name] (eats) this."

MOTHER: "You're eating it? Like a beast. It's scary. I don't like it. It's scary, like a monster. I hate monsters."

Here, the mother is essentially saying that if the child does something that violates social norms, the child is "scary." Furthermore, she is telling the child that people who behave in such ways are hated. This is an important lesson, powerfully transmitted, because it threatens a child's sense of security.

Societies function on the basis of implied principles of consensus and the restraint of conflict. People need to agree implicitly that the open display of too much conflict may prove to be socially disruptive and would impair the cohesion necessary for the viability of groups. This is perhaps most true within families but it is fundamental to any community.

Age and Gender Socialization

Children learn through their socialization that people's rights and obligations differ depending on their status and the kinds of roles they perform. The term **status** refers to one's place in a hierarchical social order. The factors that determine status vary in different societies, though age and gender are common in most social systems. Older people usually are granted more respect and deference, and children generally have little social standing. In some societies, women and men have relatively equal status, while in others, one gender has higher standing than the other. Other factors that may contribute to social status in a particular culture include class, race, ethnicity, and religion.

Social status is a factor within families as well. In familial interactions, children first become aware of different categories of people based on such characteristics as age and gender. In a society stratified by age, gender, and other factors such as class, race, and ethnicity, a child eventually learns that social rights are unequally distributed, that certain types of people have more rights or powers than others. Unequal status within families, then, is a reflection of, and reinforces, inequality in the larger society. People must learn as children how to order themselves hierarchically as adults. As onlookers and participants, children observe the varied interactions among family members. They formulate conceptions of themselves and of their place in the world according to cultural models that are enacted daily in their households.

Age. On the basis of age, children have restricted rights and limited ability to control others or even to protect themselves from other people's control. Children's lack of power is shown in several ways. First, they rarely contribute to group discussions related to community activities. In families, there is variation from culture to culture and from family to family. In some societies, it would be unthinkable for children to have a say in family decisions, while in others they might contribute significantly, especially if the discussion relates to an activity that affects them. Older children are more likely to have their opinions heard than younger children.

Second, children's behavior is more directly constrained than is that of adults. As part of the socialization process, children may be verbally reprimanded or physically punished when they violate rules of cultural appropriateness. This process teaches them that some people have the right to comment on and control the behavior of others. The rights of some to control others is one of the earliest lessons children learn.

Third, children have fewer and more restricted conversational rights than adults. For instance, children may be unsuccessful in getting the attention of adults, particularly when the adults are engaged in conversation and interaction with other adults. In a study of middle-class American families, Susan Ervin-Tripp et al. (1984) found that when children age 2 to 4 ½ years tried to get the attention of someone already involved in conversation, they were unsuccessful 94 percent of the time. Older children, age 4 ½ to 7 years, fared somewhat better but still met with a failure rate of 79 percent. Adults also often interrupt children. Although our cultural stereotypes portray children as talkative and interruptive, laboratory and natural observations of familial interactions demonstrate just the opposite (Gleason, 1987). Gender of adult and child is a significant factor in interruption. Research showed that fathers interrupted children more than did mothers, and both parents interrupted daughters more often than sons. Children replicate this gender-differentiated pattern quite early. In a study by

status
The position or rank that one occupies in a group or society that carries certain role expectations.

Anita Esposito (1979) of children (from 3 ½ to 4 ½ years of age) who were observed in male-female encounters, boys interrupted girls twice as frequently as the reverse.

Conversational power is also displayed in the context of giving and receiving commands or instructions. Giving commands is indicative of social rights to control others, and the way in which commands are stated also can signal relative social standing. Imperatives ("Sit down!" or "Close the window!") assert power overtly, whereas indirect expressions, questions, and statements of rationales soften the speaker's control and acknowledge the other person's feelings ("Why don't you sit down?" or "Would you please close the window?"). Studies of parent-child interactions indicate that adults consistently issue more commands to children than they receive. Gender difference is manifested in the type of command. Gleason (1987) found, for example, that in a study of middle-class urban families, fathers gave imperatives twice as often as did mothers. A total of 38 percent of all fathers' utterances were overt commands. In contrast, mothers tended to make requests with polite constructions and questions.

In addition, some fathers socialize sons into competitive behavior by adding threats or insults to direct imperatives. Commands such as "Don't go in there again or I'll break your head" and references such as "wise guy" or "nutcake" were sometimes addressed to sons. These encounters no doubt serve as training grounds for boys when they interact with other boys in competitive displays and challenges. Later, when they become parents, they may reproduce the same hierarchical status system with their children.

Gender.   Gender is a basic aspect of a person's individual and social identity. A child is socialized into his or her **gender identity** from the earliest age, beginning immediately after birth. Girls and boys may be treated differently, handled differently, and spoken to differently from the very beginning of life. Studies in child development indicate that in the United States, parents and other caregivers interact differently with boys and girls. These studies indicate general patterns within populations, but they do not predict any particular interactions between parents and children.

There is enormous variability in any society about expected norms and behaviors. However, research indicates, for example, that parents interact more physically with boy babies than with girls. Boys are held, touched, and stimulated more, a pattern that helps them develop stronger muscles and motor behavior. Boys also are handled more roughly than girls. In addition, when boys fuss, parents pay more attention to them than they do to girls. Through these modes of interaction, boys learn to seek attention because they get attention, while girls learn to satisfy their own needs (Ember, 1981). Fathers in particular tend to handle their sons more roughly than their daughters. And boys tend to be physically punished more than girls, especially by their fathers.

Research on expressing aggression suggests cross-sex permissiveness on the part of parents—that is, fathers may permit more aggression from daughters, and mothers may permit more aggression from sons. This pattern may encourage aggressiveness in boys. For example, physical punishment of boys by fathers could result in increased anger, but because sons cannot turn their anger toward their fathers, they displace it in aggressive behavior toward peers. In addition, mothers' greater tolerance for aggression in their sons may increase a boy's aggressive behavior.

Studies also show that girls spend more time playing at home than do boys. They are, therefore, under more adult supervision and are more likely to take on household chores, including helping to care for younger siblings. Boys, in contrast, interact more with peers. These patterns also may affect aggression. A child is likely to defer to adults and nurture younger children. Girls are more likely to develop these personality and behavior characteristics, therefore, because of their patterns of interaction at home, whereas boys develop more aggressive behavior because of their patterns of interaction both at home and with peers.

In both cases, certain human behaviors are likely to be encouraged and developed (aggression in boys, nurturance in girls) and others inhibited (aggression in girls, nurturance in boys). Patterns of treatment and interaction, therefore, help to mold a child's personality to conform to cultural norms. Females and males are born, but girls and boys (and women and men) are products of enculturation.

gender identity
The way that people think about themselves in terms of their sex, how they present themselves as men or women.

? *How are clothing styles, hairstyles, and jewelry used to challenge gender stereotypes in North America and Europe today?*

Gender Identification. Gender identity is marked in many ways, among them dress and body decoration. A common example is dressing baby boys in blue and baby girls in pink. Clothing styles, hairstyles, and the wearing of jewelry are other visual markers of gender. External modifications of the body are powerful, repetitive indications of one's gender identity and gender differentiation in one's society. Changes in cultural notions of gender may be reflected in changing habits of dress and body ornamentation.

Naming conventions are nearly universal means of distinguishing males and females. Most cultures bestow different names for boys and girls. In American English, only a handful of names are ambiguous for gender. Some of these, like Leslie and Dana, are older in the language, while others, like Kim and Tracey, are newer. Some names that may be used for both males and females have spellings that differentiate the sexes: Frances for girls, Francis for boys; Sydney for girls, Sidney for boys. English names for girls may refer to flowers (Rose, Iris, Lily), months of the year (April, May, June), and moral virtues (Prudence, Hope). Boys, in contrast, are rarely named for objects or abstractions. Certain sounds in the names also differentiate the genders: English girls' names often end in vowels, whereas boys' names rarely do. Finally, girls' names may be derived from boys' names by addition of "feminine" endings, such as -a, -ine, -ette, for example, Paula, Pauline, Paulette. This process can apply idiosyncratically to any male name, although some are more common than others. The only male name that is derived from a female name is Marion (note the difference in spelling for the girls' name Marian), derived from Mary, a name with religious significance.

Otherwise, to name a boy with a girl's name would be considered highly inappropriate and might have consequences for the carrier. Note, though, that endearing or diminutive forms of some names given to girls are the same as those used for boys: Roberta/Bobby, Geraldine/Jerry, Antoinette/Tony. In addition, boys are more likely to be named for their fathers (John Jr., for example) than girls are to be named for their mothers. This pattern symbolizes and transmits the acknowledgment of kin ties through the male line.

In traditional communities in China and Taiwan, names given to boys and girls are strongly differentiated. Chinese names function as meaningful symbolic markers of men's social distinctiveness and the social nonbeing of women. In a study of naming practices in Hong Kong and Taiwan, Ruby Watson (1986) found that both girls and boys are given personal names based on literary sources, events occurring near the time of the child's birth, or a wish for the child's future. However, boys' names have positive or prestige implications, while girls' names more often have negative meanings. For example, an eldest boy might be called "Eldest Luck," but a second or third girl might be named "Too Many" or "Little Mistake." Names with these meanings are not given to all girls, but the fact that the pattern exists indicates negative cultural attitudes toward females. In addition to differences in first names, acquisition of subsequent names also distinguishes males and females. Throughout his life, a man acquires new names that indicate social standing in his household and community and that confer prestige to him, such as a school name given by a teacher, a marriage name selected when he marries, a "courtesy" name that marks economic or social success, and a posthumous name given to honor his life.

Women, in sharp contrast, have only their personal name. Even this name is dropped when a woman marries; but rather than acquiring a new marriage name, as men do, a woman becomes known thereafter by kin terms in reference to her husband and children, for example as "Eldest Luck's wife" or "Too Many's mother." In old age, a woman is simply called "old woman" by everyone except her closest relatives. And, finally, a woman's nonbeing is forever memorialized on her tombstone where instead of personal, courtesy, and posthumous names, as are engraved for men, a woman's existence is subsumed under her father's surname and she is listed eternally as "Family of [father's surname]."

Chinese naming patterns are consistent with traditional strong preferences for sons. These preferences go back to ancient times and the establishment of Confucian philosophy, which reinforced the Chinese kinship system. The preference for sons reflects a strongly patrilineal kinship system with inheritance rules in which wealth and property are passed from father to son. In societies where men and women are thought of as equally valuable, parental preferences for girls and boys may be personal but are not generally imbalanced in the society as a whole. In some cultures where people trace their descent and inheritance through women, girls may be preferred. For example, among the Mohawk and other Iroquois nations, parents preferred girls in order to maintain the family line that in Iroquois culture descended through women. However, children of either sex were equally welcomed and nurtured. The Mohawk pattern of preference was not, therefore, the mirror image of many societies' desires for sons. Although there are numerous cultures in which girls are routinely neglected and abused, even killed, because of intense preferences for boys, there are no reported cases of cultures where boys are neglected and abused because of preferences for girls.

Boys and girls learn their future identities as men and women by observing their parents and other household members. They see how men and women treat each other, what they say about each other, and how they respond to each other. They come to understand whether men and women contribute equally to group discussions and decision making. And they see the kinds of work that women and men perform. Through these observations, children absorb attitudes about themselves, about their own worthiness, as they prepare for their rights and responsibilities as adults.

One of the ways that children acquire models of gender and social relations is through participation in family interactions. Research conducted by Elinor Ochs and Caroline Taylor (1995) focused on 100 dinnertime conversations among family members. Ochs and Taylor analyzed the content of the conversations, looking especially at which family members introduced the stories, whose activities were discussed, and who commented on the actions described. They found that a majority of the stories were characterized by what they called a "Father knows best" family dynamic in which "father is set up to be primary audience, judge and critic of family members' actions, thoughts and feelings" (p. 99). A majority or 60 percent of the stories focused on the activities of the children, while mothers were central in 23 percent of the stories and fathers featured in 19 percent. Because children's activities made up most of the narratives, they became the focus of comments and evaluations by parents. Thus, children's actions and thoughts were most open to others' scrutiny, while fathers were talked about the least, making them the least vulnerable to evaluation. Children rarely selected the topic of conversation. They introduced only about one-third of the stories about themselves. Instead, parents (especially mothers) focused the narrative on the child's actions, which could be seen as reinforcing children's lack of privacy and control over information about themselves and the scrutiny of others. Stories were told about children for the fathers' hearing, thereby setting up the father as the "family judge" with the right to evaluate others.

Rites of Passage

Enculturation also occurs in linking activities between individuals, represented by their families, and their community. Religious teachings and participation in ritual, for example, are powerful means to convey social and ideological principles to children. Myths and folktales transmit practical knowledge, historical information, and symbolic meanings as they are recounted in the informal settings of home and community as well as in the formal contexts of church and school.

In many societies, children undergo critical **rites of passage** as they move from the social role and status of child to those of adult. Other rites of passage occur at other life transitions, such as birth, marriage, and death, which are discussed further in Chapter 14. In the process of preparing for and undergoing rituals marking the transition to adulthood, children may be taught practical arts associated with their

rites of passage
Rituals that mark culturally significant transitions throughout the life cycle, including birth, puberty, marriage, and death.

The narrative dynamics of this conversation subtly teaches these children their gender roles and status through a complex play of family and interactional power and control. Mother has introduced stories about the children's activities for the father to hear. Father takes family power to act as a judge of others' actions and thoughts. Children are socialized into the ideology of unequal gender relations, both because they are witnesses to their parents' behavior and because they are chosen as central characters motivating the drama.

initiation rites
Rituals that mark a person's transition from childhood to adulthood.

future roles. They also may be instructed in knowledge necessary for their roles as parents and spouses, learning their responsibilities, obligations, and rights.

Certain types of rituals and teachings have particular effects on molding the personalities and identities of children approaching adulthood. For example, in many African societies as well as in Aboriginal Australia, boys undergo intense, prolonged, and frightening **initiation rites** as they approach manhood. The rites are held once in several years (the number of years varies from culture to culture) for groups of boys of the appropriate age. The boys are taken out of their settlements and are subjected to weeks, months, or even years of instruction and preparation for their roles as men.

Among the Kpelle of Liberia, boys are initiated by groups into a men's secret society called *Poro*. Initiations occur sporadically, perhaps once every ten or fifteen years. Boys are brought from their communities to an isolated bush area for four years. During this time, they are instructed in the knowledge and skills—farming techniques, methods of house building, and craft specialties—needed to function productively in Kpelle society. They also learn various dances, songs, and traditional histories. Finally, they learn how to behave appropriately and how to act with elders and chiefs (Gibbs, 1965). Social messages are reinforced by beatings and verbal harassment.

A number of physical changes are imposed on boys during their initiation, including circumcision and scarification. Scars formed from cuts made on a boy's back and chest are permanent, visible signs of adult status. Such scars are said to be the teeth marks of a "Great Masked Figure" who embodies a mythic spirit believed to eat the boy at the beginning of the initiation process. According to Kpelle beliefs, a boy dies when he enters the initiation camp and is reborn when the Great Masked Figure disgorges him. He then receives a new name signifying his new status. A boy's childhood name is never used thereafter. Boys who go through their initiation collectively form strong emotional and social bonds with one another. They learn to identify and empathize with the actions and needs of men in their own age cohorts with whom they have been associated in their periods of seclusion and transition. As well, they develop strong bonds of mutual assistance, interdependence, and loyalty that last throughout their lifetimes.

In contrast, some Native American people of the North American Midwest and Plains sent young boys (and sometimes girls, too) on lonely, individual quests for visions when they neared adulthood. The overt purpose of the vision quest was the acquisition of a personal spirit guardian who comes to the lonely seeker after periods (typically four days) of isolation in the woods or on the plains. During the quest, the seeker abstains from food and sleep. Guardian spirits thus acquired form a lifelong relationship with the seeker, coming to his or her aid in visions and dreams and imparting knowledge and comfort.

In addition to the spiritual lessons learned, children also learn the important lessons of endurance, self-control, self-reliance, and courage necessary to survive in harsh conditions. Through their experiences, children learn that they can endure the deprivation of food, water, and sleep. They also learn emotional resilience through the knowledge that they can survive loneliness and fear. These physical and psychological strengths are necessary for survival in nomad societies where resources are occasionally scarce and difficult to obtain and where weather may be life-threatening.

In many societies, children's initiation ceremonies include instruction in secret ritual and lore. In the Amazon, Australia, and some cultures of central and southern Africa, boys are taught sacred songs that they are told never to reveal to anyone, especially to women and uninitiated children. These rites symbolize the segregation of the genders, fundamental to their society's economic and social roles. The selective transmission of knowledge defines and reinforces gender identity.

? *What are some examples of initiation rites and other rites of passage in the United States?*

Schooling

In many societies, children's enculturation takes place in formal settings of school, where children are taught explicit lessons to acquire practical and intellectual knowledge. In early societies, children of the elites (especially boys) were sent to schools to learn the responsibilities and practical applications of their future administrative or political roles. In early literate societies, elite children were taught to read and write and do mathematics.

Case study

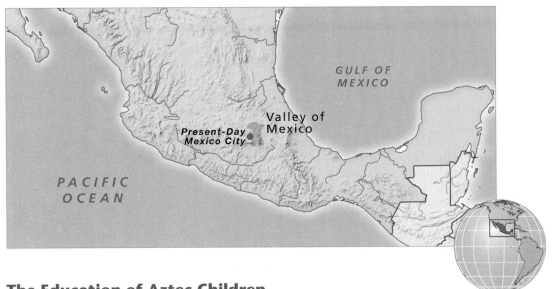

The Education of Aztec Children

The Aztecs developed a large, complex, and wealthy society in the Valley of Mexico over several centuries beginning in the thirteenth and fourteenth centuries. By the fifteenth and sixteenth centuries, they controlled vast territories with more than 5 million inhabitants. Their economy was based on intensive farming, centering on production of maize. In addition to farming, the Aztecs gathered wild plants and fruits. Because of the rapid growth of population, they overhunted their territories and then relied for animal protein on some domesticated species, especially turkeys and dogs (Fagan, 1984).

By the early sixteenth century, the Aztecs had established a centralized state government, developing complex links between cities and countryside villages. An efficient bureaucracy managed government functions and oversaw the construction and maintenance of irrigation works and large public structures such as government buildings and temples. Traders traveled throughout the empire, obtaining and distributing goods from one region to another. Ceremonial life, organized by a prestigious and powerful priesthood, was central to state government and to ordinary citizens. And a well-trained military expanded Aztec territory and controlled the outlying provinces.

Aztec society was organized on the basis of class, wealth, and power. The major social and economic division was between nobles and commoners. Nobles were the relatives and descendants of Aztec rulers. The ruler and the nobles owned the land and controlled all of the valuable resources in the territory. They received portions of the produce of commoners as tribute and also benefited from the people's required labor in mines and on farms. Nobles also functioned as government officials, governors of the thirty-eight provinces, generals, and judges. Commoners worked the land, paid tribute to landowners, participated in communal works projects organized by the state, and were subject to regulations imposed by local, regional, and central officials.

People were socialized into their various roles from early childhood. Formal education was one of the means the state used to mold individuals to accept their place in the social order and to fulfill their responsibilities. The education of Aztec children was of primary concern to their parents. Boys were under the tutelage of their fathers, and girls were trained by their mothers. The formalized structure of child care can be noted in the rations of food prescribed for children at different ages: a 3-year-old was given half a cake of maize taken at the main daily meal, children of 4 or 5 years ate one cake, children of 6 through 12 years had a cake and a half, and children of 13 or older were given two cakes. Boys and girls were fed the same amounts of food (Soustelle, 1961).

At around the age of 3 or 4, boys from commoner families were trained in their future economic roles by their fathers. Boys began to carry wood from the forests and water from the lakes to their households. They accompanied their fathers to the marketplace. Girls helped their mothers with domestic tasks, doing simple cooking and cleaning chores. When children were between 7 and 13 years of age, they learned more difficult tasks. Boys were taught to fish and to steer and maneuver boats; girls helped their mothers spin cotton, weave cloth, and grind maize into meal to be prepared as the Aztecs' staple food.

During a child's earliest years, adults treated children with kindness and affection, giving good advice and encouragement. However, once the period of more careful supervision began (at about the age of 3), children who misbehaved were treated harshly. Scoldings and physical punishments were meted out to correct children's errors. A child might be scratched with thorns of the agave plant or forced to breathe the bitter fumes of burning red peppers.

Children began formal education between ages 12 and 15. The Aztec educational system included two tracks, one suited for children who were destined for membership in the bureaucratic and elite classes of Aztec society, the other geared for children of the commoner social stratum. Schools called *calmecacs* trained the sons and daughters of the elite ruling class of Aztec society, although children of the merchant class might also attend. Some sources indicate that children of ordinary families were also sometimes sent to the *calmecac*. These schools were run by priests who themselves had attended such an institution. Each of the several temples in pre-Columbian Mexico administered a *calmecac*, where it trained children who might one day join their ranks. Overseeing all of these institutions was the head of the Aztecan religious hierarchy. Education in the *calmecac* prepared children for futures in the priesthood or in other high-ranking positions in the state bureaucracy, political organization, and military. Physical training and hard work were instilled in them as daily routines. They learned to use the weapons of war and had practical experience on the battlefield, under the protection of experienced warriors.

Training in the *calmecac* was as much personal and psychological as it was intellectual. Children were awakened early in the morning when it was still dark and then went alone into the mountains in order to make offerings of incense to the gods and to prick their ears and legs with thorns of the agave plant until they drew blood. Children fasted frequently as a sign of their humiliation and their submission to the gods. In addition, they worked on the farms and lands belonging to the temple to which their school was attached. According to the sixteenth-century Spanish chronicler Father Bernadino Sahagun, an Aztec father admonished his son upon entry to a *calmecac*: "Listen, my son, you are not going to be honored, nor obeyed, nor esteemed. You are going to be looked down upon, humiliated and despised. Every day you will cut agave-thorns for penance, and you will draw blood from your body with these spines and you will bathe at night even when it is very cold. Harden your body to the cold. And when the time comes for fasting do not go and break your fast, but put a good face upon both fasting and penance" (Sahagun, 1975, Vol. II:222). Children were taught the values of self-control and respect for others. They were taught "to speak well, to make proper salutations, and to bow." Finally, children at the *calmecac* were given religious instruction, learning to sing sacred songs and to interpret dreams. Their intellectual learning included knowing how to read Aztecan pictographs and methods of reckoning time. They read and recited poetry and oratory.

Girls who attended the *calmecac* were treated more leniently than the boys. Their training was not as rigorous nor were they punished as severely. At the *calmecac*, girls were under the supervision of elderly priestesses who taught them the graces of native etiquette. They were taught to value obedience and purity of mind and body. They participated in making ritual offerings of incense to the gods each night. Their practical learning consisted mainly of becoming skilled weavers of cloth and artisans of embroidery. Girls, too, learned songs and stories that told the history and accomplishments of the Aztec people. Through these oral traditions, people acquired their identity as Aztec and took pride in their culture and their history.

A second type of institution, called *telpochcalli*, provided a different kind of experience. Most of the children at the *telpochcalli* came from the commoner stratum of Aztec society, although some of these might attend the *calmecac*. Children at the *telpochcalli* performed physical labor, including sweeping the schoolhouse, cutting wood for the school, repairing ditches and canals, and cultivating lands belonging to the school.

These tasks prepared boys for their future economic roles and for their future public service in maintaining communal irrigation and water delivery systems. Boys in the *telpochcalli* were also trained in the skills of war. In fact, military training was central to the school program. Punishments for misbehavior were sure and harsh.

The two systems of education, that of the *calmecac* and of the *telpochcalli,* were presided over by two different gods. The god of the *calmecac* was Quetzalocatl, who was the god of self-sacrifice, penance, books, the calendar, and the arts. He was the god of learning, discipline, and culture. In contrast, the god of the *telpochcalli* was Tezcatlipoca, who was the god of war.

The two kinds of educational institutions and the learning that took place in them exemplified the two contradictory and yet complementary strands of Aztec philosophy. One strand consisted of the ethics of self-control, sacrifice, and dedication to the public good; the other strand emphasized physical prowess and the glorification of war in the service of state defense and expansion. Children who were destined by family background and inclination to become the future leaders of Aztec society were steeped in the cultural traditions of learning, literature, and the arts. They were taught social graces and the burdens and responsibilities of leadership. Punishment for misbehavior by nobles was harsher than that meted out to commoners on the assumption that with privilege went responsibility.

Finally, children of both sexes and all social strata attended a "House of Song" when they were between 12 and 15 years of age. These institutions, each one attached to a temple, instructed children in the arts of singing, dancing, and music. Led by elder men and women, the students began an hour before sunset to learn ceremonial songs and sacred narratives of the Aztecan creation and their ancestors' migrations to central Mexico. Thus, Aztec education provided training for boys and girls of all social classes. Every child was given the opportunity to learn and appreciate the history and culture of their people.

Most modern nations today have universal education where all children are required to attend school. This principle is consistent with democratic ideals that all people can aspire to productive, rewarding lives in their societies. However, in practice, children have varying access to schooling in many nations. In many countries in Latin America, Africa, and the Middle East, rates of boys' attendance at school far exceed those of girls. Boys' greater access to education is reflected in statistics compiled in 2000 by the United Nations on enrollment in schools, especially at higher levels. Unequal opportunities for education result in much lower levels of literacy for women than for men. Even in the developed world, where nearly all of the adult population is literate, girls are somewhat more likely to be illiterate than boys, except in Malta and the United States, where rates of illiteracy for males exceed those for females.

Throughout the rest of the world, however, illiteracy rates are higher overall and the gender discrepancy favoring men is much more marked. Gender discrepancies in illiteracy widen in many Asian, Middle Eastern, and African nations, where women's rates exceed those of men by 20 or 30 percent (United Nations, 2004).

In much of the developing world, girls' school enrollment has increased during the last several decades, but it still falls below that of boys. For example, a study of education in Papua New Guinea revealed that while about 70 percent of school-age boys were attending primary schools, only 58 percent of girls were enrolled, despite the government's target of full enrollment for all children (Yeoman, 1987). A significant factor is the attitude of parents, especially fathers, about the status and education of women. Of parents interviewed, 89 percent thought it important for their sons to go to school, but only 56 percent considered education for their daughters to be important. In addition to gender bias, class, ethnic, and cultural differences may also have an effect on rates of attendance and success in school. Children from different cultural backgrounds may have different expectations about the learning process and about prevailing norms of interactions with others.

GLOBALIZATION

The 2003–2004 report released by UNESCO on its Education for All program showed that, worldwide, girls are still receiving inadequate or no schooling. The twelve countries with the greatest gender inequality in education include the decolonized states of Chad, Yemen, Guinea-Bissau, Benin, Niger, Ethiopia, Central African Republic, Burkina Faso, Guinea, Mali, Liberia, and Pakistan. Most people view equal education for both sexes as a positive effect of globalization.

In Their Own Voices

Going to School in Ake, Nigeria

In this excerpt from his memoir, Ake, The Years of Childhood, *Nigerian writer Wole Soyinka recalls his impressions of school in the small town of Ake, in western Nigeria, where he grew up in the 1930s and 1940s. Wole Soyinka was awarded the Nobel Prize for Literature in 1986.*

Every morning before I woke up, Tinu was gone. She returned about midday carrying a slate with its marker attached to it. And she was dressed in the same khaki uniform as the hordes of children, of different sizes, who milled around the compound from morning till afternoon, occupied in a hundred ways.

At a set hour in the morning one of the bigger ones seized the chain which dangled from the bell-house, tugged at it with a motion which gave the appearance of a dance and the bell began pealing. Instantly, the various jostling, tumbling, racing and fighting pupils rushed in different directions around the school buildings, the smaller in size towards the schoolroom at the further end of the compound where I could no longer see them. The bigger pupils remained within sight, near the main building. They split into several groups, each group lined up under the watchful eye of a teacher. When all was orderly, I saw father appear from nowhere at the top of the steps. He made a speech to the assembly, then stood aside. One member of the very biggest group stepped forward and raised a song. The others took it up and they marched into the school-building in twos, to the rhythm of the song.

It was an unusual song too, since the main song was in English but the chorus was sung in Yoruba; I could only catch the words of the latter:

B'ina njo ma je'ko
B'ole nja, ma je'ko

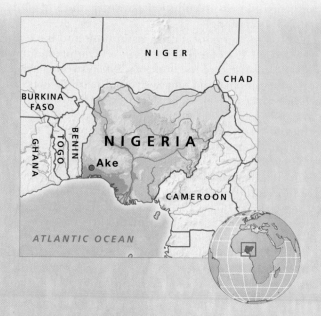

"I am going to school," I announced one day. It became a joke to be passed from mouth to mouth, producing instant guffaws. Mother appeasingly said, "Wait till you are as old as your sister."

The hum of voices, once the pupils were within the buildings, took mysterious overtones. Through the open windows of the schoolroom I saw heads in concentration, the majestic figure of a teacher who passed in and out of vision, mumbling incantations over the heads of his attentive audience. Different chants broke out from different parts of each building, sometimes there was even direct singing, accompanied by a harmonium. When the indoor rites were over, they came out in different groups, played games, ran races, they spread over the compound picking up litter, sweeping the paths, clipping lawns and weeding flowerbeds. They roamed about with hoes, cutlasses, brooms and sticks, retired into open workshop sheds where they wove baskets,

The Western model of education is based strongly on the authority of the teacher-adult, question-answer interaction, and individual achievement. Many Native American children are socialized to learn differently, however, and especially to refrain from behavior that isolates their performance in a competitive manner in front of peers. In a comparison of classroom behavior of native children from the Warm Springs Reservation in Oregon with that of nearby nonnative students, Susan Philips (1978) found that Native children were extremely reluctant to answer teachers' questions or to speak out in class. In contrast, in situations where they could have individual access carved bits of wood and bamboo, kneaded clay and transformed them into odd-shaped objects.

Under the anxious eyes of "Auntie" Lawanle, I played by myself on the pavement of our house and observed these varied activities. The tools of the open air were again transformed into books, exercise books, slates, books under armpits, in little tin or wooden boxes, books in raffia bags, tied together with string and carried on the head, slung over shoulders in cloth pouches. Directly in front of our home was the lawn, which was used exclusively by girls from the other school. They formed circles, chased one another in and out of the circles, struggled for a ball and tossed it through an iron hoop stuck on a board. Then they also vanished into classrooms, books were produced and they commenced their own observances of the mystery rites.

Tinu became even more smug. My erstwhile playmate had entered a new world and, though we still played together, she now had a new terrain to draw upon. Every morning she was woken earlier than I, scrubbed, fed and led to school by one of the older children of the house.

I got up one morning as she was being woken up, demanded my bath at the same time, ate, selected the clothing which I thought came closest to the uniforms I had seen, and insisted on being dressed in them. I had marked down a number of books on father's table but did not yet remove them. I waited in the front room. When Tinu passed through with her escort, I let them leave the house, waited a few moments, then seized the books I had earlier selected and followed them. Both parents were still in the dining room. I followed at a discreet distance, so I was not noticed until we arrived at the infant school. I waited at the door, watched where Tinu was seated, then went and climbed on to the bench beside her. Only then did Lawanle, Tinu's escort that day, see me. She let out a cry of alarm and asked me what I thought I was doing. I ignored her. The teachers heard the commotion and came into the room. I appeared to be everybody's object of fun. They looked at me, pointed as they held their sides, rocked forward and backwards with laughter. A man who appeared to be in charge of the infant section came in, he was also our father's friend and came often to the house. I recognized him, and I was pleased that

he was not laughing with the others. Instead he stood in front of me and asked, "Have you come to keep your sister company?"

"No. I have come to school."

Then he looked down at the books I had plucked from father's table.

"Aren't these your father's books?"

"Yes. I want to learn them."

"But you are not old enough, Wole."

"I am three years old."

Lawanle cut in, "Three years old wo? Don't mind him sir, he won't be three until July."

"I am nearly three. Anyway, I have come to school. I have books."

He turned to the class teacher and said, "Enter his name in the register." He then turned to me and said, "Of course you needn't come to school everyday—come only when you feel like it. You may wake up tomorrow morning and feel that you would prefer to play at home."

I looked at him in some astonishment. Not feel like coming to school! The coloured maps, pictures and other hangings on the walls, the coloured counters, markers, slates, inkwells in neat round holes, crayons and drawing books, a shelf laden with modeled objects—animals, human beings, implements—raffia and basket-work in various stages of completion, even the blackboards, chalk and duster. I had yet to see a more inviting playroom! In addition, I had made some vague, intuitive connection between school and the piles of books with which my father appeared to commune so religiously in the front room, and which had constantly to be snatched from me as soon as my hands grew long enough to reach them on the table.

"I shall come everyday," I confidently declared.

From *Ake, The Years of Childhood*, pp. 22–25, Wole Soyinka, Copyright © 1981 by Wole Soyinka. Used by permission of Random House, Inc.

CRITICAL THINKING QUESTION

How does this memoir highlight the perspective that formal education is a privilege?

to teachers, they were more likely than nonnative students to seek help, initiate questions, and engage in dialogue. The setting, not inherent interest, affected native children's learning.

Studies of working-class African American children in the United States and Afro-Caribbean children in the United Kingdom reveal that the school environment presents difficulties not experienced by middle-class children. Reacting to the demands for conformity to school authorities (teachers and principals) and to middle-class styles of learning and interaction, children from working-class or racially marginalized groups often behave defiantly, insisting on their own norms of action and speech. Sociolinguistic studies in the United States and Britain indicate that such children may reject middle-class standard speech in favor of nonstandard varieties that are distinguished on the basis of both class and race. In such communities, pressure from the peer group often supports nonconformity, noncompliance, and nonachievement. Children who excel in the school setting are sometimes teased, ostracized, or shunned by the social groups of their peers (Labov, 1972b; Cheshire, 1982; Richmond, 1986).

> **REVIEW**
>
> Enculturation takes place both informally and formally—for example, through observation, folklore, family interaction, rites of passage (such as initiation rites at puberty), and schooling. Children learn skills, values, behavioral expectations, interactional norms, and role and status based on age and gender. Through enculturation, children develop a gender identity, which strongly affects the way they are perceived and treated in their society.

PSYCHOLOGICAL ANTHROPOLOGY

Although each of us is a unique individual, anthropologists are interested in questions of cross-cultural similarities and differences among people. Some of these questions include

1. Are there psychological differences between human populations, and can those differences be described? What are the causes of such differences?

2. What are the cultural causes and consequences of psychological variations across groups?

3. How do cultural institutions affect individual development?

4. How do sociocultural changes affect individual dispositions, and vice versa?

The field of **psychological anthropology** focuses on cultural factors in the development of personality, people's beliefs and responses to psychological states, and cultural influences on perception and cognition. Although every person is an individual with a unique character and personality, there are overall cultural influences and constraints on the ways that each person's underlying nature is manifested. That is, people are products of both their internal nature and their external experiences as a member of a society and culture. Genetic factors that contribute to a person's dispositions and feelings are modified and channeled by their culture, by the ideas that parents and other caregivers have about them as children, by their interactions with older and younger family members, and by relations with peers.

Culture and Personality Traits

We think of ourselves as individuals with unique personalities, that is, with particular ways of feelings, thinking, reacting, and meeting needs. People develop their personalities in part in response to the social expectations and cultural models of behavior to which they are exposed. Behaviors and ways of seeing and reacting to the world then become so ingrained, and so unconscious, that people think of them as part of their nature rather than as a product of culture. Actions and thoughts, expectations for oneself and for others, undergo a process of **naturalization** as a result of the internalization of cultural norms. Thus, personality is, to a large extent, culturally and socially constructed.

Personality can be thought of as consistent patterns of thinking, feeling, and behaving. But the way we think, feel, and behave is influenced by complex processes of interaction between innate potentials and exposure to cultural norms and values. And it may be that the concept of "personality" is a Western cultural construct. Individuals respond to events in their lives differently. Their perceptions, thinking processes, modes of learning, and emotional reactions are distinct.

psychological anthropology
A subfield of cultural anthropology that studies the psychological motivations of behavior and the personality types prevalent in a society.

naturalization
The process of learning and incorporating attitudes, values, and behaviors so that they seem natural or part of one's nature rather than learned cultural behavior.

personality
A constellation of behavioral traits and dispositions. Some features of personality emerge at birth while others are acquired in the process of enculturation and psychological and cognitive growth.

Cross-cultural research in personality development suggests that cultures and personalities form an integrated, patterned, and adaptive system, suited to the social, economic, and political needs of societies. Put another way, people are molded (and mold themselves) to fit into the cultural contexts in which they live. Different cultures encourage and reward certain personality traits while discouraging and punishing others. Not everyone conforms to the expectations of their society, but most people seek to act in culturally appropriate ways most of the time. Internalized cultural values that affect personality may include, for example, an orientation toward cooperation or competition, an independent or interdependent self-concept, and a focus on a public or a private self.

Cooperation and Competition.   Early cross-cultural research on personality tended to focus on traits such as cooperation and competition. In all societies, people exhibit both cooperative and competitive behavior, in different contexts. All cultures, therefore, need to encourage the development of cooperation and competition in particular situations among particular individuals. Behavior must be contextualized. In addition, the labels "cooperation" and "competition" describe sets of behaviors rather than any particular behavior. Finally, competitiveness and cooperativeness are matters of degree rather than absolute qualities.

With these cautions in mind, studies based on experimental testing of children from several countries and from urban and rural areas revealed marked differences in children's willingness to compete or cooperate in achieving tasks (Munroe and Munroe, 1975). For example, children in the United States were the least willing to cooperate and continued to compete with each other even when competition led to failure and cooperation would have led to success. Even after several trials when children should have noticed that if they had cooperated they would have been successful, American children continued to compete. This pattern contrasts with that of urban Mexican children who initially competed but then quickly caught on that cooperation would aid them all and thus changed their strategy. Differences were noted within countries as well. That is, competitiveness was more typical of urban Mexicans than rural Mexicans, urban Israelis than kibbutz children, and urban Canadians than rural Canadians.

Studies of traditional or preindustrial cultures from the anthropological record indicate a common focus on cooperation. Rather than stressing individualistic and competitive goals, these cultures emphasized the interrelationships between a person and the groups to which they belong. Strongest links were established with one's kin and a group focus reinforced through child-rearing practices. Children interacted with and learned how to get along with many different people on a daily basis. They were cared for by older siblings and adults besides their parents. They saw people engaged in group activities and they learned the value of cooperation. Personality traits that were encouraged were those of communal responsibility, generosity, and even temper. According to Ruth Bunzel, writing about the Zuni,

> In all social relations whether within the family group or outside, the most honored personality traits are a pleasing address, a yielding disposition, and a generous heart. The person who thirsts for power, who wishes to be as they scornfully phrase it, "a leader of the people" receives nothing but criticism. (1932:480)

Public Self and Private Self.   Cultures vary in their focus on "private self" and "public self" (Triandis, 1989). These, too, are labels that refer to sets of attitudes rather than discrete or isolated concepts. People have notions that focus on both their private and public selves, each coming into focus in particular contexts. **Private self** is the feelings and thoughts that involve characteristics and behaviors of the person, whereas **public self** is a person's feelings and thoughts that involve characteristics and behaviors of a "generalized others' view of the self" or of the "collective self" (p. 507).

Cultural notions of the private self emphasize self-actualization; cultural notions of the public self emphasize the norms and values of the group. According to Triandis, these divergent emphases on self correlate with societal scale and economic systems. The private self is the focus in large-scale, comparatively affluent societies, where

private self
One's inner feelings and concepts of oneself.

public self
The self that one projects in public, in interactions with others.

self-concepts
Attitudes that people hold about themselves.

independent self
Concepts of individuals as self-contained, independent agents with a focus on their own thoughts, feelings, and achievements.

interdependent self
Concepts of individuals as connected to others, related to other people, with a focus on group needs rather than individual inner feelings, opinions, and attitudes.

? *How would you describe your personality? What cultural factors influenced the development of your self-concept as a person?*

individualism and personal achievement are stressed in the context of social and economic competition. The public self is the focus in smaller, more egalitarian societies, where collectivism and group well-being are stressed. Child rearing in individualistic societies emphasizes personal achievement and the value of standing out, being distinct and different. In contrast, child rearing in collectivist societies emphasizes conformity and fitting in with group norms, especially in public settings.

Culture and Self-Concept

Research suggests that people in different cultures have different ideas of themselves, or **self-concepts.** In an influential review of research, Hazel Markus and Shinobu Kitayama (1991) point to a basic distinction between cultures that have an "independent" view of the self and those with an "interdependent" view of the self. Again, these labels cover constellations of attitudes and societal emphases rather than absolute, discrete differences. In all societies, people have both independent and interdependent concepts, each appropriately displayed in different contexts. Markus and Kitayama characterize the **independent self** view as a primarily Western notion of a person with unique "dispositional attributes". . . "detached from context" (p. 225). The **interdependent self** view, in contrast, sees the self as embedded in surrounding context, or "self-in-relation-to-other." These researchers believe that the only universal aspect of self, beyond an awareness of one's physical body, is awareness of internal activity, such as dreams, thoughts, and feelings, which cannot be known directly by anyone else. An inner private self results from this awareness of "unshared experience."

An independent view of the self is individualistic, egocentric, and self-contained, whereas an interdependent sense of self is based on feelings of "connectedness" to others. In cultures where independent views of the self dominate, people are most concerned with their own thoughts and feelings and with their own achievements. In cultures where interdependent views of the self dominate, one's inner feelings, opinions, and attitudes are secondary to the needs of the groups to which one belongs. Group and community consensus and expression of solidarity are valued.

The people in this Cinco de Mayo parade are expressing social solidarity as well as cultural identity through a public event. In personality characteristics, compared to people from some other cultures, they likely would score higher on psychological measures of emphasis on cooperation versus competition, interdependence versus independence, and public selfhood versus private selfhood.

Case Study

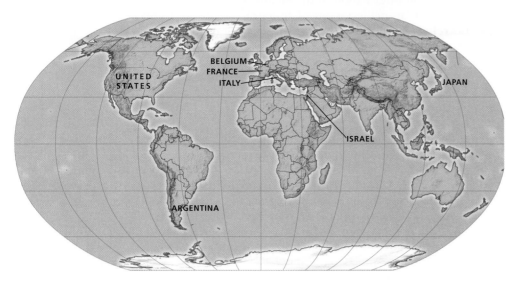

Am I a Good Mother?

A study of self-evaluations of parenting in seven industrialized countries revealed differences in mothers' statements about their own competence and focus in child rearing and about their attitudes in regard to success and failure (Bornstein et al., 1998). While these are generalizations across a culture, they do point to interesting contrasts. Researchers noted the following significant cultural patterns.

Argentinian mothers evaluated themselves as relatively low in competence and investment. They generally blamed themselves for problems encountered by their children. The mothers voiced concern about making mistakes that would lead to their child's future unhappiness. One mother remarked, "You never know for sure if you are doing a good job."

Belgian mothers reported high levels of satisfaction with their roles as parents. They expect their children to behave. However, they neither thought of themselves as especially competent or incompetent as parents. The researchers suggest a significant correlation between Belgian mothers' satisfaction and security and the existence of national health programs and support agencies available to provide families with health and educational services.

French mothers claimed relatively low investment in parenting. They, too, rely on an efficient and widely available infant and child day-care system to provide services and information. They believe that parenting "should come naturally" and that a mother who needs to exert extra effort is not a "genuine" mother.

Israeli mothers rated themselves high in parenting competence. Israeli society stresses the importance of having children, so Israeli mothers consider parenting a positive experience. But they also believe that raising children involves other people as well as the parents, wanting to connect their children to relatives and friends.

Italian mothers had a relatively low opinion of their own competence. They did not see a strong link between parenting and a child's behavior because of their belief that children develop spontaneously.

Japanese mothers saw themselves as the least competent or satisfied with their parenting. However, they reported high investment in their roles as mothers. They believe that effort is the most important attribute of a good mother. A child's failure is, therefore, thought to result from a mother's lack of effort and involvement. It may be that Japanese mothers' statements are motivated not necessarily by inner feelings of incompetence but by social norms that stress modesty when talking about oneself and one's abilities.

American mothers gave themselves relatively high ratings on competence and satisfaction. They were reluctant to attribute failures to their own abilities. Consistent with American attitudes about individuality and success, U.S. mothers consider good parenting to be an achievement of themselves and their children. Their responses may also reflect social norms against public admissions of a lack of competence or satisfaction.

Interdependent views of the self are more prominent in some cultures than others. Related values include the importance of respecting other people's feelings and adjusting one's behavior to the needs of the group. Community goals become personal goals as well. People ideally observe other people's behavior for the purpose of deducing their motives and feelings. People in societies with interdependent views of the self express strong needs for affiliation with others.

A person's identity emphasizes one's relationships and one's membership in groups of various kinds, including family and community. In-group and out-group distinctions are likely to be well marked in collectivist societies. People feel great loyalty to their own group (however defined). Self-discipline and emotional restraint may be valued in collectivist societies, whereas self-esteem and personal expression are valued in individualistic societies (Heine et al., 1999). In all cultures, though, people who conform to the expectations of their society, whether for individual accomplishments or for group cooperation, can have feelings of self-regard because they are acting according to cultural models of authenticity and appropriateness. Anthropological studies popular in the 1940s, 1950s, and 1960s focused on these cultural models as examples of **national character.**

Culture and Cognition

Cross-cultural psychological research raises some important questions about cultural impacts on styles of thinking. While it is impossible to isolate any one feature as causal, these questions can be approached from a holistic perspective, viewing cultures as integrated systems of practices, attitudes, and values. Studies with Inuit subjects from Arctic Canada and Alaska and with Kpelle subjects from Liberia illustrate cultural differences in the characteristic ways that people think.

The Inuit have a highly developed ability to make spatial judgments. In tests, subjects were required to sort out the components of their environment, separate an element from its context, and locate themselves accurately in relation to environmental features (Munroe and Munroe, 1975:82). The Inuit also demonstrate a remarkable memory for territorial features. Their success at spatial tasks is consistent with the needs of their economic and settlement patterns. In Arctic terrain, where color and shape are relatively uniform, it takes sophisticated knowledge and judgment to discern and recall significant environmental features. Such knowledge is critical to survival for people who depend on migratory animals for their food sources and who relocate their settlement sites with some frequency.

Inuit child-rearing practices encourage the development of complex spatial abilities. Children have freedom of movement and activity, but the rules that prohibit risky, life-threatening behavior are made clear and are applied consistently. The Inuit language has a rich array of terms that describe location, relations of objects to backgrounds, and relations connecting the speaker to directions, distances, and objects in the environment (Denny, 1982). Correlations between hunting and gathering economies and spatial acuity are supported by data from Australian Aborigines, who also score high on spatial judgments tests (Segall, 1979).

Recall from Chapter 4 that people classify objects and experiences according to different principles. In one study, members of the Kpelle tribe of Liberia were asked to sort twenty objects into categories. The objects included five members of four categories: food, clothing, tools, and utensils (Segall, 1979). Rather than sorting into these categories, however, Kpelle subjects sorted into functional groupings. For example, a

national character
A constellation of behaviors and attitudes thought to be characteristic of a modal personality type prevalent in a particular country.

Controversies

Is There Such a Thing as National Character?

Research on national character attempted to elucidate personality types prevalent in different cultures. Ruth Benedict's pioneering work, *Patterns of Culture* (1934), characterized tribal groups by what Benedict proposed was an overriding personality type. Working with Native American and Melanesian materials, Benedict attempted to describe contrasting cultures in terms of general, overriding thematic constructs. She suggested that every culture develops a particular configuration of behaviors and beliefs that becomes associated with specific personality types. As illustration, Benedict labeled the Kwakwaka'wakw (or Kwakiutl) of the North Pacific coast of British Columbia as "Dionysian" because of their competitive economic and ritual cycles of feasting (potlatching) and their competitive and boastful personality styles. The Zuni of the American Southwest she referred to as "Apollian" because of their nonaggressive, consensus building, and conformist social ethics. And the Dobu Islanders of Melanesia were "paranoid" because of their intense concern with witchcraft and fears of being the target of malevolent witches.

During World War II, Benedict and others attempted to characterize Japanese society, personality, and mentality through handy catchphrases, summed up by the title of Benedict's book on the subject called *The Chrysanthemum and the Sword* (1946). Some of these efforts were related to the war effort, in attempting to understand Japanese culture and specifically their motivations and actions during the war. Studies of Japanese personality focused on the contrast, as perceived by Western observers, between their peaceful, harmonious family life, serene artistic aesthetic, and violent militarism. Benedict's work was later criticized for seeming to reduce culture and personality to stereotypes.

Although it is certainly true that specific personality types may be more or less favored in different cultures, or more or less adaptive in cultural context, and, therefore, more or less nurtured in the development of children into adults, national character studies overgeneralized personality types and value orientations while overlooking actual differences that are attested. The concept of national character also risks constructing an "other" that masks the similarities among people.

These studies have lost favor in the anthropological discipline. Nevertheless, the tendency to overgeneralize and stereotype particular groups may reemerge in public discourse and social policy. For example, the profiling of racial or ethnic groups in criminal investigations, and, most recently, in cases of suspected terrorism, has become a widely known and greatly contested issue.

CRITICAL THINKING QUESTIONS

How might concepts and attributes of national character be used or misused by governments and power elites? What might be some examples from recent history?

---

knife was sorted with an orange, a hoe with a potato. When questioned about their choices, some commented that "was the way a wise man would do things." In response to an experimenter's question, "How would a fool do it?" the subject sorted the objects into "four neat piles with food in one, tools in another, and so on" (Glick, 1975:636).

Additional studies with Kpelle focused on the contextual nature of memory. Kpelle subjects had difficulty remembering objects out of context, but when they were able to classify them into functional and experiential categories, their recall ability improved. Recall also increased when items were embedded in folktales (Munroe and Munroe, 1975:87). In addition, Kpelle subjects had a superior ability to estimate quantities of some items but not of others. For example, they were accurate in estimating quantities of rice, their staple food, but not of other substances. Munroe and Munroe suggest that context-bound thought is adaptive in small-scale preindustrial societies, where "categories and processes of thought operate with what is immediately relevant—as culturally defined—and this is seldom knowledge for its own sake" (p. 89).

In contrast, cognitive processes that children learn in the United States stress intellectual functioning leading to "more and more flexible and general schemata." This type of thinking is also adaptive. It is adapted to situations of rapid change where people are confronted with numerous types of problems requiring both multitasking and specialized knowledge. Studies indicate that in all cultures, increased formal schooling correlates with increased success in memory tasks involving abstract concepts and out-of-context items. Intelligence and cognitive styles, too, prove to be adaptive.

Formal education favors decontextualized thinking, which may present difficulties to Kpelle and other children adjusting to the demands of school settings (Rogoff and Morelli, 1989). They may find it odd to be expected to answer questions out of context without any perceived need or functional goal. They also may find it odd to provide information to an adult who clearly already has the information being requested.

> ### REVIEW
>
> Personality development, self-concepts, and cognitive skills are affected by culture and the individual's internalization, or naturalization, of cultural norms. These are all topics in the field of psychological anthropology. People's personalities and cognitive skills, though highly variable, tend to be fitted or adapted to the culture in which they live. Examples of differences in personality traits include cooperative or competitive tendencies, individualistic or collectivist tendencies, and a focus on the private self or public self. This is not to say, however, that societies have a national character characterized by an overarching specific personality type.

DEVIANCE AND ABNORMAL BEHAVIOR IN CROSS-CULTURAL PERSPECTIVE

Societies differ in what is considered normal or abnormal behavior. They also differ in the ways in which abnormal behavior is interpreted and treated. Cultures teach people how to act appropriately in different situations. People learn the behavior expected of them, attuned to the contexts, the people they are interacting with, and the goals that they wish to accomplish. Most people try to act in accordance with the expectations that their cultures teach them, and most people do act appropriately most of the time.

Rules vary from culture to culture, so that what might be considered appropriate behaviors when interacting with relatives, acquaintances, officials, or strangers in one society might be considered rude, unusual, or even "crazy" in another society. In addition, cultures differ in how underlying psychological fears, tensions, and conflicts are manifested. And they contrast in their ways of interpreting people's actions and speech as normal or abnormal and in responding to or treating that behavior. What is considered **deviance** in one culture might be considered powerful in another.

Responses to "Mental Illness"

? *Do you know anyone who has been diagnosed with a mental illness? What type of treatment has been prescribed for him or her?*

In the United States, medical interpretations of psychological disorders have gained great currency among experts whose opinions influence the general population. These interpretations lead to treatments that are medical and pharmacological. People with "problems" are advised to take drugs to alleviate their symptoms. Drugs are developed by scientific researchers and prescribed by doctors with increasing frequency. Although these treatments may relieve symptoms, they may not cure underlying problems. Whatever we may think of these modalities, however, they are an improvement over the treatment common in Europe and the United States several centuries ago, when people suffering from anxiety, depression, and hallucinations were isolated in asylums where they were verbally and physically abused (Foucault, 1976).

Consider this alternative response to Black Elk, a nineteenth-century spiritual leader of the Oglalas (Neihardt, 1961). Beginning when he was a child of 9 years, Black Elk experienced periods of intense anxiety and fear, followed by his receiving of visual and auditory messages from the spirit realm. These messages were not exclusively for Black Elk but for his community. A modern American physician-psychiatrist might diagnose Black Elk as prone to anxiety attacks or panic disorder and hallucinations, but the Oglalas interpreted his experiences as powerful episodes of contact with the spirit world. Rather than ostracizing, punishing, or medicating him, the Oglalas respected Black Elk as a visionary who could receive messages from the spirit world. Oglala culture gave Black Elk a respected central role in the life of the community.

deviance
Behaviors that violate cultural norms and expectations.

Research comparing the ways that unusual or deviant behavior is treated in diverse societies uncovers both similarities and differences in specific actions and reactions and underlying attitudes. For example, the Inuit recognize a condition they deem aberrant, called *nuthkavihak*, a word translated as "crazy." It refers to a condition where "something inside the person—the soul, the spirit, the mind—is out of order" (Murphy, 1981:813). Manifestations of this ailment include talking to oneself, screaming at somebody who doesn't exist, believing that a child or husband was murdered by witchcraft when nobody else believes it, believing oneself to be an animal, refusing to eat for fear one will die of it, refusing to talk, running away, getting lost, hiding in strange places, making strange grimaces, drinking urine, becoming strong and violent, killing dogs, and threatening people. While you may recognize some of these behaviors as deviant or "crazy" in your community, others are highly specific to the Inuit culture and environment.

According to the Yoruba, some people are *were*, a word translated as "insane." Manifestations include hearing voices and trying to get other people to see their source when the other people cannot, laughing when there is nothing to laugh at, talking all the time or not talking at all, asking oneself questions and answering them, picking up sticks and leaves for no purpose except to put them in a pile, throwing away food because it is thought to contain *juju* (sorcery), tearing off one's clothes, setting fires, defecating in public and then touching the feces, taking up a weapon and suddenly hitting someone, breaking things while in a state of being stronger than normal, and believing that an odor is continuously being emitted from one's body. Again, some of these behaviors have analogs in descriptions of psychosis in Western medicine.

Inuit and Yoruba reactions to people with these conditions, which are thought to be incurable, vary with the severity of the symptoms and the danger of the behavior to the sufferer and to others. Such people may be avoided, restrained, or assaulted as the situation warrants. Both the Inuit and the Yoruba also recognize certain emotional and behavioral conditions that disturb the individual and others in the community but are not "insane." According to Jane Murphy, Westerners would describe many of these conditions as instances of anxiety and depression. Inuit and Yoruba treatment theories consider these types of ailments as curable, especially by ritual practitioners, who perform curing ceremonies that alleviate both the symptoms and their cause. However, they also recognize that some people cannot be cured and may suffer lifelong emotional stress.

Finally, the Yoruba and Inuit are aware of people who simply deviate from social norms. Each group focuses on particular aspects of inappropriate behavior that violate their cultural rules of propriety. The Yoruba call such people *arankan*, which means a "person who always goes her or his own way regardless of others, who is uncooperative, full of malice, and bullheaded" (Murphy, 1981:821). The Inuit word describing such people, *kunlangeta,* means "the mind knows what to do but the person does not do." In both societies, the negative labels are not applied to people who occasionally act in inappropriate ways, recognizing that all people violate social norms from time to time. Instead, they are used to refer to people who repeatedly offend and violate cultural norms, seemingly without remorse. In both societies, people who behave in these ways are subject to informal means of social control such as gossip, teasing, and reprimands. If their behavior continues, they may be physically punished or even killed. And in both societies, such people are considered social incorrigibles rather than illness sufferers. As a result, rituals or other treatments are not offered to them.

Culture-Specific Psychological Disorders

Researchers have noted specific psychological disorders that occur with some frequency in certain cultures but are rare or absent in others. Such **culture-specific psychological disorders** are named and recognized as aberrant behavior by members of the culture (Yap, 1969). Specific reactions to or treatments of such syndromes also may be culture-specific.

In American society, eating disorders such as anorexia and bulimia have relatively high rates of incidence, particularly among young women, although men and women of any age are susceptible. The behaviors are associated with an exaggerated concern with weight and distorted body image. Sufferers who might be very thin see themselves as

GLOBALIZATION

Using Western medical models, a study conducted by the World Health Organization in 2001–2003 focused on incidences of psychological disorders in fourteen countries: Belgium, China, Colombia, France, Germany, Italy, Japan, Lebanon, Mexico, the Netherlands, Nigeria, Spain, Ukraine, and the United States. In the findings, untreated panic attacks, phobias, and posttraumatic shock syndrome topped the list everywhere, except in the United States and Ukraine, where untreated mood disorders and depression were most prevalent. The researchers noted that culture-specific disorders, such as attention deficit hyperactivity disorder (ADHD), were not included in the study.

culture-specific psychological disorders
Psychological disorders that seem to occur with some frequency in certain cultures but are rare or absent in others.

overweight. The syndromes arise in the context of cultural obsessions with appearance, especially for women, and an obsessive fear of gaining weight, which are linked to emphasis on youth and fear of aging. Most Americans do not become anorexic or bulimic in avoiding weight gain but are sympathetic with those who do, because of shared cultural images. Some researchers argue that the majority of women in the United States has some form of eating disorder, even though they may not be anorexic (Bordo, 2004). In other societies, these preoccupations might appear to be bizarre in the extreme.

In some Southeast Asian, North African, and Siberian cultures, people may become victims of a syndrome called *latah*. *Latah* is manifested as a startle reaction, involving trembling, involuntary sudden movements, and overreacting to the behavior of others. People who experience *latah* episodes have difficulty coping with sudden sounds or movements. They become disoriented and extremely anxious. They may have phobic reactions toward common objects and may especially fear worms and certain animals. *Latah* sufferers are particularly vulnerable to repeated episodes after an initial traumatic experience. People in the grip of *latah* usually are not violent, but they may occasionally exhibit aggressive, even homicidal, impulses.

In the Pacific islands and in Indonesia, some people exhibit a syndrome referred to as *amok* (the origin of the English expression "to run amok"). *Amok* is manifested by intense outbursts of rage triggered by relatively simple frustrations of daily life and interactions with others. *Amok* sufferers often have amnesia following an episode, not remembering anything that they said or did during the incident. Extreme cases are rare but might include generalized blind rage. In such instances, sufferers may be forcibly restrained.

Among Algonkian peoples of northeastern Canada, people may be afflicted by a syndrome called *windigo*. According to Algonkian beliefs, this disorder is the result of possession by a supernatural being, called *windigo*, a cannibal spirit. Victims of *windigo* manifest depression and anxiety prior to an episode of spirit possession. Algonkians believe that if not properly treated, *windigo* can lead to murder and cannibalism, because the victim is in the clutches of the cannibal *windigo* spirit. In traditional communities, shamans treated cases of *windigo*, but if the sufferers became homicidal or cannibalistic, they were more often put to death. Fear of possible starvation during prolonged, intensely cold winters may be an ecological trigger to the development of *windigo*, given its emphasis on eating a forbidden source (another human).

In the Arctic, Inuit may experience a syndrome called *pibloktoq* (or "arctic hysteria") that is manifested by convulsive fits, sobbing, and running around in the cold outdoors without adequate clothing. Women more than men may be prone to episodes of *pibloktoq*, especially after the death of a close relative. Incidents of *pibloktoq* sometimes occur epidemically, one victim setting off the disorder in others.

Some researchers suggest a seasonal and physiological trigger for *pibloktoq* (Wallace, 1961; Foulks, 1972). Incidents tend to be concentrated toward the end of winter, when sunlight is scarce or absent and people are unable to synthesize vitamin D, a necessary factor in the absorption of calcium. Calcium deficiency may, therefore, be a factor leading to the syndrome and may also result from low amounts of calcium in the Inuit diet. Another possible reason is the disturbance of circadian or daily rhythms that influence many physiological functions, including blood pressure, body temperature, blood sugars, and hemoglobin levels. The rhythms are adjusted to light-dark cycles and are disrupted by the lack of sunlight in the Arctic winters. Lack of synchrony in physiological functioning can disturb the central nervous system, leading to irritability and anxiety. In addition, such factors as isolation, intense cold, and legitimate fears of starvation may contribute to anxiety and depression that are expressed in *pibloktoq*.

Here is a final example of culture-specific psychological disorders: In China and Southeast Asia, some

Inuit men are more likely than women to experience "kayak fright." They report feelings of dizziness and paralysis, and are afraid to go out in their boats to hunt on the open seas. Victims of kayak fright also report a fear of being abandoned. As a culture-specific psychological disorder, such fears of the dangers of open sea hunting may be both well founded and culturally adaptive. What might be some examples of culture-specific psychological disorders in American society?

Anthropology Applied

The Ethnobotany of Psychotropic Substances

Since prehistory, people around the world have used medicinal and psychotropic substances found in plants. Preserving and passing down botanical knowledge is one of the earliest specializations in human social organization, usually performed by shamans or other spiritual leaders or healers. And it is not surprising that humans would have embraced the use of mind-altering substances to enhance religious or spiritual experiences or healing effects. The study of these and other interactions of plants and people is called *ethnobotany*. Researchers interested in this subject also include medical anthropologists. Increasingly, as shamans' and their peoples' ways of life disappear, preserving and passing down ancient botanical knowledge and the species and varieties of medicinal and psychotropic plants fall to ethnobotanists and medical anthropologists.

Psychotropic (or psychogenic) substances, called *entheogens*, may be intoxicating, narcotic, depressant, or hallucinogenic. They may be absorbed through the skin, ingested, or inhaled. In South America, traditional religious sacraments, healing ceremonies, and divination involve the use of liquid or solid tryptamines derived from native plants with high concentrations of alkaloids. Tryptamines include LSD, psilocybin, and other powerful hallucinogens. Administered by

shamans, a drink—*ayahuasca*—causes hallucinations in which people, while sweating and convulsing, see jaguars, snakes, and vivid colors (Hill, 2002). Depending on the culture, *ayahuasca* may be used by everyone in the community, by males only, or by shamans only.

Tryptamines also may be administered as solids, such as ground seeds. The Otomac use a snuff called *yopo*, inhaled nasally through the hollow leg bones of birds. The Waika boil resin from the inner bark of certain trees, which is then dried and ground for use as snuff (Balick and Cox, 1996).

Transnational pharmaceutical companies and others compete for access to these and other psychotropic and medicinal plants indigenous to tropical rain forests. Also, biopiracy, stealing native plants for profit, has become a growing concern of developing countries. At the same time, governments have moved to criminalize the use of tryptamine-based entheogens, even in religious contexts. Together, these developments threaten native plants. Fearing the loss of wild plant genomes and heirloom varieties, many ethnobotanists work with other specialists in efforts to preserve the living species on which modern synthetic drugs are based.

CRITICAL THINKING QUESTIONS

Why do most modern states treat tryptamines as controlled substances? Why might it be important to preserve ancient species and varieties of plants?

men are gripped by *koro,* an intense and depersonalized fear of the retraction or shrinking of the penis. A man believes that his penis will retract into his abdomen, leading to death. *Koro* panics, which tend to occur as epidemics, may be associated with guilt over real or imagined illicit sexual encounters or over autoerotic thoughts or actions. They can also be triggered by generalized anxiety or by cold. Significant historical and cultural contexts for *koro* include the demands or perceived demands of sex in polygynous households. Husbands may be uncertain about their sexual adequacy or performance in a culture that places high value on the fathering of children to ensure continuation through the male line.

REVIEW

All societies have informal and formal ways of dealing with deviant behavior. For example, people commonly apply informal social sanctions to alert individuals that their violations of social norms are not acceptable. People also define behavior regarded as mentally ill. While there are behaviors that people everywhere identify as "insane," there also are culture-specific psychological disorders. Many of these disorders have physiological causes, but each society explains them differently based on its system of beliefs and values.

Chapter Summary

The Process of Enculturation

- Human beings are born helpless and completely dependent on adults. Infants may be helpless, but they are immediately responsive to the world around them and begin to learn their culture as soon as they are born. Gradually, they acquire the language of their society and they learn to behave in culturally appropriate ways. This process, called enculturation or socialization, takes place primarily through informal means over a period of many years.

- Child rearing differs considerably from place to place and over time. In general, a society's child-rearing practices are consistent with its core values. Child rearing includes implicit messages absorbed by children as they observe and interact with members of their family and community. And they include methods and techniques used to feed and care for children, sleeping arrangements for children, and ways in which children are held and carried.

- Attitudes toward children and child care change over time. In the United States, for example, advice given to parents and other caregivers by medical doctors, psychologists, and sociologists has varied considerably, even in the twentieth century. The advice about how to raise one's child is generally consistent with the economic needs of the nation and with the social values about family, individuality, and gender roles that are shared by members of the culture.

Formal and Informal Learning

- Children absorb cultural values, including norms of behavior, attitudes, and ethics, by observing how people act and hearing what they say in the course of their daily activities. The repetition of sayings and proverbs and storytelling are powerful symbolic means of transmitting core cultural values. Children also need to learn how to properly interact with others. This, too, they learn by observing their elders and interacting with peers, family members, and people of different social roles in their communities. In addition, children learn their place and their social role in their family and community. They learn that factors such as age, gender, and status influence the rights that people have and the ways in which they behave.

- Children are also socialized in formal settings such as schools. The ways in which schools are organized and instruction is given vary cross-culturally. Although today most nations support universal education, in practice children in many nations don't all have equal access to

schooling. School attendance and literacy rates may vary according to gender. Rates of school attendance for boys are higher than for girls, resulting in lower rates of literacy among women than among men. Class, ethnic, and racial differences may also affect rates of attendance in school as well as a child's success in school. These differences have long-term effects on an individual's adult role in society and on his or her economic potential and security.

Psychological Anthropology

- Although we tend to think of personality as an innate part of our identity, our personalities are largely shaped by environmental factors, including our culture. Personality emerges from the interaction of nature and nurture. And the anthropological study of personality demonstrates that cultural differences in underlying core values lead to differences in the kinds of personality developed in each society. Although all cultures contain and approve of some elements of competitiveness and cooperativeness, cultures do differ markedly in the emphasis that is placed on one or the other. Many postindustrial societies, including the United States, emphasize individuality and competitiveness, whereas many nonindustrial societies favor the group over the individual and value cooperation more than competition.

- Differences in personality are also reflected in differing cultural concepts of the "self." Cultures contrast in their emphasis on individualistic approaches to the self and collectivist approaches to the self. The former emphasize individual traits, experiences, and accomplishments. The latter emphasize a person's relationships with others and membership in groups of various kinds, including families and communities.

Deviance and Abnormal Behavior in Cross-Cultural Perspective

- Societies differ in what is considered normal or abnormal behavior. They also differ in the ways in which abnormal behavior is interpreted and treated. In addition, cultures differ in how underlying psychological fears, tensions, and conflicts are manifested. What might be considered deviant behavior in one culture might be considered a sign of spiritual power in another. Anthropologists have isolated a number of culture-specific psychological disorders that seem to occur with some frequency in certain cultures but are rare or absent in others.

 *Key Terms*

socialization   104
social birth   105
child-rearing
   practices   107
folklore   112
status   114

gender identity   115
rites of passage   117
initiation rites   118
psychological
   anthropology   124
naturalization   124

personality   124
private self   125
public self   125
self-concepts   126
independent self   126
interdependent self   126

national character   128
deviance   130
culture-specific
   psychological
   disorders   131

Review Questions

1. What kinds of beliefs and practices do societies have for managing the physical and social birth of new members? What is the relationship between infant mortality rates and definitions of social birth?
2. What child-rearing tasks must all societies address? How do child-rearing strategies commonly vary?
3. What are some examples of formal and informal modes of enculturation?
4. How does status and inequality within a family reflect status and inequality within a society as a whole?
5. How are age and gender socialization reflected in naming practices?

6. What are some examples of rites of passage? What social and psychological functions do rites of passage serve?
7. How do individuals acquire personality traits in the context of enculturation? What are some examples of cross-cultural differences in personal identity and self-concept?
8. What is national character, and why was it controversial as a concept?
9. What are some examples of the diverse ways in which societies deal with deviant and abnormal behavior?

CHAPTER 6

Preview

1. **In what basic ways do humans satisfy their need for food?**

2. **To what factors affecting food supply and availability must people adapt?**

3. **How does subsistence influence the size of populations and people's habitation patterns?**

4. **How does subsistence shape people's work, social organization, and social relationships?**

5. **What are some characteristics of foraging and examples of foragers?**

6. **What are some characteristics and examples of pastoralists and horticulturalists?**

7. **What are some benefits and risks of agriculture as a mode of subsistence?**

8. **How can people's subsistence strategies combine and change over time?**

*A*t first there was no earth, only sky above and water below. In the Sky-World lived a woman who was *pregnant. One day, while searching near roots of a large tree for medicines for her husband, she fell through a hole in the sky and descended toward the waters below. Animals in the sea saw her falling and decided to make a soft place for her to land. They dove beneath the water and took up some mud which they placed on a turtle's back. The woman landed unharmed and the turtle's back, covered with mud, gradually expanded to become the earth.*

The woman soon gave birth to a daughter. This daughter later became pregnant and gave birth to twin sons. One son was born in the normal manner but the second was born through his mother's armpit, killing her in the process. The woman's mother buried her and out of her body grew the plants on which people depend for their sustenance: Corn grew from her breast, out of her abdomen grew Squash, and from her fingers grew Beans. These plants are called "The Three Sisters" and "Our Life Supporters."

From Mohawk narrative relating the origin of food crops (compiled from narrative accounts, Bonvillain, n.d.).

The Mohawk lived in the woodlands of what is now eastern New York, western Vermont, and southwestern Québec, before European settlers began to displace them in the seventeenth century. Today, many of their descendants live on reservations (or reserves) in New York State and in Québec and Ontario, Canada. Although they supplemented their diet with game and wild plants, they obtained the bulk of their food from farming. Their principal crops—like those of all Native American farmers in North America at that time—were corn, beans, and squash.

In this narrative, a traditional story told today as well as in ancient times, the Mohawk account for the origin of these crops and acknowledge their dependence on them. All three emerge from different parts of the buried body of the daughter of the earth. Corn, the daily staple, springs from her chest, squash from her belly, and beans from her fingers. The symbolism in the story connects the growth of plants from the woman's body with the continuing fertility of the earth. Through her death, she gives us life because she gives us the foods that we eat to survive. The narrative also expresses the Mohawk understanding of the fundamental connection between women and food production. In Mohawk society, women were the farmers. They controlled the use of land, planted the fields, and harvested the crops.

Although men provided their families with fish and meat, women sustained their families with the crops that they grew.

ECONOMIC ANTHROPOLOGY

This chapter looks at the many strategies, farming among them, that humans have developed to meet their basic need for food. And it examines the cultural implications of each of these strategies—their influence on everything from population size to social structure. Chapter 7 continues this discussion by examining people's economic systems and systems of exchange.

Economic anthropology is the subdiscipline of anthropology that focuses on subsistence strategies and economic systems—how people meet their survival needs and make their living. Meeting survival needs requires resources and the labor and technology necessary to obtain those resources and transform them into usable foods and goods. People, therefore, need to develop practices that allow for efficient adaptations to their environments, adjusting their settlement patterns and their populations to the available resources. Economic anthropologists study the ways that people organize their labor, allocate various tasks among members of their communities, and share or distribute goods and services within their settlements as well as with people in other communities or regions. Specific subsistence strategies are generally associated with particular types of social and political life. Economic systems thus influence the ways that other cultural practices develop in order to meet physical and social needs.

REVIEW

Economic anthropology is the study of subsistence strategies—how people meet their basic survival needs—and how those strategies shape their society and culture. Basic subsistence underlies the economic system of a society and strongly influences every other social system in that society as well as people's daily decisions about living their lives.

How might events like this art exhibition be analyzed from the perspective of economic anthropology? Under the auspices of the National Science Foundation, economic anthropologist Stuart Plattner wrote an ethnography of a local art market (High Art Down Home: Economic Ethnography of a Local Art Market, 1996). He interviewed artists, art dealers, collectors, gallery operators, museum curators, and people who attended exhibits like this one. His question was, What social, cultural, and economic factors govern this market and people's decisions about participating in it?

economic anthropology
Subdiscipline of anthropology that focuses on subsistence strategies and economic systems.

UNDERSTANDING HUMAN SUBSISTENCE PATTERNS

Everyone must eat to survive, so a fundamental requirement for any cultural group is to feed its members. The way it does so—the way its people make a living—influences and constrains many other cultural traits. There are different **subsistence patterns**— methods of obtaining food—each making different use of available land and resources, each making different use of available labor and energy, and each utilizing a different technology. Other aspects of culture tend to co-occur with particular subsistence strategies. These include the size and permanence of settlements that people establish, the kinds of households that people live in, the ideas that people have about property and ownership, and even the ways that people think of themselves and other people.

Two basic modes of subsistence involve finding food (foraging, or hunting and gathering) and growing food (food production).

Foraging versus Food Production

Our early ancestors were **foragers,** or hunter-gatherers. They hunted, fished, and collected wild plants, nuts, fruits, and insects. Foraging was humanity's only subsistence strategy for countless millennia until about 10,000 years ago when people living in the Middle East began to herd animals and grow their own crops. Foragers are food collectors. They make use of the resources growing wild in their environment.

People who grow crops or manage herds are **food producers.** They transform and manage their environment in order to obtain their food. The three major types of food production are pastoralism, horticulture, and agriculture. **Pastoralism** involves raising and caring for large herds of domesticated animals as primary subsistence. Horticulture and agriculture are types of farming. Although some people still live by foraging and pastoralism, the forces of globalization are making these ways of life increasingly peripheral. And many people have multiple subsistence strategies based on mixed economies, combining farming, herding, and other methods of food production.

The earliest farming techniques were of the type referred to as **horticulture,** which refers to small-scale farming using a relatively simple technology. Later, intensive farming techniques, or **agriculture,** were developed. Today, agriculture is often combined with industrial processes that eliminate much of the need for human labor. These modes of food production are ideal types and often are combined or practiced in relation to other peoples in trading relationships. We discuss how these subsistence strategies work in the following sections.

Ecosystem, Adaptation, and Carrying Capacity

Subsistence techniques vary considerably, in part depending on available resources, climate, and topography. They are developed in order to satisfy people's needs for food, clothing, and shelter. They must also be adapted to available resources, water, land, and labor supply. Some areas of the world are rich in natural resources while others are meager, each presenting an array of possibilities and challenges for human populations.

The **carrying capacity** of any region or environment is the number of people who can be sustained by its resources. Carrying capacity, however, is not a fixed number. Rather, it varies with such factors as subsistence techniques, labor expenditure, and technological development. Some subsistence strategies and technologies are able to extract more resources from the land than others. This means that people can change a region's carrying capacity by changing their way of life. In general, for example, the same region can support a bigger population of farmers than of foragers. And as farmers work harder to cultivate more land, or develop technologies like irrigation to make their land more productive, they can increase yields and the size of the population that the land can sustain. At some point, however, new limits may eventually be reached, beyond which the productivity of the land can no longer be increased and may, in fact, begin to decline. The resulting problems are something that every society must consider in their subsistence strategies.

---

subsistence patterns
Methods of obtaining food using available land and resources, available labor and energy, and technology.

foragers
Peoples whose subsistence pattern is hunting and gathering.

food producers
Users of a subsistence strategy that transforms and manages the environment in order to obtain food.

pastoralism
A subsistence strategy focusing on raising and caring for large herds of domesticated animals.

horticulture
A subsistence strategy that focuses on small-scale farming using a relatively simple technology.

agriculture
A subsistence strategy focusing on intensive farming, investing a great deal of time, energy, and technology.

carrying capacity
The number of people who can be sustained by the resources and environment in which they live.

Culture as much as biology dictates the foods we choose to eat. Many foods that most North Americans would consider unfit to eat—such as insects, grubs, or snakes—may be considered tasty or even delicacies elsewhere in the world.

GLOBALIZATION

Anthropologists have studied the globalization of food choices, which are shaped by a vast and increasingly complex global economy. In *Tasting Food; Tasting Freedom: Excursions into Eating, Culture, and the Past* (1996), for example, Sidney Mintz explores the globalization of sugar, tea, chocolate, and the ubiquitous Coca-Cola.

settlement pattern
The way people distribute themselves in their environment, including where they locate their dwellings, how they group dwellings into settlements, and how permanent or transitory those settlements are.

Another factor influencing carrying capacity is the resources within an ecosystem that people choose to exploit. People in all cultures make distinctions between the foods that they consider to be edible and those they consider inedible, whether or not they are actually capable of consuming them. For example, different peoples regard different kinds of animals, insects, fish, or plants and seaweeds as inedible or edible because of cultural attitudes.

Communities need to keep their population size within the limits of the carrying capacity of their territory. Their adjustments to their land and resources should be attuned to productivity in good times in order to be able to sustain their numbers when conditions are not optimal. Different subsistence modes entail different kinds of strategies for adjusting population size to resources and land.

Many aspects of society and culture, including population density, the way people reckon kinship, and the way they organize their communities, may influence and be influenced by the way people feed and shelter themselves. Thus, there are relationships between subsistence and settlement patterns, population factors, division of labor, and other elements of culture. It is also important to keep in mind that people engage in a variety of subsistence modes of production, often shifting over time and interacting with people who practice other modes of subsistence. No subsistence system functions in isolation or in a timeless way unaffected by the forces of culture change.

Subsistence and Settlement Pattern

Subsistence strategies tend to be related to particular types of settlement patterns. The term **settlement pattern** refers to the way people distribute themselves in their environment: where they locate their dwellings, how they group dwellings into settlements, and how permanent or transitory those settlements are. Foragers, for example, tend to live in small settlements that fluctuate in size and location, depending on the seasonal availability of plants, animals, and water.

Foragers are usually mobile. They do not have fixed, permanent settlements but, rather, move from camp to camp to secure resources in different places at different times of the year. Pastoralists also tend to relocate their settlements throughout the year, although their movements may be more predictable than those of foragers. Pastoralists often alternate between two or three locations during the year, making use of familiar available grazing lands for their animals. The size of pastoral settlements varies significantly. Some are quite small, numbering less than 100 people, while others may be in the hundreds or even thousands.

In contrast to foragers and pastoralists, farmers often establish relatively permanent settlements. Horticulturalists might move among their gardens and groves or relocate to more fertile fields. Many farmers live in small, scattered villages and may change location every generation or so when their farmland becomes depleted of nutrients. Agriculturalists might live in large, permanent towns or cities.

Subsistence and Population

The number of people living in a community depends on the resources available and the strategies used to extract them. Foraging communities tend to have relatively few people. Some may number no more than a few dozen, whereas others may number into the hundreds. The variation in community size depends on the scarcity or abundance of resources. In places where there are more resources, larger populations may congregate; places of scarcity support fewer people. In most foraging societies, community size fluctuates throughout the year, depending on the availability of resources. People come together when resources are available to support them and disperse when resources dwindle. Food producers tend to have larger populations than foragers. The security afforded by producing one's own food, along with the possibility of producing surpluses, enables larger populations to concentrate in one settlement.

Subsistence, Work, and Division of Labor

Different subsistence strategies involve different kinds of work, allocated to different people. In foraging societies, most work is assigned according to gender. In general, men do most of the hunting and fishing and women do most of the gathering of food from plants. However, these patterns are rarely rigid. Instead, in practice, the roles of men and women overlap so that men may participate in gathering and women may assist in hunting and fishing. In farming societies, the heavy work of clearing fields is usually assigned to men. Thereafter, there are no hard-and-fast rules cross-culturally. In some cultures, women are the principal farmers, whereas in others men are. Age is also a factor in allocating work. In foraging societies, young children may contribute by gathering wild plants, and in farming societies, by helping to plant and weed fields and harvest crops.

Bedouin women of the Bani Hamida tribe in Jordan weave traditional carpets for international trade. Weaving is women's work in this society, and division of labor is also by age, for the elderly women are put in charge of the dye pots for dying the wool.

Subsistence and Social Relations

Modes of subsistence affect people's interpersonal and intergroup relationships. To some extent, all societies have subsistence strategies that result in greater or lesser equality among individuals and social groups because of the way that resources are allocated. Societies also differ in their emphasis on greater or lesser cooperation or competition in producing and consuming resources and placing greater or lesser value on **reciprocity**—principles of mutual gift giving. And societies differ in having more or less effective systems for **redistribution**—the gathering together and then reallocation of food and resources to ensure everyone's survival. The economies of all societies also have **leveling mechanisms**—practices designed to equalize access to food, resources, and wealth or to prevent the concentration of wealth in too few hands, again to ensure general survival of the larger group.

Subsistence strategies include the way that people extract resources from their environment, allocate their land, and utilize labor and technology in order to obtain food and other goods necessary for their survival. The major subsistence modes of foraging, pastoralism, and farming differ in many significant features as they relate to other aspects of behavior and attitudes. They obviously differ in their economic focus since foraging peoples obtain resources directly from their environment, pastoral peoples emphasize the herding and care of animals, and farming peoples grow their own crops.

reciprocity
Principles of mutual gift giving.

redistribution
The gathering together and then reallocation of food and resources to ensure everyone's survival.

leveling mechanisms
Cultural practices designed to equalize access to food, resources, and social prestige through a community so that no one individual can amass greater wealth or greater prestige than other people.

REVIEW

Subsistence patterns are broadly divided into foragers (hunting and gathering) and food producers (growing food). Pastoralism (herding), horticulture (keeping gardens and groves), and agriculture (growing field crops on a large scale) are three forms of food production. People's subsistence strategies depend in part on the carrying capacity of the environment they occupy, which, in turn, affects their settlement pattern, population size, and movements within a territory. The greater the carrying capacity, the more people can be supported. Subsistence strategies also shape and are expressed in people's social relationships and systems of exchange, such as reciprocity, redistribution, and leveling mechanisms.

FORAGING

Foragers depend on nature to supply them with resources, although they need to develop technologies and techniques to exploit those resources. Foraging societies once existed in all parts of the world, but today very few people, if any, remain dependent exclusively on a food-collecting subsistence strategy. Over many centuries, foraging societies have been transformed into food producers, either because they adopted new subsistence techniques on their own, in response to environmental or internal social change, or because they were forcibly absorbed by expanding agricultural or industrial societies.

Foraging survived longest in environments that have proved inhospitable to other subsistence strategies. The indigenous foraging peoples of the Canadian and Alaskan Arctic, for example, until recently lived off the scarce resources of a region that is extremely cold for most of the year. At another extreme, the indigenous foragers of the Kalahari Desert depended on the limited resources of an extremely hot and dry environment. Now, however, the indigenous people even of these regions have become enmeshed in the national economies of the countries within whose borders they live, and they no longer rely exclusively on foraging.

Ecological Factors

Because they depended on widely dispersed and relatively scarce resources, most foragers were **nomads.** They had to travel to particular sources of food as the food became seasonally available. In some cases, seasonal migration meant frequent relocations; in others, only a few. The more abundant and concentrated a region's resources, the less a foraging group had to move to exploit them. In some rare cases, such as in the Pacific Northwest of North America, resources were so concentrated and abundant that the people were able to live in permanent settlements. The need of most foragers to exploit a wide variety of plants and animals added interest and novelty to their diets and supplied a well-balanced assortment of nutrients. Exceptions to this foraging diet included the diet of people like the Inuit, which consisted almost exclusively of meat and fish because of the scarcity of vegetation in the Arctic.

To exploit successfully the resources available to them, foragers needed an intimate knowledge of their environment. They had to be familiar with the life cycles and properties of the plants and animals they depended on and adjust their own migrations to coincide with their seasonal availability. In arid environments, they also had to know where and when they could find fresh water. This crucial knowledge was gathered from experience and, along with critical skills such as fire making, transmitted from generation to generation. Even today some foragers' hearths may burn with fires made from thousand-year-old embers transported from campsite to campsite over many generations.

Optimal Foraging

Some researchers have suggested that human foraging behavior can be understood through analogies with the foraging behavior of other animals (MacArthur and Pianka, 1966; Stephens and Krebs, 1986). They use decision theory to predict the behavior of an "optimal forager," a person with perfect knowledge of her or his environment, of the survival benefits of particular food resources, and of the relative risks involved in pursuing particular food resources. **Optimal foraging theory** might be used to explain why labor is expended in certain pursuits but not in others. However, although this theory offers some intriguing insights, it may reduce human behavior to biological processes and ignore the intervention of culture. Cultural practices respond to environmental constraints and develop to ensure individual and societal survival, but they respond to cultural values and attitudes as well.

A common misconception is that foraging requires constant labor in the pursuit of food. Observations of the Ju/'hoansi of the Kalahari, however, suggest that they spent considerably less time in subsistence activities than do people living in farming or

? *What foraging have you done? How might your practices differ if your foraging was for subsistence rather than recreation?*

nomads
People who do not have permanent homes but travel to sources of food as the food becomes seasonally available.

optimal foraging theory
Application of animal studies and decision theory to human foraging.

Table 6.1 AN ESTIMATED JU/'HOANSI WORKWEEK

	Subsistence Work	Tool Making/ Fixing	Housework	Total Workweek
Men	21.6	7.5	15.4	44.5
Women	12.6	5.1	22.4	40.1
Average both sexes	17.1	6.3	18.9	42.3

industrial societies (Lee, 2003:56). As Table 6.1 indicates, the Ju/'hoansi workweek—including foraging for food, making and repairing tools, and food preparation and other household maintenance—averaged only 42.3 hours.

Although men spent more time and energy in subsistence work than did women, women provided the bulk of the calories (56 percent) in the Ju/'hoansi diet (Lee, 1982:40). Women were more productive than men because success in hunting is appreciably lower than success in food collecting. On average, men killed one animal for every four days of hunting. And on average, women gathered enough plants, fruits, insects, and nuts in a few hours' work several times a week to feed everyone in a camp each night.

Population Factors

Most foraging societies had to keep their numbers low to avoid literally eating themselves out of their territories. In addition, the size of settlements—the number of people living together—usually varied according to the seasonal availability of resources. Generally, people tended to congregate in seasons of abundance and disperse in smaller groups in seasons of scarcity. When families migrated from one location to another, parents had to carry infants and small children, yet another incentive to limit family size.

Because the availability of resources varied from year to year, as well as within the year, the ideal population size for a foraging society would not exceed their region's carrying capacity in a bad year. Failure to keep population in check could result in starvation and malnourishment, which would leave survivors with long-term physical and psychological damage, devastated by the loss of family and fearful for the future.

Foragers adopted a variety of strategies to curb population growth. These included ritually prescribed periods of sexual abstinence before, during, or after certain ceremonies or in conjunction with cleansing or purifying rites. In addition, women in many foraging societies (as in many other types of indigenous societies) often nursed their children for many years. Women are less fertile when they are nursing than when they aren't. Reinforcing this contraceptive effect, many foraging societies (like many societies generally) had taboos or restrictions on the sexual activity of nursing mothers. Some indigenous peoples knew of plants and other natural substances that may have some contraceptive or abortive effects. Finally, when all else failed, many societies permitted infanticide as a response to the need to limit population growth. Taken together, these strategies could not control fertility completely, but that was rarely a necessary goal. Rather, they helped to stabilize population growth over time.

? *What are the implications of foraging for the accumulation of material culture? What kinds of social relations would foraging tend to foster?*

Social and Cultural Factors

Foraging peoples tended not to accumulate much property. For nomadic peoples, having many possessions is a burden because they have to carry them whenever they move. Foraging peoples were rarely interested in claiming land as property. Since they could not control the resources on which they relied, ownership of land would be futile and counterproductive because it would tie people to a particular location. Instead, subsistence based on foraging required territorial flexibility. Ownership of land contradicts that principle of flexibility and might potentially stifle the freedom of movement foragers needed to survive.

Case study

Foraging Societies in the Arctic and the Kalahari

A close look at nomadic foraging societies provides insight into the cultural characteristics common to many such societies. For example, although the Inuit of Arctic Canada and Alaska and the Ju/'hoansi of the Kalahari Desert in Botswana and Namibia live in starkly different environments, they share a dependence on dispersed and seasonally variable resources.

THE INUIT AND INUPIAT OF THE ARCTIC

The Arctic regions present inhabitants with enormous difficulties. Resources are scarce, and weather conditions often make subsistence activities hazardous. The Inuit, indigenous peoples of Arctic Canada, and the Inupiat, closely related peoples of Arctic Alaska, live along the coast and until recently depended primarily on sea mammals, fish, and birds for their sustenance. Because of the nearly total lack of edible plants in the Arctic, the Inuit diet consisted almost entirely of meat and fish. Their only plant sources were the berries and mosses that grow briefly in the summertime and the plant contents of the stomachs of seals, walrus, whales, and caribou that the people hunt.

This lifestyle came to an end for different Arctic groups at different times. By the middle of the twentieth century, most people in the region had abandoned their aboriginal economic patterns. Instead, like other people in the United States and Canada, they now make their living by working in jobs in the public and private sectors. Still, some families continue to supplement the foods they buy in stores with meat and fish caught in the wild.

Because large animals found in the sea and inland regions are migratory, their annual numbers are subject to seasonal changes. Breeding patterns and disease can have an unpredictable effect on both the caribou and sea mammal populations from year to year. Fluctuations in the supply of meat made Inuit life precarious. Learning to endure periods of deprivation and harsh weather was an essential aspect of life. To survive, they developed sophisticated technology for hunting and making clothing. But even with the best equipment, the ablest hunter could fail and families starve.

Environmental and resource constraints kept Arctic settlements small. Along the coast, settlements were largest in winter when people hunted seals. These winter camps typically had no more than forty or fifty inhabitants. Inland groups tended to congregate in late autumn for collective caribou drives, when the animals were most numerous and most valuable, having fattened over the spring and summer. Fall was also the time for making and repairing clothing, so essential to survival in Arctic winters.

As spring approached, people began to disperse, setting up smaller camps usually consisting of two to several small families. Inuit families could reside with either the husband's or wife's kin, but usually preferred the husband's. Men had to cooperate with one another to hunt large animals. In general, hunting and fishing were considered men's work, and food

The explorer Martin Frobisher illustrated this Inuit family on one of his voyages. In his journals, Frobisher remarked that Inuit men and women dressed themselves to look like their prey, in sealskins for hunting marine mammals and in caribou furs for tracking caribou on their inland migrations.

preparation and the gathering of foods such as berries, algae, and birds' eggs was considered women's work.

Among some Arctic peoples, daughters as well as sons learned to hunt (Blackman, 1989; Bodenhorn, 1993). Inuit families hoped for at least one son and one daughter who could fulfill the complementary subsistence tasks associated with each sex. In Alaska, families sometimes adopted children in order to balance the size and gender composition of their households (Bodenhorn, 1988). Alternatively, parents with only boys or only girls might train one child to do both men's and women's tasks (D'Anglure, 1984). Because of their knowledge of the full range of Inuit subsistence skills, these individuals were valued as spouses.

In Alaska, whale hunting often involved a crew of men working under the direction of a leader, called *umialik,* who owned a boat and hunting equipment and recruited the crew. The men in a whaling crew were a cohesive social group, forming relationships with one another that were second in closeness only to those with their families (Spencer, 1984).

Distribution of meat from large animals was a ritualized process that underscored people's social and economic interdependence. It also ensured that everyone received adequate portions of food. And it ensured that over time people would receive different sections of the meat based on the role that they played in any particular hunting expedition. Distribution was managed by the "acquirer" of the meat (D'Anglure, 1984). If the kill resulted from individual hunting, the acquirer was the man who killed the animal. In collective seal or walrus hunting, the acquirer was the man who first harpooned the animal.

Whales, walruses, and seals were butchered into specific sections and allotted according to traditional rules. So, for instance, men in the hunting party received certain sections, women received others, and the whole community shared in a broth made from the remaining parts. In Alaska, the *umialik,* or whaling captain, directed the butchering and allocation of whale meat. The hunter who killed the animal received the hide. He and other members of the crew and any man or woman who contributed labor or equipment to the hunt were entitled to meat. The captain generally received extra shares but later distributed them at public gatherings and ceremonials rather than keeping them for his own household. Once the meat for formal distribution had been cut from the whale, any woman in the community could carve what she wanted from the carcass (Bodenhorn, 1988). In keeping with Inuit social ethics, these "leveling mechanisms" ensured that no one in the community went hungry when food was available.

THE DOBE JU/'HOANSI OF THE KALAHARI DESERT

The Ju/'hoansi live in the hot, dry Kalahari Desert in Namibia and Botswana. The Dobe are a group of Ju/'hoansi who, in the 1960s and 1970s, numbered about 400 and lived by foraging in 3,000 square miles of semidesert terrain. Water is the most critical scarce resource in the Kalahari, and its availability determined settlement size and location (Lee, 1982, 2003; Shostak, 1983). The Dobe area had ten permanent water holes, each "owned" by a resident group, which, however, did not have exclusive rights to the water hole. They had to share it with anyone who could claim kinship by birth or by marriage to any member of the resident group.

Unlike most foraging peoples, who congregated in larger groups when resources were abundant and dispersed into smaller groups when resources were scarce, the Ju/'hoansi reversed this pattern, settling around permanent water holes during the dry season and dispersing during the rainy season when water was more widely available. Dry-season camps generally consisted of eight to fifteen huts, housing twenty to fifty people. Population had to be kept small to avoid straining the resources around the permanent water holes. Rainy season settlements, located near seasonal and secondary water sources, varied in size from three to twenty huts (Lee, 2003:32).

This photo of a Dobe family suggests the effects of modern influences on the Ju/'hoansi way of life. Today, very few people sustain themselves by hunting and gathering. Most Ju/'hoansi live in small settlements, many established by the national governments. Some work as herdsmen for neighboring tribal peoples; others have jobs either in their own communities or in the cities of southern Africa.

Each camp had a core group of residents, usually siblings or cousins, with other residents related by blood or marriage to members of the core group. Camp composition was kept balanced. If a persistent imbalance emerged between numbers of males and females, for example, some families would shift residence to another camp. Similarly, families would move if the number of children in a camp became too large for the number of adults available to care for them.

In general, women's main subsistence activity was to gather wild foods. The Dobe region has more than 100 edible varieties of plants, roots, fruits, and nuts. In all, gathered foods accounted for approximately 70 percent of the Ju/'hoansi diet. Although men also gathered wild foods, their primary subsistence task was hunting (Lee, 1982:40). Men individually tracked and hunted small animals, but larger animals, especially antelope and giraffe, were usually hunted by groups of men.

The Ju/'hoansi valued meat highly. First, meat provided a more concentrated source of protein and calories than plant food, making it important to people who expended a great deal of energy in their daily activities. Second, given the relatively low rate of success in hunting, meat was a scarce resource, and scarcity contributed to its desirability. Third, and perhaps most important, meat had great social value. Whereas gathered foods were usually consumed within the gatherer's household, meat was distributed throughout an entire camp. Meat from an especially large animal might be given to residents of other camps as well. A successful hunt provided the opportunity for feasting and the display of proper etiquette in distributing portions to kin and neighbors. As among the Inuit, the distribution of meat had great social significance. As recounted in an ethnography of the Ju/'hoansi by Richard Lee:

> Distribution is done with great care, according to a set of rules, arranging and rearranging the pieces for up to an hour so that each recipient will get the right proportion. Successful distributions are remembered with pleasure for weeks afterwards, while improper meat distributions can be the cause of bitter wrangling among close relatives. (2003, p. 48)

The Ju/'hoansi had several leveling mechanisms to prevent successful hunters from gaining disproportionate wealth, status, and authority over others. For example, "ownership" of a kill went not to the hunter who shot it but to the owner of the fatal arrow. Arrows were given to hunters through reciprocity—gift exchanges called *hxaro*. An individual could give a present to anyone and thereby establish a relationship based on future reciprocity. When a man went hunting, he might use arrows that he made himself as well as arrows given to him by one or more of his *hxaro* partners. Prestige accrued to the arrow owner, who supervised the distribution of meat.

A second leveling mechanism was the practice of "insulting the meat." A successful hunter did not immediately bring his kill into camp. Instead, he left it a distance outside and returned alone. He would then announce his deed and gradually persuade other men to come and see. When the group arrived at the kill site, they made derogatory comments about the animal and voiced annoyance at the hunter for bothering them with such an insignificant kill. The hunter was expected to join in in insulting the meat and ridiculing himself. The Ju/'hoansi were well aware of the "leveling" purpose of these social rituals. An elder hunter explained:

> When a young man kills much meat, he comes to think of himself as a chief or a big man, and he thinks of the rest of us as his servants or inferiors. We can't accept this. We refuse one who boasts, for someday his pride will make him kill somebody. So we always speak of his meat as worthless. In this way we cool his heart and make him gentle. (2003, p. 52)

Social etiquette in foraging societies was often based on the principle of communal sharing. Sharing the meat of large animals was a critical way of distributing resources and making sure that everyone in the community had the same chances of surviving. People in foraging societies depended on one another in times of need, and sharing food is a way of symbolizing community interdependence just as it ensures everyone's well-being. In such societies, people understood the needs of others to be just as important as their own needs. What is good for all is good for each one. They also understood that the people whom they help feed one day might help feed them the next.

Most foraging societies were characterized by social equality. Foragers generally believed that all people have equal rights to resources, equal rights to social respect and prestige, and equal rights to a decent standard of living. In foraging societies, there was usually little differentiation among families in terms of possessions, wealth, housing, and equipment. Similarly, there was usually little differentiation among people in terms of social standing except as a reflection of individual differences in intelligence, skill, and personality. Only a few foraging societies had significant distinctions of wealth and social standing.

Finally, in many foraging societies, people had religions that included the belief that animals, plants, and some objects had souls similar to the souls of human beings. Animals were understood to be capable of thought and speech. Foraging peoples also performed rituals aimed at securing successful hunting.

Land, Labor, and Production in Foraging Societies

In most foraging societies, land and resources are generally available to all members of the group. A "group" may be defined as a family, a larger kin group, a local community, or a dispersed population who consider themselves the inhabitants of a particular territory. Each type of group tends to have certain territories and resource sites that its members utilize on a repeated basis, following usually unstated customs. Everyone acknowledges by tacit agreement everyone's customary rights to a usual territory. Individual control or ownership of land and resources is absent, but kin groups or a recognized social group may claim land or expect that their rights to land and resources will prevail. Adjustments in the balance among people, land, and resources are made informally.

Although foragers usually have open access to land, they may allocate certain key resources to specific groups. For example, among the Ju/'hoansi of the Kalahari, water is the scarcest and most valuable resource. Water holes are owned or controlled by two or three individuals related through kinship (usually siblings or cousins). Owners hold access to water holes, but they are not the exclusive users. Other people may make claims to the water through their relationships to the owners, either by blood or marriage. Individuals who need access to water owned by relatives make a direct request. When a claim is made, access must be granted. Therefore, although in principle only a few people own the water holes, the rights to use the water are widely dispersed throughout the community. No one is left without the right to have water, an obvious necessity for survival.

Similarly, among foragers of California, such as the Wintus, Yokuts, Maidus, Yanas, and Miwoks, acorn groves were owned by separate kinship groups. The acorns and their products were important food staples. However, ownership did not entail exclusive usage rights. If another group of people entered one's territory and came upon one's acorn groves, it was customary for them to ask formal permission of the owners before exploiting the resource. Formal requests for permission to use one's acorn groves had to be granted. The asking and granting of permission was automatic but symbolized one group's right to ownership and the entire community's reciprocal interdependence.

As another example, among foragers of the Pacific Northwest, salmon were the primary and most prized food resource. Particular kin groups owned streams where salmon spawned. Such groups also owned berry patches and other abundant food sites. The salmon streams and berry sites were exploited exclusively by members of the kinship group who claimed them and were acknowledged as owners. However, as you read on, you'll learn that the fish and fruit were distributed in a much wider network that included many families belonging to the same community and even to families in other communities.

In Their Own Voices

An Inupiaq Whaler's Wife

Sadie Brower Neakok was an Inupiaq woman living in Barrow, Alaska. She died on June 18, 2004, and was praised in the U.S. Senate for her work as the first woman to serve as a magistrate in the state of Alaska. Daughter of a native mother and an Anglo father, she was raised in both traditional and nontraditional ways. From her mother, who was a skilled hunter, Sadie learned to hunt and fish. And from her father, a whaler, she learned the importance of education in the "outside" world. Sadie grew up to be a social worker and magistrate in Barrow. She married an Inupiaq man, and she accompanied him on many hunting trips. In this excerpt from her life history, Sadie Brower Neakok: An Inupiaq Woman, *Sadie describes women's contributions to whale hunting.*

Being a whaler's wife is just as much work as preparing to go out with a crew. You have to see that they all have warm clothing. So your husband buys all the fur. In the olden days, it was caribou hides, ruffs, fur socks, fur pants. We didn't have down clothing, so everything was made out of caribou hide or reindeer hide and sealskin for waterproof boots. New clothing is made every year because it's tradition.

Inuit whalers.

If you want a good skin on your husband's boat, you have to hire several women to sew together six or seven ugruk hides with waterproof seams and stretch them over a frame. . . . The sewers also have to know how to make the thread; it's braided from caribou leg sinew, and then the

---

REVIEW

Foragers such as the Inuit of the Arctic and the Ju/'hoansi of the Kalahari share hunting and gathering as a subsistence strategy. They are nomadic, moving seasonally to different resources as they become available. According to optimal foraging theory, subsistence activities can be predicted on the basis of getting the most or best food for the least investment of time and energy, but cultural factors also play a role. Foragers typically have egalitarian relationships, cooperate in food getting, share food across kin groups, and do not have individual ownership of land or resources.

PASTORALISM

Pastoralism is a way of life that centers on the herding and care of domesticated animals. A very broad term, it applies to people dependent on diverse animals in diverse environmental and social contexts who exploit their animals for various products—rarely just for their meat and in some cases not even for food. Pastoralism differs from simple animal husbandry, which is the keeping of domesticated animals. It is a way of life in which a people's economy, settlement patterns, and social systems are adapted to large-scale herding. So, for example, American farm families in rural communities are not pastoralists by virtue of keeping a small number of chickens, cows, and horses. In contrast, pastoral families in Africa, the Middle East, and Asia may own hundreds of cows or sheep and goats or horses or camels whose needs for grazing land and water determine people's daily routines and seasonal movements.

part where you put the needle [i.e., eye of the needle] is made from the back sinew.

Nate [Sadie's husband] has been a whaling captain for quite a while. And in his time, I guess he has gotten about five whales. The last one was in 1984. And you could see him cutting it up, measuring it for the various parts that go to certain people.

The fluke area is for the whaling captain, and then there's a belt of about eighteen to twenty inches wide, which is for the captain's pleasure. It's up to the captain whether he wants to sell it; he talks with his crew whether they want a share of it for their own consumption or to sell it. And the captain's part is set aside by itself, to give to people at the whale catch celebration—Nalukataq time—and Thanksgiving and at Christmastime. We cut it up in thirds for all the people. That's a lot of work, cutting it up. You have to feed the whole town; that's the custom.

Everybody enjoyed our whale. There are so many people in town now—even our whites have acquired the taste of fresh maktak and meat, and they mingle in with our people—and feeding some three and four thousand in one day out of that whale, by 10:00 P.M. we were all in.

Then you do it all over again at Nalukataq time. You have to cut up meat and maktak and put it into containers to age. You cook the heart, and the kidney, and the intestines at Nalukataq time. Oh, it's a lot of excitement when it

happens. Then there's the blanket toss and the dances, but it's not like the old days anymore. People didn't work in those days when I was young. Now we have to wait till everybody gets off work to serve our big portions of whale. It starts at five.

As far back as I can remember, in the old tradition, women were out there on the ice with the men. They could go out and hunt with the menfolk; they would cook for them, or sew, or tend to their men's needs out there. But we are shying off from that today. There's not very many women who would go out and stay out there, but Nate gives our girls a chance to be out there.

When you're a whaling captain's wife, your part is just as important as the men's because you're entrusted with keeping your husband's crewmen out there comfortable and fed. You're in charge of all their care, preparing their food. . . . When the boats start chasing a whale, all you do is just listen to see who is catching it. It gets so exciting, like you are inside of the boat yourself. It's an exciting event when your crew gets a whale, a lot of work, but when all the women's work of feeding the whole town is done, then you feel like you have shared in the whale catch.

From *Sadie Brower Neakok: An Inupiaq Woman*, pp. 209–216, by Margaret Blackman. Copyright 1989. Reprinted by permission of the University of Washington Press.

Like farming, pastoralism allows people some control over their food sources. Perhaps by about 9,000 years ago, people in the Middle East were keeping domesticated sheep and goats. Pigs were domesticated in southeastern China at about the same time. And African peoples domesticated cattle as early as 9,500 years ago. Andean peoples in Peru began to domesticate animals by 7,000 years ago, keeping alpaca and llamas for their meat and wool. They also kept guinea pigs. In North and Central America, people domesticated dogs and turkeys.

Combined Subsistence Strategies

Rarely, if ever, has pastoralism been a self-contained subsistence strategy. Some pastoralists combined herding with foraging, others with small-scale farming, and still others traded for food with their settled farming neighbors. Like foraging, pastoralism is rarely the central economic strategy of any people today. Most pastoralists have adopted farming or wage work or trade as their primary mode of making a living. It has become increasingly difficult for pastoralists to keep control of a large enough territory in which to graze their animals, as the pressure on land has increased with population growth and national economic policies.

The Nuer of southern Sudan combined cattle herding with farming. They consumed milk from their animals and used dung for fuel, but ate meat only on ritual occasions or when an animal died of natural causes. Middle Eastern sheep and goat herders like the Basseri of Iran drank milk from their animals and processed it into butter, cheese, and yoghurt. They also traded milk, wool, and other animal products for grains and other crops from their farming neighbors.

Pastoral nomads of Mongolia have a mixed economy, combining subsistence bases tied to the modern Mongolian state, which achieved independence from China in 1921. Yet their way of life is similar to that of other horse-herding peoples in different cultures in other parts of the world. These similarities reflect the power of basic modes of subsistence such as pastoralism to shape peoples' ways of life as well as their daily activities.

? *What different patterns might you predict for relationships between pastoralists of the ranges and farming peoples of the valleys?*

The sheepherding Diné (Navajo) kept their animals mostly for their wool, used for weaving into blankets and clothing for household consumption and for sale. In the past, the Diné obtained food primarily through farming, hunting, and gathering plant foods. Horse pastoralists, such as the Cheyenne, Lakhota, and Crow, who dominated the North American Plains until the late nineteenth century, used their animals for transportation and warfare and to hunt the great herds of bison that roamed the plains. They also had a complex intertribal trade network, often traveling great distances by horse to exchange bison meat and hides for farm produce.

Land and Labor in Pastoralist Societies

Pastoralists' strategies for organizing and controlling land and resources differ significantly from those of foragers, because, in pastoralist societies, land and resources such as domesticated animals are controlled, even owned, by individuals or groups. Pastoralist societies closely regulate and manage rights to use land to ensure that there is enough forage for the animals. Sometimes, herds may put excessive strain on lands and resources because of overgrazing. To prevent overgrazing, pastoralists take their herds to different grazing areas throughout the year. Pastoralists make total use of their animals and allocate these crucial resources according to rules of ownership and control. For example, Nuer cattle herders in southern Sudan own livestock individually. Each animal is the personal property of a man or teenage boy who has completed initiation rituals at puberty. These people are the primary caretakers of the cattle, although a family's herd is taken to pasture collectively. Individuals or kinship groups also own pastureland. Among the Basseri of Iran, the animals are individually owned, but different groups may use the same pastureland at different times of the year according to customary cycles of use. Among the Diné, livestock is tended as a family herd on family land. In pastoralist societies, as a consequence of individual ownership, domesticated animals become objective measures of wealth, and inequalities of wealth and competitive status seeking can arise based on the size of herds.

The division of labor by gender varies in pastoralist societies but is generally not as egalitarian as in foraging societies. Men and boys generally tend to the animals while women and children do related tasks, such as milking, dressing skins, and watching over animals. Among some pastoralists, people of any age and either gender may assist with herding animals to and from grazing lands.

Pastoralists may accumulate some surpluses, based on surpluses of animals. The more animals a family owns, the more animals they may feel they need for both herd size and all the products derived from animals (hides, furs, bone) that can be used for many purposes, including the manufacture of clothing, tools, and utensils. The animals and the products crafted from them become important items in trading networks, enabling families to obtain other foods, goods, and services.

Nomadic Pastoralism

The diversity in subsistence strategies among pastoralists is associated with a variety of settlement patterns. Some pastoralists, like the Basseri, were nomadic, changing locations frequently as they led their herds to new pastures, a practice known as **transhumance,** or seasonal movements of people in search of available grazing land. Others, like the Nuer, maintained a year-round home base from which they led their herds to nearby pastures.

Despite their variety of subsistence strategies and settlement patterns, most pastoralists shared a common self-concept as pastoralists, constructing their social and personal identities around herding. Certain cultural features are commonly associated with pastoralism. For example, because pastoralists needed access to land for grazing and seasonal control over access to specific areas, they tended to define and defend their territories more vigorously than foragers. Some pastoralists, such as the Bantu-speaking peoples of southern Africa and the native peoples of the North American Plains, used the strategies of raiding and warfare to defend their territories and to expand into the grazing lands occupied by others. Nomadic pastoralists might be satisfied with customary rights to graze their animals on some defined but not necessarily exclusive territory. They might be content to share their grazing lands with other people, negotiating occasional or seasonal usage. Sedentary pastoralists, on the other hand, might require permanent and exclusive access to particular tracts of land. These tracts might be under the ultimate control of large kin groups or under individual ownership.

Population density varied in pastoral societies, depending on the size and quality of grazing lands and herds. Unlike foraging societies, measuring and accumulating wealth and property, especially in the form of animals, has been a major feature of pastoralism. Because animals are easily countable and their numbers increased by breeding, pastoral peoples generally measured wealth by the size of a family's or individual's herds or flocks. In addition, because animals or products derived from them (meat, hides, wool) can be traded for other goods, herds represent both present and future wealth. In some pastoral societies, wealth in animals became the basis for differentiating people in terms of social status. People with larger herds had higher social standing, prestige, and influence than others. In this context, competition was a successful adaptive strategy. And because in most nomadic pastoralist societies men are usually the owners of most, if not all, of the animals in the herds, systems of descent and inheritance typically follow in the male line.

Nomadic pastoralists, like nomadic foragers, are limited in the amount of property they can acquire because of the difficulties of transporting many possessions from one location to another. In contrast, sedentary pastoralists are able to build up their stores of goods, keeping extra clothing, household utensils, and tools beyond the amount necessary for their survival. Along with notions of private property in animals, competition among individuals and families may be reflected in the desire to accumulate goods and to raise one's standard of living over that of others.

Despite a focus on ownership and competition, pastoralists maintained values of reciprocity, especially sharing with relatives and the expression of generosity and hospitality. Social norms calling for generosity acted as a leveling mechanism, ensuring that richer families shared some of their wealth with poorer families.

transhumance
The practice among pastoralists of moving to new pastureland on a seasonal basis.

? *Why did pastoralism as a subsistence mode favor competition over cooperation?*

Case study

Pastoral Societies of Iran and Sudan

The following case study compares two pastoral societies, revealing some of the common features of this type of subsistence strategy as well as the differences that reflect the specific environment of each group and the kinds of animals that they herd.

THE BASSERI OF IRAN: NOMADIC PASTORALISTS

Pastoralists in the Middle East, such as the Basseri of Iran, herded sheep and goats and traded animal products for grains with nearby settled farmers (Barth, 1964). The Basseri, numbering about 16,000, were, until recently, nomadic pastoralists living in southern Iran. Today most Basseri have given up their traditional lifestyle, principally because of the pressure exerted on them by the central Iranian government. Like national governments elsewhere, Iranian authorities actively discouraged indigenous pastoralists from pursuing their economic strategies because nomadic peoples are difficult to identify and control.

In addition, central governments and their economic planners view pastoralism as an outmoded way of life that retards national economic development. This attitude is one more of ideology than of fact. The Basseri's traditional way of life was an efficient use of sparse resources and territories. Their territory—about 300 miles long and 50 miles wide—is varied in terrain, with mountains, deserts, and plains. Rainfall is light, occurring mainly in the winter. Precipitation, often in the form of snow, is heaviest in the mountains, which, as a result, have the regions richest in vegetation. The rest of Basseri territory is extremely dry and covered with only sparse grasses.

The Basseri did not have exclusive rights to their territory but instead shared it with other pastoral peoples. Each group had its own migration route and schedule, however, so that two or more groups were never at the same pastureland at the same time of year. Each route and schedule—called the *il-rah,* or "tribal road"—was the collective property of the group that followed it. Groups, not individuals, thus controlled access rights to pastureland.

The Basseri moved frequently—on average once every three days—among the pasturelands on their route. Their winter pastures were in the low-altitude southern part of their region, where snowfall is relatively light. As spring approached, they moved to middle-altitude pastures, and in summer to high-altitude pastures that are snow-covered at other times of the year. In the fall and spring, they moved nearly every day, whereas in the summer and winter, they might stay in one location for several days. Each day's trek took about three hours, with some people on foot and others on donkey or horseback. The sheep and goats were led from camp first, under the care of an adult man or a boy or girl. Usually about thirty or forty families traveled and camped together. In the winter, large groups dispersed into smaller camps to avoid overburdening pastureland.

A Basseri family usually consisted of a couple and their children. Each family had its own tent and flock. A family required a herd of about 100 sheep and goats to sustain itself. Boys and men herded the animals to their daily grazing areas, sheep and goats together. Although girls sometimes led the animals on migratory treks, they generally did not herd when their families stayed in the same location for several days. Families with many animals and few able-bodied sons might hire boys to work for them. One shepherd could usually handle about 300 or 400 sheep and goats. People kept donkeys as pack animals and as mounts for women and children. Men rode horses. The Basseri also owned some camels, which they used for heavy loads.

Milk from their animals and milk products, such as butter, buttermilk, sour milk, and cheese, were the basis of the Basseri diet. Milking was done by men and women, usually in a group. The animals were milked at least once a day and sometimes more often. Preparing foods derived from the milk was women's work. The Basseri rarely slaughtered adult sheep and goats to eat, but they did eat excess lambs and kids to keep their herds from growing unsustainably large. They used wool and hides for clothing, tent coverings, and carrying bags. They also traded hides, wool, and finished goods made from animal products to people in settled farming communities.

The Basseri had complex relations with their neighbors in settled farming communities along their migration route. They traded for grains, fruits, vegetables, and cash. During lean years, some Basseri occasionally took seasonal jobs in towns along their routes to earn money for farm goods, clothing, tools, household utensils, and other manufactured goods. Some Basseri amassed enough wealth to buy land, which they leased to farm families, receiving money or produce as rent.

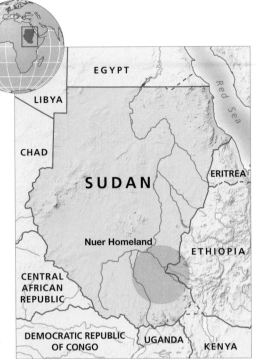

THE NUER OF SOUTHERN SUDAN: FARMING PASTORALISTS

The Nuer are a pastoral people in eastern and central Africa who combined cattle herding with the cultivation of grains and other crops. The Nuer lived in villages along the Nile River and its tributaries. They took their cattle out to pasture from the village and returned them to corrals each evening. With a total population of more than 300,000 in the 1940s, the Nuer were organized into at least ten separate tribes. They felt a strong allegiance to their tribes but otherwise had no sense of themselves as a unified people (Evans-Pritchard, 1940, 1955).

Today, the lives of the Nuer are drastically changed. Caught up as victims of civil wars in the Sudan that raged in the 1990s, most of the Nuer are refugees. Tens of thousands, possibly nearly 200,000, Nuer became refugees in camps in Ethiopia (Holtzman, 2000). Then, when fighting broke out between government and revolutionary forces in Ethiopia, many Nuer moved into Kenya, where they established their homes. Finally, about 4,000 Nuer were permitted to emigrate to the United States in the mid-1990s. According to Jon Holtzman, most of these immigrants now reside in Minnesota, where they have maintained a strong sense of community and Nuer identity, focusing on kinship and on affiliation with Christian churches.

Although traditional Nuer subsistence combined herding and farming, their ideology centered around their relationship to their herds. Significantly, boys took a personal name derived from an attribute or name of their favorite animal. Although the Nuer seldom slaughtered animals for meat, they made total use of the animals. They consumed blood—bled in small amounts from shallow incisions in their cattle, which they drank fresh or mixed with other foods. For instance, a favorite Nuer food is cow's blood mixed with warm milk and a dash of cow's urine. The people worked the animals' hides and bones into various utensils, and they used dung as fuel for fires and as plaster for the walls and floors of their dwellings.

The Nuer rigidly distinguished men's from women's work. Men (including boys of about 15 or older who had been ritually initiated into manhood) were responsible for herding cattle. In addition, men's productive roles included fishing in the many streams and rivers in the region. Fish constituted an important, year-round food source. Men also did some hunting, although game added little to the Nuer diet. Women, girls, and young boys, although not permitted to herd cattle, were responsible for milking the animals twice a day, once in the morning before the cattle were led to pasture and again in the evening when they returned to the corrals. Women also tended gardens, principally growing millet and maize.

These Nuer focus on the challenges of living as immigrants in the United States, where a pastoral way of life is not possible.

Nuer settlements varied seasonally. During the dry season, people concentrated in large villages around streams that provided permanent water sources. During the heavy flooding of the rainy season, they moved to higher ground in small camps of between fifty and two hundred residents. Villages were usually organized around relatives tracing descent through men. They were composed of extended family homesteads consisting of a cattle barn and several huts. Women, girls, and uninitiated boys occupied the huts. Men and initiated boys slept with their cattle in the barns. This pattern reflects the importance of gender and age divisions in Nuer society, and the strong bond between men and cattle in Nuer ideology.

In the Nuer view of the world, cattle are the focus of life. A family's animals are said to be owned by the male head of household, but a man's wives and sons have rights to them as well. When a man marries, he receives some of the cattle owned by his father. Brothers are, therefore, potential co-owners of cattle and are bound together both by their own blood relationship and by their ties to their family herd. And when a woman marries, her family receives cattle from her new husband's kin that are then divided among her male relatives, especially her brothers. Cattle, therefore, are essential to economic and social life, as they are used to establish and solidify social relationships.

REVIEW

Pastoralists such as the Basseri of Iran and the Nuer of southern Sudan traditionally depended on the animals they herded for all their subsistence needs. Animals also became the basis of wealth. Some pastoralists practice transhumance, moving herds to different pasturelands as they become seasonally available for grazing. Control of grazing land and rights in a herd are major concerns in pastoralist societies.

HORTICULTURE

Horticulture and agriculture are two types of farming that are not always easily distinguished. The term *horticulture* refers to farming on a small scale with a relatively simple technology consisting of digging sticks, hoes, and other handheld tools. The term *agriculture* refers to large-scale farming and the use of more complex technology, which can include, for example, draft animals. Intensive agriculture involves irrigation systems and extensive exploitation of land and labor. Some farming peoples may be horticulturalists and others agriculturalists, and still others may combine both kinds of farming.

In general, farmers, in contrast to foragers and pastoralists, require secure access to and control over specific plots of land. In some farming societies, land is owned or controlled by a group of relatives as a collective unit. In others, land may be owned by individuals for their own benefit and that of their immediate families. Because farming requires regular access to land, farming communities tend to be stable. Agriculturalists in particular usually live in fully sedentary communities. Among horticulturalists, there may be more variation. Some are permanently settled, whereas others may shift locations from one season to the next, residing near their fields during the planting season and living elsewhere, perhaps near foraging sites, at other times. Weather conditions may also dictate changes in location. So, for example, many African horticulturalists live in different settlements during the rainy and dry seasons. When there is no rainfall, people live close to the few flowing rivers, but in the rainy season they move to higher ground.

Because they live in stable settlements, farmers can accumulate more property than can foragers or nomadic pastoralists. Their houses may be more substantial because it is worth people's efforts to erect a large, solid house if it is to be their permanent dwelling. Farm families may own forms of property other than land, such as herds, ornaments, tools, and household goods. Households measure their relative wealth according to the quantity of such goods they possess. At the same time, many farming societies limit the accumulation of wealth by encouraging people to redistribute surplus food and property to needier community members.

Impacts of Sedentism and Surpluses

Horticulturalists tend to live in relatively small settlements of from one or several hundred to several thousand people. Settlements may be sedentary, depending on the amount of surplus generated. Farmers regularly try to produce more food than they need for any one season in order to have enough to sustain themselves in years of drought, during crop failure for any reason, or in the event of flooding. **Surplus** means food and other goods that are produced at a level greater than that needed for survival. Farmers usually produce enough surplus to last one or two years of bad times. In **sedentary,** or stable, **communities,** people develop methods for preserving and storing surplus produce. Horticulturalists try to produce enough to maintain a surplus as a buffer to be consumed in bad years, but their techniques rarely yield great abundance. Therefore, they need to control population size with strategies like those used by foragers: periods of sexual abstinence, lengthy periods of breast-feeding, and the use of contraceptives, abortion, and infanticide.

Slash-and-Burn Horticulture

The tasks involved in farming include preparing fields or gardens for cultivation, planting, weeding, and harvesting. The most strenuous of these is preparing new fields for cultivation. Many horticulturists, especially those who live in tropical forest areas, use **slash-and-burn,** or **swidden, cultivation** to accomplish this task. Once an area of land is selected for planting, men cut down trees and bushes and then burn them, which both clears the land and enriches the soil with nutrients. Farmers usually rotate their fields, allowing some to remain fallow intermittently in order to restore their fertility. Others may relocate from time to time, from every few years to a generation or so, when the fields around a settlement become depleted of nutrients. Relocating villages and selecting new fields is a strategy that works only when population densities are low and land is readily available.

Gender Allocation of Work

In horticulture societies, gender allocation of work typically calls for men to do the heavy work of clearing forests and woodlands to make new fields. In some societies, men continue as the primary workers, while in others, women are the farmers. In other societies, both men and women do farmwork, growing the same or different crops.

Among the Pueblo of the American Southwest such as the Zuni and Hopi, both men and women grow crops, although they employ different methods and work in different types of farmland. Zuni men plant, weed, and harvest crops in the fields surrounding their villages. Some work was traditionally carried out individually, while other tasks were

surplus
Food and other goods that are produced at a level greater than that needed for survival.

sedentary communities
Settlement pattern involving long-term, permanent settlements.

slash-and-burn (swidden) cultivation
A farming technique for preparing new fields by cutting down trees and bushes and then burning them in order to clear the land and enrich the soil with nutrients.

Swidden farmers in Borneo transform forests on marginal mountain slopes into palm groves for producing rattan, used in caning and weaving. They cut and burn the forest vegetation and plant palm canes in the ashes. In other mountainous areas of Indonesia, reclaimed forestland is cut into terraces for rice farming. Terraces depleted of nutrients are left fallow as others are farmed. Without organic or chemical fertilizers, however, depleted soils ultimately must be abandoned and more forests cut down to create new cropland.

GLOBALIZATION

The expansion of slash-and-burn farming into tropical rain forests in Indonesia and the Amazon region contribute to global deforestation, but on a smaller scale than commercial lumbering. Deforestation alters climate and weather patterns and contributes to global warming.

done collectively, usually by a group of relatives consisting of fathers, their unmarried sons, and their resident sons-in-law. Before marriage, men worked the land controlled by their mother; after marriage, they worked on land under the direction of their wife's mother.

Because of the difficulty of farming in an arid environment, the people developed a system of floodwater irrigation that made best use of available water from rainfall and from the small Zuni River and a few nearby springs. When a man cleared new land for planting, he built small dams and canals with mud walls to direct water from rainfall and from overflowing streams. The walls were constructed by packing mud over a row of stakes made of branches, rocks, sticks, and earth. In contrast to men's work, women grew some produce in "waffle gardens" along the banks of the Zuni River. Waffle gardens were divided into small square or rectangular cells surrounded by low mud walls that helped conserve water and protect the plants from wind. Women watered their plants by hand, using ladles to distribute water brought from the river or from nearby wells in water jars.

Farming families are able to utilize the labor of their children at early ages. Young children can plant seeds, weed gardens, and pick fruits and vegetables. Some people may become part-time specialists, making pottery, baskets, canoes, houses, and other items. By bartering or selling their products, artisans and other part-time specialists may free themselves from some subsistence work. Horticultural societies produce surplus crops as a buffer against hunger and starvation in years of low yield. Farmers produce surpluses by intensifying their labor and maximizing the land's productivity. People prevent the over-burdening of land and its fertility by rotating their crops or relocating every generation or so. Social norms calling for hospitality and generosity contribute to the redistribution of surpluses so that no one goes hungry.

Among the Yanomamo (ya-na-MA-mo) of the Orinoco River basin of Brazil and Venezuela, men are the principal farmers. They clear and prepare fields and plant and harvest crops. Principal crops include plantain, manioc, and sweet potatoes. Men also grow tobacco, used for chewing, and cotton, used to make yarn for weaving hammocks. Men also hunt and fish. In effect, men provide all the food for the family. Women's work, which includes food preparation and child care, is entirely domestic. Their work is considered secondary to men's work, and they have a correspondingly low status in Yanomamo society (Chagnon, 1997).

In contrast, among the Jivaro (HE-va-ro) of Peru, women were responsible for planting, tending and harvesting crops, notably manioc, sweet potatoes, and squash. These crops, supplemented by fish and game provided by men, supplied the bulk of the Jivaro diet (Meggers, 1971). Women were also responsible for performing the garden rituals that ensure a good crop. The Jivaro valued these tasks, and Jivaro women still have a higher status in their society than Yanomamo women do in theirs.

In some West African societies, horticultural work is performed by both men and women, but the crops that they plant differ. Among the Igbo of Nigeria, for example, tasks are strongly demarcated according to gender. Men traditionally plant yams, considered to be the staple crop. Rice, introduced into the region in the 1950s, is the only plant grown by both men and women. Women plant and harvest all other crops, including manioc, cocoyams, maize, beans, and okra. Women also weed their husbands' yam gardens. Even when work has a collective focus, tasks are demarcated according to gender. For example, men harvest yams, but women and children carry the yams to the household yam barn (Ottenberg, 1965; Ottenberg and Ottenberg, 1962). Other subsistence and household activities are likewise allocated according to gender. Both men and women fish, but in different places: men in nearby rivers, women in ponds and streams.

In some horticultural societies, especially in sub-Saharan Africa, farming is combined with pastoralism, as among the Nuer. Horticulturalists may keep domesticated animals for meat. For example, indigenous peoples of the Melanesian Islands of the western Pacific cultivate yams and other food crops and also keep pigs. Pigs, however, are not grazing animals like cattle, sheep, or goats. They eat the same foods as humans. Melanesian horticulturalists, as a result, grow crops to feed both themselves and their pigs. As the pig population grows, the effort to feed them becomes increasingly burdensome. Eventually, the pig population grows so large that it triggers a round of ceremonials accompanied by pig sacrifices and feasts. The pig population plummets and the cycle begins anew (Rappaport, 2000).

Case study

Mohawks: Farmers of the Eastern Woodlands

The economy of the Mohawks combined horticulture and foraging. Settlements were relatively stable, although people moved to new locations every generation or so when their farmland became less productive and they had exhausted the supply of readily available firewood. Village size ranged from about 50 to 1,000 people and averaged several hundred. Women and men performed different but complementary tasks. Men cleared new fields with slash-and-burn techniques. Then women took over as the principal farmers, planting varieties of corn, beans, and squash, the three staple crops of Native North American farmers. Using wooden hoes, women dug holes in small mounds of earth and planted seeds in them. Before planting, seeds were soaked in herbal solutions for several days to keep crows away from the crops.

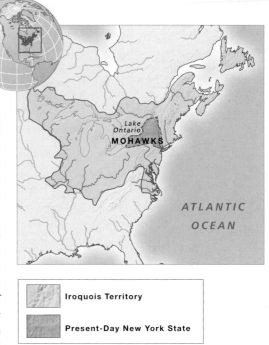

Iroquois Territory

Present-Day New York State

Corn was central to the Mohawk diet. They ate it in soups and stews, often mixed with berries, meat, or fish. Corn kernels were preserved by drying them in the sun, and later were baked into breads. In addition to farming, women gathered wild plants, fruits, berries, and nuts. In the early spring, women extracted sap from maple trees that they used to sweeten corn dishes and teas. Women also controlled distribution of the food they produced and the resources and goods contributed by their husbands and sons. They also collected and distributed supplies for public feasts and ceremonial occasions (Lafitau, 1974). Consistent with this control over resources, Mohawk women had high status within their households and communities (Brown, 1975; Bonvillain, 1980).

Men's subsistence roles included hunting and fishing to supplement the plant diet. They hunted deer, elk, moose, bear, beaver, partridges, and wild turkeys. Bows and arrows were the basic hunting gear. Hunters also used wooden traps to capture deer and spears and nets to catch birds and fish. Men and women occasionally organized communal deer-hunts in which they might kill as many as 100 animals. They walked through the woods in a long V-shaped formation shaking rattles and making other noises. The frightened deer were driven into the ever-narrowing arms of the V and killed.

Men were also responsible for trading with other peoples.

REVIEW

In horticultural societies such as the Mohawk and Yanomamo, people keep small animals, cultivate food trees, and plant gardens with staple crops. Sedentism—living in one place—requires small populations sustained on surpluses from horticultural production. Work is allocated by gender and age, in which men clear land for planting. Slash-and-burn (swidden) horticulture is a destructive process that involves a constant round of abandoning depleted land and bringing new land under cultivation.

AGRICULTURE

Pastoralism, horticulture, and agriculture are subsistence strategies that involve food production. The strategy called agriculture originated in the Middle East about 12,000 years ago. At that time, the region's climate was gradually drying, prompting people to concentrate near rivers, where resources remained plentiful. Over time, people learned to control their supplies of food by planting their own crops and domesticating their own animals (dogs, sheep, goats, and cattle). They began growing grains that could sustain large populations. The earliest crops were wheat and barley. Once

PEOPLE WERE ABLE TO PLANT, HARVEST, PRESERVE, AND STORE MORE FOOD.

Increase in surplus ⟶ increase in population ⟶ increase in accumulation of material culture

Use of grains to feed babies and young children ⟶ decline in lactation ⟶ increase in fertility ⟶ increase in population

Increase in population ⟶ increase in food production ⟶ pressure on the environment

Dependence on intensive agriculture ⟶ sedentary populations ⟶ crowding in urban centers

Dependence on grains ⟶ malnutrition ⟶ vulnerability to drought and famine

Large sedentary urban populations ⟶ decline in health standards ⟶ rapid spread of disease

Figure 6.1
Consequences of Food Production.

farming proved productive, more people settled in the region and learned the new techniques. Others acquired the skills and moved to outlying areas, gradually spreading farming knowledge to other communities. Over the following millennia, similar processes led to the independent emergence of farming in several other regions of the world, including the Indus Valley of Pakistan, the Yellow River Valley of China, the Nile Valley of Egypt, Mexico, and the Andean region of South America.

Archaeologists have proposed a variety of explanations for the origin of farming. Some suggest that increasingly concentrated populations exceeded the capacity of the fertile regions to sustain a foraging existence, while at the same time declines in wild vegetation discouraged people from dispersing into surrounding environments (Binford, 1971; Flannery, 1973). Another theory suggests that some people in foraging societies began to accumulate surpluses of storable foods to sponsor feasts and thereby raise their social status. As their desire for larger surpluses grew, they began to control and augment their accumulation of foods by protecting and then producing their own crops (Bender, 1978). These theories are not mutually exclusive. Several factors operating together may have led to the beginnings of plant and animal domestication.

Archaeologists are more certain about the consequences of food production. We know that populations increased rapidly and became sedentary because of the ability to control the growth of crops, to plant more crops, and to harvest, preserve, and store greater surpluses. Reliance on grains also allowed women to nurse their babies for shorter periods of time, because young children could be given cereals to eat. And fertility levels rose with the decline in lactation, leading to greater increases in population size and greater crowding of population centers.

Another result of food production was a general decline in health standards (Diamond, 1995). Studies of the bones and teeth of members of early farming communities indicated signs of malnutrition, probably resulting from an overdependence on only a few sources of food rather than the more typical varied range of the foraging diet. And diseases spread more rapidly among sedentary farming people.

In addition, permanent settlements made possible by farming permitted people to accumulate an increasing number and variety of material possessions.

? *How would you compare the benefits and costs of food production as a subsistence strategy?*

REVIEW

Food production based on agriculture permits greater accumulation of surplus, which sustains larger sedentary populations in villages and urban centers. Craft specialization, ownership of land and resources, social inequalities, and public health problems are among the many consequences of agriculture as a mode of subsistence.

Anthropology Applied

Interpreting Economic Activity from Archaeological Remains

Knowledge from cultural anthropology aids in the interpretation of archaeological sites, and vice versa. For example, information about diet and health and economic activities often is evident in archaeological remains. Consider craft specialization, for example, which indicates that a population had an adequate surplus of food to support people who did not contribute directly to subsistence. Craft specialization is widespread in agricultural societies, and signs of it in an archaeological site is supporting evidence that the people had a subsistence base as farmers.

Evidence of craft specialization is found at the archaeological site of Huánuco Pampa, Peru, a provincial capital of the Inca. Through excavations there, archaeologists Craig Morris and Donald Thompson (1985) found a compound of fifty buildings containing thousands of distinctive ceramic jars and spindle whorls. The buildings were manufacturing and storage sites, as well as housing for artisans involved in production. Using ethnohistorical records, Morris determined that the finds were associated with beer-making and cloth production.

Inca society had a special class of women, called *aklla* (or *aclla*), who worked for the Inca state and were segregated from the rest of the society. They were the "chosen women," or girls, who might be sacrificed to the sun god in bad times. Awaiting their possible fate, they lived and worked together in special houses making and preserving beer and weaving cloth.

Inca Ruins at Huánuco Pampa, Peru

In this case cultural anthropology was used to help interpret archaeological remains. Using ethnohistorical and archaeological evidence, Morris hypothesized that the compound found at Huánuco Pampa housed *aklla* along with the goods they produced.

CRITICAL THINKING QUESTIONS

What signs of an agricultural economy other than craft specialization might you expect to find at Huánuco? What kinds of remains might you expect to find in archaeological sites of people using other modes of subsistence? For example, what evidence of subsistence activities and material culture might you find among prehistoric pastoralists or foragers?

SUBSISTENCE AND CULTURE CHANGE

No society is locked into a particular subsistence pattern. All are in a dynamic relationship with the environment and with other societies and are subject to change from both internal processes and external sources. A change in the environment might force a change in subsistence strategy, or a change in population, or the invention of a new technology, or changing patterns of trade with neighboring societies. Subsistence strategies may also change as a result of borrowings from other peoples, either through peaceful trade or through forced elimination of traditional patterns and their replacement by foreign methods of economic production and work as a result of conquest and colonization.

Environmental change or relocation to a different area may compel people to rely on different kinds of foods or different subsistence strategies. Foragers may have their territories diminished because of incursions or invasions by farming or herding peoples and therefore abandon their traditional ways of life, adopting farming themselves or working for wages on other people's farms or ranches. Technological developments may also affect subsistence strategies. For example, as industrial techniques have led to improvements in agricultural productivity, fewer farmworkers can produce enough food for many more people, freeing up a large labor force to work in other sectors.

Small indigenous societies throughout the world have become increasingly involved in regional, national, and international economic networks in the global economy. Many of their traditional patterns have been altered. In some cases, they have been able to sell their products widely through commercial outlets. Others have found wage employment in locally expanding production and manufacturing. We will look more at the issues of changing economic systems in Chapter 7, as well as in Chapters 16 and 17, which focus on global issues.

> **REVIEW**
>
> Economic anthropologists also study changes in people's subsistence due to environmental or population changes and cultural contact, as well as the effects of those changes on society and culture.

Chapter Summary

Economic Anthropology

- Economic anthropology is a subdiscipline of anthropology that focuses on subsistence strategies and economic systems—how people meet their survival needs and make their living.

Understanding Human Subsistence Patterns

- Subsistence strategies include methods that people use to obtain food. People need to develop techniques to adapt to their environment, exploit available resources, or produce their own food. Subsistence strategies affect and are affected by environmental conditions, such as topography, climate, and available plants and animals. The techniques that people use have an impact on population size, settlement patterns, and household composition.

Foraging

- Foraging is a subsistence strategy that depends directly on plants and animals available in the environment. Foragers collect wild plants, fruits, nuts, and seeds and hunt animals and fish in the waterways of their territory. Because foragers depend on naturally available resources, they require a large territory for subsistence. Most foragers are nomadic, changing their settlement sites frequently. They usually live in relatively small communities in order to not overly burden their environment.

Pastoralism

- Pastoralism is a subsistence strategy that centers on the herding and care of large numbers of domesticated animals. Settlement patterns among pastoralists vary. Some are nomadic, moving frequently as they take their animals to new pasturelands. Others retain a home base and make daily excursions as they take their animals out to graze. Settlement size also varies, although most pastoralists live in communities numbering no more than several hundred. In most pastoralist societies, animals are owned by individuals, although they may be cared for in a collective herd.

Horticulture

- Horticulture is a subsistence strategy based on growing crops. Horticulture is small-scale farming, using hand-held tools and a relatively simple technology. Farmers need to remain near their fields during the planting season. Some horticulturalists live in permanent villages while others shift their locations in different seasons. Their settlements usually number from several hundred to at most several thousand. Horticulturalists generally produce enough surplus to last a year or two beyond their minimum requirements.

Agriculture

- Agriculture is a form of food production based on permanent settlement; large-scale farming using complex technology; and the storage, distribution, and trade of large surpluses. Agriculture arose independently in different parts of the world based on different kinds of domesticated plants and animals. Increases in population and food supply were offset by problems of poor nutrition and the spread of disease in urban centers that grew up around centers of agriculture.

Subsistence and Culture Change

- Subsistence strategies change in response to environmental changes, population migration, and conditions of cultural contact between peoples.

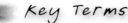

Key Terms

economic anthropology 138	pastoralism 139	redistribution 141	transhumance 151
subsistence patterns 139	horticulture 139	leveling mechanisms 141	surplus 155
foragers 139	agriculture 139	nomads 142	sedentary communities 155
food producers 139	carrying capacity 139	optimal foraging theory 142	slash-and-burn (swidden) cultivation 155
	settlement pattern 140		
	reciprocity 141		

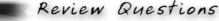

Review Questions

1. What do economic anthropologists study?

2. What are the essential differences between foraging and food production? Which is more costly in terms of time, effort, and calories? Which is more costly in terms of short-term survival?

3. What is carrying capacity, and how do people adapt to this subsistence constraint?

4. How are settlement patterns influenced by modes of subsistence? How is nomadism an example of settlement pattern adaptation?

5. How do subsistence modes influence population size, density, composition, and distribution?

6. How do subsistence modes influence a society's division of labor by age, gender, skill, and social status?

7. How do peoples' systems of roles and statuses both reflect and reinforce their subsistence?

8. What ecological, demographic, and sociocultural factors characterize foraging?

9. What is the theory of optimal foraging? How can foraging be combined with horticulture to increase survival rates?

10. What ecological, demographic, and sociocultural factors characterize pastoralism?

11. Why do many pastoralist societies avoid using their animals for food?

12. What are the impacts of greater sedentism and production of surpluses among some pastoralists and horticulturalists?

13. How does swidden farming work as a subsistence strategy? What are its advantages? Its disadvantages?

14. What are the chief characteristics of agriculture as a subsistence strategy?

15. How do subsistence patterns change over time? How can changes in subsistence cause other changes in a people's way of life?

Economic Systems

Preview

1. **What is an economic system? How is it integrated into a culture?**
2. **What are the different types of economic exchange?**
3. **How do the economic systems of foragers, pastoralists, horticulturalists, and agriculturalists differ?**
4. **How is surplus related to the different subsistence modes?**
5. **How is specialization related to the different subsistence modes?**
6. **What are the characteristics of an economy based on capitalism?**
7. **What effects has industrialization had on economies and cultures?**
8. **What are some characteristics of industrial and postindustrial societies and today's global economy?**

Three men went into the forest: one was the Cultivator, the other the Trapper, the third the Gatherer-of-Honey. Arriving in the forest, they asked themselves: "how shall we build our houses?" They said: "you, the Cultivator, build your house in the middle of the three hills." The Trapper built his house on a hill, the Gatherer-of-Honey built his on a hill. No sooner had they finished building their houses then the Cultivator had already finished growing plants behind his house. The Trapper asked the Gatherer-of-Honey to make a blood pact with him, stating that they should not make such a pact with the Cultivator. Having finished making friendship, and having killed game, the Trapper went with the meat to his friend. They did not show it to the Cultivator. The following day, the Gatherer-of-Honey passed with a jar of honey to bring to his friend the Trapper. They did not give anything to the Cultivator. And so it was every day; they made things pass at the entrance of the village of this one, the Cultivator. He said to himself that his children alone would die of hunger.

This Harvester, this Cultivator, went to sow discord between the two friends. He called in a loud voice, "you man of the rodents Mikii, you the Trapper, it is you will kill my children, never again bring rodent Mikii here at my house." The Cultivator also set out to the village of the Gatherer-of-Honey calling, "you Gatherer-of-Honey, it is the flies that you bring here that cause my children to be sick; also it is my rodents Mikii, which you eat, that makes you factor." On his side, the Trapper reflected much, stating that so then his friend had just insulted

him; on his side the Gatherer-of-Honey also thought that his friend had just insulted him. Having heard that, the Trapper and the Gatherer-of-Honey, one left from his house, the other left from his house, they met in the valley at the Cultivator's. Arriving there, they questioned each other.

One said, "you yelled to me that it was my rodents Mikii who are the reason why your children have caught the kwashiorkor, yes my rodents Mikii!" And the other said, "you yelled that because of me your children have their throat obstructed by larvas of bee." The one denied and the other denied, both at the same time. At this time, the Cultivator was dancing, while his wife beat the drum for him. This instigator, the Cultivator, took to dancing and singing:

I, the instigator Cultivator.
I just finished placing in discord those who are two.

The two friends understood, having heard the manner in which this Cultivator had placed them in discord, one against the other. Having considered that, they made a pact of friendship with the Cultivator. As such, the three became friends among each other; and they began to give meat, honey, and agricultural products, all of them giving to one another mutually.

That is why a man should never refuse the mark of friendship because the mark of friendship is a thing capable of saving the family group.

Excerpts from *Folktales Told around the World* by Richard Dorson, pp. 384–385. Copyright 1975. Reprinted by permission of The University of Chicago Press.

In this narrative, the Nyanga of Zaire dramatize the three significant elements in their economic system: hunting, gathering, and farming. They express the mutual interdependence of these subsistence strategies, and they relate the importance of trade and exchange in binding a community together.

Chapter 6 described the subsistence strategies of foraging, pastoralism, horticulture, and agriculture. This chapter considers agriculture-based economies in greater detail and analyzes subsistence techniques that involve a large investment of labor, intensive use of land, and complex technologies. Intensive agriculture and industrial agriculture result in greater surpluses than can be achieved by other economic strategies. As you will learn, these modes of production are interrelated with other cultural features, such as population growth, emphasis on accumulating wealth, and status differences within a community.

ECONOMICS OF AGRICULTURE

Agricultural production employs interrelated techniques of intensification. Specialized technology, sophisticated land-use strategies, and labor inputs result in more reliable production techniques that result in larger crop yields. Agriculturalists use plows, often pulled by horses or oxen, to turn the earth and increase the area they can cultivate productively in a certain period of time. Early agriculturists in the Middle East, China, and Central and South America built extensive, permanent irrigation systems to deliver water to outlying fields. In mountainous regions they built terraces to increase the surface area available for farming on steeply sloping terrain. People in swampy areas piled up earth (berms) to create fertile artificial islands. Because of their heavy investments in labor and infrastructure, agriculturalists maintain permanent, fully sedentary communities.

These two characteristics of agricultural societies—permanent settlements, called sedentism, and an intensive investment in labor and technology—likely emerged together in a complex and dynamic process of change. Investment of labor and material in agricultural production set the stage for permanent settlements, and permanent settlements created conditions conducive to increasing investments in labor and technology. As labor and technology intensified, the energy expended per acre increased, leading to greater yields and the accumulation of larger surpluses. These surpluses helped support an ever-growing sedentary population. The more food there was, the more people could be supported, and the more people there were, the more food could be produced.

Furthermore, unlike in foraging and pastoral societies, where most subsistence work required adult strength, skill, and judgment, agricultural societies could make productive use of the labor of young children. Thus, large families were a premium. The result was a relaxation of the birth-control practices that limited population in foraging and pastoral societies. On the contrary, agricultural societies encouraged fertility, an attitude that might be incorporated into religious doctrines that specifically encouraged women to have many children.

This dynamic set the stage for increasing population size. Eventually, however, population size would come up against the carrying capacity of a particular region at a particular level of technology. In other words, at some point, increasing the amount of labor available (by increasing population) would fail to result in increased yields. As it reached that point, an agricultural society would have to develop new, more productive agricultural technologies or secure more land. New technologies were not always readily available, however, and expanding into new territory ultimately brought a society into conflict with its neighbors.

In agriculture, the ability to put large areas of land under cultivation depends on the use of draft animals and technologies such as the plow. Archaeologists find plows, hoes, threshing devices, grinding stones or mills, and granaries in the earliest agricultural settlements.

Intensive farming communities—agriculturalists—tend to emphasize individual ownership and control of land, because of their investment in labor and technology. Building irrigation works or terraces involves enormous expenditures of human energy. Plows and other heavy equipment are a large capital expense.

Among the Inca and other Andean farmers of Peru and Ecuador, ownership of land was vested in a collective group of relatives, whereas in India, each parcel of land is owned by an individual. Private individual ownership usually permits the owner to sell his or her land, a practice impossible in most horticultural societies. The importance of ownership and control is demonstrated in patterns of inheritance in which children or other designated relatives receive the land belonging to their parents or other kin. Large-scale agrarian states also tend to foster competition among individuals and families, reflected in the goal of accumulating surpluses and consuming them within the household.

In many agrarian states, the central government may organize the redistribution of surpluses so that everyone can be maintained at some minimum level of subsistence. In addition to humanitarian goals, maintaining the population is essential in state societies to forestall dissatisfaction that might lead to rebellion. The Inca state developed an efficient system of redistribution in which district chiefs collected farm produce and woven cloth from people in their territory. Some goods were channeled into the households of chiefs and other state elites, but a portion was stored in large regional granaries and warehouses. Chiefs dispensed these goods to needy members of their communities.

A common pattern in agrarian societies is for land to be concentrated in the hands of a few. Nonwealthy individuals and families lose their control of land through misfortune—illness, poor crops, or other disaster. Motivated by values that promote competition and the accumulation of surplus, wealthier landowners enlarge their acreage by buying land from those less fortunate. Over time, a large part of the population may become landless. Landless people then hire themselves out as laborers on other people's land. In one system, called *sharecropping*, they work the land and pay rent to the landlord, either in money or as part of their harvest. Competition and accumulation of wealth lead to economic exploitation in both agricultural and industrial societies as well as in mixed or transitional economies.

A hallmark of settled, large-scale, state societies with mixed economies is the appearance of full-time specialists. Specialists, rather than doing subsistence work, instead produce tools, utensils, or crafts, or they become state functionaries, working as traders, soldiers, or government officials. Because these specialists do not perform subsistence work, they must be supported by the extra work of others. Intensive agriculture and industrial agriculture increase farm output that can be traded or sold to nonsubsistence workers. Surplus outputs may also be taken from farmers in the form of tribute or taxation in order to support nonproducers or state functionaries. In modern states, the percentage of people working as specialists has greatly increased, while the percentage of people producing food or working in food-delivery systems has greatly decreased.

Intensive Agriculture and Crop Variety

Throughout the centuries, new inventions and technological advances have contributed to a tremendous growth in agricultural productivity. **Intensive agriculture** involved the use of the plow, draft animals, and irrigation. By recent centuries, however, as worldwide population increased exponentially, the growth of cities has reduced the amount of land

intensive agriculture
Application of technology and intensive labor to farming, such as the plow and irrigation.

In this 1960s photograph, a family and their neighbors in Balakan, Azerbaijan, reel silk by hand from the piles of silkworm cocoons they have harvested from their mulberry trees. Craft specialization in transitional economies typically is risky for landless families, because their income is dependent on a stable market in which to sell their product—but market forces are beyond their control. Today silk production flourishes in factory settings in East Asia, as artificial silk has not replaced demand for natural silk as a luxury good.

In Their Own Voices

"Free to Do as You Like"

In this excerpt from his autobiographical novel, Fragments of Memory: A Story of a Syrian Family, *Hanna Mina describes the plight of sharecroppers, bound to and dependent on landlords who extract most of the profits from the farmers.*

Ever since February, Mother had been gathering the hen eggs with great care. We were living and working as day laborers in a field belonging to the village *mukhtar*. It was a small field, empty except for mulberry trees. Our only duty was raising silkworms during the silk season. It was a raw deal that Father had contracted with the *mukhtar*. . . . He didn't succeed here either but he was forced into it. . . . He had to find shelter somewhere, so he agreed to take the abandoned field. The *mukhtar* opened a page for us in his debt ledger. The first thing he put down in it, against the account of the silk harvest, was five kilos of mixed sorghum and barley, a few meters of unbleached cotton and a few articles like salt, oil, kerosene and soap. He also advised Father to be a faithful share cropper who knows his obligations and pays his debts. Father raised his hand to his forehead and then placing it over his heart said, "At your service, Mr. Elias!". . .

Our house was a rectangle built of unbaked clay bricks, divided into two parts by a wall. One part was for animals, the other for living in. Since we possessed no animals, that

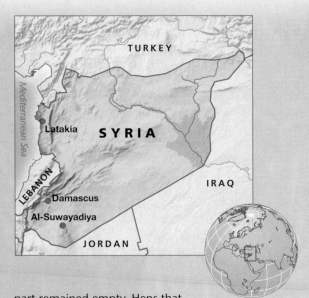

part remained empty. Hens that relatives had generously bestowed upon Mother ran around and pecked there. In one corner we piled up firewood and dung, and in another near a small window high in the wall was a hearth made of stones and clay.

Father began, with the help of the family, the cultivation of the land and the care of the mulberry trees by borrowing a neighbor's animal. Before the work was finished, a

under cultivation. The dilemma of more people to feed on less land has so far been solved by the application of industrial processes to agriculture. In much of the world, preparing fields, planting seeds, fertilizing, weeding, and harvesting have become highly mechanized. Work once done by people is now done by machinery with only minimal human participation and direction. In the United States, less than 3 percent of the population works in agriculture. In countries with less developed industrial and technological sectors, the proportion is higher but everywhere has been declining. Fewer workers and less land must now produce food for more people.

This irrigation and flood-control system in Sichuan, China, is one of the oldest surviving man-made engineering projects in the world. It controlled the direction and rate of flow of the Minjiang River. Called Dujiangyan, this waterworks is recognized as a World Heritage Site by the United Nations Educational, Scientific and Cultural Organization (UNESCO).

messenger arrived from the *mukhtar* asking for Father. So he went only to be told that he must work in his fields first and that Mother must work in the *mukhtar's* house. Father raised his hand to his forehead, lowered it and placing it over his heart said, "At your service, Mr. Elias!"

Although the parents worked hard as sharecroppers, their precarious situation worsened because synthetic silk made in India undersold natural silk. The landlord shut down silkworm production, forcing sharecroppers to leave.

So we bundled up the belongings we had left, and our parents went to inform the *mukhtar* that we were leaving.

We could have left covertly at night or in the early morning without our departure arousing anyone's attention or interest. The surrounding houses were empty, the mulberry groves were being cut down and burned or their trunks gathered for wood. The paths were filled with columns of travelers on the backs of animals or in carts drawn by donkeys or cows. The fathers who lacked these means carried their things on their backs, dragging their children along, fleeing from hunger, fear, and thieves, traveling together to be safe from highway robbers who lay in wait for them in the valleys and the foothills of the mountains.

It was possible for us, in this state of collective emigration, this mutual dissolution of contracts to forsake our mud hut and the mulberry grove, empty except for the whistling wind, and flee the whole village without letting anyone know and without anyone asking about us. But our oldest sister was with the *mukhtar.* Considering her to be payment for the debt, he had tightened his watch over her since learning that Father had returned and that we were on the point of leaving since it had become impossible for us to stay on.

Father's lengthy beseeching diatribe, Mother's tearful entreaties, and requests from those who were acquainted with our circumstances and sympathized with us, were of no avail. The *mukhtar* spurned them all. He would not give us anything to eat and could not cope with us remaining hungry. We were of no use to him as *fellahin.* So he made it known that we were free to leave, but as far as our sister was concerned, he would keep her until we paid our debt.

"You're free to do as you like!" said the *mukhtar.* The landowners had said that before him, and he said it to other *fellahin* beside us. The sweet word "freedom" had become frightening, meaning no money, no food and no concern for the unpredictable destiny of the families who had lived on raising silkworms. The arrival of artificial silk was finishing off them and the silkworms together.

Therefore the word "free" became an odious term to the *fellahin,* who came from their fields seeking aid from the owners of the fields. As a consequence, they rejected this term, bringing up the matter of their servitude being in exchange for certain conditions, among which was the stipulation that they should be sustained until winter was over and the growing season arrived.

From *Fragments of Memory: A Story of a Syrian Family* by Hanna Mina, pp. 19–20, 88–89. Copyright 1993. Reprinted by permission of the Center for Middle Eastern Studies. The University of Texas at Austin.

CRITICAL THINKING QUESTIONS

Why were Hanna and his family not really free to do as they wanted? What patterns in agricultural societies lead to social inequality?

One consequence of industrial agriculture has been a limited number of crops and varieties of crops. For example, in native North America, farming peoples such as the Iroquois in the Northeast and the Pueblo nations of the Southwest grew more than a dozen varieties of corn. Now, only a few types of corn, selected for yield and resistance, are grown. This process of limiting diversity to maximize efficiency is potentially dangerous. Different varieties of a crop often supply a different mix of nutrients, so limiting crop diversity limits nutritional variety. Furthermore, some varieties may be susceptible to diseases and infestations to which other varieties are immune. As a result, decreased crop diversity can increase the risk of catastrophic crop failure. And we cannot know what needs future generations might have that a now-lost plant variety might have met.

Industrial Agriculture

Industrial agriculture is characterized by six general features (Bartlett, 1989): (1) increased use of complex technology, leading to increased replacement of human labor with machinery and increased use of fossil fuels as sources of energy in production; (2) increased role of state agencies in farm production policies; (3) a tendency toward competition among producers; (4) specialization of crop production;

industrial agriculture
Application of industrial technology and chemicals to farming in order to increase productivity.

(5) overproduction of farm products; and (6) increased interdependence between farm units and the corporations that control machinery, sales, processing, and transport. Let's take a closer look at each of these features.

Mechanization has become part of nearly all agricultural processes, from planting to weeding and harvesting. Many small farmers cannot afford to invest in all of the new machinery available and, therefore, are threatened by large, corporate-run farms, or agribusinesses. Chemicals, too, are increasingly expensive, putting a strain on the budgets of small farmers. They pose a threat as well in the contamination of water and the destruction of ecosystems. Chemical use also harms farmworkers. A study carried out in the 1980s showed that corn farmers in Iowa and Nebraska had a 44 to 63 percent greater risk of leukemia than the general population (Bartlett, 1989). Furthermore, agricultural chemicals are potentially harmful to anyone who consumes the food treated with chemicals. The industrial conditions under which poultry and livestock are grown and slaughtered can result in outbreaks of illness from dangerous bacteria like *Salmonella* and *Escherichia coli*. The use of antibiotics in the poultry and livestock industries contributes to the emergence of immune strains of those same bacteria (Bartlett, 1989).

Genetic engineering and irradiation of foods have become standard, but controversial, processes. Genetic engineering modifies the genetic codes inherent in the foods to produce strains that have particular market advantages, such as more even textures or tougher skins on fruits and vegetables so that they will not be bruised in transport from fields to stores. According to the Centers for Disease Control, ionizing irradiation (which has nothing to do with nuclear waste) eliminates disease-causing bacteria and parasites. While some people favor these processes, others fear potential danger because of the manipulation of genetic codes for foodstuffs and the introduction of possibly harmful substances.

? *Does your local store sell irradiated or genetically engineered foods? Do you think these foods should be labeled accordingly?*

Energy usage has increased significantly in industrial agriculture. For example, although 1 kilogram of breakfast cereal provides 3,600 calories of food energy, 15,675 calories are required to produce and transport that 1 kilogram (Bartlett, 1989). The processes involved in growing, packaging, processing, and transporting food, in other words, expend far more energy than the food provides in calories.

The U.S. government influences agricultural production by implementing tax laws that favor capital investment over labor. Tax benefits are provided for investments in farming technology and research. The government also directly subsidizes agricultural research that leads to increased mechanization, genetic engineering of plants, and other scientific processes. And government programs subsidize the production (and overproduction) of particular crops. Intense capital investment and competition have led to a sharp drop in the number of farms in the United States.

In many parts of the world, industrial agriculture undermines the stability of subsistence farming. In Africa and Latin America, household farming for subsistence has become precarious, as owners of large plantations have succeeded in putting pressure on local farmers to sell their land. Smallholders are caught in the bind of needing cash to buy clothing, household goods, equipment, and food. As their household economies become insecure, people need to obtain cash either through employment or sale of their land. Employment is difficult to find in rural communities, so many people opt to leave their homes, temporarily or permanently, and migrate to towns and cities to find jobs. But rampant urban growth, especially in developing regions of the world, has led to the spread of slums, deteriorating health conditions, and increasing rates of urban crime.

Industrial agriculture increasingly replaces the intensive agriculture carried out on a comparatively small scale by families and communities.

REVIEW

Agricultural societies have larger populations and greater division of labor, along with more centralization and wider disparity of wealth and power. Intensive agriculture involves the use of draft animals, fertilizers, and irrigation works to farm on a large scale. Industrial agriculture, or agribusiness, involves the mechanization of farmwork on an even larger scale and scientific interventions in food production.

ANALYZING ECONOMIC SYSTEMS

Societies organize their subsistence strategies in ways that utilize their land and resources efficiently. Available land must be distributed among members of the community. People need to agree about methods of exploiting their resources so that everyone has at least a minimal share in order to survive. People also need to know how to organize their work, taking account of differences in age and gender and skill, as well as whatever other social variables are considered significant (such as class, race, or ethnicity). And societies must have methods of distributing food, goods, and services within and among their communities. Rarely do people consume all and only what they produce individually. Instead, they share with others or exchange their products or services for other products or services. Patterns of **consumption,** therefore, are also affected by cultural norms. In some communities, all members have similar opportunities to consume or avail themselves of resources and goods and services. In other communities, though, levels of consumption may vary considerably. Taken together, these various factors constitute an **economic system.**

Anthropologists understand economies and economic systems holistically. That is, they try to situate features of land and resource use and labor organization in the context of people's adaptation to their environment. And they try to delineate the ways that land, resources, and labor are interrelated with other features of culture, including social and political systems. Put another way, economic systems consist of practices that organize people's activities of production, distribution, and consumption.

Subsistence strategies constitute an important but not exclusive factor in economic systems. Food-obtaining techniques are central to economies, but other factors, such as production of utilitarian and luxury goods, distribution and exchange of products, and specialization of work and services, are also important aspects of economic systems. Thus, for example, different modes of subsistence generally are correlated with different principles on which economic systems are organized. Subsistence strategies that focus on foraging, pastoralism, or farming tend to have different ways of allocating land and resources, organizing labor, producing goods, and distributing or exchanging products and services.

Allocating Land and Resources

Different subsistence modes tend to foster different attitudes about land rights and access to natural resources. Foragers usually have relatively open access to the lands in their territories and to the lands' resources. This strategy is especially useful for nomadic peoples, who rely on their ability to exploit available resources seasonally. Their occupation of territory is occasional and temporary rather than permanent. Pastoral peoples may also extend rights to exploit all available land in their territory to graze their herds. However, some pastoral societies limit access to land to particular groups on either a seasonal or permanent basis. Farming peoples need to make claims to specific parcels of land that they cultivate. Among some farming peoples, land is permanently owned by an individual. In others, land may be reallocated from time to time, depending on inheritance rules and the size and composition of households living in the same area. Finally, in industrial and postindustrial societies, individuals and groups and states own land and resources and other means of subsistence and production.

As a way of allocating resources, ownership varies in different types of societies. Ownership may be vested in a community as a whole or in individuals. Among nomadic foraging peoples, individuals rarely have rights to exclusive ownership and

consumption
The use of subsistence resources, including outcomes of production.

economic system
Cultural methods of allocating natural resources, the means of exploiting the resources through technology, the organization of work, and the production, distribution, consumption, and exchange of goods and services.

In Vietnam, rice paddies are owned by individual families, and land is subdivided and passed on to sons or male relatives through inheritance. At the same time, in the transition to a market economy, rice farming has become women's work, as men leave the paddies in search of wage work. Rice farming—for both subsistence and export and often combined with duck raising—is highly labor intensive. Women and children manage most of the burden of this labor along with household tasks.

control of land and resources. Ownership of land tends to be most formalized among farming peoples, who expend a great deal of labor readying their fields for planting and need specific acreage to produce sufficient food.

Producing Goods

In addition to subsistence products, people also need other goods to ensure their survival and well-being. Systems of **production** provide clothing, shelter, tools, utensils, and weapons. People also want decorative items to adorn their bodies and their residences. And their religious practices require ritual objects, costumes, and other paraphernalia for use in public and private ceremonies. In some societies, people within a household may make all of the various types of equipment that their family requires. In others, some people develop the skills and arts that enable them to become part-time or full-time specialists in the production of specific types of goods. Specialists engage in some types of exchange in which they either sell their products or exchange them for other goods and services.

Different types of subsistence strategies are more or less likely to produce surpluses. When surpluses arise, societies use different ways to dispose of them. Sometimes people keep surpluses on hand for use when supplies are low. At other times, and in other circumstances, surpluses may be traded or sold so that the producers can obtain other goods or services that they require but do not make themselves. Surplus, therefore, is tied to patterns of distribution and exchange. In general, nomadic peoples obtain little in the way of surplus goods because of the inconvenience of carrying more than basic necessities when moving from one camp to another. Sedentary peoples, in contrast, prefer producing a certain amount of surplus to protect themselves against lean years.

In addition, surpluses serve social functions. Surplus farm produce or manufactured goods can be distributed by the wealthy to those less fortunate, stabilizing social networks and enhancing the prestige of the givers. Surplus goods also can be distributed in ritual contexts, such as celebrations of births, marriages, and funerals. Finally, in state societies, surplus wealth may be appropriated through taxation to support the various functions of government and public services.

Organizing Labor

Societies allocate the labor of their members to productive tasks through division of labor. Work roles are assigned minimally on the basis of age and gender. In addition, certain individuals may specialize in craft production or other arts and skills. Men and women are assigned different but complementary tasks. Elderly people usually retire from direct productive work, depending on the ability of the family or society to support them, although their advice may be sought because of their knowledge and experience. Young children are assigned household and subsistence tasks consistent with their physical and cognitive maturation as well as the type of economy. Whereas farm families depend on children's labor, in industrial societies children typically are prevented from competing with their parents for jobs and wages. These norms often are codified as laws. The legal age of work in the United States, for example, is 14. Nevertheless, children are widely exploited as sources of labor in the world today.

? *What do you own, and how did you come to own it? Do you control the redistribution of what you own?*

production
System of extracting resources and utilizing labor and technology in order to obtain foods, goods, and services.

Case study

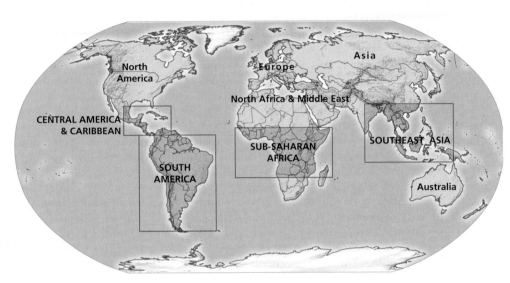

Child Laborers Today

The exploitation of child labor is an international concern today. According to a report issued in 2002 by the International Labor Office (ILO) in Geneva, Switzerland, children who work are divided into four categories: "children at work in economic activity," "child laborers," "children in hazardous work," and "children in unconditional worst forms of child labor." "Children at work in economic activity" is a broad category that encompasses most productive activities performed by children, including all market production (paid work) and some types of nonmarket production (unpaid work), such as producing goods for one's own use. Work may be in the formal sector (especially factory work) or the informal sector (street vendors, construction) and may encompass legal or illegal activities.

"Children at work in economic activity" includes children who work in a market-oriented establishment operated by a relative in the same household. It also includes children who are domestic workers in someone else's household, but it excludes children who do the same chores in their own households without pay. The ILO estimates that some 352 million children between the ages of 5 and 17 "work in economic activity." Of these, about 211 million are under the age of 14, and 73 million are younger than 10.

Boys and girls are equally likely to be engaged in economic activities. For children younger than 14, no significant gender differences are found, but for older children, ages 15 through 17, there are a greater number of boys in economic activities. This disproportion may reflect the fact that by the age of 15, many girls in developing countries are married or otherwise performing unpaid productive work in their own households (a class of economic activity excluded from the ILO conventions).

The ILO study discovered world regional differences in the numbers of children engaged in economic activity. The largest numbers of such children are found in the Asia-Pacific region (127.3 million), followed by sub-Saharan Africa (48 million), and Latin America and the Caribbean (17.4 million). In terms of the ratio of working to nonworking children, sub-Saharan Africa has the highest ratio of child workers. There, about 29 percent of children younger than 15 are engaged in economic activities. In contrast, in developed countries, only about 2 percent of children below the age of 15 are economically active.

The second ILO category, "child laborers," refers to child workers under the internationally agreed minimum ages for specific kinds of work. For example, "child laborers" are children under the age of 18 (or 16 years under certain strict conditions) who perform "hazardous work." Any working child who is younger than 12 or 13 is considered to be a "child laborer," but children between the ages of 12 and 14 may also be classified as "child laborers" if they do light work for more than 14 hours per week.

The ILO defines "light work" as work not harmful to a child's physical development and health and does not interfere with his or her attendance at school or a vocational training program. By this definition, it is estimated that there are about 186 million child laborers under age 15.

The ILO found that boys are more likely than girls to be child laborers. However, among children in the age group 5 to 14, girls and boys participate in child labor at about the same rates. The gender difference becomes pronounced in the older age group (15 to 17), where boys are more prominent. That is, of children classified as child laborers ages 15 to 17, 57 percent are boys and 43 percent are girls.

The third ILO category is that of children engaged in "hazardous work," defined as "any activity or occupation that, by its nature or type has, or leads to, adverse effects on the child's safety, health (physical or mental), and moral development." Hazardous work may also refer to excessive workloads or long or intense periods of work, even if the work itself is not hazardous. Some examples of hazardous work for children are mining, construction, working with heavy machinery, and exposure to pesticides. The category also includes work underwater, at dangerous heights, or in confined spaces.

Using these definitions, the ILO estimates that nearly 171 million children work in hazardous situations. This figure accounts for about half the total number of economically active children (48.5 percent) and more than two-thirds of the world's child laborers (69.5 percent). In all age groups, boys are more likely than girls to be engaged in hazardous work. For all groups, 52 percent of boys and 44.6 percent of girls were working in hazardous conditions.

The final category, "children in unconditional worst forms of child labor," includes human trafficking, forced and bonded labor, armed conflict, prostitution and pornography, and criminal activities. The total number of children in this category stands at about 8.4 million worldwide. About 1.2 million children are trafficked to and from all regions of the world. While boys and girls are both subject to human trafficking, there are gender differences depending on the purposes for trafficking. Boys are more often trafficked for forced labor (especially in commercial farming), petty crimes, and the drug trade, whereas girls are likely to be trafficked for commercial sexual exploitation and domestic service.

An estimated 5.7 million children are engaged in forced and bonded labor. The vast majority of these (about 5.5 million) reside in the Asia-Pacific region, although large numbers are also found in Africa and Latin America. Some 300,000 children, mostly boys, are forced to serve in armed conflict. Child soldiers are most prevalent in Africa and the Asia-Pacific region. The majority of children engaged in prostitution and pornography are girls. In total, about 1.8 million children are affected, and all regions of the world participate in this exploitation, as both tourists and domestic clients sexually exploit child prostitutes. The ILO estimates that about 600,000 children are engaged in illicit activities, including petty crimes and especially the production and trafficking of drugs.

Labor and Specialization. **Specialization of labor** based on skill, talent, or training is a common feature of large-scale societies. All societies have some degree of labor specialization within households as well. In addition, communities may value individuals skilled at making certain kinds of tools, utensils, or crafts. Others may seek to acquire their high-quality or unique or effective products or services. In some societies, part-time specialists accumulate income from their work. The more skilled the artisan, the more compensation he or she may receive because others especially prize their work. In other societies, labor specialization involves full-time specialists. These people do not participate in direct subsistence activities but instead exchange their labor and skill for food and goods obtained through the labor of others. Depending on the system of exchange and relationships between people, these products may be given away, exchanged, traded, purchased, or sold.

specialization of labor
System of allocating work in which different people perform different tasks.

Labor and Social Status.   The relationship between labor and social status is reflected in relative contributions to subsistence, which affect social prestige and influence. For example, in societies where men have higher social status than women and perform most of the subsistence work, their higher social standing may be attributed to their contributions to their households as producers. In contrast, women's lesser social standing may result from their relatively minor contributions to the food supply. Performing a major share of productive work does not necessarily translate into social prestige or power, as in the case of slavery. In the Caribbean and the southern United States, for instance, slaves in the eighteenth and first half of the nineteenth centuries were the primary subsistence workers and also produced most of the crops intended for external trade. However, they clearly did not benefit from their labor in terms of greater social prestige. The determinants of social power stem more from control over labor and the right or authority to exert control, manage productive forces, and distribute the products. For example, monarchs, nobles, and other members of elite classes control and benefit from the labor of others. Finally, in many large-scale industrial societies, some people accumulate wealth and power from the labor of others and do little or no productive work themselves.

These clam diggers belong to a maritime community in New England and are among the few who are granted commercial licenses each year to exploit this easily overburdened resource. The men work at their specialized and highly regulated trade for only two or three months of the year at daytime low tides. After inspection and cleaning, the clams are sold cooperatively to regional and national markets, but only rarely are they part of family subsistence, which is derived from the labor of others. At other times of the year, some clam diggers gather mussels or other shellfish part time, sometimes relocating to do so, but most work on a percentage basis in the fishing or lobster industries or for wages in local factories. Their clam businesses can be wiped out in a single season by storms, disease, pollution, or contamination—a risk of labor specialization.

Distributing and Exchanging Products and Services

Once goods, whether foodstuffs or manufactures, are produced, they enter into patterns of distribution and consumption. Because societies are organized on principles of interdependence in cooperation and competition, individuals must always be connected to others in networks of distribution. Systems of exchange include reciprocity, defined in Chapter 6 as giving and taking "in kind" between individuals and families, as in simple spontaneous gift exchange. Reciprocity can be far from simple, however. In traditional societies, networks of reciprocal relations may be complex and of long standing. For example, in the Trobriand Islands of Melanesia, complicated patterns of inter-island trade linked people through the exchange of ritual items (necklaces and armbands), as well as food and other goods.

Types of Reciprocity.   Members of families and households may be intertwined in recurring series of exchanges, a type of distribution called generalized reciprocity. In **generalized reciprocity,** goods and services are exchanged, but the value of the products or services given and received is not exactly or objectively calculated. There may be an expectation that goods and services will be given and received frequently and will have approximately equivalent worth, but the frequency and the amount of value are not specified. Many exchanges between parents and children, for example, are examples of generalized reciprocity. Distribution of food in traditional societies likewise involves principles of generalized reciprocity, as in the exchanges of foraging peoples such as the Inuit and Ju/'hoansi. Through generalized reciprocity over time, all families become both givers and receivers of food.

In contrast to generalized reciprocity, some exchanges are characterized by **balanced reciprocity,** in which exchanges more closely specify the value and the time at which an exchange will take place. The mutual giving and receiving of gifts at birthdays or religious holidays and the informal exchanges of clothing or objects are examples

generalized reciprocity
The exchange of goods and services without keeping track of their exact value, but often with the expectation that their value will balance out over time.

balanced reciprocity
Exchange of goods and services of a specified value at a specified time and place.

Case Study

The Potlatch as an Example of Negative Reciprocity

An unusual example of negative reciprocity, called the **potlatch,** was prevalent in indigenous societies of the U.S. and Canadian Pacific Northwest coast. The Kwakwaka'wakw (known previously as the Kwakiutl) now live on reserves and in communities in British Columbia, Canada. They formerly were a cultural and linguistic group made up of approximately thirty independent "tribes," but did not recognize any kind of central organization that united them. Each "tribe" occupied a separate territory containing at least one large sedentary village and several smaller temporary communities. They were foragers, but unlike most hunting and gathering peoples, they were not nomadic. They relied on a great abundance of wild resources, most especially fish and other sea products, as well as numerous varieties of land animals and plants, fruits, and berries. The richness of their resources allowed the Kwakwaka'wakw to live in permanent villages containing many hundreds of residents.

People of highest status constituted the informal leadership of kin groups and villages. Chiefs received portions of the animal, fish, and plant products obtained by members of their group, and they were usually exempt from most subsistence tasks. Chiefs were responsible for organizing cooperative activities, such as house building, but most hunting and fishing was done by individuals acting alone. Chiefs also were representatives of their lineages in the system of potlatching or feasting that served to validate ceremonially people's social standing.

Potlatches (from the Chinookan word for "to give") were feasts to which relatives, community members, and high-ranking chiefs were invited. They were held to celebrate life-cycle transitions (birth, naming, puberty, marriage, death), the building of new houses, and the naming of new chiefs. As part of the potlatch, the host, who had accumulated goods over many months or even years, gave food and gifts to the invited guests. High-ranking chiefs also received objects such as bowls and dishes and ceremonial objects. The host's purpose was to distribute an amount of wealth greater than that received at prior potlatches. By doing this, the host raised and secured his social standing. But the system was inherently competitive, so that the next time around, guests at one potlatch would attempt to outdo the generosity of the previous host in order to regain the highest social position.

Giving more than receiving might appear to be the reverse of negative reciprocity, but in this case a different kind of reward was being negotiated. Hosts gave away material goods in exchange for greater social prestige. Helen Codere (1950) gives perhaps one of the best definitions of the potlatch:

> "Potlatching" is more than any single potlatch. The public distribution of property by an individual is a recurrent climax in an endless series of cycles of accumulating property—distributing it in a potlatch—being given property—again accumulating and preparing. The whole potlatch system is a composition of these numerous individual potlatch cycles. (p. 63)

potlatch
Ceremonial feast, characteristic of indigenous Pacific Northwest coast societies, during which hosts distributed to guests a great deal of food and goods that had been accumulated over many months or years.

In addition to its social and symbolic value, the potlatch cycle thus served economic functions. In days of feasting, food was distributed along with blankets and other surplus wealth. People of high status could recirculate these goods when they hosted potlatches, but lower-ranking people made direct use of them in their domestic consumption. Negative reciprocity maintained the entire society.

In Sumatra today, horticulturalists still barter for manufactured goods, especially hunting tools, or even for tourists' personal objects. Is barter relevant in today's industrial economies?

negative reciprocity
Exchange of goods and services in which each party seeks to benefit at the expense of the other, thus making a profit.

barter
An exchange of products in which one person gives one type of product in exchange for another type of product.

redistributive networks
Economic systems in which food and other goods are amassed by an organizer and then distributed to community members or guests at large public gatherings.

of balanced reciprocity. Balanced reciprocity characterizes exchanges between people of equal social status who are not kin.

Balanced and generalized reciprocity are similar in their social basis and principle of equivalence. That is, items or services given or received are roughly equal in value. Furthermore, in addition to distributing food and material items, reciprocal exchanges are symbolic affirmations of social relationships. By exchanging goods and services, people enact their mutual interdependence.

A third type of reciprocity, **negative reciprocity,** characterizes exchanges in which some parties receive more than they have given. Negative reciprocity is rarely found within families or among members of small communities but is typical of trade or market exchanges in which the goal is profit. Negative reciprocity is common between strangers or enemies. However, negative reciprocity may occur among people in the same community who operate on the principle of competition. Trade exchanges called barter may be based on negative reciprocity. In **barter,** people trade a product they have in excess in order to obtain an item they need but do not produce themselves.

Redistributive Networks.   The Pacific Northwest coast potlatch is an example of a system of redistribution. In **redistributive networks,** produce and other goods are collected by an organizer and then distributed to community members or guests at a large public gathering. The occasions for redistribution are many. Ceremonial events, especially those marking rites of passage (birth, marriage, death), may provide the context for redistribution by the host to the guests, as in the potlatch. Political events, such as installations of chiefs in Melanesia and Polynesia, are occasions for redistribution as the new leaders or their relatives provide giveaways displaying their generosity and at the same time attracting loyal followers. And in some early states that had agriculture as an economic base, such as the Inca, central governments collected surplus produce and other goods, stored them in granaries and warehouses, and distributed them to needy people in times of poor harvests or other catastrophe.

In modern societies, state governments organize networks of redistribution. One of the state's functions is to collect taxes, now paid in money, from its citizens to fund and support public projects and programs. In theory, the value of these monies is returned

?Have you ever bartered services or products?

trade
System of exchange in which goods are exchanged for either other goods or for money.

market economy
Economic system in which products are traded in impersonal exchanges between buyers and sellers using an all-purpose currency.

commodity
A product that can be sold or traded in return for money or other products.

capitalism
An economic mode of production in which the goal is to amass wealth in the form of money in order to gain control over the means of production and then use this control to accumulate even greater wealth.

capital
Land, money, factories, and the like that support and supply the materials needed for production.

to citizens in public services such as road construction, water supplies, educational institutions, justice systems, and defense. In practice, however, systems of redistribution based on taxation often are flawed or work imperfectly as leveling mechanisms. For example, in the United States the progressive income tax was developed to allocate more equitably people's tax burdens so that wealthier people paid a higher percentage of their income in taxes than poorer people. The wealthiest people have many ways to reduce their tax liability, however, so poorer people shoulder a disproportionately higher tax burden.

Markets and Trade. Another form of redistribution is **trade,** in the form of either barter or market exchange. As defined previously, barter is the exchange of goods between individuals, each one supplying the other with produce, crafts, or other items. People who engage in barter usually know each other. In some cases, they may establish relatively formalized and permanent trading relationships, visiting each other's communities from time to time and exchanging their goods. A market exchange, on the other hand, is usually impersonal and is based, in principle, on fixed prices for goods. However, people buying and selling in local and regional markets in traditional societies frequently haggle over prices in an attempt to reach a compromise between the seller's desire to get as much as possible for the goods and the buyer's desire to pay as little as possible.

> ### REVIEW
>
> An economic system can be understood in terms of interdependent systems of production, consumption, allocation of land and resources, organization and specialization of labor, and exchange. In systems of exchange-based generalized reciprocity, people exchange goods and services of unequal or unfixed value. In balanced reciprocity, equal exchanges are sought, whereas in negative reciprocity, people expect to get more than they give. Systems of exchange also include redistributive networks, barter, trade, and market transactions.

MARKET ECONOMIES AND CAPITALISM

A **market economy** is a system of allocating goods and services and determining prices on the basis of market forces, such as supply and demand. Thus, items in short supply with high demand cost more to buy. In modern societies, buying and selling of goods and services is negotiated through a system of money exchange. Money, whether in the form of paper, coin, precious metals, gems, or other material object, is endowed with a specific value. Societies might have special-purpose money, such as cowrie shells, of fixed value that can be exchanged only for certain commodities, or tokens or tickets good only for a particular event on a particular day. In contrast, market economies rely on all-purpose money that can be exchanged for any product or service at any time. This money is portable, durable, divisible, abstract, and universal. Its value is calculated independently of any particular exchange, therefore, and can be used as a measure of worth in any exchange of goods, services, and labor. Money can even be used to "commodify" (make into a **commodity** to be bought and sold) essentially noneconomic things, such as people, their talents, and events in their lives. Market economies are based on these principles of measurement of the value of goods and services. Markets as physical places for the exchange of products, such as in local or regional markets, may exist in societies with other kinds of subsistence strategies, even including foraging, simple farming, or pastoralism.

    Capitalism is both an economic system based on money and markets and an ideology based on the private and corporate ownership of the means of production and distribution. Means of production include land, money, factories, and the like, collectively called **capital.** Economies based on capitalism must grow to survive, and growth is based on profits from buying and selling in diverse markets. The greatest profits are made in free markets that are unrestricted by industries or governments, and the greatest growth occurs as profits are accumulated and reinvested in businesses. Thus, capitalist economies favor business interests and state expansion for the purposes of acquiring new capital, including land, raw materials, and inexpensive labor.

Capitalism as an ideology-based economic system arose in Europe beginning in the sixteenth century, based on the principles of private property, individual rights, free trade, profit, and the amassing of wealth. By amassing wealth in the form of money, some people are able to gain control of the means of production and can then use this control to accumulate even greater wealth. The capitalist mode of production differs in many significant ways from modes of production in traditional indigenous societies. In contrast to economic relations in small-scale, kin, and community-based societies, capitalist economic relations are impersonal and institutionalized.

Capitalist production is characterized by three fundamental attributes (Plattner, 1989):

1. Workers do not control the means of production; they cannot by themselves produce the goods they need for survival. In contrast to subsistence farmers and artisans, workers in modern production are dependent on the owners of factories or industries that organize and produce goods and services.

2. Workers gain access to the means of production only through working for wages. According to the classic Marxist paradigm, because of this relationship, capitalist societies are divided into two basic classes: owners of the means of production (capitalists) and workers (proletariat). While some discussions of capitalism describe workers as "free" in the sense that they can sell their labor independently of kinship or other constraints, they are not free in that their lack of capital forces them to work for wages.

3. Workers produce value that is greater than the wage paid to them. This **surplus value** is retained by the owners of capital and contributes to their profit (above the costs of maintaining the means of production). In contrast to economic systems that strive for balance and stability in labor output and the benefits reaped, capitalist systems strive for continual increases in profits and rates of growth. Capitalists raise profits by increasing the scale of production, purchasing more machinery, increasing the efficiency of production, investing in new technology, finding inexpensive labor, and increasing labor output.

Cultural beliefs and values support the principles and practices by which economic systems operate. Ideological constructs that support capitalism include the idea that benefits accruing to owners are "natural" and legitimate. Owners deserve their wealth because they plan ahead, take risks, make sacrifices, and work hard. In contrast, people who are poor are seen as undeserving. Poverty, which actually results from fundamental social and economic inequalities, is presented as the consequences of an individual's personal failings—lack of intelligence, laziness, or even moral deficiencies. Through formal and informal enculturation and the reinforcement of political and religious beliefs, most members of capitalist societies learn to accept their "proper" roles without question. Members of elite classes expect to be privileged, to have wealth, and to exert social and political power; in turn, members of lower classes accept their comparative disadvantage.

GLOBALIZATION

Today, farm products enter into complex systems of transportation and delivery to national and worldwide markets. Some of the profits reaped from sale of produce are reinvested in newer technologies that permit the production of even greater surpluses, a cycle of profit and growth consistent with the principles of capitalist economic production.

surplus value
The amount of value produced by workers in capitalist production that is greater than the wage paid to them.

Arab traders first brought cowrie shells to Africa from islands in the Indian Ocean in the thirteenth century. The use of the shells as currency gradually spread westward, and later the Dutch and English traded them at West African ports. Africans preferred cowrie shells to gold coins and developed a standardized rate of exchange to use the shells as money.

What values, beliefs, and practices support the type of economic system in which Tokyo thrives?

REVIEW

A market economy is based on supply and demand and the use of money and other capital as mediums of exchange. A good, service, idea, or even a person is treated as a commodity to be bought and sold. Three characteristics of capitalism are that workers are dependent on owners to organize and produce goods and services; workers sell their labor for wages or salaries; and workers produce a surplus value that is retained by the owners as profit. Capitalism is based on private property and profits from the buying and selling of commodities in free markets. As in all types of economies, ideological beliefs and values justify the relationships in a capitalist society.

IMPACTS OF COLONIAL EXPANSION, INDUSTRIALISM, AND GLOBALIZATION

The growth of capitalism depended on the exploitation of land, labor, natural resources, and raw materials. Beginning in the fifteenth century, European explorers, traders, soldiers, missionaries, and settlers traveled throughout the world in an effort to acquire new territories, resources, markets, and souls. Each colonial power had its specific goals but all shared a common purpose and worldview. Their underlying purpose was to expand their national wealth and power. In the process, they had to control and conquer other lands and peoples.

Through **colonialism,** conquered or dominated peoples were incorporated into European economic systems as extractors of resources. In North America, for example, native peoples became enmeshed in trading networks directed by Dutch, French, British, and Russian merchants, delivering animal furs in exchange for manufactured goods. In Mexico and Central and South America and the Caribbean, indigenous peoples were forced to work on plantations and in mines operated by Spanish and Portuguese owners. In Africa, people were extracted as resources to be bought and sold along with gold and ivory. And many millions of other people died from warfare, overwork, and disease as the direct and indirect casualties of European colonial expansion.

colonialism
Policies in which countries establish colonies in distant places in order to exploit their resources and labor, and possibly to establish settlements of their own citizens abroad.

Culture Change

ECONOMIC TRANSFORMATION OF THE INNU AND THE TONGA

The Innu

Changes in patterns of economic organization have had cultural consequences for all peoples throughout the world, especially foragers. The Innu (or Montagnais), for example, exploited the forests, lakes, and rivers of northeastern Québec. They hunted animals, fished, and gathered wild plants and fruits. The people relocated to follow the seasonal availability of food. Access to land and the products of the land traditionally were considered common to all members of a band—a flexibly defined social and economic group inhabiting a vaguely defined territory. The principle of sharing extended from natural resources to food, clothing, and other necessities for survival, which were shared among community residents and even were given to travelers in need.

The Innu's traditional practices were transformed as a result of contact and involvement with European traders. Because of their location in eastern Québec, the Innu were among the first indigenous North Americans to meet European fishermen, traders, and missionaries. By the middle of the sixteenth century, the French had established a permanent post in Innu territory along the St. Lawrence River.

As the French presence grew in the region, the Innu's involvement in trade grew as well. Indians were especially interested in obtaining kettles and other metal tools and utensils. To obtain European products, they trapped beaver and other animals whose pelts were the medium of exchange. As reported by Paul LeJeune, a seventeenth-century Jesuit missionary, "The [Montagnais] say that the Beaver is the animal well-loved by the French, English, and Basques. I heard my host say one day, 'The Beaver does everything perfectly well, it makes kettles, hatchets, swords, knives, bread; in short, it makes everything'" (Thwaites, 1901, 6:297).

The Innu's role in the fur trade expanded as they functioned as intermediaries between French merchants and native peoples living far from trading posts. Innu territory positioned the people to exert regional influence. Through trade, the Innus gradually became dependent on European goods. As their dependence on trade deepened, the Indians wanted to control access to trade routes, which led to wars that pitted native nations against one another. As a result of their success in these wars, the Innu dominated eastern Canada.

Innu bands living closest to French trading centers came to rely on European goods as early as the middle of the seventeenth century. Because of their preference for metal, the Innu gave up making their own implements and eventually lost the skills to do so. Innu bands whose territories were more remote were more insulated from European influences. After the British gained possession of Québec in 1762, following the French and Indian Wars, economic interest in eastern Québec waned. Nevertheless, native trappers continued to bring their furs to the European trading posts for trade.

As a result of concentrating on trapping, fundamental changes occurred in concepts of property, ownership, and cooperation within families and communities. In contrast to traditional patterns, where resources were consumed quickly, participation in the fur trade required people to keep animal skins on hand for many months during the trapping season until they could visit trading posts and exchange their catch for goods. Whereas in the past all resources and goods were shared among community residents, some possessions became the restricted property of individuals (or families) and were withdrawn from social and economic networks. Rather than sharing, people began to hoard some of their property. This change also had the consequence of creating differences in wealth among families.

The people expanded the concept of individual property from objects to territory. Innu territory was no longer open for exploitation by any member of a band. Rather, families claimed some land as "hunting territories" for needs of trapping and trading (Leacock, 1954). Families owned the beaver houses located within their territory, but if members of another group were starving, they could kill and eat the beaver, leaving

Today the Innu are the most populous native people in Québec. To supplement wages, some Innu hunt caribou, the most important food source for their ancestors.

the fur and tail for the proper owners. The system of group or family ownership initially operated only during the trapping season, but by the second half of the eighteenth century, family allotments were stable, passed on through inheritance from parents to children.

Innu bands also began to alter traditional nomadic patterns, settling near trading posts and leading to the formation of "trading post bands." During the summer, people remained near the posts, preparing and trading the furs they trapped during the fall and winter. Gradually, trappers' families were less likely to accompany the men on expeditions and remained at home camps for most of the year. The social composition of bands located near trading posts also tended to become more stable and to develop more structured leadership patterns than did the more remote groups.

In the 1950s, 1960s, and 1970s, the Canadian government established Indian reserves. The Innu currently reside on nine reserves in Québec, encompassing only a fraction of their prior lands. Especially significant is their loss of the large expanse of territory necessary to continue a viable hunting and trapping economy. Although some people still obtain supplemental income from trapping and selling furs, few families can subsist in this way. Instead, they must find other employment, working for wages in small businesses, factories, and mines located in the vicinity of their reserves. But current data reveal continuing serious economic problems on all Innu reserves, with an unemployment rate of 32 percent and family incomes at the poverty level.

The Tonga

In societies characterized by inequality in social position and rank, elite groups have greater control over land than do commoners. Therefore, they have greater opportunity to exploit and amass resources, and they often control the labor of others. Such systems developed among many island peoples of Polynesia. People of the Tongan Islands, for example, developed a complex economic system based on horticulture and fishing. Tasks were divided between men and women and between chiefly and nonchiefly classes. Nonchiefly men carried out farming and fishing tasks. Nonchiefly women collected shellfish, fished, and extracted oil from coconuts. In addition to subsistence activities, men were responsible for cooking, an occupation that carried low prestige in Tongan society. Other household tasks, such as child care and house building, were not linked to gender but were performed by both women and men.

Production of crafts, utensils, and weapons was assigned according to gender and rank. Nonchiefly men made canoes and weapons. Nonchiefly women made mats, bark cloth (called *tapa*), bedding, and net bags. Chiefly people usually did not engage in food getting, but chiefly men made rope and decoration on weapons, and chiefly women made *tapa*. Craft production in Tonga was extensive, an example of the economic diversity and specialization found in most complex Polynesian societies (Sahlins, 1970).

The Tongan populace was divided into two primary social strata: chiefs (*eiki*) and nonchiefs (*tu'a*) (Gailey, 1987b). These two groups had different relationships to land as well as differences in their subsistence roles. Paramount chiefs controlled Tongan land, allocating portions to lower or district chiefs. Chiefs were perceived as guardians but not exclusive owners of land. Each chief gave the rights to use land under his jurisdiction to heads of kinship groups, usually men, who lived in the chief's district. In return for land use, families owed a part of their produce to the chiefs. This tribute helped support chiefs and their families. Chiefly people did not usually engage in subsistence activities but instead obtained food and goods from the productive work of commoner men and both chiefly and nonchiefly women. Chiefs also used surplus resources to sustain other dependents, such as attendants and warriors, who thus owed their well-being to the chief's largesse. In return, they were loyal followers. Tongan chiefs used their role as the center of networks of redistribution in order to increase their own authority and prestige.

Tongan economy was based on a strict division of labor according to gender. Two kinds of goods were produced: women's products, called *koloa* or "valuables, wealth," and men's products, called *ngaue* or "work" (Gailey, 1987b). *Koloa* items were considered more valuable than *ngaue* because they were made by women. Although the value of *koloa* reflected the social worth of women, both *koloa* and *ngaue* were necessary and fulfilled daily needs of household members.

Koloa products included bark cloth and mats made by both chiefly and nonchiefly women. The value of a particular item was determined by the status of the maker, the status of the person who ordered its production, the time involved in producing the item, and the age or history of the product.

Koloa, or women's wealth, had many uses (Gailey, 1987b). *Koloa* products could be given as barter for other items and as payment for services rendered. They could also be given as gifts on ritual or other special occasions, such as weddings and funerals. People could exchange *koloa,* both parties giving and receiving valuables. *Ngaue,* or men's products, though, could not be given in return for *koloa,* because *ngaue* items were inherently of less value (Gailey, 1980).

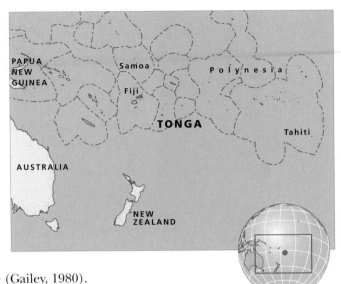

In Tongan society, one's father's sister held high social status within the family and wielded authority over her brother and his children. Rights of a sister, called *fahu* rights, included the ability to command labor and products from her brother and his wife and children. An older sister had even greater status and *fahu* rights. In addition to the *fahu* rights of a sister, a woman's children had *fahu* rights and could claim labor and products from their maternal uncles and cousins.

Transformations in Tongan economy, the organization of production, and social relations began to occur as a result of European contact, especially in the mid-1800s, when European trade and whaling in the South Pacific became more frequent and sustained. Through trade, Tongans obtained metal goods (axes, nails, knives), beads, and cloth. In exchange, they gave fish, coconuts, yams, bark cloth, and other crafts. Women, especially unmarried nonchiefly women, offered sexual services in exchange for manufactured goods from traders and sailors. Chiefs were keenly interested in trade with the British, especially wanting to obtain firearms that could be used in conflicts with one another over goals to increase their territorial control.

Expansion of trade throughout the nineteenth century changed the traditional division of labor and the value of *koloa.* At first, coconut oil, processed by women, was an

In Tonga today, the processing of coconut into copra is the only significant industry.

important trade item. It was employed by Europeans to light lamps and manufacture soap. As a result of its use as a trade commodity, women's production of coconut oil intensified, enhancing their status. Then, in the late 1800s, the world market for coconut oil declined. Instead, Europeans sought dried coconut, called copra. Because the collection and processing of coconuts was men's work, or *ngaue*, the shift to trade in copra began a realignment of traditional Tongan beliefs about the inherent value of women's and men's products. The prestige traditionally associated with the production of coconut oil (a woman's product) shifted to the production of copra (a man's product). The prestige value of products then shifted to the product itself rather than to the gender of the producer, thus undermining the very foundation of Tongan economic and social principles.

Influenced by British colonial administrators and missionaries, the Tongan legislature granted land-use rights to individual men as heads of households. The inheritance of land, formerly a sister's right to claim, became inheritance from father to son. Competing claims through fathers' sisters were dismissed by law, and the exercise of *fahu* rights by sisters was made illegal. A woman can no longer lay claims to her brothers and their families, thus altering the network of relationships that linked people to their kin.

GLOBALIZATION

The Europeans needed to develop markets to sell goods manufactured in Europe and to expand markets for materials extracted from their colonies. This dynamic produced the complex economic system that we refer to as globalization.

In Asia, European expeditions met powerful, centralized, and well-organized states that they were not able to defeat militarily. Instead, Europeans developed trading networks that brought resources and products to Asia from colonies in other parts of the world. In exchange, they obtained Asian luxury items to sell in Europe. Some indigenous peoples in all parts of the world readily and even enthusiastically welcomed European traders, wanting to acquire manufactured goods and luxury items. They willingly supplied the merchants with the resources, products, and people so much sought after in European and world markets. The participation of many other indigenous peoples was not voluntary, however.

European economic expansion was closely connected with nation building. Governments controlled much of the trade, directly or through state-appointed merchant organizations, and pursued policies of political and military intervention to promote and protect their economic interests. These policies often led to military invasions and wars of conquest, followed by the establishment of direct colonial rule. Far-flung empires were established, with European powers competing to acquire the most colonial possessions. The French and British claimed much of North America, for example, and the British claimed India.

As colonial control spread throughout the world, capitalism and market economies were introduced to peoples whose subsistence strategies were based on foraging, pastoralism, and horticulture. Transformation of their economic systems was promoted by involvement in trade, as illustrated in the culture change case studies in this chapter about the Innu and the Tonga. Because economic systems are integrated with other aspects of culture, the changes in work and landholding practices caused by colonialism and trade stimulated political, social, and ideological transformations as well. These topics are the focus of Chapters 16 and 17.

Colonialism and the Exploitation of Labor

Slavery was the most extreme form of colonial exploitation of labor of indigenous peoples. Slavery deprived the victims of all rights to determine their own labor, forced them to produce goods directed by their owners, and expropriated all their products to be distributed and consumed according to the wishes of their masters. In the Caribbean and the southern United States, slaves in the eighteenth and first half of the nineteenth centuries were the primary subsistence workers and produced most of the crops intended for external trade. However, they clearly did not benefit from their labor in either income or status.

Case study

The Spanish Mission System in California

Prior to the Spanish invasions of California in the mid-eighteenth century, native peoples had lived for millennia in the coastal, riverine, and desert environments of what is now northern Mexico and the state of California. They were foragers, gathering abundant acorns, other nuts and seeds, fruits, and plants, as well as hunting and fishing. The rich resources of the territory permitted permanent settlements, and this centralization of population contributed to their swift conquest and incorporation into a Spanish colonial presence known as the **mission system.**

After 1769, the Spanish established twenty-one missions along the coast from present-day San Diego to Sonoma, California. Missions and military forts housed tens of thousands of native people, who were rounded up, forcibly relocated, compelled to convert to Roman Catholicism, and put to work on behalf of Spain and the Church. Spanish mission economies were based on farming, ranching, and textile production. Native laborers grew corn, beans, wheat, barley, and various fruits and vegetables and tended cattle, horses, and sheep. As agricultural and livestock production grew, farm produce, livestock, and textiles were sold to settlers and to the Spanish military (Jackson and Castillo, 1995).

Inmates of the missions lived in virtual slavery. The slightest infractions or resistance were punished by beatings, solitary confinement, mutilation, or execution (Castillo, 1978). Men were beaten in public view of others to serve as examples, but, according to a French naval officer visiting the mission at San Carlos in 1786, "Women are never whipped in public, but in an enclosed and somewhat distant place that their cries may not excite a too lively compassion, which might cause the men to revolt" (Jackson and Castillo, 1995:83). Indians were prohibited from engaging in traditional subsistence activities. In 1832, the Mexican government began the process of secularizing the missions, relieving the priests of control. However, rather than freeing Indians from their plight, secular authorities established a system of peonage that replaced religious personnel with civilian overlords. Ranches that had been established by Spanish soldiers and settlers with coerced labor continued to expand and became more numerous under Mexican jurisdiction (Forbes, 1969). Missions were converted into towns, leaving the Indians destitute. Many remained in the towns or sought work at ranches because they had no land or resources.

California became part of the United States in 1846, but conditions remained harsh. In 1850, for example, the California state legislature passed a law entitled Act for the Government and Protection of Indians, providing that "any Indian able to work who shall be found loitering and strolling about . . . shall be liable to be arrested on the complaint of any resident citizen . . . and brought before any Justice of the Peace . . . who shall [authorize] him to hire out such vagrant to the best bidder . . . for four months" (Heizer and Almquist, 1971:215). After passage of the act, nearby Indians were rounded up and forced into indenture.

Excursions into the interior to kidnap children became common. According to the *Humboldt Times* in 1855: "A large number of children have been brought down and sold in the agricultural counties. They bring from $50 to $250 each" (Heizer and Almquist, 1971, p. 41). And, in 1862, an army officer named Colonel Francis Lippitt reported: "Individuals and parties are constantly engaged in kidnapping Indian children, frequently attacking the rancherias, and killing the parents for no other purpose. This is said to be a very lucrative business, the kidnapped children bringing

mission system
Pattern of Spanish colonization of the Americas in the name of the Roman Catholic Church.

good prices, in some instances hundreds of dollars apiece" (p. 43). With the government's tacit approval, raids on native communities to steal children increased at least until 1867, when the Fourteenth Amendment of the U.S. Constitution forced the California legislature to repeal the laws. But by then more than 4,000 Indian children had been taken (Castillo, 1978:109).

Another means of controlling indigenous labor was the imposition of colonial taxes, for example, mandatory **poll taxes,** or head taxes. Because taxes had to be paid in cash, people were compelled to seek wage employment in the European-controlled economic sectors in their countries—in European-owned mines, plantations, or service and construction jobs—or they grew crops for cash, removing land from subsistence farming. Their crops thus entered national and international markets under the control and distribution of colonial powers.

Ideologies that supported these practices focused on perceived benefits to the native peoples. In the words of a member of the British Parliament, speaking in 1926, "Under all circumstances the progress of natives toward civilization is only secured when they shall be convinced of the necessity and dignity of labor; and therefore I think that everything we reasonably do to encourage the natives to work is highly desirable" (Joseph Chamberlain, quoted in Wellington, 1967:250). In 1934, another British official stated, "As the natives were often reluctant to leave their homes, a little gentle pressure was brought to bear upon them with the introduction of a poll tax. This measure quite effectively stimulated their desire for earning the white man's money" (Eiselen, 1934:71). Comments such as these show how colonial powers were able to rationalize the economic exploitation of colonized peoples.

Industrial Economies

poll taxes
Taxes levied on households.

Colonialism resulted in the spread of capitalism and market-based economies, which increasingly relied on the mass production of commodities. European merchants,

This industrial employee in northern India is performing work that a preindustrial counterpart would have done at home without the aid of machines. India began its painful transformation to a modern, independent, manufacturing state during Great Britain's colonial rule. In what other ways was Indian society and culture transformed through industrialism?

desiring to increase their profits and to find new markets for their goods, promoted the invention of new technologies that would increase productivity. Demand for mass-produced goods also encouraged new technologies and the development of the factory system, a hallmark of **industrialism,** the use of machinery to produce goods. In Europe and the United States in the late eighteenth century, innovations in production began a process that transformed agricultural societies into industrial nations.

Industrial production began in Great Britain as an outgrowth of cottage piecework in the making of textiles and clothing. Women traditionally wove woolen cloth and made garments for their families, in keeping with a domestic division of labor between men and women in a farm household. Gradually, women began to produce surplus cloth and garments for sale to merchants, who bought up the products and sold them in regional and then national markets. Initially, women were paid to produce the cloth and garments in their homes. Eventually, cottage piecework shifted to factories, whose owners hired workers and directed their labor on site, away from homes and household duties. In some cases, entire families were hired to work in the factories. But many married women, to fulfill domestic and child-care responsibilities, dropped out of the labor force.

By 1820, manufacturing incorporated complex machinery and new sources of energy. These innovations enabled workers to create more products in the same amount of time, and machine production replaced handwork. Labor patterns shifted. The employment of children became inefficient because they could not operate heavy or complicated equipment. In addition, public disclosure of children's illnesses and injuries caused by long working hours and unsafe conditions led to demands for legal protections against the abuse of children. Consequently, men and young women remained the primary factory employees.

In the United States one of the first industries to develop was textile manufacturing. In Massachusetts mill towns, for example, young women from farm families worked to help their families buy the growing number of commodities, such as shoes, household utensils, and tools. Unmarried daughters were available for factory jobs because their labor was not as critical to agricultural production on the family farm as that of sons.

By the use of machines and powerful energy sources (coal, steam, electricity) to produce goods, industrial processes have vastly increased the efficiency and growth of commodity production. Increased production makes higher levels of consumption possible, and consumption creates demand, which, in turn, fuels more production. That is, the more goods that are produced, the greater the demand; and the greater the demand, the more goods are produced. Our attitudes about consumption are shaped by this cycle, which reflects the needs of a capitalist economy. We are given every incentive to consume and to believe that we need to consume more. In other words, demand is artificially created and maintained through an ideology that promotes the acquisition of material goods as the means of achieving pleasure and progress.

Social inequalities increase in capitalist economies based on industrialism. This raises the question of whose needs are satisfied by socioeconomic systems. Unlike in foraging, pastoral, or horticultural economies, in a capitalist economy the needs of some people are satisfied much more than those of others. Another question is to what extent the general affluence of capitalist economies compared to other kinds of economies gives people more leisure and security, as is commonly believed. Anthropologists have tried to answer this question. For example, in a comparison of middle-class French people and members of the Machiguenga society in Peru, Allen Johnson (1978) points out that horticulturalists like the Machiguenga spend less time in subsistence work and have more leisure time than workers in modern industrial nations. Johnson compared the ways in which French and Machiguenga people spend their time in production (of goods and services), in consumption (using consumption goods, as in eating, leisure activities), and free time (idleness, rest, chatting). Johnson found that French men spent more time in production than any other group while Machiguenga women spent the least time producing. Machiguenga men and French women spent about the same amount of time in production, less than French men but more than Machiguenga women. In addition, French people spent far more time in consumption than the Machiguenga, in fact, about three to five times as much. In contrast, the Machiguenga had much more leisure time than did the French.

industrialism
The use of machines to produce products and foods.

? *What do you think about your role as a consumer in a capitalist economy?*

Anthropology Applied

Economic Anthropologists and Consumer Behavior

Methods of cultural anthropology include ethnographic observation and interviews and recording qualitative (as well as quantitative) information about human behavior. Anthropologists also are trained in cross-cultural research. For these reasons big companies hire anthropologists to do consumer research, especially to reveal the underlying cultural and social patterns that shape consumer behavior.

People's economic behavior is shaped by their cultural identities, beliefs, and values, as well as by environmental influences. As researchers, anthropologists can take the role of the "other" and see through the other's eyes to yield insights that companies can use to make business decisions and offer new products to increase their sales. Anthropologists also might be called upon to analyze company and product brands, to conduct focus groups, and to write employee or customer ethnographies.

For example, economic anthropologists might help a company test a new product, enter a new market by appealing to an ethnic group or other demographic,

decide on the right interface for selling products online, analyze a wedding registry for consumer preferences, observe shoppers in a new setting, gather information on customer satisfaction or loyalty, predict trends in technologies for the home, or identify the contexts for people's shopping decisions, such as deciding to buy organic produce (http://www.ethno-insight.com/). Anthropologists also are involved in market research for pharmaceutical firms and professional sports teams, as well as companies such as Pizza Hut and Coca-Cola (http://www.ethnographic-solutions.com/).

Anthropologists who work for corporations also are concerned with the cultural, material, and health and safety impacts that products and services have on consumers and the company employees and their communities. In addition, they analyze the sustainability of economic growth and development in relation to people's physical, social, and cultural environments.

CRITICAL THINKING QUESTION

In applied anthropology, what might be some concerns in balancing the goals of corporations with anthropological perspectives?

GLOBALIZATION

Western consumerism has infiltrated developing countries (Dannaeuser, 1989). In Latin America, Asia, and Africa, Western-style shopping malls satisfy the demands of the rising numbers of the middle class. Products with the greatest demand include home appliances, TVs, computers, and other electronic equipment.

consumerism
Culture of consumption of goods and services.

Johnson and others have also pointed out that people's ideas about their needs and satisfactions are subjective and culturally constructed. For example, although North Americans and Europeans consume more goods and services than any other group, they often feel a shortage of time. Consumption behavior provides pleasure and excitement, but people sometimes do not enjoy consumption activities because they feel pressed for time, needing to keep busy schedules and cram in as much as possible in a day. Time itself is treated as a commodity. In English, metaphors for time as a commodity include "spending time," "saving time," "having time for [something]" (Lakoff and Johnson, 1980).

Consumerism has grown in all economic classes in all parts of the world. The expansion of consumer credit enables people without cash on hand to accumulate household and personal possessions that represent a lifestyle above their means. The extent of consumer debt in the United States and elsewhere reveals the power of culturally constructed demand, including the desire to display the trappings of wealth and prestige. For example, American households carry about $8,000 in credit card debt annually. In 2003, American consumers spent an average of 43 percent more than they earned. According to the Federal Reserve, they owed $1.9773 trillion, or $18,654 per household, not including mortgage debt. The U.S. national debt was also the highest in history that year.

An important difference in consumer spending between the developed and developing countries is the fact that the developed countries have a strong, domestic industrial base, while most of the developing world lacks national industries. Therefore, spending in the developing world pays primarily for imported goods, which tend to be more expensive. Developing countries often lack the capital and infrastructure to develop strong domestic industries, and so become dependent on other nations for

Global trends in consumerism are fueled by the advertising industry, which seeks to create and sustain demand for certain products and services. By creating a perception of need, these advertisements in Vietnam contribute to overspending and the accumulation of debt.

production and distribution of products to their citizens. Local economies may be undermined as a result, as rural subsistence farmers and artisans are put out of business by imported and mass-produced goods.

In the past 100 years, a dramatic shift has taken place in the types of work that people do. A century ago, the vast majority of people in the world worked in the agricultural sector, either owning or working on a farm. Today, in many countries only a small fraction of the population works in agriculture, as Table 7.1 shows.

Table 7.1 PERCENT OF POPULATION INVOLVED IN FOUR ECONOMIC SECTORS

	Agriculture	Industry (total)	Industry (manufacturing)	Services
Africa	63.21	11.10	6.49	25.69
Asia	61.85	16.91	12.57	21.24
Southeast Asia	59.17	13.85	10.45	26.98
Eastern Asia	64.76	17.49	12.89	17.76
Europe	12.18	36.23	25.36	51.58
North America	2.89	25.92	17.51	71.19
South America	23.32	23.75	13.45	52.93
Latin America and the Caribbean	25.39	23.60	14.15	51.00
Oceania	19.62	22.34	13.73	58.03
Australia and New Zealand	6.30	26.09	16.31	67.61

Source: International Labor Organization, 2002.

GLOBALIZATION

In a new trend, service jobs are now being exported, or outsourced, from countries like the United States to countries in the developing world, where labor costs are less. As service industries and information technologies increase, heavy industry declines as an economic past, prompting some analysts to refer to Western nations as "postindustrial."

In Table 7.1, "agriculture" includes all farming for commercial purposes as well as full-time subsistence farmers; "manufacturing" refers to heavy industry; and "services" includes secretarial, sales, and information occupations. The figures show that (1) participation in farming is lowest in the wealthiest regions with the highest standards of living—North America, Australia and New Zealand, Europe; (2) conversely, participation in farming is highest in the poorest regions—Africa, Asia; (3) levels of industrial production are in an inverse relationship with farming—where farming is high, industrial production is low and where farming is low, industrial production is high; and (4) service employment is highest in the wealthiest regions.

> **REVIEW**
>
> Native peoples across the world became enmeshed with European market economies beginning in the fifteenth century. Through colonialism and trade, the exploitation of native lands and resources and labor, and coercive practices such as poll taxes and the mission system, capitalist and industrial economies gradually came to dominate the growing present-day global economy. Foraging, horticulturalism, and pastoralism have been replaced by industrial agriculture and manufacturing in most regions of the world. Industrialism is a system of production that increases efficiency and productivity through the use of machines and automation. Increases in production lead to greater wealth, and increases in consumption and consumerism further stimulate economic growth. Over the past 100 years. service industries have replaced agriculture and industrial manufacturing as the dominant economic sector in wealthy postindustrial societies.

COMPARING SUBSISTENCE STRATEGIES

We tend to think that because of its ability to feed so many billions of people, modern industrial agriculture is superior to all earlier subsistence strategies. But, as you have seen in Chapter 6, other strategies have their advantages as well as disadvantages. Foragers do not have exclusive ownership of land and resources. Division of labor is based on age and gender, though men and women often share the same tasks. Labor specialization in foraging societies is at the household level, with individuals doing craftwork for the family. Among nomadic foragers, surpluses, when they occur, are consumed and shared with the group to reinforce social ties.

Foraging societies had the advantage of access to a complex and varied diet from resources growing wild in different ecological niches. For example, the Ju/'hoansi ate about 100 kinds of plants, fruits, and nuts in a yearly foraging cycle. Offsetting this advantage, however, was their vulnerability to malnutrition or starvation in years of severe drought or other environmental disaster. Moreover, foragers' dietary variety usually came at a price—the need to move constantly. Nomadism puts a premium on good health because it is hard for the frail, sick, and elderly to relocate frequently. It also puts a burden on pregnant women and parents with young children. The need for mobility also prevents the accumulation of surpluses of clothing, shelter, and tools and utensils.

On the other hand, the physical activity required by a nomadic lifestyle has health benefits of its own. Also, the kinds of infectious diseases that plague people living in close quarters in settled communities were rare or absent among nomadic peoples. As they moved, they left behind their garbage and bodily waste—another source of disease. The small community size characteristic of foraging societies had the advantage of minimizing pressure on resources and reducing interpersonal tensions. The need to limit household size, however, may have been a burden because of the need for aggressive birth control.

Pastoralists put more stake in the idea of land and animal ownership. Grazing land may be owned by a collective (a family or group), with individuals owning or having rights to the animals. Wealth and prestige are counted by the size of one's herd, so there really is no surplus. Division of labor is variable, but everyone's work addresses the care and herding of the animals and secondary production using animal products.

In horticultural societies, families or kin groups own and allocate land. Men clear fields, cut trees, and burn brush. The division of labor for other subsistence tasks varies from society to society. Part-time artisans are paid in goods or food. Horticultural surpluses are stored against famines and disasters and redistributed to those in need.

Horticulture solves some of the problems of foraging. Farming provides people with a stable source of food. Rather than relying on the fluctuating bounty of nature, people grow their own crops. The security of horticulturalists is not absolute, however, because drought, insect infestation, flooding, or other natural disaster may wipe out a season's produce. For these reasons, horticulturists try to obtain surpluses to rely on in bad years. Pastoralists solve the uncertain success of hunting by maintaining their own herds of animals. In contrast, hunters and fishers may or may not find the game they seek. However, pastoralists must invest more labor and resources in maintaining their herds than foragers do in hunting.

In most agricultural societies land is owned and controlled by individuals. Surpluses are more common and may be hoarded or used to pay tribute or taxes to state governments, which redistribute surpluses to those in need. Surpluses also support full-time specialists, who do nonagricultural work in arts, crafts, occupations, and professions.

Intensive agriculturists solve many of the problems engendered by other subsistence strategies, but they, too, create additional difficulties. They solve the problems of nomadism by establishing sedentary communities, but settled life also has problems. Sedentary farmers usually have a much less varied diet than foragers or people who utilize a mixed horticultural and foraging strategy. The more limited variety of crops and foods potentially leads to the kinds of diseases that result from the lack of certain nutrients. Sedentary communities are also more vulnerable to epidemic diseases. And with many people confined to one place, their communities are subject to festering tensions or open conflicts between groups and individuals. Agriculturists do, however, have a striking advantage in that they are able to use increasing numbers of people to produce larger surpluses and, therefore, except in times of natural catastrophe, they have access to a secure supply of food. This often comes at the cost, however, of back-breaking labor. Agriculturists work harder and longer than do horticulturists, pastoralists, or foragers.

The relaxation of population-control mechanisms in some agricultural societies results in rapid population growth and problems of overpopulation. As a consequence, more labor is available, but more labor is also required to feed larger populations. This process leads to greater burdens on the land and creates needs for more land for farming and living space. In addition, numerous pregnancies and births create burdens on mothers' health and increase the risks of maternal death.

Industrial agriculture solves some problems of supply. Through industrial techniques, farm output has increased enormously. There is now the ability to feed everyone in every country, but many people continue to go hungry and to die of malnutrition because of the uneven distribution of food. The complex reasons are partly economic and partly political. But industrial agriculture also has created unforeseen problems in its overreliance on harmful chemicals in food growing and processing.

REVIEW

Modes of subsistence can be compared and contrasted in terms of trade-offs in the factors that relate to the quality of human life. Those factors include security, food supply, diet, living space, living conditions, labor burdens, health risks, and life expectancies.

Chapter Summary

Economics of Agriculture

- Intensive agriculture and industrial agriculture lead to increases in population size and density, landownership, specialization of labor, centralization of authority and power, and social inequalities.

Analyzing Economic Systems

- Economic systems include strategies for allocating land, resources, and labor. People everywhere need to produce, distribute, and consume foods and other goods. They obtain their resources from their land through various modes of production. People in different cultures employ different methods to allocate land and resources.

- Societies need to allocate the labor of their members to productive tasks. Work roles are often assigned to people on the basis of age and gender. Children are usually given work to do that is compatible with their lack of strength and stamina. But the way in which gender affects work roles varies considerably in different cultures. In some, men's and women's roles are rigidly separated; in others, women and men may perform many of the same tasks and work cooperatively.

- Economic exchanges occur among family members, friends, traders, and other members of communities. Exchanges between family members or other familiars are usually of the type called generalized reciprocity, where no immediate return is expected, while exchanges between other members of communities are called balanced reciprocity, where there is usually a mutual exchange of goods. Exchanges between strangers, especially in the marketplace, are characterized by negative reciprocity, where each party tries to receive more value than he or she gives.

- Systems of exchange also include redistributive networks, barter, trade, and market transactions.

Market Economies and Capitalism

- Market economies are based on the buying and selling of commodities of fixed value, depending on supply and demand and using standardized mediums of exchange. Markets also are where these transactions take place.

- Capitalist economic production is based on the desire by owners of the means of production to increase their profit. In capitalist production, workers do not control the means of production but instead must sell their labor to owners of factories or other institutions that organize and produce goods and services. Workers sell their labor to the owners for a wage. Workers produce "surplus value" or the value of the goods produced by their labor that is greater than the wage paid to them. This surplus value becomes profit for the owners. Capitalist economic systems are geared toward an ever-increasing rate of profit. Unlike traditional indigenous subsistence economies, capitalist production is inherently unstable.

Impacts of Colonial Expansion, Industrialism, and Globalization

- In the fifteenth century, European powers began a process of economic and colonial expansion aimed at expropriating resources and labor from indigenous lands and peoples. In this process of globalization, which is not confined to Europeans historically, resources and trade items were incorporated into a worldwide economic system that led to the growth and concentration of wealth in Europe. This wealth and desire for even greater profits motivated the development of industrialization.

- In complex agrarian and industrial societies, systems of distribution have developed to circulate foods and other goods from direct producers to those who do not produce food. Members of elite classes in particular benefit from the distribution of goods. Through kinship networks or through state organization, they are able to make claims on other people's labor. Whether this is called tribute, taxes, or slavery, some segments of society are not able to control at least some of the products of their labor.

- Postindustrial societies increasingly rely on consumerism and the provision of information and services to the global economy rather than goods.

Comparing Subsistence Strategies

- In most foraging societies, land and resources are generally available to all members of the community. Foraging peoples do not think of land and resources as commodities to be owned by individuals. In pastoral societies, land and especially animals are controlled or owned by individuals or families. Pastoralists need to have either rotating or permanent access to pastureland for their animals. Domesticated animals often become a social measure of wealth, and competition may displace cooperation. In horticultural and agricultural societies, land is owned by individuals or family groups. As people's investments in labor and technology increase with the intensity of farming, the need to retain permanent and individual control of land also increases. Eventually, people developed the notion of private property in land, giving owners the right to buy and sell their land.

- In foraging, pastoral, and horticultural societies, most people, given characteristics of gender and age, perform similar subsistence work. But in complex agricultural and industrial societies, individuals are not engaged in the same kinds of labor. Instead, economic life is characterized by labor specialization. In the past century, the percentage of people engaged in producing food has declined considerably. Although there is much variation in the rates of agricultural work throughout the world, there has been a decline everywhere. In the United States and Canada, less than 3 percent of the population is engaged in farming.

 *Key Terms*

barter 175
redistributive
  networks 175
trade 176

market economy 176
commodity 176
capitalism 176
capital 176

surplus value 177
colonialism 178
mission system 183
poll taxes 184

industrialism 185
consumerism 186

Review Questions

1. What social behaviors are part of any society's economic system? How do anthropologists view economic systems?

2. What kinds of economic exchange are seen in societies? How do systems of exchange relate to modes of subsistence?

3. What are the different types of reciprocity? Why is balanced reciprocity seen in foraging groups? How is the potlatch an example of negative reciprocity?

4. How do allocations of land and labor differ among foragers, pastoralists, horticulturalists, and agriculturalists?

5. How are economic concepts, such as ownership, integrated with other cultural systems, such as kinship, social status, political power, and ideology?

6. What are the distinguishing features of a market economy? What are the impacts of capitalism on a society's systems of production, distribution, and consumption?

7. How does the rise of social inequality relate to changes in economic systems?

8. How were indigenous peoples brought into European economies? What impacts did colonialism have on those peoples and their economies?

9. Why do capitalist economies depend on ever-increasing consumerism?

Kinship and Descent

CHAPTER 8

Preview

1. **What is descent, and why is it significant in organizing human relationships?**
2. **What different types of descent are found in human cultures?**
3. **What kinds of kin groups do the various descent rules create?**
4. **How do different unilineal descent rules affect people's interrelationships?**
5. **How do kinship systems interrelate with other aspects of culture, such as economic and political systems?**
6. **How and why do kinship systems change?**
7. **What kinship terminologies do people use to classify their kin?**
8. **How do kin terms reveal the type of kinship system people have?**

Whereas I, Joseph Mygatt, of Hartford upon the River and in the jurisdiction of Connecticut in New England, have in the behalf of my son Jacob and at his request made a motion to Mrs. Susanna Fitch, in reference to her daughter Sarah Whiting, that my said son Jacob might with her good liking have free liberty to endeavor the gaining of her said daughter Sarah's affection towards himself in a way of marriage: . . . I will pay thereupon unto my said son as his marriage portion the full sum of two hundred pounds sterling. . . . And I do further engage for the present to build a comfortable dwelling house for my said son and her daughter [Jacob's bride-to-be, Sarah] to live in by themselves. . . . And [I] also give them therewith near the said house one acre of ground planted with apple trees and other fruit trees, which said house, land, and trees shall be and remain to my said son as an addition for his marriage portion, before mentioned, and to his heirs and forever. . . . And I do further promise and engage that at the day of my death I shall and will leave unto him my said son and his heirs so much estate besides the dwelling house, ground, and trees. . . . I do hereby engage and bind over my dwelling house and all my lands and buildings in Hartford. . . . And I do further engage that my daughter Mary's portion of one hundred pounds being first paid to her, I will leave to my said son and his heirs forever my whole estate at the day of my death, he [Jacob, his son] paying to my wife during her natural life twelve pounds a year, and allowing to her a dwelling entire to herself in the two upper rooms and cellar belonging to my now dwelling house, with the going of half the poultry and a pig for her comfort in each year during her said life; also allowing her the use of half the household stuff during her life, which she shall have power to dispose of to Jacob or Mary at her death. . . . And lastly I do engage that the whole benefit of the Indian trade shall be to the sole advantage of my son Jacob, and do promise that I will during my life be [an] assistant and helpful to my said son in the best ways I can, both in his trading with the Indians, his stilling, and otherwise, for his comfort and advantage.

From "Marriage Settlement of Jacob Mygatt, of Hartford, Connecticut," in *Collections of the Connecticut Historical Society*, XIV (Hartford, Conn., 1912), pp. 558–560, cited in John Demos, ed., *Remarkable Providences 1600–1760*, NY: George Braziller, 1972. Copyright 1972. Reprinted by permission of George Braziller.

This marriage contract for Jacob Mygatt and Sarah Whiting was written on November 27, 1654, in Hartford, Connecticut. It reveals a complex array of concerns common to all human societies: Among the people one lives with, to whom does one owe the greatest loyalty and support? Who among them might one marry? What will happen to one's dependents when one dies? How will they support themselves? How will one's property be divided and distributed, and to whom? Universally, these and other questions are resolved through kinship systems. This chapter compares the various ways that people define their relatives and reckon their kinship.

KINSHIP SYSTEMS

In all societies, people have ways of organizing their relationships with other people, especially their primary relationships with kin. As children, our earliest and most influential interactions are with our parents, siblings, and other relatives. We rely on our families for all of our survival needs. Our families feed us, clothe us, and provide our shelter. They also help us adjust to the world around us, teaching us the behavior and attitudes that our culture expects. And they provide emotional support in both good times and bad.

Many of our relatives continue as important economic and emotional supports throughout our lives. Even as adults, we can turn to our kin in networks of reciprocity, asking for aid in times of need. In turn, we may be asked to respond to their requests when they are in need. We may align ourselves with our relatives when they are engaged in disputes with others. And we may expect loyalty from our kin when we are in conflict with neighbors or other community members. During personal or family crises, we may expect emotional support from our relatives. Together we celebrate happy occasions such as births and marriages, and we mourn the deaths of our kin.

In large-scale societies, friends, colleagues, co-members of clubs, and other nonrelatives also function significantly to give us companionship and support. But in most societies, kinship relations permeate people's daily lives and mold their identity and their sense of themselves. In small-scale societies and in cohesive communities within pluralistic states, family members may be united in dense, complex networks. They may perform important functions in the absence of the formal institutions that regulate and organize economic, political, and religious life in large-scale societies. People identify themselves not just as individuals but as members of kinship groups.

A **kinship system** consists of connections between people by "blood," marriage, or adoption, and the beliefs and practices by which people regard and treat each other as relatives. The people may be genetically related (**consanguines,** "related by blood") or related by marriage (**affines**), or they may not be related at all. Many kin groups include adopted kin and **fictive kin,** unrelated individuals who are regarded and treated as relatives. Thus, the notion of kinship is essentially a social and symbolic idea, not based on universal objective criteria.

Among foragers, pastoralists, and horticulturalists, kinship relations were the primary regulators of social and economic life. Through kin relations, people organized their households, allocated work roles, controlled land and other property in common, made decisions affecting the group, and carried out ritual functions. In agrarian societies, kinship relations generally continued to be paramount in organizing and integrating communities, but new patterns of interaction also emerged. Gradually, as state societies developed, many of the functions carried out by kinship groups were taken over by specialists and state institutions. The state regulated intergroup trade, established formal procedures for making decisions and settling disputes, and set up institutions to carry out some social functions, replacing the critical roles of kinship groups. In postindustrial societies people may live apart from their relatives, and all of the functions of kin groups can be fulfilled through public or private institutions. Thus, fundamental differences exist between those societies where people's lives center around their kin and where social, economic, and political functions are integrated with kinship groups and those societies where ties among kin are looser and less intense and where formal institutions provide social, economic, and political functions.

Kinship systems are organized around rules of marriage (the subject of Chapter 9) and **rules of descent,** which stipulate the nature of relationships from one generation

kinship system
System of determining who one's relatives are and what one's relationship is to them.

consanguines
People related by blood.

affines
People related through marriage.

fictive kin
Unrelated individuals who are regarded and treated as relatives.

rules of descent
Social rules that stipulate the nature of relationships from one generation to another.

This family reunion, held at Monticello in Virginia in July 2004, celebrates the kinship of descendants of Thomas Jefferson and the African slave Sally Hemings. Some of the relatives at this event were meeting each other for the first time.

bilateral descent
Principle of descent in which people think of themselves related to both their mother's kin and their father's kin at the same time.

unilineal descent
Principle of descent in which people define themselves in relation to only one side, either their mother's side or their father's side.

kindred
Kinship group consisting of known bilateral relatives with whom people interact, socialize, and rely on for economic and emotional assistance.

to another. Although the notion of kinship is subjective, there are a limited number of ways in which people trace descent and organize kinship groups. Two fundamental organizing principles are bilateral descent and unilineal descent. In societies with **bilateral descent,** people think of themselves as related to both their mother's kin and their father's kin at the same time (*bilateral* means "two sides," from *bi* meaning "two" and *lateral* or "side"). In **unilineal descent** systems, people define themselves in relation to only one side, either their mother's or their father's (*unilineal* means "one line," from *uni* meaning "one" and *lineal* or "line").

? *What rule of descent is followed in your family? What is the name for the type of kin group formed by this rule?*

Bilateral Descent

Organizing one's relatives according to the principle of bilateral descent creates a large, potentially limitless group of people to whom one may claim relationship. People usually do not interact with everyone in this large kinship group. Rather, they tend to know, socialize with, and depend on a smaller group of relatives within the wider network. This smaller group of bilateral relatives is called a **kindred** (see Figure 8.1).

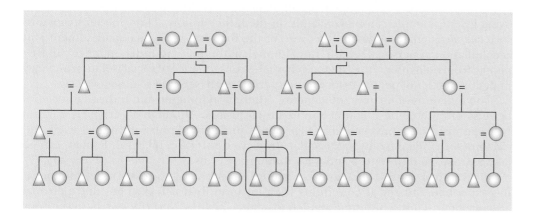

Figure 8.1
A Kindred. A group of people, traced through bilateral descent, related to the brother and sister shown at the bottom row, center.

The San of the Kalahari reckon their kinship bilaterally, tracing relationships through both father and mother. They depend on their kin for aid and support in times of need. This reality reinforces traditional social ethics that stress generosity, hospitality, cooperation, and loyalty.

? *What are the names of the people you regard as members of your kindred? How are they related to you?*

GLOBALIZATION

The increasing prevalence of bilateral descent in the world today is partly an outgrowth of the adaptive functions of bilateral descent groups in industrial societies and partly a result of the globalization of culture based on Euro-American power and influence.

Reckoning one's kin through bilateral descent is common in modern industrial societies, but it is also found in many small foraging societies. Kindreds are adaptive in both kinds of cultures, but for different reasons. In foraging societies, bilateral descent allows people to make claims on a wide group of people for economic assistance and emotional support. This strategy is adaptive, especially when resources are scarce. In times of need, people may ask relatives for aid, based on the principle of reciprocity. At different times people are both givers and receivers of support. They are at an advantage if they can call on the help of many others in times of need. They are also likely to be asked for help, but in the long run, having diffuse reciprocal networks is an efficient and reliable adaptive strategy.

Bilateral descent is also adaptive for people in modern industrial countries, where it functions to loosen kinship ties. Thus, the same system of descent can have different outcomes and serve different purposes, depending on people's needs as they adapt to specific ecological, social, and economic conditions. While bilateral descent provides a large number of people with reciprocal obligations and responsibilities, it also creates a loosely organized kin group without definite social limits or boundaries. By loosening kinship ties, people establish greater individual autonomy, freeing themselves from claims that other people might make on them. Individuals and small family units can advance themselves economically, accumulate more wealth, and raise their standard of living if fewer people can make claims on them for support. Thus, modern capitalist societies favor bilateral descent because of the focus on individual achievement and accumulation of personal wealth. But although autonomy and independence can free people from obligations, they may also have the consequence of social isolation and may limit the number of people from whom a person might seek aid in times of need.

The functions of bilateral descent are different in foraging and industrial societies because of both cultural context and cultural history. Although a particular cultural behavior may be adaptive, its advantage can be understood only within the society and circumstances. That is why a particular strategy, in this case, bilateral descent, can be advantageous in different societies for different reasons.

In historical context, bilateral kin groups in industrial societies reflected changing economic and social conditions favoring individual achievement and personal advancement. These conditions tended to weaken kin ties. Nevertheless, both the poor and the wealthy can benefit from membership in bilateral kin groups. Carol Stack's

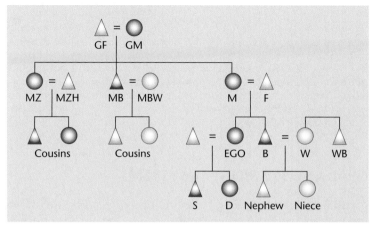

Figure 8.2
Matrilineal Descent. Brown triangles and circles are ego's kin group. Diagrams of kinship terminology systems use the following conventions: Circles represent females, triangles represent males, horizontal lines link siblings, vertical lines link generations, and equal signs link husband and wife. Abbreviations used to designate kin in a kin diagram are M = mother, F = father, Z = sister, B = brother, D = daughter, S = son, H = husband, and W = wife. Using combinations of these symbols anthropologists can describe all kin relations in any kinship system.

research in African-American urban families (1975) and Rhoda Halperin's study of rural Kentuckians (1990) demonstrate that low-income people and people living in rural areas tend to maintain large networks of kin, which diversifies and widens their possibilities of support in times of need. The very wealthy, meanwhile, can shelter their money in trusts distributed among their kin (Marcus, 1992). And they rely on each other for political support based on shared interests and goals.

Unilineal Descent

Unilineal descent has two principal forms: matrilineal and patrilineal (see Figures 8.2 and 8.3). Other variants, discussed later in this chapter, are far less common. In both forms, kinship is traced through descendants on one side only, either through the mother or the father. But they differ in the side through which descent is traced or whether a person may choose the side with which he or she wants to affiliate, or even whether both sides may be taken into account. In **matrilineal** societies, people reckon descent through their mothers. That is, a child belongs to the kinship group of his or her mother. In **patrilineal** societies, people reckon descent through their fathers, so that a child belongs to the kinship group of his or her father.

matrilineal
Descent system in which kinship group membership and inheritance pass through the female line.

patrilineal
Descent system in which kinship group membership and inheritance pass through the male line.

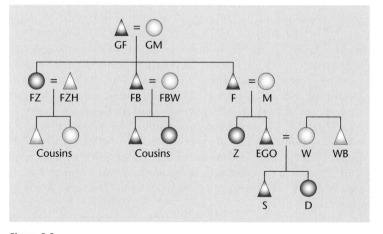

Figure 8.3
Patrilineal Descent. Brown circles and triangles are in ego's kin group.

? *If your kinship system were matrilineal, who would be in your kin group? Who would be your closest relatives if your kinship system were patrilineal?*

> **REVIEW**
>
> A kinship system consists of the beliefs and practices by which people regard and treat each other as relatives. The people may be genetically related (consanguines) or related by marriage (affines). As well, they may be unrelated, adopted, or fictive kin. Rules of descent stipulate the nature of kin relationships from one generation to another. Two ways that people trace their descent are bilateral descent (tracing relationships through both parents and both sets of their parents) and unilineal descent (tracing relationships through either the mother's kin or the father's kin). Bilateral descent groups are called kindreds.

MATRILINEAL AND PATRILINEAL SYSTEMS

Although in unilineal systems people belong to one particular line of descent, social bonds with people belonging to other kinship groups are also recognized. For example, in patrilineal systems, a child belongs to the father's kin group but still knows that he or she is also related to people on the mother's side. Nevertheless, people feel the strongest ties to members of their own group, in this case, the father's.

Prevalence of Matrilineal and Patrilineal Descent

Of known cultures whose kinship systems were organized on principles of unilineal descent, the great majority were patrilineal. Possibly only about 15 percent were matrilineal (Aberle, 1961:663). Matrilineal societies were concentrated among peoples whose economies were based on horticulture, especially those where women were responsible for the farmwork. Because women were the primary subsistence workers and helped one another with both child care and farmwork, they benefited from the existence of stable and cooperative units. Tracing descent through women in such societies stressed the communal and permanent bonds among women and between women and their children, especially their daughters. Most horticultural societies were patrilineal, however, even those that relied on women's labor.

The proportion of matrilineal societies was highest among horticulturalists of West Africa and Native North America (Aberle, 1961:665). Patrilineal societies were most prevalent among nomadic foragers and pastoralists, who rely on men's cooperative labor. Although subsistence plays an important role in shaping patterns of kinship, it is not sufficient to explain these patterns. Exceptions to patterns show that other cultural variables are involved.

Matrilineal and Patrilineal Societies Compared

A comparison of Figures 8.2 and 8.3 shows that the structure of matrilineal descent is the mirror image of the structure of patrilineal descent. In practice, however, there are several important differences between them, particularly in the kinds of bonds people maintain with their own kinship group after marriage. These differences stem from one main cause: In matrilineal societies, women bear their own lineal descendants; in patrilineal societies, women bear the lineal descendants of the men into whose group they marry.

In patrilineal systems, particularly those in which married couples live with the husband's family, women tend to leave their own kin group after marriage. Their separation is in part residential, because they usually move to their husband's household, and in part structural and psychological. The intensity of a woman's separation from her own kin group and incorporation into her husband's group varies among patrilineal cultures. Separation is strongest in societies where men control descent, inheritance, and social power. Such societies are said to be patriarchal. In patriarchal societies, women typically lose much contact with and support from their own relatives. **Patriarchy**—rule or dominance by men in social, economic, and political life—is not the same as patrilineality—descent traced through men. One term refers to power and the other to descent.

In contrast, in patrilineal societies with greater gender equality, women may maintain strong emotional bonds with their families, especially with parents and siblings,

patriarchy
Social system in which men occupy positions of social, economic, and political power from which women are excluded.

even if they change residence after marriage. For instance, among the Tewa of New Mexico, daughters leave their natal family when they marry, but emotional ties to their kin remain strong. Women continue to visit their relatives often, to participate in family rituals and other important events, and to take part in discussions about matters of communal interests. And, in times of conflict with her husband or in-laws, a woman can expect that her family will be her allies.

In patrilineal systems, it is in the interests of kin groups to establish secure marital ties, because it is through marriage that a patrilineal descent group obtains its children. That is, through marriage, a man is able to claim the children his wife bears. For this reason, divorce tends to be difficult to obtain. The couple's relatives may exert pressure on both husband and wife to remain in an unhappy union. Even where divorce is possible, some social criticism attaches to the couple after divorce, especially to the wife.

In parts of rural India that are strongly patriarchal, once a woman marries and moves to her husband's household, she cannot expect emotional or financial support from her birth family. Even if she becomes a victim of psychological or physical abuse by her husband or his relatives, her parents are unlikely to respond to her complaints. Parents also are unlikely to welcome a daughter who seeks divorce or tries to return home.

These conditions, common in patrilineal systems, are absent in matrilineal societies or appear in different form and function. Matrilineal kinship groups obtain new members (children) from women of their own group, so the marriage tie is often not as intense or secure. Divorce may be more easily obtained by either spouse and carries less social stigma, if any.

Although matrilineal societies have practices and attitudes that support women, none is matriarchal in the sense that some patrilineal societies are patriarchal. That is, there are no known examples of societies where descent, inheritance, and social and political power are controlled exclusively by women. There are no societies in which men's voices are silent and their interests are ignored. Issues of relationships between men and women in a society are discussed more fully in Chapter 10.

In matrilineal systems, especially where married couples reside with the wife's kin, men often have split loyalties. Their identification with and integration into their wife's household may be rather loose, particularly in the early years of marriage. Men often maintain strong emotional, economic, and ritual ties to their family of birth. They may function as representatives of their natal family to outsiders and may have important decision-making roles within it.

Influence and Inheritance in Unilineal Descent Groups

Matrilineal descent groups characteristically differ from patrilineal descent groups in several important ways (Schneider, 1961). For instance, matrilineal descent groups depend for their continuity and operation on retaining control over both male and female members. In contrast, women are peripheral members of their own patrilineal descent groups because they bear children for their husbands' group. In matrilineal systems, women give birth and care for future members of their own kin groups. Men retain interests in their descent groups through ties that are not completely severed when they marry. They may continue to have some control over resources allotted to their kin group. They may be required to give economic support to their mothers and especially to their sisters. And they may play a role in the upbringing of their sisters' children, who, by virtue of descent, are members of their kin group (their own children belong to the kinship group of their wives, the children's mothers).

For example, among the Trobriand Islanders of Melanesia, men are responsible for supplying their sisters (and their sisters' husbands) with yams (Weiner, 1976, 1988). Although yam gardens are tended by men, the "owner" of the produce is the man's sister. A man begins planting a yam garden for his daughter with the understanding that one of her brothers will take over the responsibility and continue to supply her and her family with yams after she marries. A man also assumes the role of authority

In Their Own Voices

Wedding Songs from North India

The poignancy of women's separation from their kin is vividly dramatized in North India at the moment of departure, when a newly married woman first leaves her natal home in the company of her husband and his male kin. Both men and women are apt to shed tears at the sight of the heavily veiled young woman being carried to a waiting vehicle. The women of the bride's village sing "departure songs" at the doorway. Many of these songs are commentaries on the fragile position of a woman in her husband's household and on her relationships with her blood relatives and her in-laws.

1. Refrain [bride's kin speaking]

   Dear girl, today you have left your father's house, today you have become "other".

   The streets in which you spent your childhood have today become "other".

   [Bride speaking]

   My grandfather cries, my grandmother cries, the whole family cries.

   My younger brother cries, your sister born from the same mother has left and gone away.

   [Verses are repeated with bride speaking, using different kin terms]

2. Two water pots are on my head

   A beautiful golden pendant is on my forehead.

   Call me back quickly, Mother.

   Beg with folded hands.

   My heart is not here in my husband's mother's house.

   My heart is not here with this foreign man.

   Call me back quickly, Mother.

   Beg with folded hands.

   My friends still played with dolls together.

   But I went off to my in-law's house.

   Call me back quickly, Mother.

   Beg with folded hands.

   [The first verse is repeated a number of times, changed only by the substitution of the names of other ornaments worn by married women.]

   _____

   From Gloria Goodwin Raheja and Ann Grodzins Gold, *Listen to the Heron's Words: Reimagining Gender and Kinship in North India.* Copyright © 1994 The Regents of the University of California. Reprinted by permission.

---

inheritance rules
Rules for the passage of land, wealth, and other property from one generation to the next.

and disciplinarian to his sisters' children rather than to his own, because it is his sisters' children who are members of his own matrilineal kin group.

Inheritance rules are strongly related to rules of descent. In societies with matrilineal descent, for example, resources and property are inherited through women. However, men may still control the allocation and disposition of resources, so that inheritance passes from one man to another within the matrilineal kin group. In such societies, the role of the mother's brother is enhanced, because inheritance passes from one's mother's brother to one's sister's son. For example, among the matrilineal peoples of the Pacific Northwest of North America, such as the Tlingit, resources that are owned by matrilineal kin groups and used by men pass from a man to his sister's son rather than to his own son.

Thus, matrilineal descent groups do not require the statuses of father and husband. Because of the matrilineal descent rule, children belong to the kin group of their mother. Women do not need to be married, and the identity of the father is not relevant to descent. In contrast, in patrilineal systems, the statuses of father and husband are critical in the determination of descent and the legitimacy of the offspring. Marriage is necessary for men because it is through marriage that a man as husband claims the status of father to his wife's children. And marriage is necessary for women in patrilineal systems because it is through marriage that a woman's child may claim membership in a kin group and thus be granted legitimacy.

The institutionalization of strong, lasting, intense ties between husband and wife is not compatible with the maintenance of matrilineal descent groups. In matrilineal societies, women's loyalties must remain primarily with their own kin group and not with their husband. Men's loyalties, on the other hand, are split between the kin group of their wife and children and the kin group of their own family of descent. Men

These Trobriand Islanders are sorting yams from a patch that their father planted for their sister. It is a brother's responsibility to supply his sister and her husband with yams.

often are needed by their own kin group to perform economic, ritual, and political functions, and thus must remain identified with and loyal to that group. In contrast, as noted earlier in this chapter, women in patrilineal societies may lose all or most attachments to their own kin group, and, once married, they no longer have economic obligations to their family of origin.

The matrilineal Diné of the American Southwest recognize a man's continuing bonds and responsibilities to his natal family, especially to his mother and sisters. His integration into his wife's household is gradual and limited. His role in decision making in his own household is only slowly recognized and remains limited in scope. In contrast, the patrilineal Yanomamo of the Amazonian rain forests of Brazil and Venezuela emphasize men's control over their own households, wives, and children.

The bonds that may develop between children and their father may compete with the authority of the children's matrilineal descent group. Thus, in matrilineal systems, fathers may develop strong, intense, and lasting emotional bonds with their children, but their authority over their children is usually weak. Instead, men in the mother's kinship group, especially the mother's brothers, tend to exert authority over the child. The Diné and the Trobriand Islanders exemplify this pattern. In both groups, men are affectionate toward their own children but are not authority figures for them.

In matrilineal descent groups, the emotional investment of the father in his own children is a source of strain because he owes his primary allegiance to the children of his own kin group, namely, his sister's children. And in patrilineal descent groups, emotional ties between the mother and her children may be a source of strain. Because of children's early bonds with their mothers and a mother's affection for her children, a child may not always identify with his or her father's group. Indeed, in strongly patrilineal societies, a mother and her children may form intense emotional ties as a buffer or refuge against the father's control. Nevertheless, these emotional ties do not directly threaten the father's dominant position as head of household.

In Japan, mothers encourage the development of strong, enduring emotional bonds, called amae, *with their children, especially their sons (Sofue, 1984). The son benefits from the emotional involvement and protection offered by his mother, and the mother benefits from the loyalty of her son. Each can call on the emotional support of the other when in conflict with an authoritarian father.*

Table 8.1 A COMPARISON OF CULTURAL CHARACTERISTICS IN MATRILINEAL AND PATRILINEAL DESCENT

	Continuity	Status of Father and Husband	Strength of Marital Bond	Male Authority	Father-Child Relationship	Kin-Group Relationship
Matrilineal Descent Groups	Women bear their own descendants and are crucial members of their descent group.	Not required.	Weak	Weak in marital household, often strong in sister's household.	Strong emotional bond, little authority.	Father's kin group retains important ceremonial functions.
Patrilineal Descent Groups	Women bear their husbands' descendants and are secondary members of their own descent group.	Required for legitimacy of offspring.	Strong	Strong in marital household.	Great authority.	Mother's kin group relinquishes attachments and obligations.

In matrilineal societies, strong bonds between fathers and their children might threaten the mother's authority and the important position of other men in the children's matrilineal descent group. Men and women in the father's kinship group also play important roles, however. Among the Zuni of the American Southwest, for example, a baby's father's mother performs critical birth ceremonies honoring and protecting the child (Gill, 1982). Immediately after a baby is born, its paternal grandmother comes to the home and recites protective prayers. She then bathes the baby, rubs ashes on its body, and remains with the mother and child for eight days. At sunrise on the eighth day, after washing the baby's head and sprinkling it with cornmeal, she takes the baby out to greet the rising sun, again reciting protective prayers.

Women also play an important role in funerals. At the end of life, the sister of a deceased's father has the responsibility of preparing the body for burial. She bathes the body, rubs cornmeal on it, and dresses it in new clothes, thus preparing the deceased for the journey to the afterworld.

The ritual participation of men's relatives dramatizes the connections between people and their paternal kin in a matrilineal system. Table 8.1 compares matrilineal and patrilineal descent groups in terms of the cultural and relational characteristics discussed in this section.

double descent
Kinship principle in which people belong to kinship groups of both their mother and father.

parallel descent
Kinship principle in which descent and inheritance follow gender-linked lines so that men consider themselves descended from their fathers and women consider themselves descended from their mothers.

Other Forms of Unilineal Descent

While most societies with unilineal descent trace kinship through either matrilineal or patrilineal principles, some societies reckon descent according to both patrilineal and matrilineal principles. In this system, called **double descent,** people belong to kinship groups of both mother and father. Some kinds of property might be inherited along matrilineal lines and other kinds patrilineally. For example, the Yako of eastern Nigeria have a double descent system in which property is divided into patrilineal and matrilineal ownership (Fox, 1984:135). Patrilineal descent groups own farmland and grazing pastures while matrilineal descent groups own cattle and other livestock. People inherit these two different kinds of resources, one permanent and inalienable and the other consumable, from each of their parents.

The Inca of Peru had a system of **parallel descent,** in which descent and inheritance followed gender-linked lines, so that men considered themselves descended from their fathers, and women considered themselves descended from their mothers (Silverblatt,

1987). Inheritance of property and rights to use land typically followed these parallel lines as well. That is, men inherited from their fathers; women inherited from their mothers. Parallel descent and inheritance created strong gender identity and solidarity. Principles of parallel descent made sibling bonds important in kinship unity. Inheritance could flow through men from a mother's brother to sister's son and through women from a father's sister to brother's daughter.

Finally, some peoples have systems of **ambilineal descent,** in which individuals may choose to affiliate with either their mother's kinship group or with their father's group. Each person makes this decision based on a strategic consideration of the territory, wealth, and social prestige of each group he or she is eligible to join. In societies of the South Pacific where such systems operate, a person can affiliate only with one group during his or her lifetime, but the person's offspring may choose a different affiliation. In societies with ambilineal descent, as in the Pacific Northwest of North America, a person could make claims to be a member of multiple descent groups. For example, among the Kwakwaka'wakw (or Kwakiutl) of British Columbia, people could inherit material and ceremonial wealth, as well as access to food resource sites, through claims to multiple kin groups.

> ## REVIEW
>
> Unilineal descent rules include matrilineal (reckoned through one's mother's line), patrilineal (reckoned through one's father's line), ambilineal (reckoned through either parent's line), parallel descent (reckoned by women through their mothers and by men through their fathers), and double descent (reckoned through both one's mother's line and one's father's line). A patriarchy is any society, especially one organized by patrilineal descent, in which men have dominant power and authority. Inheritance rules generally follow principles of descent. For instance, in societies with patrilineal descent, men hold wealth and when they die pass it to their sons.

UNILINEAL DESCENT GROUPS

Unilineal descent systems usually organize people into more structured groupings than are formed by bilateral descent rules. Four kinds of unilineal descent groupings are lineages, clans, phratries, and moieties. Some cultures have all four types; others have only one or two. All have in common a focus on lineal descent, following either the mother's or the father's line, so that the specific descent group may be a matrilineage or patrilineage, or a matriclan or patriclan, respectively.

In some cultures, lineages and clans have corporate functions, owning or controlling land and resources in common. Lineages and clans have continuity independently of their specific membership at any one time. Their structures and functions are perpetual, and their membership is continually replenished with the births of new members. Lineages and clans also usually regulate marriage, favoring some unions or forbidding others between members of the same or related groups. Other social functions of unilinear kin groups vary from culture to culture, such as making communal decisions, settling disputes, selecting leaders, and performing ritual obligations.

Lineages

The smallest kinship unit is a **lineage,** or a set of relatives tracing descent from a known common ancestor. In a matrilineal system, a matrilineage may consist of a female ancestor, her sons and daughters, her daughters' children, and her daughters' daughters' children. A patrilineage may consist of a male ancestor, his sons and daughters, his sons' children, and his sons' sons' children. The depth of lineages varies in different cultures. In some societies, people know the names of their lineage members for only a few generations, whereas in other societies lineages may have a known depth of nine or more generations. In some West African societies the names and deeds of lineage members are memorized and passed on by word of mouth from generation to generation, in some cases covering 200 years or more. Written records create greater time depth. The Old Testament of the Bible, for example, contains a chronology of ancient patrilineages.

ambilineal descent
Principle of descent in which individuals may choose to affiliate with either their mother's or their father's kinship group.

lineage
A set of relatives tracing descent from a known common ancestor.

? *What do you know about the history of your descent group? How is this knowledge preserved?*

exogamy
Marriage principle in which people cannot marry members of their own lineage or clan but instead must forge alliances with members of other groups.

endogamy
Marriage principle in which people marry members of their own group.

parallel cousin
A child of one's mother's sister or of one's father's brother.

cross-cousin
A child of one's mother's brother or of one's father's sister.

clans
Named groups of people who believe that they are relatives even though they may not be able to trace their actual relationships with all members of their group.

matriclans
Clans formed through descent and inheritance from women of their group.

? *Does your kinship system distinguish between cross-cousins and parallel cousins?*

Among the Kwakwaka'wakw of British Columbia, lineages are named groupings that control access to resource sites such as ocean coastline, salmon streams, berry patches, and other foraging locations. Lineages also own ceremonial objects such as masks and crests and sacred songs and dances. Each lineage has a founder shrouded in myth and a story of origin from an animal ancestor. Although membership in a lineage follows principles of descent, individuals can choose to affiliate with the group of their mother, father, or one of their grandparents. In the past, choices were made as they might best advance a person's social position. So, for instance, if one's maternal grandfather were a renowned chief, a person would choose to affiliate with his lineage. This is an example of the way that people can manipulate their positions in systems with ambilineal descent.

Siblings belong to the same patrilineage or matrilineage, depending on the descent rule in effect. New lineages are formed after the death of the senior parent. At that time, surviving sons in patrilineal systems and surviving daughters in matrilineal systems establish themselves as the heads of new groups. In societies where seniority contributes to one's social standing and prestige, sibling order determines the relative status of each new lineage. That is, an individual who is a member of the lineage of an elder son has higher status than an individual who is a member of the lineage of a younger son.

Exogamy and Endogamy

As mentioned previously, in some societies lineages have corporate functions. That is, they hold land in common, apportioning land and resources to member households. They may have formal procedures for selecting leaders and settling disputes among members or with members of other lineages. And they regulate marriage, forbidding unions between certain members. Most unilineal kin groups practice **exogamy,** or marrying out. In exogamy, people cannot marry members of their own lineage or clan but must forge alliances with members of other groups. Lineages and clans are usually exogamous.

A less common marriage rule is **endogamy,** or marrying in, as, for example, in parallel cousin marriage. A **parallel cousin** is one's mother's sister's child or one's father's brother's child. In parallel cousin marriage, one of these sets of children would be one's preferred marriage partners—the mother's sister's children in a matrilineage and the father's brother's children in a patrilineage. Parallel cousin marriage is prevalent among Middle Eastern Arab societies with patrilineal descent. In patrilineal systems, brothers belong to the same patrilineage or patriclan, and descent is traced through men. Thus, through the endogamy rule, it is desirable for the children of brothers to marry. This "patrilateral" parallel cousin marriage conserves wealth within the patriclan. Thus, land, wealth, and resources stay within the kinship group rather than being dissipated or fragmented through inheritance among a wider group of claimants. Endogamous marriage patterns also solidify and strengthen bonds between brothers and avert conflicts over inheritance.

The opposite of a parallel cousin is a **cross-cousin:** one's mother's brother's child or one's father's sister's child. In cross-cousin marriage, these children would be preferred as one's marriage partners. As in parallel cousin marriage, this form of endogamy functions to strengthen a unilineal descent group and to concentrate resources within it. Figure 8.4 shows the types of cousins. Notice that cross-cousins are related through opposite-sex siblings (father's sister, mother's brother), whereas parallel cousins are related through same-sex siblings (father's brother, mother's sister).

Clans

Many cultures with unilineal descent organize their members into clans. **Clans** are named groups of people who believe that they are relatives, although they may not be able to trace all the actual relationships with clan members. Clans differ from lineages in this feature. That is, members of lineages can trace their exact relationship to all other members of the same lineage, but members of clans, which are much larger kin groups, can trace relationships only to close relatives.

Clans recruit new members through the birth of children. **Matriclans** obtain new members from women of their group (a child belongs to the clan of its mother),

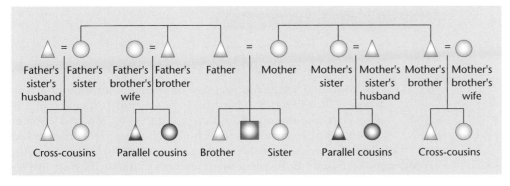

Figure 8.4
Distinctions between Parallel and Cross-Cousins.

whereas **patriclans** recruit new members from men of their group (a child belongs to the clan of its father). Depending on the size of a society, clan size may range from several hundred members to many thousands. Although clan members cannot know all their relatives, because clans are named groups members can always determine if a stranger is related to them by asking the person to identify his or her clan.

The conventions for naming clans vary cross-culturally. In some societies, clans are named after animals or plants; in others, they are named for locations. Where clans are named after animals, people often have beliefs about some mythic connection between the originators of the clan and the animal for which they are named. The origin myth might describe how the clan animal saved the human ancestors from some calamity or mated with the human ancestor to found the clan.

In some societies, clans are totemic. A **totem** is an animal or plant with a special spiritual connection to the members of its clan. Ritual prohibitions, or taboos, mark the relationship between clan animals and members of the kinship group. For example, people may not hunt or eat the animal that is their totem. By observing taboos, people express their respect for their ancestors. Totems also identify people in terms of their eligibility for marriage. In societies with clan exogamy, for example, two people with the same totem would not be allowed to marry.

Thus, clans, like lineages, not only establish and organize relatives but also regulate social relations, especially marriage. Clans usually are exogamous, that is, a person cannot marry someone belonging to his or her own clan. Such a marriage would be

Australian Aborigines believe that in mythic times, called the Dreaming or Dreamtime, human ancestors rose out of the earth and had encounters with ancestral animals who protected them and endowed them with spiritual knowledge (Hume, 2000). As the people procreated and survived, they honored these relationships by naming themselves after their animal protectors.

Case study

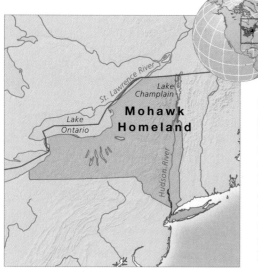

Iroquois Territory

Present-Day New York State

A Matrilineal Society: The Mohawks

The Mohawks were, and are, one of the member nations of the Iroquois Confederacy. Organized on kinship principles of lineage, clan, and moiety (Bonvillain, 2001:69–70), Mohawk descent is reckoned matrilineally so that children belong to the lineage and clan of their mothers. In former times (until about 200 years ago), residence was based on the ideal that members of a matrilineage live together. Therefore, a household typically consisted of an elder woman, her husband, their daughters and daughters' families, and the couple's unmarried sons. Each nuclear group of parents and children had its own quarters within a large house separated by bark partitions. Matrilineages had a depth of three or four generations, depending on the age of the eldest female member. If a woman survived to be elderly, she might live to have great-grandchildren and be the head of a lineage of four generations. In other cases, a lineage might have a three- or possibly even only a two-generation depth. The deeper the lineage, the more respected was its leading woman.

Mohawk society is divided into three matrilineal clans named after animals: Bear, Wolf, and Turtle. In former times, clans regulated marriage through rules for exogamy, stipulating that people could not marry members of their own clan. These rules created linkages between kinship groups through marriage alliances. Today, restrictions on marriage choices have largely been abandoned. However, Mohawks who want their marriage ceremony performed in the indigenous Iroquois religion now known as the Longhouse Religion must belong to different clans.

Mohawk clans controlled and distributed farmland to their members. Land was held in common but was allocated and farmed by lineages working collectively. Land was said to be owned by the leading woman of the matrilineage, not as her personal property but as collective control. Women in the household were given portions of land that they planted and harvested. Finally, clans owned the large communal houses in which their members lived. Today, the corporate functions of clans have disappeared and they no longer own land in common. Instead, due to the changes in Mohawk culture as a result of European and American influences, land is owned individually. And most households consist of parents and children, although some grandparents may reside with the basic family group. The collective labor of clan relatives has been largely replaced by private property and individual economic pursuits.

Mohawk clans continue to have leaders, both women and men. Leading clan women, now usually referred to as clan mothers, are chosen informally through public recognition of their intelligence, sound advice, and personal charisma. They lead by example and play a central role in protecting Mohawk lands, culture, and language. Clan mothers select the men who serve as clan chiefs. The women make their choices based on a man's intelligence, good judgment, even temper, and charisma. Clan chiefs represent their groups in community meetings and at meetings with representatives from the other Iroquois nations.

Clan mothers nominated men of their clan to function as chiefs. The chiefs attended councils to discuss and make decisions about issues of importance to their communities. Clan mothers continued to give advice to the chiefs and could depose chiefs who lost public support. Clan mothers are influential members of their communities today.

The Mohawk nation is divided into two moieties. The Wolf and Turtle clans form one moiety and the Bear clan is the other. Like clans, moieties were formerly exogamous. Today, as in the past, moieties have mainly ceremonial functions, the most important of which is to prepare and conduct funerals for members of the opposite group. This custom reflects the Mohawk belief that people from the deceased's clan or moiety are too overcome by grief to be able to conduct a proper rite. Viewed as a feature of social structure, the reciprocal exchange of funerary duties symbolizes and enacts the mutual interdependence and unity of all members of the Mohawk nation.

considered incestuous. Marriage rules may also preclude people from marrying into the clan of either parent. For example, according to marriage restrictions among the matrilineal Diné, a person cannot marry someone of his or her own clan or father's clan, even though by rules of matrilineal descent people are not members of their fathers' groups. An even wider proscription bars people from marrying anyone whose father is a member of one's own father's clan. These rules may be a reflection of an early Diné pattern of bilateral descent that prevailed before their arrival in the Southwest and the change from a nomadic foraging society to one based on semisedentary farming. According to bilateral principles, one's mother's and one's father's relatives are treated the same.

The Diné talk about clan relations by saying that a person is "born in" or "born to" his or her mother's clan and "born for" his or her father's clan. Therefore, two people who are "born for" the same clan are not permitted to marry. According to the Diné view, such a marriage would be incestuous. The importance of Diné clan membership is also reflected in the etiquette of self-introductions. When introducing themselves to another person, the Diné first identify their mother's clan and then mention their father's clan. These identifications precede a statement of one's personal name. This practice reflects the importance of situating oneself within a network of kin. Kinship relationships are the most critical influences on one's social being.

In addition to social features, clans often have corporate functions. In some societies, these functions may be similar to those of lineages, whereas in others, they may be more highly structured and formalized. Clan members may hold land in common, apportioning fields or resource sites to their members individually or by household. Clan-held territory can be periodically reapportioned to adjust to changes in resources as well as to changes in the size of households.

? *Does your descent group have corporate functions?*

Clans usually have structured means of decision making and problem solving. They have recognized leaders who may be informally selected by public opinion and consensus or formally chosen by representatives of households or lineages. Such leaders have various functions in different societies. In some, they may serve as spokespersons for their clan when interacting with similarly structured groups. They may meet with leaders of other clans to make decisions that affect the whole community, to resolve interclan disputes, and to act as a unified body when dealing with outsiders. Clan leaders may also adopt strategies to help foster community cohesion and cooperation by exhorting members to behave properly and to help one another.

Among the matrilineal Iroquois nations of New York State (the Mohawks, Oneidas, Onondagas, Cayugas, Senecas, and Tuscaroras), chiefs were chosen to represent their clans on the basis of their intelligence, generosity, even temper, and other desirable personality traits. The men were selected by leading women of matrilineages within the clans. The chiefs represented their clans in village councils that debated issues of common interest. They made decisions, or at least recommendations, that affected their members. They helped settle disputes between their members and members of different clans. Clan chiefs also represented their groups in intertribal meetings, calling together all of the nations in the Iroquois Confederacy. In that body, issues of trade, intertribal relations, and war and peace were discussed and decided.

In some societies, clans and lineages are organized in a complex hierarchical structure in which different levels of the hierarchy have different social or political

Case study

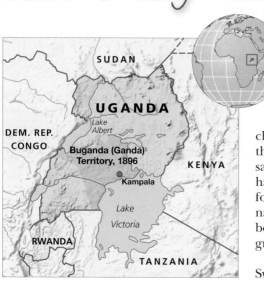

A Patrilineal Society: The Ganda of Uganda

The Ganda are a horticultural people who live in small villages in Uganda. Each village has between thirty and eighty homesteads. Homesteads contain several huts and yards in between huts are used for socializing and tending domesticated animals, especially chickens and goats. Most households consist of husband and wife, although some men have more than one wife. Co-wives usually reside in the same household, each having her own bedroom, but women sometimes have separate huts within the homesteads. Some men establish residences for their several wives in separate villages. In any case, women leave their natal village when they marry to live with their husband. The marital bond tends to be somewhat unstable today, although in the past, men had greater authority and control over their wives (Southwold, 1965:105).

The people's principal subsistence crop is bananas or plaintains. Sweet potatoes, yams, peanuts, and a variety of leafy vegetables, roots, and fruits are also grown. Men clear the fields for planting when needed, but women do most of the subsistence farmwork. In the past, men hunted and fished to supplement the diet, but today men grow cash crops, especially cotton and coffee.

Ganda society is organized around membership in clans and lineages. Descent is patrilineal, so children belong to the lineage and clan of their father. Clans are exogamous, husband and wife belonging to different kinship groups. There currently are forty-eight named clans, derived from an original six clans of mythic times (Southwold, 1965:95). Each clan is composed of several lineages, organized in a hierarchy of segments, or "segmentary lineages." Among the Ganda, there are four levels of segmentary organization: a clan, a segment of a clan is called a *ssiga*, a segment of a *ssiga* is called *mutuba*, and a segment of a *mutuba*, the smallest segment, is called *lunyiriri*.

In daily life, one's patrilineal kin are prominent in social interactions and share economic and personal responsibilities toward one another. People secure rights to use land and plant their gardens on the basis of membership in patrilineal clans. Men obtain these rights through descent from their fathers. Women obtain rights to gardens through marriage. That is, a woman plants her crops on her husband's land. After marriage, a man chooses his place of residence from among the villages in which he has rights through patrilineal affiliation, selecting acreage in clan-controlled territory.

Men prefer to marry women from villages other than their own in order to expand their network of relatives and allies. They also prefer not to live in either their father's village or in their wife's father's village but, rather, to make a new homestead near more distant kin (Southwold, 1965:96). Ganda men wish to establish their independence from their fathers and also to avoid conflict with their brothers. Ties to other male relatives provide men with the aid and allegiance they expect from kin. Families may move to new villages periodically as their needs or inclinations change.

Ganda clans have a number of corporate functions. Each clan and lineage has a leader who is responsible for administering his group. He is assisted by a council made up of the heads of subordinate lineage segments. They settle disputes after hearing testimony from both sides. Decisions made by councils can be appealed to the council of the next higher segment in the lineage and clan hierarchy. In the past, final appeals could be made to the highest authority or king, called *kabaka*. After independence from Great Britain, leaders of the republic appointed the *kabaka* of the largest ethnic group—the Buganda—as the constitutional monarch of the new state of Uganda.

The corporate nature of clans is demonstrated in formal obligations that each clan owed to the *kabaka*, or hereditary king. For example, clan members supplied bark cloth to the *kabaka* and herded his cattle. They also performed services for the *kabaka*'s mother, a person of great authority and prestige in her own right. And each clan provided boys to serve in the king's household. Today the king's power has diminished.

Clan councils and clan members are responsible for supervising the activities of their group. If anyone commits an offense, it is up to the clan to settle disputes and punish their members if judged to be in the wrong. In the past, a clan could also suffer collective punishment if one of their chiefs committed an offense against the *kabaka*. In such cases, the *kabaka* might order the execution of all clan members.

In addition to their administrative role, clans and lineage segments own land in common. Each clan has an allotted territory in which its members have a right to live. Prominent members also have a right to be buried in clan territory. Residence on clan land is complicated by the fact that each clan owns territory in several areas. People, therefore, may make diverse claims to residential land, adjusting their needs to available acreage. People also base their decisions on the qualifications of political leaders who control each territory, choosing to affiliate where they might seek an advantage. Personal and political allegiance, then, contributes to settlement patterns as much as kinship connections do (Southwold, 1965:102).

In earlier times, clans controlled the distribution and inheritance of movable property from a deceased male clansman to his successor. The successor was formally chosen and ceremonially installed, taking the place of the deceased in kinship networks. He adopted the deceased's name and was called by kin terms appropriate to the deceased. And he received most of the dead man's property. Succession was inherited through kinship, but a man's eldest son was not eligible. In fact, there was a preference to bypass a man's sons altogether and instead choose a more distant patrilineal relative. This preferential pattern had the effect of dispersing kinship ties and creating linkages with more distant relatives, broadening one's alliances. The traditional rules of succession were changed in the late nineteenth century so that a man's son could succeed him. Today, father to son inheritance is preferred. Clan power has been reduced by the practice of making wills setting out one's wishes for the inheritance of one's property. Still, clan leaders influence the process through their high prestige.

Collective principles underlying clan organization include the obligation to be hospitable to all members of one's clan. Men who move to new villages could expect to receive banana shoots from their resident clansmen in order to start their gardens. People are expected to be helpful to clansmen in economic difficulty or to help pay a fine for some offense that a clansman committed. Similarly, clansmen had the obligation of avenging an injured or murdered member of their group. Thus, despite many changes in the postcolonial era, clan membership remains fundamental in defining one's identity, organizing social relations, restricting marriage choices, and promoting ethics of hospitality and collective responsibility.

functions. Several peoples in Sudan, for instance, were organized into clans composed of **segmentary lineages** hierarchically ranked according to the number of generations they encompassed. The Nuer, for example, were organized into about twenty patrilineal clans (Evans-Pritchard, 1955; Sahlins, 1961). Each clan was subdivided into four levels of lineage segments. The first subdivision was into large units, called maximal lineages. Each maximal lineage was segmented into smaller groups, called major lineages, and these were divided into still smaller groups, called minor lineages. Finally, the smallest segment, referred to as a minimal lineage, consisted of a group of relatives descended from a common great-grandfather or great-great-grandfather. In other words, a minimal lineage had a depth of four or five generations. Members of these smallest segments interacted frequently, lived near one another, and shared resources in times of need. Seniority in a lineage conferred influence and prestige. Lineage segments could temporarily become allies in times of conflict, but there was no established leadership beyond the smallest lineage and no permanent structure that united them. However, when disputes arose, the parties concerned could appeal for support to members of structurally similar units in wider and wider networks. Therefore, the segmentary system was a flexible solution to the problem of resolving disputes within and between the twenty clans.

segmentary lineages
Lineages organized in a hierarchical structure, ranked according to the number of generations they encompass.

phratries
Groups of linked clans that are usually exogamous.

moieties
Groups of linked clans that divide a society into two halves, usually exogamous.

avoidance relationships
Patterns of behavior between certain sets of kin that demonstrate respect and social distance.

Phratries and Moieties

Clans may combine to form larger organized kinship units, such as phratries and moieties. **Phratries** are groups of linked clans that usually are exogamous: in a phratry, a person cannot marry someone belonging to a clan associated with his or her own clan. The phratry may or may not be named. Unlike clans, phratries rarely have corporate functions. In a phratry system, there are always three or more linked groups.

Like phratries, **moieties** are groups of linked clans, but they differ in that there are only two of them. A moiety system divides a society into two halves (*moiety* comes from the French word meaning "half"). Thus, in such a system, all clans are apportioned into two groups. Like clans and phratries, moieties are usually exogamous, although in some cultures people can marry within their moiety even though they cannot marry within their clan. Moieties generally are named groups. They may or may not have corporate functions such as owning land, resource sites, and other property communally. In some societies, moieties may have ceremonial functions.

> ### REVIEW
>
> Four levels of descent organization are lineages (relatives who trace descent from a known common ancestor), clans (groups of people who believe but do not know that they are relatives), phratries (groups of linked exogamous clans), and moieties (two groups of linked clans that divide the society). Depending on the unilineal descent rule in effect, a lineage may be a matrilineage or a patrilineage, and a clan may be a matriclan or a patriclan. Segmentary lineages are subdivisions of lineages that are hierarchically ranked. Most unilineal kin groups practice exogamy, or marrying outside of one's lineage or clan, which broadens kin ties. Clan membership and marriage eligibility often are defined through the use of totems and taboos. Forms of endogamy, or marrying in, are parallel cousin marriage (one's mother's sister's children or one's father's brother's children are preferred marriage partners) and cross-cousin marriage (one's mother's brother's children and father's sister's children are preferred). Endogamy keeps resources within a kin group rather than broadening kin ties.

PATTERNS OF RELATIONSHIPS

In addition to establishing structured groupings of relatives, kinship systems also define and enforce expected behaviors among kin. Members of every society share ideas about appropriate attitudes and actions between any set of individuals, especially relatives. For example, we may be taught to be respectful of our elders and gentle with younger siblings. We learn how to behave with our relatives, what to say to them, and what not to say to them. We learn our rights with respect to them, and we learn what obligations we owe them. We learn that toward some relatives we must behave with respect, deference, and obedience, whereas we can exert influence and authority over others. With some relatives, we learn to comply with their wishes and in other ways acknowledge their dominance. With others, we may joke, tease, and act informally.

As with other social rules, or norms, there is great cross-cultural variation in the types of behaviors prescribed between relatives, and there may be variation within a society as well. Factors of gender, age, and class may have an effect on people's attitudes and actions. The more homogeneous a society is, the more likely people will agree about appropriate behavior, whereas in heterogeneous, or pluralistic, societies, there may be less consensus. Still, we can recognize general social values even if we as individuals do not behave in accordance with them.

Two common patterns that anthropologists observe in many cultures are avoidance relationships and joking relationships. Some societies focus on relationships of avoidance or respect. Gary Witherspoon (1972), writing about the Diné, also refers to this behavior as "bashfulness." In some societies, **avoidance relationships** characterize the relationship between parents-in-law and their sons-in-law or daughters-in-law. For example, among the Diné, a man does not speak directly to his mother-in-law and avoids being alone with her. If he needs to make a request of her, he asks his wife to intercede on his behalf. He defers to his mother-in-law, complies with her wishes and requests, and makes himself helpful and cooperative.

GLOBALIZATION

Within the past century, the economies of preindustrial peoples worldwide changed from subsistence activities to wage work, and the production of food and goods for cash and export to national and international markets. How have these changes transformed people's kinship behavior and relationships?

This kind of behavior is fairly common between men and their mothers-in-law in matrilineal societies. In such societies, men usually leave their natal homes when they marry and take up residence with or near their wife's kin. Circumspect, deferential, and "bashful" behavior helps minimize potential conflict that may exist between a man and his mother-in-law in matrilocal households. A new husband does nothing that could be interpreted as a challenge to her authority or of anyone else in the household. After many years of a stable marriage, a husband's behavior may be modified and he may begin to assert himself more with his wife's relatives. Eventually, he may take on leadership roles in the household.

Avoidance and respectful behavior on the part of a daughter-in-law toward her father-in-law is especially expected in patrilineal societies, where the married couple lives with the husband's kin. In this situation, a daughter-in-law lives in a household dominated by her father-in-law. Here, too, avoidance behavior mitigates any potential conflict. Rarely would a daughter-in-law have authority in such a household, but rather the potential conflict might concern the emotional allegiance of her husband, their son. To avoid forcing the husband to choose sides between his parents and his wife, the wife acts with deference and respect. In strongly patriarchal societies, daughters-in-law are expected to be acutely aware of their subordinate status and act with extreme deference and obedience to their husbands' parents.

The pattern of **joking relationships** between certain sets of relatives involves reciprocal joking, teasing, and playfulness. Joking may take the form of flirtation, sexual innuendo, and even explicit sexual remarks. This type of behavior is found most commonly between certain kinds of cousins, as between cross-cousins in societies in which cross-cousin marriage is preferred. Joking behavior also may be common between an individual and his or her spouse's same-sex sibling. For example, a woman may joke with her husband's brother, and a man may joke with his wife's sister. In many cultures, these in-laws are potential spouses. They may be preferred marriage partners in the event of the death of one's own husband or wife. So, joking relationships between some types of relatives (cross-cousins, spouse's siblings) acknowledge the potential sexual or marital relationship that might be established between the individuals.

joking relationships
Patterns of behavior between certain sets of kin that involve reciprocal joking, teasing, and playfulness, sometimes taking the form of flirtation and sexual innuendo.

? *Do you have avoidance relationships and joking relationships among your kin?*

REVIEW

All societies identify specific behaviors as appropriate for specific sets of relatives. Two common patterns of relationship are avoidance relationships and joking relationships. In patrilineal societies, bashful behavior and avoidance are common for daughters-in-law toward their fathers-in-law, whereas in matrilineal societies, these are seen with sons-in-law toward their mothers-in-law. In some cultures, avoidance may also be prescribed for siblings. In some societies joking relationships are common among cross-cousins or spouse's siblings or others who may be potential sexual or marital partners.

PATTERNS OF CHANGE

One would think that the way we reckon our kin would be a permanent feature of our culture. As you have read, however, even kinship systems respond to changes in the way people make their living or adapt to their environment. One pattern of change, for example, involves shifts from matrilineal descent to other rules of descent, based on changes in men's and women's subsistence roles. Forces of cultural contact and change also bring about changes in the way people reckon their kin, identify their kin group, and interact with relatives.

When studying changes in kinship systems, we can see how sensitive these systems are as indicators of cultural transformation. Principles of kinship reckoning are consistent with other cultural practices. When behavior changes, kinship systems respond by altering the way that kin groups are organized. Changes may come from internal dynamics within a society as adjustments are made to environments and new ways of living are developed and transmitted. And they may come from external sources when societies come into contact with others, either learning and adopting new systems voluntarily or being forced to adapt to more powerful peoples.

Culture Change

CHEYENNE DESCENT

The Cheyenne currently reside on two reservations. The Northern Cheyenne live on one in Montana and the Southern Cheyenne on a reservation that they share with the Arapaho in Oklahoma. These lands are the last refuge of people with a complex history in North America. Examination of this history sheds light on the ways that changes in economic systems and adaptations to one's environment affect social life, even systems of descent (Eggan, 1966).

The Cheyenne originally lived in the woodlands surrounding the Great Lakes in what is now the state of Minnesota. By the middle of the seventeenth century, the Cheyenne were well established in fertile valleys along the upper Mississippi River west of Lake Michigan and Lake Superior. They were met in that region by the French explorer Sieur de La Salle in 1680. At that time, the Cheyenne were living in small villages with perhaps 200 or 300 residents. Their economy was based on foraging. Women gathered the wild rice that grew in abundance along the shores of lakes and in marshes near rivers and streams. They also gathered many other varieties of plants, tubers, fruits, and nuts. Men caught fish in nearby lakes and rivers, hunted deer and small animals in the dense woodlands, and caught large quantities of waterbirds.

Although documentary evidence is lacking, it is likely that their social systems revolved around families and kinship groups organized by principles of bilateral descent, consistent with the usual practice of foraging peoples in the northern woodlands. These patterns are adaptive for situations of resource flexibility and nomadic settlement patterns. Suggestive evidence also comes from related peoples of the region, speaking languages in the same Algonkian family, who reckon descent bilaterally.

The Cheyenne began to leave their region in the late seventeenth century because of conflict with eastern and northern neighbors who were being pushed westward by the increasing numbers of British and French traders and settlers in North America. Eventually, by the early 1700s, the Cheyenne settled in eastern North Dakota in the northern prairies. They arrived as foragers, hunting, fishing, and gathering wild foods. Soon, however, borrowing from other native peoples in the region, they began to grow some of their own crops, especially corn, beans, squash, and tobacco. Along with borrowing productive techniques from their neighbors, the Cheyenne adopted the descent systems of the nearby Mandans and Hidatsas. Like them, the Cheyenne began to trace descent through matrilineal kinship ties. According to this rule, children belonged to the kin group and clan of their mother. The Cheyenne also adopted preferences for residence with the wife's family after marriage, consistent with matrilineal descent.

The Cheyenne soon began to trade with French merchants who had opened a post in southern Manitoba, not far from Cheyenne territory. From there, the Cheyenne obtained manufactured goods in exchange for buffalo hides and deerskins. Then, sometime after 1750, the Cheyenne obtained horses from other native peoples, such as the Crow. The horses made an enormous difference in the Cheyenne economy, enabling people to travel far distances to hunt and trade and enabling them to more easily transport their possessions.

By the late 1700s, conditions on the prairies worsened. Native peoples from the east and mid-west were pushing into the central prairies because of increased pressure from Europeans and American colonists who were taking more and more land. As eastern peoples moved westward, they came into Cheyenne territory, competing for the natural resources of the region. By the early nineteenth century, the Cheyenne were building settlements west of the Missouri River on the plains of South Dakota. They spread west and south, expanding their territory to the Rocky Mountains. There, the Cheyenne established a way of life quite different from the one they left behind on the prairies. They no longer lived in permanent villages, but moved their camps several times each year. They no longer planted crops but instead they hunted animals, especially buffalo, and gathered wild plants. And they more fully exploited the advantages offered by horses for hunting on horseback and as beasts of burden (Jablow, 1950).

As a consequence of the changes in their economy and settlement patterns, Cheyenne social systems were also transformed. The people gradually abandoned their system of descent based on membership in matrilineal clans and began to trace descent through bilateral relations. As an adjustment to their new way of life, bilateral affiliation became adaptive in the context of increased mobility. The need to maximize alliances, to widen one's network of kin, and to be able to shift membership in local and territorial units led to the disappearance of matrilineal clans and the reemergence of bilateral descent.

Nevertheless, the Cheyenne continued to live in groups of households of families linked by relationships through women, and couples continued to reside with the wife's family after marriage. Each nuclear family resided in its own lodge, but groups related through women generally built their dwellings near one another. Such residential groupings often consisted of an elder couple, their unmarried children, married daughters, and the daughters' husbands and children. In addition to being a residential unit, the family grouping cooperated economically, sharing resources and foraging tasks. Men hunted together and provisioned the co-residential group. Most of the men working together were unmarried brothers still living with their parents or the brothers-in-law brought in after marriage to daughters of the group. Women worked with their sisters and daughters, gathering wild foods and sharing the responsibilities of cooking and child care.

One of the benefits of a bilateral system is that it allows for an emphasis on generations rather than on lines of descent. That is, whereas unilineal descent separates members of a generation according to their degrees of descent from specific ancestors, bilateral descent focuses on similarities among the members of each generation across lines of descent. The kinship terms that the Cheyenne used emphasized these generational relations, as well as the social equivalence of people. For example, kin terms made no distinction between siblings and cousins other than by relative age (Hoebel, 1978), and only elder siblings were distinguished by gender. Rather than referring only to a small set of relatives, the Cheyenne system extended the concept of family to many people.

> **REVIEW**
>
> Patterns of change in kinship systems are based on the functions of kin groups in relation to environmental adaptations. Foragers tend to develop bilateral descent rules, for example. Kinship also changes in response to cultural adaptations. For example, people may adopt the kinship system of another people with whom they come into contact.

KINSHIP TERMINOLOGY SYSTEMS

The Cheyenne called siblings and cousins by the same kin term, using separate terms only for elder brother and elder sister. Younger siblings of both sexes were called by the same term, a fact that further indicates the importance of seniority in Cheyenne society. Relatives in one's parents' generation were called by terms that distinguished between paternal and maternal relatives and between the genders. The same term was

The Cheyenne used a system of naming relatives called the Iroquois system, which focuses on the criteria of generation and age as distinguishing principles.

kinship terminology system
System of terms used to address and refer to relatives.

Iroquois system
Kin terms that emphasize the difference between one's parents' same-sex siblings and parents' opposite-sex siblings, classifying parallel cousins with one's own siblings.

Eskimo system
Kin terms making distinctions between the nuclear family and all other types of relatives and on gender.

used for one's father, father's brothers, and his male cousins, while another term was used for one's mother's brother and mother's male cousins. A parallel set of terms was used for female relatives. Grandparents were distinguished only by gender—one term for all the men and another for all the women. The terms used for one's children were extended to the children of one's same-sex siblings and cousins. So, for example, a woman used the same kin terms for her son and daughter and the children of her sisters and female cousins. A man used these terms for his son and daughter and for the children of his brothers and male cousins. A different set of names was used for children of one's opposite-sex siblings and cousins. On the generational level of one's grandchildren, all related children were called by the same term regardless of gender or relationship.

The Cheyenne pattern of naming kin is an example of a type of **kinship terminology system** known as the Iroquois system. There are six types of terminological systems, and all people worldwide have a system of kin terms that fits one of these types. Each type is named for the culture in which it was first described. Kinship terms are more than just words for people, however; they define types of relationships. The **Iroquois system,** for example, emphasizes the difference between one's parents' same-sex siblings (MZD, MZS, FBD, FBS) and parents' opposite-sex siblings (MBD, MBS, FZD, FZS). As Figure 8.5 shows, one's parents are classed with their siblings of the same sex, and parallel cousins are classed with one's own siblings. Separate names for cross-cousins identify them as potential marriage partners. Children of anyone whom one calls mother and father are called sister and brother.

The Eskimo and Hawaiian Systems

The Eskimo and Hawaiian types of kinship terminology systems make the least distinctions among kin. The **Eskimo system** focuses on distinctions between the nuclear family and all other types of relatives and on gender distinctions. This system is likely to be associated with bilateral descent and is prevalent in both modern industrial and foraging societies.

As Figure 8.6 shows, the Eskimo system has separate terms for mother, father, sister, and brother. Siblings of one's parents are distinguished by gender, but whether they are related through one's mother or one's father is ignored. Relatives of one's own generation outside of the nuclear family are all called by the same term: cousin. There are separate terms for one's own children and the children of one's siblings, based on gender: daughter, son; niece, nephew. And children of one's cousins are also called cousin, although some speakers may note different degrees of relationship.

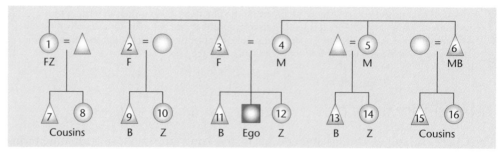

Figure 8.5
Iroquois Kinship System. According to the Iroquois system of kinship terminology, the father's brother (2) is called by the same term as the father (3); the mother's sister (5) is called by the same term as the mother (4); but the people numbered 1 and 6 have separate terms for themselves. Those people numbered 9–14 are all considered siblings, but 7, 8, 15, and 16 are cousins.

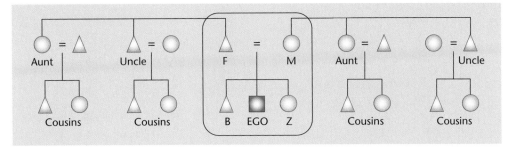

Figure 8.6
Eskimo Kinship System. The Eskimo system of kinship terminology emphasizes the nuclear family. Ego's father and mother are distinguished from ego's aunts and uncles, and siblings from cousins.

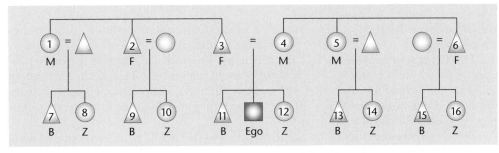

Figure 8.7
Hawaiian Kinship System. Ego calls the men numbered 2 and 6 by the same term as father (3) and the women numbered 1 and 5 by the same term as mother (4). All cousins of ego's own generation (7-16) are considered brothers and sisters.

The Eskimo system of terminology distinguishes among kin primarily by generation and gender. It highlights a distinction between the nuclear family and other relatives, but whether they are related through the mother or father is irrelevant. These terms are consistent with a social system that centers on the nuclear family as an independent, mobile, and potentially self-sustaining unit.

The **Hawaiian system,** in contrast, has even fewer terms than the Eskimo system, because it makes distinctions only of generation and gender. For this reason, it is sometimes referred to as a generational system. As Figure 8.7 shows, all male relatives of the parental generation are called father and all females are called mother. Similarly, all male relatives of one's own generation are called brother and all females of one's generation are called sister. Sons and daughters include one's children and the children of anyone that one calls brother or sister.

The Hawaiian system is found in many societies of the Pacific and among speakers of Malayo-Polynesian languages. It is often associated with ambilineal descent, in which people can choose to affiliate with the kinship group of either their mother or father. In the Hawaiian system, marriage with cousins is impossible because all cousins are classified as siblings.

The Crow, Omaha, and Sudanese Systems

The Crow system is similar to the Iroquois system for the parental generation (see Figure 8.5). That is, father and father's brother are called by the same term and mother's brother is named separately; similarly, mother and mother's sister are called by the same term and father's sister is named separately. As Figure 8.8 shows, parallel cousins are called by sibling terms.

The **Crow system** is used by some matrilineal peoples. Its key feature is that it extends the terms for father and father's sister to include cross-cousins on the paternal side—that is, the children of father's sister—and then continues the terms for father and father's sister in the female paternal line. Thus, the children of father's sister are

Hawaiian system
Kin terms making distinctions only of generation and gender.

Crow system
Kin terms used by some matrilineal peoples that extend the term for father and father's sister to include cross-cousins on the paternal side.

Omaha system
Kin terms used by some patrilineal peoples that extend the term for mother and mother's brother to include cross-cousins on the maternal side.

Sudanese system
Kin terms that give separate words for all kin relationships.

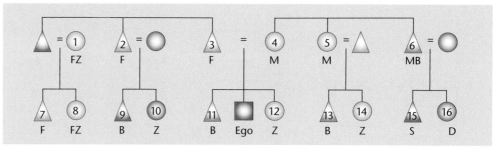

Figure 8.8
Crow Kinship System. The Crow system is obverse of the Omaha system. Those numbered 4 and 5 are merged under a single term, as are 2 and 3. Ego's parallel cousins (9, 10, 13, 14) are considered siblings, while the mother's brother's children are equated with the children of a male ego and his brother.

called father and father's sister. The effect of the Crow system is that it distinguishes descendants in the female line on one's father's side.

The Crow system also extends the terms for son and daughter to include cross-cousins on the maternal side, the children of mother's brother. That is, the children of one's mother's brother are called son and daughter. So, although one's cross-cousins are of the same biological generation as oneself, these relatives are given terms otherwise applied to one's own children.

The **Omaha system** follows the same principles as the Crow system except that it applies the generational skewing pattern to the descendants of mother's brother instead of father's sister. The Omaha system is found in some patrilineal societies where its purpose is to identify descendants of male members of the maternal side of the family.

Both the Crow and Omaha systems have a generational skewing pattern that focuses on lineal relatives not in one's own clan. So, in the matrilineal Crow system, it is the father's sister and her descendants who are singled out because these are the people in one's father's clan. Similarly, in the patrilineal Omaha system, it is the mother's brother and his descendants who are singled out because these are the people in one's mother's clan.

In the **Sudanese system,** which is rare, all kinship relationships are given separate terms. There are separate terms for members of the nuclear family, a distinctive word for mother's brother and another for father's brother, and separate words for mother's sister and for father's sister. Parallel cousins and cross-cousins are called by different terms. The Sudanese system allows individuals to negotiate their relationships with others and to affiliate with either side of their family, depending on their circumstances or personal inclinations.

Comparing Kin Terms in English and Seneca

Cross-cultural comparisons of categories of kin terms can sometimes reveal basic similarities and differences in worldview and experience. For example, people's social relations can be inferred from their kin terms (the words people use to identify relatives). North Americans generally use the following words for relatives: grandmother, grandfather, mother, father, aunt, uncle, sister, brother, cousin, daughter, son, niece, nephew, granddaughter, grandson. Analysis of these words reveals systematic meanings. First, North Americans distinguish between generations: grandmother/mother/daughter/granddaughter. Second, they note the sex of relatives: mother/father, sister/brother. Third, they distinguish between direct or lineal relatives and collateral relatives (those who may have a common ancestor but are not lineally related): mother/aunt, son/nephew. These three sets of contrasts—of generation, sex, and lineality—define the features of their kin that are meaningful to North Americans.

Other cultures may select other aspects of kinship relationships to emphasize, revealing different priorities through a different set of contrasts. For example, the Seneca name the following kinds of relatives, using an Iroquoian system of terminology (Lounsbury, 1964).

? *What organizing principles seem most important for Seneca kinship? How do those principles differ from those used in your kinship classification system?*

Anthropology Applied

LINKAGES Genealogy Projects

When doing ethnography in the field on any subject, cultural anthropologists gather kinship data for the people they are among. Then they link these data into a local genealogy. Anthropologists use this information to know who people are and how they relate to one another. As you have seen from reading this chapter, understanding a society's kinship system is also a key to understanding the way people organize their communities, subsistence activities, and leadership. Kin relations are the building blocks of human social organization. But what can ethnographic and historical genealogies of particular people tell us about what it takes to build self-sustaining human communities?

LINKAGES is an international network of researchers concerned with the long-term assessment of populations in relation to the impacts of economic development and culture change on those populations. These researchers create database sets of recorded kinship data and track long-term changes in those data. By doing so, the researchers hope to show how knowledge of kinship must be taken into account when planning social policy and economic change. In addition, the knowledge gained from large-scale, long-term comparisons of kin networks may help local communities to participate more effectively in changes that affect their lives and the sustainability of their cultural ecologies.

The data sets that LINKAGES maintains are diverse; among them are Alyawarra kin networks in Australia; kinship in the village of Tlaxcala, Mexico; genealogies of U.S. presidents; Muslim elites in an Indonesian village; Old Testament patriarchs; Mbuti Pygmies of the Ituri rain forest of Africa; genealogical censuses for many band societies; and many others (for example, !Kung of Africa, Chechu of India, Ainu of Japan, Vedda and Semang of Indonesia, Inuit of North America). Affiliates of LINKAGES around the world have established long-term field sites for tracking changes in kinship. Data are displayed in maps and graphs generated by special software, such as Large Network Analysis and Genealogical Information Manager. Studies on such a large scale have been made possible only though recent advances in computer technology and the Internet (http://eclectic.ss.uci.edu/linkages/).

CRITICAL THINKING QUESTIONS

What do you know about your families' genealogies? How far back do they go? How might information about long-term changes in your networks of kin contribute to LINKAGES's goals?

Seneca Kin Terms

Grandmother (and her sisters)
Grandfather (and his brothers)
Mother and mother's sister
Father and father's brother
Mother's brother
Father's sister
Older sister
Younger sister
Older brother

Younger brother
Cousin
Daughter
Son
Niece
Nephew
Granddaughter
Grandson

As in English, Seneca kinship classification is organized by generation and sex. Unlike English, the Seneca language uses separate terms for older and younger siblings. Seneca also treats what we call "aunts" and "uncles" differently. That is, a mother's sister and a father's sister are called by different names, as are a mother's brother and a father's brother. Furthermore, a mother's sister is given the same name as that for mother, and a father's brother is given the same name as father. As a result, some relatives whom we would call cousin actually fall into the categories of sister or brother:

Mother's sister's daughter = sister
Mother's sister's son = brother
Father's brother's daughter = sister
Father's brother's son = brother

Thus, a child of anyone called "mother" or "father" is called "sister" or "brother."

Differences in kinship terminology are not merely linguistic but reflect societal attitudes toward one's relatives. Individuals called by each kin term are understood to stand in particular social relationships and to have certain rights and obligations. The meanings of words, then, reflect one's social universe.

REVIEW

Kinship terminology system refers to how relatives are classified. It identifies a specific kind of relationship and the rights and obligations that that relationship entails. In the Eskimo system, which generally uses bilateral descent, the nuclear family is distinguished from other relatives. The Hawaiian system makes distinctions with gender and generation and is oftentimes associated with ambilineal descent. The Iroquois system distinguishes between one's parent's same-sex and different-sex siblings and also between parallel and cross-cousins. The Crow system, used in matrilineal societies, is similar to the Iroquois system except for the terminology referring to cousins. The Omaha system, found in patrilineal societies, is similar to the Crow system, with maternal cross-cousins called "mother" and "mother's brother" and paternal cross-cousins called "son" and "daughter." The Sudanese system is rare and unique in that every individual has a distinct term. Differences in kin terms reflect differences in people's social systems.

 Chapter Summary

Kinship Systems

- In every society, people have systems for tracing descent and organizing kinship groups to which they belong.

Bilateral Descent

- In many cultures, people consider themselves related to both their mother's and their father's families. In such systems of bilateral descent, the most significant kin group is that of the kindred, a loosely defined network of relatives who interact on a regular basis and acknowledge mutual rights and obligations to one another. Systems of bilateral descent are commonly found in many foraging societies as well as in modern industrial nations. Bilateral descent is adaptive in societies where mobility is a premium. In small-scale foraging societies, people are able to make claims in a wide network of kin in times of scarcity and need, whereas in modern industrial countries, people can loosen their kin ties in order to promote their economic independence.

Matrilineal and Patrilineal Descent

- The second major kinship system is one of unilineal descent. In this system, people acknowledge relationships on either their mother's (matrilineal) or their father's (patrilineal) side. Through unilineal descent, people form kin groups that restrict membership to particular people who can trace relationships through only either their mother or father. Unilineal descent is commonly found in farming and pastoral societies. Of the groups that can trace relationships through unilineal principles, about 15 percent are matrilineal and the remainder are patrilineal.

- A few societies have (or had) systems of double descent, in which people could belong to kinship groups of both their mother and father. And some had systems of parallel descent, in which men were considered descended from their fathers and women from their mothers. Finally, some peoples have systems of ambilineal descent, allowing them to affiliate with either their mother's or their father's kin group.

Unilineal Descent Groups

- Unilineal descent systems usually organize people into structured groupings of related people. The smallest such unit is a lineage, a specific set of relatives that trace descent from a known common ancestor. A matrilineage consists of a female ancestor, her children, her daughters' children, her daughters' daughters' children, and so on. A patrilineage consists of a male ancestor, his children, his son's children, his son's son's children, and so on.

- Many cultures with the unilineal descent organize their members into clans, named groups of people who believe they are relatives but cannot trace the actual relationship that they have with all members of their clan. Whereas members of lineages can prove their common descent from a specific ancestor, members of clans stipulate or claim relationship. In addition to establishing relationships, clans often regulate marriage by forbidding marital or sexual unions between their own members. Clans also often have some corporate functions: holding land in common and apportioning fields or resource sites to their members. They may have recognized chosen leaders who speak for their group. And they may have acknowledged methods of making decisions and settling disputes.

- In some societies, clans join together to form larger groups of related people. Phratries are groupings of linked clans that may or may not be named but serve primarily to regulate marriage by forbidding unions between members. Moieties are even larger groupings, dividing the society as a whole into two groups or halves. Typically, people cannot marry members of their own moiety. Moieties are usually named groups that may or may not have corporate functions, but some do control land, resource sites, and other property. And some have ceremonial functions as well.

Patterns of Relationships

- Kinship groups sometimes have preferences for the kind of marriage that their members may make. Clans are often exogamous, their members marrying people of other groups. Endogamy, in contrast, is a pattern of preference for marriage with a member of one's own group. In some societies, there are preferences for marrying particular types of cousins, either cross-cousins or parallel cousins. Marriage patterns tend to be consistent with other rules that organize social groups.

- Members of every society share ideas about attitudes and actions that are deemed appropriate between any set of relatives. In some societies, there are highly structured behaviors appropriate between certain relatives. At one end of the behavioral spectrum, some people are in a "joking" relationship, allowing them to tease each other and make critical or sexual remarks, while at the other end, people may be in an "avoidance" relationship, barring them from teasing or criticizing but instead encouraging them to be "bashful," avoiding eye contact, and refraining from speaking directly to or even being alone with a dominant person.

Patterns of Change

- Kinship changes as a result of changes in the environment affecting people's economic systems. Contact between people and the forces of globalization also cause people to change the way they reckon their descent and their rules for inheritance and kin relations.

Kinship Terminology Systems

- Kinship terminologies are words that people use to refer to and address their relatives. Worldwide there are a small number of such sets of terminologies. Anthropologists are keenly interested in kinship terms because they are more than just words. Rather, they are labels that symbolize relationships, including the rights and obligations that relatives have for one another. The kinds of systems used reveal the kinds of distinctions that people make, identifying some relatives as similar in status and relationship while distinguishing others.

Key Terms

kinship system 194	patriarchy 198	clans 204	kinship terminology
consanguines 194	inheritance rules 200	matriclans 204	system 214
affines 194	double descent 202	patriclans 205	Iroquois system 214
fictive kin 194	parallel descent 202	totem 205	Eskimo system 214
rules of descent 194	ambilineal descent 203	segmentary lineages 209	Hawaiian system 215
bilateral descent 195	lineage 203	phratries 210	Crow system 215
unilineal descent 195	exogamy 204	moieties 210	Omaha system 216
kindred 195	endogamy 204	avoidance	Sudanese system 216
matrilineal 197	parallel cousin 204	relationships 210	
patrilineal 197	cross-cousin 204	joking relationships 211	

Review Questions

1. What is bilateral descent? What are some cultural correlates of this descent rule in societies that practice it?

2. What are the two types of unilineal descent? With what kinds of societies is unilineal descent associated?

3. How would you compare and contrast the descent groups that are created by the application of descent rules? How are kindreds different from lineages?

4. What are the distinctions among lineages, clans, phratries, and moieties?

5. What patterns of relationships among kin group members do anthropologists observe?

6. How, and why, do kinship systems change?

7. What are the six methods of classifying relatives? What are the distinguishing characteristics of each?

8. How are kinship systems and rules of descent functionally interrelated with other social systems, such as the economic and political systems?

Marriage and the Family

Preview

1. **How do anthropologists define marriage and family?**
2. **What are the characteristics of nuclear families and extended families?**
3. **How do residency patterns relate to other aspects of a culture?**
4. **How do marriage rules extend kinship while observing incest taboos?**
5. **What are some theories about the origins of the incest taboo?**
6. **In what ways is marriage a rite of passage?**
7. **What are some social functions of marriage?**
8. **What forms of marriage are known to exist?**
9. **How is marriage a form of political alliance and economic exchange?**

A woman had an only son who became grown up and had not been married yet. She wanted to find him a bride, but he always told her, "Later, not now," and things like that. One day his mother said to him, "Listen, my son, I've grown old and become tired of household work. You must get married before I die."

He said to her, "Well! Find me a good girl from a good house."

She looked until she found him a girl from one of the most notable houses in their town and he married her.

When the wedding [party] was over and after seven days or so, he went back to his shop to work, while his mother stayed with his wife. "Listen, in this house [you] don't open what is closed or close what is opened, nor uncover what is covered or cover what is uncovered, nor unwrap what is wrapped or wrap what is unwrapped, nor unfold what is folded or fold what is unfolded. Do you understand?"

The girl, his wife, said, "Yes."

Days passed with things like that. His mother is everything in the house; his wife works all day while his mother orders her around. When the man returns home, his mother would set the dinner for him and if he would say "[Let us] call [his wife] to eat with me," his mother would answer him, "This can't be. She is still new in the house. She would get bold with us. Wait for a few more days."

After a few more days her son would say, "Let her come and eat with me."

His mother would say, "She hasn't been broken to our house yet. She does not need to eat for she has been eating all day."

He would say to his mother, "May God extend his grace upon us. Let her eat as much as she wants," and [he] used to eat only until he was half-full and leave some of the best food to his wife. His mother would hide it and would give her only hard bread and water.

The girl grew sicker and weaker by the day. Whenever her husband asked her, "What is the matter with you?" she would answer, "Nothing."

One day he said to one of his friends at the store, "By God, my wife is becoming sick. Every day she is getting thinner and paler. I am afraid she doesn't want me. Ever since she set foot in my house, she doesn't speak to me, and she is always sad."

His friend said to him, "I'll tell you what to do to see whether she wants you and wants to stay in your house, or whether she hates you and would like to return to her father's house. After dinner swear by God that she joins you and your mother for the coffee, then break wind. If she laughs at you, she doesn't care for you and you should send her back to her father's home. If she doesn't, then she is ill."

That same day after the man ate his supper and thanked his God, he said to his mother, "Call [his wife] to have coffee with us." He swore by God, and his mother *went to call her. As they were drinking their coffee, he broke wind. His mother laughed, but his wife didn't and kept on drinking until she finished her cup. . . .*

The following day he told his friend about what had happened. His friend said to him, "Your wife is hungry. Your mother is starving your wife."

He built a new house for his wife and moved out of the old one and got his mother a servant.

Excerpts from *Folktales Told around the World* by Richard Dorson, pp. 166–168. Copyright 1975. Reprinted by permission of the University of Chicago Press.

household
A group of people occupying a common dwelling.

This narrative from Iraq tells of the conflict and tensions between a new bride and her mother-in-law who live together in a household. In the story, the young husband is beset with divided loyalties. His respect for his mother is tempered by his concern for his wife. The wife, knowing her place, is obedient and deferential to the older woman. The narrative raises issues of power for women in patrilineal and patriarchal households. The mother tries to exert power over her daughter-in-law, but in the end she has less authority than her son because he is the man, the recognized head of the family. And in this story, the son chooses to protect his wife's interests and allies himself with her.

This Iraqi family unit was formed not only through rules of descent but also through marriage rules. The family unit at the household level consisted of a man, his widowed mother, his wife, any children borne by his wife, and the man's unmarried siblings. This chapter explores marriage and the family and how they interrelate with other elements of culture in a society.

Kinship systems and family arrangements are basic elements in all societies. They are among the topics of central concern in anthropology because they help structure people's daily lives and lay the foundations for the ways that individuals are integrated into their communities. But societies differ greatly in how families are formed, who constitutes a family, and what are the rights and obligations of family members toward one another. As we shall see, variations in family organization are not random but are consistent with economic and social needs. Thus, different types of families are preferred in different types of societies.

DEFINING MARRIAGE AND FAMILY

People are social beings. We live together in groups, work with others, and form emotional bonds with other people. Although at any given time in every society, there are some individuals who live alone, most people live with others during all or most of their lives. Most people who live together are members of families. In everyday speech, we use the word *family* casually to refer to our relatives without specifying how we are related to these people. Even anthropologists do not agree on a single or concise definition of family.

Anthropologists tend to make a distinction between family and household, although people often use the two words interchangeably. A **household** refers to a group of people occupying a common dwelling. The Iraqi man, his wife, and his mother are members of a household. The term *homestead* refers to multiple dwellings occupied by related and interacting people.

As you read in Chapter 8, members of families are related either through descent (consanguines) or marriage (affines). For example, one's grandparents, parents, aunts and uncles, siblings, children, and cousins are all consanguinal relatives, whereas one's spouse and all the people called in-laws are affinal relatives. North Americans differ in the ways they apply the word *family* to many of these relatives. Some people use the word to encompass all their relations, but others restrict the term to refer to close relatives with whom they interact regularly.

These roommates share a household. Unlike family households, roommates typically do not share all economic resources and have no expectations of mutual obligation or of an enduring relationship.

A useful starting definition of **family** is one given by anthropologist Kathleen Gough (1975:52). She defines the family as a "married couple or other group of adult kinfolk who co-operate economically and in the upbringing of children, and all or most of whom share a common dwelling." In this definition, a family is more than just a couple. Gough's definition includes several important features of family, stressing the cooperative links among members who share social and economic responsibilities. On this basis, the Iraqi man, his wife, and his mother constitute a family.

There are other definitions of family, however, and family members need not occupy the same household. Some members of polygynous families may occupy different households within an area. In addition, although marriage is the most common bond that creates families, marriage itself is not a required component of family. Heterosexual or gay couples who are not married also constitute families. And the single-parent family of parent and child is perhaps the smallest family unit (Fox, 1984).

Although issues of family composition, family life, and "family values" are controversial in the current climate of North American social and political discourse, the American Anthropological Association has taken a strong position supporting the legitimacy and viability of all family types. In its statement, issued in 2003, the association said,

> More than a century of anthropological research on households, kinship relationships, and families, across cultures and through time, provide no support for the view that either civilization or viable social orders depend upon marriage as an exclusively heterosexual institution. Rather, a vast array of family types can contribute to stable and humane societies.

The family is a basic unit of economic cooperation and stability. Members of families usually perform at least somewhat different economic tasks, a pattern that highlights the interdependent relationships among family members. And they pool all or at least some of their resources for the survival of the group.

The family serves social needs as well, providing members with companionship, emotional support, and assistance. And families function in the propagation and survival of society. They provide the context for biological reproduction and for the training and enculturation of children. Families function universally as vehicles for socialization of children, their own or adopted, into expected roles and goals. Children learn what is appropriate by observation of adults and by overt instruction and practice of skills for roles they will assume as adult women and men. In the context of their families, children learn their gender identity and their role in households and communities. Through observation of social relations between their parents or among all adults in their households, they learn whether men and women have equal rights to contribute to discussions and decision making. They also deduce social rights through the ways that conflicts are resolved. Girls and boys also learn whether they can expect emotional and economic support from their natal kin groups once they reach adulthood and form their own families.

In addition, families are decision-making groups. Members of families consult with each other, make decisions together, and may function as political units with others in their communities to establish and provide leadership. In some societies, positions of leadership are inherited within families. But everywhere, inheritance of property and the transmission of cultural knowledge take place within family units.

All societies contain units recognized as families, but there are differences in the ways in which families are formed. Throughout the world, most families are formed through marriage. *Marriage* is another word that we use casually with reference to a union between a man and a woman, but anthropologists have not

family
A married couple or other group of adult kinfolk who cooperate economically and in the upbringing of children, and all or most of whom share a common dwelling.

? *Based on your experience in your family, what are some specific expressions of the functions of the family as a social institution?*

These Mexican families are celebrating the Day of the Dead. In many cultures, households and families perform religious functions. Ceremonies celebrating family members at birth, puberty, marriage, and death may be organized and enacted on the basis of household units, with or without the participation of larger community groups.

? *What do you think might be some sources of disagreements about the definitions of marriage and family?*

settled on an uncontested definition of marriage. There is even some debate in the field about whether marriage and the family are universal constructs. Still, even if we accept that marriage is a recognized social status in most, if not all, cultures, there are differences in the ways that marriages are contracted and in the relationships between the spouses.

Marriage is generally understood as a socially recognized, enduring, stable bond between two people who each have certain rights and obligations toward one another. These rights and obligations vary from culture to culture, but are likely to include some common features. For example, married partners have the right to expect to have a sexual relationship with each other, although the number of partners may vary. In plural marriages, for example, a person may have more than one spouse. In most societies, husbands and wives have obligations to assist one another in the rearing of children and the provisioning of their household. They share economic resources and provide shelter, clothing, and household equipment. And marriage establishes bonds between groups of kin (the wife's relatives and the husband's relatives), who also have rights and obligations toward each other.

It is through marriage that men and their kinship groups may claim rights to children. For this reason, as pointed out in Chapter 8, there is a fundamental difference in the emphasis on marriage in patrilineal groups, where descent and inheritance are traced through men, and matrilineal groups, where they are traced through women. In matrilineal societies, kinship groups obtain new members when the women of the group give birth to children. A mother's child automatically becomes a member of her own kin group, whether she is married or not. In contrast, patrilineal kinship units cannot obtain children from their own women, because a child does not belong to its mother's kin group but to its father's. In this case marriage serves the purpose of securing a stable relationship between men and women from outside their kin group. Marriage also provides for the establishment of what Kathleen Gough calls "social fatherhood." **Social fatherhood** may or may not be the same as biological paternity. One's social father is the man who fulfills the responsibilities of parenting, just as stepparents and adoptive parents are social parents.

REVIEW

A family is a group of people related by blood (consanguines) or by marriage (affines) who live together, raise children, and share economic and other social responsibilities. A household consists of relatives and, often, nonrelatives who live together and share economic responsibilities. In all societies, enculturation of children and the inheritance of property and status take place within families. In most societies, families are formed through marriage, a public acknowledgment of a couple's commitment and a new alliance between kin groups. Marriage enables men in patrilineal societies to add children to their kin group, whereas in matrilineal societies, children are automatically in their mother's group. Marriage also allows for social fatherhood.

FAMILIES AND IDEAL TYPES

Anthropologists differentiate between one's family of orientation (the family one grows up in) and one's family of procreation (the family one founds as an adult). In addition, anthropologists have long used a classification of ideal family types that is generally descriptive of different family structures. Many real families diverge from these types in some way or to some degree. Nevertheless, the types are useful because they broadly correlate with other aspects of culture. The nuclear family, extended family, joint family, and single-parent family are some of these types.

Nuclear Families

Among nomadic foragers and members of industrial societies, most families are of the type that anthropologists call "nuclear." A **nuclear family** consists of one or more parents and their children, although another relative, such as a grandparent or an unmarried sibling of one of the parents, may reside in the same household for a time. The nuclear family is the characteristic family form of societies with bilateral descent, which, as discussed in Chapter 8, are typically either foraging or modern industrial societies.

marriage
A socially recognized, stable, and enduring union between two adults that publicly acknowledges their rights and obligations and forms a new alliance between kin groups.

social fatherhood
The status of a man who fulfills the responsibilities of parenting, a role that may or may not be the same as biological paternity.

nuclear family
Family consisting of parents and their children.

A nuclear family structure provides certain benefits. For instance, it has the advantage of mobility. The relatively small number of people in a nuclear family unit can easily separate themselves from the larger community in which they live. In foraging societies, nuclear families aid in survival in conditions of scarcity. If there are insufficient resources to support a large group, nuclear families can go their own way, dispersing into a large territory and exploiting meager resources. In industrial societies, nuclear families allow for economic independence and promote the loosening or weakening of wider kinship bonds. This pattern is advantageous for societies where competition and individual advancement are goals.

This Japanese nuclear family is enjoying a day out like other nuclear families around the world.

Comparatively small families are an advantage for people in both foraging and industrial societies. Family size is limited among foragers in order not to exceed the carrying capacity of the environment. In addition, infants and young children need to be carried when traveling, which favors the spacing of births. And because foragers lack grains and animal milk as foods for babies, mothers nurse their children for as many as three or four years. Therefore, closely spaced children have a low chance of survival. As well, frequent pregnancies and deliveries have a negative impact on the health and long-term survival of mothers. In industrial societies, small nuclear families have the mobility necessary for leaving larger kin groups and moving from job to job and region to region. Distant relatives are unlikely to make claims for assistance, and if they do, families can easily avoid contact with them or deny their requests for aid. Small families are an advantage because dependent children are economic liabilities in modern industrial economies where work requires strength, stamina, and skilled training and where laws forbid or restrict child laborers.

single-parent family
Family consisting of one parent (either mother or father) and her or his children.

extended family
Family formed with three or more generations, for example, parents, children, and grandparents.

Nuclear families risk social isolation. Family reunions in industrial societies may be seen as equivalent to seasonal gatherings of larger kin units among nomadic foragers. **Single-parent families** in industrial societies are formed as the result of divorce or the death of a spouse and parent. Others develop when the parents do not marry or live together. In the United States, most single-parent households consist of mother and children. According to U.S. Census statistics for 2000, 12 percent of all households were headed by a single mother; 4 percent had a single father as head. Single-parent households, especially those headed by women, are more likely to have incomes near or below the poverty line. Their economic difficulties stem from a common problem of nuclear families: Economic independence accrues only to people with resources and jobs. For people with meager incomes, the isolation of single-parent families increases the difficulty of seeking support from kin. In contrast, in extended family systems, people who lose or lack a spouse can rely on a large network of relatives for assistance.

Extended and Joint Families

Family systems based on an extended family principle are more common worldwide. Extended family arrangements are especially prevalent in farming and pastoral economies. **Extended families** consist of three or more generations of people, extending the family vertically. Typically, an extended family unit is composed of an elder parent or couple, their unmarried children, some of the married children, and the children's spouses and children. As you read in Chapter 8, rules of descent determine which adult married children remain with the parents. That is, in patrilineal systems where descent and inheritance are traced through men, it is more often the sons who remain with their parents, whereas daughters leave home after marriage to reside with their husbands' families. In matrilineal societies, daughters remain with their parents after marriage, but married sons leave to join their wives' families.

This four-generation extended Polish family, grouped around their 96-year-old matriarch, is characterized by vertical ties between generations.

Culture Change

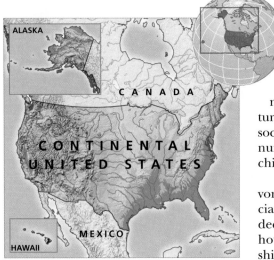

THE CHANGING AMERICAN FAMILY

Family types are responsive to changes in productive modes and general social values. In the United States, the percentage of family units conforming to the idealized model of husband, wife, and children has declined considerably since the mid-twentieth century. The idealized nuclear family model is itself a product of economic needs and adjustments made during the nineteenth and twentieth centuries as capitalist and industrial production dominated North American society. Other kinds of family units have now become more common. The number of blended families, based on remarriages and the combining of children from previous marriages, also has increased.

Single-parent households also have risen with growing rates of divorce. As women have gained more economic independence, the financial need to remarry after divorce or the death of a spouse has somewhat declined. The number of people who never marry has increased. Many households consist of a man and woman involved in a long-term relationship who, however, choose not to marry. Such couples may or may not have children. Another less common but not unusual type of household consists of two people of the same gender who share a sexual relationship, economic responsibilities, and other attributes of family life such as child rearing.

Statistics collected in census reports indicate changes in U.S. household composition, marital status, and numbers of children over the last several decades. The following tables present some of the relevant data.

MARITAL STATUS OF THE U.S. POPULATION 1980–2003 (AS PERCENTAGE OF TOTAL, BY SEX)

	1980		1990		2000		2003	
	Male	**Female**	**Male**	**Female**	**Male**	**Female**	**Male**	**Female**
Never Married	27.3	21.1	32.1	22.5	32.3	23.4	35.8	24.6
Married	67.1	64.3	60.9	62.4	59.7	60.7	56.7	61.1
Widowed	1.6	7.1	1.5	6.5	1.6	6.5	1.4	5.5
Divorced	4.0	7.6	5.5	8.5	6.4	9.3	5.9	6.7

Source: U.S. Census Bureau, *Statistical Abstract of the United States, 2001,* Table 49; *2003,* Table 63; *2004–2005,* Table 51.

As the figures in the table indicate, the percentage of people "Never married" has steadily risen between 1980 and 2003, and the percentage of people "Married" at the time of the census has declined. Similarly, the percentage of people "Widowed" has declined, and the percentages of people "Divorced" has increased.

Census reports also indicate that the size of families has decreased between 1980 and 2002. More couples are having fewer children than in the past. Indeed, there has been an increase in the number of childless couples, as the table at the top of the next page demonstrates.

Another finding is an increase in the number of cohabitating unmarried couples. In 1980, there were 1,589,000 such couples, but by 2000, there were 4,486,000 unmarried couples (U.S. Census Bureau, *Statistical Abstract of the United States, 2001,* Table 52).

Number of Children	1980	1990	2000	2002
No children	48%	51%	52%	52%
One child	21	20	20	20
Two children	19	19	18	18
Three or more children	12	10	10	10

Source: U.S. Census Bureau, *Statistical Abstract of the United States, 2001,* Table 58; *2003,* Table 71.

Looking at family statistics on composition of households, we can also see changes from 1990 to 2002.

Type of Household	1990	2000	2002
Family Household	71%	69%	68%
Married couple family	56	53	52
Single father	3	4	4
Single mother	12	12	12
Nonfamily Household	29	31	32
Living alone	25	26	26
Males	10	11	11
Females	15	15	15

Source: U.S. Census Bureau, *Statistical Abstract of the United States, 2001,* Table 53; *2003,* Table 65.

Size of families has changed since 1980, indicating a general decline in the number of persons per family.

Size of Family	1980	1990	2000
Two persons	39%	42%	44%
Three persons	23	23	22
Four persons	21	21	20
Five persons	10	9	9
Six persons	4	3	3
Seven or more persons	3	2	2

Source: U.S. Census Bureau, *Statistical Abstract of the United States, 2003,* Table 67.

The U.S. Census Bureau also reports data on households consisting of same-sex partners. States with the largest numbers of same-sex households were California, New York, Texas, Florida, and Illinois. Census figures indicate a sharp increase in the number of such households between 1990 and 2000. This increase may reflect both a real growth in same-sex households as well as a greater likelihood that members of such households self-report. In 2000, there was a total of 594,391 households consisting of same-sex partners. Of these, 301,026 were male couples and 283,365 were female couples (U.S. Census Bureau, *Statistical Abstract, 2003,* Table 69).

Anthropology Applied

Anthropologists as Expert Witnesses

Testifying in a courtroom is not thought of as being within the realm of cultural anthropology. However, cultural anthropologists often are called to testify in court cases involving possible cultural misunderstandings on issues ranging from landownership to family law and child custody. Other kinds of cases in which anthropologists play an important role as expert witnesses involve tribal rights, criminal investigation, and forensic science.

In her article "Infighting in San Francisco: Anthropology in Family Court, Or: A Study in Cultural Misunderstanding," anthropologist Barbara Jones (1998) outlines a custody dispute in which she was an expert witness. The dispute was between a mother seeking custody and the father, with whom the child was living. The mother had remarried a fourth time, was pregnant, and planned to leave the country. The father was single but closely tied to an extended family network. A psychologist, who was hired by the court and assumed to be unbiased, examined both households and concluded that the mother should have sole custody of the child. Jones believed that the psychologist's conclusion was based on a lack of understanding about the benefits that the father and his extended family could offer the child.

Jones was invited to explain these benefits to the court. She observed that the child had been interacting almost daily with loving grandparents, cousins, aunts, and uncles. In addition, the father had hired a full-time nanny to assist in daily care of his daughter while he worked. Contrary to the psychologist, then, Jones concluded that the extended family of the father provided greater benefits to the child than the mother's situation would allow.

CRITICAL THINKING QUESTION

What perspectives do anthropologists have that might make them valuable contributors to the adjudication process?

? *Which ideal type best characterizes your family? What are some benefits and challenges of life in this type of family in relation to the larger culture?*

A family that is extended laterally rather than vertically is referred to as a joint family, which is much less common. A **joint family** typically consists of siblings who combine their families to share work and resources, such as two or three brothers, their wives, and their children.

Extended and joint family systems have the advantage of establishing a more or less stable group of people who can share resources, household tasks, and subsistence work, and provide emotional support and material aid. However, because many people live together, conflicts may develop. Intergenerational tensions may arise because of the authority of the eldest couple over their adult children, or sibling rivalry may develop in a joint family compound. Conflicts over authority, inheritance, and loyalty are common. In addition, extended and joint family systems may lead to social difficulties for in-marrying spouses. Women moving in with their husbands' kin, for example, may face demanding mothers-in-law. Economic cooperation and interdependence is a prominent feature of extended and joint families. For this reason, people in industrial societies may form this type of family unit on a temporary or permanent basis when they are unemployed or otherwise lack resources.

joint family
Family consisting of siblings with their spouses and children, sharing work and resources.

REVIEW

Ideal family types include nuclear, single-parent, extended, and joint families. A nuclear family consists of parents and their offspring and occasionally another relative. This type is commonly found in both foraging and industrial societies. Single-parent families have a mother or a father and children as a result of single status, divorce, or the death of a parent. The majority of single-parent families are headed by women. Extended families, found in many societies, consist of parents, their unmarried children, married children and their spouses, and their grandchildren. Joint families extend the family unit horizontally among siblings rather than vertically across generations. Extended and joint families are most prevalent among agrarian and pastoralist societies.

Explaining the Incest Taboo

The origins of the incest taboo are much debated. One theory proposes that the incest taboo arose out of an instinctive aversion toward sexual relations within the nuclear family. The problem with this theory is that incest is known to occur fairly widely in human societies, so avoiding it could not be an instinct. Another biological theory is based on the fact that inbreeding can increase the incidence of undesirable or harmful (as well as desirable and beneficial) genetic traits in a population. This theory suggests that the incest taboo is a learned, cultural response to the possible negative biological consequences of inbreeding. However, this theory assumes that ancestral human groups understood the relationship between mating and the variability of traits in their population, and that this cultural adaptation then spread to all human societies through diffusion or contact to become a universal element of culture or, alternatively, that human societies in different areas independently invented an incest taboo.

A theory championed by anthropologist Bronislaw Malinowski, based on the work of Sigmund Freud, focused on the origin of the incest taboo as a response to the need to lessen sexual competition within the nuclear family unit. This theory might account in part for the ban on sexual relations between parents and their children, which would strain the marriage bond between husband and wife. However, this psychological theory does not account for the near-universal prohibition on marriage between siblings. Sibling marriage occurred among the emperors of ancient Peru, Egypt, and Hawaii but was not defined as incest. Marriage between a brother and sister at the highest level of the state functioned to consolidate power and minimize struggles over succession. However, sibling marriage was not permitted among ordinary citizens.

Many anthropologists favor understanding the incest taboo as a means of ensuring survival by forcing people to make alliances with others outside the nuclear family. This "marry out or die out" theory emphasizes that marriage within a small unit will lead over time to the isolation and genetic homogeneity of the group, which makes it more vulnerable to population loss or even extinction. Mating outside the nuclear family reduces this risk and also leads to the formation of social alliances and bonds of reciprocity with other people. Reciprocal social networks are critical in times of scarce resources and other dangers to survival.

We may never know why the incest taboo started, but the fact that it is universal indicates its importance. All these theories add interesting dimensions and clues to the debate.

CRITICAL THINKING QUESTION

Which theory or combination of theories about the origin of the incest taboo do you favor, and why?

ENDOGAMY, EXOGAMY, AND THE INCEST TABOO

As discussed in Chapter 8, marriage serves as a means of extending kinship within a particular group (*endogamy*) or extending kinship to other groups (*exogamy*). All societies ban marriage—and condemn sexual relations—within the nuclear family, particularly between parents and children and also, with very few exceptions, between brothers and sisters. This ban is referred to as the **incest taboo.** The incest taboo is essentially a rule of nuclear family exogamy, forcing people to marry outside their families. The incest taboo is universal, but beyond the nuclear family the "forbidden" relatives are different in different societies. For example, in some societies one set of cousins is preferred for marriage, whereas other sets of cousins are forbidden under the incest taboo.

Effects of Exogamy on Social Organization

The marriage rules of endogamy and exogamy are predicated on the incest taboo. And both exogamy and endogamy reflect and reinforce the structure and organization of a

incest taboo
A ban on sexual relations or marriage between parents and their children and between siblings.

class
Social grouping usually determined on the basis of a combination of birth and achievement.

caste
Social grouping whose membership is determined at birth and is generally inflexible.

society, the subject of Chapter 11. For example, village exogamy is the norm in societies in which people contract marriages with residents of other villages. Through intervillage marriages, people create alliances over a broader geographic area, thereby widening their networks of allies and supporters. In areas of frequent warfare, such marriages also give some protection against raids, because people are less likely to attack villages where they have relatives.

In addition, some stratified societies practice exogamy, stipulating that members of identifiable social groups or strata need to marry outside their own group or **class,** a social grouping whose membership is usually based on a combination of birth and achievement. For example, the Natchez of the south-central United States were divided into two major classes—nobles and commoners. These groups had different, unequal access to resources, services, and power. The nobility consisted of three graded ranks: Suns, Nobles, and Honored Persons. Descent was matrilineal. The chief was the highest ranked member of the highest ranked matrilineage, the Suns. The Suns were never able to consolidate their power and wealth, however, because the Natchez social system required that all members of the nobility practice class exogamy. That is, they had to marry commoners. The Sun matrilineage was perpetuated through children of Sun women who were Suns themselves, but children of Sun men, including children of the Great Sun, were not members of that chiefly lineage. The children and more distant relatives of Sun men became Nobles and Honored Persons, whose male children were commoners through membership in their mothers' lineage. On the other hand, children of male commoners became members of the nobility if their fathers married noble women. Commoners could also raise their status through exemplary services to the nation, such as serving in the military, which raised wives' status as well (Bonvillain, 2001:132–133).

Effects of Endogamy on Social Organization

Many stratified societies also practice endogamy, in which people marry within their class or rank in order to maintain social, economic, and political distinctions. Endogamous marriages solidify and preserve the privilege of elites by consolidating wealth and power. Recall the examples of parallel cousin marriage and cross-cousin marriage, described in Chapter 8.

A strong form of endogamy occurs in caste systems (described further in Chapter 11). **Caste** is an ascribed social category identifying a group by status or by occupation. At birth, a person automatically becomes a member of the caste of his or her parents and remains in that caste throughout life. In India, for example, people traditionally must marry other members of their own caste. Caste exogamy (marrying someone of another caste) is, in principle, forbidden, although it does occur.

Informal class endogamy is widespread in stratified societies, simply because people with similar backgrounds tend to associate with one another and marry within their group. Members of the same class tend to socialize together, attend the same schools, live in the same neighborhoods, perform the same social activities, and so on. Therefore, even in the absence of a strong marriage rule, proximity and informal sanctions against marrying down tend to lead to class endogamy. Other marriage preferences that follow informal social norms include the tendency for people in pluralistic societies to marry within their own racial or ethnic group and to choose partners who speak the same language and observe the same religion.

Brahmans, like the one in this photograph, traditionally were teachers and spiritual leaders. Brahmans are the highest of four main castes identified in ancient Hindu sacred writings. Castes are tied to specific ranked occupations. India's many tribal societies and ethnic minorities were not included in the caste system and thus became "outcasts."

REVIEW

The incest taboo, universal in human societies, is a general ban against sexual relations between individuals within a nuclear family. Explanations for the origins of the incest taboo include biological and psychological explanations and hypotheses based on cultural adaptations to survival factors. Marriage rules affect the organization of a society. Village exogamy, for example, links villages in political and economic alliances. Examples of impacts of endogamy on social systems include the caste system of India, alliances created through cross-cousin marriage, and class systems with preferential marriage based on shared membership in a social, racial, or ethnic group.

FORMS OF MARRIAGE

Marriage rules define the forms that marriages can take, and these forms vary. For example, norms concerning the number of spouses that can constitute the marital unit differ in different societies. In most societies, marriage is a union between two people—**monogamy**—but in some societies the marital unit may consist of three or more people—**polygamy,** or plural marriage. Monogamy is the most common form of union today, even in societies where plural marriages are possible. Societies that permit remarriage after the death of a spouse or divorce practice **serial monogamy,** meaning that a person can be married to only one person at a time, although individuals may have two or more spouses during their lifetime.

Polygyny and Polyandry

There are two forms of polygamy. **Polygyny** is marriage between a man and two or more women, and **polyandry** is marriage between a woman and two or more men. Polygyny is far more common than polyandry as a form of plural marriage, but even in societies where plural marriages are possible, most couples live in monogamous unions. A common type of polygyny is a pattern in which a man marries two or more sisters, usually wedding one first and the other years later. This system is called **sororal polygyny.** Sororal polygyny has the advantage of minimizing potential conflicts between wives, because the women have close emotional and supportive bonds as sisters. When co-wives are not related, there may be tensions between them, each vying for favoritism from their common husband to benefit themselves and their children. Different societies favor different kinds of residence patterns for plural marriages. In some, the entire unit of husband and several wives lives together in one dwelling. In others, each wife of a polygynous homestead has a separate hut for herself and her children.

Polyandrous marriages may occur in societies where there are shortages of women. For example, in some communities in the Indian Himalayas and Chinese Tibet, such as the Nyinba and the Pahari, brothers may jointly contract for a wife. This fraternal polyandry permits all men to be married, and also promotes economic cooperation among brothers for their mutual benefit. Rather than fragmenting a family's property through inheritance by numerous and possibly conflicting heirs, polyandrous unions solidify wealth, property, and social status and raise people's overall standard of living (Levine, 1988). And where resources are scarce, it may limit population growth. Finally, in societies where men frequently travel for trade or military expeditions, polyandry ensures that households will likely have at least one man at home to accomplish male economic tasks. Although most of the relatively few societies that practice polyandry are in South Asia, it has been reported elsewhere, as among the Inuit of Arctic Canada and the Iroquois of New York State.

Explanations of Polygyny

Polygyny develops in different societies for different reasons. In communities where women greatly outnumber men, polygyny helps correct imbalances in the sex ratio. Among the Innu of eastern Canada, for example, polygyny, limited to two or three wives, ensured marriage for all women in a society with a scarcity of men. Male mortality

Increases in rates of multiracial marriage and in numbers of mixed-race children in many parts of the world can be seen as an extension of the process of globalization. In many countries, including the United States, interethnic marriage also contributes to the spread of English.

monogamy
Marriage rule that stipulates a union between two people.

polygamy
Marriage in which the marital unit consists of three or more people.

serial monogamy
Marriage pattern that stipulates that a person can be married to only one person at a time, although individuals may have two or more spouses during their lifetime. Subsequent marriages may be formed after the death of one spouse or after divorce.

polygyny
Marriage between a man and two or more women.

polyandry
Marriage between a woman and two or more men.

sororal polygyny
Marriage between a man and two or more women who are sisters.

In this West African family, each co-wife has her own hut, which she occupies with her children. To prevent jealousy and competition, the most senior wife is often given the highest status. In other cultures, co-wives are treated and supported equally. Economic changes in African societies put pressure on this form of marriage, however. Today only the wealthiest of men can afford many wives.

GLOBALIZATION

The shared practice of polygyny fostered the rapid spread of patriarchal Arab culture and Islam to African nations. It is well known that culture change occurs more rapidly and more completely when peoples in contact share basic cultural characteristics such as forms of marriage and family.

rates were comparatively higher than female mortality rates because of the dangers for men in hunting and warfare. As the seventeenth-century French Jesuit missionary Paul LeJeune observed, after lecturing the Innu about the evils of plural marriage: "Since I have been preaching among them that a man should not have more than one wife, I have not been well received by the women; for, since they are more numerous than the men, if a man can only marry one of them, the others will have to suffer. Therefore this doctrine is not to their liking" (Thwaites, 1906, vol. 12:165). In the case of the Innu, polygyny prevented population decline by maintaining an effective rate of reproduction.

Polygyny also occurs in some strongly patriarchal societies in which women are viewed as property and a source of status. Men who can afford to support a greater number of wives and dependents are seen to have greater wealth, power, and prestige in their communities. Historically, hereditary high chiefs of polygynous Central African kingdoms boasted hundreds of wives and concubines. In pre-Communist imperial China, wealthy men measured their status and good fortune in the number of wives they accumulated. Daughters became mediums of exchange between men seeking to form alliances with each other.

Polygyny also develops as an adaptation to economic needs or goals because of the important economic roles women serve. For example, as the economy of the Plains Indians shifted to dependence on the buffalo by the middle of the nineteenth century, men wanted to obtain the economic services of more than one wife, because women were responsible for tanning the buffalo hides and thus turning a raw product into a marketable item. To advance themselves in trade networks that were supplied by the labor of women, men wanted several wives.

In some farming societies, polygyny also serves the purpose of supplying additional labor of women and their children. For example, among the Tswana and Herero, two cattle-herding and horticultural societies of southern Africa, men with more than one wife were able to accumulate greater farm surpluses because of women's key roles as subsistence farmers. Also, the more wives a man had, the more children he acquired. His children raised his social standing because they contributed to the growth of his patrilineage and patriclan. A man's sons helped care for his cattle, and his daughters brought cattle to the family as wedding gifts from their husbands' kin.

Men living in foraging societies also may reap benefits from the labor of more than one wife. Among the Tiwi of Australia men want to have several wives because the Aboriginal foraging economy centers on the collection of wild plant resources, work that is generally done by women. As one Tiwi reported, "If I had only one or two wives I would starve, but with my present ten or twelve wives I can send them out in all directions in the morning and at least two or three of them are likely to bring something back with them at the end of the day, and then we can all eat" (Hart and Pilling, 1960:34).

Tiwi husbands benefit from polygyny both economically and socially. A man with several wives can accumulate enough food surplus to give to others, raising his prestige by his generosity. Australian Aborigine men also value their wives because of their desire to have many children, a condition of marriage. The Tiwi traditionally practiced reciprocal polygyny, with men sometimes agreeing to marry each other's sisters or each other's daughters.

"Ghost Marriage" and Other Adaptive Forms

Cultures demonstrate a great deal of variety in the ways that people think of sexual relations, marriage, and family. Marriage might even be entirely symbolic and not involve procreation. Yet, even in rare forms of marriage, principles of descent, patterns of residence and household composition, and ways of establishing bonds with others form systems of relationships and meaning that integrate individuals into families and communities.

In some African societies with patrilineal descent, marriages can be contracted in ways that emphasize the importance of descent and the continuity of patrilineal kin groups. Among the Nuer, for example, if a married man died without sons, one of his younger brothers married his widow. The children of the new couple, though, were considered heirs of the deceased (Evans-Pritchard, 1955). Nuer **ghost marriage** thus permitted an elder brother to maintain his patrilineage even after his death. In Nuer society, seniority in a lineage was an important criterion for determining relative social status, so allowing descent to follow from an elder sibling, dead or alive, was a strategic practice. In this way, children born to the younger brother but claimed by the dead older brother would have seniority over members of junior lineages.

Another Nuer marital option was allowed when a lineage failed to produce a male heir. In that event, a woman in the lineage could take the role of husband and be married to another woman. The woman who became a husband refrained from having sex, because husbands cannot conceive. The "wife" conceived by having sex with a chosen man from any lineage other than her own. The children borne to the "wife" belonged to the "husband's" lineage, thus supplying the line with heirs (Evans-Pritchard, 1955:108).

In marriages between women, the woman who acted as husband was transformed into a legal man. As a "man," she could receive bridal payments given in marriages for her kinswomen, and she could inherit cattle from her father. She also could be compensated with cattle if her "wife" had an adulterous affair without her consent. Nuer practices of marriage between women and "ghost marriage" both create social fatherhood for the purpose of securing the continuation of patrilineages.

In another rare form, the matrilineal Kwakwaka'wakw (Kwakiutl) of British Columbia developed a marriage option that created daughters for men who had none. Such a strategy was necessary because status, wealth, and named titles were transmitted from men to men through women. In practice, men needed daughters because wealth and titles passed from a father to his daughter's children. To accommodate men who had no daughters, several types of marriage could be arranged. According to George Hunt, a Kwakiutl chief, a man "turned the left side of his son's body into a woman and gave ['her'] the name belonging to the oldest daughter of his line" (quoted in Boas, 1966:55). Then another man proposed marriage to the first man's "daughter." After they were married, the first man was able to acquire the titles belonging to "her" lineage and could pass these on to children whom he had with a subsequent wife. If a man had no children at all, according to Hunt, "the father may call his foot or one side of his body, his daughter. The marriage ceremony is performed as though these were the women married, and the names are transferred in the usual manner." This was called "taking hold of the foot" (Boas, 1897:359). These marital options allowed for the transmission of wealth and status in a society where man controlled wealth but the wealth passed through women.

The Nayar, a matrilineal people living in Kerala, South India, have concepts of marriage that differ from most peoples' (Mencher, 1965). Nayar kinship centers on matrilineal relatives, organized into matrilineal descent and residence groups called *taravad*. The *taravad* consists of sisters and brothers, the sisters' children, the sisters' daughters' children, and so on, all descended from a female ancestor. They hold land and other property in common, managed by the senior man. And they care collectively for children born to their female members. Shortly before a girl reaches puberty, she is married to a man chosen by her family. However, the man and woman have no social or economic responsibilities toward one another and do not live together. However, when the man dies, the woman honors him in mourning ceremonies.

The man and woman have a succession of lovers over the years. A lover acknowledges and legitimizes his sexual relationship with a particular woman by giving her gifts three times a year for as long as the liaison lasts. Children produced from these unions belong to the *taravad* of the mother, and her family takes responsibility for the economic care of children. Fathers have no economic obligations for their children, but establishment of paternity is critical to the social standing of mother and child.

ghost marriage
Marriage practice among the Nuer of Sudan in which a widow marries her dead husband's brother and in which the children ensuing from the second marriage are said to be the children of the first, dead husband.

In May 2004, Massachusetts legalized gay marriage, and on that day 265 gay couples, like the couple pictured here, were married statewide.

same-sex marriage
Marriage between two men or two women.

One of the lovers publicly declares himself the father of a child by giving a gift to the mother and to the midwife who assisted in the birth.

The Na, an ethnic group of Yunnan province in southern China, do not recognize marital ties or obligations at all (Hua, 2001). Households consist of siblings and the children of female members. Sexual encounters, termed "visits," can be proposed by men or women but always take place at night in the woman's house. The couple have no mutual obligations or rights and do not expect to have exclusive sexual access to one another. Nor do they contribute to a joint household. Children belong to the kin group of the mother, but there is no acknowledgment of paternity or social fatherhood. Instead, children are raised by their mother and her male and female kin.

Same-Sex Marriage

Although most marriages in most cultures are unions between men and women, some societies allow marriage between individuals of the same sex. This is not the same as the **same-sex marriages** practiced by the Nuer, in which a woman is legally defined as a man for purposes of marriage to another woman. In this case, the couple does not have sexual relations. Rather, the female wife has sex with a man in order to bear children for her female husband.

Same-sex marriage was an option in many Native American societies as late as the early decades of the twentieth century. Especially in cultures of the Great Plains, the Southwest, and California, two women or two men might marry, have sexual relations, and share household and family responsibilities. These people, now often referred to as "Two-Spirits," were publicly recognized as forming legitimate couples. Chapter 10 discusses in greater detail the Two-Spirits and their roles in their communities.

In North America today, growing numbers of lesbian and gay couples agitate for the right to marry in ceremonies that have legal standing. Advocates note that same-sex couples fulfill all of the same obligations and responsibilities toward each other as do heterosexual couples. They share their resources, make joint decisions, and make commitments to exclusive sexual relationships. Many also raise children together. Opponents of lesbian and gay marriage claim that the traditional cultural concept of marriage, based on religious precepts, applies only to the union of one man and one woman. Growing tolerance for homosexual marriages in the United States and Canada is a measure of social and culture change.

> **REVIEW**
>
> Monogamy, which is most common, is the marriage of one man and one woman, either for life or for a given time (serial monogamy). Polygamy, or plural marriage, can be in two forms: polygyny or polyandry. Polygyny is marriage between one man and two or more women. Marriage between a man and two or more sisters is called sororal polygyny. Explanations for the development of polygyny relate to population sex ratios, the status of women, and economic adaptations. Polyandry, marriage between one woman and two or more men, often brothers, is rarer. Other rare forms of marriage include ghost marriages, foot marriages, and same-sex marriages.

MARRIAGE AS ALLIANCE AND ECONOMIC EXCHANGE

The relationship established through marriage is not only social but economic as well. Each spouse usually has certain obligations to the other and to their children to supply basic needs such as food, clothing, and shelter. The economic factor in marriage may also be expressed through exchanges of goods and services prior to, during, or after

Some of these Botswana cattle may be destined to become bridewealth for sons from the owner's family to give to the parents of their prospective wives. The bridewealth is offered as symbolic compensation for the woman's loss to her own family and as material compensation for her family's loss of an important economic asset.

marriage rites. In most Native American cultures, gifts were mutually exchanged before and during a marriage ceremony. Relatives of the bride and groom gave each other foods, clothing, and ornaments as a sign of their mutual respect and support.

Bridewealth and Brideservice

In some places, substantial gifts may be given, not mutually by both sides, but more often by one side to the other. In patrilineal societies, for example, **bridewealth** is given from the husband's group to that of the wife. Among the Nuer and most of the cattle-herding societies of eastern Africa, bridewealth was primarily in the form of cattle. In the plains of North America, people gave horses as bridewealth. The number of cattle or horses given was taken to be a reflection of the wealth and prestige of the husband's kin and an indication of the esteem in which they held the bride and her family. Offering too little, then, could be an insult.

In societies where a married couple lived with the husband's kin, the transfer of goods from the husband's group to that of the wife was symbolic compensation for the woman's loss to her family. Bridewealth was also recognition that after the wedding, the husband's family benefited from the bride's labor while her own kin would be deprived of it. In addition, bridewealth was a means of legitimizing the couple's children and their membership in the husband's patrilineal group. Bridewealth typically was returned if a couple divorced, so the wife's kin often had a large stake in discouraging the dissolution of the marriage.

In another form of gift giving, called **brideservice,** men are obligated to perform services for their wife's parents. A period of brideservice may predate the marriage ceremony, or the period may extend for many years after marriage. During this period, the future or newly married husband contributes his labor to his parents-in-law. Depending on the subsistence strategies employed, he may give all or a portion of animals he has caught and help with planting and harvesting crops. In addition, the husband may help construct his parents-in-law's dwellings, fetch wood or water, and perform other domestic tasks.

Dowry

In some societies, goods of value are given by the bride's family rather than the groom's family. These gifts are given to the newly married couple and/or to the husband's kin

bridewealth
Presents given by the husband's family to the wife's kin before, during, or after the wedding ceremony.

brideservice
A period of months or years before or after marriage during which the husband performs labor for his wife's parents.

Culture Change

DOWRY IN INDIA

Dowry was the traditional marital exchange in India. There, a woman's family had to amass wealth in jewelry, fine cloth, and money to present to the husband's family before the marriage took place. The amount of wealth given was an indication of both the bride's status and the esteem of the husband's kin. A great deal of property was given by wealthy parents, but even poor families made every effort to collect as many valuables as they could so as not to shame their daughter and themselves.

The economic burden of dowry contributed to a preference for sons over daughters, because girls were a financial liability while boys brought in dowry wealth when they married. Thus, the custom of dowry contributed to female infanticide and the neglect of the health of daughters in India and Bangladesh. However, dowry was not the only factor involved in preferences for sons and the consequences of such preferences. Rather, the constellation of behaviors and attitudes grew out of a context of kinship based on patrilineal descent and inheritance, of subsistence strategies emphasizing intensive agriculture with farmwork primarily the responsibility of men, and of male control over land. All of these practices place value on men and undermine the worth of women.

Today, asking for and giving dowry is illegal in India, but there are reports that the custom is still practiced and may be gaining in popularity. Although outlawed by the Dowry Prohibition Act (1961, amended in 1984 and 1986), dowry often is demanded by a husband's family (Ghadially and Kumar, 1988:175). Such demands specify amounts of cash or goods necessary to contract a marriage. Young men of high status, good education, and favorable employment prospects command large sums. In many cases, dowry demands are made after a marriage is contracted and even after a wedding.

Public controversy over dowry has arisen in India because of increasing incidences of deaths of young wives whose families have not satisfied the dowry demands of their in-laws. Rehana Ghadially and Pramod Kumar (1988) report a study indicating that of a registered 179 "unnatural deaths" of young married women in Delhi in 1981–1982, 12 to 16 percent were dowry-related (Ghadially and Kumar, 1988:167). In two-thirds of these cases, young women committed suicide; the remaining one-third were murdered by their in-laws. The families involved were of all social classes, educational levels, and occupations.

Ghadially and Kumar (1988), also report a study conducted in the Indian state of Maharashtra concluding that dowry deaths rose from 120 in 1984 to 211 in 1985, an increase of 64 percent. By the mid-1990s, dowry deaths, including bride burnings, had climbed to an estimated 5,800 incidents a year. Many cases of "unnatural deaths" of women are classified as "kitchen/cooking accidents" and "stove-bursts," a common method of killing unprofitable daughters-in-law. Retaliation against wives whose families fail to meet dowry demands takes many forms, from verbal abuse to beatings, burns, hanging, poisoning, and strangulation.

A disturbing finding in studies of dowry abuse and death is the fact that the wife's parents are sometimes aware of the violence perpetrated against their daughter but do nothing to give her emotional or legal support. The abused daughter is told to endure her situation rather than stir social controversy that would negatively affect her family's reputation.

Dowry and the related mistreatment and deaths of women gave impetus to the birth of the feminist movement in India. Beginning in 1979, women's groups staged public protests to bring the issue of dowry harassment out in the open. As a result, many families of abused and murdered daughters came forward to give testimony and ask for redress. The Indian government responded in 1980 with passage of laws against dowry-related crimes, mandating police investigation of the death of any woman who had been married less than five years at the time of her death. Legislation passed in 1983 strengthened the first law, making "cruelty to a wife a cognizable, non-bailable offense" and stipulated that "cruelty" included both mental and physical harassment (Kumar, 1995:68). Cases reported as suicides (frequently involving death by dousing and burning) could be investigated as "abetment to suicide," shifting the burden of proof to the woman's husband and his family. In addition, amendments required autopsies of women who died within seven years of marriage.

The latest studies, however, indicate increases in dowry demands. For example, the All India Democratic Women's Association conducted a survey in 2002, questioning 10,000 people in eighteen of India's twenty-six states and found "an across-the-board increase in dowry demands" (Brooke, 2003). And government statistics report that, in 2001, nearly 7,000 women were killed by husbands or in-laws angry because of small dowry payments. In 2003, a well-publicized case brought the issue of dowry demands to national attention. A bride called police on her wedding day when her in-laws demanded an additional $25,000 in cash. The refusal of her father to pay caused a scuffle and prompted the young woman to summon the authorities. The husband was eventually arrested and made to serve fourteen days in jail for violating laws against dowry (Brooke, 2003).

prior to or upon the marriage. This type of exchange is called **dowry.** Dowries are prevalent in some patriarchal cultures that stress the prestige of men and their families. In theory, dowries are a kind of insurance that protects the interests of a wife in a patrilineal and patriarchal society. In practice, however, dowry wealth is often appropriated by the husband and his family.

In Europe, from medieval times until well into the nineteenth century, well-to-do families bestowed dowries on their daughters when they married. The ability to give large amounts of money, property, and annual incomes was a sign of a family's wealth, enhancing their prestige as well. In turn, fathers who could afford handsome dowries could bargain for wealthy and powerful sons-in-law. Through marriage exchanges of dowries for husbands with property and status, men acquired a host of affinal relatives as personal and political allies. The legacy of the European dowry system is preserved today in the custom of collecting fine clothes and linens in a bridal hope chest.

Marriages are economic transactions, but they are also occasions for celebration. What is celebrated is not simply the union of two people, but the alliances formed between two families, lineages, or clans. When marriage takes place between a man and a woman who come from different villages, the wedding may symbolize extended networks and alliances between two communities.

REVIEW

As well as creating alliances among families and larger social units, marriage has important economic functions, and economic exchange is a common feature of marriage arrangements. Gifts are exchanged in many societies to represent the new economic obligations the spouses now have to each other and their in-laws. Bridewealth, found in patrilineal societies, consists of forms of wealth or objects of value given to the bride's family by the groom's family. Brideservice consists of work that the groom does for his in-laws. In the dowry system, the family of the bride pays or promises to pay wealth to the family of the groom in exchange for the marriage of their daughter.

MARRIAGE AS A RITE OF PASSAGE

For individuals, families, kin groups, and communities, marriages are crucial rites of passage. Because of the importance of the alliances formed by marriage, in many societies, marriages, especially first marriages, are arranged by one's parents or other

dowry
Gifts given by the wife's family to the married couple or to the husband's kin before, during, or after the wedding ceremony.

In Their Own Voices

"I Hear That I'm Going to Get Married!"

Florence Edenshaw Davidson, a Haida woman from Vancouver Island, British Columbia, Canada, was 14 when her parents told her that she would be married to Robert Davidson. As was proper in this matrilineal society, the proposal was made by Robert's kin to Florence's parents. Her father deferred to his wife's brother (Florence's mother's brother), who was a senior member of Florence's matriclan. These are Florence's recollections about how she came to be married to her husband.

I was still going to school yet when several people came into my dad's house to propose for my husband-to-be. I was wondering what was going on when all these people came in. The women all belonged to C'al'lanas, my husband's tribe [lineage], and the men all belonged to my husband's dad's tribe, Stl'ang'lanas, except for my husband's brother. They were all streaming in and I didn't know what was going on . . .

"Don't say anything when I tell you something," my mother said to me. "Those who came in last week proposed to you." I didn't know what to say. Propose! Why? I thought. I was just a kid yet. I didn't know what to say and mother advised me not to say anything about the proposal because they were high-class [y'a Yet] people . . .

"They want you to marry Robert Davidson." "Did you say yes?" I asked her. "No, your dad sent them to your uncle. [Florence's mother's brother]. Your dad says he's got nothing to do with it; it has to go through your uncle. You have more respect for your uncle than for us," she told me. "That's the only brother I have." "You're going to make me marry," I said. "Yes, you're going to marry him." "I'm not going to marry him," I said. "Don't say that, Florence, he's a real prince [y'a Yet]."

It bothered me so much. For a long time I couldn't sleep when I went to bed. Every day I bothered my mother. "I'm

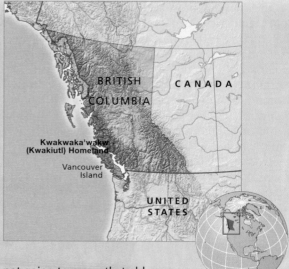

not going to marry that old man. I'm not. If you make me marry him, summertime I'll run away. You won't see me again." My mother didn't say anything, though every day I used to bother her. My dad didn't say a word to me about it. Finally, my mother said, "Don't say anything dear. Your uncle thinks it's best for you to marry him. He's a prince. He's going to respect you all your life and if you don't want to marry him you're going to feel bad all your life. He belongs to clever people; you're not going to be hard up for anything. We need a young man's help, too. You must remember that. We belong to chiefs too and you're not supposed to talk any old way. You have to respect yourself more than what you worry about." I don't want to say any more because my mother said I'd be sorry for the rest of my life if I didn't marry him. I made up my mind not to say anything much as I disliked it.

From *During My Time: Florence Edenshaw Davidson, A Haida Woman* by Margaret Blackman, pp. 95–96. Copyright © 1982. Reprinted by permission of the University of Washington Press.

---

arranged marriages
Marriages that are arranged by the parents or other relatives of the bride and groom.

relatives. A proposal of marriage may be made from one side or the other, although it is more common worldwide for the future husband's kin to approach the family of the intended wife. This is true whether the people follow patrilineal or matrilineal rules of descent.

A proposal of marriage may be a simple, short process, or it may be a long, drawn-out, ritualized exchange of greetings, proposals, counterproposals, and gift exchanges before the hoped-for marriage is finally settled upon. Among the Lohorung Rai of Nepal, for example, the marriage proposal process may take many years to accomplish. After the husband's family makes the initial contact, there follow numerous exchanges of refusal and counterproposal before a final date is set for the wedding.

And these are the recollections of James Sewid, a Kwak-waka'wakw man from Alert Bay, British Columbia. He, too, was married when he was nearly 14 to a girl he knew only by sight.

And that's when the big day came. It was late in the fall and I was going on fourteen. . . . I had been out late that night to a dance with my friends and when I came in I lay down on the couch. That was when I heard Jim and Mary Bell talking about me to Ed and Rachel Whanock and my mother and stepfather. One of them was saying, "You might as well go and see her parents because I think he should get married because we don't want him running around like this.". . . I lay there and pretended that I was sleeping and pretty soon my grandparents walked out. So as soon as they had gone I got up and said to my stepfather, "Let's go take a walk. It's pretty warm in here." I used to be very good friends with him and we were just like pals. "All right," he said, "we'll go for a walk." When we got outside and were walking along the road I asked him, "What was going on in there? I heard the people talking about me." "Well," he said, "you're going to get married." "Well," I said, "I can't get married! I'm too young!" "Oh that's all right," he said. "We'll look after you. I think it is the best way for you, to get married now, because if you're not going to get married now you might go haywire." "Well," I said, "who is this girl anyway?" And just then we happened to be passing by the house where Moses Alfred lived, and David said, "It is the girl that lives here." I didn't know what to say. I used to see her around the village but I didn't know her.

Well, it was the Indian custom for someone to go to the parents of the girl and ask their consent. That is where my grandparents had gone that night when they walked out of the house. So I just waited for the answer that this girl's parents would give to the old people who went to talk with them. I was careful after that not to listen anymore because I didn't like to butt in on what was going on. A few days after that I was alone with my mother, just the two of us, I said to her, "I hear that I'm going to get married. You know that I'm too young to get married." "Oh, no!" she said. "Don't talk like that. We want you to get married. You are going to marry Flora Alfred. It has already been arranged with her parents and it's all right. Now you have to go and see the minister so it can be announced in the church and published in the band." "Well," I said, "I don't think I should get married. It isn't that I don't want to get married, but what am I going to do if I have children?" "Well," my mother said, "we'll look after you some."

After that I went to see my old grandmother, Lucy. She had already heard about it. I went in and sat down and said, "Well, they say I'm going to get married." "Yes," she said, "I heard about that and I think it's a wonderful thing. I would really like to see it. I want to see you get married and have children before I die. There is nothing better that I wish to see than your children before I go." Well, that is what made me kind of give in. I didn't want to get married but of course I had no business to my own personal opinion. I had no business to try and argue or anything like that because I knew that the older people knew what was right for me; that's what I figured. I never did like to argue with anybody that was older than me but I always liked to respect what they said to me.

From *Guests Never Leave Hungry: The Autobiography of James Sewid, a Kwakiutl Indian* by James Spradley, pp. 66–67. Copyright © 1972. Reprinted by permission of Yale University Press.

Although both Florence and James voiced serious reservations about their arranged marriages, especially concerning their young age and fears about taking on adult responsibilities, they gave up their objections in the interests of their families. As James said, "I had no business to my own personal opinion." As it turned out, they both had successful marriages, long and loving relationships with their spouses.

CRITICAL THINKING QUESTIONS

Would you be willing to have your family arrange your marriage? Why, or why not? What might be some of the benefits and risks of doing so?

Arranged marriages symbolically emphasize the fact that such unions are not simply relationships between a woman and a man but are more fundamentally alliances between families. Each side measures their own worthiness in relation to the social standing and resources of the other side. Their willingness to promote a marital union is an indication of their trust in their future affines.

Weddings are rites of passage in which the participants change their status from single to married. In societies without arranged marriages, preparation for marriage usually involves some form of **courtship,** in which a couple tests their attraction and compatibility as well as the acceptability of their union to others who are important in their lives. Mate selection is the common goal of courtship, and weddings mark the

courtship
Period prior to marriage when a couple tests attraction to and compatibility with each other.

Case study

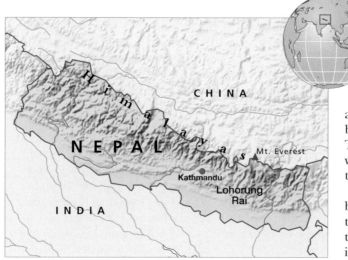

A Wedding in Nepal

In societies of larger communities and settled populations, especially where lineages are important kinship, economic, and political units, marriages may be complex, lengthy procedures. Among the Lohorung Rai of eastern Nepal, marriage involves a ten-step process (Hardman, 2000). The most complex aspect of the marriage is the negotiation that takes place between the families of the intended husband and wife. These negotiations underscore the social and economic as well as spiritual alliances created between two families, their clans, and their villages.

Most Lahorung Rai marriages are arranged when the boy and girl are young, beginning with an initial presentation of a gift of liquor brought to the girl's parents by the boy's kin. The boy's emissaries recount his good qualities and those of his family. It is not uncommon for the girl's family to refuse the initial request, returning the gift to the boy's relatives. Typically, a second visit is undertaken, and several trips may be needed before the girl's parents accept, drink the liquor offered, and tell the boy's relatives how much meat they will need to distribute to their kin.

Subsequently, additional gifts are brought by the boy's kin to those of the girl. Eventually, the final gift of a live pig, some rice, and liquor are presented to the girl's kin. This final gift, referred to as a "ransom," marks the formal betrothal of the couple and commits the families to the certainty of the marriage. The wedding, lasting all night, takes place at the bride's home. The groom proceeds there accompanied by his cousin (father's sister's son). The rite not only celebrates a marriage but also marks the transition of a male from boyhood to manhood.

After the wedding, the bride accompanies her husband to his parents' home, but the following day she returns to her own parents' home, bringing additional gifts from her husband's family. She returns to her husband's home sixteen days later but remains for only a few days, not finally taking up residence there for perhaps as long as a year. Several years later, usually after the birth of her first child, she returns to her parents' home for a final rite of separation, receiving gifts from her brothers.

The lengthy and complex Lohorung Rai marriage process not only solidifies an alliance between two families but also symbolizes and enacts the difficulty of a young woman's separation from her family in a society where postmarital residence is in the husband's locality and usually involves village exogamy. The woman's family demonstrates their reluctance to lose her by their hesitation in accepting the initial gifts offered, and she shows her difficulty in leaving by repeatedly returning to her parents' home.

At this Nepalese wedding, both sets of relatives express the difficulties that they had to overcome to achieve the desired marriage, praising each other. At the end, the bride's relatives accept gifts of gold, clothing, silver bangles, and necklaces that all symbolize the marriage.

passage from courtship to marriage. The bases on which people choose their mates may include personal compatibility, desired personality traits, likelihood of reliability and economic contributions, and physical attraction. In most societies, the Western concept of romantic love is not a prerequisite for courtship or marriage, although these feelings may develop when people begin to live together, adjusting to one another and sharing their lives. The stories of Florence Davidson and James Sewid, given in the "In Their Own Voices" feature, illustrate that feelings of caring and love can follow, but do not necessarily precede, a successful marriage.

In small-scale societies, especially among foraging and horticultural peoples, a wedding ceremony is usually a simple affair. Among the Mohawk, a marriage traditionally was proposed by a young man's family to the family of the intended bride, or a couple announced their plans to marry. Before the wedding, the couple separately presented gifts to their future mothers-in-law. The future husband gave his bride's mother a gift of deer meat, and the future bride gave her husband's mother a gift of cornbread. These presents were symbolic of the economic roles of men as hunters and women as farmers, thus representing the interdependence of spouses and households.

A Mohawk wedding involved a feast sponsored by the bride's family for relatives, clan members, and villagers. The father of the bride made a formal announcement of the couple's marriage and bestowed the family's approval. Then followed speeches from a number of respected elder guests who exhorted the couple to behave properly, responsibly, and kindly to each other.

This couple married through mutual consent after declaring their love for one another, and their families were the last to know about their plans. The rite of passage in which this couple is participating is a variation on an ancient theme. Originally, a groom fed his bride to symbolize his ability to support her. Here the bride and groom feed each other.

REVIEW

Weddings are rites of passage that publicly confirm the changes in marital status and kinship status of the participants. Societies that place high value on kinship and community relations often have arranged marriages, and others have courtship practices in which individuals choose their own marriage partners. Weddings also extend the alliance and economic transaction functions of marriage.

PATTERNS OF RESIDENCE AFTER MARRIAGE

The elaborate Nepalese wedding process described in the Case Study is partly a result of postmarital residence patterns that call for a bride to separate herself from her relatives. In all societies, after people get married the new couple follows norms dictating where they should live. They may live with or near the husband's or the wife's family; they may alternate their residences between families; or they may establish a place of their own apart from any of their relatives. Their choice may depend on factors such as the amount of resources available or the composition of existing households. Societies vary in the patterns of postmarital residence that they encourage. Particular postmarital **residence rules** often are associated with different descent systems and specific economic strategies.

Matrilocal and Patrilocal Residence

Arrangements in which a married couple lives with or near the wife's family are termed **matrilocal residence.** Usually (but not always) matrilocal residence is associated with matrilineal descent. That is, societies that reckon descent matrilineally usually prefer that couples live with the wife's family. Because children resulting from marriage belong to the lineage of the mother, matrilocal residence ensures that kin group

residence rules
Rules that stipulate where a couple will reside after their marriage.

matrilocal residence
Pattern for residence after marriage in which the couple lives with or near the wife's family.

uxorilocal
Living with or near the wife's parents.

patrilocal residence
Pattern of residence after marriage in which the couple lives with or near the husband's relatives.

virilocal
Living with or near the husband's parents.

avunculocal residence
Patterns of residence after marriage in which the couple lives with or near the husband's mother's brother.

bilocal residence
Patterns of residence after marriage in which the couple alternates between living with the wife's kin and the husband's kin.

neolocal residence
Pattern of residence after marriage in which the couple establishes a new, independent household separate from their relatives.

members remain together. Matrilocal households typically consist of an elder couple, their daughters, their daughters' husbands and children, and their unmarried sons. Married sons live with their wives' kin. This kind of residence pattern is also called **uxorilocal**—living with the wife's family.

Patrilocal residence refers to arrangements in which a married couple lives with or near the husband's family. Patrilocal residence usually occurs in societies that reckon descent patrilineally. Because children resulting from marriage belong to the father's lineage, patrilocal residence creates stable, interacting groups of patrilineally related kin. Patrilocal households, therefore, consist of an elder couple, their sons, their sons' wives and children, and their unmarried daughters. Married daughters live with their husbands' relatives. This kind of residence pattern is also called **virilocal**—living with the husband's family.

Avunculocal Residence

In some societies with matrilineal descent and inheritance, an arrangement called **avunculocal residence** is preferred (from the Latin word *avunculus* meaning "mother's brother" and origin of the English word *uncle*). In these cases, a married couple lives with the husband's mother's brother. Avunculocal residence is found in societies where inheritance follows matrilineal descent but wealth, property, and social status are held by men. According to rules of matrilineal descent, a man's wealth and status cannot be passed to his own son because his son is a member of his wife's kinship group, not his own. Wealth, therefore, passes from a man to his sister's son. From the inheritor's point of view, a man gains wealth and status from his mother's brother. Avunculocal residence establishes a residential and emotional bond between a man and the person from whom he will inherit.

Bilocal and Neolocal Residence

In **bilocal residence,** married couples live alternately with the husband's and the wife's families. Bilocality has the advantage of flexibility, adapting residence to economic and resource conditions. When resources are scarce, couples can make adjustments by relocating from one household to another. Bilocal patterns also are adaptive in realigning living arrangements depending on the composition of households. That is, if households grow too large by the addition of in-marrying spouses and their children, then some people can leave and align themselves with their spouse's kin.

In societies with **neolocal residence,** a married couple establishes a new household independently of the residence of either the husband's or the wife's kin. Such systems typically are found in modern industrial and postindustrial societies, where couples tend to form new households immediately after marriage or within a year or two. Neolocal residence has the feature of independence, another reflection of the loosening of kinship bonds advantageous in capitalist economies. Neolocal residence separates people from larger kinship groups, allowing them to ignore claims from relatives who might want to share their resources.

Correlates of Residence Patterns

Among foragers, postmarital residence tends to be fairly diverse. Although couples generally live with relatives, the choice of wife's or husband's family depends on the composition of the households, the availability of resources, and personal preferences. According to Kathleen Gough (1975), approximately 60 percent of foraging societies tended to live patrilocally, whereas 16 to 17 percent preferred matrilocal residence. The remaining 15 to 17 percent were bilocal, choosing location with the family of either spouse. In farming societies with unilineal descent systems, postmarital residence tends to be consistent with principles of descent. Societies with matrilineal descent usually prefer matrilocal residence, whereas those with patrilineal descent prefer patrilocal residence. In societies whose economies are based on intensive agriculture, descent is nearly always patrilineal and residence is nearly always patrilocal. The patterns are consistent with men's primary responsibility for farming and their control over the allocation and use of land.

? *What residence rule is observed in your culture? Are there different historical patterns in residence that relate to people's cultures of origin?*

Like the Yanomamo of the Amazon, the Dani of the New Guinea highlands were patrilineal horticulturalists who engaged in frequent internal warfare.

internal warfare
Warfare between closely situated villages or communities.

external warfare
Warfare that takes place at some distance from home communities, requiring warriors' absence from their homes for extended periods of time.

Residence patterns have been observed to correlate with other cultural patterns. For example, in a classic study anthropologists found that in societies with frequent **internal warfare,** household groups are likely to be organized patrilocally (Ember and Ember, 1971). Internal warfare is characterized by frequent raiding among neighboring or nearby settlements. Because men act as warriors who defend their households and communities against the threat of attack by others, it is advantageous for them to live near male relatives they trust. In contrast, **external warfare,** fought against people from other societies, does not favor a particular residence rule, though external warfare that takes warriors away from home for extended periods may shift economic burdens to women in a way that favors matrilocal residence.

The Iroquois of North America and the Yanomamo of South America provide contrasting examples of the connection between types of warfare and postmarital residence patterns. Iroquois society was based on matrilineal descent, with people organized into matriclans. Iroquois economy centered on horticulture, an occupation for women, supplemented by hunting and fishing provided by men. By the seventeenth and eighteenth centuries, men were involved in frequent and prolonged external warfare with Europeans and with other native peoples, spending many months away from home. Matrilocal residence, the traditional preferred pattern, was strengthened by men's absence from home communities. In contrast, the Yanomamo reckon descent patrilineally. They are horticulturalists whose subsistence is provided nearly entirely by men. Yanomamo men engage in frequent internal warfare, raiding neighboring villages and defending their own homes against attacks by others. Consistent with the Embers' predictions, postmarital residence is strongly patrilocal.

REVIEW

Residence rules tend to ensure that people belonging to the same kin group remain close to one another. Matrilocal patterns, in which the couple lives with or near the wife's parents, are common in matrilineal societies. Patrilocal patterns, in which the couple lives with or near the husband's parents, is common in patrilineal societies. In avunculocal residence the couple moves in with the husband's mother's brother. Bilocal residency allows for the couple to live with either the husband's or wife's family, depending on the resources available. Neolocal residency allows the couple to establish their own independent household. Residence patterns may relate to other cultural patterns. For example, societies with frequent internal warfare tend to have patrilocal residence rules, whereas societies with frequent external warfare may strengthen matrilocal residence rules.

Case study

Residence in Rural North India and Sudan

RURAL NORTH INDIA

Households in rural villages in North India are made up of large extended or joint families. Village economies center on farming, although people living within a village may have a variety of occupations. Descent follows patrilineal principles, that is, people belong to the kinship group of their father. Marriages are arranged by parents. Men typically marry when in their early twenties to young women in their teens. Girls may be betrothed as young children. Postmarital residence is generally patrilocal. Residential groups, therefore, consist of a couple, their sons and sons' families, and their unmarried daughters. Women move to their husbands' homes upon marriage and subsequently have infrequent contact with their own kin. Because girls usually marry shortly after puberty, they may be in their early teens when they leave their parental homes. A wife who relocates at such a young age to her husband's household generally accepts her subordination, as it is based on age as well as on gender. She is thus easily dominated by her husband and especially by his mother. As many researchers of Indian culture have noted, wives often experience their greatest difficulties at the hands of their mothers-in-law rather than of their husbands (Chitnis, 1988).

Wives' domination by their mothers-in-law is due, in part, to the uncertain quality of relationships between spouses. Rarely are newlywed couples acquainted prior to marriage, and unions are arranged without consent from either the bride or the groom. Once married, couples actually have little interaction. The husband is himself a young man and lives under his father's authority. As a subordinate in his father's household, he takes great care not to shift away from his first allegiance to his parents. Because wives are perceived as potentially destabilizing to established familial order, married sons refrain from showing too much affection or even concern for their wives, especially early in their married life. Couples rarely interact publicly or have extended conversation when other family members are present. A wife thus spends most of her time in the company of other women in the household. These women, unmarried daughters and in-marrying wives, are all under the supervision of the elder woman. A new daughter-in-law is typically met with some degree of hostility by her husband's mother and sisters. As a result, authoritative statuses are immediately established and reinforced.

SOUTHERN SUDAN

Among the Nuer of southern Sudan, couples traditionally shifted residence at critical stages in their marriage. Homesteads consisted of a number of huts inhabited by related nuclear families. Plots for growing crops, principally women's work, and land for grazing cattle, principally men's work, were located outside the cluster of houses. Couples initially lived in the homestead of the wife's family, although the wife took up residence in a separate hut where her husband visited. After the birth of the first child, a husband moved in with his wife. They continued to live in the wife's compound until their child was weaned, then relocated to the husband's family compound (Evans-Pritchard, 1955:72–74).

This pattern of initial residence with the wife's kin is not uncommon in patrilocal societies. Beginning the marital experience with the wife's relatives provides the woman with some emotional support as she acclimates to her new role. In addition, when she eventually moves to her husband's family, she is not only a wife but a mother, having borne a child for

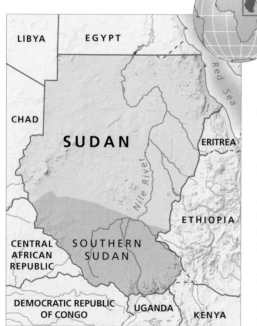

her husband's kin group and thereby gaining in status. When she shifts to her husband's household, she is a mature wife and mother.

Despite the normative preference for patrilocality, matrilocal residence was not uncommon among the Nuer (Gough, 1971:84, 91). According to Kathleen Gough's (1971:110) review of settlement lists compiled by Evans-Pritchard for the Nuer, less than half of the men surveyed lived in their fathers' villages. However, the gradual shift from wife's to husband's residential area reflects traditional Nuer attitudes toward marital stability. During early years of marriage a union is considered unstable. The insecurity of marriage, which is felt to deepen after birth of a child, is symbolized by a husband's residence in his wife's hut. The final move to the husband's compound is made a few years later.

levirate
Marriage preference rule in which a widow marries her deceased husband's brother.

sororate
Marriage between a widower and his deceased wife's sister.

WIDOWHOOD AND DIVORCE

All societies have strategies intended to preserve kin ties, marriage bonds, and household units. All cultures have patterns of beliefs and behaviors for dealing with widows and orphans, for example, and for regulating divorce and remarriage. These cultural patterns reveal the underlying principles of kinship, marriage, and family that are most important in a society. For example, the importance of family alliances is highlighted by marriage preference patterns that anthropologists refer to as "levirate" and "sororate."

The Levirate and Sororate

In the levirate and sororate marriage patterns, if a spouse dies, the deceased's family of origin supplies a younger sibling to marry the surviving spouse. So, for example, in the **levirate,** if a husband dies, his (usually younger) brother will marry the surviving widow. In the **sororate,** a younger sister of a deceased wife will marry the surviving widower. These kinds of marriages symbolically stress family alliances, because they say in effect that once two families are joined through marriage, it is in the families' interests to maintain the established alliance. Because the death of a husband or wife potentially disrupts the bond between families, a sibling of the deceased spouse perpetuates the alliance by marrying the survivor. The "ghost marriage" of the Nuer is a type of levirate, since a younger brother marries the widow of his elder brother. It differs from the more common pattern only in that children of the subsequent union are considered the offspring of the dead brother.

Divorce

Societies vary in their views about the dissolution of marriages. In some societies, divorce is a common outcome of an unhappy union, whereas in others, it rarely occurs because of social or religious restrictions. In some societies, either husband or wife may seek divorce; in others, only one of the parties (usually the husband) may initiate a breakup of the marriage. The ways in which marriages are dissolved also vary across cultures.

In general, matrilineal societies have more lenient attitudes toward divorce than do patrilineal societies because of the differences in principles of descent and the resulting claims that kinship groups have over children. It is nearly universal (although there are exceptions) that young children continue to live with their mothers after a divorce. Because children belong to the kin group of their mother in matrilineal societies, divorce does not cause a contradiction between location and kinship. In contrast, the dissolution of a marriage in patrilineal

In Saudi culture, children belong to the father, his patrilineage, and his patriclan. He automatically would retain custody of them in the event of divorce, which, until recently, was a prerogative only of men. Saudi society and the religion of Islam reinforce the relative confinement of women and strict regulation of their sexual and social behavior.

societies causes a problem, because it is through marriage that patrilineal descent groups are able to make claims over children produced by the wives of their male members. In addition, patrilineal societies generally exert more control over women's sexual behavior than do matrilineal societies, because they need to establish paternity to ensure a child's legitimate place in the father's kinship group.

Small-scale foraging and horticultural societies most often have flexible attitudes toward divorce, regardless of the type of descent system in their culture. In native North America, for example, with few exceptions, either husband or wife could initiate a breakup of their marriage. Divorce was fairly common, especially in the early years of a marriage and especially if the couple had no children. Acceptable grounds for divorce included adultery, failure to provide or fulfill domestic obligations, or simply personal incompatibility. Few societies had formal procedures for divorce. Rather, the couple would separate, each returning to his or her natal family, or the in-marrying spouse would leave. A divorce could be the result of a joint decision by husband and wife, or it could be initiated by one or the other.

In some Native American societies, there were publicly recognized ways to signal one's wishes for divorce. For example, among both the Mohawk and the Diné, two matrilineal, matrilocal societies, if a woman wanted a divorce, she might remove her husband's personal belongings from the house when he was away and place them outside. When the husband returned, he would collect his belongings and go back to the home of his mother or sister. If the husband initiated the divorce, he would simply take his possessions and leave. No social stigma was attached to either husband or wife after a divorce.

Among the Lakota and some other peoples of the Great Plains, a divorce could be jointly agreed upon by both parties. However, a man had a public way of signaling his wishes to end their marriage that was not available to a woman. He would beat a drum at a warrior society dance and proclaim that he wished to "throw away [his] wife" (Hassrick, 1964:130). Through this strategy, a man not only ended his marriage but publicly humiliated his wife as well. Although men did not suffer social criticism if their marriages ended, divorced women were shamed.

There are economic deterrents to divorce. For example, exchanges of bridewealth tend to lessen rates of divorce. The husband's kinship group does not favor divorce because a couple's children, although belonging to the husband's kin group in patrilineal societies, usually stay with their mother and therefore leave the husband's household if divorce occurs. A wife's family may also be reluctant to sanction a divorce, because when couples break up, the wife's kin must return the goods that they received as bridewealth. Therefore, they may pressure an unhappy wife to remain with her husband. Conflicts over bridewealth and its return in cases of divorce may result not only in the end of family alliances but lead to interfamilial tension and conflict.

In extreme patriarchal societies, such as in some villages in India, in pre-revolutionary China, and in many Middle Eastern nations, women rarely have the right to divorce, whereas men are free to break up their marriages, usually on grounds of their wives' disobedience, laziness, or adultery. In some societies, a woman's failure to produce sons might also be a cause for divorce. In such cases, great social criticism is heaped on a divorced woman and on her family as well, although little if any criticism is leveled at the husband.

In some cultures, religious beliefs are used to strongly condemn and even outlaw divorce. Today, Roman Catholicism, Islam, and Orthodox Judaism place barriers to the breakup of marriages. In these belief systems, because a marriage was sanctified in the wedding ceremony, people have no right to dissolve the union. In strict Islamic and Orthodox Jewish communities, it is very difficult for women to initiate divorce, but men may seek divorce in religious councils if they cite acceptable grounds.

REVIEW

The levirate and the sororate marriage patterns maintain alliances between families after the death of a spouse. Marriage is not only a relationship but an economic obligation to the other party as well. Divorce is viewed, and occurs, differently across societies. Patrilineal societies generally have more strict rules concerning divorce than do matrilineal societies.

Case study

Marriage and Divorce among the Kpelle of Liberia

Marriage patterns among the Kpelle, a farming society of Liberia, provide several options of payment and service that lead to differences in the strength of bonds between couples and the rights that a man exercises over children born of the union (Gibbs, 1965). The ideal form of marriage involves transfer of bridewealth from a husband's kin group to that of his wife. This is the standard type of union. It permits a husband and his lineage to claim children produced by the marriage. A second form involves performance of brideservice rather than payment of bridewealth. In this type of marriage, a couple resides with the wife's family for a fixed period of time agreed upon by the parties concerned. During this period, the husband performs labor for his in-laws. Children born to the couple during the years of service belong to the wife's lineage rather than to the husband's. Once the period of brideservice is completed, the children become members of the father's patrilineage.

A third marital option is "male concubinage." In this option, the status of the couple is somewhat ambiguous. It involves an economic and sexual union between a poor man and one of the wives of a chief or wealthy man. Although the woman remains the legal wife of the patron, her relationship with the client is publicly recognized and sanctioned. Such a marriage provides benefits for two kinds of men. A poor man who would otherwise have few marital prospects can marry and ally himself with the wealthy person. And a wealthy man who is either already a chief or wishes to become one can gain a client in a dependent relationship. The client's dependence is turned into political support for the patron. Since the client and patron's wife farm land controlled by the patron, the latter obtains products of their labor that he can sell for cash income or can distribute to others and thereby gain their support as well. Finally, since the woman remains the legal wife of the patron, children born to the client couple belong to the patron's lineage rather than to that of their biological father.

Kpelle marriages, then, are basically differentiated in terms of the legal status of women and the rights that husbands and their lineages may claim over a woman's children. If a woman is a full legal wife, that is, in standard marriages with payment of bridewealth, her children belong to her husband's patrilineage. If a woman's legal status is in transition, as during the period of brideservice, her children belong to her patrilineage and cannot be claimed by her husband. And if the woman is the legal wife of a patron even though she lives with another man, her children belong to the patron.

Although marriage is the usual and preferred state for adults, rates of divorce are reported to be "moderately high" (Gibbs, 1965). Divorces are granted by formal courts under the jurisdiction of local chiefs. Proceedings involve public hearings to determine the party at fault. Women usually initiate divorce, in part because fixing of blame is most often placed on the initiator and men are reluctant to be publicly criticized for ending their marriages. Even though women are characteristically blamed for failed marriages, their request for divorce is usually granted. A man who wishes a divorce may mistreat his wife so that she will seek a formal divorce in court. In this manipulative manner, he obtains his objective but is not publicly faulted.

Kpelle divorce benefits both wife and husband in an unhappy marriage. A wife who seeks to divorce is given her freedom and thus is personally satisfied. A husband, whether or not he wants to be divorced, retains two prerogatives: He receives the return of bridewealth that he had given to his wife's kin when he married, and he retains rights as father to his children. Such rights significantly include the privilege of receiving bridewealth for his daughters when they marry.

Defining Marriage and Family

- Families serve economic and social functions. Members of families usually reside together and provide for biological reproduction and for the training and enculturation of children. Families provide people with companionship, emotional support, and assistance, and are the basic unit of economic cooperation and interdependence. Families, particularly households, work together to complete the daily tasks necessary for survival. They are also decision-making groups. Members consult together and make decisions regarding joint actions. In many societies, families perform religious functions, planning and carrying out rituals that celebrate significant events in members' lives.

- Marriage is the most common way in which families are formed. Marriage is a socially recognized, enduring, stable bond between people who each have certain rights and obligations with respect to one another. Husbands and wives can expect to have an exclusive sexual relationship and assist one another in the raising of children and in the provisioning of their household. Through the marriage bond, men are able to claim "social fatherhood" by establishing themselves as the husband of the mother.

Families and Ideal Types

- Although the family is a universal cultural construct, the types of families found in different kinds of societies vary. Nuclear families consist of parents and their children, whereas extended families consist of a larger number of relatives, usually representing at least three generations. Nuclear families are often found in modern industrial societies, which stress economic independence and promote the loosening of wider kinship bonds. They are also found in many foraging societies because they are adaptive to survival in conditions of resource scarcity. In the context of insufficient resources, nuclear families can splinter off and disperse into a large territory.

- Extended families are more common in farming and pastoral societies. They have the advantage of perpetuating the social unit, sharing resources and work, and providing emotional support and material aid. Members of extended families can rely on each other for help in their work, in childcare, and in support in times of crisis or conflict with other groups.

- Family types are responsive to changes in productive modes and general social values. In the United States and Canada, as well as in many countries throughout the world, the idealized model of husband, wife, and children has declined in frequency throughout the twentieth century. Many households consist of single parents and their children, others consist of unmarried couples,

and still others consist of stable unions between same-sexed partners. Numbers of children per household have declined throughout the century.

Endogamy, Exogamy, and the Incest Taboo

- The incest taboo universally forbids marriage between parents and their children and between siblings. In some societies, the incest taboo is extended to include other relatives as well. For example, marriage may be forbidden between cousins or between aunts/uncles and their nieces/nephews.

- Anthropologists and other researchers have offered various explanations about the origin of the incest taboo. Suggested theories include an instinctual revulsion and aversion toward sexual relations within the nuclear family, the biological consequences of inbreeding that may increase frequencies of undesirable physical and mental traits, a reduction in the fitness of a population through genetic homogeneity, a response to the need to diminish sexual competition within the nuclear family unit, and a means of forcing people to make alliances with others in order to survive.

Forms of Marriage

- Societies differ in the expected or permissible number of spouses that a person can have at any one time. Marriage between one man and one woman is called monogamy; marriage between more than two people is called polygamy. There are two kinds of polygamous marriages: Polygyny is the marriage between one man and two or more women, and polyandry is the marriage between one woman and two or more men.

Marriage as Alliance and Economic Exchange

- Marriage often involves an economic exchange either preceding, during, or following the wedding ceremony. The term *bridewealth* refers to a gift given by the husband or his family to that of his intended wife. Bridewealth is most often given in patrilineal, patrilocal societies as a symbolic compensation to the woman's family for the loss of her economic labor. Instead of or sometimes in addition to a gift, a husband may be required to perform services for his wife's parents, a custom called *brideservice*. He may hunt for them, construct their homes, fetch wood or water, or fulfill other household tasks. Finally, in some societies, economic goods or wealth are given by the bride's family to the new couple or to the husband's kin prior to or upon the marriage. Such gifts are called *dowry*.

Marriage as a Rite of Passage

- Marriages may be arranged by parents or by the couple themselves through courtship. The marriage ceremony publicly sanctions marriage and symbolizes the rights and duties of couples to each other and to their families after marriage.

Patterns of Residence after Marriage

- Societies tend to have preferences for where couples reside after they marry. In some societies, a couple resides with or near the husband's relatives (patrilocal residence), and in others, a couple resides with or near the wife's kin (matrilocal residence). Bilocal residence refers to living arrangements where married couples live alternately with the husband's and the wife's families. In some societies with matrilineal descent and inheritance, a couple may live with the husband's mother's brother (avunculocal residence). Finally, some societies, such as our own, prefer neolocal residence, in which couples establish a new household of their own, separate from either group of kin.

Widowhood and Divorce

- In some societies, the emphasis on marriage as an alliance between families is highlighted by marriage preference patterns called levirate and sororate. In these marriage patterns, if one spouse dies, the deceased's family of origin supplies a younger sibling to marry the surviving spouse. In the levirate, a deceased husband's brother (usually younger) marries the surviving widow; in the sororate, a younger sister of the deceased wife marries the surviving widower.

Key Terms

household 222	caste 230	brideservice 235	avunculocal residence 242
family 223	monogamy 231	dowry 237	bilocal residence 242
marriage 224	polygamy 231	arranged marriages 238	neolocal residence 242
social fatherhood 224	serial monogamy 231	courtship 239	internal warfare 243
nuclear family 224	polygyny 231	residence rules 241	external warfare 243
single-parent family 225	polyandry 231	matrilocal residence 241	levirate 245
extended family 225	sororal polygyny 231	uxorilocal 242	sororate 245
joint family 228	ghost marriage 233	patrilocal residence 242	
incest taboo 229	same-sex marriage 234	virilocal 242	
class 230	bridewealth 235		

Review Questions

1. What definition of marriage would cover all the marriage types discussed in this chapter?
2. How is subsistence related to family forms? How can changes in marriage and family reflect adaptations to changes in subsistence?
3. How do endogamy and exogamy affect a society's social organization?
4. What are some hypotheses about the origins of the incest taboo?
5. What are the benefits of polygamous marriages? What are the drawbacks?
6. What are common forms of political and economic exchange in marriage, and what types of kinships are associated with those forms?
7. How are postmarital residence patterns related to kinship? How are residence rules related to women's and men's status in a society?
8. What are some reasons that marriages are arranged? Why is divorce discouraged in arranged marriages?
9. How are levirate and sororate different? Why do societies have these practices?

Gender

CHAPTER 10

Preview

1. **What is the difference between sex and gender?**
2. **How do gender roles and gender relations vary cross-culturally?**
3. **How does subsistence strategy relate to gender roles and relationships?**
4. **How do gender constraints relate to a culture's ideological system?**
5. **What are some outcomes of male dominance or of gender equality for a society?**
6. **What global factors affect women's participation in the work force?**
7. **How have ideologies affected gender constructs in the industrial and postindustrial eras?**

A man and a woman were once making a hard journey through the bush. The woman had her baby strapped upon her back as she walked along the rough path overgrown with vines and shrubbery. They had nothing to eat with them, and as they traveled on they became very hungry.

Suddenly, emerging from the heavily wooded forest into a grassy plain, they came upon a herd of bush cows grazing quietly.

The man said to the woman, "You have the power of transforming yourself into whatever you like; change now to a leopard and capture one of the bush cows, that I may have something to eat and not perish." The woman looked at the man significantly, and said, "Do you really mean what you ask, or are you joking?" "I mean it," said the man, for he was very hungry.

The woman untied the baby from her back, and put it upon the ground. Hair began growing upon her neck and body. She dropped her loincloth; a change came over her face. Her hands and feet turned into claws. And, in a few moments, a wild leopard was standing before the man, staring at him with fiery eyes. The poor man was frightened nearly to death and clambered up a tree for protection. When he was nearly to the top, he saw that the poor little baby was almost within the leopard's jaws, but he was so afraid, that he couldn't make himself come down to rescue it.

When the leopard saw that she already had the man good and frightened, and full of terror, she ran away to the flock of cattle to do for him as he had asked her to. Capturing a large young heifer, she dragged it back to the foot of the tree. The man, who was still as far up in its top as he could go, cried out, and piteously begged the leopard to transform herself back into a woman.

Slowly, the hair receded, and the claws disappeared, until finally, the woman stood before the man once more. But so frightened was he still, that he would not come down until he saw her take up her clothes and tie her baby to her back. Then she said to him, "Never ask a woman to do a man's work again."

From *African Folktales* by Roger D. Abrahams, pp. 148–149. Copyright © 1983 by Roger D. Abrahams. Used by permission of Pantheon Books, a division of Random House, Inc.

This narrative of the leopard woman from Liberia transmits attitudes about the proper work of women and men. Women perform the tasks of farming and fishing, and men are responsible for hunting. But the story also tells of the dangers of violating social norms about gender. These are powerful lessons, meant to instruct through example, drama, and humor. This chapter explores the cross-cultural study of gender and gender relations, about which every human society has something to say. People's norms for gender behavior vary widely; yet common patterns exist. These patterns of thought and behavior relate in part to the way people make their living and the ideologies that support those ways.

gender
The roles that people perform in their households and communities and the values and attitudes that people have regarding men and women.

sex
Biological differences between males and females.

gender construct (gender model)
The set of cultural assumptions about gender roles and values and the relations between the genders that people learn as members of their societies.

cultural constructs
Models of behavior and attitudes that a particular culture transmits to its members.

SEX AND GENDER

As anthropologists use the word, **gender** refers to the roles that people perform in their households and communities and the values and attitudes that people have regarding men and women. Thus, gender is a cultural category. It is not the same as **sex,** which is a biological category. That is, females and males are born, but women and men are products of their culture's definitions of how females and males should act.

The term *gender identity* refers to how people internalize and enact those attitudes and expectations that are associated with their gender category. Gender identity is conveyed, for example, by the way people dress, walk, and speak. And it is shown by the kinds of activities that people engage in and the attitudes they have about themselves and others. The term **gender construct (gender model)** refers to the set of cultural assumptions about gender roles and values and the relations between the genders that people learn as members of their societies. Unlike sex, gender is in every way "culturally constructed."

People in every culture maintain and transmit ideas about the roles that are appropriate for women and men to fill, the rights they have in relation to each other, and the values associated with their activities. These gender constructs are based in part on sex differences between males and females, but they vary widely across cultures. In many societies, however, the contrasting activities of men and women are constrained by the reproductive role that is exclusive to women. For example, during periods of childbearing and nursing it is difficult for women to engage in physically stressful or dangerous activities.

The Cultural Construction of Gender Identity

Gender as a social or cultural construct is a primary aspect of one's personal and social identity. It develops in earliest socialization through the ways that a baby is handled, treated, and spoken to. **Cultural constructs** are models of behavior and attitudes that a particular culture transmits to its members. These constructs are shared beliefs and values that become taken for granted as guiding principles. Childhood learning teaches appropriate behavior and molds personality to conform to cultural norms. Girls and boys learn skills and attitudes that make them functioning members of their community. In addition, most (but not all) cultures use two sets of personal names, one appropriate for females and one appropriate for males. In Chapter 5, we discussed the importance of naming in constructing a person's social and gender identity.

Ideological messages about women's and men's places in their families and communities and about their social value may be conveyed through religious beliefs and practices, language, and daily interactions between men and women in their families, communities, and wider social arenas. Rights to make decisions, to speak, and to participate in particular activities reflect cultural valuations and privileges allocated to people. In our discussion of language (see Chapter 4), we considered examples of the differences in how English-speaking women and men use language not only to communicate their ideas and feelings but also to transmit their gender identity. For example, we noted that women tend to be more polite, deferential, and attentive to others, whereas men tend to be more assertive and interruptive when speaking with others.

One universal expression of gender identity is the signaling of gender differences by bodily adornments and comportment. For example, men and women generally wear different kinds of clothing or jewelry. They may fashion their hair in different styles, or use body

Gender identity in conservative Islamic societies is both unambiguous and complex. This veiled figure is easily recognized as a woman in Saudi Arabia. According to many women, wearing the veil is a privilege of becoming a marriageable adult and represents a woman's responsibility to her family, whose identity and social standing depend upon the morally correct behavior of all its members.

decorations such as tattoos or makeup. In North American and European countries, it is only since the middle of the twentieth century that pants was considered appropriate attire for women. And even so, styles, colors, and designs used for women's clothing may differ from those commonly used for men. Moreover, while it may be acceptable for women to wear garments styled like men's pants and shirts, in most American settings it is not at all acceptable for men to wear dresses and skirts. It was not until 1995 that **transvestism,** or cross-dressing to look and act like someone of the opposite gender, was removed from the official list of mental illnesses.

> **transvestism**
> Dressing in the clothes usually worn by members of the opposite gender.

Other kinds of gender-differentiating behavior are subtler and less conscious but just as powerful. Social presentation includes dynamics of walking, sitting, and general body posture. Speech styles employed by women or men are also often distinct. Nonverbal communication, such as gestures, smiling, eye contact, and touch, may be differentially employed.

Gender and Sexuality

Although we commonly think of our sexual feelings and practices as part of our nature, they, too, are shaped by our culture. Our culture teaches us what kinds of sexual feelings and practices are "normal" or "natural" and what kinds are "deviant." We learn who are appropriate sexual partners, when and where sexual relations are appropriate, and the proper ways to engage in sex. With few exceptions, these expectations are culturally constructed.

As discussed in Chapter 8, all societies institute some form of the incest taboo that bans sex between members of the nuclear family and certain other relatives. Many societies also set an appropriate age to begin sexual relations. In the United States, for example, it is illegal for an adult to have sex with someone younger than 16, a crime called statutory rape. This obviously does not mean that no one under the age of 16 has sex, but it does formalize cultural attitudes and criminalize specific behaviors. American society also has gender-based attitudes about the relative ages of men and women engaging in consensual sex. In many "normal" couples, a man may be fifteen or twenty years older than the woman, but it is rare to hear of a couple in which a woman is significantly older than the man. One reason may have to do with reproductive potential. That is, an old man can still have children with a young woman, but a young man cannot have children with a much older woman. Nevertheless, negative attitudes about younger men who choose much older women reveal cultural values about both sex and gender.

Another cultural element in attitudes about sexuality is the accepted relationship between sex and marriage. In American society, public discourse regards sex between unmarried people as inappropriate or less appropriate than sex between a husband and wife. Actual practice contradicts public morality, but the fact that political and religious leaders are reluctant to condone sex outside of marriage indicates the strength of underlying cultural constructs.

In contrast, in many other societies, it is considered normal and natural that unmarried people engage in sex. In some societies, proving one's ability to conceive is a prerequisite for marriage. And while no society encourages extramarital sexual activities, the punishment for adulterers varies widely and is not everywhere severe. In addition, patriarchal societies often have a double standard about these issues. Men are permitted and even encouraged to have premarital sexual experiences, while women are taught to remain chaste before marriage. In some patrilineal societies, a woman's virginity is a prerequisite for marriage, and adultery may be more severely punished if committed by a woman than by a man. In some Islamic countries, adultery is a capital offense for both partners. In others, only the woman is singled out for punishment. In 2003, for example, a divorced Nigerian woman, Amina Lawal, was condemned to death by stoning by an Islamic court for bearing a child out of wedlock; the man, who denied he was the father, received no punishment. However, an appeals court acquitted and released Lawal later that year, in large part because of international pressure.

Gender and Homosexuality

Attitudes about homosexuality are a further reflection of cultural learning. Judeo-Christian-Islamic teachings convey negative messages about homosexuality, considering

The complementarity and interdependence of genders are represented in this ancient symbol of yin (femaleness) and yang (maleness). This symbol, based on astrological observations of the changing solstices, comes from the Han period (207 B.C.E.-C.E. 9). The light area represents the greater sunlight of the summer solstice, which is associated with maleness; the dark area represents the greater moonlight of the winter solstice, associated with femaleness. The small circles within the arcs of color show the mutual interdependence of yin and yang, as each is "born" within the other.

? *Why do you think that third gender roles such as the* hijras *exist?*

it to be a violation of natural law. Many nations dominated politically by religious thinking have laws that criminalize homosexual conduct and institute policies that discriminate against homosexuals. In the United States, as recently as 1986, the U.S. Supreme Court, in the case of *Bowers* v. *Hardwick*, upheld the right of the state of Georgia to make private sexual relations between consulting adult homosexuals a crime punishable by imprisonment. This ruling was superseded, however, in 2003.

Attitudes about homosexuality are continuously debated, most recently over gay marriage. In the United States, Vermont was the first state to permit the legal recognition of civil unions between homosexuals, so long as they did not call it "marriage." In 2003, the Anglican Church installed an openly gay priest, Gene Robinson, as bishop of New Hampshire. And in 2003, the Supreme Court of Canada ruled that Canadian marriage laws allow homosexuals to wed, joining Belgium and the Netherlands as the only countries where same-sex couples can legally marry. In the following year, the state of Massachusetts became the first in the United States to legalize same-sex marriage, not simply to recognize same-sex civil unions.

Antihomosexual attitudes are far from universal. In India, for example, Hindu belief regards homosexuality as one of the possible expressions of human desire. Hindu mystic stories portray both heterosexual and homosexual experience as natural and joyful. In addition, the pantheon of Hindu deities includes some who are sexually ambiguous, combining aspects of maleness and femaleness, or who transform themselves from one gender into the other. Finally, some Indian male homosexuals and transvestites adopt the role of *hijras,* people thought of as "neither man nor woman" (Nanda, 1990). Although *hijras* are sometimes feared and ridiculed, they also are considered sacred, combining and mediating between female and male aspects believed to exist in all humans.

As another example, the Etoro and several other horticultural societies in New Guinea insist on male homosexual activity to ensure a man's physical growth as well as to enhance his physical and spiritual strength. According to Etoro beliefs, people have a kind of spirit essence called *hame* that is needed to develop and maintain one's energy and vitality. At birth, only a small amount of *hame* is placed in a child, not enough to protect it for a long, healthy life. So, as people mature, they must try to augment their store of *hame* or life force. They must also protect it from potential sources of depletion, and one of the major causes of depletion is heterosexual intercourse. Men protect themselves from depleting their *hame* by avoiding sexual intercourse with women during periods associated with farming and trading cycles, estimated by anthropologist Raymond Kelly (1976) to amount to between 205 and 260 days per year. Protection against depletion is not enough, however, because the Etoro also believe that boys lack semen, which contains *hame.* Youths can acquire *hame* only by receiving semen from adult men. Boys orally consume a man's semen after manipulating his penis to the point of ejaculation.

In contrast to men, women are thought (at least by men) to have a limited amount of *hame,* thus explaining their relative weakness compared to men. Women's beliefs about *hame* were not collected by Kelly, however, because "a male anthropologist cannot develop an informant relationship with a female" (p. 47). Although Etoro men claimed that "only the women know what the women do," they believe that women engage in some form of homosexual activity through which adult women may transmit menstrual blood to young girls to initiate their reproductive capacity.

Case study

Two-Spirits: A Third Gender

Although the division of humans into two gender categories is the most common cultural pattern, other possibilities exist. For example, many native cultures in North America recognized a third gender category as well. The concept of a third gender was based on separating the social being (the gender category) from the biological body (the facts of sex). The third gender was a social concept that included biological males and females who assumed social roles other than (or sometimes in addition to) the roles usually associated with their sex. This third gender was a distinct gender category, different from woman and man. Western observers formerly misused the term **berdaches** to refer to third-gender individuals in a derogatory way.

According to documentary evidence reviewed by Charles Callender and Lee Kochems (1983), 113 native North American societies provided a third gender status as a possibility for their members. Lack of mention of third genders, now often called **Two-Spirits,** in other cultures does not necessarily mean that they were absent. Rather, their existence may not have been noted by Euro-American observers. In any case, third genders were well established in most regions of North America, especially in the west, from the Great Lakes to California. Callender and Kochems find no correlation between types of social or economic systems and the use of third genders, except that Two-Spirits were least likely to be found in societies that relied heavily on hunting.

People became Two-Spirits as a result of personal inclination, spiritual calling, or parental selection. From an early age a young girl or boy might take an interest in the occupations and demeanors usually displayed by members of the other gender. Parents thereafter trained the child in the subsistence skills appropriate to his or her chosen role. Among some groups, parents who had no sons might choose one of their daughters to learn hunting skills so that she could contribute directly to household subsistence as a son would.

A second, more common mode of recruitment was to receive a spiritual calling through a vision or dream. Dreaming to assume the third gender gave both spiritual and social validation to a male's or female's gender transformation. Two-Spirits who came to their status through a spiritual calling were often thought to have extraordinary powers to heal and to foretell the future.

A Two-Spirits' social role was formally validated with rituals that publicly marked their special status. Among the Kaska of Yukon Territory, when a female Two-Spirit reached the age of 5, her parents tied a bear's dried ovaries to her belt to protect her from becoming pregnant. And at puberty, female Two-Spirits of the Cocopa had their noses pierced like men rather than tattoos on their chins like women. Among the Mohave, when a male Two-Spirit was about 10 years old, he participated in a public ceremony in which he was led into a circle surrounded by an audience and a singer. When the singer sang initiation songs, the Two-Spirit danced as women did and was proclaimed an *aylha* (Two-Spirit) after the fourth dance. He/she was then ritually bathed, given a woman's skirt, and announced a new woman's name for him/herself.

Two-Spirits typically performed economic duties usually appropriate to the opposite sex, sometimes in addition to those associated with their own biological sex. Female Two-Spirits were hunters, trappers, and occasionally warriors as well. Male Two-Spirits contributed their labor as farmers (where economies included horticulture) and were trained in domestic skills, such as sewing, embroidery, and food preparation.

Where warfare was a significant activity, male Two-Spirits generally did not participate. However, in some societies, male Two-Spirits did join war parties, either as active fighters or as carriers of supplies. Among the Cheyenne, male Two-Spirits accompanied war expeditions, serving critical religious functions as healers of the wounded and

berdaches
Male Two-Spirits in some Native American societies who adopted some of the economic and social roles of women.

Two-Spirits
In Native American societies, males who adopted some of the social and economic roles of women, and females who adopted some of the social and economic roles of men.

George Catlin made this drawing in the 1800s during an expedition among the Sac and Fox Indians. It shows warriors dancing to a male Two-Spirits. According to the observer, while the warriors are making fun of the Two-Spirits, who appears in women's attire, they are also competing to attract his/her attention, which is seen as a sign of good fortune. (Smithsonian American Art Museum, Washington, DC/Art Resource, NY)

guardians of scalps obtained in battle. They also had charge of the Scalp Dances that followed victorious raids. Although female Two-Spirits did not always participate as warriors, they were not barred from doing so, and some became famous for their military and tactical skills.

Two-Spirits are often described in the literature as unusually prosperous in comparison with other members of their community. They had economic advantages due to their ability to perform both women's and men's work. In some societies, Two-Spirits had sources of income not available to any other people because they performed ritual functions specifically assigned to them. For example, Lakota Two-Spirits bestowed secret, spiritually powerful names on children, receiving horses in payment for their services. In several California groups, Two-Spirits were responsible for burial and mourning rituals. And in societies such as the Diné, Cheyenne, and Omaha, they functioned as go-betweens between men and women by resolving conflicts between spouses or arranging liaisons and marriages, usually receiving payment for their services (Williams, 1986:70–71).

One of the consistent features of third-gender tradition was that members wore clothing and hairstyles associated with their chosen social role rather than with their biological sex. The significance of this pattern is that it demonstrates that gender distinctions are given symbolic as well as practical value. In a literal as well as figurative sense, people wear the markings of the gender with which they are associated. In some cultures, Two-Spirits who performed both men's and women's occupations changed their clothing to reflect the gender identity of the work. For instance, Western Mono Two-Spirits wore men's clothing when hunting and women's dress when gathering, and male Osage and Miami Two-Spirits wore men's clothing when they joined war expeditions but dressed like women when they returned home. Deceased male Zuni Two-Spirits were buried in women's dress and men's trousers (Williams, 1986:454).

The social and sexual lives of Two-Spirits were consistent with their gender roles. Sexual activity and marriage usually involved relationships with members of the opposite social gender. That is, female Two-Spirits had sexual relations with and might marry women, and male Two-Spirits had sexual relations with and might marry men. Two-Spirits often were highly desired as mates because of their economic prosperity and productive skills and their spiritual knowledge and abilities. According to recorded accounts, they had little difficulty marrying and establishing successful households. The wives of female Two-Spirits sometimes had children fathered by men but claimed by the Two-Spirit husband in an expression of social fatherhood. In some societies, Two-Spirits might marry either men or women. Significantly, Two-Spirits never married other Two-Spirits, because two people with the same social gender could not marry.

Native Americans did not view sexual relations between Two-Spirits and their mates as either homosexual or heterosexual because Two-Spirits were not men or women. They were a distinct third gender. Symbolic transformation made gender, not biological sex, the important factor. Two-Spirits' sexual activity, like all their behavior, was seen as private and specific to them as members of a distinct third gender. In Native American worldviews, this privacy was extended to all sexual activity, including homosexuality and heterosexuality.

Gender equality is a prerequisite for the respect and high status most often conferred on Two-Spirits, because it meant that neither males nor females gave up or acquired social prestige by abandoning roles usually associated with their sex and instead assuming other roles. Euro-American observers did not understand this underlying gender equality, however. They could not understand why males chose not to identify as men, interpreting this choice as a voluntary decline in status. In contrast to Euro-American values, in most Native American societies males did not give up dominance by abandoning men's roles, because men's roles did not include rights to dominate. Most examples of men's dominance over women occurred in native societies that had already been transformed by contact with European and American traders, officials, and missionaries.

By the late nineteenth and early twentieth centuries, the number of Two-Spirits declined due to voluntary or forced adoption of Euro-American attitudes and practices. These insisted on only a two-category system of gender, denigrated males who dressed like women or assumed women's roles, and proclaimed homosexuality to be a violation of natural and divine laws. Agents of the U.S. and Canadian governments who supervised native reservations with varying success tried to force male Two-Spirits to wear men's clothing and short hair. In the words of a Lakota religious leader speaking of events that occurred in the 1920s:

> When the people began to be influenced by the missions and the boarding schools, a lot of them forgot the traditional ways and the traditional medicine. Then they began to look down on the *winkte*, Two-Spirits, and lose respect. Some changed their ways and put on men's clothing. But others, rather than change, went out and hanged themselves. (quoted in Williams, 1986:182)

Female Two-Spirits also were forced to abandon their social and sacred roles. Despite decades of concerted social and ideological pressures, however, Two-Spirits continue to exist in some Native American societies.

REVIEW

Gender, cultural constructs that refer to the roles people perform in their households and communities, differs from sex, which is a biological category. Gender identity is expressed in clothing, makeup, personal names, speech, nonverbal communication, economic roles, and the way people are enculturated into appropriate behaviors for men and women. Attitudes and practices concerning homosexual and heterosexual sexual behavior are also culturally constructed. Gender constructs also include third gender roles, such as Two-Spirits and berdaches, people who are biologically male or female but take on the cultural and economic roles of the opposite gender.

GENDER ROLES AND RELATIONS

In all societies, certain behaviors and activities are deemed appropriate for women and others for men, with some overlap for both genders. Constellations of behaviors that are culturally associated with each gender are referred to as **gender roles.** Gender roles include the kind of work typically assigned to men and women, the familial roles that people play, the positions of leadership at home or in the community, and the ritual practices in which they engage. In some societies, women's and men's roles may be quite distinct with little overlap, whereas in others, gender roles may be flexible.

Men and women carry out their gender roles in relation to one another, interacting in their households and their communities in nearly every aspect of life. Even in activities in which women and men are separated from each other, same-gender groups usually act in a way that is mindful of the other group. Coming of age rituals for girls and boys, for example, may be organized around gender differences.

Gender relations consist of interactions between men and women, which may reflect differences in the relative status, prestige, and power of women and men. In some societies, gender equality generally prevails. Women and men are thought of as equal, having the same rights to respect, autonomy, and independence. Although men and women may have different roles in their households and communities, their work and activities are equally valued and socially rewarded. In other societies, the genders are not considered equal, and some degree of male dominance prevails. Men are thought of as superior to women, as more capable, intelligent, or spiritually endowed. Men occupy more prestigious roles in their societies as leaders and decision makers. In their homes, men may have control over the activities of their wives. Extreme forms of male

gender roles
Constellations of rights, duties, attitudes, and behaviors that are culturally associated with each gender.

gender relations
Norms of interaction between men and women, which may reflect differences in the relative status, prestige, and power of women and men.

dominance may be reflected in physical abuse and rape. These behaviors tend to be more acceptable in strongly patriarchal societies, where men hold positions of authority and power to the exclusion of women. As mentioned in Chapter 8, there are no known examples of matriarchal societies in which women have exclusive power.

Division of Labor by Gender

As you read in Chapters 6 and 7, in all societies some form of division of labor by gender influences the range of daily work that an individual carries out. Men's and women's work is often complementary, both contributing to the maintenance of their households by providing food, shelter, clothing, and necessary equipment. There is a great deal of cross-cultural variation in the allocation of work according to gender, but certain patterns tend to be found in most societies. Table 10.1 summarizes some of these frequent associations between tasks and gender.

Inferences about division of labor by gender can be made from data concerning nonhuman primate behavior and traditional foraging societies whose cultural patterns are well documented. Such data led Lila Leibowitz to postulate that a division of labor was not necessary when human ancestors engaged in "unspecified and undifferentiated" production (1983:123). Our early hominid ancestors, like modern nonhuman primates (chimpanzees, gorillas), spent their days in the same pursuits. They moved from one resource site to another, gathered and ate fruits and plants, and socialized together. Male and female tasks were not differentiated except for childbearing, nursing, and caring for the young, all obviously female responsibilities. However, at some point in our ancestral past, a division of labor developed when people began to engage in more specialized economic techniques, requiring more complex skills and learning. A division of labor was efficient because it allowed different people to learn different sets of skills, enabling them to specialize, refine, and deepen their knowledge and proficiency.

A division of labor based on gender contributed to coordinating a group's activities, due to the fact that women were restricted in their mobility because of their reproductive roles. That is, unlike other mammals whose young are able to walk and feed themselves fairly soon after birth, human infants remain dependent on adults for a protracted period of many years. As a consequence, caregivers are limited in their own activities. Pregnancy, childbearing, and nursing limit women's ability to travel during significant periods of their lives. Travel becomes more burdensome and also more dangerous to a mother's and child's survival. In almost all cultures, women are allotted the care of infants and young children. Presumably as an extension of these duties, women generally perform other caretaker activities, such as preparing family meals and caring for the sick or disabled or aged individuals within the household.

The division of labor based on gender is also an efficient allocation of human resources and energy in cultures where different kinds of labor require different outputs

Table 10.1 TASKS AND GENDER

Tasks Usually Performed by Women	Tasks Usually Performed by Men
Gathering plants, seeds, fruits, nuts	Hunting animals
Caring for children	Fishing as a primary responsibility
Caring for the sick and elderly	Herding large animals
Keeping up dwellings	Clearing fields for planting
Making clothing	Conducting warfare
	Conducting long-distance trade

Variable Gender Assignment or Cooperative Tasks	
Hunting small animals	Making crafts: pottery, basketry, tools
Fishing as a secondary resource	House building
Herding small animals	Conducting local trade
Planting/harvesting crops	

of energy and strength. Furthermore, it is efficient to teach people skills they are going to use during most of their lives. Skills needed to recognize and utilize edible plants, roots, herbs, and fruits or to track, locate, and kill animals require many years of careful instruction and practice. Therefore, specialization by gender and other factors such as age is efficient and provides for the survival of all.

As you read in Chapter 6, in contemporary or recent foraging societies, women gather wild plants, fruits, and nuts and may also hunt small animals. In contrast, men are allotted economic roles that include travel away from home settlements, requiring a man's absence all day or over a period of days or longer. Hunting and trading with other groups are typically the work of men. Anthropologists extrapolate from these data to make assumptions about the lives of prehistoric peoples.

In addition to considerations of energy and mobility, foraging societies may assign home-based activities to women and external hunting and traveling to men because of the need to protect women against possibilities of accidents and deaths that might occur away from local settlements (Friedl, 1975:135). Because the survival and continuity of a community depend on the successful reproductive life of women, protecting them from unnecessary danger is adaptive. At the same time, cooperative labor may include both men and women within a community. For example, communal hunting and farming might involve adults and youths of both genders.

In addition, gender roles change as economic and material factors change, for example, when foragers become agriculturalists. Cultural forms arise in specific conditions and are changeable when those conditions no longer obtain. Although gender roles may have arisen because women and men have different reproductive functions and different energy and mobility requirements, when productive work is historically transformed and can be performed equally well by women or men, the adaptive basis of earlier division of labor by gender is lost. However, more than economic and material factors are involved. For example, in modern industrial societies, most jobs can be accomplished equally well by women or men, but many jobs are held predominantly by one gender or the other. Men or women equally could be brain surgeons or typists, but most brain surgeons are men and most typists are women. Therefore, we need to explain gender roles in noneconomic terms as well.

One explanation is the social organization of households. As you read in Chapter 8, all societies structure households on the basis of families, regardless of family composition and household organization. Economic cooperation helps sustain family units, because members perform different kinds of work that complement each other's tasks, becoming interdependent in providing basic necessities. Households are established and maintain stability on this basis, so the gender division of labor remains a convenient method of organizing household production even when it is no longer an economic necessity.

Another explanation is that attitudes about work and its association with gender are part of the background ideologies that members of a society take for granted. These beliefs and attitudes are naturalized and thought of as human nature rather than understood as endowments of one's culture. Ideological processes, then, contribute to the maintenance of a gender division of labor, regardless of economic or other considerations.

One aspect of these ideologies is the evaluation of some work roles as inherently more attractive or fitting for men and others as inherently more appropriate and appealing to women. For example, women are thought to make good nurses because they have an innate desire to be nurturing. And they make good elementary school teachers because they like to work with children, an extension of their motherly roles. Men, in contrast, are thought to make good leaders and heads of corporations because they are innately assertive and like to be in control. Nurturance and dominance, however, are learned behaviors. Nevertheless, positive judgments

What socioeconomic and sociocultural changes in the United States permitted the changes in gender roles that this photograph represents? What are some economic, structural, and ideological sources of changes in the gender division of labor in U.S. society?

gender equality
A constellation of behaviors, attitudes, and rights that support the autonomy of both women and men.

gender inequality
The denial of autonomy and equal rights to one group of people based on their gender.

male dominance
A constellation of behaviors and attitudes that grant men access to roles of prestige and reward and deny the same to women.

become associated with the proper performance of one's gender roles, while people who resist assuming their culturally prescribed gender identities are negatively viewed.

Gender and Status

Gender roles are complicated by the fact that work and other tasks assigned to men and women may not be considered equivalent or equally valuable. In theory, gender relations may be characterized on a continuum from approximate equality to the complete domination of members of one gender by members of the other. In practice, whenever there is gender domination, as in strongly patriarchal societies, it is always the domination of women by men.

Gender equality refers to a constellation of behaviors, attitudes, and rights that support the autonomy of both women and men. In a gender equal society, women and men may have different economic, social, and political roles but the rewards given to them are roughly similar. For example, in Mohawk communities, women did most of the farmwork and household tasks while men hunted, fished, and traded. Although their activities were distinct, their work and contributions to their households were equally valued. Both men and women could hold positions of prestige and influence in their communities. Gender equality is more likely to exist in foraging and small horticultural societies, where all individuals make important contributions to subsistence and where hierarchical leadership is absent or minimal.

In contrast, **gender inequality** refers to denial of autonomy and equal rights to one group of people based on their gender. Gender inequality tends to be most marked in large-scale societies with strong economic specialization, where social and political stratification affects the allocation of rights and privileges among social categories, including class and gender. In patriarchal societies, for example, in India, Pakistan, and many Middle Eastern countries, women generally do not occupy positions of authority and are restricted in many of their daily activities. In these and other male-dominated societies, men contribute most of the productive labor that supports their families. They make most of the important decisions that affect their families, and they serve their communities as political or religious leaders.

Cultural values and social rewards mold people's attitudes about themselves and their relations to others. In societies where **male dominance** is pervasive, men learn to disvalue women and to assume rights to control women's activity. Women in these cultures learn to disvalue themselves and accept male domination. These gender models often are conveyed nonconsciously and go unquestioned. They are automatically accepted and followed and thus strengthened in the society.

? *How does a religion with which you are familiar define the status and roles of women and men?*

In all societies, ideological constructs support and perpetuate existing ways of living. For example, as is discussed in Chapter 14, religion often provides explanations and justifications for existing social relations. Religious beliefs sanction the status and roles of women and men, explaining divine origins for personal freedoms or restrictions, for differences in the prestige or power of men and women, and for the rights and obligations that they have. Myths of creation may give greater or lesser prominence to male or female deities, justifying the social value of human women and men (Sanday, 1981). For example, religious practice affects gender by allowing or restricting the ability of men and women to perform rituals. Barring women from sacred roles limits their status and prestige.

These Orthodox Jewish men are praying at the Wailing Wall in Jerusalem. Judaism, Roman Catholicism, and Islam are male-dominated religions. These religions make women equal in the eyes of God, but women are not permitted to worship in mosques, and in Orthodox synagogues they may be seated together in a separate section. Controversies in American Jewish and Christian denominations over the ordination of women bring to the surface underlying issues of gender and ideology.

Is Male Dominance Universal?

Anthropologists long maintained that, in all societies, the status of women was at least to some extent subordinate to that of men (Friedl, 1975:7; Rosaldo, 1974:17). In other words, although women's status varied from society to society, in no society were they fully equal to or superior to men. But an important question remains: Are there (or were there) genuinely egalitarian societies? From the data, it seems that the answer to this question is yes. But this is a complex issue, for several reasons. One is that there has been a long history of Western male bias in reporting behavior and beliefs in non-Western cultures (Leacock, 1981:17; Rohrlich-Leavitt et al., 1975:110–111). Explorers, missionaries, soldiers, and travelers in early periods of European colonization of the Americas, Africa, Asia, and the Pacific were almost exclusively men, who interpreted the cultures of native peoples through their own ethnocentric worldviews.

Later observers, including anthropologists, economists, and historians, also were predominantly men. Notwithstanding their supposed objectivity, they brought with them, as all people do, biases and frames of reference dominant in their own cultures. They usually asked for the opinions of men, partly because it was difficult for a foreign man to interact with women, but also partly because male investigators considered men's opinions to be more significant than the opinions of women. It is well to be reminded of the admonition made by Joseph Lafitau, a French observer of Native American cultures, who commented in 1724 that "authors who have written on the customs of the Native Americans concerning the rights and status of women have formed their conceptions, in this as in everything else, on European ideas and practices" (1974:344).

In addition to the inherent problem of obtaining a truly objective view of another culture, colonial contact often swiftly and dramatically altered traditional gender relations by transforming the indigenous cultures of colonized peoples (Leacock, 1981; Etienne and Leacock, 1980; Gailey, 1987; Wolf, 1982). Economic roles were radically changed in response to trade. Emphases on external trade rather than household production and consumption undermined women's contributions and enhanced male control over resources. As a result, the allocation of productive roles changed.

Changes in production often were accompanied by rapid realignments of indigenous political formations to meet colonizers' demands. Among the northeastern Iroquois, for example, British, French, and American officials bypassed the authority of women and ignored their opinions, dealing instead only with male chiefs. As described in Chapter 12, however, among the Iroquois, female heads of matrilineal clans were responsible for choosing men of their group as leaders and appointed spokespersons to voice their opinions in council meetings.

In Africa, too, the European colonizers bypassed female chiefs and warriors in favor of male leaders. Among the Igbo of Nigeria, for example, villages traditionally had a male leader for men and a female leader for women, but the power of the female leaders was undermined. Subsequent changes in traditional political organization following European colonization usually led to enhanced public prestige of men, which, in turn, was leveraged into greater control over their localities and families.

CRITICAL THINKING QUESTIONS

How could changes in gender relations caused by colonialism be interpreted as proof of the theory of universal male dominance? Why would that interpretation be wrong?

Even in societies that restrict women's public participation, however, women nevertheless have some power and informally control much of what happens in their households. Women's lives are sometimes described as focused on the "domestic sphere" and men's lives taking place in the "public sphere." This distinction may be fitting for some societies, especially large-scale agrarian or industrial states where labor tasks are highly specialized and gender roles are rigidly defined. But the distinction loses its value when applied to small-scale foraging or horticultural societies (Lamphere, 2001). In these societies, there is little differentiation between a public and private domain. Most activities take place communally, often out in the open or indoors in dwellings inhabited by

GLOBALIZATION

Beginning in the fifteenth century, European explorers and colonizers directly and indirectly altered the gender roles, status, and relations of people in the societies with which they came into contact. Europeans imposed their own cultural beliefs and attitudes on those peoples, devaluing women and regarding men as dominant.

? *Would you say that gender equality exists in the United States? How would you defend your answer?*

multiple family groups. Much work requires the cooperative efforts of men and women. Although there are certainly gender distinctions in these societies as well, a demarcation of domains is generally less rigid.

Women are sometimes able to exert influence, even in the most rigidly segregated communities, through direct personal religious experiences. In Ethiopia, for example, women may be possessed by spirits known as *zars,* whose presence is manifested through ecstasy and out-of-body experiences. Women who are possessed by spirits must attend a communal ceremony in the company of other afflicted individuals. At these rituals, held regularly about once every month, healers cure the women in an atmosphere of festivity and abandon (Boddy, 2001). In addition to the ritual functions of *zar* beliefs, afflicted women have the opportunity to socialize together away from the control and supervision of their fathers or husbands. *Zar* spirits may possess any individual, but their most frequent targets are married women. It has been hypothesized that in the context of a male-dominated society, *zar* beliefs and practices provide married women with an outlet for frustrations, a release from restrictions imposed upon them, and an escape from household responsibilities (Lewis, 1989).

In societies with gender equality, men and women are equally able to occupy positions of prestige and authority in their communities. Both contribute to making decisions that affect themselves and their families, and their rights to act independently and autonomously are equally respected. Gender equality does not necessarily mean that women and men do the same kinds of work or have the same social roles and responsibilities but that their contributions are equally valued. In addition, attitudes about males and females reflect positive evaluations. In family and personal life, women and men have the same opportunities and rights. Attitudes toward male and female sexuality are comparable. If premarital sex is permitted for men, it is permitted for women as well. If men can initiate divorce, women may also end their unhappy marriages.

While the status of men is generally secure in most societies, the status of women varies greatly across cultures. Anthropologists attempt to explain this variability by drawing attention to economic, structural, and ideological factors. A basic feature of society and influence on gender status is the productive contribution that women and men make to their household and community economies. Ownership or control over resources interrelates with participation in economic production. And risk taking in hunting and warfare further influences the relative status of men and women.

In general, women's status is higher in societies where their labor contributes the major share of food that their family consumes. For example, among foragers such as the Ju/'hoansi of Namibia and Botswana, the plants, roots, and nuts that women gather make up about 70 percent of the people's yearly caloric intake (Lee, 2003). And, significantly, women's social rights are respected and their independence is secure. In contrast, in foraging societies such as the Inuit of the Alaskan and Canadian Arctic, where the percentage of food obtained by women's direct labor is relatively low, women's status is correspondingly lower.

In farming societies, a generally consistent relationship can be seen between the amount of farmwork that women do and their social and political rights. For example, among the northeastern Iroquois, women's labor, planting and harvesting crops, supplied most of the food that people ate, supplemented by meat and fish brought in by the men. In addition to their direct labor, women controlled the allocation of land through the matrilineages that they headed. And they controlled the distribution of food to families within their kinship groups. All these responsibilities in production and distribution gave women a secure basis for their high social status. In contrast, among the farming and hunting peoples of the Amazon region in South America, women's relatively low status can be understood partly as consistent with their minor roles in obtaining food, as most of the planting, hunting, and fishing is done by men.

As you read in Chapter 7, historical evidence shows that when relations of production are transformed in a way that limits women's participation, then women's social and political rights become restricted and their social value declines. Recall from Chapter 9 that patterns of postmarital residence also play a role in women's security and independence. Matrilocal societies provide women with continued emotional support from their kin, whereas patrilocal residence patterns remove women from

Anthropology Applied

Advocacy for Women

Anthropologists work in organizations that champion women's rights, economic independence, and quality of life. For example, anthropologists conduct and report research on the impacts of economic development on women as well as on their households and communities. It has been found that women play an important role in the economies of developing countries as both producers and consumers, even in strongly patriarchal societies that tend to ignore women's contributions outside the home.

International organizations involved in advocacy for women include, for example, the Women's Environment and Development Organization (WEDO), the International Center for Research on Women, and the Women's Rights Project of EarthRights International. Through the efforts of organizations such as Earth-Rights International, rural Burmese women had an opportunity to address the United Nations about human rights abuses against women in their country. They reported on their dislocation, forced labor, abandonment, and abuse related to the construction of the Burma-Bangladesh-India natural gas pipeline. The International Fund for Agricultural Development (IFAD), another example, is concerned with ending poverty for rural people. IFAD attempts to strengthen the roles of women in their communities by ensuring that they serve as advisers in projects and as intermediaries between women's organizations and the government. IFAD also attempts to construct projects so that both women and men are involved in the outcomes, thus avoiding the tendency for development projects to favor men's interests.

A contention of IFAD is that gender inequality helps to perpetuate poverty. To break the cycle of poverty,

Female delegates from the Karenni ethnic minority look on during the opening of the Myanmar Constitutional Convention.

IFAD attempts to increase women's access to resources (including food, water, and education) and enable women to attain political positions. IFAD also seeks to involve men in the new roles of women, because women cannot become empowered to change their roles and status without the support of men. The idea is that with equal access to resources, women and men in poverty will be able to help each other and their society together.

CRITICAL THINKING QUESTIONS

How does gender inequality perpetuate poverty? As a cultural anthropologist, how might you conduct research to determine if goals like those of IFAD are viable?

---

their kin groups and the support they can provide when conflicts arise. In addition, social and political complexity and the patterns of community leadership also affect gender status.

The degree and type of warfare in a region also influence gender constructs. Success in warfare usually confers social prestige on men. However, men's ability to translate their military achievements into control over women in their communities is in part related to the frequency of warfare and to characteristics of warfare. Where warfare is frequent and directed against distant enemies, warriors are absent from home for long periods of time and are less able to dominate the households they leave behind. Women in these societies have higher status. Warfare directed against nearby settlements, however, creates conditions in which warriors can extend their military dominance to other aspects of social life, including gender dominance. Furthermore, frequent internal warfare endangers noncombatants, affirming men's roles as defenders and protectors.

> ### REVIEW
>
> In some societies gender roles are strongly segregated, whereas in others, common activities are performed by both men and women. Gender roles strongly affect gender relations. Societies exhibit either gender equality or gender inequality, which is almost always in the form of male dominance. All societies have some division of labor by gender, which allows people to specialize in a few skill areas rather than having to master all the survival skills of their culture. All societies also have cooperative labor. Gender division of labor reflects biological as well as economic and cultural realities. The status of women in a society is based in part on the importance of their roles in the production of goods or provision of food; on their importance as householders, depending on the type and frequency of warfare; and on their access to kin support based on postmarital residence patterns.

GENDER AND SUBSISTENCE

As you have read, modes of subsistence relate to gender roles, gender status, and gender relations. Foraging societies tend to have gender equality and egalitarian gender relations, except where men's economic or political roles are critical to the survival of the group, a situation that favors male dominance. Horticultural, pastoral, and agricultural societies tend to have greater gender inequality, depending on the control of subsistence resources and other factors, with the likelihood of some degree of male dominance. This pattern, however, varies considerably. Industrial societies, with economies built on agricultural bases, tend to retain ideological male dominance while gradually enlarging economic opportunities for women and extending legal and institutional equalities to both genders.

Foragers and Gender

In many foraging bands, women's and men's interdependent contributions to their households were (and in some cases still are) reflected in equality of social relations and social status. However, among others, male dominance is apparent. We can compare two foraging societies, the Ju/'hoansi of southern Africa and the Inuit of the North American Arctic, to understand similarities and differences. Both these small, nomadic societies were traditionally organized around bilaterally related kin groups. Economic roles were defined according to gender, but flexibility and overlap also were found. The productive labor of both women and men was essential for survival and was socially recognized and rewarded. Formal political structures and formalized leadership were absent. Settlements were politically and economically autonomous.

In Ju/'hoansi and Inuit societies, marriages are usually monogamous, although polygyny and polyandry occur infrequently. Initial postmarital residence is matrilocal, providing a young wife with support from her kin until children are born and her marriage becomes stable. Divorce, though, is common, particularly in the early years of marriage, and can be initiated by either spouse. Fathers in both cultures take an active role in child care and are affectionate and playful with their children. In general, attitudes toward premarital sexual activity are permissive for both girls and boys. And, although adultery is not condoned, its only punishment is gossip and criticism. Despite these similarities, important differences in the two cultures also exist that help us understand the conditions under which egalitarian gender relations are maintained and, conversely, some of the conditions that promote male dominance.

In contrast to Ju/'hoansi society, where annual caloric intake consisted mainly of plant products, the Inuit diet was almost exclusively based on meat and fish. Because men supplied these resources primarily, their labor was seen as more directly producing conditions for survival. Women's contributions, although substantial and essential, were seen as supplements. An emphasis on male labor among the Inuit led to preferences for patrilocal residence following an initial period with the wife's kin. Camp affiliation was commonly based on kinship bonds among men. Collective male labor was essential for many economic pursuits, especially among coastal peoples engaged in hunting sea animals.

Culture Change

TRANSFORMATION OF GENDER STATUS IN TWO FORAGING SOCIETIES

The role of subsistence in gender constructs can be seen clearly in well-documented cases of culture change. Economic and political changes experienced by the Ju/'hoansi and Inuit, for example, have had significant impacts on gender roles, relationships between women and men, and cultural evaluation of the genders. Ju/'hoansi society has been affected by modern technology, involvement in wage work by large segments of the population, and incorporation into national states that first surrounded and then engulfed Ju/'hoansi territory. These changes occurred over a relatively short time. Beginning in the 1960s, the majority of Ju/'hoansi in Botswana and Namibia became involved in pastoral and farming activities, first as laborers for Herero and Tswana villagers and later as owners of their own herds and fields (Lee, 2003:157–158). Most Ju/'hoansi today live in sedentary villages where subsistence is based on farming and herding. Men carry out these tasks, whereas women's work consists mainly of domestic tasks and occasional foraging for wild foods (Draper, 1975:101–103).

Three factors have led to transformation of gender relations among the Ju/'hoansi. First, while men and women formerly contributed roughly equal amounts of labor and time to subsistence, in modern villages men's contributions are much greater, both in terms of the amount of labor expended and the quantity of food produced. Second, where once both women and men had individual control over the use and distribution of resources, now it is primarily men who own herds and fields. And third, the division of labor by gender has become rigid, so that working with livestock is a male domain along with the heavy labor involved in clearing fields for planting, erecting fences, and harvesting crops (Draper, 1975:103). Perhaps because women's work has declined in visible social value, men are extremely reluctant to carry out any tasks identified as "women's work" (Draper, 1975:96).

As a consequence of economic changes, settlement patterns and the flow of daily life have been altered in ways that also affect gender constructs. Villages now consist of permanent houses spaced at greater distances from each other rather than the casual shelters previously built in the bush. Women spend more time and energy on upkeep of these new larger and more permanent structures. Domestic responsibilities keep women indoors more and apart from other villagers. Women engage in foraging activities for shorter periods of time and remain closer to their settlements. In contrast to decreasing mobility for women, men have become more mobile, leaving their villages for substantial periods and engaging in herding, farming, and trading with other peoples. Greater social prestige accrues to men because of their involvement with other peoples and cultures. Ju/'hoansi men are frequently bilingual and often serve as intermediaries in bringing technological innovations into Ju/'hoansi communities. In addition, many Ju/'hoansi men are now employed for wages in nearby towns and even as far away as the gold mines in South Africa (Draper, 1975:103; Lee, 2003:159–160).

Notions of private ownership of property by individuals have become incorporated into Ju/'hoansi ethics. Goats and cattle in Ju/'hoansi herds are owned separately by men. Houses are also said to be "owned" by the male head of household. Particular men who have amassed greater material wealth than others are even said to be "owners" of a village (Lee, 2003:98). Because property that constitutes wealth is identified more with men than with women, men are endowed with greater status.

The transformation of Inuit economies and gender relations took a different course. Trade with Europeans, Canadians, and Americans encouraged Inuit men to

Inuit

spend more time and energy trapping animals for furs wanted by traders, causing a shift from subsistence hunting. Men who engaged in trade could accumulate valued manufactured goods, especially items related to men's work, such as fishing nets, metal fishhooks, guns, and ammunition (Graburn, 1969:107–108). In the twentieth century new equipment in the men's domain was added, such as steel traps, modern boats, and outboard motors (Graburn, 1969:129–130). As Arctic economies focused on trapping, families congregated near trading posts, becoming more dependent on the goods and foods they received in exchange for furs. In the twentieth century, Canadian and U.S. authorities accelerated this relocation by establishing administrative offices, schools, and nursing stations in settled villages.

Inuit attitudes toward ownership changed. Formerly, land and the resources were not controlled by individuals but were shared by anyone in the area. Later, trapping lines and the animals they snared were considered individual property. Because inspecting trapping lines and retrieving animals were accomplished individually rather than collectively, cooperation in most economic activities became unnecessary. Emphases on individual property and accumulation of wealth enhanced the status of young men who were successful trappers.

After World War II, the pace of change throughout the Artic accelerated. Towns grew through consolidation of neighboring communities, influx of people from distant camps, and natural population increases. Exploration for oil, particularly in Alaska, by transnational corporations created numerous jobs and stimulated immigration of thousands of non-natives to the region (Chance, 1990).

Today wage work is available to some Inuit women and men, often in gender-linked occupations. Men typically are employed in construction, mining, building maintenance, and work at Canadian and U.S. military bases. Women find employment in service occupations and as nurse's aides, teachers, and school aides. Since the 1980s, however, women have joined men in technical, managerial, and professional fields (Bodenhorn, 1993:184). Both men and women also gain income from skilled craftwork, including sculpture, painting, and basketry. Contemporary Inuit women have increased economic independence, leading to gender equality as they participate more directly in wage-earning activities.

The Inuit situation contrasted with that of Ju/'hoansi economies. Ju/'hoansi hunters were respected and socially rewarded, but Ju/'hoansi women were also recognized for contributing to and controlling the major food supply. The Inuit division of labor that required men to leave their camps for individual or collective hunting resulted in the physical separation of men and women. Primary social interactions were with members of one's own gender. In contrast, physical and social separation of women and men was not common among the Ju/'hoansi. Conversational and interactional groupings form casually without regard to gender.

The conditions under which men pursued their economic roles added to their prestige because of the risks involved. The Arctic environment presents severe constraints, and a man's efforts, however skilled and fearless the hunter, were likely to fail. Daily risks to survival, compounded by the likelihood of failure, encouraged hunters' effort to establish some control over their situation. Their religious beliefs revolved around ritualized precautions, taboos, and prayers to forestall disaster. The greater risks they took were rewarded with greater social prestige. Arctic survival depended on men's ability to control resources in dangerous situations involving violent acts against large, aggressive animals (Sanday, 1981). This control extended to dominance over women. In a society where interpersonal aggression was condemned and where cooperative, friendly, and hospitable behavior was preferred, men were permitted to act violently toward women. Wife beating and rape were not uncommon (Briggs, 1982).

These Mbuti Pygmy women live in a foraging society in the Ituri rain forest of Zaire. Like the Ju/'hoansi of the Kalahari Desert, they enjoy greater gender equality than groups with more hostile environments. Gender division of labor gives men and women different economic and social roles. In Mbuti society, women are valued artists. They gather materials to make pigments and express in art the key themes of Mbuti culture. These themes center on the rain forest as the parent, birthplace, provider, arbiter, resting place, and god of all. As their canvas, the women use barkcloth, their bodies, and the bodies of their children.

Gender in Pastoral and Horticultural Societies

In pastoral and horticultural societies, control over the distribution of produce and goods influences gender status. In societies that are generally egalitarian, women exert their rights to make decisions concerning economic activities. In Iroquoian economies, for example, women performed most of the farmwork, including planting and tending crops and harvesting. In addition, women gathered a wide assortment of fruits, nuts, and roots and were responsible for domestic tasks and child care. Men's subsistence roles included hunting and fishing to supplement the basic plant diet. Trading with other native peoples for animal skins and utilitarian and luxury articles was also the work of men (Thwaites, 1906:15:155). Both women's and men's work was highly valued, socially recognized, and rewarded.

Women not only were responsible for food production but also controlled distribution of both the food and the resources contributed by their husbands and sons. This control over resources was a crucial factor in Iroquoian women's high status in their households and communities (Brown, 1975:236; Bonvillain, 1980:50). In addition to allotting food for daily consumption, women collected and distributed supplies for public feasts and ceremonial occasions (Lafitau, 1974:318). Their economic roles in household production and as resource distributors were thus extended into public domains.

Household organization centered around matrilineal clans that formed the basis of Iroquoian kinship. Matrilocality was the preferred residence pattern, so a house typically consisted of an elder woman, her husband, their daughters and daughters' families, and the couple's unmarried sons.

Iroquoian behaviors and attitudes related to sexuality and marriage reflected the independence and autonomy of women and men. People freely chose to engage in sexual relationships and to form marriages. Marriages were monogamous. Violence against women in the form of wife beating or rape was unheard of (Bonvillain, 1980).

Iroquoian women's prestige was strengthened through many features of their roles within clans. Senior women of matrilineages composing each clan had responsibility for overseeing domestic tasks performed in their households and for allocating farmland to their kinswomen (Lafitau, 1974:69). And clan mothers chose lineage and clan chiefs from among prominent men in their kin groups. Thus, both men and women made important, socially valued contributions to their society and had ultimate control over their own behavior.

In contrast, among the Igbo of Nigeria, both men and women contribute to subsistence through their farm labor, but men control land and resources. Preferred postmarital residence is patrilocal, consolidating bonds between fathers and sons and between brothers. And men occupy most major decision-making and influential roles in political life. However, women dominate village and regional trade. Therefore, although Igbo culture contains overtly expressed attitudes of male superiority, Igbo tradeswomen control market exchanges and benefit both economically and socially from their expertise in this sphere of life. Women's control over local trade is key to their ability to establish a high degree of autonomy in a culture that otherwise is dominated by men.

Igbo subsistence is based on horticulture. Tasks are strongly demarcated according to gender. Men plant yams considered to be the staple crop. Rice, a product introduced in the early twentieth century, is the only crop grown by both men and women. Women plant and harvest all other crops and weed their husbands' yam gardens. Even when work has a collective focus, tasks are performed according to gender. For example, men harvest yams, but women and children carry the yams to the household yam barn (Ottenberg, 1965:7; Ottenberg and Ottenberg, 1962:119).

Other subsistence and household activities are likewise allocated according to gender. Men obtain fish from nearby rivers; women fish in ponds and streams. Men make bamboo frames for houses, women collect and carry mud for house walls; men put mud on the frames, women smooth it when dry. Gender differentiation is extended to craft production as well: Women are potters, men make mats (Ottenberg, 1965:9–10).

Most Igbo women engage in trade, as do the women of a majority of cultures throughout West Africa. Men also trade, but their participation was traditionally less extensive than that of women. Women's marketing expertise encompasses men's products as well, since women usually sell agricultural products grown by their husbands in addition to those in their own domain. Most Igbo women are not full-time traders but engage in marketing as an extension of their roles in agricultural production. However, some women do engage in more complex trading activities, functioning as intermediaries and buying from local producers and reselling produce in regional markets. Others buy in large quantity from markets and then resell to villagers who do not go to market (Ukwu, 1969:177). Through these various efforts, women function as catalysts for wide redistributive networks.

Tradeswomen's husbands avoid interfering with their activities or making too many demands on their labor. Successful women have the income and prestige to manage on their own and, therefore, are able to leave an abusive or domineering husband. If divorced or widowed, successful tradeswomen do not feel compelled to remarry, because they know that they can support themselves and their children.

Nigerian women conduct trade in the markets.

In contrast to the Iroquois and Igbo, among the Yanomamo of Amazonia, women are excluded from direct productive work. This exclusion is then used as justification for their social subordination. Yanomamo culture sanctions men's dominance over women in every feature of ideology and practice (Chagnon, 1973, 1997). Settlement patterns, social systems, subsistence activities, and village leadership are all dominated by men. These conditions of Yanomamo society have been strongly influenced by economic changes as a result of culture contact (Kellman, 1982), a subject taken up further in Chapters 16 and 17.

Residence patterns are patrilocal, based on affiliation among patrilineal kin. Marriages are usually arranged by men, a father giving his daughter to be wed to a man with whom he wishes to forge an alliance. Young girls, often as young as 8 or 9 years old, are married to men in their 20s or 30s. Polygyny is common and desired by all men but not economically possible for everyone. A man may contract multiple marriages through establishing alliances with several men who have daughters. Men also obtain wives by capture when raiding other villages.

Prestige in Yanomamo culture is principally based on success in two roles held exclusively by men: warrior and shaman, a type of ritual practitioner who makes contact with the spirit world and performs ceremonies to heal the sick and protect warriors. Successful warriors also function as influential village leaders. Warfare is common and is characterized by raids against nearby villages with the aim of killing as many inhabitants as possible. Young women, however, are often captured and brought back to become wives.

Although men are more likely than women to die as the result of raiding, there is still a relative lack of women in most communities because of the practice of female infanticide, a dramatic reflection of the unworthiness of females. This artificially created scarcity of women is a motivation for warfare, giving men the opportunity to capture a wife from a neighboring village (Harris, 1974). Warfare creates a dangerous situation for noncombatants, enhancing men's status in their role as defenders. Thus, men's success is rewarded by both high social prestige and the subordination of women. Women's subordination is demonstrated by frequent violence in the form of beatings and rapes.

Finally, in an area of scarce resources, practices may develop in order to disperse populations (Siskind, 1973). The scarcity of women, created by female infanticide and polygyny, helps limit population growth and also generates conditions of warfare conducive to forcing people to relocate away from centers of conflict.

Gender in Agricultural States

Agrarian states are complex societies with centralized political systems that maintain some degree of control over local areas within the state. They have economies based on intensive farming and produce surpluses that are used to support a ruling elite. There is marked segmentation of the population into classes that occupy different positions in society, have different kinds of occupations, and different standards of living. Many such societies are (or were) characterized by male dominance in gender relations. As in other types of societies, however, the degree of male dominance varies widely, depending on economic, political, and historical factors, as well as on patterns of kinship, marriage, and family.

Industrialism, Postindustrialism, and Gender

In Europe and the United States of the late eighteenth century, innovations in productive modes began a process that transformed agricultural societies into industrial nations. Industrialization began in the manufacture of textiles, using mainly women's labor for the first several decades and then marginalizing women as manufacturing became fully established as the dominant productive mode. During the early nineteenth century, the independent self-sufficiency of farming families was gradually eroded by the need to purchase commodities. At the same time, transformations of production in manufacturing resulted in owners' need to hire workers for the burgeoning industrial sector. These two processes coalesced in the growth of industrial production.

Textile manufacture, centered in Massachusetts, was one of the first industries to develop in the United States, as it had been in Great Britain as well. Manufacturing began in the early 1800s and became well established by the 1820s. Young women, the daughters of farmers, constituted the bulk of mill operators. Unmarried daughters were available for outside

Mill life reproduced the patriarchal relations that existed in households. Men were owners and supervisors, controlling the organization of production, whereas young, unmarried women labored as subordinate workers. On average, mill workers in the mid-nineteenth century worked for four and a half years, most leaving to marry (Matthaei, 1982:150).

Male Dominance in Traditional Chinese Culture

Traditional Chinese culture was intensely patriarchal. Patriarchal gender relations were developed through several millennia of Chinese history. Centralized imperial dynasties took hold in the eighth century, succeeding one another after wars among rivals. To stabilize and expand political and military power, ruling classes adopted philosophies that supported the legitimacy of state control. The thoughts of Confucius (551–479 B.C.) and his disciples were especially influential. A cornerstone of Confucianism is the notion of "filial piety" that ordains obedience to one's social superiors. Thus, all Chinese owed obedience to the emperor, sons to their fathers, and women to their husbands.

Male dominance was manifested in numerous social, economic, political, and religious spheres. Households consisted of members of patrilineages, headed by the eldest male. His wife, unmarried children, married sons and their wives and children—all were under his authority. The rule of a head of household was potentially harsh, involving culturally sanctioned beatings of wives and children. Because postmarital residence was patrilocal, wives could rarely depend on their relatives for support in times of conflict with their in-laws (Wolf, 1974:158). A wife experienced subordination within her husband's household, especially when young and not yet the mother of sons to carry on her husbands' lineage.

Mothers-in-law often acted as "surrogates for male authority" (Diamond, 1975:376). They had little authority in relations with their own husbands and instead asserted authority over their sons' wives. Wives had few, if any, allies in their husbands' households. In keeping with notions of filial piety, a man's allegiance was first and foremost to his parents. His wife was secondary and could not depend on him for social support. Women began to receive deferential treatment after they reached middle or old age and had adult sons. Sons were a woman's main allies, and mothers could attempt to control their sons through strong emotional bonds (Wolf, 1974:168). With stern authoritarian relationships with their fathers, sons gravitated toward their mothers' emotional warmth.

Patriarchal attitudes were reflected in a marked preference for sons. Sons were necessary for the social, material, and spiritual well-being of their parents. Through sons, patrilineages maintained their continuity. And the economic division of labor contributed further justification for preferring sons to daughters. According to gender-assigned tasks, men were primarily responsible for agricultural production. Women's work was usually confined to domestic household tasks. When additional labor was required for farmwork at harvest time, women, especially among poor families, helped in the fields.

Women living in prosperous households were restricted to domestic labor and often to the physical confines of the home. The Chinese word for wife, *neiran*, literally means "inside person" (Croll, 1982:224). By keeping one's wife in the home, a man demonstrated his wealth and the fact that he did not need his wife working in the fields. Thus, women's social subordination was justified, in part by their economic dependence on men (Wong, 1974:234).

Marriages were arranged by fathers of the prospective couple without consulting the bride or

With four sons, this traditional Chinese family has a strong future. Families depended on sons for labor and crucial religious functions.

groom. Girls generally were married when in their late teens but were often betrothed as children. These betrothals solidified alliances between men. Girls' chastity before marriage was absolutely essential to maintain the honor of the girl and her family, but men were not constrained by premarital restrictions. Men frequented brothels to gain sexual experience before marriage (Wong, 1974:236–237). This double standard about sexual activity was another instance of male privilege.

Traditional customs related to divorce further discriminated against women. Only husbands could initiate divorce, often because of a wife's disobedience or failure to produce a son (Wong, 1974:234). Divorce carried no stigma for a husband, but a divorced woman was shamed.

Ideally, widows were not supposed to remarry, but poor men who were unable to find suitable women for marriage sometimes sought them (Wong, 1974:236). Because widows had few alternatives, they often agreed to such unions to escape the social stigma and economic hardships of widowhood.

From an outsider's viewpoint, the practice of foot binding symbolized restrictions on girls and women in traditional Chinese society. The feet of young girls at the age of 4 or 5 were tightly bound with cloth so that their toes curled under their feet. As the girls grew to adulthood, their feet became more deformed and normal walking became impossible. Adult women took tiny, faltering steps on feet as small as three inches long (Wong, 1974:232). Only among the very poor, where women's agricultural labor provided a necessary financial contribution to family survival, did daughters escape this practice.

In the early twentieth century, some customs began to change because of the influence of Chinese intellectuals and administrators, as well as British and French colonial agents (who had defeated the Chinese military in the Opium Wars of 1839–1842). Although British and French societies were certainly dominated by men, colonial influences had a beneficial effect on women's status in China. For instance, foot binding was outlawed in 1902, although the ban was widely ignored until the 1950s, when the new Communist government undertook a vigorous campaign to eliminate the practice.

After coming to power in 1949, the Chinese Communist government enacted several laws that attempted to transform social and familial relationships between women and men. The Marriage Law of 1950 declared that the "New-Democratic marriage system is based on the free choice of partners, on monogamy, on equal rights for both sexes, and on the protection of the lawful interests of women and children" (quoted in Wong, 1974:242). Additional laws banned child-marriage and dowry.

However, patriarchal attitudes continue in a preference for sons, even in the face of government reforms and programs for population control. To limit population growth, the Chinese government began a "One-Child Certificate Program" in 1979. A couple who pledge to have only one child receives substantial benefits in the form of cash bonuses, preferential housing, job assignments, and educational opportunities for their child. According to a 1986 study conducted by Fred Arnold and Liu Zhaoxiang (1986), 37 percent of Chinese couples with one child enrolled in the program, but a disparity exists between those with one son and those with one daughter. Of all holders of One-Child Certificates, 60 percent have sons, whereas only 40 percent have daughters (Arnold and Liu, 1986:227–228). Although the program has been a significant success in reducing population growth, a matter of critical importance in China, the gender disparity is significant for future opportunities of men and women.

employment because their direct productive contribution to their families was not as critical as that of sons. In the farming economy, daughters generally helped in farmwork and housework, but sons were central to agricultural production since they, along with their fathers, contributed the major share of labor on the farms.

American women's participation in mill work began to decline by the 1840s, when working conditions in the mills deteriorated due to competition from abroad and the desire of mill owners to cut costs. Women at mills in Lowell, Massachusetts, went on strike in the 1830s, but their efforts to protect their jobs and improve work conditions

GLOBALIZATION

Culture change through government mandate is a force in the process of globalization. As in the case of China, central governments that have unified or expanded their countries through revolution or territorial conquest often have the power to compel obedience to laws that affect gender and other relationships.

failed because the owners were able to find immigrant, especially Irish, women and men willing to work for lower wages. Except for textiles, native-born men also made up a large percentage of the work force in the growing industries of the northeastern and central states (Goldfield et al., 2004). But they, too, faced competition from immigrant workers willing to work for lower pay.

Women were marginalized in the industrial sector through intersecting links between gender segregation in employment and unequal pay. Some occupations were considered appropriate for women and others for men. For example, industrial jobs requiring operation of large, heavy machinery were open to men, whereas women were employed in industries that relied on handwork and small machinery that produced such items as soap, hats, and cigars (Hartmann, 1979). Even where both men and women worked in the same industry, they were differentiated according to specialization. In the manufacture of boots and shoes, for instance, men were employed as cutters and finishers and women were stitchers and sewers (Matthaei, 1982:189).

In addition, women generally received lower wages than did men, even when both performed the same jobs. This differential in pay, or **gender gap,** as it is now called, was—and is—often masked by the segregation of work and workplaces. Men's social dominance can then be justified by the fact that they earn more money than do women. And paying women lower wages was justified by an ideology that women were only interested in working until they married and would leave the labor force to become wives and mothers.

In the early and mid-nineteenth century, a cultural construct currently referred to as the **cult of domesticity** became popular and justified separation of the genders, relegating women to the domestic sphere. Its popularity grew throughout the nineteenth century and remains in one form or another as a gender construct in American society. According to this cultural ideal, separate roles and domains are appropriate for women and men. Men provide material support for their families; women are suited to perform domestic tasks. Married women who joined the labor force as an economic necessity were told that by working outside the home they were neglecting their proper duties to nurture their husbands and children. Husbands of working women were similarly made to feel derelict in their duty. Since the ideal man was one who supported his wife and children, a man whose wife worked was less than a real man.

Labor leaders also used these attitudes to restrict women's involvement in wage work as competition between employed women and men intensified at the beginning of the twentieth century. Although ostensibly dedicated to bettering conditions for all workers, most unions in the nineteenth and early twentieth centuries discriminated against women, barring them from membership or relegating them and their interests to auxiliary status (Berch, 1982). When men were faced with competition from women, who often were willing to work for lower wages, unions had two possible responses: They could advocate equality of pay for all workers, to remove the financial incentive for employers to hire women rather than men; or they could advocate restrictions on women's employment as a strategy for maintaining men's advantages. They chose the latter course.

In another response to competition from women workers, labor leaders and public figures advocated enactment of "protective legislation," to protect women from harmful conditions on the job. Hours for women were decreased, night work in some occupations was forbidden, and exposure to dangerous chemicals, materials, or machinery was banned. But the same protections were not extended to men. Although the rules protected women from dangers on the job, they carry hidden costs, rendering women less attractive as employees and, therefore, hurting their chances of being hired.

Despite strong pressures to keep women in the home, some women sought to obtain higher education and to participate in the work force, spurring social changes in gender roles and expectations. And their political activism also increased. As early as the mid-nineteenth century, women sought political rights equal to men. Organizing at the Seneca Falls (New York) Convention in 1848, Elizabeth Cady Stanton and Lucretia Mott (later joined by Susan B. Anthony) issued a Declaration of Sentiments and Resolutions modeled on the U.S. Declaration of Independence calling for equal rights for women (Sapiro, 1986). The women's suffrage movement culminated in 1920 in ratification of the Nineteenth Amendment to the U.S. Constitution, which gave women the right to vote.

gender gap
The difference in wages and income earned by men and women for comparable work.

cult of domesticity
Constellation of beliefs popular in the late nineteenth and early twentieth centuries that promoted the notion that women were, by nature and biology, suited to the domestic tasks of nurturing and caring for their husbands and children.

Culture Change

TRANSFORMATION OF AMERICAN WORK IN THE TWENTIETH CENTURY

Many factors came together to change the economic and social roles of men and women in the twentieth century. New demands for workers, rising standards of living, and growing awareness of inequalities all led to increased participation of women in paid employment. During World War I (1914–1917), women replaced men who had joined the military, obtaining jobs that had previously been barred to them and including managerial positions and jobs in heavy industry. Patterns of employment among women changed as well. As white women were increasingly hired as office workers, teachers, saleswomen, and telephone operators, black women moved into domestic and service occupations (Amott and Matthaei, 1991).

After the war ended, many women left the public sector and returned to home life, but many others remained in the work force. Economic needs of families continued to grow as inflation rose and real wages fell. Expansion of consumer goods provided another incentive for women to increase their family's income and raise their standard of living. And many mothers worked in order to support children through college.

The years of the Great Depression, beginning in 1929, witnessed another cycle of shifts. Industrial and construction jobs were hardest hit, throwing millions of men out of work. Wives of unemployed men were, among others, vocal in their attacks against married working women. Some states passed laws barring employment of married women.

The depression was shortly followed by World War II, a period of change yet again. Millions of men entered the military, leaving millions of jobs unfilled. Women again heeded the call to do their patriotic share by joining the work force. Job opportunities for all women improved during the war. Black women obtained work in industries that had previously been closed to them (Bose, 1987:279). Not only was there a large increase in the numbers of married working women, but women with young children also entered public labor. After the war, men returned to reclaim their jobs, pushing women out of work or at least out of the positions they had occupied. Many women, though, remained in the work force, motivated by the dual factors of economic necessity and personal interest.

Each increase in women's employment in the nineteenth and twentieth centuries was fed by workers from different social categories. At first, young unmarried women made up the bulk of workers. Then immigrant women, single and married, entered the work force. Married, native-born women constituted the next contingent, entering and staying in paid employment in large numbers in the 1940s. Subsequently, most married working women were older women whose children had grown up. Since the 1960s, however, working mothers with young children have taken jobs in addition to their domestic responsibilities (Fox and Hesse-Biber, 1984:27–28).

Rising costs of living make it necessary for married women and for mothers to earn money so that their families can maintain their standard of living. Thus, the two-worker family has become commonplace. In addition, many mothers are without husbands, either as a result of divorce or of never having married. And many women choose to work even without economic necessity because of their interests in pursuing a career or escaping the social isolation of their homes.

By 2000, about 57.3 percent of all women were in the labor force, and 70.1 percent of men were working (U.S. Bureau of the Census). Rates varied for different age cohorts, with highest levels for men and women between the ages of 25 and 55. Younger people (between the ages of 16 and 19) had somewhat lower rates, and people over 60 had the lowest rates of employment.

A majority of women with children at all ages were in the labor force in 2002 (U.S. Department of Labor). That is, about 72 percent of mothers with children under the age of 18 were working. This is a large increase since 1975, when only 47 percent of mothers with children under 18 were working. The increase comes primarily from mothers with very young children. In 2002, 61 percent of mothers with children younger than 3 years of age were in the labor force (up from about 34 percent in 1975). However, those with younger children tended to work fewer hours than those with older children.

Despite the growth in the number of women who are in paid employment, discrimination in wages and lack of access to some jobs still hinder women's equality as workers. The gender gap in pay continues to be an ever-present source of inequity for women, even though in most occupations, the wage gap has grown narrower in the last several decades. According to the Bureau of Labor Statistics, reporting for 2002, full-time women workers earned 78 percent of men's salaries. Women are paid, on average, less than men in all occupations and for all age cohorts. When salaries are compared for women and men with comparable education and comparable number of years of experience, the gender gap remains. Although the gender gap in pay exists for all races, black and Hispanic women's wages are closer to those of men of their own group than is true for whites. Black women earn 91 percent of black men's wages, and Hispanic women's wages are about 88 percent of Hispanic men's earnings. However, these data reflect the relatively lower wages of nonwhite men rather than higher wages of nonwhite women.

Women continue to face occupational segregation in the types of jobs for which they are hired. Table 10.2 gives percentages of women in selected occupations (U.S. Department of Labor, 2002).

Table 10.2 WOMEN AS A PERCENTAGE OF WORKERS IN SELECTED OCCUPATIONS, 2002

Managerial and Professional Specialties		**Professional Specialties**	
Medical and health managers	78.4	Teachers, kindergarten	97.7
Accountants and auditors	59.4	Registered nurses	92.9
Postmasters	50.0	Teachers, secondary school	58.1
Construction inspectors	5.0	Teachers, college and university	42.7
Service Occupations		Actors and directors	38.2
Child-care workers	97.6	Musicians and composers	36.4
Police and detectives	15.5	Physicians	30.6
Firefighters	3.4	Lawyers	29.2
		Computer analysts and scientists	27.8
Precision Production, Craft, and Repair		Athletes	25.8
Machine operators, assemblers	35.3	Dentists	19.4
Mechanics and repairers	4.4	Clergy	14.1
Construction trades	2.4	Engineers	10.8
Technical, Sales, and Administrative Support		**Transportation Workers**	
Dental hygienists	98.1	Bus drivers	48.4
Secretaries, stenographers, and typists	97.6	Truck drivers	4.9
Sales workers, apparel	77.7	**Farming, Forestry, and Fishing**	
Electricians	19.1	Animal caretakers	68.1
Sales workers, motor vehicles and boats	11.3	Farmers	25.5
Airplane pilots and navigators	4.2	Timber cutters and loggers	1.6

Source: U.S. Department of Labor, 2002.

Women who remain at home and fulfill the traditional ideal of domestic roles are involved in the important work of social reproduction. **Social reproduction** entails the care and sustenance of people who will be able to contribute productively to society. Necessary tasks include obtaining and preparing food, maintaining the physical premises of the home, purchasing clothing and other material goods, tending family members when they are ill, and planning and supervising the education of children. However, the worth of labor contributed by stay-at-home wives and mothers is socially devalued, reflected, for example, in the phrase "just a housewife," which women themselves often use as a self-definition. But the work of social reproduction performed by such women is vital to society and to the economic system. Although nonemployed wives are perceived as dependent on their husbands, husbands also depend on their wives. Just as men contribute their wages to support their families, women contribute their unpaid labor to family survival.

social reproduction
The care and sustenance of people who will be able to contribute productively to society.

? *Why is housework devalued? What role does household labor play in statistics about the productivity of the American economy?*

> ### REVIEW
>
> Relationships between subsistence and gender relations vary depending on the allocation of power and control of resources and other factors. Foragers such as the Ju/'hoansi were egalitarian, whereas others, such as the Inuit, tended toward male dominance. Some horticultural societies, such as the Iroquois, had gender equality, whereas others, such as the Yanomamo, have male dominance in every facet of their culture. Agrarian societies, such as imperial China, were generally male dominated. Industrialism brought about changes in gender relations. Segregation and a gender gap (unequal pay) developed in factory wage work. More women entered the American work force when needed during wartime, and at other times a cult of domesticity called for women to stay at home, responsible for social reproduction. Unemployed women who stay at home came to be seen as nonproductive, an attitude contributing to the subordination of women.

GLOBALIZATION AND GENDER

Agricultural and industrial development programs sponsored by national governments or international agencies aim to strengthen economies, raise living standards, and improve health in impoverished rural communities. Development theory emphasizes the importance of modernizing in technology, agricultural production for trade, and industrialization dependent on a mobile labor force. When measured by gross national product (GNP), median family or household income, and longer life expectancy, advances can be demonstrated, but researchers still question the impact of economic development on different sectors of the population.

When the differential effects of development on men and women were first systematically explored, evidence suggested that modernization contributed to a decline in women's status, especially in Africa and Asia (Boserup, 1970). In Africa, landownership has passed from the collective control of kinship groups to individual control, increasingly concentrated in the hands of men. And as land utilization has changed from an emphasis on subsistence to production for trade in national and global markets, women have seen their role in subsistence farming diminished. And as their centrality in family production shrinks, their status has also declined. In Asia, mechanization and technological advances in farming have tended to favor male farmworkers.

An additional element in weighing the changes in women's status is their role in social reproduction and the gender division of labor in the household. The domestic labor that women do helps support family members and makes their participation in agriculture or industry possible. This element is often ignored by policy planners and analysts of economic development (Beneria and Sen, 1986). Furthermore, in societies where attitudes about gender limit women's ability to participate in work outside the home, their social status declines as societal value is placed on wage-earning activities.

Women's actual contributions to the world economy are often distorted and rendered invisible because of the inadequacy of research and statistics on labor force participation in the public sphere and because women's economic contributions in the home are ignored. Productive work or "active labor" is generally interpreted as participation in income-earning activities. Because much of women's work is in subsistence

GLOBALIZATION

European colonization had a significant impact on gender roles and attitudes. European traders preferred to deal with men and thus ignored or subverted the economic contributions of women. Missionaries affected gender relations directly and indirectly by redefining marriage and family in terms of European principles. Colonizers also tended to legitimate men's political authority and diminish women's public political roles.

In Their Own Voices

Tsetsele Fantan on Women and AIDS in Botswana

In this address from a 2003 conference on Botswana's Strategy to Combat HIV/AIDS, Tsetsele Fantan, from the African Comprehensive HIV/AIDS Partnership, talks about the cultural constraints affecting HIV/AIDS prevention and treatment programs in Botswana. She talks about attitudes about sex, marriage, and women's roles that hamper the effectiveness of these programs. And she emphasizes the need to involve men and women working together to achieve change. Africa is the world region hardest hit by HIV/AIDS. In Botswana, 67 percent of HIV infected people ages 16 to 49 are women. In addition, women are the principal caretakers for AIDS sufferers in their households. And since farming is primarily the work of women (eight out of ten farmers are women), their illness and death from AIDS affect their entire communities.

Globally, women are exposed to HIV transmission because of four main vulnerabilities: the social/cultural context, economic subordination, sexual subordination, and the female biological makeup. As far as the social/cultural context in Botswana is concerned, boys and girls are socialized differently, predominantly along traditional norms that emphasize female subordination throughout the lifecycle. This is also emphasized when young women get married. We remind them that they need to honor and obey. This becomes extremely difficult when women are abused in marriage, because as they go to uncles and aunts for counsel, they are reminded of their marriage vows. This gender power differential is compounded by age differences.

As far as economic subordination is concerned, poverty does force some women to adopt economic strategies, survival strategies, such as transactional sex. As far as sexual subordination is concerned, women are expected to have one lifetime partner, while male deviation is condoned, generally expected, or even encouraged. Women are also vulnerable to coerced sex, including rape and other sexual abuse, both inside and outside of the family, including marital rape. Young women and girls are increasingly targeted by older men seeking safe and/or subservient sexual partners, or just sexual adventure.

In addition to all the education that is being given about HIV and AIDS, I would like to mention three areas where I

---

agriculture, home craft production, or the "informal" labor sector in urban environments (peddling, domestic service), their economic contributions are often seriously underestimated. In addition, census classifications of workers according to their "main" occupation tend to ignore women's economic contributions because they are classified as home workers without detailing their specific contributions to subsistence and also to extra household income such as making foods or crafts for sale. Finally, development programs often focus on the generation of work itself rather than on the reasons that women are not qualified, rooted in their lack of training and education because of discriminatory attitudes.

Women's Roles in Urban and Rural Economic Development

In some countries, industrial development favors women's employment in certain sectors. For example, in Malaysia, Singapore, and Taiwan, national and multinational corporations have established factories, especially in electronics and garment assembly, that employ mainly young women. According to some estimates, about 80 percent of workers in light manufacturing plants worldwide are women between the ages of 13 and 25 (Moore, 1988:100). In Singapore, labor force participation rates for women have increased dramatically since the government embarked on rapid industrialization, providing tax incentives to foreign investment and curtailing labor union organizing (Wong, 1986:208). By 1995, women's economic activity rate had risen to 51 percent (United Nations Division for the Advancement of Women, 2000). Factories in Malaysia have also increased the wage-earning opportunities of young women believe work needs to be done. The first is a need to redefine traditional gender images. There is an urgent need to redefine images of masculinity and femininity through culturally relevant public education, and this is an area where the media can play a very important role. We need to emphasize the role of men, not only as breadwinners, but as ensuring the protection of the health of themselves and their families. We need to clearly articulate the imperative for men to change attitudes and behaviors in a nonthreatening way. We need transformational programs that acknowledge that men are partners in the fight against HIV and AIDS. Secondly, we need to engage men in the empowerment of women. We need to recognize and come to terms with the realities of women in Botswana, and the realities of our social circumstances in Botswana, and recognize that women's empowerment cannot be realized without full involvement and engagement of the men. We therefore need to develop initiatives, innovative community-based programs that empower grassroots men to work with women. We need to develop programs that assist men and women to effectively negotiate for space, recognition, and acknowledgment of each other. To develop targeted programs for men that utilize informal, traditional structures, led by traditional and opinion leaders in the districts.

We need to develop gender and culturally sensitive programs and support services that address the vulnerability of women to HIV and AIDS. We need to develop women's entrepreneurial skills, as well as giving them or facilitating their access to credit, because acquiring skills without the capital to start a business which has a market will not change much.

Attitudes and practices that are deeply rooted in culture are unlikely to change in the short term. Programs to address this will require long-term commitment from development partners. Local traditional leaders must be empowered to advocate for and effect these changes at the community level. This should be done through proper dialogue. We need to identify and liberate the positive aspects of culture for gender sensitive prevention initiatives. Lastly, we need to make sure that the valuable elements in our culture must be preserved and passed on to the next generation.

From Center for Strategic and International Study HIV/AIDS Task Force, *Botswana's Strategy to Combat HIV/AIDS, Empowering Women and People Living with HIV/AIDS,* November 12, 2003. Reprinted by permission of the Center for Strategic & International Studies, Washington D.C.

CRITICAL THINKING QUESTIONS

What aspects of traditional culture encourage the spread of HIV/AIDS among women in Botswana? What features of traditional culture can best address the challenge of preventing this spread?

(Ong, 1983). There, and in other Asian and Latin American countries, rural women leave their homes to improve their skills and chances of economic advancement. Their needs are especially acute in the context of increasing poverty in the countryside and the resulting dislocation. In the decade of the 1970s alone, shortly after the government began its industrialization program, the number of Malay women factory workers increased dramatically, from about 1,000 to more than 60,000 (Ong, 1983:429).

Young women benefit from their job opportunities by earning an income that gives them some economic independence and greater status in their families. They also escape the intense control traditionally exerted over them in their households, and they meet friends and socialize in the industrial centers. The wages they earn are higher than available in other jobs. However, the companies take advantage of the workers' poverty, lack of skills, and few alternative opportunities, paying them relatively low wages and offering few benefits.

Today, economic development increasingly affects small, relatively isolated communities. For example, the Pacific islands of Melanesia and Polynesia have become incorporated into national and global export networks. The production of copra (dried coconut) as a cash crop on the Melanesian island of Vanuatu (formally called New Hebrides) has gradually involved villagers in globalization while also maintaining a diversified subsistence and cash economy (Rodman, 1993). The people of Vanuatu first became involved in coconut production in the 1930s, but by the early 1980s, world prices for copra declined, and the local market collapsed. At that time, the Vanuatu government sponsored a fisheries development program to diversify sources of income and employment.

The shift from copra to fishing has had an impact on gender relations and contributions to household economies. Although most land under copra production was owned or controlled by men, both men and women worked cooperatively in the fields. The fisheries industries, however, tend to recruit men because deep-water fishing is an occupation reserved to men. Still, women continue some traditional roles by marketing the fish locally. In addition, although people have become involved in the global economy, they have also continued subsistence farming, fishing, and craft production. Melanesion women have thus been able to maintain much of their traditional status and equality.

In Polynesia, Tahitian women also have been able to retain or even enhance their status in the context of economic change, because cultural values supporting gender equality have remained intact. Local governments initiated agricultural development projects oriented toward growing potatoes and green vegetables. These programs are largely successful, involving both men and women by granting financial support and technological training to all. By the early 1990s, approximately 43 percent of potato farmers were women (Lockwood, 1997:511–512). Women's involvement in farming represented a break with the traditional division of labor that had limited women to performing domestic tasks. But they were able to use their customary access to communal land and their new access to government programs to produce crops for export. In addition, women's crafts, such as woven mats, hats, and quilts, have become major income-generating occupations, allowing women's economic contributions to be seen as central to the welfare of their families. And women's rights are protected by the traditional view that people control the products of their labor and the income received.

Women in Changing Socialist States

Most socialist nations have made great strides in a relatively short time in increasing women's participation rates in paid employment. Full employment is an underlying principle both for national economic growth and social equality of all citizens. Universal education has helped women acquire the necessary skills and training for industrial and professional occupations. However, serious discrepancies remain between the wages received by men and women for comparable work. For example, women agricultural workers in four socialist societies (the Soviet Union, China, Cuba, and Tanzania) are concentrated in less skilled, nonspecialist, low-paying, and low-prestige jobs (Croll, 1986). And women's contributions to total economy are minimized by the official definitions of "economically active" that omit family subsistence production, a sector in which women are concentrated (Kruks and Wisner, 1989). Furthermore, women often perform the major share of household responsibilities, leading to the "double day" typical of women in many industrial societies.

Although women work in all sectors of the industrial and professional economy, occupations in which women are concentrated tend to have low prestige. And while most socialist governments officially advocate policies aimed at combating discrimination against women, in varying degrees they all fail to recognize the critical link between public production and social or household reproduction. Women's roles in their households make it more difficult for them to enter the public work force as equals.

The fragility of the advances made by women in socialist countries in terms of economic participation, legal protections, and social equality is demonstrated by changes that have taken place in the former Soviet Union and Eastern Europe since the collapse of the socialist systems at the beginning of the 1990s. In the former Soviet Union, for instance, a market system has, among other things, resulted in drastic reductions in employment. Although all sectors of the economy have experienced declines, women have suffered disproportionately. For example, in 1993, approximately 70 percent of people officially listed as unemployed were women (Waters and Posadskaya, 1995:353). Because of fears of population decline and falling birth rates (so low that Russia now experiences a negative birth rate), pressure on women to become full-time mothers and housewives has increased considerably. The resurgence in defining women as childbearers and homemakers indicates that changes in social attitudes necessary to protect advances in women's status have not been realized.

Swedish Prime Minister Goran Persson and Foreign Minister Laila Freivalds sign the European constitution for Sweden in 2004. The underrepresentation of women is universal in all national governments. Sweden and Norway have the highest percentage of women in elected parliaments (about 40 percent) (United Nations Division for the Advancement of Women, 2001). In only twenty-one other countries do women constitute 20 percent or more of elected representatives.

A further indicator of the fragility of women's status in the former Soviet Union is the fact that women's political representation on the national level has plummeted. In the 1980s, women constituted approximately 33 percent of the deputies in the Supreme Soviet (the highest government body in the USSR) and approximately 50 percent or more in lower-level government organizations. After the elections of 1991, however, women accounted for only 5.6 percent of national deputies and were even less represented in regional and local governing bodies (Waters and Posadskaya, 1995:352–353). Similar dramatic declines in women's political representation and increases in unemployment rates have occurred throughout Eastern Europe.

Impacts of Ideology on Gender Constructs

Ideological influences can be seen clearly in the history of American women's participation in the labor force. Since the nineteenth century, each increase in women's participation evoked an ideological attack by supporters of patriarchal values. At first these attacks focused on beliefs about the divine and innate origins of the gender division of labor. Following World War II, ideological bias socialized men and women to want to do different kinds of work. Interest in popular psychology spread the ideas that men were inherently aggressive and driven to competition and domination, whereas women were passive, docile, and wanted to be dominated. It was widely believed that attempts to behave in ways that contradicted one's innate gender roles were not merely futile but also produced warped, destructive personalities.

Mothers' responsibility for their children's mental health became paramount. A mother's job, then, consisted of selfless devotion to the interests of her children. Mothers who, by poverty or through divorce or widowhood, were compelled to work

Table 10.3 TYPES OF FAMILY COMPOSITION, 1970–2000

Type	1970	1980	1989	2000
Married-couple families	86.7	81.7	79.2	77.0
Wife in paid labor force	—	41.0	45.7	51.0
Wife not in paid labor force	—	40.0	33.5	22.0
Male householders, no spouse present	2.4	3.2	4.4	5.0
Female householders, no spouse present	10.9	15.1	16.5	17.0

Sources: From U.S. Bureau of the Census, cited in Ries and Stone (1992:253); U.S. Bureau of the Census (2000).

outside the home received some sympathetic understanding, but middle- and upper-class women who sought professional careers were thought to be selfish and destructive.

Attitudes change to reflect realities, and a reality today is that a majority of households is composed of people in quite different circumstances than the earlier cultural ideal. Couples who both work, unemployed husbands, separated or divorced people, widows or widowers, single parents, and unmarried people living alone constitute a larger percentage of households. Table 10.3 presents data on various types of family composition, indicating a trend toward both fewer married-couple families and fewer households with nonemployed wives (Ries and Stone, 1992:253).

Government statistics thus indicate that, in 2000, less than 80 percent of American households consisted of a married couple (77 percent). And of these, more than half of the wives were in the paid labor force. Therefore, less than one-third of all American households consisted of a husband and nonemployed wife. And, according to figures released by the U.S. Department of Labor for 2001, 59 percent of married-couple families were supported by the incomes of both husband and wife. This figure shows an increase from 1967, when only 44 percent of married couple households had incomes from both spouses (U.S. Department of Labor).

As women's roles have been transformed, men's roles have also changed. Husbands are no longer the sole supporters of their families, relieving them of an intense economic and psychological burden. They no longer need to feel that their wives and children are completely dependent on their incomes but can look to their wives for support as well. Some men have taken on the role of "house-husband" or "stay-at-home dads," adopting many of the care-taking responsibilities formerly identified with mothers. This new alignment of roles within the households frees both men and women and enables them to do what suits them best as individuals. Another change has been around issues of child custody in cases of divorce. Courts are no longer automatically granting custody to mothers but instead are weighing multiple factors in their decisions, sometimes assigning custody to fathers.

Although gender roles and relations in any given culture can be analyzed at specific historical periods, it is crucial to understand the forces of change that transform people's behavior and their concepts about themselves and others. The possibility of change always exists, and this is what makes culture a dynamic rather than a static system. Gender relations can become more or less equal or hierarchical, depending on the specific context and operative forces experienced by members of each social category.

The relations between ideology and behavior are extremely complex. Although ideological systems develop in response to structural conditions, changes in these structural conditions usually occur much more rapidly than do changes in the ideological constructs that validate them. People's beliefs may continue despite changes in the contexts that produced them. Therefore, people sometimes have difficulty accepting a new social order and new social concepts.

Additional difficulties in changing ideologies derive from the fact that ideological constructs often are embedded in powerful systems of religious teachings and in attitudes expressed through daily interactions. Individuals usually experience their own behavior as "normal" and "natural" rather than as motivated and mediated by cultural constraints. They are, therefore, largely unaware of the underlying rationales influencing their actions and responses.

Analyses of gender roles and constructs in societies throughout the world demonstrate the diversity of possibilities of human life. People are not forever bound by traditional beliefs and practices. They can accept changes in their actions and they can adopt new ideological concepts relevant to their own experience. Just as we can uncover and understand the transformative dynamics that have occurred in the past, we can also witness and appreciate changes occurring in the present and into the future.

REVIEW

Cultural ideologies are used both to maintain and to change gender constructs as needed. Ideological attacks on women in the U.S. labor force were designed to discourage participation, just as later ideological inducements encouraged participation during wartime. Contact with Europeans influenced many indigenous groups to adopt more patriarchal or male-dominant ideologies and behaviors. In other instances, European contact brought about positive changes in the status of women. Ideological frameworks create, maintain, and change gender roles and constructs that are viewed as acceptable in a society. Changes in behavior, though resisted, usually happen before changes in ideology occur.

Chapter Summary

Sex and Gender

- Gender is a cultural construct that assigns an identity and appropriate roles to people based partly on sexual differences and partly on cultural beliefs about sex and behavior. Gender models make use of sexual differences between males and females, but cultures vary in the roles that women and men perform, the rights they have in relation to each other, and the values associated with their activities. People learn their gender identity from their earliest socialization in infancy through their childhood, learning appropriate behavior and molding personality to conform to cultural norms. Females and males are born, but women and men are products of their culture.

- Most cultures organize their concepts of gender into a dual division of man and woman. However, some cultures provide a third possibility, a third gender. In these societies, found in Native North America, India, Indonesia, and some other cultures, males and females could choose to identify as a third gender. The specific roles and behaviors appropriate to members of the third gender varied in different cultures. Two-Spirits in North America and *hijras* in India might perform the work usually associated with the opposite sex. Two-Spirits often had significant ritual roles that granted them prestige in their communities.

- Although we commonly think of our sexual feelings and practices as part of our nature, they are shaped by our culture. Our culture teaches us what kinds of sexual feelings and practices are "normal" and what kinds are "deviant." We learn who are appropriate sexual partners, when and where it is appropriate to have sexual relations, and the proper ways of engaging in sex. Another cultural element in attitudes about sexuality is the accepted relationship between sex and marriage. Attitudes about homosexuality are a further reflection of cultural learning. In some societies, homosexuality is viewed as unnatural or sinful or criminal, whereas in others, it may be regarded as one of the possible expressions of human desire.

Gender Roles and Gender Relations

- In all societies, some form of division of labor by gender influences the daily work of an individual. Women's work always includes caring for young children, performing household tasks, usually including cooking and cleaning, although in some South Pacific societies, men do the daily household cooking. Men's work always includes large animal hunting and warfare. Other economic activities, such as farming, small game hunting, and fishing, might be done by men, women, or both. As with other elements of culture, gender roles change as economic and material factors change.

- In some societies, men and women are considered equal, each having rights to autonomy and independence, each permitted and encouraged to participate in decision making, productive work, and prestigious roles in their societies. Gender equality is likely to exist in foraging societies where all individuals make important contributions to subsistence and where hierarchical leadership and control is absent or minimal. In other societies, male dominance may be reflected in men's control over access to resources, economic production and distribution, household and community decision making and leadership, and ritual activity. The most intense forms of male dominance tend to occur in agricultural states. However, in male-dominated societies, women may have some degree of independence and power in some spheres of life, as in the case of West African women who control local and regional trade.

- Some anthropologists suggest that some form of male dominance exists in all societies, whereas others point to the variation that occurs in known societies in which women and men have or had equal rights and privileges and their economic, social, and political roles were equally valued. Rapid culture change brought about by European colonization led to greater subordination of women, as Europeans favored men as individuals and as a group, thereby enhancing their status and power to the exclusion of women.

Gender and Subsistence

- Egalitarian relationships develop among foragers and in industrial and postindustrial societies. In the United States, women were central to the industrializing economy in the late eighteenth and early nineteenth centuries, as farmers' daughters went to work in textile mills. At first, young unmarried women worked for wages in many types of industries, but later married women and even those with young children joined the work force. These women were compelled by economic conditions to contribute their salaries to the growing needs of their families. However, although many women worked outside the home, they remain marginalized in the industrial sector by gender segregation in the workplace and by unequal pay. The "gender gap" in pay between men and women continues to this day.

- During wartime, women were encouraged to work outside the home to contribute to the war effort. In peacetime, however, many women were pressured to leave the public sector and return to home life. Many remained, though, in the work force. Economic needs of families grew as inflation rose and real wages fell. Some women continued to work because of their desire for personal gratification and professional development. By 1996, more than half of women with children of all ages were in the work force.

Globalization and Gender

- Globalization has affected men and women differently as national and international agencies have introduced agricultural and industrial development projects in rural and poor communities. Women often lose their central roles as subsistence farmers when land is taken out of household production and dedicated to growing crops for national and global trading networks. Multinational corporations build light manufacturing plants that employ predominantly young, unmarried women at low pay. These jobs offer advantages to the employees, who gain an income and some degree of independence, but they also have disadvantages.

- In most socialist and former socialist societies, public policies promoted women's full participation in production and equal legal rights. However, working women continue to be burdened by a "double day," combining paid employment with household responsibilities. Women's unemployment has been disproportionately high in Eastern Europe and the former Soviet Union as socialist economies have changed to a free-market economy. In most countries, women constitute only a small fraction of elected officials or appointed administrators with decision-making powers.

Impacts of Ideology on Gender Constructs

- Despite the significant contributions of women to U.S. economic development and to their families, a range of ideological pressures continues to undermine gender equality. Some people promote the nineteenth-century "cult of domesticity," claiming that men and women are suited for different kinds of roles because of their different biological needs, psychological orientations, and social wants. It is claimed that men are inherently aggressive and assertive while women are innately nurturing and passive. However, many other people support the goal of gender equality, working toward equal rights for women and men, shared work and household responsibilities, and equal participation in public life.

 *Key Terms*

Review Questions

1. What are cultural constructs? How are they used to define gender in societies?

2. Cross-culturally, what are some economic roles typically undertaken by women, and how are those roles different from those undertaken by men?

3. What is a third gender identity? How do third gender concepts relate to sexuality? To homosexuality?

4. How do contributions to production, postmarital residence, and warfare patterns affect the status of women in a society?

5. How are gender roles and relations related to the subsistence strategy of a group?

6. Why would economic developers of business enterprises in Nigeria be wise to give Igbo women a key role in planning and implementation?

7. How did gender relations among the Ju/'hoansi, Inuit, Iroquois, and Chinese change in part as a result of both external contact and internal change?

8. How do ideologies affect changes in gender constructs?

Equality and Inequality

CHAPTER 11

Preview

1. **What is social stratification? How does inequality arise in human societies?**

2. **What are three basic types of social organization? How do they work?**

3. **How do caste and class systems differ as two forms of stratified societies?**

4. **What are some determinants and indicators of social standing in stratified societies?**

5. **How are societies stratified by gender, race, and ethnicity?**

6. **Why is the concept of race controversial?**

7. **How and why do people create, accept, maintain, reject, and change their ethnic identities?**

8. **How do ideologies reinforce systems of stratification?**

9. **What can we learn from an anthropological perspective of class, ideology, ethnicity, and race in American society?**

On a bright Sunday morning some peasants sat on the door-step, chatting about their affairs.

The village shopkeeper went up to them and began to boast that he was this, that and the other, and had been in the lord's own chambers.

One of the peasants, the poorest of the lot, sat and scoffed.

"Pooh, that's nothing. I could dine with the lord if I wanted to."

"What—you? Dine with the lord? Never in all your life!" cried the rich shopkeeper.

"But I will, just to prove it."

"No, you won't."

They argued on until the poor man said:

"Let us lay a wager. If I dine with the lord, I win your black and your bay; if I do not, I shall work three years for you for nothing."

The shopkeeper was mighty pleased.

"Very well, I bet you my black and my bay with a calf thrown in for good measure. Let these good men stand witness."

And they shook hands on it before the witnesses.

The poor man went to the lord.

"I should like to ask you in secret—what might be the price of a gold nugget the size of my cap?"

The lord said nothing. He just clapped his hands.

"Ho, there! A drink for this man and myself! Be quick about it. And serve us dinner, too. Sit down, sit down, my man, make yourself at home. Help yourself to all that is on the table!"

The lord treated the poor man as he would an honored guest, and all the time he was agog with impatience. There was nothing he wanted so much as to lay hands on that gold nugget.

"Now, my man, go quickly and fetch the nugget. I will give you a sack of flour and a piece of silver for it."

"But I haven't got any nugget. I was just asking what a nugget the size of my cap would be worth."

The lord flew into a rage.

"Get out, you fool!"

"How can I be a fool when you yourself have treated me as such an honored guest and the shopkeeper owes me two horses and a calf for this same dinner?"

And the peasant went home happy as a lark.

From Alex Alexander (1975), *Russian Folklore: An Anthology in English Translation*, pp. 216–218. Belmont, CA: Norland Publishing.

wealth
Economic resources, whether in land, goods, or money.

power
The ability to exert control over the actions of other people and to make decisions that affect them.

In this tale from Russia, differences in people's wealth and status are at the center of the narrative action and resolution. The story turns on the success of the lowly peasant who, by his cleverness, is able to outwit the wealthy lord. In doing so, he also succeeds where the rich shopkeeper has failed. The story acknowledges the system of class that existed in pre-revolutionary Russia, dividing people and granting privileges to some and disadvantages to others. The story sides with the peasants. Peasants are generally looked down upon because of their poverty, but it is the peasant who prevails by his wit. While the narrative acknowledges the system of class, it can also be read as a form of resistance to the dominant ideology of inequality. And although poor, the peasant shows his worthiness by outsmarting the rich shopkeeper and the wealthy landlord. This story, then, exposes the prevailing system of inequality but with a subversive message.

"Four score and seven years ago our fathers brought forth, upon this continent, a new nation, conceived in Liberty, and dedicated to the proposition that all men are created equal." This is the opening sentence of the Gettysburg Address by President Abraham Lincoln, one of the most famous and most often quoted excerpts from American oratory. But the world of 1863 was quite different from the world implied in this speech. Presumably Lincoln meant that the founders of the United States intended to establish a nation where all people were free. But the United States in its beginnings was a country with slavery and founded on land appropriated from indigenous peoples. In contrast, an ideology of equality, stated in the Declaration of Independence, in Lincoln's Gettysburg Address, and in countless political speeches ever since, has permeated American public discourse for centuries. Through this discourse, people come to believe in an equality of opportunity that did not, and does not, exist.

EQUALITY, INEQUALITY, AND SOCIAL STRATIFICATION

In previous chapters, we encountered societies in which everyone has equal access to resources, livelihood, and respect. We also encountered societies in which access to resources, livelihood, and respect is given more to some people than to others. The first type of system, based on principles of equality among members of communities, is called egalitarian. The second type, based on social, economic, and political inequality, is called stratified. In this chapter we are particularly concerned with systems of social and political inequality.

Before we begin, though, several important distinctions must be made clear. Although people in egalitarian societies have equal access to resources and to positions of prestige and respect, all people are not equal in ability. Individuals everywhere differ in that some have more talent, intelligence, skill, or valued personality traits than others. And, of course, those people with more desirable characteristics are more respected, appreciated, and liked than those people lacking such positive traits. Nonetheless, everyone may make use of the group's resources, secure subsistence, and live a decent life more or less comparably to other people in their community.

In contrast, some people in stratified societies achieve positions of respect, influence, and power that grant them privileges and opportunities denied to others. We will be examining the bases on which stratified societies make social distinctions and the differing rewards and benefits available to some.

Three categories of culturally valued resources are wealth, power, and prestige (Fried, 1967). **Wealth** refers to economic resources, whether in land, goods, or money. **Power** refers to the ability to exert control over the actions of other people and to make

This African king shows his wealth in a grand festival. In any stratified society, wealth, power, and prestige confer privileges, along with opportunities to amass greater wealth, power, and prestige.

decisions that affect them. **Prestige** is a social resource. It is reflected in other people's good opinion, in their respect, and in their willingness to solicit and to listen voluntarily to one's advice. According to Max Weber (1968, 1981), prestige, or honor, as he called it, is central to the establishment and maintenance of status. Weber related honor to the notion of personal charisma. People strive to be well thought of because they then can influence other people. In stratified societies, prestige is linked to wealth and power. Since social values emphasize the worthiness of accumulating wealth, wealthy people are considered successful and looked to as models to emulate. Prestige, then, built on wealth, can be used to obtain and exercise power.

Another set of terms relevant to our discussion of egalitarian and stratified societies has to do with various statuses and roles. Some of these are achieved and some are ascribed. An **achieved status** is one that people attain on the basis of their own efforts and skills. An **ascribed status** is one that a person occupies simply by birth or through a culturally determined right. In our society, leadership is an achieved status; we elect our mayors, governors, and presidents, presumably because of their abilities. In monarchies, leadership is an ascribed status; a king occupies his position simply because he is the eldest son of the previous king.

Finally, the distinctions among societies are not absolute, discrete types but, rather, form a continuum from egalitarian to stratified. Many societies contain elements of both, combining principles of equality in certain contexts with principles of inequality in other contexts. Indeed, there is a type of society, called ranked, that exhibits characteristics of both. **Ranked societies** differentiate individuals or, more usually, kinship groups along a continuum from lowest to highest, based partly on achieved status and partly on ascribed status. The benefits of high rank are social rather than economic or political. People of high rank have prestige and respect but they do not have a living standard significantly better than that of people of lower rank. And although they may have influence in their communities, they do not have the power to control the activities of others.

Egalitarian Societies

Egalitarian societies are ones in which all people have equal access to valued resources. Everyone has available land and natural resources to supply the food that they need to survive. Everyone can achieve positions of respect and influence. And while people may seek the advice of respected individuals, no one is able to exert control or dominance over other people. Egalitarian social systems are usually found in cultures with economies based on producing for subsistence and use rather than to accumulate large surpluses and wealth. Small foraging societies tend to be egalitarian in their social and ethical principles. Many horticultural societies are also egalitarian. This does not mean, however, that there are no forms of inequality in such societies. There are the inequalities of intelligence, skill, and personality that render some people more respected and influential than others. There are also attribute inequalities, such as age and gender, that may affect one's position in the household and society. Older people may be consulted and asked for their opinions about personal or community matters because of their greater experience in life.

The importance of age may be reflected within the household as well. Some of the authority and influence of parents derives from their age as well as from their genealogical relationship to their children. And, in some societies, the importance of seniority among siblings may be reflected in kinship terms that distinguish older and younger siblings and in behavior where younger siblings act deferentially toward their elders.

In addition, gender may be a factor in the respect and authority that people exert. If men and women are thought of as equal, both have influential roles in family and community decision making, conflict resolution, and group action. In male-dominated societies, however, men's opinions have paramount weight in these matters and women's voices are muted. Other kinds of inequalities derived from kinship relationships may exist as well. Heads of lineages or clans may have important, decisive roles, certainly within their families and often in wider social contexts. In some societies, lineage or clan leaders may form village or district councils to discuss matters of community concern.

? *What is an example of one of your achieved statuses? What is an example of one of your ascribed statuses?*

prestige
A social resource reflected in others' good opinions, respect, and willingness to be influenced.

achieved status
A social position attained by a person's own efforts and skills.

ascribed status
A social position that a person attains by birth. A person is born into an ascribed status.

ranked societies
Societies in which people or, more usually, kinship groups are ordered on a continuum in relation to each other.

egalitarian societies
Societies in which all members have equal access to valued resources, including land, social prestige, wealth, and power.

Despite all of these possible forms of inequality, "status tends to be individual or situational rather than categorical" (Berreman, 1989:8). That is, a person's prestige and influence are based primarily on his or her personal qualities and relationships. Finally, people with influence do not use their advantages for personal material gain. The reward for being respected, for being skilled, and for being charismatic is social prestige, not wealth or power.

For example, among the Innu, an egalitarian society of northeastern Québec, social ethics stressed generosity, hospitality, cooperation, and loyalty. People were expected to share resources and to aid each other in household and community work. Coupled with responsibilities to kin and community members, individual autonomy and the rights of all men and women to make decisions and act independently were valued. Coercion of others, either within households or in camps, was not tolerated and, given the strong negative reactions against such behavior, it was rarely attempted. Group leadership was diffuse, flexible, and dependent on personal qualities and subsistence skills. People looked for advice to those who were intelligent and successful in the particular endeavor requiring assistance or consultation—for example, skilled hunters were consulted regarding hunting. However, a man's or a woman's influence was temporary, fitted to the given occasion. Advice, therefore, was sought among local "experts," but such people could not exert authority or control. Decisions were made jointly by all involved. No formal leadership existed.

Ranked Societies

In systems of rank, every person—or, more accurately, every lineage or kin group—has a different position in the social hierarchy. Each rank is ordered in relation to all others. People of higher ranks have more social prestige than people of lower ranks, but they do not have significantly greater wealth or power. Their rewards are social, manifested in the respect given to them and the influence allowed them. If people follow their advice and direction, it is only because they have earned respect by their intelligence, behavior, and sound judgment. Ranked positions are established and maintained through a complex interplay of economic resources, political alliances, personal demeanor, and charisma, all leading to the formation of people's opinions of others.

Ranked systems are not static. Indeed, they are inherently extremely dynamic, even potentially volatile types of social organization. People can raise their status by their behavior and achievement and by the support of their relatives. But one's status can also fall. In order to move up the metaphoric "ladder of success," people have to mobilize public opinion because it is public opinion that legitimates one's place in the system. People attempt to increase their economic wealth, forge alliances and attract dependents or clients, and act in ways that convey self-respect and conform to social norms of personality and attractiveness. In order to be successful and achieve these results, people need the support of their kin. And because of the competitive nature of ranked systems, competition within the family might prove disruptive if members of the family itself vied with each other for access to rank. Therefore, many such systems include the rule of primogeniture, or inheritance by seniority, so that the eldest child has the privilege of representing the family by occupying a position of rank. (In some societies, only men may hold rank; in others, women or men might occupy status positions.)

? Have you been a member of a ranked social organization? How would your experience compare with living in a ranked society?

Stratified Societies

In **stratified societies,** people do not have equal access to valued resources. Because of their ability to accumulate all three elements of culturally valuable resources—wealth, power, and prestige—in stratified societies, some people have more economic resources than others. They have more land, food, and possessions, and their standard of living is superior to that of other people. Some people have more power than others, and they are able to exert control over the actions of other people by making decisions that affect them with or without their consent. And as a consequence of having more wealth and power, they also have more social prestige. People respect them and regard them with envy. In stratified societies, some wealth, power, and prestige accrue to people because of their achievements, hard work, and personal

stratified societies
Societies in which people have differential access to valued resources, including land and property, social prestige, wealth, and political power.

Case study

The Kwakwaka'wakw as a Ranked Society

Kwakwaka'wakw social organization, introduced in Chapter 7, was based on ambilineal descent, centering on a lineage system that allowed people to affiliate with either their mother's or father's group (see Chapter 8; Boas, 1966). People could also claim membership in lineages of their grandparents. Because people could affiliate and claim rights in at least four different groups, choices were made as to how they might best advance a person's social and economic position.

The lineages collectively owned the houses in which their members lived, as well as access to fishing sites, berry patches, and other resource areas. Ritual property, such as songs, dances, and ceremonial gear, were also owned by lineages. Members of lineages had unrestricted access to the sites controlled by their group, but members of other groups were barred from utilizing the resources without permission. Some resource areas were more productive than others, resulting in some advantage to different lineages over others. However, because each group might control more than one resource area, relative disadvantages tended to equalize over the whole of each group's holdings. Some resource sites, however, were considered common property, exploitable by any of the tribes. In addition, people whose territory lacked a particular resource could trade for it with those more strategically located.

All Kwakwaka'wakw tribes and all of their constituent lineages were ranked in relation to all others. In addition, each lineage possessed a number of names that were also ranked in relation to each other. Each name was held by a particular individual, although people could hold more than one name at a time. Names were inherited from parents or grandparents and could also be acquired through marriage. Inheritance of ranked positions followed rules of primogeniture to the firstborn child, whether boy or girl. Although the rule of primogeniture was absolute, rivalries between siblings sometimes surfaced. When a woman was the chosen inheritor, she generally received a man's name and transmitted her social position to her own eldest son as soon as he was grown. It was common for holders of rank to choose their successors and pass on their names before their death, often beginning the process of transfer when the child was young.

Most marriages took place between people of different lineages. The higher one's social position, the more necessary it was to marry one's social equal or, even better, to marry someone of higher rank. However, since high-status people did not want to marry beneath them, it was unlikely that a person of low rank could achieve social advancement by marrying far up the social scale.

The Kwakwaka'wakw social system differentiated among three groups: nobles or chiefly people, commoners, and slaves. The first two groups were not discrete classes but gradations of relative rank. Slaves, in contrast, were socially distinct and had no social mobility. The difference between slaves and the rest of society was a distinction of stratification, not rank.

Most slaves were acquired in warfare or were the descendants of slaves. They generally performed menial subsistence and productive tasks. Their major constraint was that they could not be part of the system of social rank and prestige that was fundamental to society. The contrast between commoners and nobles was much more complex. These were not fixed categories but were on a continuum from lowest to highest social standing. People of highest status constituted the informal leadership of kin groups and villages. Chiefs were recipients of portions of animal, fish, and plant products obtained by members of their group. They were usually exempt from most subsistence tasks. Chiefs were responsible for organizing cooperative productive activities such as house building. They acted as representatives of their lineages in the system of potlatching or feasting that was the occasion for ceremonial validation of one's social standing.

Potlatches functioned to redistribute wealth and to claim status. Wealth was related to status, but wealth was accumulated in order to give it away publicly. The potlatch system demonstrated leveling mechanisms that barred the concentration of extreme wealth in any individual or family. Potlatching also confirmed status and contributed to social solidarity. For instance, to be invited as a guest at a potlatch given by a high-ranking person was a public acknowledgment of one's own high social status. Chiefs needed others of comparable standing to raise their own social rank. And chiefs needed their own kin to amass the goods distributed at feasts. In these ways, potlatching served to unite families and lineages. One's own social status rose and fell with the social status of other members of one's family and larger kin groups.

social stratification
Divison of society into two or more groups, or strata, that are hierarchically ordered.

elites
Members of a social group in a stratified society who have privileges denied to the majority of the population.

characteristics. But some of their good fortune comes to them because of their birth. They are the children of wealthy and powerful people. Prestige, wealth, and power, therefore, are both ascribed and achieved.

Social stratification refers to a division of society into two or more groups, or strata, that are hierarchically ordered in relation to each other. Within each stratum, members are all of more or less equal social standing. While there are differences among individuals in stratified systems, people in the same stratum have equivalent opportunities, privileges, and standards of living, at least when compared to people in other strata.

One of the significant features of all systems of stratification is that the highest group is usually, if not always, a numerical minority. Why, then, is it that the majority of people are willing to accept a system that does not benefit them? There are many and complex explanations. One reason is that the elite group controls the means of forcing compliance with their wishes. Because the **elites** control social, economic, and political resources, they are in a position to use political (and often military) power against those who resist their control. But the use of force is costly, not just in economic terms. When force is used against people, especially if they constitute the majority of the population, it is likely that sooner or later they will rebel against a system that disadvantages them. So, instead, social attitudes and beliefs are developed to induce conformity. People are taught to believe that the system they live in is just. And, if not entirely just, it is, at the least, legitimate.

There are many ways of creating and transmitting such attitudes or ideologies. Religious teaching, for example, is an effective means of instilling obedience to the rulers. People may be taught that their leaders have been chosen by the deities or that the system they live in has divine approval. Or they may be pacified by the hope that divine beings favor them, an idea conveyed by the biblical phrase "The meek shall inherit the Earth." In addition, social ideologies transmit the notion that elites are more capable, more intelligent, and in other ways superior to common people. Common people absorb these ideologies through their socialization and through exposure to public discourse that is controlled by the elites.

Thus, many fail to see that poverty and wealth are part of the structure of our society. And they fail to see that our capitalist economic system depends as much on the existence of poverty as it does on the existence of wealth. The wealth of some people depends on the labor of other people, many of whom work for low wages. In addition, the existence of a group of unemployed and underemployed people exerts a downward pressure on all wages because there are more people wanting work than there are

This woman is one of many working poor who earn minimum wages in the United States. In some stratified societies, common people accept inequality because they believe that with hard work and diligence, they, too, can achieve success and social mobility.

jobs available. This situation leads to competition among workers for jobs and creates a situation where even low-paying jobs become attractive.

Explaining Social Stratification

Social stratification is a characteristic of complex state societies. Among other traits, states have economies based on intensive agricultural production, resulting in a large surplus. This surplus can be used to support ever-growing populations and to free some people from agricultural work. Labor specialization develops so that some people work as farmers, others as artisans, traders, soldiers, or government officials. States are also characterized by unequal access to resources. Some people accumulate more goods, land, and other property than others. Rather than distributing their wealth to community members in need, they use their property for themselves, raising their standard of living and living better than people with fewer resources. Over time, inequalities in standards of living become entrenched as children of wealthy parents are born with advantages and opportunities lacking to the children of poor people. (Characteristics of state societies are discussed further in Chapter 12.)

Several types of explanations are offered to explain the existence of stratification. Functional analyses emphasize the fact that different sectors of the population perform different roles in society. Rewards are given to those people who are more capable and hardworking than others. In functionalism, people who are leaders, traders, and officials, performing important functions for the community as a whole, are acknowledged and permitted to accumulate wealth, social prestige, and power. These benefits are believed to be just compensation for their societal contributions.

Although there is merit in this argument, because it points out the various roles of different people in systems of economic specialization, it fails to take into account several important factors. People with wealth are not necessarily more capable than others. Some people inherit their wealth without any effort or achievement of their own. Also, some leaders are incompetent. In monarchies where the eldest son of the king automatically becomes the next ruler, there is no guarantee that the person so promoted is the most capable. Hard work does not necessarily translate into wealth, prestige, and power. As an extreme example, African slaves in the United States and the Caribbean certainly contributed great effort, and often gave their lives, in the production of wealth but received no benefit at all from their work. The value of their labor was extracted and used by their owners. In modern societies as well, the hard work and long hours of, for example, factory workers, secretaries, and nurses are not reflected in luxurious standards of living.

A second set of explanations for social stratification emphasizes the conflicts between members of different strata or classes. These analyses, following Karl Marx, focus on the processes that create groups in opposition to each other. Members of different classes have different class interests. They develop a consciousness of their class and strive to protect and expand their interests. Members of elite classes try to influence economic and political policies that will benefit themselves. Although members of lower classes may also try to influence leaders to implement policies that will aid them, they are generally less successful, in part because the leaders tend to come from or identify with the elites.

These explanations focus on societies as dynamic systems. They emphasize the processes of struggle between members of opposing groups. It is through these struggles that societies can be transformed. And then new types of group formation and new types of opposition and conflict lead to further series of changes and adaptations. Of course, although complex societies are composed of groups with different, often conflicting, interests and goals, societies also attempt to build consensus and foster cooperation among groups. Therefore,

GLOBALIZATION

Systems of stratification based on the control of capital and the concept of social mobility have spread throughout the world as a consequence of globalization. Stratification based on class membership is rapidly replacing other forms of stratification, as well as ranked and egalitarian societies.

Karl Marx explained social stratification as an outgrowth of class conflict over the control of resources and wealth. Neo-Marxist approaches to the study of social stratification focus on conflicts between different groups in a society.

How might a functionalist explain homelessness in a stratified society such as the United States? What explanation based on conflict might a Marxist offer?

functional and Marxist explanations for social stratification both offer insights that can be useful in analyzing societal structures and processes.

REVIEW

Societies become stratified through the unequal distribution of wealth, power, and prestige, which attach to the different ascribed statuses (inherited) and achieved statuses (acquired) in a society. In ranked societies, different groups are ranked hierarchically on the basis of both ascribed and achieved statuses. Egalitarian societies provide equal access to resources, whereas in stratified societies some individuals and groups have more resources and others less. Structuralism, functionalism, Marxism, and other theoretical perspectives offer alternative explanations for social stratification.

CASTE AND CLASS

Hindus revere many deities, including the goddess Lakshmi, here being worshipped at the rice harvest.

A caste is a social group whose membership is hereditary. Castes are endogamous. That is, people must marry within their caste, and their children are also members of the same group. Thus caste is an ascribed status with automatic, involuntary, and unchanging membership and identity. Separation on the basis of caste may be manifested by restrictions on living spaces, occupation, style of dress, and demeanor. In caste systems, each group is assigned a particular order of prestige relative to the others on a scale from lowest to highest. Unlike rank, caste order cannot change.

Determinants of Class

Systems of class are also ways of grouping people in a hierarchical order. But whereas castes are differentiated according to the sole criterion of ancestry, class may be defined in various ways. One way to talk about class is to talk about economic factors, primarily income, education, and occupation. These factors tend to go together, so that people with the highest

 *Culture Change*

CASTE IN INDIA

In India, there are hundreds of discrete castes (called *jati*), all ranked in relation to one another (Koller, 1982). The caste system unifies constituent groups into four large groupings (called *varna*), each containing numerous castes that are perceived to be somewhat similar in their origin, function, and especially in their ritual purity. Members of the highest varna, called the Brahmins, were traditionally the priests and scholars. The second-highest category are the Kshatriyas, who were the warriors. The merchants and traders constitute the third varna, called Vaishyas. And the fourth varna are the Shudras, or artisans, carpenters, blacksmiths, barbers, farmers, and menial workers. Finally, there is a fifth group, ranked below all the others: the untouchables. Untouchables are people considered ritually impure, fit to do only the most menial work, such as cleaning toilets. According to Hindu religious and ethical beliefs, a member of one of the higher castes can become ritually polluted by touching or being touched by an untouchable.

Caste in India is an example of a comparatively closed system of stratification. Although in practice some social mobility is possible, people traditionally are born into a particular caste and remain in that caste for the rest of their lives. Rural villages often are divided into caste neighborhoods, and occupations are determined by caste. In the most traditional contexts, there is little, if anything, one can do to change one's circumstances. Even if a person were to move to another community and not reveal his or her heredity, a person's way of talking and behaving would probably be telltale signs of the person's ancestry and, by implication, his or her caste identity.

The behavior of people in different castes functions as a barrier to social interactions, acting as boundary markers. People belonging to different castes should not eat together and certainly should not have sexual relations with each other. Members of higher castes may avoid taking food offered by members of lower castes. Higher caste people are more likely to be vegetarians and to refrain from drinking alcoholic beverages. Members of different castes may have somewhat different ways of speaking, including their pronunciation of sounds and in some cases their choice of words. The most stringent restrictions are placed on the behavior of untouchables. In rural villages, untouchables must reside in their own section and cannot take drinking water from wells used by the higher castes.

The most prestigious group, the Brahmins, is thought of as ritually pure and need to maintain their purity through social distance. But while many Brahmins have respected occupations and earn high salaries, many do not. Brahmins are not necessarily wealthy. For example, Brahmins may work as cooks in restaurants because members of all castes may eat food touched by the highest group.

Although Indian castes are perceived to be primarily social and ritual categories, they also have economic functions. High caste people cannot perform important subsistence and productive functions for themselves because of the polluting nature of these activities, such as working with wood or making pottery. These goods and services are provided by lower caste people, who in return receive food, clothing, and money. A permanent and stable relationship between patron and client may become established over the years, providing for an exchange of goods and services between the two parties. The patron-client relationship may pass to the descendants of the originators, continuing important economic exchanges through the generations. In this way, both groups receive significant benefits.

Caste economic relationships serve both divisive and integrating functions. They are divisive because people are restricted to performing caste-specific economic roles, but at the same time they are integrating because they create necessary interdependence among people of different castes. However, despite the advantages of stability and security obtained by lower caste people from their patrons, it is still true that the

mobility
A principle that people can move from membership in one social group to another.

system as a whole stigmatizes them and takes more from them than it gives. As in any system of social stratification, higher ranked people benefit most.

Finally, Indian castes were intimately associated and intertwined with political power. The structures of caste functioned in villages and regional territories to both segment and articulate various kinship groups and residential communities. They formed the basic structure of political alliances and political control. Much of the political significance of castes was ignored and obliterated by British colonial administrators beginning in the nineteenth century. By reinventing caste significance as primarily ritual, the British were able to pretend that India lacked "genuine politics," in effect providing a rationale for British control (Dirks, 2001).

The system of caste in India is not as static as it is often described, however. Since India's independence in 1948, a number of laws have been enacted that affect restrictions on caste behavior. People belonging to different castes can now legally marry and cannot be prosecuted for engaging in sexual relations. Family and community opinion, however, still often frowns on such unions. It is currently illegal to discriminate against untouchables. Indeed, the government specifies that certain jobs and a percentage of openings in universities must be reserved for members of the lower castes. And all people have the right to vote, a right that carries with it the potential, if exercised, to seek wider political changes to improve the economic and social position of the lower castes.

In modern India, especially in the cities, caste ranking is not immutable. Upward mobility for the caste as a group is possible if members have achieved a degree of wealth and prestige. But upward mobility pertains to the group; it is not a narrowly individual process. However, striving for upward mobility does not necessarily undermine the system of stratification, as it merely results in a change of the ordering of groups rather than in a challenge to the legitimacy of the existing social principles on which the system is based. It is still possible that, over time, fluidity in caste may lead to fundamental challenges to the system. Members of the Untouchable caste are especially vocal opponents of the system, calling for laws that ban discrimination. Many thousands have converted from Hinduism to Buddhism as a protest against the injustices of caste hierarchies.

incomes usually have the most advanced education and the most prestigious jobs. However, cases can easily be cited that contradict this general tendency, such as occupations requiring advanced education but earning lower incomes than other occupations with lower educational requirements. In this economic meaning of class, the groups are not closed, discrete units but, rather, are categories differentiated along a continuum. These categories form social layers or strata that are ranked in relation to one another. There are no absolute boundary markers between them; they differ only in relative terms.

Unlike caste, class is an achieved status because the criteria for determining class membership are subject to achievement by individuals as well as to change. Also, unlike caste, where a person's identity is rigidly determined, the factors used to determine class membership are less easily and less consistently specified. And, unlike the fixed and closed nature of caste, systems of class are open and allow for mobility from one group to another. Class **mobility** may be either upward or downward.

Another way of talking about class is to talk about relations of production. In this Marxian sense of class, there are two contrasting groups—the group that owns the means of economic production and controls the distribution of products and the group that does not own the means of production. These two groups, or classes, can be simplified as owners and workers. Owners control production and distribution and profit from the productive labor of others, and workers sell their labor to the owners for a wage. In modern corporate capitalism, the distinction between owners and workers is more complicated than was true in the late nineteenth century, when Karl Marx developed his insights about the European capitalist economic system.

? *How does your social class influence your life experiences? How does your culture reinforce the class system of which you are a part?*

In North American discourse on class, there are strong pressures against public discussion of class interests and underlying class conflicts. Rather, we are led to believe that anyone can grow up to be president. Nevertheless, members of different classes, however defined, occupy different places in society and their life experiences are fundamentally different.

Social Class and Language

Class differences are revealed and reinforced by patterns of language use. When we speak, we consciously and unconsciously use forms (pronunciations, words, grammar) that identify who we are. People can immediately tell something about us—where we come from, how old we are, what gender we are, and what social group we belong to. Our class, race, and ethnicity are some of the social factors that we reveal when we speak. And when we hear other people speak, we make judgments about them based on their language.

These Saudi royals experience privilege in their living standards, their health, and the control they have over other people. They may influence ordinary citizens through the laws they enact, the policies they implement, and the media outlets (television, radio, and newspapers) they regulate.

While all speakers may employ both the standard and nonstandard forms, middle-class speakers use the standard forms more frequently and lower-class speakers more often use the nonstandard forms. In the United States and Great Britain, instead of the standard pronunciation of "thing" and "the," lower-class speakers might say "ting" and "de," replacing the "th" sound with "t" or "d" (Labov, 1966, 1972b; Trudgill, 1974, 1983). Class-related variations in these sounds are documented in the English language in both Great Britain and the United States as early as the seventeenth century.

Research in Belgium conducted by Jef van den Broeck (1977) also showed differences in the speech of working-class and middle-class speakers. Van den Broeck discovered that middle-class and working-class speakers showed no significant differences in sentence complexity in informal situations, but a marked distinction in formal contexts. In formal situations, middle-class speakers used more complex constructions than in informal situations, but working-class formal grammar was less complex than working-class informal style. Van den Broeck suggested that in formal situations middle-class speakers want to distinguish their style from that of the working class. They use linguistic mechanisms as an "act of conspicuous ostentation, a marker of social distance." Working-class speakers, on the other hand, through their speech, may reflect their feelings of relative powerlessness in formal situations.

Slavery

Slavery, the most extreme form of stratification, is an ascribed status. People become slaves either by being born into slavery or by being captured in warfare or slaving raids. Slavery is thus forced upon a person, either through accident of birth or through the deliberate actions of others. And the slave group, like castes and classes, is endogamous. Slaves usually marry other

slavery
An ascribed status forced on a person upon birth or through involuntary servitude.

A group of slaves gather under a tree as they wait for freedom in southern Sudan. On July 4, 2001, three African American ministers and a Harvard student, with funds from Christian Solidarity International, bought the freedom of 2,035 slaves in Sudan. The price they negotiated for each slave on this "redemption mission" was less than the cost of one healthy goat, about $40. Slavery and the slave trade were outlawed in the United Nations Universal Declaration of Human Rights in 1948, but today an estimated 27 million people in the world are enslaved.

Anthropology Applied

Working against Human Trafficking

In both government and nongovernment organizations, anthropologists are among those combating international human trafficking. Human trafficking includes buying and selling women and children into indentured servitude or slavery, illegally transporting migrants, and marketing body parts. The United Nations and various national governments publish reports on the effectiveness of nations' measures against human trafficking. In the summer of 2004, the U.S. State Department's report on human trafficking named ten countries—including Sudan, Myanmar, and North Korea—as among the world's most negligent in protecting human rights. A second tier of nations with inadequate measures against human trafficking included forty-two countries, Japan among them. Japan is a destination for Asian, Latin American, and East European women and children trafficked for forced labor and sexual exploitation by the *yakuza,* Japan's organized crime groups. Other countries on the tier 2 watch list include Russia, Thailand, Vietnam, the Philippines, Pakistan, India, Zimbabwe, Greece, Mexico, and Peru (Sakajiri, 2004).

Anthropologists may work against human trafficking in different ways. For example, anthropologists working for HimRights (International Institute for Human Rights, Environment and Development), a watchdog organization, in Nepal conduct preventive educational campaigns and help monitor Himalayan border crossings to detect and report suspected trafficking and protect Bhutanese and Tibetan refugees. They may help rescue and repatriate trafficked persons. And they provide data for the region to the United Nations Commission on Human Rights (www.inhured.org/download/HimRights_brochure.pdf).

In addition, human rights work often involves surveillance (or observation) and documentation, which are the skills of an ethnographer. The underworld trafficking of human organs for transplants was exposed largely through "undercover ethnography." This kind of work, which raises serious ethical issues for anthropologists as well as for the medical profession, led to the discovery of an extensive network of "outlaw surgeons, kidney hunters, and transplant tourists" engaged in trade for human body parts (Scheper-Hughes, 2004).

CRITICAL THINKING QUESTIONS

Why might anthropologists disagree about becoming involved in human rights work? What might be arguments for and against undercover ethnography?

---

slaves, not necessarily because of their preferences but because nonslaves are unwilling to marry them. Slavery generally entails the loss of a person's independence and autonomy. At the least, slaves work at the direction and the behest of their owners. They cannot control their own labor, and they do not benefit materially from the goods that they produce. In addition, slaves cannot leave and find homes and work elsewhere. With low social status, slaves cannot hope to achieve any position of prestige or influence in their society, except within the community of other slaves. Social attitudes attribute negative qualities to slaves. They are thought to be inferior and incapable of valued achievements.

The quality of a slave's life varies across cultures. We are familiar from the history of the United States with a form of slavery in which slaves had no rights of any kind. In other societies with slavery, the life of a slave was not necessarily much different from that of ordinary people. For example, among the Kwakwaka'wakw and other indigenous societies of the Pacific Northwest, slaves lived in the homes of their owners, ate the same kind of food, and wore the same kind of clothing. They usually performed menial tasks and suffered the indignity of low social status, but they could be ransomed by their relatives and returned to their own communities.

GLOBALIZATION

A dark side of globalization today is widespread trafficking of women and children for the sex trade and illicit trade in human body parts for transplants. These and other transborder crimes feed on a global service economy.

REVIEW

Societies may be stratified by caste—a hierarchy of hereditary, endogamous, closed system of social strata defined by occupation and concepts of religious purity. Societies also may be stratified by class—a hierarchy of social strata based mainly on achieved economic status, in which people may be upwardly or downwardly mobile but tend to marry within their own group. Class membership typically is identified by lifestyle factors and the use of language. Slavery is an extreme form of social stratification, based on ascribed status, in which people are defined and treated as commodities.

RACE AND ETHNICITY

Like caste and class, **race** is a social, not a biological, category. There are no absolute biological differences among people that would allow for an objective categorization of human beings into discrete, nonoverlapping groups. Rather, so-called "racial" distinctions focus on a particular set of external physical traits that are then used to identify different "races." In the United States and elsewhere, these traits most especially include skin color, hair color and texture, and facial features. However, it is obvious that all of these characteristics appear in human populations on a continuum. The classification, labeling, and valuing of these differences as races are entirely arbitrary.

These Amerasian children of mixed descent would be regarded as outcasts in their home countries in Southeast Asia. These children's status as outcasts would have affected their chances of survival, health, education, occupation, quality of life, and longevity. Many Amerasian children were airlifted from South Vietnam as a humanitarian gesture when Saigon fell and later when diplomatic relations between the United States and Vietnam were reestablished after the Vietnam War.

In the process of constructing race as a cultural category, people are identified as belonging to different "races" based on supposed biological differences. Social ideologies are then developed to justify the system. The next step associates certain constellations of behavior with each group. So, for example, members of one race are said to be more intelligent, more honest, more capable than members of another race. These associations and the social foundation on which they are based privilege some groups and disadvantage others. The group that controls the social, economic, and political structures of the society thinks of itself as superior and of different others as inferior. Whether a majority or minority of the population, the group in power has the ability to control the ideological grounds on which the social order rests.

Race as Caste

In its artificiality, race is very much like caste. In both systems, particular groups are said to have separate ancestral origins, thus explaining their appearance, behavioral characteristics, and place in society. Both caste and race are ascribed statuses and both are closed systems. Like castes, racial groups tend to be endogamous because people usually marry members of their own race. In some racialist societies, marriage between members of different races is legally forbidden, but even where there are no legal boundaries to intermarriage, people generally choose to marry members of their own group for a number of social and emotional reasons. Finally, race is like caste in the attribution of purity to superior groups and impurity to inferior groups who are often thought of as "unclean" in some ways. Contact between the races is thought to pollute those of higher status. For example, in some southern American states, African Americans were legally barred from drinking from the same public water fountains as whites, from using the same rest rooms, and from sitting in the same sections on buses and trains. Although these laws were repealed in the 1950s and 1960s, their underlying symbolism has not been entirely eradicated in some communities.

Race in the United States

In the United States, the races are ordered in a hierarchy that is arbitrary and culturally derived. Attitudes toward members of the different races are learned and transmitted without any basis in fact, although holders of these attitudes believe that they are factually true. In addition, races tend to be endogamous, partly because people tend to live near, go to schools with, and socialize with people of their same racial background, but also because of lingering attitudes about racial separation. Although it is true that many workplaces are racially mixed, occupational stratification often contributes to boundaries between the races. Attitudes toward members of the disadvantaged groups are fraught with negative stereotypes and prejudice.

race
A cultural category that groups people according to so-called "racial" distinctions.

Case study

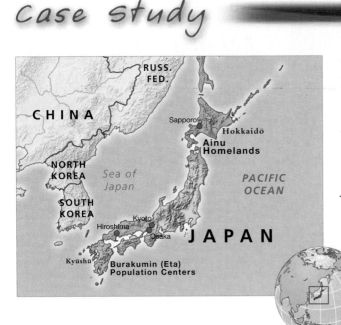

Outgroups of Japan

In Japan, people adhere strongly to notions of belonging to a homogeneous racial and cultural group. They believe that they are physically similar and look quite different from other Asian populations. They also believe that to be "Japanese" is an identity that is ascribed and cannot be acquired. As George De Vos and Hiroshi Wagatsuma state, "In the Japanese mind only those born of Japanese parents are genetically Japanese—nobody can become a Japanese" (1995: 268). People who live in Japan but are not defined as "Japanese" face overt and covert forms of discrimination even though their ancestors have lived in Japan for thousands of years.

According to De Vos and Wagatsuma, about 4.5 percent of the population in Japan belongs to "minority" groups. Some are citizens of the country, but others are denied citizenship. The largest minority group socially defined as "not Japanese" are the Burakumin. Numbering about 3 million, the Burakumin are descendants of an ancient group of outcasts. In the traditional stratified social system, there were four ordered classes of Japanese below which the Burakumin were ranked as a defiled pariah group. The official name of this group, called Eta, is written with characters meaning "full of filth" (p. 274). Their traditional occupations included work that was thought to be ritually polluting such as slaughtering animals, disposing of the dead, and making musical instruments (containing leather and other animal products). The Burakumin, literally "village people," originally lived in separate villages, but now they may also live in certain neighborhoods in large towns and cities. Despite no supporting evidence, the majority of Japanese believe that there are racial distinctions that set the Burakumin apart.

The Buraku community is as heterogeneous as any other in a modern state. Class distinctions exist, based principally on occupation and income. Some Burakumin continue to work in their traditional occupations, but others own land and property. Some members of the group accept their minority status and actively identify as Burakumin, but others attempt to "pass," principally by learning new occupations and changing their place of residence. However, changing one's residential identity is not as simple in Japan as elsewhere because past addresses are maintained in official population records and can be investigated by teachers and employers, among others.

In the past, the Burakumin were the only Japanese to eat meat, in violation of Buddhist principles, but now many Japanese eat meat. As a somewhat self-conscious marker of identity, some Burakumin wear a distinctive type of sandal called *setta zari*. Otherwise, Buraku dress is perceived to be informal and "careless," a negative characteristic. Finally, Buraku speech is generally more "informal" and "less refined" than that of the general population (p. 277). Most Burakumin work in their own communities, employed by or working with relatives or people familiar to them in the community. But many Burakumin are unemployed or underemployed and rely heavily on government assistance programs. A high rate of endogamy exists within the Buraku community because of both their own preferences and the prejudices among other Japanese.

Because the Burakumin are not distinguishable from ordinary Japanese in their appearance, it is possible to "pass" in public situations simply by avoiding the dress styles and speech patterns considered distinctive identity markers. Middle-class Burakumin have stronger pressures to pass than do poor people because they hope to give their children educational and financial advantages that would allow them to become white-collar and professional workers. The major impediment to "passing" is the record of residence that betrays one's origin.

Negative stereotypes about the Burakumin are widely held by many people in Japan. The Burakumin are thought to have personality traits that violate general social norms.

They are considered impulsive, volatile, hostile, and aggressive (p. 279). Especially given the premium on polite behavior and an even-tempered demeanor so highly regarded in Japan, the behavior attributed to the Burakumin is especially disvalued. In addition, the Burakumin demonstrate less conformity and deference to authority than ordinary Japanese. Openly deviant behavior, especially toward authority figures, is tolerated and may even be somewhat rewarded within the community as a challenge to the discrimination experienced by the people. Finally, the Burakumin are more open about engaging in and talking about sexual activity than is the acceptable norm in Japan. The fact that some Burakumin continue in behaviors that they know the majority Japanese criticize may be an example of a subversive challenge to dominant ideologies.

The Ainu, descendants of the indigenous people of ancient Japan (pictured here at a Thanksgiving festival), live in a few small villages on the northern island of Hokkaido, where they were driven when Japan invaded their territory. Today they are often considered "quaint or primitive" (De Vos and Wagatsuma, 1995, p. 273). Many people of Ainu ancestry have intermarried with the general Japanese population, but some maintain a sense of their unique cultural identity.

Interviews with officials in family courts in the city of Kobe revealed that the small Buraku minority contributed disproportionately to the number of cases brought before the courts because of family problems and delinquency (p. 282). Partly because of actual records of criminal problems and partly because of negative stereotypes, ordinary Japanese claim to be fearful of the Burakumin. Similar attitudes are often found in other cultures with hierarchical social systems. Disadvantaged groups frequently bear the brunt of derogatory suspicions and fears that undermine their own self-esteem and that serve to justify the majority's discrimination against them.

In addition to the Burakumin, several other groups, supposedly distinguished racially from the Japanese, face discrimination as well. The Okinawans, Taiwanese, and Koreans are considered foreigners even though they have lived in Japan for many generations. These include Okinawans, Taiwanese, and Koreans who were relocated as a result of earlier Japanese military expansion. Most remain noncitizens living in large urban ghettos (p. 273). Koreans in particular are thought to be "inherently uncouth and uncivilized" (p. 287). Because of the discrimination they face, many Koreans live in poverty. But rather than their being considered victims of discrimination, they are seen as deserving the negative attitudes toward them. To become citizens, some people of Korean or Taiwanese ancestry have hidden their origins by taking on Japanese names. As in other cultures with racial or ethnic discrimination, children of mixed marriages are considered to be tainted and impure.

Another group of people who face negative attitudes are the *hibakusha*, survivors of the atomic bombs that were dropped by the United States on Japan in 1945 during World War II. These victims of war are considered "irrevocably contaminated" because of their physical illnesses and deformities. And children of marriages or sexual relationships between Japanese women and American soldiers stationed in Japan during the U.S. occupation also face some types of discrimination. According to De Vos and Wagatsuma, "More than any other minority group in Japan, offspring of Japanese and non-Asian foreigners are maliciously stereotyped in mass media, including popular literature, films, and comic books" (p. 273).

Attitudes about race in Japan are in some ways very similar to those in the United States. So-called minority groups are thought to be physically different from the majority population no matter how erroneous this assumption and no matter how little evidence there is to support it. In addition, negatively viewed personality traits and behavioral norms are attributed to them, again with little supporting evidence. The conditions of poverty in which disadvantaged and stigmatized groups live actually result from discrimination but are used to prove the people's lack of merit and thereby justify the negative stereotypes that are applied to them.

In Their Own Voices

The Souls of Black Folk

W.E.B. DuBois was born in Great Barrington, Massachusetts, in 1868. He received his undergraduate degree from Fisk College and his Ph.D. in sociology from Harvard University. Having grown up in western Massachusetts, DuBois was shocked at the overt racism that he experienced when he went to college in the South. He taught school for several years in Georgia, where he again confronted racist bigotry. In this excerpt from his influential book, The Souls of Black Folk *(1903), DuBois writes about the lives and destinies of two men, one black and one white.*

The white folk of Altamaha, Georgia voted John a good boy,—fine plough-hand, good in the rice-fields, handy everywhere, and always good-natured and respectful. But they shook their heads when his mother wanted to send him off to school. "It'll spoil him,—ruin him," they said. But full half the black folk followed him proudly to the train station.

Up at the Judge's they too had a John—a fair-haired, smooth-faced boy, who had played many a long summer's day to its close with his darker namesake. "Yes, sir! John is at Princeton, sir," said the Judge every morning as he marched down to the post-office. "Showing the Yankees what a Southern gentleman can do," he added.

Thus in the far-away Southern village the world lay waiting for the coming of two young men, and dreamed in an inarticulate way of new things that would be done and new thoughts that all would think. And yet it was singular that few thought of two Johns,—for the black folk thought of one John, and he was black; and the white folk thought of another John, and he was white. And neither world thought the other world's thought, save with a vague unrest.

John grew slowly to feel almost for the first time the Veil that lay between him and the white world; he first noticed now the oppression that had not seemed oppression before, differences that erstwhile seemed natural, restraints and slights that in his boyhood days had gone unnoticed or been greeted with a laugh. He felt angry now when men did not call him "Mister," he clenched his hands at the "Jim Crow" cars, and chafed at the color-line that hemmed in him and his.

It left John sitting so silent and rapt that he did not for some time notice the usher tapping him lightly on the shoulder and saying politely, "Will you step this way, please, sir?" A little surprised, he arose quickly at the last tap, and, turning to leave his seat, looked full into the face of the fair-haired young man. For the first time the young man recognized his dark boyhood playmate, and John knew that it was the Judge's son. The White John started, lifted his hand, and then froze into his chair; the black John smiled lightly, then grimly, and followed the usher down the aisle.

While these attitudes no doubt are changing, members of disadvantaged races are still burdened by unfair treatment, lack of equal opportunity, and a marginalized role in public life.

It is apparent to most North Americans that racial groups in the United States are ordered hierarchically with "white" as the privileged group. Stating that whites are privileged does not mean that all white people live well and have power. Clearly, this is not the case. Many white people are poor, unemployed, undereducated, and endure many kinds of hardships. Most white people lack social and political power because they, like members of the minority groups, do not control the means of producing wealth and influence. However, although individual whites suffer from poverty and lack of opportunity, their suffering is based on class, not race. Poor whites are marginalized in a class system that disadvantages them, but poor African Americans, Native Americans, and Hispanics are marginalized by both class and race, compounding their structural powerlessness. The antagonism that pervades and obscures issues of class and race surfaces in attitudes toward affirmative action programs, for example. Working-class and middle-class whites who oppose affirmative action are expressing an anger that stems from competitive relations underlying capitalist economies, turned instead toward people who are even more disadvantaged than they.

[When John arrived back in his segregated hometown, he applied for a job teaching at a school for Black children.]

The Judge plunged squarely into the business. "You've come for the school, I suppose. You know I'm a friend to your people. I've helped you and your family. Now I like the colored people, and sympathize with all their reasonable aspirations; but you and I both know, John, that in this country the Negro must remain subordinate, and can never expect to be the equal of white men. In their place, your people can be honest and respectful; and God knows, I'll do what I can to help them. But when they want to reverse nature, and rule white men, and marry white women, and sit in my parlor, then, by God! We'll hold them under if we have to lynch every Nigger in the land. Now, John, the question is, are you, going to accept the situation and teach the darkies to be faithful servants and laborers as your fathers were."

"I am going to accept the situation, Judge Henderson," answered John, with a brevity that did not escape the keen old man. He hesitated a moment, and then said shortly, "Very well,—we'll try you awhile. Good-morning."

[As a teacher, John instructed his students well, teaching them to read and write but also teaching them to think about their lives and the world in which they lived.]

"John, this school is closed. You children can go home and get to work. The white people of Altamaha are not spending their money on black folks to have their heads crammed with impudence and lies. Clear out! I'll lock the door myself."

The great brown sea lay silent. The air scarce breathed. The dying day bathed the twisted oaks and mighty pines in black and gold. There came from the wind no warning, not a whisper from the cloudless sky. There was only a black man hurrying on with an ache in his heart, seeing neither sun nor sea, but starting as from a dream at the frightened cry that woke the pines, to see his dark sister struggling in the arms of a tall and fair-haired man.

He said not a word, but, seizing a fallen limb, struck him with all the pent-up hatred of his great black arm; and the body lay white and still beneath the pines, all bathed in sunshine and in blood. John looked at it dreamily, then walked back to the house briskly, and said in a soft voice, "Mammy, I'm going away—I'm going to be free."

He leaned back and smiled toward the sea, whence rose the strange melody, away from the dark shadows where lay the noise of horses galloping, galloping on. With an effort he roused himself, bent forward, and looked steadily down the pathway.

Amid the trees and in the dim morning twilight he watched their shadows dancing and heard their horses thundering toward him, until at last they came sweeping like a storm, and he saw in front that haggard white-haired man, whose eyes flashed red with fury. Oh, how he pitied him,—pitied him,—and wondered if he had the coiling twisted rope. Then, as the storm burst round him, he rose slowly to his feet and turned his closed eyes toward the Sea.

And the world whistled in his ears.

From W.E.B. DuBois, *The Souls of Black Folk* (Signet Classics, 1903/1995), pp. 246–263.

CRITICAL THINKING QUESTIONS

What contrasts does DuBois draw here? What conclusions does he make about race relations in the United States?

Despite the successes of social movements, there are still barriers between racial groups. One reason is the reluctance of North Americans to acknowledge issues of class. Of course, although most members of the highest classes are white, there are wealthy African Americans, Hispanics, and Native Americans. Focusing attention on race helps hide distinctions of class that account for much of the disadvantage experienced by many members of minority groups. In addition, racial antagonisms are used to create barriers to the formation of multiracial interest groups based on class. Members of privileged groups benefit from a system that pits poor people against one other based on race, each group believing that its problems are caused by members of other racial groups rather than by members of other classes.

Although racial categorization springs from and is connected to issues of control and oppression, "race" identity can also be a means of mobilizing and countering oppression. In the words of Manning Marable:

"Race" for the oppressed has come to mean an identity of survival, victimization and opposition to those racial groups or elites which exercise power and privilege. What we are looking at here is not an ethnic identification or culture, but an awareness of shared experience, suffering and struggles against the barriers of racial division. These collective experiences, survival tales and grievances form the basis of an historical consciousness . . .

this sense of racial identity is both imposed on the oppressed and yet represents a reconstructed critical memory of the character of the group's collective ordeals. Definitions of "race" and "racial identity" give character and substance to the movements for power and influence among people of color. (1995:365)

Race in Brazil

In Brazil, there is the same mix of races as in the United States, with people whose ancestry stems from indigenous groups, Africa, and Europe. However, there is not the same rigidity of categories, and there is much greater public recognition of multiracial ancestry. Brazilians employ some 500 different labels to identify a person's race, many more than the dual division of black/white that dominates U.S. racial discourse (Harris, 1970). Not everyone knows and uses all of these labels, but in a study of a small village in northeastern Brazil, about forty different racial terms are used (Kottak, 1999). Most of these terms make fine distinctions about skin color, hair color and texture, eye color, eye shape, shape of the nose, and shape of the lips. The same person might describe himself or herself or someone else using different labels in different contexts. The terms selected are based on comparisons with other people present, for example, whether someone were lighter or darker, had lighter, darker, or redder hair, and so on. People in the village also disagree about the proper labels to use for specific individuals.

While the Brazilian system might appear to be more flexible, a hierarchy of race-based privilege exists nonetheless. Although this system is also more flexible than that in the United States, the wealthiest and most powerful elites, whether measured in economic or political terms, tend to be light-skinned and/or of European ancestry. In fact, the distribution of wealth in Brazil is even more unequal than that in the United States. The gap between rich and poor in income, education, standard of living, and social and political power is enormous (Andrews, 1992). In general, the ranks of the poor are made up largely of nonwhites.

Ethnic Identity

Like race, **ethnicity** is a social category. Its definition includes a complex mix of ancestry, culture, and self-identification. Ethnicity is largely based on a "shared cultural heritage" (Berreman, 1989). This heritage may include language, religion, family and household structure, preferences for foods and clothing, and a general perspective and worldview. In small homogeneous societies of the type that anthropologists formerly studied, all members of the group shared their basic cultural heritage. But in modern, complex societies, where people of many different backgrounds are united within the same nation, cultural differences can be significant. Ethnicity, as a social category, is a feature of such societies. In many modern nations, ethnic groups are ranked relative to one another. Some groups have higher status, and therefore greater privilege and power, than others.

Ethnicity, unlike race and caste, is not an entirely closed or ascribed status. Although ethnicity is based on ancestry, it is also based on identification with a cultural group. For example, if a person is a recent immigrant in another country, his or her ethnic identity is automatically assigned, but if that person is the child or descendant of immigrants, there may be more flexibility in his or her identity. Under most circumstances, people who are not themselves immigrants may choose to either retain or abandon the cultural traits that identify them as members of a particular ethnic group. The process of relinquishing one's cultural heritage is called assimilation. Immigrants may want to positively identify with their new country, but they may also want to distance themselves from the social stigma attached to their immigrant status. Contrasting ethnicity and race in the United States, Gerald Berreman points out that "the American 'melting pot' works for ambitious ethnic groups because they can assimilate by relinquishing their heritage; it does not work for race groups because their status is an unalterable consequence of birth that they cannot relinquish (i.e., are not allowed to relinquish), and hence they cannot assimilate (this is the very essence of racism)" (1989:16).

ethnicity
Social category based on a complex mix of ancestry, culture, and self-identification.

Case study

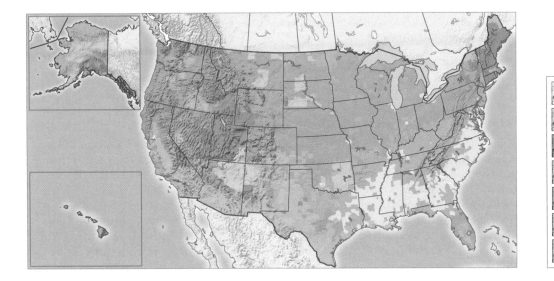

	African American
	American Indian
	English and Irish
	French
	German
	Hispanic, Mexican, Puerto Rican
	Other

Ethnic Identity in the United States

Because of their growing numbers, particularly since the middle of the twentieth century, people of Spanish origin or ancestry, variously referred to (and self-referred) as Hispanic or Latino, have received prominent attention (Fears, 2003). Some members of this group are the descendants of people who were early colonizers and settlers in North America, but the vast majority are immigrants or descendants of more recent immigrants, mainly from Central and South America rather than from Spain. However, "Hispanic" is clearly an ethnic, not racial, label inasmuch as Hispanic people may be white, black, or Native American.

The complexity of categories of race and ethnicity is reflected in recent federal census questionnaires. In the 2000 census, respondents were asked to identify their "race" using the labels listed below. Significantly, people were given the option of choosing "one or more" of these identifications: White; Black, African-American, or Negro; American Indian or Alaska Native (print name of enrolled or principal tribe); Asian Indian; Chinese; Filipino; Japanese; Korean; Vietnamese; Native Hawaiian; Guamanian or Chamorro; Samoan; Other Asian (print race); Other Pacific Islander (print race); Some Other Race (print race). In addition, people were asked to state whether they were "Spanish/Hispanic/Latino." If they responded affirmatively, they were then asked to identify their "group" from among the following: (1) Mexican, Mexican-American, Chicano; (2) Puerto Rican; (3) Cuban; (4) Other.

U.S. Census Bureau statistics, compiled in 2001, revealed the following percentage makeup of the U.S. population: white: 70 percent; Hispanic: 13 percent; African American: 12.7 percent; Asian: 4 percent; Native American: 0.9 percent. For the first time, the number of Hispanics was greater than the number of African Americans. The Hispanic population experienced the fastest growth, increasing at a rate of nearly 5 percent since the 2000 census. This growth is a result of high fertility rates and increased immigration from Central and South America. Both factors are projected to continue into the future with a continued growth in both absolute numbers and percentages.

Significantly, similar counting procedures are not used for Native Americans. In fact, the government's practice of ignoring mixed racial and ethnic identification and instead categorizing many respondents with mixed Indian ancestry as whites, African Americans, or Hispanics contributes to the undercount of native peoples. According to Jack Forbes (1990), a more accurate assessment of the number of people with Indian ancestry should include people with "Hispanic" identification, as well as the

30 to 70 percent of African Americans who various studies report to be part Indian. In the 1990 census, the official native population stood at 1.9 million, but by the year 2000, the U.S. census reported nearly 8 million people with American Indian ancestry. The large growth in the reported number can be accounted for by changes in census questionnaires and counting people who claimed either American Indian identity or American Indian ancestry.

GLOBALIZATION

Pan-Africanism refers to various movements in Africa that have sought to define African ethnic, racial, and transnational identity at the continental level. Starting in 1900, these movements had the common goal of unifying Africans against colonialism and colonial influences. The great diversity of peoples and interests prevented that unity. In 1963 the Organization of African Unity (OAU) was founded as a forum for discussing problems in Africa and achieving shared goals. The OAU was replaced in 2002 by the African Union (AU), modeled on the European Union (EU).

In some contexts, ethnic identification is irrelevant and not thought about; in other situations, ethnicity may be a key feature of one's personal identity. In multiethnic nations undergoing rapid social change, identifying with and asserting one's ethnicity may be an important means of group formation. In Africa, for example, the search for identity has complex meanings attached to different ethnic symbols, depending on the contexts and frames of reference used. According to Victor Uchendu (1995), the search for an African identity takes place on four contrasting planes: continental, racial, national, and tribal. A continental-wide identity as "African" contrasts Africa with other continents. As Uchendu observed, "Continental identity became an instrument for decolonization and a weapon for post independence international diplomacy" (p. 129). Racial identity contrasts black Africans with other groups living on the continent, that is, Arabs and whites. National identity refers to the quest for the formation of a cohesive identity within a given country. This goal is often problematic in Africa because of the artificial national boundaries created by colonial European powers for their own interests. And finally, the search for tribal identity takes place within the newly independent and emerging multiethnic African nations.

Until the 1960s and 1970s, when African nations won their independence from their European colonizers, African peoples did not identify as "African" even though Europeans identified them as such. Self-identifications were tribal and ethnic. Today, people choose from among numerous possibilities for self-identification based on circumstances. For example, "Nigerian students in London or New York are more likely to identify themselves as African than as Nigerian unless the situation clearly indicates that identification of country is expected or required. To another Nigerian, they are most likely to identify themselves with state or region; if they are speaking to a co-ethnic, they are likely to name the provincial or administrative headquarters to which they belong. Thus, identity is likely to change as the frame of reference changes" (Uchendu, 1995:131).

Ethnic allegiance also has different meanings in rural and urban settings. According to Uchendu, tribal identity is paramount in rural Africa because "the tie to the tribal, communal, or lineage land, often phrased in the idiom of filial loyalty to ancestors, is still an important social and economic asset" (p. 129). Although such ties are not significant in urban areas, ethnic loyalty may be advantageous in the context of "the competition for jobs, the uneven distribution of government patronage, and the insecurity of urban employment" (p. 129). Through ethnic identification, a person can claim membership in a cohesive community that provides economic, social, and emotional support.

In many countries, the inherent stratification of ethnic groups in relation to each other can come to crisis in times of economic and political stress. In these situations, ethnic groups can be pitted against one another in struggles for prestige and power. Loyalty to one's ethnic group then becomes a paramount factor in taking sides, only exacerbating underlying tensions and furthering the processes of ethnic identification and conflict.

Just such a crisis developed in the 1980s and 1990s in the former Yugoslavia. Although the causes of the breakup of Yugoslavia need much more study and reflection, political leaders on all sides used long-standing ethnic animosities to gain support in their own identifiable ethnic enclaves. According to Mary Kay Galliland (1995), most of the people residing in a "midsize town" in eastern Croatia on the border with Bosnia were "relatively unconcerned about ethno-national identity" during the 1980s (p. 201), thinking of themselves primarily as citizens of the unified country of Yugoslavia. Their primary concerns were economic: food shortages, inflation, lack of jobs and housing. After the death of the longtime Yugoslav president, Josip Broz (known as Tito), in 1982, the government instituted an austerity program aimed at limiting imports and increasing exports in order to gain hard currency needed to repay Yugoslavia's large debts to Western nations. The government also rationed domestic products, such as gasoline, coffee, and laundry detergent (p. 206). The basic Yugoslav currency, the dinar, was devalued, resulting in a precipitous decline in real wages as prices soared. Shortages of many foods and domestic products also became widespread. All of these conditions contributed to feelings of uncertainty and instability.

Each group saw itself as victims of economic and political policies promulgated by other groups. According to Galliland, "Serbs [a minority in Croatia] blamed Croats for their own lack of economic development; the Western portion of the former Yugoslavia, they said, had gained at Serbian expense. Croats turned the argument around; they had been supporting the less-developed regions with the products of their own hard work. Worse, they had also been paying for a growing military and corrupt [federal Yugoslav] government bureaucracy heavily dominated by Serbs" (p. 203).

As tensions mounted and incidents of interethnic violence occurred, nationalist politicians and the media contributed to the "production of fear" that characterized much of Yugoslav discourse. Although the causes of the violence are complex, ethnic nationalism clearly played a role in solidifying group identity and creating rigid boundaries among the various ethnic groups. By culturally constructing groups in opposition to each other, people came to see themselves and their group as distinct from all others. In addition, people began to speak more openly about the past, redefining the past as they talked about it. No longer did they remember Yugoslavian unity but instead recalled incidents that provided reasons for distrust and animosity. Although throughout much of the postwar period these memories were not considered important, they were lying beneath the surface, "waiting to be called into action, if the times were right, if someone wanted to make use of them, and if the means of communication were available" (p. 216). Nationalist Serbian and Croatian political leaders tapped into this reservoir of memory, exploiting it in order to mobilize followers and gain power. But by intensifying people's fears, political leaders unleashed a wave of hatred and violence that ended by destroying a nation and creating new reasons for people to distrust one another.

> **REVIEW**
>
> Although people exhibit biological differences, race is a social and not a biological classification. Race and ethnic identity are culturally constructed and are stratified differently in different societies. Racial or ethnic minorities, such as the Burakumin in Japan and native Indians in Brazil, may be viewed negatively and experience discrimination. Ethnicity is based on identification with a cultural or ethnic group.

CLASS, RACE, ETHNICITY, AND IDEOLOGY IN AMERICAN SOCIETY

As in other stratified societies, the system of inequality in the United States that grants privilege to members of some groups and denies opportunities to others is supported by ideological beliefs that members of high-status groups, whether based on class, race, or ethnicity, deserve their advantages. In contrast, it is believed that members of low-status groups are responsible for their plight because of their lack of motivation and initiative. But some hope of achievement and advance is held out to less privileged people in order to diminish their anger and resistance. Many people are nurtured by the "American Dream," convinced that if they work hard enough and are sensible and practical, they can achieve a better standard of living for themselves and their children.

The dream of the rewards of hard work, elusive though it may be for most people, is based on the fact that class, at least theoretically, is a social ordering that allows for mobility. It is the hope of upward class mobility that helps alleviate the burdens of class disadvantage and blunts potential anger on the part of the lower classes who might otherwise challenge the legitimacy of the system. And issues of class and class interests are masked behind an ideology of equality. Even to talk about class may be considered disruptive and antagonistic, especially in political campaigns and media rhetoric.

However, it is clear that members of the upper classes act in their class interests. They may not talk about their identity as a class, at least not publicly, because to do so would violate the ideology of classlessness that makes up the American Dream. However, their actions in formulating economic and political policies do indicate their awareness of class solidarity. And even the trend toward living in gated communities translates class segregation into architecture. In contrast, members of the middle and lower classes generally do not understand their social position as part of the structure of a hierarchical social order. Those that do, perceive it as temporary, amenable to change if they persist.

There are, in addition, other difficulties in uniting as a class. Among these are antagonisms that develop between members of groups defined in ways other than by class, such as race, ethnicity, and gender. These three factors are employed as part of the hierarchical structure to divide members of nonelite classes in order to keep them from recognizing and acting on their common interests.

Talking about race also is perceived as divisive. Much of the popular discourse on race focuses on the partial successes of the civil rights movement of the 1950s and 1960s that led to passage of legislation mandating equal treatment and recognition of the civil rights of all Americans. One can point to vigorous programs to end segregation in schools, to bar the most overt forms of racial discrimination, and to redress underrepresentation of nonwhites in many occupations through affirmative action policies. Nonetheless, these programs and policies have not created full racial equality. Members of nonwhite groups remain disadvantaged in terms of income, employment, quality of education and health care services, and political representation. But race was supposed to be eliminated in the vocabulary of a "color-blind" society, proven so by the fact that some African Americans could achieve wealth and status (Baker, 1998).

Despite the hope of upward class mobility, most people do not experience improvements in their class standing. Indeed, there are the opposite experiences of some members of the middle and upper classes who experience downward mobility. As the work of Katherine Newman (1989) has documented, since the 1980s in the United States, a large but largely unpublicized number of Americans have been catapulted from comfortable and rewarding lifestyles after they lost their jobs. Newman found that people "fall from grace" for a variety of reasons. Some lose jobs as well-paid executives or managers in large corporations when the firms "downsize." Others lose jobs in factories when the plants move to "more profitable and business-friendly" regions of the United States or to foreign countries in a trend toward outsourcing that is becoming increasingly frequent, with dire economic consequences for many North American workers. And still others are fired when they participate in strikes. When plants close down or workers in small communities go out on strike, the economic effects can be disastrous to more than just the people immediately involved. Whole communities may suffer when residents no longer have money to spend in stores, restaurants, and local entertainment.

The extent of downward mobility is much greater than most Americans realize. The true picture certainly does not square with the mythology of the American Dream that many people adhere to. And it doesn't square with media coverage of the U.S. economy. Newman uses several indices to measure downward mobility. A person who experiences a decline in income or is employed in a job having less prestige or status than his or her previous job can be a victim of downward mobility. In a national survey taken every year by the National Opinion Research Center, approximately 25 percent of respondents claimed in the 1980s that their financial situation had worsened during the year they were questioned (Newman, 1989:21). Federal

? *To what extent and in what ways are you upwardly mobile? In what circumstances could you become downwardly mobile, and what are your chances of this?*

statistics indicate that individual real income (adjusted for inflation) declined 14 percent between 1972 and 1982. The rate of decline accelerated so that between 1978 and 1982, 56 percent of the population was falling behind inflation, a clear indicator that their standard of living declined. Economic decline affects families in all socioeconomic groups. And many families experiencing downward mobility are not just "sliding" but are actually "plunging." In the 1970s, studies indicated that nearly one-third of the American population experienced a drop in family income of 50 percent or more (p. 23).

Job loss affects all economic sectors but is most severe in manufacturing and heavy industry. Plant closings often occur in order to save money by relocating to areas of the country that are less heavily unionized (especially the South) or to foreign countries where wages are lower and job protection is nearly absent. The plight of displaced industrial workers is compounded by general economic trends resulting in the decline of manufacturing in the United States. In addition, managers and professional, technical, and administrative workers have also been displaced in high numbers. Women have a harder time finding new jobs than do men. And African Americans and Hispanics have longer periods of unemployment than do whites. Using government statistics, Newman concluded that job displacement in the 1980s caused nearly 6 million people to become downwardly mobile (p. 27).

Finally, divorce has a deleterious effect on women's income and often is the catalyst that propels them into a downward economic spiral. Divorced women with children, particularly when they have little or no continued financial support from their husbands, usually experience downward mobility. Many divorced women who were not working at the time of their divorce have great difficulty finding employment. But even those who work do not earn as much money as their husbands and therefore cannot support themselves and their children at their previous standard of living.

People who experience downward mobility suffer socially and psychologically in addition to their economic losses. They may have to give up spacious houses and a comfortable lifestyle. They may lose their friends because they can no longer afford to socialize in the ways they had in the past. Economic problems may put strains on marriages, resulting in separation and divorce. And people feel ashamed because of what they perceive to be their lack of success. They feel that they have not lived up to their own and others' expectations.

Although people who experience downward mobility are actually disadvantaged by a hierarchical social system, there are many ways that social ideologies about the American Dream blunt people's awareness of class as a major determinant of their lives and their opportunities. Rather than becoming angry at a system that not only tolerates inequality but is in fact built on necessary inequality, they feel disappointed and ashamed. Rather than understanding their predicament as part of the integral structure of capitalist economies, they make a judgment about their personal deficiencies.

> **REVIEW**
>
> Social, political, economic, educational, and religious ideologies serve to justify and maintain a society's system of social stratification. Thus, people learn to believe that social inequalities are normal or necessary. Furthermore, ideologies have great power over people's sentiments and behaviors, such that people readily believe in things that are not true and act on those beliefs.

 Chapter Summary

Equality, Inequality, and Social Stratification

- Societies differ in respect to people's access to resources, livelihood, respect, and prestige. In egalitarian societies, all individuals have equal access to whatever resources are available and have equal likelihood to achieve positions of respect and prestige in their cultures. Although people's different skills and talents are rewarded, no one is denied opportunities and the possibilities of achievement. Small foraging societies and some horticultural societies are likely to be egalitarian in their basic social and ethical principles.

- In social systems based on rank, individuals and kinship groups occupy different positions in the social hierarchy. Each position is ranked in relation to all others. Occupying a high rank gives people economic, social, and political advantages. In some ranked systems, high-ranking individuals are freed from subsistence activities. They are supported by the productive work of others through claims that they may make through kinship ties and through the inherent rights of high rank. High-ranking individuals benefit socially by being awarded prestige and by the inherent influence that follows from high rank. And, finally, people of high rank wield political influence through their roles in decision making as leaders of kinship groups and in some cases of territorial units. However, despite the significant privileges of rank, no one is denied a basically decent standard of living, sufficient food, clothing, and housing. In fact, although high-ranking people have rights not granted to others, they also have the responsibility of distributing goods to members of their kin groups. Indeed, generosity is one of the necessary personal attributes of high-ranking people.

- In stratified societies, people are differentiated on the basis of certain attributes that they have at birth. These differences allow some people to have greater access to resources, wealth, and positions of prestige, influence, and power than other people. The granting of privileges and opportunities to some people effectively denies them to others. Many traditional agrarian societies and all modern industrial states are highly stratified. Unlike systems of rank, in stratified societies some people may go hungry, may be poorly clothed, and live in substandard housing. The gap in the standard of living between rich and poor may be quite wide.

Caste and Class

- A caste is a closed social group whose membership is hereditary. That is, a person is born into a particular caste and remains so for life. Caste membership, then, is an ascribed status. The various castes are ordered hierarchically in relation to one another from highest to lowest. Just as one caste identity is unchangeable, the hierarchical order of castes is also fixed. Mobility is not possible. Members of higher castes have rights and privileges denied to members of lower castes. They have better standards of living, greater opportunities for achievement, and are more likely to occupy positions of influence and power in their society. In India, for example, caste membership not only dictates social group but also regulates marriage, occupation, and area of residence. People must marry members of their own caste. Each caste is associated with a specific set of occupations. And in traditional villages, castes have their own assigned neighborhoods.

- Some stratified systems are organized into classes rather than castes. Class systems are, at least theoretically, based on achieved factors including education, occupation, and income. However, in practice, access to better education and with it to occupations and income is more readily available to people whose parents have greater wealth and are in higher classes. In addition, although mobility is, at least in theory, a characteristic of class systems, most people do not change their class membership but remain more or less constant in their position within society. In fact, downward mobility is as likely as upward mobility.

Race and Ethnicity

- Race is a social construct, focusing on a particular set of external physical traits but having no biological basis as separate, discrete categories. Physical traits that are used to demarcate the races, including skin color, hair color and texture, and facial features, appear in human populations on a continuum, not as consistent markers of groups. But race, once identified on the basis of physical characteristics, becomes projected onto social and personal behavior. The races then are ranked hierarchically in relation to each other. Obviously, the group that controls the social, economic, political, and ideological structures of society thinks of itself as superior and projects negative qualities on to other groups thought of as inferior.

- Ethnicity is a feature of cultural identification. Cultural traits that often are used to define group membership include language, territorial residence, food habits, items of dress, and body ornamentation. In some ways, ethnicity is an ascribed status in that people are born into a cultural group. In other ways, ethnicity is an achieved status because people can choose either to identify with their ethnic group of origin by maintaining the cultural traits associated with it or they can give up identifying cultural behaviors and become assimilated into the mainstream society, however that is defined.

Class, Race, Ethnicity, and Ideology in American Society

- In the United States, an ideology coalescing around the American Dream obscures the actual facts of the structure of class and of class privilege. While elites who control policies promulgated by government agencies obviously act in the interests of their class, barriers are created that hinder the formation of class consciousness among disadvantaged groups. People who are poor, uneducated, and unskilled are blamed, and blame themselves, for their disadvantages instead of recognizing their imposed structural position in a hierarchical system. People may also feel that their low position in the socioeconomic system is temporary, amenable to change if they dedicate themselves and try harder to achieve. Other barriers that divide people include racial, ethnic, and gender differences.

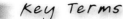

Key Terms

wealth 286
power 286
prestige 287
achieved status 287

ascribed status 287
ranked societies 287
egalitarian societies 287
stratified societies 288

social
  stratification 290
elites 290
mobility 294

slavery 295
race 297
ethnicity 302

Review Questions

1. What core concepts are used in the analysis of systems of social stratification?

2. What are some ethnographic examples of egalitarian, ranked, and stratified societies? How are these forms of social stratification different?

3. What are three basic theoretical explanations for the existence of systems of social stratification?

4. What are the differences between caste and class? What role does social mobility play in caste and class societies?

5. How can ideologies be used to socialize conformity to the social order, to reinforce the system of social stratification, and to challenge the system?

6. How does language reveal class membership? What are some other indicators of social class?

7. How are race and ethnicity social constructs? In what contexts can race and ethnicity be seen as a form of caste?

Political Systems

Wolf Face

CHAPTER 12

Preview

1. **What do political anthropologists study, and why?**

2. **What are the five main types of political organization in human societies? How are they different?**

3. **What forces cause political systems to change, and how do those forces operate?**

4. **What are the origins and characteristics of political entities known as states?**

Long ago, a girl named Short Woman lived with her parents and her brother on the plains at a distance from a large *Cheyenne camp. One day the father, named Bull Looks Back, killed his wife and deserted his two young children. The children wandered about for a time trying to find the main camp to seek shelter and food. Finally, they came upon the camp and entered a lodge. There they were told that they were the children of Bull Looks Back, who was then also in the camp. When the father heard that his children had arrived, he said aloud: "Those monstrous children of mine killed their own mother and ate her flesh. That is why I left them. They should be staked to the ground and abandoned."*

And so the people did as he said. The girl and boy were bound by leather ropes and left to die on the plains. But a dog approached at nightfall and chewed on the straps binding the girl. When she got free, she untied her brother and both ran swiftly away. They were met by a stranger who told them that the girl had a power to kill buffalo by looking at them. At first she did not believe the stranger's words, but when a large herd of buffalo appeared, she looked up and they all fell dead.

After she butchered the animals, the girl told a crow to carry some meat to the Cheyenne camp where she and her brother had been abandoned. She said to the crow: "Tell those people the meat is from the children they left on the plains to die." The people then understood that the children were alive and that the girl had special powers.

Then the girl sent for the people to come to her. She told them, "We are going to make chiefs. You know I have been accused of killing my mother. That is not true. Now, we shall make chiefs, and hereafter we shall have a rule that if anyone kills a fellow tribesmember they shall be ordered away from one to five years, whatever the people shall decide."

The girl chose the first chiefs. She told them, "You will swear that you will be honest and care for all the tribe."

The girl told the chiefs how they should act and gave them a pipe of peace to smoke. She taught them songs and prayers to guide and protect them. Then she said, "My brother and I will leave this earth. We may go up into the heavens. Yet I shall always be working for the people. I may be a star."

From *The Cheyennes: Indians of the Great Plains* by E. Adamson Hoebel, pp. 45–49. Copyright © 1978. Reprinted with permission of Wadsworth, a division of Thomson Learning: www.thomsonrights.com. Fax (800) 730-2215.

In this narrative, the Cheyenne of the American plains tell the story of the founding of their system of governance. It tells of the creation of the Council of Forty-four, a council that united the ten Cheyenne bands into a system of tribal government. The council had forty-four members chosen from the ten constituent bands (Hoebel, 1978). Members served ten-year terms. They met only during the summer, when the nation as a whole gathered for communal buffalo hunts. Council members were responsible for settling internal disputes and organizing and overseeing communal hunting. As the narrative relates, the members of the council were selected because they were men of sound judgment and good moral character. The story also relates that wrongdoers were punished by banishment from their communities, a punishment that might have severe consequences because other bands would be reluctant to take in strangers or people who were suspected of antisocial behavior. Systems of leadership and decision making are mechanisms that help unify and integrate community members into a relatively cohesive society.

POLITICAL ANTHROPOLOGY

In every society, indeed, in every social group, actions need to be planned, decisions need to be made, and procedures for organizing group activities need to be drawn up. Societies differ in the ways in which people organize their interactions and integrate themselves into a cohesive community. And in every society, in every social group, different people have different roles to play. Some people have more influence than others when group decisions have to be made and assume leadership responsibilities when actions have to be undertaken. These features of society are the components of each group's **political organization.** Political systems, then, include procedures for making decisions, organizing group actions, choosing leaders, and settling disputes both within the group and with other groups. All societies have some form of political organization, but not all have formal governments familiar to people living in modern states.

Political anthropology is the branch of anthropology that studies these cultural dynamics. Political anthropologists focus on the mechanisms people use to solve the basic problems that confront them as a group. Although every person has individual interests and needs, social groups are formed on principles of cohesion, of sharing, and of reciprocity. People know that no matter what their individual inclinations, they need to adjust their actions in ways that enable their group to survive and thrive. Political anthropologists are concerned with understanding these mechanisms and with analyzing how they develop and are implemented. They are interested in understanding differences in the degree of influence, authority, or power that leaders may wield in different types of society. Of course, not everyone in any community agrees with group goals or conforms to group wishes. So political anthropologists also study the ways that community decisions are reached and conflicts are resolved. In this chapter, we examine questions of community organization and leadership, and in the next, Chapter 13, we will be concerned with conflict and conflict resolution.

political organization
The ways in which societies are organized to plan group activities, make decisions affecting members of the group, select leadership, and settle disputes both within the group and with other groups.

political anthropology
The study of the ways that communities plan group actions, make decisions affecting the group, select leadership, and resolve conflicts and disputes both within the group and with other groups.

> **REVIEW**
>
> Political anthropology is the branch of anthropology that studies political organization—the roles and processes that societies have for making decisions, mobilizing action, choosing leaders, settling disputes, and enforcing social norms.

TYPES OF POLITICAL ORGANIZATION

It has become commonplace to describe political systems in a four-part typology of band, tribe, chiefdom, and state. This typology, introduced by Elman Service (1962), is based on distinguishing different kinds of sociopolitical organization in terms of types of leadership, societal integration and cohesion, decision-making mechanisms, and degree of control over people. Although the typology might seem to make too sharp distinctions among societies, it is a useful tool in discussing cultural differences. It is important to remember, though, that few societies are ideal "types," but, rather, there are features within them that overlap from one set in the typology to

On June 28, 2004, U.S. Administrator Paul Bremer (left) ceremoniously transferred state sovereignty to Iraq's interim President Ghazi al-Yawar (right), as Bremer's deputy David Richmond applauded. Political anthropologists recognize that the transfer of power in Iraq was delayed by violence and foreign occupation.

Anthropology Applied

Anthropologists and the NGOs

NGOs—nongovernmental organizations—include charities, research institutes, churches, professional associations, and advocacy or lobby groups. These private organizations may be international, national, or community-based. They often work with governments and with international umbrella organizations such as the United Nations. NGOs may be involved in defending a particular cause, such as land rights or refugee resettlement, or in designing and implementing large-scale economic development programs. Most NGOs serve people in disadvantaged or developing countries, based on values of social justice (http://docs.lib.duke.edu/igo/guides/ngo/).

Oxfam, CARE, and Save the Children are examples of international public charities. Private-sector NGOs include, for example, the Mennonite Central Committee and World Vision, a Christian relief organization. An example of a professional organization operating as an international NGO is Partners in Health (PIH), a Boston-based public charity that serves people in poor countries. PIH medical teams, working with anthropol-ogists and local community leaders, treat people with HIV in Haiti and people with multidrug-resistant tuberculosis in Peru (Castro, 2004).

NGOs employ anthropologists to help them fulfill their missions as nonprofit organizations. Because of the focus on development and social justice for disadvantaged groups in poor countries, anthropologists play key roles in NGOs. They may conduct research, advise organizations, protect the interests of aid recipients and their communities, and serve as liaisons or mediators (Hursey, 2001). Because of their training, anthropologists know to question the cultural assumptions and power structures that restrict people's access to health care, education, housing, and so on. They also have the background to understand how NGOs, as transnational carriers of culture, act as instruments of globalization.

CRITICAL THINKING QUESTIONS

In what ways might recipients of NGO aid sometimes find "strings attached"? How should negative impacts of globalization be balanced with the needs for help that NGOs meet?

---

another. It is best to think of the types as constellations of varying features rather than as absolute cases. It is important not to overgeneralize. The different sociopolitical types of societies tend to co-occur with particular kinds of subsistence activities, economic modes, settlement patterns, and kinship systems.

Bands

Bands are generally small, loosely organized groups of people. Their leaders are selected on the basis of personal qualities and skills. They lead by example and influence but lack authority to enforce their opinions on the community. Decision making is relatively informal and open to the participation of all competent members. Until a few centuries ago, band societies could be found in many parts of the world, but by the middle of the twentieth century, the remaining band societies were located only in marginal areas of the world, such as the Arctic, the desert regions of Africa and Australia, and the dense forests of South America (see Table 12.1). Bands generally have (and had) relatively small populations. The smallest groups have perhaps only twenty-five to fifty people, while larger bands might have as many as several hundred members. Individual settlements were generally dispersed throughout a wide territory; consequently, population densities were low.

Most bands relied on foraging as their primary, if not exclusive, subsistence strategy. Consistent with foraging, bands were nomadic, utilizing various resource sites within a familiar territory. Today, some bands are seminomadic, moving their settlements between several relatively fixed locations on a yearly basis. Bands are often no more than territorial units, occupying common territory that may be well defined or that may be only vaguely delineated in relation to other comparable groups.

Bands are held together by informal means. Families or households are the significant units of the band. Membership within one band rather than another is generally based on kinship ties, through either descent or marriage, to other people in the

bands
Small, loosely organized groups of people held together by informal means.

Table 12.1 EXAMPLES OF BAND SOCIETIES

Americas	Europe	Africa	Asia	Pacific
Netsilik of Arctic Circle	Lapp (Saami) of northern Scandinavia	Mbuti (Pygmies) of Congo Basin	Ainu of Japan	Tiwi of Australia
Inuit of eastern Canada			Chenchu of India	
Apache (historical) of western United States		Ju'/hoansi of Botswana	Semang (Negritos) of Malaysia	
Mi'kmaq of Nova Scotia			Vedda of Sri Lanka	
Ojibwe of Great Lakes region, United States and Canada				
Yahgun of Tierra del Fuego				

group. Choice of band membership may also be based on loyalty to and approval of the band's leader. But band leadership is also informal. It is based on the personal abilities of the leader, including intelligence, subsistence skills, charismatic personality traits, and in some cases spiritual knowledge. The leader contributes as much, and in some cases more, to the band's subsistence than anyone else. He (or she, although most leaders of bands are men) lives no differently than other members of the band and receives no financial economic rewards.

The reward of leadership is prestige. But leadership also carries with it greater responsibilities because the leader is thought to be responsible for the well-being of the group. While the band's success increases the prestige of its leader, the band's failure is similarly attributed to the leader's weakness or faults. A leader who proves unsuccessful risks losing his position. The band members will simply choose another among themselves to be the leader or will leave the settlement and relocate to another group. Band leaders, therefore, have only influence, not power. That is, they can use their oratorical skills to persuade people to remain with them and to follow their advice, but they have no means of enforcing their decisions. In fact, in many band societies, leaders who even attempt to control the actions of others would immediately disqualify themselves as leaders. Authority roles tend to be limited to the family, and even in that context, the authority of parents over children or of one spouse over the other is generally weak.

Other features of band societies are not necessarily components of a sociopolitical system but derive from the kind of subsistence and production generally found in bands. So, for example, the small size of settlements follows from the principle of carrying capacity—that is, the number of people that can be supported by the land and its resources (see Chapter 6). In addition, notions of private property are generally weak or absent. Land is never individually owned but is understood to be the common domain of band members. In some bands, specific resources or resource sites may be controlled by kinship groups but never by individuals. And people in band societies do not accumulate significant surpluses of resources or personal possessions. These concepts about land and property derive from a foraging economic system and a nomadic or seminomadic settlement pattern. Band societies, and foraging societies generally, are usually egalitarian in their social system. Their egalitarian ethics are reflected in people's equal access to resources, equal potential access to prestige, and generally equal gender relations.

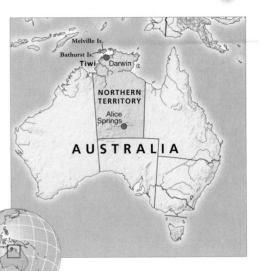

Case study

Two Band Societies: The Tiwi of Northern Australia and the Mi'kmaqs of Nova Scotia

The Tiwi of northern Australia and the Mi'kmaqs of Nova Scotia, Canada, were aboriginal band societies. They shared some similarities of economic, social, and political organization but also differed in important respects as well. Present-day Tiwi are indigenous foragers living on Bathurst and Melville islands, off the northern mainland of Australia. Both islands have inland rivers, marshlands, and extensive ocean coastlines. And both islands have dense forests and abundant natural resources. Until recently, the people obtained their food by hunting, fishing, and gathering wild plants. Most of the Tiwi annual diet was derived from the vegetable foods that the women gathered. Men in their prime did most of the hunting and fishing.

Tiwi camps consisted of a number of related families or perhaps just one large family. If the camp contained more than one family unit, the groups were usually related through men. During the rainy season, November through April, people needed protection against the heavy rains. They built small dwellings made of wooden poles covered with bark. In the dry season, May through October, only protection from the sun was needed. Dwellings then were made with leaf-covered branches tied together to give shade.

Households were the basic functioning units of society. Members of households cooperated and coordinated their activities to hunt and gather food for their group. Households and camps were linked informally into larger units or bands. These bands typically had about 100 members, although people did not necessarily identify with the same band from year to year. They might even change their band allegiance within the year, and households within a band might disperse to exploit seasonal resources.

Band membership and residence overlapped. Every adult owned land, usually in the place where they were born and lived. But land was not divided into individual parcels. Rather, a particular area, now referred to as a "country," was owned collectively (Goodale, 1971). All of the owners of a particular country were communally responsible for its well-being, including its physical and spiritual protection. Women and men inherited landholding rights from their fathers. A person could hold land through his or her father in several countries if the father had lived and was buried in a place other than his own land. Since 1976, when the Tiwi were officially recognized as the legal owners of their land, the Tiwi Land Council regulates and registers the owners of countries and holds them responsible for protecting the land.

The Tiwi kinship system is based on membership in matrilineal clans. All clans are linked into four larger units, or phratries, that are exogamous—that is, a person cannot marry someone belonging to a clan in one's own phratry. Clans and kinship groups generally have informal leaders. These people, usually men, have influence in their families and communities because of their intelligence, skills, and sound judgment. Although in theory every man can aspire to high status, men with large families have advantages because of the loyalty and support of their kin.

Men enlarged their families, and, therefore, their influence, by marrying more than one wife. Prestige and leadership were thus intertwined with marriage customs. In traditional Tiwi society, all females had to be married from birth to death. Girls were betrothed immediately upon their birth, sometimes even before birth. Fathers arranged their daughters' marriages to men with whom the father wished to form an alliance. The men were usually in their 20s or 30s and had shown promise by their hunting skills and personality. The actual marriage ceremony did not take place until the girl reached puberty, but the future son-in-law helped his future inlaws by supplying them with meat, rendering other aid, and acknowledging his father-in-law's influence. And fathers were guaranteed support in their old age. Thus, fathers used their daughters strategically to gain economic support and social prestige.

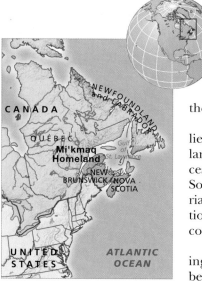

As often happened, given the age difference between a young wife and her first husband, women were usually widowed one or more times during their lives. Immediate remarriage was expected. Often, a middle-aged or even elderly widow would marry a much younger man who had not been able to contract a favorable marriage. An older woman benefited a younger man because she had extensive kinship relations who could help advance her young husband. Eventually, he could marry other women and form alliances with their fathers.

Tiwi women also could aspire to positions of influence and prestige in their families and communities. A woman gained in prestige as she aged and accumulated a large family through her own children and grandchildren. Her experience as a successful householder and matron of a large family earned her support and authority. So men's and women's leadership was intertwined in this system of kinship and marriage. No one wielded absolute control over anyone else, however, and no one's position of authority was automatic. Rather, leadership and influence were available to all community members and could be manipulated by the most skilled and intelligent.

Like the Tiwi, the Mi'kmaqs had an economy based on foraging. Meat from hunting and fishing supplied the major portion of the aboriginal diet. Men hunted deer, beaver, muskrat, otter, moose, bear, and elk. Sea mammals and many kinds of fish were caught in the Atlantic Ocean and in the numerous rivers and lakes in Mi'kmaq territory. To supplement the diet, women gathered wild roots, nuts, and berries.

Migration and settlement patterns were based on resource availability. The people followed an annual cycle of moving to where animals and fish were seasonally abundant. Most of the year, their livelihood was varied and relatively secure, with only occasional times of scarcity. The size of settlements was adjusted to best exploit the resources, in keeping with the principle of carrying capacity. There were ecological constraints on population size. From the beginning of the fall hunting season until the start of spring fishing, people lived in small camps composed of several nuclear families, generally linked through men on the basis of kinship or friendship. In the spring, large groups, numbering 200 or more, formed in villages along coasts or on the banks of rivers where fish and waterfowl were caught. Each group or band had its accustomed site along the coast or river where they camped. Residents of such settlements were usually related through bilateral kinship ties, by marriage, or by friendship. Band composition varied from year to year, so that membership in any given group changed over time.

Community cohesion and leadership were diffuse, but each band had a leader or **sagamore,** a man with some control over a small territory. Band leadership tended to be inherited from father to son. Mi'kmaq sagamores had a role in economic redistribution. They were able to accumulate extra provisions through the labor of unmarried young men, who gave their leaders all the products of their hunts. After marriage, men gave the sagamores only a portion of their catch. When new members joined the band, they gave the sagamore gifts as well. Sagamores used these extra provisions to make distributions to all members of the band at public feasts and religious ceremonies. Leaders, therefore, functioned as the centers of redistributive networks and were rewarded with greater prestige through their generosity.

Sagamores had some control over territories that their groups inhabited or used as hunting regions. Mi'kmaq territory was divided into seven named districts, each inhabited by bands. Therefore, a band was more a territorial than a social unit. It was composed at any one time of people who hunted in a given district and camped together in the spring and summer. Some districts were the habitual territory of only one band while others contained members of several bands. Composition of the bands was unstable as people shifted membership, depending on availability of resources, marriage alliances, and personal choices. A number of the bands were represented by symbols, such as a salmon or a cross-like design, which were carved into canoes or painted on clothing as a mark of identification.

One of the responsibilities of sagamores was to apportion territories to each band for its use during the current hunting season (Prins, 1990). According to a French Jesuit missionary who visited the Mi'kmaqs in the seventeenth century, "The occupation of this chief was to assign the places for hunting and to take the furs of the Indians,

sagamore
A leader of a Mi'kmaq band who had some degree of control over a small territory and had some role in economic redistribution.

giving them in return whatever they needed. It is the right of the head of the nation to distribute the places of hunting to each individual. It is not permitted to any Indian to overstep the bounds and limits of the region which shall have been assigned to him in the assemblies of the elders. These are held in autumn and spring expressly to make this assignment" (LeClercq, 1968:235, 237).

In the summer, sagamores from several bands met to settle disputes and to discuss issues of common interest, such as relations with other nations, trade, and war. They concluded treaties with other groups. In addition to summer meetings, councils were held whenever the appropriate situation arose. Sagamores who met at councils were all on an equal footing. In their discussions, each was free to say what he wanted and could expect others to listen. Decisions were consensual. Sagamores did not have coercive power, however. As LeClercq remarked, "All his power and authority are based only on the good wail [will] of those of his nation just insofar as it pleases them" (LeClercq, 1968:234). People could, and did, shift location and loyalty when it suited them to do so.

These two examples, the Tiwi and the Mi'kmaqs, illustrate some of the possibilities in band leadership organization. In both societies, leaders are selected informally on the basis of intelligence, skills, and personality, but no one is forced to comply with their decisions. Membership in bands may fluctuate seasonally or yearly, depending on available resources and the popularity of leaders. People may leave a band and join another if they are dissatisfied with its leadership. A leader who ends up with no followers is no longer a leader. The influence of a leader is personal and persuasive, not coercive.

Comparatively, there is less violence in band societies. Because of the informal links between band members and the instability of group composition, people can react to disputes by leaving the band and joining another. Tensions that might otherwise erupt in violence can be relieved by the departure of a party to a dispute. Violence between bands in neighboring territories is also infrequent because there is little to fight over. Land and resources are not owned and surpluses are not amassed, so conflicts over property have no basis. And because bands are widely dispersed within a large territory, even personal conflicts with neighbors are unlikely to arise.

Tribes

Tribes differ from bands in the degree of structure and organization contributing to group cohesion and community integration. Tribal societies may have more formalized organizational procedures than those found in bands. For example, they may have highly structured councils with greater authority whose members meet and deliberate regularly. The Cheyenne narrative that opens this chapter describes such a council. In addition to their roles as influential advisory bodies, councils may have some coercive powers in some contexts. Tribal chiefs with enforcement powers may be selected in more formal ways than the casual and informal recognition of band leaders. However, the powers of tribal chiefs and councils are limited by the underlying egalitarian social ethics prevalent in most tribal societies. And often there are structured ways to ignore or depose leaders who try to exert too much authority.

tribes
Societies with some degree of formalization of structure and leadership, including village and intervillage councils whose members regularly meet to settle disputes and plan community activities.

By 1900, Mi'kmaq families in Nova Scotia like this one had largely transformed many traditional practices.

Table 12.2 EXAMPLES OF TRIBAL SOCIETIES

Americas	Europe	Africa	Asia	Pacific
Penare of Venezuela	Scottish clans (historical)	Berbers of the western Sahara	Bani Khalid of Saudi Arabia	Dani of New Guinea
Kayapo and Yanomamo of Brazil	Druids of France (historical)	Kababish of northern Sudan	Munda of India	Marquesans (Tahiti island group)
Blackfeet of Montana	Celts of eastern Europe (historical)	Samburu and Maasai of Kenya	Hmong of Southeast Asia	
Hidatsa of North Dakota		Amhara of Ethiopia	Miao of China	
Cheyenne of the Great Plains		Ibo of Nigeria		
Passamaquoddy of Maine				

Like leveling mechanisms that prevent overcentralization of wealth, structured ways to ignore or depose leaders are leveling mechanisms that prevent overcentralization of power. Examples of tribes are given in Table 12.2.

A number of cultural correlates tend to be associated with tribes, although subsistence patterns vary considerably. Some tribes have economies based on foraging, some on pastoralism, and still others on horticulture. Many tribal societies have mixed economies, combining resources derived from foraging, farming, and animal herding.

Settlement patterns and sizes vary as well. Some tribal groups are fully sedentary, remaining in stable villages for many years. Farmers are especially likely to be sedentary, locating near their fields. Some farmers, though, shift locations, alternating between two or more residences each year. Foragers and pastoralists are less likely to remain in stable settlements due to the necessity of gathering wild plants and hunting animals or finding grazing land for their animals. Sedentary villages may consist of many hundreds of people, whereas less permanent settlements tend to be much smaller.

Regardless of size, tribal societies often have mechanisms to unite the group at certain times of the year or at regular intervals. At those times, larger concentrations of people congregate to socialize, discuss issues of common interest, trade with each other, and celebrate religious occasions through group ritual. The Cheyenne communal buffalo hunts, for example, referred to in the opening narrative, took place every year in the summer and brought together large groups of people to hunt, perform rituals, socialize, plan group actions, and exchange products and gifts.

Intergroup trade is common in tribal societies. People exchange foods and specialized handcrafts with others to obtain resources not found in their own territories or not produced by their own artisans. Well-established trading networks can carry resources and other goods over many hundreds, if not thousands, of miles either through long-distance trade or through local and regional exchanges.

Concepts of territoriality and private property tend to be more significant in tribal than in band societies. Farming and pastoral people delineate commonly recognized boundaries encompassing their territories. Status differentiation based on wealth occurs in some tribal cultures. However, great imbalances in wealth and standards of living do not develop because tendencies toward accumulation are countered by the values of generosity and hospitality. People aspiring to positions of prestige and influence must cooperate with others and generously give away whatever surpluses they may have. People are especially obligated to help and support their kin materially as well as emotionally. In tribal societies, networks of kin are the primary arena of social action and social responsibility.

Kinship relations in tribal societies are usually organized according to some unilineal principle, either patrilineal or matrilineal. However, some tribal societies reckon descent bilaterally. Where they exist, unilineal kinship groups, such as patriclans, are often corporate political bodies, controlling access to land and resources. Kinship groups may become differentiated on the basis of the amount or value of the resources they control. Some social inequality may arise as members of some kin groups have higher status than members of other groups. Although kinship is the most important factor in organizing social interactions and responsibilities, many tribal societies also develop nonkin sociopolitical **associations** that link people in a community on the basis of shared interests and skills. These associations may have social, economic, ritual, or military functions. Membership may be voluntary or it may be assigned on the basis of specific criteria. And membership may be temporary or permanent. By drawing members from diverse kinship groups, associations integrate or ally people on a basis other than kinship and descent. Modern state societies also have such associations, such as political clubs, religious groups, and hobby groups.

Some tribal societies have a system of age grades or age sets, associations of people of a similar age. An **age grade** is an assigned sociopolitical association—a grouping of people of more or less similar ages who are given specific social functions. Members of the same age grade consider themselves to have a kin-like relationship. They are expected to aid one another in times of need, to share resources when necessary, and to give each other emotional support. When disputes arise between members of different age grades, the members of each are expected to rally behind their own. Although their functions are very different, modern state societies also have age groups, as in school categories, for example, freshmen, seniors, or the Class of 2006.

Confederacies

In some tribal societies, formal systems of leadership and decision making may develop that link separate tribes into political systems aimed at coordinating activities and arriving at decisions that affect all members. People may choose leaders and set and follow procedures for decision making. In such societies, intertribal unity is an important goal and an important factor in the people's survival. A well-organized political apparatus may develop in response to perceived external threats. A form of political organization in which tribes and bands join together under common leadership to face an external threat is referred to as a **confederacy.** A prime example is the Iroquois, a group of five distinct but closely related indigenous nations living in what is now New York State, Vermont, and the Canadian provinces of Québec and Ontario. The Iroquois developed a highly structured confederacy that created internal unity and protection from external threats.

The five nations that came to be known as the Iroquois (Mohawk, Oneida, Onondaga, Cayuga, and Seneca) came together in a league or confederacy to preserve peace among members and to act as a unified body in dealing with other nations, either in peace or war. On the whole, these goals were achieved, although internal conflicts were not unknown. The founding of the Iroquois Confederacy predated the arrival of Europeans in North America. While some historians and anthropologists assume a fourteenth- or fifteenth-century origin, Iroquois datekeepers contend that the confederacy began much earlier. Using the arguments of the datekeepers, archaeological data, astronomical data of the eclipses, and historical sources, researchers have dated the League's origin to 1142 (Mann and Fields, 1997).

Employing the kinship metaphor of family, the confederacy was symbolized as a great longhouse, stretching from east to west across Iroquois territory. In this longhouse, the Mohawk were referred to as "Keepers of the Eastern Door" and the

associations
Sociopolitical groups that link people in a community on the basis of shared interests and skills.

age grade (age set)
A sociopolitical association of people of more or less similar age who are given specific social functions.

confederacy
A form of political organization in which tribes and bands join together under common leadership to face an external threat.

GLOBALIZATION

Many indigenous peoples established confederacies prior to the globalization stimulated by the colonial era. The earliest written records report confederations for commerce and war. However, many confederacies sprang up as defensive measures against the spread of European dominance and control. Today independent states in Central America, the Caribbean, and West Africa, for example, have established political confederacies to further regional economic interests.

Case study

Age Grades among the Hidatsa and Age Sets among the Maasai

The Hidatsa were a farming people who resided in villages and hunting territories near the Missouri River in present-day central North Dakota. Their kinship system was organized around matrilineal clans and moieties. Membership in households revolved around a stable core of lineally related women. Kinship informed most daily interactions, but nonkin associations also figured prominently in village community life.

Most adults belonged to age-grade societies that had social, economic, and ceremonial functions. Both men and women began their participation in the age-grade system when they were in their early teens and proceeded from one age grade to the next until they retired in old age. The age-grade system was a means of uniting individuals that cut across families, clans, and moieties. Members aided each other when communal work or support in emergencies was needed. And members presented food and gifts to relatives of a deceased age-mate. Certain women's and men's societies were linked as "friends," and their members gave reciprocal aid and assisted in rituals and feasts.

Rights to membership in an age-grade society were purchased collectively by people advancing to the appropriate group because of their age and achievements. The relationship between the buyers and sellers was phrased as a relationship of parent and child (mother/daughter, father/son). Purchase of membership included transfer of spirit powers and sacred objects associated with the group. Women gained spirit powers directly from the previous holders, but men needed the assistance of their wives to finalize the transfer. As part of the ritual of purchase, wives of the buyers invited the sellers to have sexual intercourse with them in the belief that the spirit power of the elder men was passed to the woman in the sex act and that she later transferred it to her husband when they had intercourse.

Twelve age-grade societies existed for men and four for women. Most of the male societies were connected in some way to military participation. One of the major male associations was the Black Mouths, who served as police, enforcing decisions of the village council of elders. In addition, Black Mouths attempted to arbitrate disputes and to dissuade victims of assaults or the kin of a murdered relative from exacting blood revenge for the crime. Because of the Black Mouths' community control functions, the Hidatsa considered it crucial that men not be advanced to the society until they were mature and showed sound judgment. Consequently, most Black Mouths were between 30 and 45 years of age (Bowers, 1992). Members of the most senior male age grade, called the Bull Society, formed the council of elders, who made decisions concerning community matters and chose village leaders. The Bull Society also had the important task of performing "buffalo calling" rituals of renewal and thanksgiving for the buffalos.

The most prominent of the women's associations were the Goose Society and the White Buffalo Cow Society. The Goose Society was composed of mature women, usually between the ages of 30 and 40. Members performed planting rites in the spring when the first waterbirds appeared in the region, celebrating the renewal of the earth and the fertility of crops. They also performed dances during the summer whenever villagers so requested. Their aid was sought during droughts to bring rain and protect crops. And the Goose Society performed rituals at the time of the fall migration of waterbirds in thanks for successful harvests. The eldest women's association was the White Buffalo Cow Society. When the people moved to their winter settlements, members performed rituals to attract buffalo near the camps so that they could be caught easily during that difficult season.

Each Hidatsa village had a council composed of mature men who were beyond the age of membership in the Black Mouth Society. Anyone could speak at council meetings, but the influence of the participant varied with his or her age and achievements.

Still, the goal of community consensus was paramount. Representatives of all households in the village were asked to express their opinions about important community matters before decisions were made. Approval by all households was critical if the decisions were to have any weight. Unanimity at tribal meetings was paramount. If a unanimous decision could not be reached, action was postponed to attempt to sway the minority. If eventual agreement were not possible, the matter was dropped.

Village councils chose a mature man to be the village leader, alternating between a summer and a winter incumbent. Fortunate occurrences during any leader's term of office, such as successful summer buffalo hunts, victorious raids, the appearance of buffalo near the camp in winter, and the general health and good fortune of the community, were all attributed to the practical and spiritual abilities of the leader. Similarly, any failures were attributed to his lack of power. Personality traits of generosity, intelligence, even temper, and compassion were critical requisites for being chosen for leadership. Spirit power was also a necessary adjunct to civil and military success. However, as one assumed greater responsibilities, spirit powers eventually waned. In fact, the more responsibilities one had, the greater was the loss of spirit power. These beliefs functioned to limit people's authority to remain in office for any considerable length of time. In this way, power sharing reflected the egalitarian basis of Hidatsa society.

The Maasai, cattle herders living in Kenya and Tanzania, have a system of age sets that organize military, political, and ritual life for men (Spencer, 1988). Passing from one named age set to another is automatic upon reaching the proper age and achievements. Men collectively move from one group to the next, beginning their age-set careers when they are teenagers.

Boys undergo ritual circumcision in preparation for their entry into the youngest age set. Thereafter, each subsequent "graduation" to the next age set requires a ritual of initiation. The first age set is that of the Warriors. While a Warrior, young men learn the skills of warfare and cattle raiding. They live together in a warrior village where they form close, cohesive bonds that last throughout their lives. They learn to depend on each other and to help each other in all endeavors. These economic and emotional bonds of reciprocal support are sustained later after they leave the Warrior stage, marry, and eventually become respected elders. The Warrior stage usually lasts about 15 years. Then the Warriors participate in a ceremony of transition to the next group where they retire from active military engagement. The third stage comprises the elders who function as village political and religious advisers and leaders.

In recent years, the Maasai age-set system has become obsolete. The governments of Kenya and Tanzania have banned cattle raiding and warfare, the major functions of the Warrior age set. Young men in the Warrior set have difficult adjustments to make, because their separate villages have been disbanded. By tradition, they are too old to live with their mothers but not yet considered eligible to marry.

Seneca were "Keepers of the Western Door," reflecting their geographic locations as the easternmost and westernmost nations. Leadership was vested in clan heads, their advisers, and respected elders. Clan chiefs were men chosen by leading women of their group. Chiefs ideally retained their office for life, but if a chief's behavior was deemed inappropriate or contradicted local opinions, he could be demoted and replaced by another of his clan. Each chief had assistants or advisers, men and women who also could be demoted if their behavior was considered unacceptable.

Political integration and expression of public opinion took place in councils that were structured by territory and by social identity. Three types of councils were held in villages: those of the elder men (including but not limited to clan chiefs), those of

In Their Own Voices

Constitution of the Iroquois Confederacy

The Iroquois Confederacy was founded by two great leaders as an organization dedicated to establishing peace among the five original member nations—the Mohawk, Oneida, Onondaga, Cayuga, and Seneca. The two leaders, one known as the Peacemaker and the other named Hayonhwatha, devised the plan and then brought it to the council of each nation for consideration. The following is an excerpt from the founding narrative of the Iroquois, translated into English.

The Peacemaker then said, "My junior brother, your mind being cleared and you being competent to judge, we now shall make our laws and when all are made we shall call the organization we have formed the Great Peace. It shall be the power to abolish war and robbery between brothers and bring peace and quietness."

Hayonhwatha [Hiawatha, a historical figure but not the subject of the poem by Henry Wadsworth Longfellow] then said, "What you have said is good, I do agree."

Then the Peacemaker said, "My younger brother, we shall now propose to the Mohawk council the plan we have made. We shall tell our plan for a confederation and the building of a house of peace. It will be necessary for us to know its opinion and have its consent to proceed."

The plan was talked about in the council and the Peacemaker spoke of establishing a union of all the nations. He told them that all the chiefs must be virtuous men and

be very patient. Then the speaker of the Mohawk council said, "You two, the Peacemaker and Hayonhwatha, shall send messengers to the Oneida and they shall consider the plan."

When the tomorrow of the next year had come, there came the answer of the Oneida council, "We will join the confederation."

So then the Mohawks sent two messengers to Onondaga asking that the nation consider the proposals of the Peacemaker. The next year when the midday came and the Onondaga council sent messengers who said, "We have decided that it would be a good plan to build the fire and set about it with you." So then at the same time the Peacemaker and Hayonhwatha sent messengers to the Cayuga nation and the answer was sent back. The next year at midsummer the Cayugas sent their answer and they said, "We do agree with the Peacemaker and Hayonhwatha."

Now the Senecas were divided and were not agreed because there had been trouble between their war chiefs, but messengers were sent to them but the Senecas could not agree to listen and requested the messengers to return the next year. So when the messengers returned the councils did listen and considered the proposals. After a year had passed they sent messengers to say that they had agreed to enter into the confederacy.

The Peacemaker requested some of the Mohawk chiefs to call a council, so messengers were sent out among the people and the council was convened.

women, and those of young men. Members of each council deliberated together and eventually came to a unanimous opinion concerning the matter at hand. Then each group chose a speaker, who presented the group's decisions in a unified meeting. Chiefs delegated one of their number to speak for them; women and young men appointed representatives who made their opinions publicly known. These representatives were often chosen among prominent senior men, but in some cases a woman or a young man was the selected delegate. If decisions varied, further discussion was necessary in *caucus* (a word of Native American origin referring to a meeting for the purpose of achieving consensus). The process of deliberation and consensus was repeated in tribal (or national) and confederacy forums, finally arriving at a universally accepted position.

Chiefdoms

chiefdoms
Stratified societies organized by kinship.

Chiefdoms are stratified societies organized by kinship, although the degree of difference among the various strata varies cross-culturally (see Table 12.3). They have structured methods of choosing leaders from within kin groups. These leaders, or chiefs,

The Peacemaker said, "I, with my co-worker, have a desire to now report what we have done on five successive midsummer days, of five successive years. We have obtained the consent of five nations. These are the Mohawks, the Oneidas, the Onondagas, the Cayugas and the Senecas. Our desire is to form a compact for a union of our nations. Our next step is to seek out Adodarhoh [an Onondaga chief]. It is he who has always set at naught all plans for the establishment of the Great Peace.

Now the Peacemaker addressed the council and he said, "I am the Peacemaker and with me is my younger brother. We two now lay before you the laws by which to frame the Ka-ya-neh-renh-ko-wa or the Great Peace. The titles shall be vested in certain women and the names shall be held in their maternal families forever." All the laws were then recited and Hayonhwatha confirmed them.

Therefore the council adopted the plan.

Then the Peacemaker himself sang and walked before the door of Adodarhoh's house. When he finished his song he walked toward Adodarhoh and held out his hand to rub it on his body and to know its inherent strength and life. Then Adodarhoh was made straight and his mind became healthy.

The Peacemaker addressed the three nations. He said, "We have now overcome a great obstacle. It has long stood in the way of peace. Now indeed may we establish the Great Peace."

"Before we do firmly establish our union each nation must appoint a certain number of its wisest and purest men who shall be rulers, Rodiyaner. They shall be the advisers of the people and make the new rules that may be needful. These men shall be selected and confirmed by their female relations in whose lines the titles shall be hereditary."

So then the women of the Mohawks brought forward nine chiefs who should become Rodiyaner and one man as war chief.

So then the women of the Oneidas brought forward nine chiefs who should become Rodiyaner, and one man who should be war chief.

So then the Onondaga women brought forward fourteen chiefs who should become Rodiyaner, and one man who should be war chief.

The Peacemaker then said: "Now, today in the presence of this great multitude I disrobe you and you are not now covered by your old names. I now give you names much greater." Then calling each chief to him he said: "I now place antlers on your head as an emblem of your power. Your old garments are torn off and better robes are given you. Now you are Royaner, each of you. . . . You must be patient and henceforth work in unity. Never consider your own interests but work to benefit the people and for the generations not yet born. You have pledged yourselves to govern yourselves by the laws of the Great Peace. All your authority shall come from it."

Then did the Peacemaker repeat all the rules which he with Hayonhwatha had devised for the establishment of the Great Peace. Then in the councils of all the Five Nations he repeated them and the Confederacy was established.

From *Parker on the Iroquois: The Constitution of the Five Nations* by Arthur C. Parker, edited and with an introduction by William N. Fenton, pp. 24–29. Copyright 1968 Syracuse University Press. Reprinted by permission.

CRITICAL THINKING QUESTIONS

What tribal principles of leadership and decision making guided the creation of the Iroquois Confederacy and the Great Peace?

Table 12.3 EXAMPLES OF CHIEFDOMS

Americas	Europe	Africa	Asia	Pacific
Timucuan of Florida	Mycenae of Middle Bronze Age, Greece	Ashanti of Ghana	Buyeo of Manchuria (prior to Chinese conquest)	Trobriand Islanders (Boyowans)
Natchez of the Mississippi Valley		Bamileke of Cameroon		Tongan Islanders
Olmecs of Mexico (historical)		Zulu of South Africa		Maoris of New Zealand
Kwakwaka'wakw of British Columbia				Tikopians and Tahitians of Polynesia

perform both political and economic functions. Chiefs and their families have higher status than other people. In some chiefdoms, they are not markedly distinguished from other people except in their social prestige, whereas in other chiefdoms, higher status people have economic, social, and political privileges. In all cases, however, higher status chiefs and their families have authority but not power. That is, because of their position, chiefs have some ability to control economic production and labor and the distribution of resources. However, their position and influence depend on the voluntary compliance of members of their kin groups and communities. Chiefs cannot coerce other people, whether relatives or nonrelatives, to do their bidding. They can only advise, cajole, encourage, and request the labor and support of others, and they lead more by example and goodwill than by control.

Despite the marked stratification in chiefdom societies, ethics of egalitarian relationships underlie daily interactions and community activities. Although the chief and his family are privileged, notions of equality and the responsibility of kinspeople to each other remain strong. These ethics are demonstrated in the redistributive networks and functions of the chief. Chiefs know very well that they owe their position to the voluntary loyalty of their kin and others in the community. They solidify their support through their generosity, through attending to emergency needs of members of their community, and by showing respect and consideration to all. In essence, then, chiefs are embedded in kinship networks and are burdened with the responsibilities and obligations that come from expectations of reciprocity and fair treatment.

In contrast to band and tribal societies where leadership is diffuse and spontaneous, chiefdoms have some centralization of authority. However, this centralization does not extend to the whole society but, rather, to local kinship groups such as lineages and clans. There are, therefore, many chiefs in a chiefdom, not one paramount leader, and each chief owes primary allegiance to his or her kin group. Chiefs usually are chosen by seniority. In some, the eldest child of either gender ascends to the position of chief when the incumbent dies. In other chiefdoms, succession is not automatic. A person aspiring to the position of chief needs the requisite skills, intelligence, and personality traits as well as the support of kin. In some parts of the world, particularly in Melanesia and Polynesia, chiefs are sometimes referred to as "Big Men." A Big Man earns his prestige and status by maneuvering within his kin group, displaying generosity by sponsoring pig feasts and other redistributions, and forming strategic alliances with other high-status and influential people.

With only a few exceptions, chiefdom economies are based on farming, either horticulture (gardens and groves) or agriculture (fields). The aboriginal chiefdoms of the Pacific Northwest in Canada and the United States were exceptional because their economies were based on foraging. However, like the farming chiefdoms, they were able to amass a surplus because of the abundance of natural resources in their environment. This points out an important characteristic of chiefdoms: They are surplus-producing economies, able to extract or produce more than enough food for their subsistence.

The distribution of surplus goods, both in food and material items, is the special prerogative of chiefs in such societies. As heads of their lineages and clans, chiefs redistribute resources among their members and throughout their local communities. They arrange and host feasts periodically, celebrating harvests, successful hunts, and ceremonial events such as marriages or deaths. They might also host feasts that celebrate victorious raids or sporting competitions. In preparation for feasts, chiefs encourage their kinspeople to work hard to produce surplus crops and to amass large stores of foods. Then entire communities and sometimes neighboring villages as well are invited to the feasts. The visitors receive part of the bounty of goods produced and collected by the host lineage or clan. They thus benefit economically and also bear witness to the generosity of the chief. The potlatch, described in Chapter 7, is a classic example of the redistributive functions of chiefs and the complex meanings of the feasts that they sponsor.

Because of their role at the center of redistributive networks, chiefs and their close kin have access to strategic resources not available to other people. In some chiefdoms, the chief and chiefly families do not benefit at all economically from their position. They work just as hard as other members of the community. But in other chiefdoms, the chiefs and their kin are able to retain a disproportionate amount of surplus brought in for feasting occasions. They use this surplus, both of foods and goods, for their own economic and social benefits. Their standard of living is higher or more elaborate than that of other people in the community. Their houses are larger, their clothing and ornaments finer, and their foods more exotic. In addition to economic benefits, chiefs and their kin use their access to strategic resources to attract followers. Through their redistribution of goods and their generosity in both formal and informal contexts, chiefs secure the loyalty of their followers.

Although chiefs and their families are privileged economically and socially, their position is inherently unstable. Chiefs compete with each other for followers in attempts to solidify and expand their spheres of influence. These underlying tensions create competition because each chief and chiefly lineage continuously has to reinforce their position in the face of competitors.

A number of other cultural correlates are associated with chiefdom societies. Concepts of territoriality and landownership tend to be well developed. The boundaries between neighboring chiefdoms are usually marked and recognized by both residents and outsiders. Ownership or control of other resources is also strongly identified. Some property might be deemed private and individual and other types might be considered a communal heritage of kinship groups as collective bodies. Where property is held communally, the chief becomes its guardian and titular owner (owner by title). Most chiefdoms have fully sedentary settlements with economies based on farming or pastoralism. Populations tend to be larger than in band or tribal societies. Methods of economic production allow for the accumulation of surpluses that can be used to support a growing population.

People in chiefdoms tend to have a strong sense of belonging not only to their own kinship group but to wider political and social associations as well. This sense of identity may promote rivalry and competition. Rivalry may be friendly, expressed in competitive sporting events, or, in some cases, lead to raiding and warfare. Warfare tends to occur more frequently in chiefdoms than in band and tribal societies. The goals of warfare may involve factors relatively rare or unknown in band or tribal warfare, such as the goal of economic gain by looting or confiscating enemy property. Warfare may also include raiding for captives. Warfare in chiefdoms also tends to be more deadly than in band or tribal groups, as killing one's enemies becomes a goal.

Tikopian society is ranked with chiefs having the highest status. Chiefs of patrilineages (maru) are elders directly descended from lineage ancestors, while clan chiefs (ariki) are descended from the common ancestor of the lineages (Firth, 1970).

An important function of the chief is as a mediator in disputes. Conflicts within a lineage or clan are often brought to the chief for advice and mediation. Some chiefdoms have councils of leaders that intervene to settle disputes between people belonging to different kinship groups. Ultimately, the chief or the council has only an advisory function, lacking the ability or power to force their decisions on adversaries in a dispute.

Chiefs and their families may be associated with ritual and spirit power. They may function as leaders of ceremonies that help bind members of the community together. And in some chiefdoms, the chief may be thought to possess special spirit powers or even to be a descendant of divine beings. Religious beliefs, discussed further in Chapter 14, therefore, can be seen to enhance the status and authority of the chief. Among the Maori of New Zealand, for example, *mana* is a kind of power and knowledge derived from the spirit world that can be controlled and manipulated by human beings and human action (Mataira, 2000). A person's control of *mana* is demonstrated by his or her success and achievements. Chiefs, who have the highest status and greatest success, are assumed also to have greater control of *mana*.

In some chiefdoms of Polynesia, including Tikopia and Tahiti, contact with a chief's powerful *mana* could cause harm to an ordinary person. Commoners, therefore, were not permitted to approach a chief too closely, to look at him directly, or to speak to him without an intermediary. Such beliefs isolated the chief from ordinary people.

Culture Change

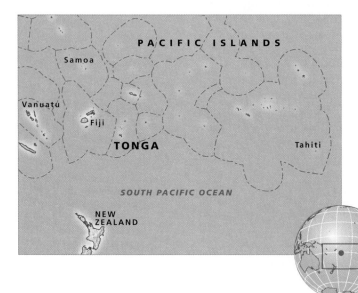

GLOBALIZATION AND THE TRANSFORMATION OF A TONGAN CHIEFDOM INTO AN ISLAND STATE

The Tongans, introduced in Chapter 7, are islanders of the South Pacific. In former times, they were organized into a highly stratified and complex chiefdom. Their social system was based on ranking in which no two individuals were of equal rank. Three principles were used to determine an individual's status relative to others. These included seniority: an older person outranked a younger; gender: a man outranked a woman; and sisterhood: a sister outranked her brother (Gailey, 1987b). Application of principles of status obviously could lead to variable ranking between, for example, an older woman and a younger man or an older brother and a younger sister. Actual determination of rank was open to maneuvering and personal claims.

The Tongan system of stratification divided the populace into two primary social strata: chiefs and nonchiefs. These two groups had different relationships to land and different roles in subsistence. Land was controlled by paramount chiefs, who then allocated portions to lower or district chiefs. Chiefs were guardians of the land.

Chiefs had prestigious titles through membership in high-ranking lineages. Succession to a title was awarded on the basis of several criteria. Although a chief's oldest son was a likely successor, other men could make rival claims based on kinship connections through the previous chief's sister, as well as through personal wealth, ability, and charisma. Descent through a sister was especially important if the prior chief had no surviving children. Because sisters were of higher status than brothers, a chief's sister's son outranked his brother's sons. But claims through sisterhood could be made even in opposition to a chief's own sons, particularly if the sister were senior to the deceased chief.

Chiefly people obtained food and goods from the work of others. Chiefs commanded collective labor by men, who farmed the chief's fields, and by women, who produced mats, bark cloth, and other valuables. Although most rights and obligations in Tongan society stemmed from kinship relations, the right of chiefly people to obtain support from commoner households was a reflection of their dominance over nonkin.

The Tongan social system included two groups intermediary between chiefs and commoners who functioned as buffers between the two social strata. One group, known as *matapules*, included artisans, warriors, administrators, and attendants to chiefs. They were internally ranked, depending on the particular job performed. For example, chiefs' attendants were of higher rank than artisans. Attendants and administrators oversaw cooperative work commanded by the chiefs. They also called together assemblies of commoners to advise them of chiefs' directives. The second intermediary group, called *mu'as*, were offspring and descendants of intermarriages between chiefs' families. They watched over young members of chiefs' families to ensure that the youths conformed to norms of public etiquette and morality. Although high rank clearly brought substantial privileges, it also incurred obligations to act in a suitable manner.

The various strata tended to be endogamous. Although lower rank people certainly preferred to marry someone of higher rank, those of higher rank looked upon such unions as disadvantageous to their own status. Chiefly people used marital alliances to consolidate high rank. At the highest levels, among paramount chiefs, marriage between a brother and sister was the most direct form of exclusion of counterclaims. This violation of the usual incest prohibitions set the chiefs apart from the rest of the population, but it also served to solidify alliances and consolidate wealth. Another strategy that the most powerful chiefs used to secure their dominance and exclude rivals was to arrange marriages of their sisters to foreigners. By such marriages, the chiefs simultaneously forged alliances with other leaders and eliminated competition from their sisters' sons, who instead became chiefs in their fathers' communities.

Seeds of political and social transformation were inherent in the Tongan chiefdom, as individual chiefs vied with each other for power and control. But contact with Europeans accelerated processes of change and channeled subsequent cultural shifts in particular directions. Among the consequences was an increase in men's authority over women's social, economic, and political claims.

Tongans first encountered European traders and explorers in the seventeenth century, with only sporadic contact throughout the eighteenth century. Chiefs were keenly interested in trade with the British. They especially wanted to obtain firearms. Acquisition of a substantial number of weapons intensified Tongan disputes over succession to chiefly titles, disputes that sometimes led to warfare. By the middle of the nineteenth century, reasons for warfare widened to include quests for land under jurisdiction of rival chiefs (Gailey, 1987b). Such competing attempts led to a transformation of the Tongan political system from a chiefdom to a **kingdom** under the leadership of one paramount ruler. This far-reaching change became institutionalized in 1845, when a paramount chief named Taufa'ahau assumed the title of king.

Coconut oil, processed by women, was originally an important trade item because Europeans used it to light lamps and manufacture soap. Women's production of coconut oil increased to fill the growing demand, and their importance in commerce enhanced their status (Gailey, 1980). However, after the middle of the nineteenth century, the world market for coconut oil declined. Instead, Europeans wanted copra, which was traditionally processed by men. The shift to trade in copra began a realignment of Tongan beliefs about the inherent value of women's and men's products.

As copra production increased throughout the rest of the nineteenth century, men spent more time in this endeavor and less time in fulfilling other subsistence and domestic tasks. Women were compelled to engage in work, such as farming and cooking, that carried low status, rather than producing *koloa*, valuables used in social, economic, political, and ritual contexts. Women also occasionally helped in copra production (men's work) to amass a greater supply destined for trade. Although women's participation increased their households' income, it further altered the traditional division of labor.

Women's work was also affected by the importation of European manufactured cotton and wool cloth, replacing traditional bark cloth, one of the most highly valued *koloa* items. And because cotton cloth was purchased with cash, men's access to money from copra production changed Tongan concepts of value. Women's wealth was thus undermined in a dual process of material replacement and ideological change.

Economic changes and political changes went hand in hand. Codification of laws and enactment of a constitution in the mid-nineteenth century solidified the state's power and men's authority over women. New laws also granted land-use rights individually to men as heads of their households. After the establishment of the Tongan kingdom in 1845, Tongan land was owned by the king, who allocated its use to men. Inheritance of land rights passed patrilineally from father to son. A woman could no longer lay claims to her brothers and their families. This shift resulted in women's dependence on their husbands, because other means of support were eliminated. In addition, a woman could no longer inherit chiefly titles from her father unless she was the firstborn child with no brothers. Even in this case, if her father had a brother, the brother's claim took precedence.

Thus, historical transformations stemming both from internal competition and external pressures from British colonial authorities resulted in benefits for men of the chiefly stratum. Women lost rights relative to chiefly men, and nonchiefly people of both genders experienced a decline in their economic and political autonomy.

kingdom
A centralized political organization with the king as the paramount leader.

Tongan chiefs often welcomed foreigners. They embraced the new opportunities for acquiring wealth and power made available through European trade. The Tongans were not passive victims of colonization but active participants in developing a new kind of society.

Although separation between chiefs and commoners was phrased as necessary for the protection of the commoners' well-being, it was the chief who was protected from contact with and the demands of ordinary people. Through these processes, religious beliefs serve to mystify the person of the chief and to render his actions and statements beyond the questioning of common people.

REVIEW

Foraging societies tended to form small, mobile, loosely defined bands. At the band level of political organization, leadership, like that of the sagamores of the Mi'kmaqs, was informal, temporary, and consensual. The political organization of tribes, whether horticultural, agricultural, or pastoral, was based on kin groups such as clans, which might be ranked. Tribal people also formed groups that crosscut kin ties, based on associations such as warrior societies or age grades. Confederacies, such as the Iroquois, were bands and tribes that joined together for mutual benefit and protection from external threat. Chiefdoms were stratified societies based on kinship and the inheritance of social status. Chiefs were chosen more formally and served as the heads of redistributive networks. Chiefdoms became kingdoms when ruling power and authority came to be inherited through a single paramount chief.

CHARACTERISTICS OF STATE SOCIETIES

states
Highly organized, centralized political systems with a hierarchical structure of authority.

republics
State societies with elected rather than inherited leadership.

States are centralized social and political systems with formal governments organized into a hierarchical structure of authority. Ultimate authority and power rest with the head of state, whether called a president, a king, or an emperor. The head of state delegates responsibilities to advisers and assistants. State government systems include procedures for formally selecting leaders. In **republics,** presidents and prime ministers are elected by some segment of the citizenry for a set period of time. In some republics, officeholders may seek reelection for an additional term or terms, whereas in others, they are barred from succeeding themselves. Factors of age and gender may affect a person's right to vote.

In kingdoms, or monarchies, the successor to the king or queen is chosen by traditional patterns of inheritance, usually **primogeniture.** The eldest child, or more often the eldest son, automatically becomes the next monarch upon the death of the previous holder of that title. Another difference between a monarchy and a republic is that in monarchies the king or queen, once installed, remains in the position until death or voluntary abdication.

Based on principles of sovereignty, or self-rule, state systems usually demarcate their territory and divide it into jurisdictions or districts and subdistricts. The size and complexity of these units vary considerably, but often each unit has some degree of independence and coordination of functions. Each territorial unit is administered by officials chosen locally or delegated by central authorities. These officials are in charge of implementing government policies in their region, acting as conduits for central powers and sometimes as intermediaries between local residents and state officials. The larger the unit over which they have control, the greater their power and prestige. Thus, states are based on political unification, often with a national identity, and the centralization and delegation of power within a sovereign territory. Expanding state societies become **empires,** enlarging their territory and power through conquest.

State societies have much larger populations than bands, tribes, or chiefdoms, and continuous population growth leads to the development of labor specialization. Unlike other types of societies where all members, given characteristics of age and gender, perform at least some direct subsistence work, in state societies there are many people who do not engage in economic production. Some people work as artisans and craft specialists making pottery, baskets, clothing, woodwork, and all manner of necessary tools, equipment, and utensils. These goods are obtained by other people either in exchange for money or for barter with foods and other resources.

In addition, state societies have the need for many different kinds of officials and bureaucrats who help organize and run projects that involve many people. Some of these are public works projects, such as construction and maintenance of roads, water delivery systems, and other infrastructure. Some bureaucrats keep track of the populace, taking census and collecting tribute or taxes. Other people work for the state as members of a police force that controls the resident population, or as a military force that defends the state from its enemies and conducts offensive warfare to expand the borders or influence of the state. Still other specialists work in commerce, facilitating the flow of raw materials, foods, and manufactured goods from one area of the state to another, as well as to other states. And some members of society are full-time religious practitioners, conducting private and public rituals. Finally, some segments of the state society do no work at all but are fully supported by the labor of others.

Labor specialization intersects with systems of social stratification. All states are hierarchically stratified societies in which some people have greater access than other people to property of all kinds and to other strategic social and economic resources. States are divided into at least two strata: elites and commoners. Elites make up a minority of the population but reap disproportionate wealth and disproportionately occupy positions of social prestige and political power (Mills, 1956). Elites have important economic functions in society but rarely enter the labor force as workers. They are sustained directly or indirectly by the tribute, rents, and taxes paid by commoners. For example, elites may own land that is farmed by peasant workers, receiving part of the harvest as tribute. State societies usually develop urban areas where populations are concentrated. These urban centers become the seats of centralized government functions. Cities are the sites of monumental architecture that celebrate the power of the state. Large buildings house government and administrative offices. Wealth is displayed in the size and opulence of homes.

Just as in chiefdoms where chiefs manage and organize redistributive networks, elites in state societies control the production and distribution of foods and other resources for consumption. However, unlike chiefs, elites retain the majority of surplus, improving their standard of living as a class while other people live in situations of comparative disadvantage. The degree of inequality between elites and commoners varies in different states. The greater the disparity in wealth, the greater the likelihood that elites will exert control over commoner classes, as commoners may come to resent the fact that the elite lifestyle is supported by their own labor. Therefore, as noted in

primogeniture
A system of inheritance of leadership in which the eldest child (usually the eldest son) automatically inherits the position of leadership from his or her parent.

empires
States expanded into larger units through conquest and the occupation or annexation of new territories.

GLOBALIZATION

Imperialism is the empire-building process by which expanding state societies gain more land and resources and control more labor, either directly through conquest or indirectly through power and influence. Imperialism has been a major contributing factor in the process of globalization that we see today.

? *How is the society of the United States stratified? What ideologies support your status in this system?*

Controversies

Origins of the State

How did sovereign states or nations develop? Anthropologists have long argued this question. Many theories have been suggested for the origin of the state. One of the most widely accepted theories is that offered by Robert Carneiro (1970). According to Carneiro, a critical factor in state development is what he calls *environmental circumscription.* This term refers to the fact that under certain circumstances, economies continue to expand and intensify production in territories that are limited by natural barriers, such as mountains, oceans, or surrounding deserts. The problem faced by people in such circumstances is the natural limitation on access to more land as populations increase.

This theory of state origins is related to theories about population growth and its interrelationship with economic production and surpluses. That is, as you may recall from Chapter 6, when economies expand and people produce more food, they are able to relax restrictions on population growth. Surplus food and population growth are intertwined. As people produce more food, they are able to support larger families and communities. And then, as there are more people available to work, even larger surpluses can be produced, again leading to population growth. This is a cycle of rising economic production and population that can continue to the point where the carrying capacity of the land is reached and threatens to be surpassed. At that point, new methods of increasing production must be developed and additional land must be obtained.

Where there is enough land, people can expand into the surrounding territory, cutting down trees and brush and cultivating the open land into farm fields. But, according to Carneiro, people living in environments where their access to additional land is curtailed by natural surroundings, populations may continue to increase to the point where competition among neighboring peoples for scarce land leads to open raiding and warfare. Unlike warfare in band, tribal, and even chiefdom societies, warfare in developing state societies is aimed at the confiscation of land and the control over inhabitants of conquered territories. These inhabitants may be forced out of their original territory or relegated to a subordinate status within the state as captives, slaves, or indentured workers.

The processes that lead to increased production, population growth, and the need for new land are never-ending. State societies, therefore, exist in a condition of instability. As populations continue to grow, land shortages intensify, leading to renewed cycles of expansion, competition, and war. The more intense and rapid these cycles are, the greater is the need for centralization and control over economic and political functions. Successful states continue to expand beyond their original boundaries as they move into the territories of smaller independent societies. As they do so, they confiscate land and disrupt the lives of inhabitants by incorporating them into the expanding state society under the control of the central authorities. Such expanding state societies may become *empires.*

Carneiro's theory of state origins also addresses the fact that states have come about in areas without environmental circumscription. According to Carneiro, states may arise in situations where natural resources are concentrated in a relatively small area and where available land elsewhere is not rich in resources. People, therefore, congregate and populations grow in these small areas of resource abundance. High population densities may also lead to the development of state societies without environmental circumscription.

An earlier theory addressing the issue of state origins is the *hydraulic hypothesis,* proposed by Karl Wittfogel (1957). According to this theory, states originated precisely in certain environments near rivers when institutions arose to organize the construction of large-scale irrigation systems. Wittfogel, therefore, saw state organization as responding to the internal need for increasing agricultural production as populations increased. Whereas Carneiro's theory emphasizes the political and military pursuit of wealth, Wittfogel's ideas stress the structural bureaucratic mechanisms that help organize communal activities in large populations. These theories do not necessarily contradict each other but, rather, emphasize different aspects of state functioning. However, one problem with the hydraulic hypothesis is that it does not account for the existence of productive irrigation without state control, for example, in early Mesopotamia and Peru (Adams, 1982), or for the existence of state bureaucracies before the development of large-scale irrigation systems (Johnson, 1973).

CRITICAL THINKING QUESTIONS

How does Carneiro's theory interrelate population and environment? What might be a specific example of environmental circumscription as a motivating factor in state expansion? How does the hydraulic hypothesis differ as an explanation for the emergence of states?

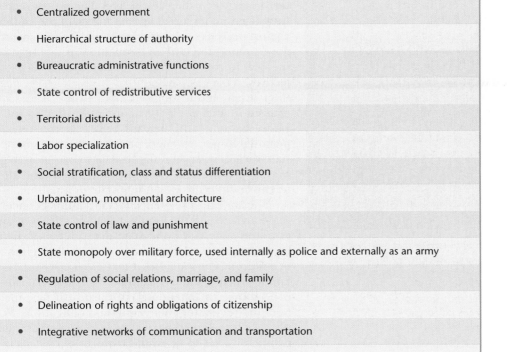

Figure 12.1
Features of state society

- Centralized government

- Hierarchical structure of authority

- Bureaucratic administrative functions

- State control of redistributive services

- Territorial districts

- Labor specialization

- Social stratification, class and status differentiation

- Urbanization, monumental architecture

- State control of law and punishment

- State monopoly over military force, used internally as police and externally as an army

- Regulation of social relations, marriage, and family

- Delineation of rights and obligations of citizenship

- Integrative networks of communication and transportation

- Ideological support through religious and social ideologies

Chapter 11, ideologies arise in state societies that legitimate the status and privileges that elites receive.

In addition to ideological control, state societies have mechanisms of force that can be brought to bear on an unruly populace. Laws are codified and standardized that regulate behavior and declare certain actions criminal offenses punishable by state authorities. Court systems determine the guilt or innocence of individuals accused of crimes and punish those deemed guilty. A police force is used as an agent of **social control.** In the codification of rules of conduct and in the punishment of wrongdoing, the state replaces kinship groups as the regulators of social behavior. These and other characteristics of state societies are itemized in Figure 12.1.

In bands, tribes, and chiefdoms, social relations are enmeshed in networks of kin. People's behavior conforms to the principles of reciprocity and ethical standards valued among relatives. But in state societies, kinship groups lose their control over members and are replaced by mechanisms of the state. Individual and personalized loyalties and affections are replaced by anonymous and depersonalized procedures and personnel. The loosening of the bonds of kinship is a slow process that is never complete, for in all societies, people have responsibilities and loyalties to their kin, as well as to other people and other entities. And in state societies, powerful extended family systems continue to thrive, especially among the ruling classes. Networks of kin among the elites help solidify their power and maintain their distinctiveness.

The state, through its police force and court system, supervises decision making and sanctioning. Individuals are deemed solely responsible for their actions, in contrast to the collective responsibility of kin groups for the behavior of their members in bands and tribal societies. State governments assume the right to enforce decisions that they make in the name of the society at large. These decisions affect internal functioning, law and order, and procedures that regulate many of the activities of private citizens. Other decisions affect external relations with other societies. The existence of capital punishment is an example of the state's monopoly on power. It demonstrates that only the state can legally kill.

In external relations, the state also monopolizes rights to conduct warfare against others. Private citizens cannot legitimately take up arms against a foreign country without the cover and sanction of a state-declared war. In fact, we now label such behavior

social control
Informal and formal mechanisms in society through which people's actions are controlled and social norms or laws are enforced.

? *How is terrorism a factor in the maintenance and expansion of modern states today?*

Early state societies included the first seats of civilization that were based on intensive agriculture in such places as the Indus Valley, the Fertile Crescent of Mesopotamia, the Nile Valley, and the Yellow River valley of China. All the characteristics of a state society described in this section also can be seen in the example of the Inca of South America. Here, the ruins of Machu Picchu mark one of the last sacred outposts of the Inca Empire, conquered in 1535 by Spanish invaders.

terrorism. According to the U.S. Federal Bureau of Investigation, terrorism is "the unlawful use of force against persons or property to intimidate or coerce a government, the civilian population or any segment thereof, in the furtherance of political or social objectives" (U.S. Department of Justice, 1999). From their origin and throughout their history, states specialized in warfare. Unlike band and tribal societies, where raiding and warfare were carried out for personal honor, revenge, prestige, or ritual goals, in state societies wars are undertaken to conquer neighboring peoples and to incorporate them and their territories into the expanding state population.

The state also regulates social relations concerning marriage and the family. Through religious sanction and state rules, the state determines eligibility for marriage, grounds for divorce, and the legitimacy of children. The state thus intervenes in personal and familial relations and decisions. States also determine procedures for extending citizenship to new members and regulating their rights and obligations. People may be assigned particular work to perform and tribute or taxes to be paid. Privileges of citizens may include the right to some level of support in times of need, protection against foreign invaders or domestic disorder, and access to training or education. Obligations of citizens to the state may include contributing to communal efforts and obeying authorities. In some early states, officials organized a complex system of public warehouses that kept stores of foods and other necessities to dispense to the populace if crops failed. States vary considerably in their provisions for social welfare.

States are integrated through networks of communication and transportation. The larger the population and territory, then the more likely it is that complex systems of record keeping and notation will develop. Specialist bureaucrats are trained to keep track of the settlements and movements of populations within the territory, tribute and taxes collected, public labor organized and expended, and services required and rendered. Routes of trade and commerce also link urban centers with one another and rural villages to regional and urban markets. Networks of long-distance trade transport products and resources throughout the state. Regional specializations, therefore, develop, enabling each locality to become efficient producers of foods and other goods in their territory.

State systems are often supported by religious ideology. A unifying state religion may develop that legitimates and rationalizes the system, including its social inequalities. A trained and specialized priesthood may ally itself with civil authorities, both groups benefiting from their consolidation of power. Religious specialists may define right and wrong, encourage obedience to authority, and claim divine origin or sanction for the political system. Many early states were **theocracies,** ruled by religious leaders or by rulers thought to be divine or divinely sanctioned to rule.

terrorism
Acts of violence perpetrated by private citizens against groups within their own country or against a foreign country without the cover and sanction of a state-declared war.

theocracies
Societies ruled by religious leaders, in which the social order is upheld through beliefs in its divine origin or sanction.

REVIEW

States are centralized social and political systems with formal governments that are hierarchically organized. These governments replace or supersede kin groups in many social functions and have other complex features. Theories of the origins of states include environmental conscription, in which states arose through a mutually reinforcing spiral of economic production and population growth within a territory, and the hydraulic hypothesis, in which states developed to ensure the regulation of intensive agriculture through irrigation. State societies are stratified, with ruling elites exercising power and authority. States enforce formal systems of social control and regulate warfare. Terrorism includes acts of war that are not state sanctioned. State systems are justified through ideologies and religious teachings. Many early states were theocracies, led by religious or divine rulers.

Case study

The Inca of Peru and Ecuador

The Inca of Peru and Ecuador developed a complex, multiethnic, centralized agricultural empire over many centuries, growing out of indigenous Andean cultures centered around Cuzco, Peru. The Inca were members of two dominant kinship groups that gradually increased their wealth and power over others, eventually transforming Andean cultures into a hierarchical state society. The state did not remain limited to its area of origin but expanded in the fifteenth century to encompass an estimated 6 million people living in what are now Peru and Ecuador. The empire grew by incorporating and transforming local cultures. The social and political features of Inca society are consistent with the general patterns of agricultural societies. Villages, towns, and cities were permanent and varied in size, depending on their location and importance to the Inca Empire. Small settlements numbered only a few hundred, but major cities contained many thousands of inhabitants. Social and economic roles were highly differentiated with a strong tendency for specialization. People were also segmented according to social status and power.

Inca Empire

The Inca state was headed by a supreme ruler who maintained his power through a complex network of agents, bureaucrats, armies, and priests. These various people transmitted demands of elites to local communities and ensured that they were fulfilled. Administrative power was exclusively a male domain. Most of the emperor's closest advisers and aides were chosen from among the men in his lineage. Succession to the position of emperor was not rigid, but the current ruler usually selected and trained one of his sons to assume the post.

The ruler's wife, known as *coya,* or "queen," was his own sister. Marriage between a brother and sister at the highest level of state functioned to consolidate power and minimize struggles over succession. Marriage between siblings was absolutely forbidden to all except the emperor and *coya.* The *coya* had substantial public influence. She participated in Inca public life in both economic and administrative capacities. She owned land and could dispose of its produce, but she redistributed some of the surplus delivered to her, holding huge public feasts as demonstrations of her generosity. *Coyas* had special lands that they used for experimentation with new strains and varieties of crops (Silverblatt, 1978). Also, they occasionally wielded political power, governing from Cuzco in the absence of their husband.

Andean land was under the control of localized kinship groups called *ayllus.* An *ayllu* consisted of people living within a particular territory. It was a corporate entity and exercised control over allocation of land to households. *Ayllu* leaders periodically reassigned allotments to adjust to changes in household composition. Land was apportioned to male heads of households on the basis of family size. Each married man received one measure (*tupu*) of land for himself and his wife. For each of his sons, he received an additional *tupu* and for each daughter, one-half *tupu.* When a son married, he was allotted the portion of land originally given to his father on his behalf. In most cases daughters relinquished their share of land upon marriage (Silverblatt, 1978, 1980).

Agricultural work was performed by both men and women, working singly or together. They cultivated more than forty species of plants (Rowe, 1950), with regional variations depending on altitude, climate, and topography. Basic crops were potatoes, maize, various grains, berries, chili peppers, squash, beans, peanuts, tomatoes, and coca. In addition to farm produce, people kept many species of domesticated animals, especially llamas, alpacas, dogs, guinea pigs, and ducks. Guinea pigs supplied the people with most of their meat. Foraging and hunting were relatively unimportant.

Communal rights to resources within an *ayllu* were recognized and enacted through redistribution of foods and goods to community members. If a family or individual were in need, they received aid from others. This system of redistribution was based on egalitarian ethics and limited the possibility of individuals' accumulation of wealth.

However, despite the fact that all people had rights to resources and sustenance, some individuals were of higher social status than others. These people, known as *curacas*, had political influence in their communities and constituted a governing body (Silverblatt, 1980:153). Although there were both men and women *curacas*, it is uncertain whether the women had solely economic privileges or whether they also had roles in decision making and leadership of their communities (Silverblatt, 1987:16–18). *Curacas* had economic privileges, including rights to obtain products from the labor of others. In return for goods received from common people, *curacas* were obligated to be generous to those in need.

In addition to agricultural work, common people were obligated to perform other kinds of labor, known as *mita* service. Men were enlisted to construct and maintain public works projects, such as palaces, temples, forts, irrigation systems, and roads. Some men were conscripted into army units under Inca command. And others were trained from childhood to serve as runners in an elaborate postal system, carrying messages throughout the empire. Women were compelled to spin and weave cotton and wool cloth for garments or for trade to other areas.

Burdens of giving tribute in labor or goods to the Inca elite were assigned not to individuals but to households. Each household was treated as the unit that had collective responsibility to fulfill its obligations. Work was assigned within a household depending on individuals' availability and skills. Although men and women performed different kinds of work, some flexibility was possible when people were called to state service or when illness or absence required a shift in tasks.

Although Inca society was highly stratified and power rested exclusively with the upper class, chiefly generosity was expected. In addition, basic survival requirements of all people were met by maintenance of granaries and warehouses from which *curacas* could obtain supplies for members of their *ayllus* in times of famine. These goods were derived from surpluses originally taken by elites from the labor of commoners. The Inca system reveals the ethics of reciprocity underlying social relationships and uniting people in kin-based societies. As in other state societies, these ethics were kept alive even as the Inca extended their empire.

INTERNAL POLITICAL CHANGE AND STATE SOCIETIES

State societies are the largest, most complex, and highly centralized political systems. The first states arose in the Middle East in Mesopotamia around 8,000 years ago. Other states developed slightly later in the Nile region of Egypt. States also arose independently in the Indus River valley of India, in China, in Meso-America (Mexico and Guatemala), and in the Andes of Peru. Today state societies exist in every part of the world, replacing other kinds of society and dominating the world scene.

Political systems also change through internal processes. State societies, for example, change through factionalism and revolution. Disagreements about community actions occur from time to time in all societies, but they can lead to entrenched **factionalism** as various interest groups vie for control of decision making and leadership roles. If a powerful faction is able to assert its will, this can lead to fundamental social changes. For example, in the early 1900s, two contentious factions developed in the Hopi community of Oraibi in Arizona over whether or not to participate in federal educational programs for Hopi children. Some people believed that knowledge of the English language and American culture would benefit the Hopi, but others feared that any but the most tangential contacts with American culture would lead to the destruction of Hopi lifeways.

Conflicts between these two factions intensified and grew increasingly bitter, eventually spilling into other issues and even dividing family groups. Finally, in 1906, the Hopi in Oraibi decided that they could not all live together in the same community. Using the quasi-ritualistic means of a "tug-of-war" across a line etched in the dirt, the two

factionalism
The tendency for groups to split into opposing parties over political issues, often a cause of violence and a threat to political unity.

sides dramatized their inability to coexist. The group who lost (called the "Hostiles," because of their opposition to American assimilationist policies) was forced to leave, later founding a new village, Hotevilla. The faction known as the "Friendlies" remained at Oraibi and continued their more accommodating approach toward American cultural innovations (Titiev, 1992). Today, the two groups have achieved a greater degree of cooperation toward community goals, although disagreements reemerge from time to time about policies affecting internal development and direction, as well as about attitudes toward dealing with outsiders.

In large stratified societies, political change can come about as a result of rebellion and revolution. These are complex processes that take different forms in different contexts. In colonial situations, residents of the colonies may eventually decide that they no longer want to live under foreign domination. They may rebel in wars of independence to oust their rulers. A successful rebellion may enable indigenous people to return to some form of traditional life. Or the colonists themselves may rebel against their country of origin to set up an independent nation. The American Revolution is an example. It was a revolution in its focus on eliminating what had come to be seen as a foreign, distant power controlling people in the colonies. And it was revolutionary in its transformation from a monarchy to a republic with ultimate power in the hands of elected officials. The French Revolution of 1789 had the additional goal of overturning a whole social system, eliminating the class privileges of wealthy and aristocratic elites. These goals were never fully met, demonstrating how difficult it is to break completely with the past.

In the twentieth century, new movements for social and political change occurred in many places in the world. The Mexican Revolution of 1910 and the Russian Revolution of 1917 were attempts to change the stratified social systems that created economic and political inequalities. Following the end of World War II, many countries in Africa that had been colonized by Europeans gained their independence. These movements were successful both because of internal resistance to colonial control and external pressure from growing international anticolonialism. Internal and external forces of cultural change are discussed further in Chapters 16 and 17.

More recently, movements for internal democratic change have also taken root worldwide as people in stratified societies with imbalances in wealth and power have attempted to claim a more equitable share of their country's resources. Elites do not give up their power and privilege easily, however. They may resist openly by using the police force at their disposal to put down revolutionary movements or by using the legal apparatus to arrest and punish leaders and participants. They may also resist by ideological means, claiming the moral authority and legitimacy of the prevailing system. In the end, movements for social and political change succeed when supported by a large and dedicated segment of the population. The civil rights movement in the United States in the 1950s and 1960s and the anti-apartheid struggles in South Africa in the 1970s and 1980s eventually won fundamental political transformations, despite strenuous opposition from those in power.

Today, the crises in the Middle East have spawned movements for social and political change within many countries in the region. Middle Eastern monarchs have implemented or begun to talk about steps toward democratization of their political processes. For example, King Mohammed VI of Morocco, installed in 1999, has broadened citizens' access to political participation and given more power to elected representatives in an attempt to respond to people's desire for a voice in their own society. And King Fahd bin Abdul Aziz of Saudi Arabia, head of one of the most autocratic governments in the world, has hinted at the possibility of reforms to allow more popular participation. These governments are responding to forces of globalization that have begun to affect their own citizenry and, perhaps, to fears of the spread of Islamic fundamentalism, which feeds on deep popular resentment.

In the late 1960s, China's Cultural Revolution, under the leadership of Mao Zedong (seen on the banner here), transformed Chinese society from a Soviet-style communist state to a modern "people's republic." This transformation was accomplished through the mobilization of urban Chinese youths into the Red Guards. The Red Guards persecuted teachers, intellectuals, and people who practiced traditional arts and ways of life, which were seen as "bourgeois." The Cultural Revolution turned violent as the Red Guards broke into factions, and many people were killed in purges.

GLOBALIZATION

Some political anthropologists trace the spread of Euro-American political concepts and institutions. These concepts, such as democracy, and institutional behaviors, such as elections, tend to accompany the economic influences of those regions on world cultures. Political ideas and behaviors also may be forced on other people through conquest or other dominating influence.

REVIEW

Internal patterns of change in political systems include, among others, factionalism, in which groups split on issues and vie for power, and revolution, in which citizens rebel against their colonial rulers, government, or ruling elites.

Chapter Summary

Political Anthropology

- Political anthropology is the branch of anthropology that focuses on the ways that societies are organized to select their leaders, make decisions affecting the group, provide community functions and services, and resolve conflicts and disputes. These cultural mechanisms help integrate a community and help direct and maintain relations with other communities.

Types of Political Organization

- Bands are generally small, loosely organized groups of people. Communities in band societies usually have relatively small populations, dispersed throughout a wide territory. Bands are held together by informal means. Membership within one band rather than another is typically based on kinship ties to other people in the group. Band leadership is also informal, based on the personal abilities of the leader. Such leaders have influence but they do not have power to control the actions of others. Bands are usually egalitarian societies, and individuals' rights to resources and access to positions of influence are respected.

- Tribal societies differ from bands in the degree of structure and organization and in their group cohesion and community organization. Tribal societies may have more formalized organizational procedures, such as highly structured councils whose members regularly meet and deliberate. Tribal chiefs may be selected in more formal ways and may have some ability to reinforce their decisions. However, the powers of tribal chiefs or councils are limited by egalitarian social ethics. And there are often structured ways to ignore or depose leaders who try to exert too much authority.

- Voluntary associations and age-grade or age-set organizations are common in tribal societies. These systems unite people within a community across lines of kinship. Members of the same age grade consider themselves to have a kin-like relationship. When disputes arise between members of different age grades, members are expected to rally behind their group.

- Some tribal societies link themselves in confederacies. A confederacy is a formal, well-organized political apparatus that is structured to counteract perceived external threats. Confederacies have formal procedures to select leaders, to debate issues, arrive at group decisions, and plan and execute group actions.

- Chiefdoms are stratified societies organized by kinship, although the degree of difference among the various strata varies cross-culturally. Within chiefdoms, groups with the most prestige are the chiefs and their families. Higher status people generally have economic, social, and political privileges. However, chiefs and their families have authority but not power. They have some ability to control economic production and the distribution of resources, but their position and influence depend on voluntary compliance of their kin groups and communities. Chiefs cannot coerce other people to do their bidding. In chiefdoms, there is some centralization of authority but there is not one paramount leader. Each chief owes primary allegiance to his or her kin group. Although there may be some tendency toward inheritance of chiefly rank, a person aspiring to the position needs to have the requisite skills, intelligence, and personality traits that make them appropriate heirs.

- Chiefs are often the centers of redistributive networks. They direct the production of economic surpluses and extract some of the surplus to help support themselves and their families and to redistribute resources among members of their local communities. They do this by periodically arranging and hosting feasts.

Characteristics of State Societies

- State societies are the largest, most complex, and highly centralized political systems. The first states arose in the Middle East in Mesopotamia around 8,000 years ago. Other states developed in the Nile region of Egypt, in the Indus River valley of India, in China, in Meso-America, and in the Andes of Peru. State societies exist in every part of the world, replacing other types of societies and dominating the world scene.

- State governments are organized in a hierarchical structure of authority. Ultimate authority and power rests with the head of state, whether president, king, or emperor. State government systems include procedures for formally selecting leaders and their assistants. State systems usually divide their entire territory under their jurisdiction into districts and have economic systems characterized by labor specialization. Some people produce food and others work as artisans, traders, bureaucrats, police force, and religious practitioners. States are stratified societies in which some people have greater access to property and resources than other people.

- State societies develop and promulgate ideologies that legitimate the status and privileges that elites receive. In addition, they have mechanisms of force that can be brought to bear upon an unruly populace to maintain the status quo. Laws are codified and standardized, regulating behavior and assigning punishments to criminal offenses. The state monopolizes the right to control and punish wrongdoers through a system of police and courts. And the state also monopolizes the right to conduct warfare against others. States pursue political and economic ends through warfare by expanding their influence and control of people living in other lands.

Internal Political Change and State Societies

- State societies, like all types of social formations, are subject to change. States are inherently expansionist because of the desire on the part of elites to increase their wealth and power. Therefore, states expand territorially and absorb the population and resources of conquered lands. Change can also result from external pressures as one state conquers another and imposes its political will. State conquest always has cultural components as basic systems of family organization, economic productive relationships, and religion may be altered to conform to the practices and beliefs of the conquering state.

- States may also be transformed from within as various interest groups or factions compete for prominence. Reform movements may develop in response to perceived inequalities and injustices in the system. Revolutionary movements may also develop to effect more fundamental changes in state systems. Attempts at revolutionary transformations may or may not be successful, depending on the support they receive from the populace. Although revolutions are met with state and military resistance initially, some revolutionary movements have proven to be unstoppable. The worldwide movement of decolonization beginning after World War II is one such phenomenon. And global movements toward democratization have more recently gained momentum in many parts of the world.

Key Terms

political organization 312	tribes 317	kingdom 327	social control 331
political anthropology 312	associations 319	states 328	terrorism 332
bands 313	age grade (age set) 319	republics 328	theocracies 332
sagamore 316	confederacy 319	primogeniture 329	factionalism 334
	chiefdoms 322	empires 329	

Review Questions

1. How might a political anthropologist approach the study of factionalism or domestic terrorism in a present-day state society? What kinds of questions might he or she ask to determine the nature, causes, and consequences of these behaviors and ideologies in the society?

2. How are bands, tribes, chiefdoms, confederacies, and states different? What is a specific ethnographic example of each "ideal" type?

3. What roles do kinship and associations play in each type of political system?

4. Do bands, tribes, chiefdoms, confederacies, and states represent steps in the development of political systems? If so, how? If not, what determines which form of political organization a society is likely to have?

5. How do the characteristics of state societies relate to social stratification?

6. What have been some impacts of colonization on people's sociopolitical systems? Of globalization?

7. How do political systems change?

Conflict and
Conflict Resolution

CHAPTER 13

Preview

1. **What are the sources of aggression and conflict in primates?**

2. **What mechanisms do individuals and societies have for preventing, avoiding, or reducing conflict?**

3. **What are the sources, goals, and expressions of conflict in and among groups within a society?**

4. **What are the sources, goals, and expressions of conflict between societies?**

5. **What measures or mechanisms do people have for mediating and resolving conflicts?**

There was once a time of great famine, and Tortoise, like everyone else, was busy seeking food for his children. He bought much maize and made up a good load. On his way home he came to a fallen tree lying across the road, and he could not get over it. He walked up and down along the trunk of the tree, and at last his load slipped off and fell down the other side. Just then a monitor lizard happened to pass, and, seeing the load, exclaimed— "Well look what I have found." Tortoise (having by this time finally made his way around the tree) said to him, "That's mine—it just slipped off my head and fell on this side." Monitor Lizard replied, "I don't know about that; all I know is that I picked it up. Finders keepers, losers weepers." Tortoise said, "Let us go to the elders and have them judge what to do."

When they came to the elders, Tortoise explained what happened: "I came from gathering food and there was a fallen tree blocking the road. My load of food slipped off and fell on the other side of the tree. Then Monitor Lizard saw it and claimed it." The elders said to Tortoise, "You know that the finder of such things is permitted to keep them. That is our rule." So Tortoise went his way, and Monitor took up what he had "found" and carried it to his children.

Now, it happened one day that Tortoise and his companions went hunting, and they made a fire to lure prey into their trap. In the grass that they had set on fire, Monitor was sleeping. He woke up and ran here and there, and found a small hole in which to hide, but his tail stuck out of it. Tortoise, seeing Monitor's tail exposed, put out his hand and seized it, saying, "Finders keepers, losers weepers."

Monitor said, "You have got hold of my tail, my friend, let me alone." Tortoise said, "I did not touch your tail, I have found something to which I am entitled, a beautiful sword." Monitor begged, "My friend, this is my tail, you cannot claim it as a spoil." Tortoise said to him, "Let us go to the elders." When they arrived, Monitor said, "I was running away from a fire and I entered a small hole, but my tail was outside; then this person came along and said, 'It is a sword,' and I said, 'It is my tail,' but he would not listen." Tortoise said, "Today you are surprised. Lately you took my food gathering, and you thought nothing of it." Monitor said, "It was only food I took that day. Wait, my friend, I will fetch what I took." Tortoise said, "Today is today." The elders said to Monitor, "Give your companion his sword." Monitor said, "But it is not a sword, it is my tail." They said, "Give it to him," and the tail was cut off. Tortoise said, "Cut it high up, that I may have a good handle." So Monitor's tail was cut off, and given to Tortoise, and half-way home he threw it away, saying, "I only wanted to be even with him." Monitor wriggled and died. If a person does harm to one another, he should remember what may happen to him another day.

From *African Folktales* by Roger Abrahams, pp. 147–148. Copyright © 1983 by Roger D. Abrahams. Used by permission of Pantheon Books, a division of Random House, Inc.

positive sanctions
Recognition and rewards for observing social norms.

negative sanctions
Punishments for offending social norms.

informal sanctions
Rewards and punishments expressed through praise, ridicule, gossip, and the like.

formal sanctions
Rewards and punishments administered by persons in authority, the state, or the law.

dominance hierarchies
In primate groups, social hierarchies established on the basis of sex and age.

In this story, the Bondei people of Tanzania dramatize the issue of conflicts that arise when people think only of their own interests and fail to acknowledge the rights of others. It also describes social norms or rules that people affirm when they want to make a claim justifying their own behavior. And the story highlights the critical role of mediators in settling disputes or resolving conflicts.

In all societies, communities, and even families, there is potential for conflict. Conflicts may occur over issues of family life, household responsibilities, or roles within communities. Such issues may arise in any family from time to time and be settled fairly quickly and amicably. Disputes within communities may be about interpersonal issues or rights to property and other resources. These problems also may be settled amicably, but they may involve more complex negotiations and mediation to reach a resolution. Conflicts occur between communities or, in the modern context, between nations. Such conflicts have the potential of leading to protracted antagonisms and even to warfare. But families, communities, and societies have methods of avoiding or stemming the eruption of conflict in some situations and of resolving those conflicts that do arise.

Societies differ as to what causes conflict and in their ways of settling disputes and reestablishing peace or harmonious relationships. Societies also differ in their mechanisms for applying sanctions that influence or control people's behavior. **Positive sanctions** are recognition or rewards, either in the form of material benefits or social prestige, granted to people who behave according to social norms. **Negative sanctions** are formal or informal methods of discouraging people from behaving improperly. **Informal sanctions** include teasing, ostracizing, or gossiping about wrongdoers. **Formal sanctions** consist of fines and other punishments meted out by leaders or other legal authorities or systems of adjudication, such as village councils, juries, and judges. Thus, norms and sanctions establish the basis of social order.

EVOLUTIONARY PERSPECTIVES ON CONFLICT

Evolutionary biologists and psychologists have recognized the primate origins of behaviors that help avoid conflict and restore peace after incidents of open aggression between animals. In primate groups, social hierarchies are established, usually along lines of sex and age. Males and females learn their place through socialization into their groups. However, the **dominance hierarchies** are inherently unstable. Although some animals seem to accept their position in the hierarchy, others vie for prominence and attempt to oust the dominant male or female from their positions of leadership. One of the ways that conflict can be avoided is for subordinate animals to demonstrate acceptance of their position in the hierarchy through the display of submissive gestures and actions.

Primate gestures of dominance and subordination have certain similarities to human behavior. Studies of nonverbal communication demonstrate that in encounters between two social unequals, the subordinate person smiles more, averts the eyes when looked at by the dominant person, and attempts to take up less space by contracting the body and lowering the head. Subordinate people also get out of the path of dominant people, giving way to them on the street or in any enclosed space. All of these behaviors seek to avoid conflict by signaling one's acceptance of subordinate status.

However, despite mechanisms that minimize aggression, conflicts occasionally arise. But although

Primate gestures of submission include crouching to make oneself relatively small, baring one's teeth in a smiling facial expression, getting out of the way of an oncoming dominant animal, and species-specific submissive vocalizations. The chimpanzee on the right is clearly signaling submission.

conflict within a primate group is disruptive of the social unit while it occurs, the aggression does not do permanent damage to the group's cohesion. Studies of our close primate relatives, the chimpanzees, reveal patterned behavior that occurs immediately after conflict has erupted and taken its course. Animals who have just been involved in aggressive actions with one another may kiss, hold out a hand, or embrace, accompanied by submissive vocalizations. These are practices that Frans de Waal refers to as **postconflict reconciliation** (2000:17). De Waal also observed behaviors that he calls "consolation" between a recipient of aggression and a third individual. Chimpanzees may approach one another, hold out a hand, and embrace in order to reassure each other. In addition, de Waal suggests that some common primate behaviors, such as mutual grooming and body contact, function to reduce aggression and promote interpersonal and group stability.

According to evolutionary psychologists and primatologists, how might this fight have been avoided? How does the boys' aggression toward one another affect their social group? How can their conflict be resolved and future aggression prevented?

Studies such as those of de Waal and his associates bring into question models of primate behavior that focus on aggression and competition. Instead, they stress the critical importance of shared interests to create solidarity among members of a stable social group. Avoidance of aggression is then only partly explained as an outcome of weighing the risks of injury to oneself. Chimpanzees and other primate species may avoid aggression also because of the importance of cooperation and the risk of the social damage that conflict would cause.

Seen in this light, aggression and the avoidance of conflict are both enmeshed in their social context. **Conflict avoidance** has the positive value of maintaining social harmony. And behaviors characterized as reconciliation and consolation have the effect of restoring and repairing social relationships. The greater the value that individuals attach to their relationships, the less likely that disagreements and disputes will erupt into open conflict. But when they do, reconciliatory behavior helps repair those relationships critical to personal and community stability. De Waal poses a central paradox that emerges in the study of primate social behavior: the need to "integrate fully the vertical (hierarchical) and horizontal (affiliative networking) dimensions of social organization" (2000:30). As we shall see, this paradox also exists among humans and is critical to an understanding of conflict and conflict resolution in human societies.

? *In what ways is your postconflict reconciliation behavior similar to that of chimpanzees?*

REVIEW

Social norms and sanctions—informal and formal and positive and negative—establish the basis of social order, but in all primate groups and societies conflicts arise. Using an evolutionary perspective, we can see the roots of conflict and conflict resolution in primate dominance hierarchies and behaviors associated with dominance and subordination, postconflict reconciliation, and conflict avoidance. Both aggression and the avoidance of conflict are mediated through social and cultural contexts.

postconflict reconciliation
Patterned behavior that occurs immediately after conflict has erupted and taken its course, to restore some measure of social harmony.

conflict avoidance
Prosocial behaviors, such as reconciliation, consolation, politeness, or apology, to repair social relationships without aggression.

AVOIDING CONFLICT

In human societies, people develop ways to express disagreement while avoiding open conflict. In some societies, the emphasis on deferring to others, not stating one's opinions directly, and generally shunning people who are angry are efficient means of lessening the possibilities of conflict and creating social harmony within families or small communities. In his overview of conflict management strategies, Douglas Fry (2000) lists a number of cultural prevention mechanisms that are both social and psychological. One technique is self-control and restraint in the expression of anger.

Among many groups living in small settlements, people learn to control the expression of strong negative feelings. They learn that negative feelings, including anger, envy, and jealousy, can be socially disruptive, especially when everyone has frequent face-to-face interaction with everyone else in the community. In such societies, group mechanisms develop to squelch negative emotions from continuing and becoming dangerous. These mechanisms of social control include teasing someone who acts inappropriately, gossiping about his or her behavior, or avoiding the person—giving the "cold shoulder." Negative sanctions confront a person about his or her disruptive behavior and encourage the person to act according to social norms. These informal sanctions are especially effective in small communities where people interact frequently. Being teased, gossiped about, or avoided in such contexts can be psychologically painful, a constant reminder of one's inappropriate actions and of the negative view in which one is held by community members.

Another technique of conflict management in Fry's list is to control aggression once it erupts, preventing it from becoming too dangerous. For example, among the Ju/'hoansi of the Kalahari Desert in Namibia, if two people are engaging in verbal abuse, others quickly intervene and try to distract the disputants (Lee, 2003). If the verbal abuse escalates into pushing and shoving, onlookers immediately disengage the people by pulling them apart and trying to calm them down. In Ju/'hoansi camps, disagreements rarely escalate beyond the stage of pushing and shoving except in situations where alcohol is involved.

The Ju/'hoansi techniques are related to another of Fry's conflict prevention measures: the intervention of **peacemakers.** In the Ju/'hoansi case, nearly everyone in the community is a potential "friendly peacemaker," attempting to squelch a conflict from erupting into dangerous combat.

Still another conflict prevention technique is what Fry refers to as "attention to the satisfaction and needs of others." In many societies, people develop personalities that exhibit values emphasizing the importance of keeping other people happy or satisfied. They focus on sharing and supporting other people, not only in economic terms but in emotional terms as well. Toleration of other people's behavior, even if unpleasant or provocative, also contributes to maintaining peaceful, if not entirely harmonious, relationships. In this category one could include linguistic and nonverbal means of conveying politeness or **deference** to others.

Politeness

Politeness consists of a constellation of words and actions that demonstrate a person's consideration of the feelings of others and deference to their wishes and needs. The cultural mechanisms through which one expresses politeness vary considerably. Every language has polite words or expressions and polite ways of phrasing one's thoughts. And every culture has its norms about how politeness is shown and about who deserves to be the recipient of polite behavior (Brown and Levinson, 1987).

Politeness strategies function to mute antagonisms and avoid overt hostility by affirming common bonds and recognizing another person's rights and feelings. In addition to techniques that calm or pacify the other person, an individual who has committed a social wrong or has erupted in anger can prevent further antagonism and conflict by showing remorse or apologizing. Apologies function to maintain or reestablish rapport between participants. They are occasioned by actions that are perceived to have negative effects on others and for which speakers take responsibility.

Channeled Aggression

In some societies, specific social mechanisms help prevent conflict or channel aggressive behavior in socially acceptable forms. An example of channeled aggression is the Inuit practice of men challenging each other to **song duels** to vent their anger and jealousy without resorting to physical combat. Sexual jealousy was a common precipitating factor in song duels. Men who were competing as suitors for a particular woman engaged in a public display of verbal wit. The two men faced each other in front of an audience consisting of community members. They took turns beating on a drum while

peacemakers
Individuals with a specialized social role of preventing conflict from erupting into dangerous combat.

deference
Nonthreatening verbal and nonverbal behaviors that convey respect or subordination to others.

politeness strategies
Behaviors designed to mute antagonisms and avoid overt hostility by affirming common bonds and recognizing another person's rights and feelings.

song duels
Inuit contests in which conflict is expressed and resolved through public response to music.

Case study

Conflict Avoidance Strategies in New Zealand and Japan

In the words of the influential sociologist Erving Goffman, by apologizing, a speaker "splits [him-/herself] into two parts, the part that is guilty of an offense and the part that dissociates itself from the delict [offense] and affirms a belief in the offended rule" (1971:143). Naturally, what counts as a deed or intent necessitating an apology depends entirely on cultural models of offensive or regrettable behavior. In Janet Holmes's study of 183 apologies collected ethnographically in New Zealand (a country culturally dominated by people of British descent), the most typical offenses that triggered apologies were instances of inconvenience, infringements on space, talk, time, or possessions, and social gaffes (1990:177). More serious breaches triggered more elaborate apologies.

Comparison with other cultures reveals some similarities and differences in apology routines. For example, Japanese social norms require apologies in more situations than would be expected in Western societies. According to Florian Coulmas (1981), citing the Japanese sociologist Sugiyama Lebra, Japanese people are highly conscious of their effects on others and are concerned with not infringing on others' rights and needs. They strive to avoid embarrassment either to themselves or to their hearers. Not only are apologies frequently issued for offenses, they are also "used to line other speech acts such as greetings, offers, thanks with an apologetic undertone" (p. 327). In fact, a common utterance, *sumimasen* (literally: "this is not the end" or "it is not finished"), can be translated as either "I'm sorry" or "Thank you" and is used to express apology or gratitude. And in contexts such as leaving someone's home, where a Westerner might say, "Thank you for a wonderful evening," a Japanese guest often says the equivalent of "I have intruded on you" (literally: "disturbance have done to you"). As in Western societies, Japanese speakers typically respond to apologies with polite downgraders, for example, "No, no, don't mention it."

Japanese norms for interaction require explicit recognition of people's effects on each other in the form of apology for actual or implicated intrusions, disturbances, and infringements. Apologies are perceived as polite, considerate, and deferential according to Japanese models of social rights. Serious breaches and formal situations invoke more elaborate apologies.

composing insulting and derisive songs about their opponent. The audience typically reacted with laughter to both contestants.

According to Inuit social etiquette, the man who bested his rival in the song duel was rewarded with marriage to the woman in dispute. Although these contests provided a safe venue for open hostility between the men involved, they may or may not actually have settled the issue at hand. The woman might decide not to marry the victor. And the emotions revealed and dramatized during the song duel may be so strong that at a future date they led to actual violence. But the social mechanism was aimed at alleviating the conflict and stopping it from escalating to violence.

Case study

Conflict Resolution among the Semai of Malaysia

The Semai are a farming people who live in mountainous regions of the Malay Peninsula. Numbering about 1,500, they live in small villages or bands that are politically autonomous. In the past, their villages contained populations of approximately 100. Semai society is based on an egalitarian social system. No one can exert power or compel someone to do something against his or her will or wishes. In addition, Semai men and women are considered equal. Gender roles are not rigidly defined, so that men and women can do whatever work is necessary in the household and the fields. Significantly, the Semai believe that the social personalities of men and women are the same, making no differences in the emotional attributes or intellectual abilities of the two genders. Although everyone is considered to have the same rights and opportunities, some degree of moral authority is vested in a headman, usually a man recognized by the community because of his intelligence, oratorical abilities, and sound judgment. Although men are usually chosen as leaders, there is no prohibition against women occupying the role, and occasionally they do so.

The Semai make a significant distinction between in-group members and outsiders (Robarchek, 1997). The contrast between kin and nonkin is extended into a distinction between members of one's own band and outsiders. In-group members, whether in one's kin group or band, relate to each other with support, nurturance, and security, but outsiders are viewed with suspicion and fear.

The Semai perception of human relations is mirrored in the dichotomies that they impose on the universe as a whole. Whatever is known and familiar is thought of as helpful and supportive, but the unknown is fraught with danger. The Semai also make a distinction in the spirit world between protective spirits that are considered to be kin or like kin and malevolent spirits that are the source of misfortune, illness, and death.

Human beings, therefore, must be ever alert against the harmful actions of malevolent spirits. They protect themselves from dangers by reciting protective prayers, avoiding dangerous places or actions, and carrying out rituals that guard against misfortune and death. In this context of danger and unpredictability, the Semai look to their relatives and fellow band members for security and protection. They are bound together in strong networks of reciprocal aid and support. And people can call upon their protective spirits to come to their aid.

The values of Semai social living center on nurturance both in the form of material aid or emotional support and affiliation or the maintenance of harmonious relationships among relatives and community members. According to Semai ethics, "goodness" is characterized by helping, giving, and sharing, and "badness" is characterized by becoming angry, quarreling, and fighting (Robarchek, 1997:53). Therefore, people who are helpful, generous, and cooperative are good; those who are angry and violent are bad.

In this social and ethical climate, conflict is, by definition, bad and threatens the stability of Semai society. When psychologist Clayton Robarchek gave a sentence completion test to Semai respondents, for the sentence prompt "more than anything else, he/she is afraid of . . .," the most common response given was "a conflict (more common than evil spirits, tigers, and death combined)" (1997:54).

When conflict does erupt, or threatens to, the Semai have a formal mechanism to contain its intensity and scope. A meeting, called a *becharaa'* is organized, attended by the entire community. The meeting is aimed at airing grievances and allowing all interested parties to voice their concerns and opinions. In principle, kinship groups are likely to support their own members in disputes, but rather than be divisive this "taking sides" actually integrates the community because the Semai reckon descent bilaterally. Most people are related to many other people within the settlement through blood or marriage, so individuals are likely to have relatives on both sides of the dispute. Therefore, it is to the advantage of all community members to settle conflicts as amicably and quickly as possible. People are held responsible for creating problems for their relatives and thus they are under some pressure to avoid conflict and, when it occurs, to settle it without further disruption.

At the beginning of the *becharaa'*, people congregate in the headman's house and discuss mundane events of interest but not the dispute itself. After a while, an elder member of one of the disputants' kin group delivers a long oration about the importance of community interdependence and harmony. After he concludes, several other prominent people give similar speeches emphasizing the importance of unity and the need to resolve the dispute under question as quickly as possible.

At that point, one of the disputants takes the floor and argues his or her case, stating facts, explanations, justifications, and accusations against the other. When the first adversary completes the presentation, the other disputant follows suit, stating his or her interpretation of the facts, justifications for actions, and counteraccusations. Following these presentations, relatives of the principal disputants enter the proceedings, arguing for their own kin. These orations are followed by any other interested members of the community who may respond, offering interpretations and opinions. Of utmost significance, it is considered inappropriate for anyone to display anger or strong emotion in recounting events and in justifying his or her own or other people's actions.

The *becharaa'* may last several hours or, more likely, continue uninterrupted for several days and nights. The hosting headman provides food for all in attendance during the many hours of the proceedings. From time to time, people sleep for short intervals and then rejoin the discussion. The *becharaa'* continues "until finally a point is reached where there is simply nothing left to say" (p. 55). At that time, the headman takes over and delivers a summary and consensus of the community. The headman then discusses the guilt of one or both of the disputants, offers alternatives to how they should have behaved, and admonishes them never to repeat their offending actions or words. Fines may be imposed on one or both of the principals. Finally, the *becharaa'* ends with long speeches by elders of both kin groups admonishing their relatives against improper behavior and again stressing the importance of community cohesion and harmony.

As Robarchek points out in his analysis of the Semai *becharaa'*, this mechanism deals with the affective, substantive, and social components of conflict. The Semai deal with the affective or emotional aspects of conflict by their extensive discussion of every angle of a dispute. By talking, retalking, and, one might say, overtalking the issues, an emotional catharsis and release is achieved for the disputants. At the end of the *becharaa'*, they are no doubt exhausted, not only physically but emotionally as well. Through nearly endless talk, the emotional aspects of conflict are dissipated. The substantive issues of the conflict are also talked over endlessly until "there is nothing more to say." Every angle is examined in the most minute detail possible. And, finally, the social content of disputes is addressed through the repetitive emphasis at the beginning and end of the *becharaa'* on the importance of community, cohesion, and harmonious social relationships.

According to Iranian cultural norms, parent-child relationships are imbued with special expectations whose violation, particularly if perpetrated by the child, lead to practices called *qahr* and *ashti* (Behzadi, 1994). The parent who feels hurt or somehow slighted by the child conveys *qahr*, an intention to withdraw from further interaction until the rift is mended. *Qahr* indirectly expresses a constellation of complex feelings of hate, anger, dislike, and hurt and at the same time evokes in the other person another complex set of feelings of guilt, shame, regret, compassion, and love. Recipients of *qahr* are prompted to correct their behavior and seek reconciliation. They may do this directly to the person offended or through intermediaries. The

? *In your culture or group, what are some examples of ways that aggression may be channeled to avoid conflict?*

cultural practice of *ashti* is this stage of mediation and reconciliation. The word itself can also be used to mean "to end a war," "to compromise with someone," and "to forget disappointment and resentment about someone" (Behzadi, 1994:322). The successful use of *qahr* and *ashti* depends on people's sensitivity to interpersonal signals that are not directly stated, especially in family relationships or close friendships where people expect others to respond appropriately without overt cues.

Role of Reciprocity in Conflict Avoidance

In some societies, it is expected that antagonisms and conflicts will surface in the context of specific occasions, giving people opportunities to vent feelings of anger, rivalry, and envy in a culturally controlled manner. For example, among the Toraja, a farming and livestock-raising people of South Sulawesi, Indonesia, anger and strong negative emotions are avoided in most daily contexts, but they are likely to arise at ritual occasions when sacrificed animals are butchered and distributed to the participants. According to Toraja etiquette, the person who distributes meat must pay heed to the relative status and prestige of the recipients (Hollan, 1997). However, because relative status and prestige in Toraja society are flexible and inherently unstable, the meat distributor may inevitably hurt the feelings of some of the recipients who believe that they should have received larger or more prestigious shares than other recipients. A person's expression of anger or resentment in such contexts is considered normal, even predictable.

What are the main sources of conflict in your family, group, or community? What do you do to counteract conflict and limit damage?

Outside these ritualized contexts, however, the overt expression of anger is considered dangerous and threatening to community stability. When disputes over other issues arise, they are handled through a number of intersecting cultural norms that are aimed at avoiding or at least limiting the intensity and scope of conflict. Incidents that may stir anger and lead to disputes often involve people's feelings of having been shamed. Such incidents include a spouse's adultery or failure to fulfill domestic responsibilities. In addition to spousal concerns, people are vigilant about making or receiving requests for resources or services from other villagers. People are careful about making requests of others because of the shame involved in being turned down. And they are hesitant to grant requests because they worry that their offer will not be reciprocated at some future time when they are in need. In essence, these interpersonal matters hinge on the principle of reciprocity, defined in Chapters 6 and 7 in the context of economic exchange. In any context, reciprocity refers to the expectation that people can depend on one another for material and emotional support. Among the Toraja, additional conflicts may arise over resources, particularly land. The most intense disputes, some leading to physical aggression, arise over disputes involving land.

To counteract conflict and limit community damage, Toraja culture transmits critical values and patterns of behavior. People learn to avoid others with whom they have disputes or even potential conflict. Confronting another individual directly is highly inappropriate. It is the Toraja's belief that when conflicts and anger erupt in ritualized contexts such as ceremonial meat distributions, the anger that is revealed should not be carried over into any other daily context. In addition, people who are the targets of someone's anger must not appear to hold a grudge against the person expressing hostility. Furthermore, the Toraja believe that a person should refrain from showing anger even if it is legitimate anger caused by a wrong committed by another. According to Douglas Hollan, "A person who publicly berates or humiliates someone for being a thief is criticized more than the act of theft itself" (1997:64). Finally, if disputes arise, village elders act as mediators in order to resolve conflicts. They lecture the parties about proper behavior and restore at least the appearance of social harmony.

REVIEW

Human strategies for avoiding conflict, in addition to systems of social control, include special social roles for peacemakers, deference behavior, and the principle of reciprocity. Deferential behavior includes expressing politeness and making apologies. Societies also have socially accepted or ritualized ways of channeling aggression, such as the Inuit song duels, as well as procedures for settling grievances and disputes.

WITCHCRAFT AND RITUAL IN CONFLICT RESOLUTION

In some societies, rituals may provide the means of avoiding or resolving conflicts and breaches of proper behavior. For example, among the Taita, a farming and cattle-herding people of Kenya, anger is dealt with in a complex ceremony that links anger with illness. Negative emotions, especially anger, are thought to be one of the most common causes of illness. But it is not the angry person who becomes ill. Rather, it is the person at whom the anger is directed who suffers misfortune or illness. If a person has been slighted, insulted, or wronged by someone else, the person who has been wronged naturally becomes angry and resentful. The Taita believe that although anger may be justifiable and legitimate, unresolved and brewing anger is what is most likely to cause illness.

This !Kung Ju/'hoansi man, N!eisi n!a, throws discs to divine the future in Botswana.

When a person becomes ill, a diviner asks for anyone to come forward who feels he or she might be the cause of the patient's illness because of the anger the person harbors toward the patient. It is no shame to come forward, because an admission of responsibility helps solidify community values and restore individual and social harmony. Finally, a person admits his or her anger toward the patient and agrees to participate in a ritual cure. During the cure, the angry person "casts out anger" (Harris, 1986). He or she ritually takes in a mouthful of water and then spits it out while calling blessings and good fortune upon the sick person. Through this dramatic enactment of anger and its expulsion, the patient and the person causing the illness are reunited and reconciled.

Because the ritual takes place publicly, it also enacts and dramatizes the importance of understanding and forgiveness. Both parties have behaved badly; the sick person is judged to have wronged the person who harbors the anger, and the angry person has violated social norms by holding grudges. And while the anger is understandable and legitimate, it needs to be expelled so that both the community and the patient can be healed. Thus, Taita rituals emphasize the importance of restoring community and interpersonal harmony.

Beliefs about **witchcraft** may function both as methods of social control and as channels for anger toward others. Witchcraft beliefs include the notion that people can use spirit powers to cause harm to others, leading to illness, misfortune, and death. Belief in witchcraft serves to control anger in a complex interplay of fears of being both a target of witches and a target of accusations of witchcraft. That is, in most societies with witchcraft practices and beliefs, people attempt to control angry outbursts and demonstrations of interpersonal antagonisms because they fear that they might offend, knowingly or unknowingly, a person who practices witchcraft. The witch has the power to retaliate and cause misfortune, illness, or death. But people also attempt to control their anger and jealousies because an angry, jealous person is likely to be accused of being a witch. These are informal sanctions controlling or responding to people's behavior.

In a study of witchcraft accounts given by respondents from the Cibecue settlement of the Western Apache in Arizona, Keith Basso (1989) recounts the ways in which occurrences of misfortune are attributed to the action of witches and the ways that accusations are used to channel anger and hostilities between community members. People who become ill after being the target of someone's angry outburst often accuse the latter of being a witch and having caused them harm. Such an accusation is difficult to shake off unless the accused person can excuse the behavior by saying that he or she was drunk and therefore not in control or responsible for words spoken.

In addition, accusations sometimes come from men directed at their mothers-in-law. Apache society is matrilineal and postmarital residence is frequently matrilocal, a

witchcraft
A belief system that functions as a mechanism of social control by channeling anger toward others.

pattern even more prominent in the past. But whether or not the married couple lives with the wife's family, a woman's mother continues to have influence over her daughter's actions.

In the current context of changing norms about household structure and gender roles, men sometimes resent what they consider to be interference from their mothers-in-law in their conjugal relationship. Acknowledging the strong ties between mother and daughter, however, married men often feel that they cannot directly challenge the mother-in-law's authority. Accusing the woman of witchcraft accomplishes the goal of criticizing her in a traditional way, that is, through witchcraft accusations. The elder woman can counter the accusation by stressing her kindness, responsibility, and adherence to sound ethical principles, noting her generosity and helpfulness to the couple and their children as well as her general good character. Still, whether or not the accusation is believed by community consensus, it allows the son-in-law a way to channel his anger and give it at least temporary voice.

REVIEW

Through religious or spiritual beliefs and practices, people ritually treat feelings of anger and aggression that underlie conflict. Diviners may magically remove negative feelings or causes of conflict, for example. Witchcraft is a powerful mechanism of social control because people fear being accused of these practices as much as they fear being victims.

PATTERNS OF FAMILY AND COMMUNITY CONFLICT

Although there are many cultural-specific and individual causes of conflict, there also are some overall general patterns in the content of disputes. Within families, disputes may arise over personal preferences and styles of interaction. There may be arguments over the proper course of action when decisions have to be made. When parents arrange marriages for their children, there are obvious possibilities of disagreement between the parents as well as with their children whose lives are being affected. Such conflicts tend to be worked out through the give-and-take of conversation, deference to others, and respect due certain family members because of their status and authority.

This Pakistani woman sought refuge in a women's shelter after her husband burned her two years ago.

In societies with polygynous or polyandrous marriages, there can be jealousies aroused by any favoritism shown by the central spouse to his or her wives or husbands. Co-wives or co-husbands in plural marriages may compete with each other and harbor resentments if they perceive that they have been unfairly treated or slighted. But co-spouses often get along well, finding friendship and mutual support with work and emotional stress. Particularly in patrilineal, patrilocal households, co-wives may become allies, aiding each other with housework and child care and giving emotional support.

Family Violence

In patriarchal family structures in India and elsewhere (see Chapter 9), young wives marrying into patriarchal households often face verbal and physical abuse from their mothers-in-law and other senior relatives while they are being integrated into the husband's family. Women in such situations must live with a great deal of resentment, anger, and shame caused by the treatment they receive and by their own powerlessness. The potential for domestic violence is greatest in strongly patriarchal societies. A jealous husband or rejected suitor in Pakistan may seek revenge against a woman by throwing acid on her face and body, disfiguring her and making her ineligible for either infidelity or marriage. In India, in a phenomenon known as "dowry death," young brides may be murdered, set ablaze by their husbands or inlaws, who then arrange for another marriage with another dowry. Reform movements to modernize law codes in these countries address these and other "traditional" crimes against women. (These issues are addressed further in Chapter 10.)

In societies where property is valued and accumulated, siblings may compete to establish themselves as preferred heirs, especially if there are no automatic rules of inheritance. Again, with rural India as an example, brothers may try to curry favor with the father, hoping to inherit the largest or best-located section of family landholdings. But because conflict among brothers is considered inappropriate and violates the ethics of family solidarity, their wives are often blamed for causing friction in the household. The women are already in a vulnerable social position, having moved away from their parental home, so they are easy scapegoats.

Families, and especially kin groups organized as lineages and clans, often have both informal and formal mechanisms for dealing with disputes among members. The heads of families and the heads of lineages or clans are aware of conflicts among their members and have the authority to mediate and resolve disputes. Lacking coercive power to have their judgments enforced, they can nonetheless influence the parties concerned to follow their advice because of the prestige of their position.

In Native American societies, disputes were settled in different ways, depending on the relationship between the people involved. Within families, disagreements were worked out by advice given by other family members, especially senior men and women in the household or in the clan. Disagreements tended to arise within families over personal matters. Because individuals did not own land and resources, people did not argue or disagree over inheritance of property or over rights to use communal territory.

Conflicts in Bands and Tribes

In foraging band societies, because land and other resources are usually not owned by individuals, conflicts over property are unlikely to emerge. The conflicts that do arise tend to be caused by jealousies, often of a sexual nature. Disputes or antagonisms may surface between rivals for a person's affections or between suitors hoping to marry the same woman. Such jealousies may lead to physical assaults, but this rarely happens in most band societies. Instead, people may attempt to use magical means such as witchcraft and harmful spells to deter or injure rivals.

In tribal societies, in addition to conflicts with personal motivations, people may engage in disputes over property. Where land and other valuable resources are owned by individuals, people may accuse others of theft or destruction of property. Even where land and resources are controlled by kinship groups communally, there may be accusations of trespass onto kin-owned resources by outsiders.

In some tribal societies, social etiquette regulates the behavior of neighbors and even of strangers in other people's territories. For example, among the Eastern Pomo, a foraging society of northern California, certain resource sites were communally owned by residents of villages or members of kinship groups. Villages owned hunting territories in surrounding areas and marked off their borders by twisting the branches of oak trees. In addition, some trees, said to belong to particular families, were marked in an identifiable design recognized by everyone in the village. Landings on lakes from which people fished were also the property of individual families and were so marked. Coastal Pomo owned sections along the streams that flowed to the sea, but no part of the ocean shoreline was considered private property.

Any claim to property was publicized throughout the community. However, if a family's resource areas were unproductive in any given year, they might ask permission to gather plants or to hunt and fish in areas claimed by a relative or neighbor. Such requests were customarily granted. The Pomo, therefore, recognized individual or communal claims to land and resources, but the needy could make use of the resources to sustain themselves in hard times. Taking resources from someone else's land was not considered theft as long as permission had been requested and granted. This social etiquette forestalled the likelihood of a dispute arising over resources.

In many tribal societies, disputes are mediated by a council of village elders. Membership in these councils may be determined by lineage or clan affiliation, or the

GLOBALIZATION

A result of globalization is that many international nongovernmental organizations have arisen to address problems of family and community conflict. For example, the International Women's Rights Action Watch (IWRAW) and the International Child Abuse Network (ICAN) monitor and report on the status of women and children, respectively; and university-affiliated programs such as the Sustainable Community Network (SCN) and the Center for International Development and Conflict Resolution (CIDCR) help communities and regions to resolve conflicts. Appreciating cultural similarities and understanding cultural differences are essential to these efforts.

Leopard-skin chiefs worked to prevent blood feuds among the Nuer by mediating conflicts.

members can be drawn from any segment in the village. Leaders tend to be selected on the basis of community consensus because of their intelligence, success, sound judgment, and moral character.

Blood Vengeance and the Feud

In tribal societies where the stakes of conflict are high, there may be specific people who function as mediators and employ a combination of interpersonal and ritual skills. For example, among the Nuer, a cattle-herding and farming people of southern Sudan, conflicts over cattle frequently arose over the rightful ownership of the animals. Cattle raiding was not uncommon, leading to accusations and counteraccusations. There was always the danger that these conflicts could lead to physical violence and even to murder. And once a kinsman was murdered, it was the responsibility of his kin group to seek revenge by killing either the original antagonist or another member of his kinship group. One revenge killing would then necessitate another round of **vengeance** on the part of the kinship group of the next victim, leading to a series of killings and eventually to a state of **blood feud.**

The Nuer instituted a process to forestall the escalation of a conflict to murder and blood feuds. Certain men functioned as "leopard-skin chiefs." They were ritual practitioners who controlled spirit powers that could be used against any person who failed to comply with their advice in a conflict. But essentially the leopard-skin chief was a mediator who functioned as an intermediary between the two rival kinship groups. Since he belonged to neither of the antagonists' kinship group, he was not identified as an ally of anyone involved but, rather, was an objective negotiator. He went from one group to another and back again, carrying messages and demands. His role was to negotiate a settlement, usually a payment in cattle between the two disputing parties. In cases of murder, he attempted to convince the kin group of the murdered man to accept reparations as settlement for the crime rather than to seek bloody revenge.

Although leopard-skin chiefs had no power to enforce their decisions, except for the threat of supernatural harm, their advice was generally taken after protracted negotiations. These mediators were skilled orators, able to persuade people to come to agreements that were in the interest of the entire community. And the lengthy negotiations allowed the wronged kinship group to save face by initially putting up a stiff resistance. But in the end, they came around to accepting the leopard-skin chief's advice for the good of restoring social harmony in the community.

> **REVIEW**
>
> Patterns of family conflict tend to arise from tensions in marital, co-wife, and in-law relationships. Domestic violence against women is widespread in some societies. Conflicts over property and land are much more common in chiefdoms and states than in bands or tribes. Common patterns of tribal conflict include raiding, vengeance, and blood feuds among kin groups. These communities have special bodies to hear grievances and try to prevent bloodshed.

PATTERNS OF CONFLICT BETWEEN GROUPS

vengeance
Aggression against others based on the principle of revenge.

blood feud
Ongoing conflict between kin groups or communities, based on vengeance.

As discussed, many indigenous communities traditionally had both informal and formal means of resolving disputes. Village leaders, usually informally selected through community consensus, helped mediate disputes by appealing to all parties concerned and stressing the importance of community harmony and stability. Through both private and public efforts, leaders typically tried to create a climate in which mediation and agreement could be successful. But community leaders had no coercive powers; they could not enforce their opinions or decisions on people. Rather, they were skilled orators with powers of persuasion and personal charisma.

If conflicts continued and the parties refused to come to a negotiated settlement, a person had the option of leaving the band or village and joining another group. Because band and village membership was flexible, people could decide to take up residence elsewhere. Because kinship was a fundamental organizing principle, people often had relatives in several communities, and people related by blood or marriage were obligated by the ethics of kinship support to provide assistance and hospitality to one another.

If disputes arose between different villages, the leaders attempted to resolve the disputes through mediation and negotiation. When these efforts failed, disputes continued to fester, sometimes leading to physical assault or murder. Then a spate of revenge killings could ensue, leading to blood feuds and prolonged antagonism. Conflicts could escalate into raiding and warfare between communities in different tribes. These conflicts, because they are between different groups acting as collective units rather than as individuals, tend to be more deadly, escalating into warfare when diplomacy fails.

Warfare

Armed aggression and hostilities between groups can occur anywhere, but the causes and character of **warfare** vary in different types of societies. In warfare, armed and organized fighters attack specified enemies with the intent of causing injury or death and possibly destroying property or the means of sustenance, thus harming survivors as well. Warfare is least likely and least destructive in bands than in any other kind of society. The reasons are multiple and interrelated. People in nomadic bands usually do not have a strong sense of territorial ownership and control, so fighting over land and resources is not likely. And because nomadic peoples do not have many possessions, they have little desire to raid neighbors for their property, though raiding sometimes occurs between groups belonging to different bands. Blood feuds may develop following the murder of a member of one band by an outsider as the victim's relatives seek revenge against the assailant and his or her band. While such hostile actions can lead to cycles of raiding and killing, the number of people affected is relatively few. And while the death of any one individual is a loss to the person who dies and is deeply mourned by the person's relatives, such practices are not necessarily disruptive on a societal level.

In tribal societies, raiding and warfare may exact a deadlier toll on the population and be more disruptive. Motives for hostilities may include trespass on tribal territory for the purpose of exploiting tribal resources. Killings and revenge counterkillings are also contributing factors. But because of the ways in which tribal societies are organized, and because of their communal orientation, raiding and warfare generally do not have economic motives. Although some property may be stolen in a raiding expedition, and human captives may be brought back to the home community, tribal warriors rarely have the goal of ousting their enemies from territory and taking over lands and resources.

Tribal warfare is generally small scale, involving relatively few fighters. The organization of the war expedition tends to be based on voluntary association. Men may join in the war if they agree with the goals and if they perceive the leadership and organization to be sound. For example, among the Choctaw, an indigenous nation of Mississippi, raiding was occasionally carried out against neighboring groups. The goals of warfare were essentially ritual and social rather than economic, although booty was taken from the enemy if possible. In addition, enemy captives were brought back to the home villages. Male captives were sometimes burned to death, but women and children were usually adopted into Choctaw families.

Raiding had a social component because successful raids enhanced the status of the participants, especially the war leader. Raids were considered successful if warriors returned home with captives and booty to be divided among their number. Victorious warriors were greeted with cheers and feted with dances and feasts. However, if warriors returned home having suffered many casualties, the raid was considered a failure even if the enemy had been harmed. Lack of success often led to the dismissal of the war chief and another taking his place.

Although by far the majority of Choctaw warriors were men, women sometimes went on raids as well, especially if they were seeking revenge for relatives killed in previous campaigns. Women warriors, however, did not undergo the same ritual preparations

warfare
Armed aggression and hostilities between groups.

Choctaw warfare was surrounded by ritual protections and interpretation of omens. Once war was declared, the warriors participated in a war dance that lasted for eight days. They fasted and rubbed their bodies with spiritually powerful medicine. The Eagle Dance, shown here, was one of the dances that might be performed to welcome back warriors. (George Catlin [1796–1872]. "Eagle Dance, Choctaw," Oil on canvas, 19½ x 27½ in. Gift of Mrs. Joseph Harrison, Jr. Smithsonian American Art Museum, Washington, DC. Photo Credit: Smithsonian American Art Museum, Washington, DC/Art Resource, NY)

GLOBALIZATION

Traditional native approaches to conflict resolution were transformed as peoples were contacted and then overwhelmed by European colonizers. Fatalities increased in feuds and raids as bands and tribes replaced their wooden and stone arrows with iron and steel weapons and guns. Causes of warfare also changed from personal or group revenge to economic and political motives as groups vied with each other for access to trade and later fought to hold on to their remaining territories.

and protections as their male comrades did (Romans, 1962; Swanton, 1946). If any warrior had a dream of disaster, he or she was likely to return home. And if the war leader had such a dream, the raid would be abandoned. Warriors among the Choctaw had high social status, but other Native American groups viewed war as a sometimes necessary but never noble alternative to the peaceful, mediated resolution of disputes and conflicts.

Both the Choctaw and the Pomo examples (see Case Study) demonstrate common patterns in tribal societies. There were no standing armies; rather, volunteers joined a war party because of their own inclinations and goals. The reasons for a conflict were primarily social and ritual, especially seeking revenge for previous wrongs done to the community. Once the conflict ended, the principal goal was restoration of harmonious relationships rather than humiliation and subjugation of the losers.

Impacts of Globalization on Warfare

Throughout time, technological, material, and organizational inequality between peoples has led to rapid social and culture change. Beginning in the sixteenth century, for example, European contact contributed to both greater unity and greater conflict among indigenous peoples. European technology made that conflict more lethal, and European technological superiority in warfare made overall conquest likely.

Prior to European contact, most Native American societies lacked formal mechanisms of dispute management in conflicts between different tribes. Perhaps the most formalized system was that of the Iroquois Confederacy, which was founded to eliminate conflicts among five nations. The arrival of Europeans at first prompted the Iroquois Confederacy to compete with other native groups for access to trade and influence. For more than a century, the Iroquois were able to expand their domain of power through skillful negotiation and military prowess, reaching as far south as the Carolinas and as far west as Lake Superior. But then the growing population and military might of the United States led to the confederacy's loss of influence and power shortly after the American Revolution. Elsewhere on the continent, the presence of Europeans stimulated open hostilities and warfare among Native Americans. The cultural contexts of warfare and tactics and goals also changed.

Case study

Pomoan Warfare

Among the Pomo of northern California, war might erupt when trespassers gathered resources or hunted in another group's recognized territory without permission. But more often such conflicts were motivated more by the desire to seek revenge for an alleged poisoning death of a member of one's community. There were no established war leaders, but any man might organize a group of followers. War leaders were temporary figures who were looked to because of their military skills but were not universally admired. They were referred to as "good bad men" (Loeb, 1926:200).

Pomo battles with neighboring tribes usually entailed confrontations between the two groups organized into lines, perhaps consisting of about 100 in each, standing about 30 yards apart. They shot arrows, threw stones, and hurled insults at one another but did not engage in direct contact. Women and boys sometimes accompanied the warriors and assisted on the sidelines by picking up arrows and stones that had been thrown, resupplying their own warriors. The battle might end as soon as anyone was seriously wounded, or it might continue, but fighting always ceased at night. Also, raids were sometimes carried out against an enemy village, generally resulting in higher casualties than in the formal line battles.

The Pomoan attitude toward war as a sometimes necessary but unfortunate breach in social harmony was reflected in the rituals practiced once a conflict ended. Chiefs of the victorious party acted as peacemakers, bringing a peace offering of clamshell beads collected from their villagers to the community of their defeated foe. Negotiations were prefaced by sending a messenger to the enemy village, often a person related to them through marriage. When the chief arrived, he made a formal speech apologizing for the suffering that had been caused. The chief of the defeated village accepted the reparation and made a speech voicing hope that peace would be restored. The beads received from the victors were divided among the mourning families who had lost men in battle. Through these procedures, reconciliation of the two former foes was achieved. And, significantly, it was the victorious community that paid damages to the losers as compensation for the deaths that they had caused.

The increase in the incidence of warfare was due to two interrelated processes. First, as the crowns of France, Britain, the Netherlands, and Spain engaged in wars against each other both in Europe and in their colonial adventures, the European powers attempted to forge alliances with various native groups to aid their own governments. And when the Europeans fought each other, their native allies became embroiled in these conflicts. When Indians fought with and for their European partners, they were fighting against both European enemies and the tribes with whom those enemies were linked. New animosities, therefore, developed between native groups.

A second reason for the growth of intertribal conflict was the emergence of competition over land and resources. By the mid-seventeenth century, European powers sought land for settlement in addition to their earlier goals of obtaining trade goods and resources from North America. As the Europeans expropriated Indian land and resources, native groups competed to hold on to their territories. As they lost access to their lands, people competed for the remaining land and resources, often through direct confrontation and warfare. Wars in the northeast and southeast increased from the early seventeenth until the late eighteenth century. As trade and European settlement moved steadily westward in the eighteenth and nineteenth centuries, Indians

Culture Change

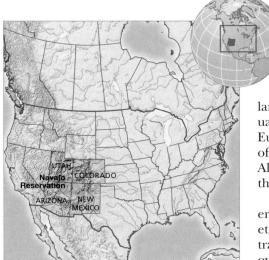

DISPUTE RESOLUTION AMONG THE DINÉ THEN AND NOW

After the establishment of the United States, American officials used the army to "pacify" Indian nations who were fighting against each other, particularly in the Great Plains, where many groups were converging as they were being pushed out of their more easterly lands. Once the new country was organized, officials opposed the continuation of intertribal warfare even though it was originally instigated by Europeans and their descendants. Turmoil in the plains stood in the way of the westward expansion of the United States, so it had to be stopped. Although intertribal warfare had benefited Europeans and Americans in the beginning of the colonial era, it had outlasted its usefulness.

Once all native groups were forcibly settled on reservations, the federal government imposed its laws and procedures on indigenous societies. Traditional systems of leadership were bypassed and eventually traditional systems of conflict resolution and mediation were officially overridden by federal legislation. In a far-reaching statute, Congress passed the Major Crimes Act in 1885. This act allowed federal courts to claim jurisdiction over Indians who committed specific crimes on Indian reservations. Until that time, Indians who committed crimes on their own reservations would be dealt with by tribal court systems, where they existed. The Major Crimes Act specified federal jurisdiction over seven crimes: murder, manslaughter, rape, assault with intent to kill, arson, burglary, and larceny (Bacheller, 1997:10).

In 1976, the U.S. Congress passed the Indian Crimes Act, specifying an additional seven crimes to be dealt with by federal courts: kidnapping, assault with intent to commit rape, assault with a dangerous weapon, assault resulting in serious bodily injury, robbery, incest, and statutory rape (sexual intercourse with a female under the age of 16) (French, 2003:58–59). Any Indian accused of one of these major crimes is tried and sentenced in federal courts. On reservations where a tribal court system operates, the tribal court has jurisdiction over lesser crimes. On smaller reservations that lack their own court system, Indians accused of any offense are dealt with by federal authorities.

Some indigenous peoples in North America are returning to traditional practices. A number of tribes across the country have reinstituted practices of *banishment* for chronic wrongdoers (*New York Times*, 2004). In former times, individuals who committed wrongs, assaulted people repeatedly, or violated other social rules might be exiled, forced to leave their own villages. Sometimes they were taken in by another community, but if their past history were well known, it would be unlikely that any other group would accept them, fearing that they might cause more trouble. Now some tribes are returning to the imposition of banishment, usually as a last resort, especially in cases of drug or alcohol abuse (*Indian Time*, 2003). Few other avenues are open to tribal courts for repeat offenders, as federal laws only permit tribal courts to impose sentences of no longer than one year in jail and no more than a $5,000 fine. Some tribal councils see banishment as a particularly effective means of dealing with non-Indians who are causing trouble on the reservation.

As part of efforts by some Native Americans to reestablish effective traditional practices in their communities, the Diné (Navajo) reintroduced its peacemaker processes of conflict resolution. American-style systems of justice were forced upon the Diné by federal policy in 1892, about twenty-five years after the people had been released from four years of roundup and virtual incarceration in an army base at Fort Sumner, New Mexico, from 1864 until 1868. For about ninety years, therefore, the Diné were under federal guidelines for adjudicating both criminal and civil offenses. The U.S. model of justice is essentially adversarial, where a court divorced from the social network of community ascertains the guilt or innocence of a person accused of wrongdoing. In the legal process before the court, each side argues its own point of view, contradicting or explaining facts introduced by its adversary. The court's decision renders a defendant either guilty or not guilty of the offense.

These procedures, and the moral theory on which they are based, contradict traditional Diné ethics. In the Diné view, conflicts are disturbances of the harmony that should exist within a person and between one person and others, with the environment, and with the spirit world. In 1982, the Diné nation established its Navajo Peacemaker Court to coexist with the American-style adversarial system. (French, 2003). According to Robert Yazzie, chief justice of the Navajo Nation, the Anglo-American court system is a "vertical system of justice where judges possess a tremendous amount of power to affect human lives, either to harm them or bring goodness to them. This vertical system relies on coercion to control and force people to do and not do something. . . . In the adversarial system the goal is to punish wrongdoers and teach them a lesson" (1992, p. 2).

Yazzie contrasts this system of justice with the Diné Peacemakers: "Traditionally, Navajos used a peacemaker to mediate disputes. Peacemakers help preserve ongoing relationships, within both immediate and extended families. The parties settled their disputes in a forum where they could talk and settle their problems by consent. In this way harmony was restored" (p. 3). Yazzie describes the Navajo Peacemaker system as horizontal system in contrast to the vertical system of Anglo-American justice.

The Navajo goals of peacemaking differ markedly from those of the Anglo-American system of crime and punishment. According to Yazzie,

> In the peacemaker process, the mediator aims at one goal, and one goal only—restoring true justice among individuals, families and the larger community and society. This is done by allowing the wrongdoer and the victim "to talk things out." Navajos have always believed that the more individuals are restored to harmony, the more the family, community, and society will live and function in a harmonious fashion. The ultimate goal of the Peacemaker process is to restore the minds, physical being, spirits, and emotional well-being of all people involved. (p. 4)

When the Navajo government reestablished the Peacemaker process, it set out procedures governing the Peacemakers and their duties and powers. Peacemakers may call people to meetings if they consider that those individuals might have a bearing either on understanding the nature of the problem or contributing to a resolution. However, they can only use cooperative and voluntary measures. They have no power to force individuals to participate, nor can they force a resolution on either party (French, 2003).

The Diné nation is divided into eighty-four districts or chapters. Residents of each chapter elect a member to represent its interests at the tribal council. Each chapter also has at least one officially recognized Peacemaker to serve that community. Anyone can be nominated and selected. The people chosen are generally leading, influential members of their communities and are of intelligence, sound judgment, and solid moral character.

The Peacemaker court does not have regularly scheduled meetings but convenes whenever requested by a member of the community. Any individual may ask for assistance from the court for problems in his or her family or community. While any type of issue or dispute may be brought for mediation, the Peacemaker court manual emphasizes its use for everyday problems, such as those arising between spouses, between married couples and their in-laws, between parents and children, and between neighbors. The court is not formally established to handle serious criminal offenses, such as murder, assault, and rape, but according to Chief Justice Yazzie, it may serve a purpose in such situations as well. He notes that the Diné and other native peoples of North America formerly had community-oriented systems of justice and conflict resolution where perpetrators of violent crimes could be compelled to pay compensation to the relatives of the person harmed. Some groups are experimenting with these traditional procedures to determine if they are as effective today as they were in the past.

Today Diné Peacemakers are mediators whose goal is to arrive at a common agreement among contending parties. Peacemakers utilize traditional Diné moral teachings, religious beliefs, and practices to restore harmony. Here Chief Justice Robert Yazzie of the Navajo Supreme Court speaks about Navajo culture and law prior to presentation of oral arguments to the court.

along the Mississippi River and its tributaries were affected. Intense wars of survival pitted native groups against one another. By the middle of the nineteenth century, inhabitants of the Great Plains also saw their territories crowded by Euro-American settlers and other Indians fleeing west from the sprawling conflicts in their own homelands.

Unlike most early warfare, wars of the later centuries were primarily generated by economic motives or the need to defend one's own community from invaders. Native warfare changed not only in frequency and motive but also in tactics. Warriors began to destroy the homes and fields of their enemy, leaving survivors with no means to sustain themselves. The goal of annihilating one's enemies or forcing them to flee in order to take land and resources was rare before the Europeans brought fundamental transformations in warfare.

Warfare in State Societies

In state societies, warfare has primarily economic and political goals. As discussed in Chapter 12, state societies are usually born through warfare and depend on armed combat or indirect pressure to compel neighboring groups to come under the jurisdiction of the expanding state society. States expand both territorially and politically by enlarging their spheres of influence and control. And the major means of accomplishing this expansion is through armed conflict or the threat of war.

The organization of warfare in state societies differs fundamentally from warfare in other types of cultures. State societies have standing armies composed of men (in some cases, also women) who are either part-time or full-time specialists. Fighters sometimes volunteer for that role, but in other cases they may be compelled to join the armed services. Warfare in state societies is organized and controlled by full-time leaders who plan the military campaigns and have absolute control over the soldiers and operations of battle. Unlike band or tribal warriors, state soldiers have little discretion in their actions. They must follow the lawful orders of their superior officers. The entire operation is structured hierarchically, in keeping with the hierarchical nature of all government functions in state societies. In some state societies, monopoly on the use of force is exerted internally as well as by the use of capital punishment to control internal enemies or violators of law.

Again, unlike band and tribal warfare, the goals of state warfare are either the total annihilation of the enemy or its humiliation into surrender and submission. Land and other property belonging to the loser may be confiscated by the victorious side. The inhabitants of the defeated communities may be forced to capitulate to the winners, becoming citizens of an expanding state but as a subjugated people. And in contrast to some tribal societies, such as the Pomo, it is the loser who pays tribute or reparations to the winner.

Not all wars end decisively but may instead have a negotiated end that gives some advantages or concessions to both sides. In modern warfare, losers are usually permitted some face-saving options so that their economic and political losses and their public humiliation do not breed deep resentment against the winners. Such seething resentment might be counterproductive from the winner's perspective because it might turn the losers into perpetual resistors against the winner's control and influence. After World War I, the German government felt that provisions of the Treaty of Versailles were humiliating, providing one of the complex causes of the rise of extreme nationalist and fascist sentiment that led to Nazism and to World War II.

Even though many countries in the world today spend large sums of money on armaments, both in absolute terms and relative to other spending, there are several exceptional examples of countries that control military spending and the influence of the military on their government. Following World War II, both the Japanese and the German governments restricted the use of military forces following their defeat and humiliation in the world community. The Japanese constitution does not permit the country's soldiers to fight in wars outside of the territory of Japan. The purpose of the military is exclusively defensive. In Germany, laws also limit the roles of German soldiers to defensive operations within Germany or to strictly peacekeeping functions abroad.

The small Central American country of Costa Rica abolished its army in 1948. Its constitution, written in 1949, expressly prohibits the creation of an army. Remarkably, Costa Rica has survived as a demilitarized state without civil unrest or discord, although surrounded by neighbors such as Honduras, El Salvador, and Nicaragua, where civil war, repressive government action, and external military involvement have destabilized the countries for several decades (Arias, 1997). The example of Costa Rica is an exception, however, in today's world.

Despite efforts to develop international mechanisms to resolve disputes through peaceful means, many armed conflicts continue to erupt throughout the world. And while every continent has been a battleground, some regions have seemingly intractable problems. In Africa, for example, since 1990 civil wars over control of the central governments have broken out in Liberia, Sierra Leone, Ivory Coast, Rwanda, and Burundi. A long, ongoing war over resources, especially diamonds, is causing havoc in the Democratic Republic of Congo. In all of these conflicts, civilians have been killed and tens of thousands of survivors have been routed from their homes. In North Africa, civil wars and struggles for internal regional independence have shattered Algeria, Morocco, Ethiopia (Eritrea), and Sudan.

In the Middle East, the Israeli-Palestinian crisis continues unabated. Both sides accuse the other of terrorist acts against civilians. And both sides refuse to compromise on key points of disagreement, although it is clear that the only way to reach a lasting peace is mutual recognition of each other's legitimate claims for security and autonomy. The war being waged by Israelis and Palestinians also has a destabilizing effect on both the region and the world. The growth and intensity of Islamic fundamentalism can be traced, in part, to the geopolitics of the Israeli-Palestinian conflict and the perceived role of the United States as a staunch ally of Israel.

Members of some Islamic fundamentalist factions conduct campaigns within Middle Eastern countries, attempting to undermine the governments and establish regimes dominated by conservative religious authorities. Some of these countries have moderate leadership (Jordan, Egypt), and others are ruled by autocratic monarchs (Saudi Arabia). And although Al Qaeda is not solely a religious fundamentalist organization, it effectively recruits among such groups because of its anti-American stance.

In Their Own Voices

Testimony from South Africa's Truth and Reconciliation Hearings of 1998

Following the end of apartheid in South Africa, the newly elected government, led by the African National Congress (ANC), established the Truth and Reconciliation Commission in order to confront and help resolve past tragedies with the goal of uncovering the causes of racial violence and establishing a unified country. The commission held hearings in 1998 to determine whether individuals who had committed politically motivated racial killings and assaults during the decades of civil war deserved amnesty for their crimes. Persons requesting amnesty had to testify at the hearings, confessing their crimes, explaining their motivations, and conveying their remorse. On the basis of their testimony, putting great weight on their sincerity and their insights into their crimes, members of the commission decided whether or not the person deserved amnesty and release.

The commission was established because South Africans decided that revenge against the perpetrators of racial crimes would create division and hostility for generations to come. In the words of one of the commission's members, "It is natural to want revenge but we need to rebuild a nation."

In these excerpts, perpetrators of racially motivated crimes give testimony, explaining their deeds. In the first, a black South African discusses his role in the killing of Amy Biehl, a U.S. citizen who was in South Africa working in the antiapartheid movement. In the second excerpt, two white policemen discuss their role in the killing of four members of the African National Congress. The questioners are all members of the Truth and Reconciliation Commission.

Testimony of Ntombeko Ambrose Peni, one of the men who killed Amy Biehl

MR BRINK: You had absolutely no idea of what Amy Biehl's political views were, isn't that the situation?

MR PENI: I did not know.

MR BRINK: And your evidence here was that you participated in this murderous attack because the aims of your organisation was to bring back land to the African people, now what I want to know is, how would the killing of an unarmed, defenceless woman possibly help you to achieve that aim?

MR PENI: We believed that the minority White people ruling the country would realise that we wanted our land back. We also believed that they were going to give up this land back to the African people.

MR BRINK: Is it your evidence that by murdering, in the most brutal fashion, Amy Biehl, the African people would get their land back?

MR PENI: Yes it's my evidence.

First of all I would like to rectify something, gender was not significant. Our aim was to attack each White person and go forward.

JUDGE WILSON: But it was not the aim of the PAC at that time to kill every White person they saw, was it?

MR PENI: It could not happen that every person be killed, but there was one slogan: *'One Settler, one bullet'.*

JUDGE WILSON: Do you agree it was not the policy of the PAC to kill White persons on sight, which is what you did on this afternoon, do you agree with that?

Underlying many Middle Eastern conflicts is the geopolitics of oil, because of world dependence on oil as a principal energy source. Oil-rich countries, whether in the Middle East, Asia, or South America, are able to affect the economies of nations that rely on their supplies by lowering or raising output, thus influencing prices on the world market. This in turn leads to political reactions by world powers, which try to control the oil-producing governments so that officials will make decisions beneficial to them.

MR PENI: It is true that the PAC could not have killed everybody that they saw, however, the PAC was aware that killing each White person the land would come back to the African people.

MR BRINK: Mr Peni, isn't it the position that on that dreadful afternoon you were involved in a mindless, savage attack on this young woman, and that it was not politically motivated at all?

MR PENI: Our killing Amy Biehl had everything to do with politics.

Testimony of Mr. Du Plessis, a security police officer, who helped set up and kill the Cradock 4, members of the African National Congress

MR BOOYENS: Did you have anything personal against any of these four persons?

MR DU PLESSIS: I can state this unequivocally, absolutely not.

MR BOOYENS: To the extent that you were involved in the fact that they lost their lives ultimately, why were you involved?

MR DU PLESSIS: Because I felt or had the opinion that it would prevent the anarchy, that it would disempower the state of anarchy. . . . They were definitely members of the ANC. I don't have precise facts about their activities any more, but I know that they were all buried under the flag of communism.

MR BOOYENS: Very well. And for which reason did you personally become involved in these matters?

MR DU PLESSIS: In this case I received an order to become involved. I also felt that it would be the only way to attempt to stop the onslaught.

MR BOOYENS: Mr Du Plessis, today it is almost 15 years since what happened. How do you feel now about what happened?

MR DU PLESSIS: One is indeed sorry and I am speaking for myself that a person as a result of one's job, was compelled to such steps.

For us who believed in the struggle of the National Party, we also believed that if the ANC/SACP alliance were to take over, it would signify the end of the white in Africa.

Right or wrong, that is what we believed. It is a great pity that two political parties such as the NP and the ANC could not sit down and discuss this matter and sort it out. And as a result, some of us and some of them died in the struggle.

I am sorry, especially for the families. I am sincerely sorry, not only for the sake of the families, but for the families of the members of the Security Branch to which we had to give orders.

CHAIRPERSON: Do I understand correctly that if it had not been for the nature of the work, that none of this would have happened?

MR DU PLESSIS: I was placed in a situation where I believed that this was the only way out. If I had been in a different position, perhaps I would have regarded the situation differently and believed something different, but I can tell you in all earnesty that that is what I believed to be the only viable solution.

Testimony of Mr. Taylor, another of the policemen

MR POTGIETER: Was it wrong if black people demanded human rights?

MR TAYLOR: Mr Chairperson, if you can give the opportunity to answer the question fully. It wasn't a question of the whole black population of South Africa, it was about the activation of radicals and mass activities and this demand for human rights was about the question of housing, schools, accommodation, books, to vote etc., etc. In other words it was part of the whole liberation struggle, yes. And I wish to reiterate that is how I thought and believed in 1985.

MR POTGIETER: And you thought it was wrong?

MR TAYLOR: Yes.

MR POTGIETER: But now you think it's right?

MR TAYLOR: Of course.

You must remember that if I have to admit, at that time I had been indoctrinated, I was politicised and for me all of these things were part of the struggle to overthrow the government and at time I thought that way and I felt that way.

The circumstances and the climate of that time, the feelings among the people, all these things have changed and we can see it now in 1998 that everything has changed.

From South African government Website:
www.doj.gov.za/trc/trc_frameset.htm.

CRITICAL THINKING QUESTIONS

What do the three testimonies have in common? Do you agree with the assertion that events must be interpreted in their historical and cultural contexts? To what extent do you think that public discussion is effective as a means of postconflict reconciliation?

Mixed in with these issues is the desire to control the proliferation of nuclear weapons. Although all the permanent members of the Security Council of the United Nations (United States, Britain, France, Russia, and China) have had nuclear weapons for decades, they lead the effort to prevent other nations from acquiring them. Other countries resent this stance, which they see as a hypocrisy. Many developing nations believe that attitudes about the proliferation of nuclear weapons discriminate against

Flames and smoke pour from a building at the Pentagon on September 11, 2001. Al Qaeda operatives are responsible for numerous deadly terrorist attacks throughout the world, including the destruction of the World Trade Center and the partial destruction of the Pentagon.

GLOBALIZATION

In modern times, as weaponry has become increasingly sophisticated and deadly—nuclear warfare and biological warfare—and as wars have embroiled larger numbers of countries, international efforts have been directed at establishing formal mechanisms for conflict resolution. The United Nations and the World Court, formed after World War II, are two international groups that mediate conflicts.

them. These reactions persist and cloud the basic issue of the danger posed to all peoples by the very existence of nuclear weaponry and the threats to use them.

Internal disputes and civil wars can damage societies for generations, leaving animosities and desires for revenge. In South Africa, for example, decades of clandestine and then open armed struggle of blacks and progressive whites were waged against apartheid laws that curtailed the legal rights of the majority blacks, forced residential and occupational segregation, and left most blacks in dire poverty. These struggles were met with the full military force of the government until the authorities recognized that the end of their power was inevitable. In 1992, Nelson Mandela, a leading member of the African National Congress, was sworn in as the first president elected after all South Africans were granted the right to vote. The new government understood that it needed to confront the conflicts of its past in order to resolve disputes and arrive at peaceful reconciliation. It did not ignore the past injustices directed at the majority blacks, but it also did not ignore the legitimate claims of the minority whites.

South Africa today is a very different country than it was before 1992. The majority black population has equal legal rights and full representation in governing institutions. The African National Congress is the country's major political party, winning most local and national elections. However, problems of economic justice continue. The majority of blacks are still poor, living in substandard housing, lacking adequate educational and medical services, and suffering high rates of unemployment. Despite government attempts, racial animosities continue to plague the country, especially in the countryside where black farmers and rural residents live in poverty with little hope of immediate improvement. White farmers fear that they will be the targets of racially motivated attacks. While these fears are perhaps exaggerated, they are based on real occurrences. And in both rural and urban areas, rates of violent crime are among the highest in the world. Rape and domestic violence against women are especially frequent crimes, with rates that are again among the highest worldwide. The efforts of the government sometimes fail because of a lack of resources and because of the damaging legacies of racial tension and economic and political injustice.

Anthropology Applied

Legal Anthropology

Applied legal anthropology touches all aspects of law, especially in the areas of international human rights, indigenous rights, and intercultural criminal law. Anthropologists serve as expert witnesses in court cases involving human remains, cultural artifacts, and cultural beliefs and practices. Anthropologists with law degrees serve as tribal public defenders and represent tribal governments or other indigenous groups in disputes with national governments. Such disputes may involve natural resource policy, treaty defense, sovereign immunity, jurisdiction, zoning, family law, land claims, commercial rights, environmental protection, religious freedom, criminal justice, contract violation, and other legal areas.

Sometimes justice is hard to obtain. In the mid-1990s, investigations began into the U.S. government's intentional exposing of people to radiation during the 1950s and 1960s, including some Inupiat in Alaska, Navajo uranium miners in Nevada, and Marshall Islanders whose home, Bikini Atoll, is still off limits to them because of above-ground nuclear bomb testing there. In one case, anthropologists assisted seventy Inupiat of the original eighty-four subjects who participated in an iodine-131 experiment without their knowledge. The suit against the government called for health care services to which they otherwise would not have access (www.eh.doe.gov/ohre/roadmap/). A special presidential commission was established in 1995 to research these cases.

Also in the 1990s, legal anthropologists assisted the Tonggom, Wopkaimin, and other peoples of Papua, New Guinea, in bringing suit against Broken Hill Proprietary (BHP), Australia's biggest mining corporation—and won. For more than a decade, BHP's copper and gold mine had released mine tailings and waste into the headwaters of the Ok Tedi and Fly rivers, polluting the water, killing or driving off subsistence species, and forcing people to relocate. The case drew international attention. In 1996, BHP settled out of court, agreeing to clean up the river, pay affected villages $28.6 million, and close the mine by 2010. In 2002, the company transferred its 52 percent equity in the mine to the newly created Papua New Guinea Sustainable Development Program Company (Ghazi, 2004).

CRITICAL THINKING QUESTIONS

What knowledge and skills can legal anthropologists bring to issues of social justice? Why do indigenous peoples need their services?

REVIEW

Patterns of conflict between groups include warfare, which varies among different types of societies. Intertribal warfare is small scale and waged by members of voluntary warrior societies. Societies may mediate conflict and prevent war through political marriage, banishment, or adjudication. The goals of warfare in chiefdoms and states may be to conquer people, annex territory, or control resources using standing armies. Warfare has spread through the forces of globalization.

Chapter Summary

Evolutionary Perspectives on Conflict

• In all societies, communities, and families, conflicts arise. They may occur over issues of family life, household responsibilities, or roles within communities. Disputes within communities may be about interpersonal issues or rights to property and other resources. Conflicts may also occur between communities or, in the modern context, between nations. Such conflicts have the potential of leading to protracted antagonisms and even to warfare. There are, therefore, mechanisms in place to avoid or resolve conflicts. Societies differ in what they consider to be causes of conflict and in how they settle disputes and reestablish peace or harmonious relationships.

• Evolutionary biologists and psychologists study the primate origins of behaviors that help avoid conflict and restore peace after incidents of open aggression between animals. One of the ways that conflict is avoided is for subordinate animals within group dominance hierarchies to demonstrate acceptance of their position through the display of submissive gestures and actions. When conflicts do arise, animal behavior reveals practices that occur immediately after the conflict has erupted and taken its course. Such postconflict reconciliation behavior includes approaching one another, holding out a hand, and embracing in order to reassure the other animals. Mutual grooming and body contact function to reduce aggression and promote interpersonal and group stability.

Avoiding Conflict

- In human societies, people develop means of expressing disagreement while avoiding open conflict. Deference to others or stating one's opinion indirectly are methods of creating social harmony even while managing disagreement. Self-control and restraint are positive personality traits that help avoid conflict. Informal sanctions such as teasing, gossiping about, or ostracizing wrongdoers also function to squelch disruptive behavior. Conflict management may take the form of control of aggressive behavior once it erupts. Friendly peacemakers may intervene when disputes arise. Deferential behavior and politeness strategies are also means of avoiding conflict.

Witchcraft and Ritual in Conflict Resolution

- In some societies, specific social mechanisms help prevent conflict or channel aggressive behavior in socially acceptable forms. For example, the Semai organize meetings to discuss and thereby contain the intensity and scope of conflicts that arise between community members. The Inuit have ritualized song duels that men may engage in to channel their anger and aggression toward one another, particularly sexual jealousies. Beliefs in witchcraft may also channel aggressive impulses and control people's behavior, because angry or aggressive people may either become the target of witchcraft or be accused themselves of being witches.

Patterns of Family and Community Conflict

- Within families, interpersonal conflicts may erupt over personal preferences and styles of interaction. People may also disagree about decisions that need to be made regarding household responsibilities, marriage choices, and involvement in their communities. In societies where property is valued, siblings may compete over inheritance.

- In societies where the stakes of conflict are high, there may be specific people who function as mediators in order to resolve disputes before they become deadly. Such conflicts may potentially lead to attacks, counterattacks, and revenge, festering through a series of killings and eventually resulting in blood feuds. Mediators may be appealed to because of their skill as orators and their ability to persuade people to come to agreements that are in the interest of the entire community.

Patterns of Conflict between Groups

- When conflicts erupt between communities, societal mechanisms may develop to negotiate a settlement that avoids or lessens the degree of hostility. While armed aggression and hostilities between groups can occur anywhere, the causes and character of warfare vary in different types of societies. Warfare is least likely and least destructive in nomadic bands than in other kinds of societies. In tribal societies, raiding and warfare may exact a deadlier toll on the population and be more disruptive. Tribal warfare is generally small scale, involving relatively few fighters.

- In state societies, warfare has primarily economic and political goals. Indeed, state societies are usually born through warfare and generally depend on armed conflict or other coercion to expand their borders and their influence. The organization of warfare in state societies differs fundamentally from warfare in other types of cultures. State societies have standing armies made up of people who are either part-time or full-time specialists. The goals of state warfare are either the total annihilation of the enemy or its humiliation into surrender and submission. In modern warfare, losers are usually permitted some face-saving options so that their economic and political losses and their public humiliation do not breed deep resentment against the winners.

- Despite efforts to develop international mechanisms to resolve disputes through peaceful means, armed conflicts continue to erupt throughout the world. Internal disputes and civil wars can damage societies for generations after they have ended. But some governments have responded by limiting their military spending, eliminating standing armies altogether, or instituting formal mechanisms for resolving disputes. International organizations sometimes step in to help disputing parties arrive at peaceful reconciliations within countries that have been devastated by civil wars and internal antagonisms.

 ## Key Terms

positive sanctions   340
negative sanctions   340
informal sanctions   340
formal sanctions   340

dominance hierarchies   340
postconflict
   reconciliation   341
conflict avoidance   341

peacemakers   342
deference   342
politeness strategies   342
song duels   342

witchcraft   347
vengeance   350
blood feud   350
warfare   351

Review Questions

1. Is it human nature to exhibit aggressive behavior? Are there universal features in all human societies that lead to conflict?

2. How do primates avoid conflict? How do they structure conflict? How do they reconcile following conflict?

3. What are the social contexts of conflict in primate societies? From an evolutionary perspective, what is the adaptive value of both conflict and conflict avoidance?

4. What are some informal and formal mechanisms of social control in human societies?

5. What are some examples of saving face, politeness, apology, and channeled aggression as four common strategies for avoiding conflict?

6. How are principles of kinship duty and reciprocity involved in both conflict avoidance and aggressive conflict?

7. In what ways can witchcraft function as a system of social control?

8. What are some ethnographic examples of family and community conflict and conflict resolution strategies?

9. How are conflicts between groups different from conflicts within groups? How do patterns of conflict differ between bands, tribes, and states?

10. How does conflict lead to warfare? How can warfare lead to culture change?

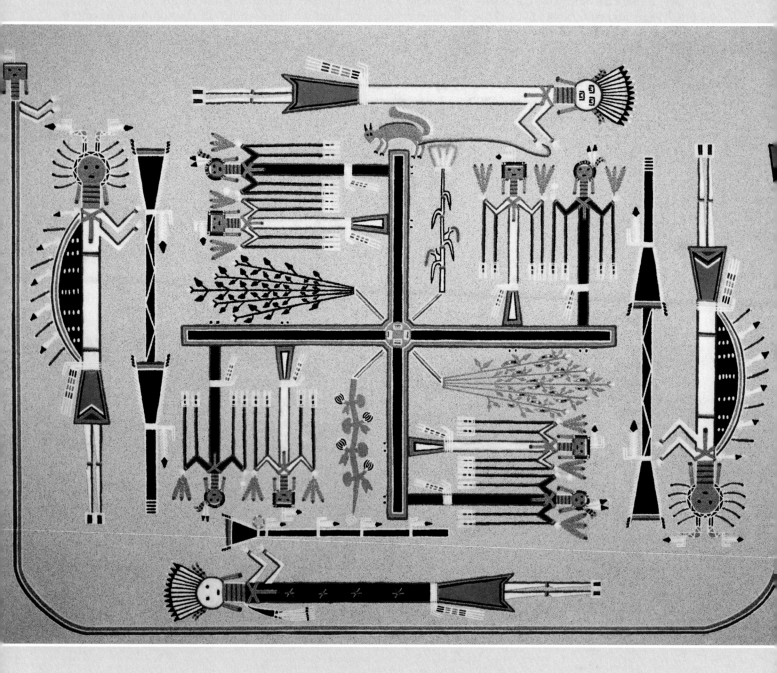

CHAPTER 14

Preview

1. **What is religion?**
2. **What perspectives do anthropologists take in studying religion?**
3. **What types of spirit entities and powers or forces do people believe in?**
4. **Who are religious practitioners, and how do they reflect their society and culture?**
5. **What are the main types of religious practice?**
6. **What are some psychological, social, and cultural sources and functions of religion?**
7. **How do religions help maintain the social order? How do they both instigate and reflect culture change?**

The surface of the fourth world was unlike the surface of any of the lower worlds. For it was a mixture of black and white. The sky above was alternately white, blue, yellow, and black, just as it had been in the worlds below. But here the colors were of a different duration. As yet there was no sun and no moon; as yet there were no stars.

When they arrived on the surface of the fourth world, the exiles from the lower worlds saw no living thing. But they did observe four great snow-covered peaks along the horizon around them. One peak lay to the east. One peak lay to the south. One peak lay likewise to the west. And to the north there was one peak.

It was now evident to the newcomers that the fourth world was larger than any of the worlds below.

Twenty-three days came and went, and twenty-three nights passed and all was well. And on the twenty-fourth night the exiles held a council meeting. They talked quietly among themselves, and they resolved to mend their ways and to do nothing unintelligent that would create disorder. This was a good world, and the wandering people meant to stay here, it is said.

[Eventually the people were visited by the gods or "Holy People" who gave them instructions about how to prepare themselves to live in the fourth world. The Holy People promised to give them advice and to teach them to live properly.]

Proceeding silently the gods laid one buckskin on the ground, careful that its head faced the west. Upon its skin they placed two ears of corn, being just as careful that the tips of each pointed east. Over the corn they spread the other buckskin, making sure that its head faced east.

Under the white ear they put the feather of a white eagle. And under the yellow ear they put the feather of a yellow eagle. Then they told the onlooking people to stand at a distance.

So that the wind could enter.

Then from the east the white wind blew between the buckskins. And while the wind thus blew, each of the Holy People came and walked four times around the objects they had placed so carefully on the ground. As they walked, the eagle feathers moved slightly. Just slightly. So that only those who watched carefully were able to notice. And when the Holy People had finished walking, they lifted the topmost buckskin. And lo! The ears of corn disappeared.

In their place there lay a man and there lay a woman.

The white ear of corn had been transformed into our most ancient male ancestor [First Man] and the yellow ear of corn had been transformed into our most ancient female ancestor [First Woman].

It was the wind that had given them life: the very wind that gives us our breath as we go about our daily affairs here in the world we ourselves live in. When this wind ceases to blow inside of us, we become speechless. And we die.

In the skin at the tips of our fingers we can see the trail of that life-giving wind. Look carefully at your own fingertips. There you will see where the wind blew when it *created your most ancient ancestors out of two ears of corn, it is said.*

From *Diné Bahané: The Navajo Creation Story* by Paul Zolbrod, pp. 45–51. Copyright 1984. Reprinted by permission of the University of New Mexico Press.

Creation stories from various cultures express different ideas about how people were given life and how people relate to their physical and social universe. And the stories express different worldviews about themselves and their relationships with their environment, other people, and the spirit world. The narrative told by the Diné (or Navajo) describes the physical environment in which the people come to be. It is a world surrounded by four sacred mountains. And it is the fourth world in which people now live. The fact that it is the fourth world surrounded by four sacred mountains is no coincidence. The number four is the sacred number for the Diné and for most Native Americans. When the people emerged into this fourth world, they saw that it was beautiful and well formed. The three previous worlds had also been beautiful and well formed, but the people had made those worlds dangerous and frightening by their own behavior. Because of their lying, adultery, and greed, they had rendered their worlds uninhabitable. Through their own wrongdoings, they created worlds of disorder. Now, arriving in the fourth world, they hoped, as the narrative says, "to do nothing unintelligent" so that they could live in peace and harmony in this beautiful new world.

The gods, called the "Holy People," created First Man and First Woman out of ears of corn, the most potent and sacred of all Diné symbols of life. These sacred ears of corn, white symbolizing maleness and yellow symbolizing femaleness, came to life through the breath of wind that animates all living things. The narrative is an origin story, explaining why we breathe and why our fingertips have whirls.

The Diné story sets out a physical and moral landscape for the people to live in. They learn the importance of proper behavior, of goodness, so that the inherent harmony of the world can be maintained. Disorder comes through wrong behavior, whereas harmony, balance, and order come through ritual and right thinking. And it ties the people to a specific place, giving explanations for their surroundings, as well as linking their lives to an ancient and sacred past.

religion
Thoughts, actions, and feelings based on belief in the existence of spirit beings and supranormal (or superhuman) forces.

WHAT IS RELIGION?

Religion is thoughts, actions, and feelings based on beliefs in the existence of spirit beings and supranormal (or superhuman) forces. It includes constellations of beliefs and practices about the spirit world and its relationship to everyday existence. Religious beliefs and practices also give people ways to contact spirit beings and forces to show them honor and respect, as well as to invoke their blessings and protection.

Spirits may be thought to inhabit a realm different from our own, or they may be ever-present, although usually unseen. People believe that the spirit world, whether visible or invisible, is connected in some ways to humans, influencing the course of human life and the outcome of human activities. To

The Creation of Adam shows the bearded figure of God touching the finger of the first man. In the book of Genesis from the Judeo-Christian-Islamic tradition, the first humans are created in the image of God and instructed to "replenish the earth," so that people will live in every habitable place, not one specific locale as in the Diné story. (Michelangelo, "The Creation of Adam," 15-08-1512. Fresco, ceiling (restored), Sistine Chapel, The Vatican, Rome. Photograph © Nippon Television Network Corporation, Tokyo)

obtain the help of spirit beings and to harness spirit forces, people perform rituals that convey their desires and intentions.

Although we often speak of the spirit world as "supernatural," this term may be misleading and not fitting for all cultures. People in some cultures believe that the spirit realm is ever-present as part of their natural world and informs their daily lives in significant ways. For them, the spirit world and spirit forces are not distinct from, but rather are intertwined with, everyday life.

Religion includes both beliefs and practices. Beliefs are a people's ideas about the spirit world, the kinds of beings and forces that have spirit power, and the ways in which the universe is created and continues to be. Religions also embody worldviews that teach people ethical values and attitudes. And sacred rituals dramatize people's beliefs and allow them to actively express those beliefs. Through ritual action and speech, people make contact with the spirit world and manipulate spirit power for their own purposes.

Anthropologists analyze religious beliefs and rituals using etic and emic perspectives, reviewing objective conditions and subjective experiences. What do people's beliefs and practices mean for them? How do people interpret their world and their experience? How does participating in rituals affect them, and what meanings do they ascribe to the rituals? Also, how are people's religious beliefs and practices consistent with other aspects of their culture? How do people's economies and modes of subsistence influence the meanings and actions of their rituals, for example? How do their political systems or systems of social stratification frame the ways they structure their beliefs about the spirit world?

Variations in religious practices and beliefs sometimes correlate with other aspects of society. In egalitarian, stateless societies, for example, relationships between deities or spirit beings tend to be egalitarian as well. Just as all individuals have more or less equal access to economic resources and social prestige, they also have the potential to acquire spirit powers. In contrast, in societies with hierarchical social structures, people are more likely to believe in the existence of a ranked pantheon of deities. The Greek and Roman gods and goddesses are a good example of such a system. Zeus (in Greece) or Jupiter (in Rome) stood at the apex of a pyramidal structure of power. Each was allied with a spouse, Hera and Juno, respectively, with whom they formed a conjugal unit, a reflection of the household structure of ancient Greece and Rome.

Monotheistic religions with their single supreme deity reflect political systems having central supreme leaders—a king or emperor. In the past, rulers of these societies were thought to be divine or to derive their authority directly from a god. Thus, many of the first state societies are referred to as theocracies, literally, governments by god. The relationships of gods and their activities are thus metaphors for ways of life on earth but on a more heroic, larger-than-life scale.

Religious behavior is both practical and symbolic. Performing rituals is doing something to achieve practical results, but these actions also have symbolic meanings. **Religious speech**—invocations, prayers, prophecies, songs of praise, curses—is a powerful means of transmitting messages about the world, and it also creates the world as well.

religious speech
Invocations, prayers, prophecies, songs of praise, and curses that are powerful means of transmitting messages about the world and also creating the world.

The hierarchical relationships among these Roman gods reflect the social structure of the society that invented and worshipped them.

These gospel singers illustrate the concept of religious speech. The anthropology of religion seeks to understand what people believe; how they embody, structure, and express their spiritual beliefs; and how these beliefs intersect with other aspects of their society and culture.

? *In what ways does your life philosophy reflect the religious and secular values of your society?*

Religious speech attempts to change a state of being, to exert agency or control over people or over events or natural phenomena. Through both speech and action, people express their ideas about causality, about how things happen and how human and other powers affect the world.

Religious beliefs are subject to change and respond to change in the social system, partly because of their underlying ambiguity and mystery. The mystery stems from the impossibility of proof, replaced instead by the certainty of faith. Ambiguity arises in religious speech, in which messages are layered with meanings. These messages must be interpreted and reinterpreted. And it is in reinterpreting religious messages that people refer to their wants and needs to weave together a meaningful philosophy of life.

> **REVIEW**
>
> Religion is thoughts, actions, and feelings based on beliefs in the existence of god(s), spirit being(s), or supernatural force(s). Religious beliefs and practices give people ways to contact such beings or forces, to honor and respect them, and to invoke their blessings and protection. Anthropologists analyze religious beliefs and behaviors using the perspectives of comparison and cultural relativism. As social institutions, religions tend to reflect the structure of the societies in which they arise.

SPIRIT BEINGS AND FORCES

Spirit beings and forces have extraordinary, more than human, powers. They typically are eternal or indestructible; they know more than an ordinary person can know; and they are able to act in ways that humans cannot. Thus, people seek contact with them to gain their protection and aid. Spirits may have the shape of animals, humans, or other, unusual forms and may change their shape at will. Sometimes they imbue inanimate objects with special powers. A supernatural force may be a vague spirit essence that pervades the universe.

Animism and Animatism

One common, nearly universal form that spirit takes is the soul. Souls are the eternal aspect of living things. In some belief systems, such as Judaism, Christianity, and Islam, only human beings have souls. But in many cultures, people believe that animals and plants—all living things—have souls as well. The soul is seen as the animating aspect of living things. It gives life to the body that it inhabits. When the body dies, the soul leaves and exists eternally in some other form or in a nonmaterial state. The belief in souls is called **animism;** and the belief that all things are endowed with some spirit form or essence is called **animatism.** For example, people with animatistic beliefs might ascribe consciousness and personality to a thunderstorm, a tree, or a rock.

Gods and Heroes

Some religious traditions have many spirit beings in human form—gods—with specific attributes, powers, and functions. Belief in numerous deities, called **polytheism,** is widespread throughout the world. In Hinduism, with its hundreds of millions of followers, as well as in the belief systems of small subsistence societies numbering in the

animism
Belief in the existence of souls.

animatism
Belief that all things are endowed with some spirit form or essence.

polytheism
Belief in the existence of numerous deities that have specific attributes, powers, and functions.

hundreds, polytheistic spirit worlds are inhabited by multitudes of beings, each with a name, identity, genealogy, history, and domain of influence. In contrast, in **monotheistic religions** people believe in one supreme deity who has powers and knowledge that affect all aspects of life. In addition, there may be other, lesser spirit beings and important mortal heroes as well.

Ancestors, Ghosts, and Demons

Other types of spirit beings include the spirit forms of deceased ancestors. Ancestral spirits have a particular connection to their living descendants, who honor them through prayer and ritual. In return, the spirits bestow blessings, health, and good fortune on their surviving kin. But if people fail to perform the rituals, ancestor spirits can bring illness and misfortune.

In Japan, after a death, especially of a man, the eldest son prepares a mortuary tablet that commemorates his father (Morioka, 1984). These tablets are kept in a household altar for at least several generations. They are honored and given offerings from time to time in commemorative rituals. Eventually, the tablets of the eldest ancestor may be retired, either buried or broken and discarded. This ritual or ceremony is sometimes referred to as **ancestor worship.** In the past, reflecting Japan's patrilineal descent and patriarchal society, tablets for women usually were discarded after only one or two generations, but tablets for men were kept for a longer time. Today, however, a bilateral principle governs ancestor worship, and mothers and grandmothers are honored along with fathers and grandfathers. And any member of the family, not just the eldest son, can carry out the rituals. These changes reflect shifts in Japanese household composition from extended family to nuclear family forms.

Among the Ju/'hoansi of the Kalahari, ancestral spirits, called *gangwasi*, are thought to cause illness and misfortune. People are wary of their ancestral spirits, avoiding contact with them in the night and hoping to be spared misfortune. They periodically perform dances to prevent ancestral spirits from attacking them and causing harm. Most important is treating people right while they are alive so that after death their spirit will not seek out offenders to harm them.

The Hopi of Arizona believe that ancestral spirits join the kachinas, powerful beings who bring rain. When a person dies, his or her spirit becomes mist and clouds that return to the people in the form of rain, helping to sustain crops in an arid environment. The Hopi view themselves as eternally linked in cycles of life and death, and they pray to and honor their ancestors so that they will be blessed with rain. Representational wooden carvings of spirits, called kachina dolls, are conduits to the spirit world.

In many cultures, people believe that deceased individuals may return or appear in the form of a ghost. Ghosts may have human shape or they may be only a shadow. Ghosts may be welcomed or feared, and they may return to the living to cause mischief or harm or to transmit messages of great importance. In some societies, ghosts are cast as demons. Among New Guinea natives, for example, village compounds must be ritually protected against wandering demons.

Mana, Totems, and Taboos

In addition to or instead of believing in spirit beings, many people believe in the existence of a pervasive spirit power. This power or essence endows people, animals, other

This Japanese woman honors a dead ancestor by presenting offerings at an altar in her home.

monotheistic religions
Belief systems that hold to the existence of one supreme deity who has powers and knowledge that affect all aspects of life.

ancestor worship
Belief in the importance of ancestors as they affect the lives of their survivors, protecting their descendants in return for rituals of honor performed to show them respect.

? *How are ghosts viewed in American popular culture today?*

mana
A force, power, or essence that endows people, animals, other living things, and possibly inanimate objects with special qualities or powers.

totemism
Belief system in which people believe they are descendants of spirit beings.

secret societies
Organizations that control the use of special objects used in religious rituals.

living things, and possibly inanimate objects with special qualities or powers. This force has its own name in every culture, but in the anthropological literature on religion it is often referred to as **mana,** from Polynesian languages where it was first described. A belief in mana is a form of animatism. Having mana gives a person special knowledge and power or an object special properties and qualities. Perfectly grown yams may be said to have mana, for example. Spirit powers are sometimes held in talismans or fetishes to give the wearer good luck. A rabbit's foot held or worn for luck, for example, is an expression of animatism.

In some cultures of Australia and the Pacific Northwest of North America, people believe that they are the descendants of spirit beings or ancestors, a belief called **totemism.** Totemic ancestors may have human or animal form. From ancient times, they gave protection or lifesaving advice to human beings in need or in danger. Thus, they are the primordial protectors of the people. Ancestral totems may also be identified as the actual progenitors of the present-day people. In either case, people owe them gratitude and respect and perform rituals in their honor so that they will continue to receive protection and guidance.

Totemism celebrates the solidarity of social groups. Australian Aborigines believe that each clan is descended from a specific animal in the mythic past or "the Dreaming" (Hume, 2000). At some time in an earlier realm of existence, the mythic animal ancestor was transformed into a human being and continues to be connected to its human descendants. The descendants honor their animal ancestor, or totem, by performing rituals in its honor and by refraining from eating its flesh. The totemic figure functioned to unite Aborigines, who, because of their nomadic lifestyle and dispersed populations, rarely came into sustained contact. Spirit links among people have survival value, because they create bonds of mutual acknowledgment, interdependence, and obligations to extend hospitality and share resources.

Spirit forces and beings are dangerous if contacted in the wrong way, in the wrong place, or at the wrong time. Some spirits inhabit particular locales that may be dangerous if entered without spiritual protection. Objects used in rituals also may be dangerous if touched or used when a person is not prepared. Societies that believe in these dangers may have organizations, known as **secret societies,** that control the special

The familiar totem poles of some Pacific Northwest Native American groups are representations of the spirit beings known as totems. The poles depict the record of a kin group and its relationship with its spirit ancestor—in the form of a mammal, bird, or other animal—as well as the key characters and events in that record.

places or the use of special objects. For example, among Australian Aborigines and Amazonian Indians, only men may touch special musical instruments or ritual objects. If women come into contact with these objects, they may be seriously harmed or even killed by the spirit forces associated with them. Even to hear the sounds of the music or the singing of the men may be dangerous to women.

Restrictions such as these are called taboos. A tabooed object or place is one that can cause harm if contacted or entered. Its danger derives from its power. A dangerous person, object, or place may not be regarded as evil, however, because spirit power in itself is neither positive nor negative. Rather, it is the use to which the power is put that renders it good or bad. Individuals may use their spirit powers to become healers, fortune-tellers, or other ritual practitioners, serving their communities in important ways. Others, however, may seek to acquire spirit powers to do harm.

An example of taboos is seen in rituals surrounding pregnancy and birth. In many cultures, expectant mothers, and sometimes their husbands as well, avoid eating certain foods or engaging in certain kinds of activities. Many of these restrictions are geared toward ensuring a safe pregnancy and easy delivery. Inuit parents were not to tie their belts tight lest the placenta strangle the baby during birth. Haida mothers refrained from eating sticky substances, such as salmon eggs, to ensure a smooth and quick delivery.

Pregnancy taboos symbolize the dangers of pregnancy and birth and the uncertainty of outcomes. Through taboos, people express their fears and their desires to control essentially unpredictable events. In addition, taboos allow people to explain both positive and negative results. If the birth goes well and the baby is healthy, parents can feel that their behavior contributed to the happy occasion. However, if the baby is sickly or dies, parents can find the reason for their misfortune by recalling taboos that they failed to observe.

> ### REVIEW
>
> Spirit beings and forces include gods, ancestors, ghosts, demons, totems, mana, souls, and spirit powers that may be evidenced in good or bad luck. Animism is belief in souls, and animatism is the belief that animals, plants, and inanimate objects are endowed with souls or personalities and have special spiritual powers. Some religions are monotheistic (one god) while others are polytheistic (many gods). In totemism, living people trace their descent from animal ancestors and observe ritual taboos to protect the ancestral spirits. Spiritual power, such as mana, may be positive or negative, depending on how it is used. Potentially dangerous or contaminating spiritual power may be managed through secret societies or through individuals' observations of taboos. Religious rituals and religious speech often are aimed at giving people agency or control over forces and events that affect their lives. Shared religious beliefs and practices also contribute to people's social solidarity.

RELIGIOUS PRACTITIONERS

Most religions have individuals or groups who function as either part-time or full-time specialists or practitioners. Sometimes a person receives a calling from the spirit world to become a religious specialist. The calling could be received in a dream, a waking vision, or an omen or sign. Some societies believe that particular individuals inherit spiritual abilities from one generation to the next. In other cases, a person decides to become a religious practitioner because of his or her interests or experiences or wish to benefit the community through ritual practice. Some people may be drawn to ritual practice because of its creative and aesthetic qualities that give outlet for artistic expression through music, song, dance, and drama. And religious specialists may enlist others to take the training necessary to become a practitioner. Mediums, healers, shamans, diviners, and priests are all religious practitioners.

Mediums, Diviners, and Healers

Mediums are believed to have special gifts that enable them to make contact with the spirit world and with spirit beings or spirits of the dead. They usually establish a direct

mediums
Persons having special gifts to make contact with the spirit world, often in a state of trance.

? *How do mediums and diviners practice in your society or community today?*

diviners
Persons with the power to predict the future through messages and omens from the spirit world.

healers
Religious practitioners who acquire spirit power to diagnose the spirit cause of illness and effect cures.

shamans
Part-time religious practitioners who make contact with the spirit world through prayer, ritual, and trance.

relationship with a particular spirit or group of spirits. Through rituals they perform, mediums become conduits or channels between ordinary people and the contacted spirit beings. They often conduct these rituals in a state of trance—an altered state of consciousness in which they are not fully conscious of their surroundings. Trance states can be achieved through various means, including meditation or mental concentration; and once in a trance, a medium can pass messages between individuals and members of the spirit world.

Diviners have the power to predict the future through messages and omens they receive and interpret from the spirit world. They use various divination techniques to obtain the spirit's guidance or answers to specific questions or problems. For example, they may recognize patterns or designs that tell a story, as in reading tea leaves or tarot cards. In some African societies, diviners roll chicken bones to read a person's fortune or examine animal entrails to predict a family's best course of action. In some Central American societies, diviners tell fortunes by throwing corn kernels into a bowl and finding meaning in the pattern the kernels make. In Native North America, diviners threw fruit pits to read patterns in the way they fell. Diviners may also look at the stars or gaze into water to retrieve omens and warnings.

Healers are religious practitioners who acquire spirit power to heal. They can diagnose the spirit cause of illness and effect cures through the performance of rituals. In North America, many people heed the advice of "faith healers," some of whom have large followings of enthusiastic believers. Traditional healers usually have some practical knowledge of human anatomy and physiology, pharmacology, and pharmaceutical substances in their environment. Healers may use this practical knowledge in their cures in addition to religious rituals. In some societies, healers may be suspected of sometimes using their control of spirit powers to cause harm rather than to cure illness. As you read in Chapter 12, beliefs and practices of sorcery or witchcraft constitute powerful sources of social control.

Ritual healers are usually called in to treat a patient when the illness is protracted or life-threatening. The following account, related in 1918 by a Fox woman, describes her experience with a healer called to assist her in the difficult birth of her first child.

This female shaman, or mudang, is conducting a kut ceremony in a village in present-day Korea. In a kut ceremony, the shaman summons forth the spirit world to promote harmony, heal, bring messages to the living, or appease the dead. Shamanism was a key feature of the traditional religion of Korea before the arrival of Buddhism, and it continues today in rural areas.

When that woman [the healer] came, she at once boiled some medicine. After she had boiled it, she said: "Let her sit up for a while. You must hold her so that she will not fall over." After I was made to sit up, she spat upon my head; and she gave me the medicine to drink. After she had give me the medicine, she began singing. She started to go out singing and went around the little lodge singing. When she danced by where I was, she knocked on the side. "Come out if you are a boy," she would say. And she would again begin singing. When she danced by she again knocked the side. "Come out if you are a girl," she would say again. After she sang four times in a circle, she entered the lodge. And she gave me medicine to drink. "Now it will be born. She may lie down." Lo, sure enough, my baby was born. (Michelson, 1920:319)

Shamans and Priests

Shamans are part-time religious practitioners who contact the spirit world through ritual, prayer, and trance. They may use masks that represent spirit beings. Shamans are similar to mediums in many respects, except that they may not channel with a particular spirit being. Rather, they enter trance states to receive visions and messages from the spirit realm. Their work tends to be on behalf of the community as a whole. Shamans may also perform healing rituals or rituals seeking spirit protection, advice, and support. Ecstatic experience, whether through trance, visions, or dreams, is central to the way that shamans make contact with the spirit world. Shamanism may be quite ancient in the origins of religions (Goodman, 1990).

Some societies have full-time religious practitioners called **priests,** who lead religious organizations and officiate at rituals but are not necessarily expected to be able to communicate directly with gods or the spirit world. The category of priest includes spiritual and ritual leaders of formally institutionalized religions with places of worship, such as churches, mosques, or congregations, including ministers, rabbis, and mullahs, in addition to Roman Catholic or Greek Orthodox priests. Priests work on behalf of their religious organization, as well as their community and its members. Priests often preside at rites of passage, such as those that mark birth, puberty, marriage, and death.

REVIEW

Religious practitioners include mediums, healers, diviners, shamans, and priests; and for some religious practitioners, these roles may overlap. A shaman, for example, may also be a diviner and a healer. Mediums enter trance states to serve as channels for communication between individuals and the spirit world; diviners tell the future or enter trance states to receive omens or advice from the spirit world. Healers use both spiritual and practical means to treat illness. Priests are full-time specialists who work for religious organizations and lead congregations in religious ceremonies and rituals. Unlike shamans, priests are not expected to have spirit power or communicate directly with divine beings.

RELIGIOUS PRACTICE

Religious practices, or **rituals,** are demonstrations of belief, putting belief into action. Rituals may be formal and public with many well-rehearsed participants and performers. They may also be informal and private, carried out by individuals or small groups. Rituals, including those involving religious speech, play a central role in most religions. They are the means by which believers make contact with the gods or spirit world; express honor and respect for spirit beings; obtain blessings, health, prosperity, or success; and achieve particular personal or communal goals. Rituals also can have specific ends, such as purification (spiritual cleansing), sanctification (making something sacred), veneration (worshiping something), or absolution (giving spiritual forgiveness). Individual rituals may be linked together in a ceremonial, a series of interconnected rituals.

Rituals usually involve the visual and performing arts. The aesthetic impact and spiritual meaning of rituals transport participants to a mental, emotional, and spiritual state of being that is different from their ordinary lives. Participants may adorn themselves with special clothing, masks, or face and body painting. They typically employ special objects made with precious metals, or such objects may be carved and painted or decorated with jewels, feathers, or stone in designs that incorporate religious symbols. Religious art and iconography (the meaning of symbols and design) thus reveal a people's aesthetic values. Rituals also involve poetic language and the arts of music, song, and dance, the subjects of Chapter 15.

Sacred and Secular Rituals

Secular life is full of rituals or ritualized activities, but these are not the same as sacred rituals. **Sacred rituals** are dedicated to the spirit realm and the expression of religious faith. Secular rituals may also be important culturally. For example, secular holidays such as Independence Day (in the United States) and Canada Day (in Canada) are times to display national symbols such as flags, sing national songs, and hear patriotic speeches. Sporting events also may be marked by ritualized protection, such as wearing team insignia or colors and cheering. The players may practice personal rituals to bring success, such as wearing good-luck gear in the game. These

priests
Full-time religious practitioners who lead a religious organization and officiate at rituals but are not expected to be able to communicate directly with the spirit world.

rituals
Activities, including religious speech, ceremonies, and behaviors, that are demonstrations of belief.

sacred rituals
Activities, places, or objects that are connected to the spirit realm and are imbued with power.

The Nuna and Bwa peoples of Burkina Faso use wooden painted animal masks and dances to make the spirit world come alive, as the butterfly dancer shows here. Geometric patterns in the masks depict moral principles. Zigzag lines, for example, represent the difficult life paths that the ancestors had to follow, and checkerboard patterns represent opposing moral forces, such as knowledge and ignorance.

rites of renewal
Rituals performed with the goal of renewing the bounty of the earth.

prayer
Religious speech or thought through which believers transmit messages to spirit beings.

sacrifice
Offerings made to spirit beings in order to show gratitude and honor.

behaviors and attitudes involve magical thinking not unlike practices associated with religious beliefs, but their purpose is secular rather than spiritual.

In many societies, seasonal or annual rituals with both sacred and secular elements are held to celebrate the earth's bounty. Celebrations serve both as a thanksgiving for the past year's plants and animals and as a request to the spirits for renewed generation and continued supplies. These are examples of **rites of renewal,** also called rites of intensification.

Prayer and Sacrifice

Prayer is both a private and a public ritual. Through **prayer,** believers transmit messages to the spirit beings or to particular deities or ancestors. Prayers are meant to honor the spirits, ask favors of them, or win future blessings. Some religions emphasize the memorization and correct verbatim repetition of prayers. Without correct recitations, prayers may not be effective. Other religions permit or encourage private prayers that individuals make up as they pray.

Believers also transmit messages to the spirit realm through the **sacrifice** of offerings that honor spirit beings by giving up something important. Offerings may consist of foods that the deities are

Flying from the Potala Palace in Tibet, former home of the Dalai Lama, are prayer flags, each representing a blessing to all beings, carried everywhere on the wind. Buddhist sacred texts and symbols are printed or painted on the flags, and colors symbolize aspects of nature. Thus, prayers are sacred messages invoking global peace and harmony that are intended to link each person to the universe. The flags are never removed, but new flags are continually raised to ensure the future.

Case study

Renewal Rituals in North America

In many Native American cultures, people pay homage to animals by thanking the animals' spirit protectors, the spirit form of the living animals. Among northern Algonkian foragers of eastern and central Canada, for example, killing a bear required special rituals. Hunters addressed the dead bear's spirit with words generally used for kinspeople. Thus, through language, they called forth the reciprocal bonds between humans and animals. They dressed the slain bear in ceremonial clothing and erected a wooden pole nearby on which they hung the bear's skull and offerings of tobacco. After the bear was butchered, its bones were placed on a raised platform so that dogs and other scavengers would not disturb them. Algonkians and others "buried" their deceased kin in the same way.

This practice, showing the animal the same respect as one would show a relative, served as a symbolic link between bears and people. Algonkians believed that the spirits appreciated these signs of respect and responded by allowing more bears to be caught. As a man from the Saulteaux nation (one of the Algonkian-speaking groups of Ontario) explained:

> The bears have a chief, and the orders of this chief must be obeyed. Sometimes he orders a bear to go to an Indian trap. When offerings or prayers are made to the chief of the bears, he sends more of his children to the Indians. If this were not done, the spirit of the bear would be offended and would report the circumstances to the chief of bears who would prevent the careless Indians from catching more. (Skinner, 1911:162)

Farming peoples also perform ceremonies to honor and thank the spirits who gave them the knowledge to grow their crops. These ceremonies are often scheduled to coincide with calendar times for planting and harvesting and are, therefore, referred to as **calendric rituals.** For example, contemporary Mohawks continue to celebrate traditional calendric rituals marking Midwinter, Maple Festival, Strawberry Festival, Green Bean Festival, Green Corn Festival, and Harvest Festival at specific times throughout the year.

Seasonal ceremonies may be held to celebrate renewal of the community, express thanks for good fortune, and create or strengthen solidarity. The Sacred Arrow ceremony of the Cheyenne of South Dakota and Wyoming brought together all of the Cheyenne bands who lived during most of the year in small, dispersed communities. Thousands of people congregated at the annual event to celebrate Cheyenne history, socialize, and symbolically renew the Cheyenne nation. The renewal rite involved unwrapping a sacred "medicine bundle"—a collection of religious objects wrapped in a buffalo skin. The medicine bundle contained four sacred arrows, two with power over buffalos and two with power over human beings. The arrows were cleansed, prayed over, and blessed by a ritual specialist called an Arrow Keeper. Then the Arrow Keeper received small willow sticks given by each family, which he held over a fire burning sweet incense. The smoke purified each stick, thus blessing the family that it represented. On the last day of the four-day rite, the sacred arrows were displayed in a central lodge and viewed by all the boys and men. Through their collective presence and participation, hunters and warriors were ensured success, communal bonds were strengthened, and the well-being of the Cheyenne nation was assured.

calendric rituals
Ceremonies performed at specific times during the year, for example, agricultural rituals performed for planting, growing, and harvesting crops.

Less extreme than the Aztecs, the North American Plains Indians incorporated sacrificial acts through self-torture by male participants in the Sun Dance. Young warriors like the one pictured here sacrificed small parts of their bodies in honor of their spirit protectors. The flesh was pierced on the chest, a long tether was tied to a stretch of skin, and the tether was then attached to a specially dedicated pole. During the all-day Sun Dance, the warrior danced slowly around the pole in an ever-widening circle until strips of flesh were torn from his body. Participants in the ritual were honored by their communities for their courage and spiritual dedication.

? *As an ethnographer, how might you describe a puberty rite, funerary rite, or other rite of passage that you have observed?*

puberty rites
Rituals performed to mark the passage of an individual from childhood to adulthood; also called initiation rites.

funerary rites
Rituals performed to mark a person's death and passage to the afterworld.

thought to prefer or valuable objects. People may also fast, refrain from sleep, or subject themselves to some kind of ordeal as a kind of sacrifice. Offerings may also include animals given in rituals of blood sacrifice in which the animals are slaughtered. Societies where people keep domesticated animals may use their stock in sacrificial offerings.

Blood sacrifice centers on the killing of a valuable domesticated animal, but some societies practiced human sacrifice. Perhaps the best-known example was the human sacrifice performed by the Aztecs in central Mexico in the fifteenth and sixteenth centuries. Aztecs believed that the sun god (also the war god), called Huitzilopochtli, needed to be fed so that he would have the energy to travel across the sky from sunrise to sunset every day. He was nourished on human blood from daily sacrifices. This practice eventually contributed to the downfall of the Aztec Empire: As the need for more sacrificial victims increased, the priesthood demanded sacrifices from defeated groups forcibly incorporated into the expanding Aztec state. Those groups thus became even more hostile toward the Aztec state and aided the Spanish invasion of the Aztec Empire in the early sixteenth century.

Rites of Passage

As you read in Chapter 5, in most societies, people perform rituals to celebrate socially significant transitions in an individual's life cycle. Such rites of passage are typically conducted to mark birth, puberty, marriage, and death. Rituals may also mark other aspects of the life cycle, such as naming or initiation into an association. According to anthropologist Arnold van Gennep (1961), rites of passage ritualize three aspects of change in life status: separation, transition, and reincorporation. That is, individuals separate from their families, learn new knowledge and skills, and return to their communities as new people. Let us apply this model to two rites of passage: puberty rites and funerary rites.

Puberty Rites. Van Gennep's model can be applied to **puberty rites,** also called initiation rites, which celebrate the transition from childhood to adulthood. In some cultures, puberty rites are held for only girls or only boys; in others, both boys and girls receive ritual recognition. The Jewish and Christian faiths have rituals that mark a child's growth and maturation. The Jewish bar mitzvah (for boys) and bat mitzvah (for girls) incorporate the child into the adult community of believers. In the Christian ceremony of confirmation, children pledge themselves to their faith and join the congregation of their own volition. Children are usually around 10 or 11 years old when they are confirmed, an age associated with cognitive maturation. In some Christian denominations, christening marks religious as well as social birth, baptism consecrates the person in the faith, and confirmation welcomes the individual into the community of believers. The Western Apache of New Mexico and the Suku of Zaire conduct elaborate ceremonies when girls and boys, respectively, reach puberty (see the Case Study).

Funerary Rites. Funerals, or **funerary rites,** mark the final stage of life and are usually solemn. Death rituals serve purposes both for the living and the dead. According to many belief systems, the proper performance of a funeral allows the soul of the deceased to depart in peace. At death, the soul, which is the activating, invigorating, life-giving aspect of a person, leaves the body and eventually travels to the afterworld. Usually, though, the soul does not make its final journey until after the funeral. And if the funeral is not properly conducted, the soul may never be fully released. It may hover near the living or wander aimlessly, possibly causing mischief and harm.

After a death, the body is usually cleansed, decorated, and dressed in special clothes by relatives or by specialists hired to perform the task. After a set number of

Case study

Puberty Rites among the Apache and the Suku

The Western Apache emphasize themes of fertility and power associated with girls' puberty. The ritual occasioned by a girl's first menstruation, or menarche, is thought to benefit both the girl and her entire community (Basso, 1970). The name of the ritual, *nai'es,* or "preparing her," "getting her ready," signifies one of its focal themes. It readies the pubescent girl for adulthood and motherhood. Preparations for the ceremony, always held in the summertime, begin immediately after menarche. The girl's parents choose a woman as sponsor for their daughter. The sponsor must not belong to the girl's matrilineal clan or that of her father. Thereafter, the sponsor and the girl's parents establish a lasting reciprocal bond, aiding one another as if they were kin.

The *nai'es* ceremony is a public event attended by everyone in the community. It begins shortly after sunrise, a time considered spiritually powerful. The rite consists of eight phases, each highlighting a different theme or activity believed to endow the girl with spiritual and material benefits. In the first phase, the girl dances on a public dance ground to attract supernatural powers from a deity known as Changing Woman. Changing Woman is a symbol of fertility and benevolence, and Apaches believe that during puberty rites the girl is transformed into Changing Woman and acquires her qualities and powers.

Apache Homelands

Apache Reservations Today

The next to last phase is one of "blessing her." The young girl and her sponsor dance in place and are both blessed by each person at the ceremony. Anyone who so desires may request aid from the powers of Changing Woman that reside in the girl. Basso (1970, p. 68) recorded several specific requests made at one rite, including the following:

To have a good crop of corn and beans
To make my sick wife get better
My cattle, to get fat for sale time
To cure my daughter
Rain
My son in Dallas learning to be a barber, not get into any trouble

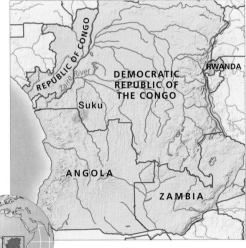

The ritual ends when the girl shakes out the buckskin blanket on which she has been dancing and then throws it toward the east, the sacred direction of the rising sun, and then toward each of the other three cardinal directions. After the ritual, the spiritual powers of Changing Woman remain in the girl's body for four more days during which time she can cure illness or bring rain.

Among the Suku, a farming people of southwestern Congo, boys traditionally undergo a rite of circumcision in groups when they are between 10 and 15 years old (Kopytoff, 1961). The ritual takes place in the summertime, the dry season. Following their circumcision, the boys are taken to a ceremonial hut located outside the village, where they remain for several weeks. In the past, the seclusion lasted several months, but today it is shortened so that the boys can return to school in September. During the summer, the initiates are taught ritual songs and dances and receive rough physical and verbal treatment from the elder men who are charged with the boys' training. At the end of seclusion, the boys go to the river to cleanse themselves and put on new clothing. They take new names by which they will be known henceforth, and then return to the village, where they are greeted joyously by relatives and neighbors. The boys have become men. They have learned their superior status to women and uninitiated boys, and have developed ties of loyalty and camaraderie with the other initiates.

Funerary rites in India end in the above-ground cremation of the deceased in a funeral pyre. In the past, widows were permitted or even encouraged to commit suicide (a practice called sati) *by throwing themselves onto the pyre of their deceased husband. Through self-immolation, Hindu widows directly enacted the reality of their low social status and lack of autonomy. Outside of marriage, women essentially had no social identity or even a right to live. Both voluntary and involuntary sati was made illegal by the British colonial government in 1829. However, the practice has not disappeared entirely, and has even increased in some areas.*

days, the funeral takes place. Cultures vary widely in the degree of elaboration of funerals and the amount of time spent on them. For example, foragers spend less time and resources on funerals than people in settled populations. In some cultures, funerals are a time for the display of solidarity or interdependence among kin. For example, Mohawk funerals were arranged and conducted not by members of the deceased's own clan and moiety but by people belonging to the opposite moiety. Mohawks thought that close relatives of the deceased were too overcome by grief to be bothered with funeral details; but the exchange of roles also symbolized interdependence, unity, and societal balance.

In addition to marking the departure of the deceased, funerals serve to underscore family solidarity and allow for people's expression of sorrow and loss. Funerals are usually followed by a period of mourning during which close relatives of the deceased may wear special clothing, eat or avoid eating certain foods, refrain from engaging in some activities, and act out their grief in culturally prescribed ways. The duration of the mourning period varies widely. In some patriarchal cultures, widows may be expected never to remarry.

Healing or Curing

In every culture, people have theories about health maintenance, causes of disease, and strategies for treatment. In many cultures, health is thought of as a state of harmony or balance. Health depends on the orderly functioning of a person's body, a person's relations with other people, the environment in which a person lives, and the spirit beings and forces with which a person interacts. When this balance is disturbed, illness and misfortune may follow.

Most people make a distinction between illnesses with natural causes and those caused by spirit beings or forces. Natural illnesses include minor aches and pains, accidents, and transitory ailments such as the common cold. These ailments are typically treated with natural remedies, such as medicinal plants and animal or mineral substances. If problems persist or worsen, spiritual causes may be suspected that call for ritual diagnosis and treatment. Patients then seek the aid of religious specialists who can diagnose the cause and recommend or perform the cure. Diagnosis may be achieved through divination or revelation in a dream or vision. Spirit causes can include soul loss, object intrusion, spirit possession, or the violation of taboos.

Many Hispanic and Latino people living in North, Central, and South America believe that illness may be caused by the sudden departure of a person's soul, a condition known as *susto.* Since the soul is the activating, life-giving part of a person, soul loss is obviously a serious, potentially fatal, illness. Soul loss may cause fearfulness, listlessness, loss of appetite, loss of interest in social activities, and a general lack of enthusiasm and vitality (Rubel, 1977). *Susto* is usually triggered by sudden fright resulting from natural disasters, such as earthquakes or thunderstorms, car accidents, or emotional shocks, such as the sudden and unexpected death of a loved one. In treating *susto,* with the help of spirit messages from dreams or visions, a specialist is able to locate the missing soul and coax it back into the patient, thus effecting a cure.

Object intrusion may be the diagnosis when a person experiences a sudden, localized pain in some part of the body. It is believed that a spirit, witch, or malevolent person somehow shot a foreign object into the patient's body, causing pain and distress. The object may have a specific shape, such as a pebble, grain of sand, feather, or animal tooth, or it could be an amorphous substance or liquid. The specialist ritually extracts the foreign object by "cupping" (pressing with the hands) or by sucking at the site of the pain. After the object is extracted, it is ritually disposed of to prevent further harm.

Spirit possession may be welcomed as a positive experience or spiritual gift or as evidence of faith in some religions. In other religions, it is considered a symptom of illness. In all societies with this belief, signs of spirit possession commonly include convulsions or loss of muscular control, erratic and rapid changes in mood, or insomnia. People possessed by spirits seek treatment aimed at removing the spirit or enticing it to leave the person's body. Techniques of exorcism range from cajoling, bargaining with, threatening, or punishing the spirit to make it leave.

In Korea, women are most commonly the targets of spirit possession. When such a diagnosis is made, a shaman, also usually a woman, entreats the spirit to leave the afflicted person. The shaman gives offerings and promises that the patient will, in the future, erect a shrine in the spirit's honor and furnish it periodically with food and drink. Spirits choose to possess women who experience tension in their households, usually from conflicts over their roles as dutiful daughter, wife, and mother. These women may feel burdened by excessive demands, and spirit possession may be an outlet for them to express frustration about their life circumstances, as well as a means of extracting themselves from their daily burdens (Harvey, 1979; Kendall, 1984). The woman is not blamed for her predicament, but other members of her household may be held responsible for her unhappiness.

In Haiti, both men and women may be possessed. Male spirits generally possess women and female spirits possess men. The spirits are attracted to their targets by physical or personality characteristics. To persuade the spirit to leave the body, the afflicted person may agree to establish a lifelong conjugal relationship with the spirit. In some cases, a formal marriage ceremony is performed between the patient and the possessing spirit. Thereafter, a separate bed is kept to which the patient retires for one or two nights each week to have conjugal visits with his or her spirit spouse (Lewis, 1989).

Religious beliefs, such as spirit possession, allow for emotional release. Brazilian practitioners of macumba, which combines West African, Roman Catholic, and Native American beliefs and practices, enter a trance induced by a deity or *orisha,* a Yoruba term. In large public gatherings held several times a week, spirit mediums are serially possessed by four different deities. These include the Old Black Slave, the Indian, and two trickster deities, the Child and Eshu, a Yoruba trickster figure. In the macumba belief system, spirits possess people to impart advice and protection to the mediums as well as to their clients. Clients seek help making decisions or finding solutions for problems of illness, social tension, emotional distress, or difficulties such as unemployment. But possession also provides mediums with an outlet for behavior that would otherwise be deemed inappropriate. When possessed by "the child," for example, adults may act silly, play with toys, perform pranks, giggle for no reason, and in

spirit possession
Belief that spirits can enter a person's body and take over their thoughts and actions.

In Their Own Voices

Macumba Trance and Spirit Healing

In these excerpts from the film Macumba Trance and Spirit Healing, *two practitioners talk about their feelings when possessed by several of the macumba orishas: the Old Black Slave, the Indian, and the Child. Moisir, a lawyer, and his daughter Beje, a schoolteacher, have been participating in macumba ceremonies for about ten years, attending several times every week. In these group rites, dozens of mediums become possessed by four different spirits in succession. The mediums can then receive messages from the spirit world, giving advice to people who are sick, depressed, or in need. The experiences of Moisir and Beje reflect their direct contact with the spirit world, a contact that gives them emotional release and a prestigious role as healer or adviser in their community.*

MOISIR: Coming out of Senior Tupan (the Indian), my guide is annoyed, then I fall to the floor on the knees with one inside the other. He beats the floor twice with the hand opened and three times with the hand closed. They are strong blows, even violent enough to injure the hand. With this the recovery is complete.

BEJE: I feel that weight. Such a heavy weight. That once I am on my knees, as much as I want to, I can't get up. It's like I'm carrying something on my shoulders. Although the possession of the Old One is easy, coming out of it is a horrible thing. I think my head will leave my body. I begin to feel weak. Now, the Children are another story; they just say goodbye. With the Indian, the entrance and departure are equal. We feel tired to a degree but with a rested head. I have the impression of it being a little like a catharsis, you know, you get everything bad out and bring in a great deal of peace and tranquility.

MOISIR: The possession of the Old Black leaves the person very well. In spite of it being slow and difficult for the medium, it leaves the person feeling very well afterwards. Possession by the Old Black makes me feel very differently from the one by the Indian. In the possession of the Old Black, instead of feeling vibrations in the upper region, I feel it in both of my legs. My legs begin to get cold and a kind of pain comes into the knee and ends up knocking me on the floor. Upon feeling knocked down on the floor, I am nearly unconsciousness. I don't have the ability to reason, to talk for myself, to know people. I have a certain lack of consciousness in my work as the Old Black.

BEJE: The two possessions are totally different, not at all similar. For example, with the Indian, my hand begins to tremble, tremble, it keeps trembling, trembling, trembling until I feel the vibrations and fall to the knees. With the Old Black, I don't feel anything. Bam, bam, I'm on the floor.

MOISIR: As for coming out of the Old Black, it is very difficult. It really hurts when he leaves the medium. After, you feel a pleasant sensation as if you've come out of a sauna. You feel very tranquil, serene, without pain or preoccupations.

I don't like to call these "consultations" because we are not doctors. We simply give advice as to what people should do to better their spiritual and material lives. They look for jobs and they don't know what to do with all this desperation we are experiencing today. So we raise their morale. The Old Blacks have this objective, they are very much alive in material worlds.

From *Macumba Trance and Spirit Healing*, 1984. Written, produced, and directed by Madeleine Richeport. Richeport Films. Distributed by Filmakers Library, New York.

? *How can spirit-caused illnesses give people outlets for expressing their needs for order, balance, and security in their lives? How do healers address those needs?*

other ways express childish exuberance. It has been suggested (Lewis, 1989) that through the ecstatic experience, people give vent to their frustrations in a socially channeled and acceptable form. They are able to air their grievances in a way that does not disrupt or undermine the social order.

Illness may result when a person commits some ritual transgression. For example, people become ill if they fail to adhere to taboos, trespass on territory protected by spirit beings, or come in contact with powerful ritual objects. To be cured, the patient needs to undergo purification and ritual rebalancing. Most spirit causes of disease are metaphors for imbalance or disorder.

Religious, ritual, and practical approaches to illness and health go hand in hand, even in societies with medical treatment models based on modern science. Spiritual and magical treatments are especially effective if people believe in them at the same time as other factors are at work, such as the use of pharmaceuticals, the therapeutic

Anthropology Applied

Medical Anthropology and Ethnomedicine

Medical anthropologists apply the holistic and cross-cultural approaches of anthropology to understand and respond to questions of human well-being, health, and disease. How are illnesses caused, experienced, and spread, and how can they be prevented and treated? What healers, healing substances, and healing processes do people use, and what beliefs and values inform those uses? How is human health related to social structure, the health of other species, and the environment?

Medical practitioners use information from medical anthropology in treating their culturally diverse patients. For example, reaching a diagnosis and prescribing effective treatment is not based strictly on the scientific model but involves understanding people's perceptions and interpretations of their bodies and bodily processes and their beliefs about illness. Those perceptions, interpretations, and beliefs are culturally constructed, because what is considered pathological is culturally defined. It is even the case that some diseases are culture-specific.

At a broader level, medical anthropologists may study epidemics, endemic diseases that persist in a society, or disease vectors that cause the spread of disease. They may study the distribution of disease in the world and the disparities in health among different populations. Some focus on the relationships between people's health and health care and the political and economic factors in societies. Others focus on particular problem areas, such as child and maternal health, eating habits and nutrition, or sanitation in a world where 1,400 children die each day from diarrhea.

A branch of medical anthropology is ethnomedicine, the study of traditional medicine in cultural groups or in preindustrial societies. Beliefs and practices in different human groups include ideas about hygiene, disease prevention, and healing properties of objects in their environment. An example is the study of Maasai ethnomedicine, based on their use of the tree bark and roots for digestive health (Ryan, 2000). The Maasai use an infusion of the bark from a kind of acacia tree to add to food as a stimulant. It is used as a digestive aid during ceremonies that call for the consumption of huge quantities of meat. The Maasai also use the bark from a kind of albizia tree as an emetic. The root can be boiled and mixed with milk to get rid of or prevent intestinal parasites, and they use this drink to deworm their animals as well.

According to the World Health Organization (2004), 80 percent of the population of Africa relies on traditional medicine to meet daily health requirements. In Asia and Latin America as well, reliance on traditional medicines and practices may be more culturally acceptable and psychologically satisfying than those based on the Western scientific medical model. In addition, modern medicine, which is also the subject of ethnomedical research, may be inaccessible to the majority of people in a developing country. However, traditional medicines and practices may be just as effective. Plants that preindustrial people used to treat illness include the sources of aspirin, morphine, ephedrin, and penicillin.

CRITICAL THINKING QUESTIONS

What are some of your beliefs and values about health and illness? Where do those beliefs and values come from?

---

effects of receiving treatment, and the curative passage of time. A critical factor in the efficacy of ritual treatments is the patients' psychological state and beliefs. Patients become the center of attention of their family and community and benefit psychologically from the knowledge that people care about them and want them to recover. The patient's belief in the healer, whether shaman or physician, and in the treatment also affect the outcome of the cure.

Magic and Witchcraft

In addition to spirit causes of illness, witchcraft (also called sorcery) may be suspected in cases of illness, death, or misfortunes such as crop failure or infertility. Witches are people who employ spirit powers to cause harm to others, the opposite of healers. They are usually thought to be motivated by anger, jealousy, or simply the desire to see other people suffer. Their targets may be people with whom they have quarreled, but

imitative magic
Magic that operates on the principle of "like causes like."

contagious magic
Magic that operates on the principle that positive and negative qualities can be transferred through proximity or contact.

they may also harm someone randomly. As you read in Chapter 12, witchcraft also is used as a form of social control and a means of achieving social justice. It is effective partly because people believe in it. For example, the literature cites many cases of healthy young people sickening and dying upon learning that a sorcerer has placed a curse on them.

Witches employ different forms of magic to produce a specific and connected result. **Imitative magic,** for example, operates on the principle that "like causes like" or that "life imitates art." Thus, depictions and enactments of harmony may predispose a community toward harmony. Manipulating drawings or replicas of individuals may cause good or harm to come to those individuals in life. Witches may use imitative magic by cursing or damaging images or objects that represent their targets.

A practice known as *couvade* is an example of benign imitative magic. In Amazonian cultures, men leave the village when their wives are about to give birth, retiring to the forest. There they imitate the actions of women in labor. They may clutch their abdomens, writhe in pain, and scream out as though in physical distress. These actions are intended to attract evil spirits who lurk about in hopes of attacking newborns. These spirits are lured to the men, allowing the expectant mother to give birth in safety.

Contagious magic operates on the principle that positive and negative qualities can be transferred through proximity or contact, like an infection. Thus, one can become more sanctified or blessed by touching something holy. In pre-Christian Europe, contagious magic was used as a palliative for pain. The cure for toothache, for example, was to nail a lock of one's hair to an oak tree, known for its strength, and then to pull one's head away. The pain of the toothache passed through the hair to the tree, where it remained. Gaining power or immunity by touching or wearing objects made powerful or immune through ritual, such as amulets or shrunken heads, are also examples of contagious magic. Witches use contagious magic by secretly collecting a victim's nail clippings, hair, urine, or excrement and saying a spell over it to harm their target.

In some cultures, witches are thought to sprinkle harmful substances in people's food or drink, on their bodies while they sleep, or along the thresholds of their houses. People may believe that witches are capable of extraordinary physical feats, making things appear or disappear, transforming themselves into animals to lurk near a victim's house, or transporting themselves great distances in an instant.

Witchcraft may be a vehicle for the conscious or unconscious expression of anger and envy. For example, patterns of witchcraft accusations may follow lines of social tensions. Among the Cewa of Zimbabwe, accusations of witchcraft are usually preceded by quarrels, especially among matrilineal kin (Marwick, 1967). Cewa society has formal mechanisms for airing and resolving disputes between matrilineal groups but not within them. When conflict arises between members of the same matrilineal group, accusations about witchcraft may emerge as outlets.

Thus, beliefs in witchcraft are also expressions of people's fears, revulsions, and suspicions about the unusual behavior of others and about the sources or causes of misfortunes. It is also an expression of people's desires and intentions in situations over which they have no direct control. Because of the secrecy of witchcraft, very little is known about its actual frequency. However, magic is not confined to societies with witchcraft. All religions incorporate principles or practices that can be understood as magic.

? *Do you practice magic or magical thinking in your daily life? Are there principles or practices in a religion in your society that could be understood as magic?*

REVIEW

Religious practices include ritual, prayer, and sacrifice—ways of mediating between people and their spirit world or spiritual forces. Rituals, both sacred and secular, may include rites of renewal or intensification, calendric rituals, and rites of passage, such as puberty or initiation rites and funerary rites. Rituals are also used in curing ceremonies for illnesses with spirit causes, such as soul loss, object intrusion, spirit possession, or the violation of taboos. Imitative magic or contagious magic may be used in curing ceremonies and in other contexts, such as the couvade. Witchcraft or sorcery, which has complex social and psychological functions, also involves the use of magic.

THE ORIGINS AND FUNCTIONS OF RELIGION

It is impossible to know when or where religious beliefs first appeared in human societies. Archaeologists have discovered ancient human burials and can infer ritual practices that may have had religious meaning, such as the use of red ochre, grave goods, caches of ritual objects, and reliquaries or shrines. But we cannot know what was in the minds of those ancient peoples. Did they have some feeling of community and family ties that made them want to memorialize the burial places of their kin? Or did they have some beliefs in an eternal soul that made them want to give their relatives a respectable interment? Did they include grave goods with the burial so that the deceased could use them in an afterlife? Possible evidence of religious practices also comes from ancient cave paintings and rock paintings discovered in France, Spain, southern Africa, and Australia (Peregrine, 2003). Most of the paintings in these venues are of animals. Why?

Explaining the World

People often turn to their religion to seek explanations for events whose causes seem unknown or uncontrollable. Their beliefs help them gain some sense of control over what is ultimately unexplainable, unpredictable, and uncontrollable. People may wonder why their efforts are sometimes successful and sometimes not, why the same effort on different occasions may lead to a positive outcome and sometimes not. Why are some hunting expeditions successful but others fail? Why are some babies born healthy but others are sickly? Why do people die? Through ritual, people attempt to impose order and control over the outcomes of their efforts. Through ritual, they appeal to spirit forces to aid them in their endeavors and to ensure successful outcomes and to avoid misfortune.

Some researchers suggest that cave paintings such as this one are expressions of magical beliefs (Wallace, 1966). The painters drew pictures of animals that they wanted to hunt. Was this imitative magic in the belief that images of desired results would lead to actual occurrences? Others suggest that human beings were not included in paintings because of beliefs that a person could be harmed through their image by contagious magic.

The explanatory power of religious beliefs also helps people understand why the world is the way it is, why the earth has the shape it has, why the animals and plants have the form they have, and why people look and act the way they do. In most religions, there are thought to be creator or transformer deities who gave the world and all the creatures in it their present shape. These creator deities may also be responsible for imparting knowledge to people, teaching them how to plant, to hunt, and to organize their social life. They may be responsible for the origin of kinship groupings and of political structure. They may be responsible for setting out the kind of work that people do, the roles that men and women fill, and the values and ethics that people live by. In this way, religious beliefs are not only explanatory but also serve to legitimate a particular social or political system. For example, social inequality may be explained as part of a divine plan. A loved one's death may be explained as god's will.

Science and technology serve many of the same functions of explaining, predicting, and attempting to control the world. But in science, the underlying premises about cause and effect are different. The scientific approach is based on empirical observation or modeling of effects that are believed to have physical causes. Religious interpretations of observations are based on the belief that ultimate causes are spiritual processes and forces.

Solace, Healing, and Emotional Release

Religious faith provides psychological support in times of anxiety and stress, and religious practices can be emotionally therapeutic for individuals and groups. Confession of wrongdoings enables people to express their remorse, shed their guilt, and feel rehabilitated in their own eyes, in the eyes of their community, and in the eyes of the deities who may see their actions, judge them, and bestow forgiveness or mercy. Psychological functions of religion may be seen, for example, in visionary experiences or spirit quests. The profound emotional catharsis that can result from prayer, participation in rituals, and contact with the spirit world may have a healing effect by comforting a sufferer, releasing tension and worry.

Social Cohesion

Religious beliefs and practices often function to support cohesive communities. Most rituals involve, in addition to individuals, their family, wider kinship grouping, and social networks that connect them to others. Some rituals, such as seasonal or annual celebrations, unite an entire local population or tribal group.

Religious beliefs and practices can further function to justify the existing social order. Relationships among deities may reflect the sociopolitical nature of the human society. In stratified societies, the leader (whether chief, emperor, or king) may be thought to be a descendant of the divinity, endowed with divine power, or chosen directly by the deities. In the Polynesian chiefdoms, central and southern African kingdoms, European monarchies, and the Inca Empire, the head of state was thought to rule by divine right.

Teachings conveyed by spirits, especially in stories of creation and transformation, also legitimate the existing social order. Gender roles, for example, and the relations between women and men may be mandated through divine teachings or modeled through the relationships of male and female deities. For example, in the Hindu pantheon of deities, gods and goddesses have important and powerful roles and are equally as likely to be worshiped by believers. However, there is a striking difference in the personalities of married and unmarried goddesses. When married, goddesses are nurturing, benevolent, and trustworthy; when unmarried, they are aggressive, dangerous, and unpredictable.

In contrast, Diné **cosmology**—belief system concerning the origin and nature of the universe—presents many deities as interdependent and complementary male and female pairs. First Man and First Woman are important creator and transformer deities. Twilight Man and Twilight Woman and Dawn Man and Dawn Woman are deities of the daytime cycle. Although they play different roles, male and female deities have similar powers, personalities, and effects on the lives of humans.

Social Control

Rituals often function as formal and informal mechanisms of social control. In some stratified societies, codified criminal and civil laws, judicial processes, and punishments or penal sanctions are based on religious doctrines, customs, or texts. The function of social control can also be subtle, however. In some cultures, for example, the time of puberty is marked by role reversals in which socially disapproved behavior is permitted briefly in ritual context. Amish teenagers completing high school are permitted to drink beer and have noisy parties before settling down to a serious and devout life, for example. Similarly, central African teenagers are permitted to act in ways considered deviant—publicly speaking obscenities or acting lewd. They may also engage in gender reversals, boys dressing and acting like girls and girls mimicking the behavior and language of boys. Such ritualized permission to act inappropriately may temporarily ease tensions in societies where norms of proper behavior are strictly followed. They also serve to highlight social values through the transgression of norms.

Economic Adaptation

Another function of religion is to give people additional means to adapt to their environments and changes in their circumstances. Anthropologists using cultural materialist or ecological perspectives analyze religious practices as means of adapting to one's environment. Recall from Chapter 3, for example, Marvin Harris's interpretation of the sacred cow in India as protection against the slaughter of cattle in light of their

? *What do texts in a religion with which you are familiar teach about gender roles and relationships? What social order do those teachings tend to support?*

cosmology
Religious worldview of a people, including beliefs about the origin of the world, the pantheon of deities that exist, and their relationships to the spirit realm.

Case study

Pigs for the Ancestors

The Tsembaga of New Guinea, numbering about 200 people, participate in an interrelated system of rituals, economic production, social activity, and warfare. The Tsembaga practice a combination of horticulture and animal husbandry. Women are the principal farmers, planting and harvesting yams that feed the people and the many dozens of pigs that each family maintains. The Tsembaga live in balanced competition with neighboring tribes. Intergroup relations involve mutually beneficial trading exchanges and social interactions that lead to marriage alliances and military support for raids. Raids help balance the ratio of people to land and resources. Raids also function to create buffer zones of uninhabitable land that is left fallow to regenerate. However, too frequent raiding would upset this balance by disturbing people's ability to farm and raise their pigs. Therefore, a complex set of practices has developed to control the frequency of warfare, and these practices are couched in beliefs about people's obligations to their ancestors and the spirit realm.

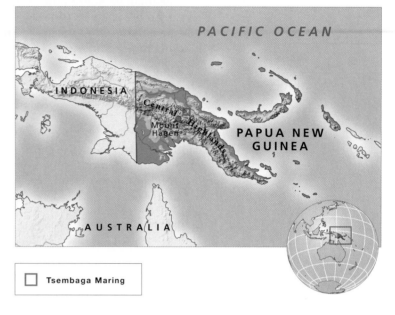

Tsembaga Maring

The cycle of practices may last as long as twenty years. At the end of a period of hostilities, Tsembaga ritually plant a shrub, called a *rumbin,* in their territory. The act of planting the *rumbin* communicates the group's symbolic and real connection to their territory. An elaborate feast is then held, centered around the slaughter of nearly all of the group's pigs. Only juvenile pigs are spared, to ensure future supplies. The pigs are slaughtered as a sacrifice to the ancestors who assisted the group in warfare with its neighbors and helped attain a successful outcome.

No matter how many pigs are sacrificed, however, the people think that the ancestors are not satisfied and obligations to the ancestors remain partly unfulfilled. People then make solemn pledges to the ancestors that they will offer future sacrifices. And until that time, hostilities must cease, because, according to Tsembaga belief, it is improper to renew hostilities until all obligations to the ancestors have been discharged. Thus, episodes of warfare are regulated by the amount of time it takes to increase the pig population to the number needed for a proper sacrifice.

Complex factors are involved in people's judgments about whether or not they have enough pigs to offer to the ancestors. When the pig population is relatively small, the animals can be fed without too much human effort, but after awhile the women gardeners must turn over a good portion of land that would otherwise go into production for human consumption and use it to grow food for the pigs instead. For instance, during Rappaport's fieldwork in the 1960s, about 36 percent of active farmland was used to produce food for the village's 170 pigs.

Eventually, a woman's complaints to her husband about the undue burdens on her labor reach a critical point, and he becomes willing to speak to other men on her behalf. By that time, most of the men in the village are receiving similar complaints from their wives. Once people experience the burdens of maintaining a large number of pigs, they acknowledge their readiness to make sacrifices to the ancestors.

The next episode of the cycle commences with the uprooting of the *rumbin,* signaling the beginning of a year-long festival. During the festival, friendly neighboring groups are invited to visit the village to socialize and feast on the sacrificed pigs. Social and economic goals may be pursued during these festivals. Pork is distributed to one's allies, and other articles of trade are exchanged. In addition, young men hold dances to signal their interest in and availability for marriage. Eligible young women attend the dances and have a chance to observe the physical and social qualities of eligible men. The young men's presence is also interpreted as a willingness to aid the hosts as military allies in future conflicts.

The final segment of the cycle begins after the festival period has drawn to a close. Raiding one's enemies (one's competitors for scarce land) may now resume. When the hostilities have temporarily resolved underlying tensions, the *rumbin* is replanted, marking the end of one cycle and the beginning of the next.

central importance in the economy of farmers. In another classic study, Roy Rappaport (1969, 2000) demonstrates how a complex ritual cycle relates to the economy and environment of the Tsembaga of New Guinea.

> **REVIEW**
>
> Whatever their origins, religious beliefs and practices provide explanations for the world as it is, for the way people are, and for major events in people's lives. Religion also helps give people solace in times of trouble and sorrow, allowing for emotional release and providing emotional support. In addition, religious beliefs and practices function to bind communities together into cohesive networks. As ideologies, they can both support and change the existing social order and, as in the case of the Tsembaga, people's adaptations to their environment.

RELIGION AND CULTURE CHANGE

? *What is an example of a belief or practice in a religion that you know about that has been changed or abandoned?*

Religious beliefs and practices, like every other aspect of culture, are responsive to changes in society. Social, economic, political, and historical developments have an impact on religions. Changes in other areas of their lives may cause people to think about their relationship with the spirit world in different ways, altering some practices or even abandoning them altogether. People may begin to rethink the roles of religious practitioners, possibly changing the criteria for choosing them or how they are trained. Ritual practice may change as new ceremonies are adopted and older ones are modified or discarded. Although religion seems like a timeless tradition, like any other system of ideology and practice it is subject to transformation.

Religions are dynamic systems, incorporating new ideas either from external sources or from the innovative creativity of believers. Some religions may be inherently more receptive to change. Polytheistic religions, for example, usually do not have a single standardized doctrine. They allow for additions of new ideas or ritual elements that appear to be effective and the elimination of those that no longer achieve desired results. New rituals might be borrowed from neighbors or from the religions of more distant people met in travel or trade. People observe each other's rituals, listen to religious narratives, and adopt practices that they find beautiful, compelling, or effective. New deities may be incorporated into a local pantheon as believers find them appealing or useful. This process is more common in religions that lack central texts whose interpretation can be argued or even fought over. People tend to borrow stories and mythic characters readily, often changing details to suit their own circumstances and attitudes. This process of combining and modifying elements from different religions is called *syncretism*, a term first defined in Chapter 2, and is a process inherent to all religions.

GLOBALIZATION

Syncretism is a common result of political processes, especially in situations of conquest and colonization. As state societies have expanded throughout history, conquerors have imposed their religious beliefs and practices on defeated populations.

Defeated populations, seeing the conquerors' gods as superior, may willingly adopt their religious systems. In many situations, however, conquered people resist change and resist abandoning their own religious beliefs and practices. They may hold even more tightly to their own traditions, keeping their rituals as acts of resistance and self-empowerment. In this context, new religious traditions may arise that give former practices new meanings and interpretations.

Revitalization Movements

A source of new religious traditions is revitalization movements—religion-based responses to societal crises. Revitalization movements arise in times of social and political upheaval, often in situations of invasion, conquest, and control, when people are confronted by a loss of their rights and restrictions on their freedom. Such movements also may arise as a response to increasing social and political inequalities within a society among people who lack rights or advantages. They are aimed at restructuring power relationships within a society or between conquered peoples and their rulers.

Revitalization movements frequently begin after an individual receives direct messages from the spirit world telling him or her to convey divine teachings to the community. Referred to as **prophets,** such individuals become the conduits for communication between the spirit world and ordinary people. Essentially, the messages point out how people have become demoralized by straying from the right path and abandoning their traditional values and ethics. Although external forces may be causing people's suffering, the people themselves contribute to their troubles. The prophets teach that the people must return to traditional ways, stressing the values of hospitality or civility, generosity, cooperativeness, and solidarity with relatives and community members. Leaders of revitalization movements proselytize others, always seeking to enlarge the community of followers and establish a network of believers.

There are several kinds of revitalization movements. **Nativistic movements** attempt to rid the society of foreign elements, returning to what is conceived to be a prior state of cultural purity. The late nineteenth-century Ghost Dance cult of the Plains Indians (see Chapter 2) is an example of a nativistic movement, inspired by the prophet Wovoka. **Revivalistic movements** stress the importance of reviving cultural and religious practices that express core values but have been marginalized or abandoned. **Millinerian movements** incorporate apocalyptic themes, prophesying an abrupt end to the world as we know it by a specific time or date in the future, leading to the establishment of a new way of life or form of existence. **Messianic movements** stress the role of a prophet or messiah as a savior for his or her people. Some religion-based social movements combine aspects of these revitalization themes.

Although revitalization movements are religious, they also have social and political messages. They are always at least potentially revolutionary and can develop into direct challenges to the established order with the aim of transforming or overturning social and political systems. Historical factors affect whether political movements develop. If authorities recognize the political potential of revitalization themes, for example, they may brutally suppress the movement. However, the leaders of the movement may direct people's energies away from political action to protect them from attack. Messages might call for accommodating external situations, or they might postpone the rewards for faith to some distant time in the future, even until after death. These kinds of messages also direct people away from political rebellion.

Cargo Cults

A different kind of revitalization movement arose in Melanesia in the early twentieth century. Referred to as **cargo cults,** these movements were a response to British colonial control, the expropriation of native land, and the relegation of indigenous peoples to roles as menial laborers and second-class citizens. Cargo cults arose at various times and in various places in Melanesia, most notably in New Guinea (Worseley, 1967, 1968). Prophets received spirit messages telling people to perform rituals, based on traditional principles of magical cause and effect, that were supposed to result in the arrival of material wealth ("cargo") for the native people.

Cargo cult followers built loading docks along the coast and, later, landing strips for airplanes in the bush, intending to make landing sites for ships and airplanes. They had seen these vehicles bringing in goods for the colonial Europeans; and they believed that if they acted as if the goods were coming, life would imitate art. On this principle of magic, the people imitated European behavior that they thought was responsible for the arrival of the cargo: They wore European-style tophats, neckties, and jackets, and sat around tables and scribbled on pieces of paper that they then put into boxes—all in imitation of having meetings and sending orders for goods.

prophets
Religious leaders who receive divine inspiration, often in a vision or trance.

nativistic movements
Revitalization movements attempting to rid society of foreign elements and return to what is conceived to be a prior state of cultural purity.

millinerian movements
Revitalization movements incorporating apocalyptic themes, prophesying an abrupt end to the world as we know it, leading to the establishment of a new way of life or form or existence.

messianic movements
Revitalization movements stressing the role of a prophet or messiah as a savior for his or her people.

cargo cults
Revitalization movements arising in Melanesia in the early twentieth century with the aim of obtaining material wealth through magical means.

Cargo cult activities appeared foolish to the Europeans, but these activities were consistent with the native worldview. According to Melanesian principles, wealth was obtained by a combination of hard work and ritual. Native people never saw Europeans doing what the Melanesians regarded as work, yet the foreigners received wealth from across the ocean or from the sky, so, clearly, their rituals were powerful. The preliterate Melanesians imitated what they took to be European rituals involving costumes and actions such as writing. Eventually, rituals were abandoned as they failed to attract cargo, until another prophet came with a new set of instructions on what to do. Waves of cargo rituals emerged and dissipated in the 1930s and 1940s. In contrast to the repressive responses to the Ghost Dance of the American Plains, however, the colonial government in New Guinea ignored the cargo cults because they posed no threat to colonial power. Eventually, the cargo movements dissolved because they failed to achieve the desired results. Note that cargo cults and the imitation of European behavior also demonstrate the political message underlying revitalization movements.

Role of Founders in Buddhism, Christianity, and Islam

Some of the most widely practiced religions in the world today began as revitalization movements. Buddhism, Christianity, and Islam originated with individuals who received divine inspiration. These founders essentially reacted against human suffering and the social and political inequalities in their societies, giving as their message the need for all people to establish freedom, equality, justice, and peace. These messages ultimately became institutionalized in formal religions under the control of ecclesiastical elites who serve as intermediaries and interpreters of divine messages.

Siddhartha Gautama, later referred to as Buddha, or "Enlightened One," was born about 525 B.C. in India, the eldest son of a local prince, destined to inherit his father's position. But Gautama rejected the privilege to which he was entitled by birth, choosing instead to leave his parents, wife, and son to seek inner wisdom and the end to physical and spiritual suffering (Koller, 1982). Buddha's message was in part a reaction against inequities in the caste system maintained through Hinduism. That system consigned people at birth to specific inherited occupations, social standing, and degrees of ritual purity. Hinduism also emphasized people's role in an inescapable cycle of reincarnation with its inescapable cycle of suffering. The message of Buddhism is that people can escape caste duty through right thinking and right action to achieve spiritual enlightenment, equality, and oneness with the universe. And eventually a person can escape the cycle of reincarnation by attaining perfect knowledge and self-control.

Jesus, whose teachings led to the founding of Christianity, was born sometime after the death of Herod in 4 B.C. Biblical scholars have different interpretations of the life of Jesus, and those interpretations reflect the social and political beliefs of the analysts (Meier, 1991). Some scholars emphasize Jesus' role as a prophet of "restoration theology," predicting the divine destruction of the imperial order imposed by Rome on Israel and the establishment of a world of justice and mercy (Sanders, 1985). In this view, Jesus' spiritual prophecy was central and within the tradition of Jewish law and interpretation. Other scholars emphasize his role as a teacher and somewhat subversive commentator on the life of his times (Mack, 1988). Still others stress the social context of Jesus' life and see his message as relating fundamentally to sociopolitical conditions (Borg, 1994; Crossan, 1994). According to this view, like Buddha, Jesus was appalled by inequalities in the prevailing social system of his day. He was also angered by the cooperation of some members of the inner circles of power in the Hebrew state with their Roman invaders and conquerors. While the common people chafed under increased control and demands for labor and tribute, the local secular and religious elites benefited from their favored positions as puppets of Roman colonial rule. This dynamic is not unique to that area but, rather, occurs in most colonized societies.

According to one modern interpretation (Crossan, 1994), Jesus' critique of his own society focused on inequalities within the family, particularly the privileged role of the father in a patriarchal system of male dominance. Because hierarchical relations begin with lessons on dominance and subordination within the family, Jesus advocated the equality of women and men (Fiorenza, 1983). Jesus used the metaphor of "open commensality"—the practice of eating at the same table—to undermine norms that segregated people according to rank and gender (Crossan, 1994). The "open table," where everyone—men and women, beggars, lepers, and all types of social outcasts—were welcome and could eat together, became a powerful symbol of the egalitarian society Jesus envisioned. In addition, Jesus urged his followers to create the kingdom of God on earth through social and religious transformation.

The founder of Islam, Muhammad, was born in Mecca around A.D. 570 of poor family. The Arabian Peninsula at the time was home to many small tribal groups who practiced polytheistic religions with an array of nature deities (Guillaume, 1986). During a solitary meditation, Muhammad experienced a vision of the angel Gabriel, who told him that God is the one and only God whom people must obey. Muhammad began to preach his message of a monotheistic religion, initially attracting only a small following of mostly slaves and poor people. He was attacked as a sorcerer, but he continued to proclaim his message for all Arabs. His mission, then, was to unite the Arab world under the mantle of one religion with its one God. However, unity came with the price of war: If people did not join the faith on their own, they had to be compelled through force to believe, thus unleashing a holy war of proselytizing religion through conquest.

In Buddhism, Christianity, and Islam, following the deaths of the founders, disciples or followers began to spread the faith to others. Over the centuries, increasingly centralized "churches" were organized to pull together a body of worship, setting out practices and doctrine. Eventually, ecclesiastical elites took control not only of priestly functions but also of standardized religious doctrines. People who had divergent interpretations of religious texts were deemed dissidents, and at various times in the history of Buddhism, Christianity, and Islam, religious authorities harassed and punished dissidents as heretics. According to some views, these authorities moved away from the original messages, replacing them with doctrines of obedience to the state, hierarchical family systems, and a controlling priesthood.

Religion and Globalization

As state societies expand their borders and influence throughout many parts of the world far from their centers of origin, they have spread their religious beliefs through proselytism. **Proselytism** is the attempt to convert a person or group from one religion to another. State societies throughout history have brought their religions to the people they have conquered. Various denominations of Buddhism, Christianity, and Islam have gained millions of converts through this process. As missionaries spread their religions to all parts of the world, some locally indigenous religious beliefs and practices have been modified and others have been abandoned and replaced by the new religions. And in some cases, people have modified foreign rituals and developed different interpretations of standard beliefs.

Diffusion of beliefs and practices and their absorption by distant peoples have resulted in marked contrasts between local practices and those in the centers of origin. For example, in Africa and the Caribbean, Roman Catholic saints are identified with tribal African deities, and rituals dedicated to indigenous deities are merged with Roman Catholic practice. Spirit possession, a phenomenon marginalized in mainstream Roman Catholic doctrine, is given central importance in Haiti, Brazil, and many African indigenous churches. Similarly, Native American Christians may incorporate traditional practices, especially prayers to the Great Creator and such offerings as the burning of sage or cedar.

Buddhism, Christianity, and Islam, the major proselytizing religions, have been successful in part because their practice is not tied to a specific locale. They can be transplanted anywhere and incorporate local beliefs and practices. This characteristic contrasts with religions whose cosmologies are tied to specific places, such as those of the Diné or Australian Aborigines.

In the world today, as in the past, global economic and political processes have affected religious practices and interpretations of sacred texts. Some revitalization movements within Christianity and Islam have led to an increase in religious fundamentalism. **Fundamentalism,** a term coined in the United States in 1920, means a commitment to do battle to defend traditional religious beliefs. In the United States,

proselytism
The attempt to convert a person or group from one religion to another.

fundamentalism
A term coined in the United States in 1920 meaning a commitment to do battle to defend traditional religious beliefs.

Culture Change ▬▬▬▬▬▬▬▬

THE DEVELOPMENT OF RELIGIOUS DENOMINATIONS

The major world religions have changed many times and continue to change. The development of various Hindu, Buddhist, Judaic, Christian, and Islamic denominations follows local practices and beliefs. People in different places at different times interpret central texts in their own ways, adapting them to their cultures and their circumstances. Religions also change because of philosophical or ethical issues of importance to their followers. As times change, as social norms are transformed, religions respond by altering emphases in their practices and beliefs.

Some current controversies demonstrate these processes. Among Jews, the distinction among Orthodox, Conservative, and Reformed branches focuses partly on issues of dietary rules and gender roles. Orthodox Jews, for example, adhere strictly to biblical dietary restrictions, principally taboos on eating pork and shellfish. Kosher rules also prescribe the separation of meat and dairy foods, extended to the necessary separation of cooking utensils, dishes, and cutlery associated with them. In contrast, Reformed Jews do not adhere to kosher dietary regulations. In Orthodox synagogues, men sit on the main level of the building, while women sit in a balcony above, symbolizing and enacting the segregation of the genders. Rules of ritual purity and contamination also demand that women take purifying baths, called *mikvas*, at the end of their menstrual periods. These practices, highlighting gender differences and the polluting effects of women, are abandoned in Reformed practice. In addition, women may be ordained as rabbis among Reformed Jews; they are barred from such roles among the Orthodox.

Christian churches and denominations are distinguished on the basis of doctrine and practice. One major doctrinal difference between Roman Catholics (and Eastern Orthodox churches) and Protestants concerns the meaning of the rite of communion. Roman Catholicism and Eastern Orthodoxy teach that the wafer and wine taken at communion have inner forms that become the body and blood of Jesus when blessed and consumed. Protestantism treats the wafer and wine only symbolically, if at all, representing but not actuating Christ's body. Protestant denominations also tend to believe that individuals and groups are free to read and interpret the Scriptures for themselves rather than receive correct interpretations from religious authorities. In addition, women may be ordained as ministers in many Protestant denominations but are barred from the Roman Catholic priesthood.

In Islam, the major Shi'ite and Sunni branches, among others, differ in their acceptance of religious authority, interpretation of the Qur'an, and application of religious law to secular activities. Sunnis, the majority, believe that any devout man can become a religious leader and that the Qu'ran should be taken at face value and not be subject to interpretation. Shi'ites, on the other hand, believe that religious leaders, imams, must be descended from Muhammad or divinely appointed and duly praised, and that they are authorities on interpreting the Qur'an to address current events.

Strict adherence to religious doctrines is strongest in countries such as Saudi Arabia, where Islam is the state religion, and among groups such as the Taliban, a militant Islamic group that took over Afghanistan in 1995 and enforced a strict Muslim code of behavior. In regions far from the centers of Islamic origins, beliefs and practices are more strongly influenced by local traditions and worldviews. For example, in Indonesia, the most populous Muslim country in the world, people rarely conform to strict interpretations of Islamic law as it relates to social practices.

members of some Christian fundamentalist movements advocate a return to both religious and social orthodoxy. They keep to a literal interpretation of the Bible and tend to believe in the divine origin of gender roles differentiating the work and family roles of women and men. They also tend to support an ideologically conservative political agenda and to place religious authority above secular authority in life matters. Fundamentalists organize against abortion rights, for example, and against gay marriage. They oppose the teaching of evolution in schools. Some fundamentalist groups have become associated with beliefs in white supremacy.

Fundamentalist organizations and lobbies have become a powerful influence in American politics. Other church groups, such as Americans United for the Separation of Church and State, advocate separation between religious and political agendas. Some religious organizations work for progressive social and political change and are outspoken members of peace and antinuclear movements. Within the Roman Catholic church, clergy and lay workers associated with liberation theology have been in the forefront of movements for social, economic, and political justice and equality, particularly in Central and South America.

Islamic fundamentalism has become increasingly popular and dangerous. In some countries of the Middle East and Africa, Islamic fundamentalists have taken over local or national governments, imposing a strict interpretation of the Qur'an on social and political policies. In Iran, for example, and in several states in Nigeria, public laws must conform to Islamic principles, and crimes and punishments are defined according to sacred texts. Religious authorities double as political leaders, whether by election or proclamation. In other Middle Eastern countries—for example, Iraq—as well as in Indonesia and the Philippines, Islamist movements have contributed to the destabilization of local and central governments and are attempting to overthrow elected or appointed authorities and institute Islamic law.

Some analysts attribute the upsurge in Islamic fundamentalism to the global spread of Western influence, chiefly from the United States. American social behaviors and social values are seen as immoral. Fundamentalist movements have gained popularity as proponents claim to resist American influence on internal affairs and foreign policies. This resistance has become increasingly violent. Al Qaeda, a terrorist network with cells in more than fifty countries, is an extreme expression of Islamic fundamentalism. Its members are both anti-Western and opposed to Arabic governments that do not espouse its own version of strict Islamic principles. On September 11, 2001, members of Al Qaeda killed more than 3,000 people by flying aircraft into the twin towers of the World Trade Center in New York City.

GLOBALIZATION

In 2003, the number of adherents of Christian religions worldwide was estimated at more than 2 billion, about a third of the world population. European state expansion, missionism, colonialism, economic and political hegemony, and imperialism have contributed to what some observers refer to as the globalization of Christianity. Islam, another strongly proselytizing religion historically associated with state expansion and consolidation and with economic and political domination, has about 1.3 billion adherents worldwide.

REVIEW

Religious practices and beliefs change over time through internal and external forces of transformation. In syncretism, new religions are created by combining parts of older ones. Revitalization movements emphasize core beliefs and values as a means of adapting to undesired changes. Nativistic, revivalistic, millinerian, and messianic movements, as well as cargo cults, are all forms of religion-based adaptations to change. Major world religions such as Buddhism, Christianity, and Islam began as revitalization movements of some kind. Religions have spread through forces of globalization and the practice of proselytism. Religious fundamentalism is a powerful force in the world today.

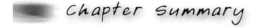

Chapter Summary

What Is Religion?

• Religion is actions and feelings based on beliefs in the existence of spirit beings and supranormal (or superhuman) forces. Religious beliefs and practices give people ways to contact spirit beings and forces and to show them honor

and respect as well as to invoke their blessings and protection. Anthropologists analyze religious beliefs and behaviors using perspectives of comparison and cultural relativism. They try to understand people's ideas about the spirit realm from the people's own point of view. And they focus on the ways that religious beliefs and practices are consistent with other aspects of culture. Religions tend to reflect the structure of their society. For example, in societies with hierarchical social structures, people are more likely to believe in the existence of a ranked pantheon of deities.

Spirit Beings and Forces

- Spirit entities and forces have extraordinary, more than human, powers. They are typically eternal or indestructible. They know more than a person can know, and they are able to act in ways that humans cannot. Thus, people seek contact with them to gain their protection and aid.

- One common, nearly universal, form that spirit takes is the soul—the eternal aspect of living things. In some beliefs, only humans have souls. Souls are seen as the animating aspect of living things. And when the body dies, they escape and exist eternally in some other form or in a nonmaterial state. The belief in souls is called animism; the belief that all things are endowed with some spirit essence is called animatism.

- Some religious traditions have many spirit beings in human form with specific attributes, powers, and functions. Polytheism, belief in numerous deities, is widespread throughout the world. In monotheistic religions, people believe in one supreme deity with powers and knowledge that affect all aspects of life, although there may be other, lesser, spirit beings and important moral heroes as well. Other types of spirit beings include, for example, the spirit forms of deceased ancestors.

- Some peoples believe in mana—a spirit power or essence that endows people, animals, objects, or events with special qualities or powers. In some cultures of Australia and North America, people believe that they are descended from human or animal spirit beings called totems. Totems are the primordial protectors of the people to whom people owe gratitude and respect.

- Spirit beings and forces are dangerous if they are contacted in the wrong way, in the wrong place, or at the wrong time. Restrictions on places or objects are called taboos. A tabooed object or place can cause harm because the spirit power within it can become dangerous.

Religious Practitioners and Specialists

- Most religions have individuals or groups who function as either part-time or full-time religious specialists. In some cases a person receives a calling from the spirit world to become a religious specialist, or he or she inherits spiritual powers from someone in the previous generation. In other cases, a person decides to become a religious practitioner for personal reasons or because ritual practice gives outlet for artistic expression.

- Mediums are specialists who make contact with spirit beings or spirits of the dead. Through ritual and trace, they become conduits for messages between ordinary people and the spirit world. Diviners have the power to predict or shape the future through messages and omens they receive and interpret from the spirit world. Healers diagnose the spirit cause of illness and effect cures through the performance of rituals. Shamans are part-time religious practitioners who make contact with the spirit world through ritual, prayer, and trance. They receive visions and messages from the spirit realm and may serve as diviners and healers. Some societies have full-time religious practitioners called priests who lead religious organizations and officiate at rituals but are not expected to be able to communicate directly with the spirit world.

Religious Practice

- Rituals are a fundamental aspect of all religious practices and include prayer, a public and private ritual through which believers transmit messages to spirit beings. Believers also transmit messages through offerings they make of foods or animals given in rituals of sacrifice. Rituals mark events in religious and secular calendars.

- People also perform rituals to celebrate socially significant transitions in an individual's life cycle. Such rites of passage mark birth, puberty, marriage, and death. Rites of passage ritualize three aspects of a change in life status: separation, transition, and reincorporation. Puberty rites mark sexual maturity and the transition from childhood to adulthood. Funerals mark the departure of the deceased and reinforce family and community solidarity as people share the expression of sorrow and loss.

- People adhere to theories of health maintenance, causes of disease, and strategies for treatment. Health is often thought of as a state of harmony or balance that depends on the orderly functioning of a person's body, relations with others, the health of the environment, and relations with spirit beings and forces. When this balance is disturbed, illness and misfortune may follow. Serious illness is often attributed to spiritual causes needing ritual diagnosis and treatment with the aid of religious specialists. Spirit causes can include soul loss (the sudden departure of a person's soul), object intrusion (a foreign object shot into the patient's body), spirit possession (the invasion of a person's body by a spirit), or the violation of taboos. Curative rituals attempt to restore balance through magic, practical remedies, therapeutic effects, social validation, and the passage of time. In combination, spiritual treatments can be especially effective when people believe in them.

- Witchcraft may be suspected in cases of illness, death, or misfortune. Witches or sorcerers employ spirit powers to cause harm to others. They are usually thought to be motivated by anger, jealousy, or simply the desire to see other people suffer. Witchcraft may be used as a form of social control and a means of achieving social justice. Witches, like healers, employ imitative and contagious magic. Magic is an expression of people's desires and intentions in situations over which they have no direct control.

The Origins and Functions of Religion

- Specific origins of religious beliefs are unknown. Religions give people solace in times of trouble and sorrow, and religious beliefs and practices bind communities together into cohesive networks. They give ideological support for the existing social structures, including family organization, social stratification, and political inequalities. Anthropologists using cultural materialist or ecological perspectives analyze religious practices as a means of adapting to one's environment.

- Social, economic, political, and historical developments have an impact on religions. Changes may cause people to think about their relationship with the spirit world in different ways, altering some practices or even abandoning them altogether. Religions incorporate new ideas from either external sources or the innovations of believers.

Religion and Culture Change

- Revitalization movements are religion-based responses to societal crises. They arise in times of social and political upheaval, often in situations of invasion, conquest, and colonial control. Revitalization movements are aimed at restructuring power relationships within a society or between conquered peoples and their rulers. They are begun by individuals who receive direct messages from the spirit world telling them to convey divine teachings to the community. Nativism is aimed at ridding society of foreign elements, returning to what is thought to be a prior state of cultural purity. Revivalism stresses the importance of reviving cultural and political practices. Millinerian movements incorporate apocalyptic themes and an abrupt end to the present world and establishment of a new world. Messianic movements stress the role of a prophet or messiah as a savior for his or her people.

• The major world religions have changed many times and continue to change, following local practices and beliefs throughout the world. As times change and social norms are transformed, religions respond by altering their practices and beliefs. These changes can lead to the development of distinctive religious sects and denominations within the world religions, differentiated on the basis of both belief and practice.

• As state societies have expanded their borders and influence throughout the world, they have spread their religious beliefs through proselytism, converting people or groups from one religion to another. Various denominations of Buddhism, Christianity, and Islam have gained millions of converts through this process. Revitalization movements within Christianity and Islam have led to an increase in religious fundamentalism. In the United States, Christian fundamentalists advocate a literal interpretation of the Bible and tend to support an ideologically conservative political agenda and to place religious authority above secular authority in life matters. Islamic fundamentalism includes terrorism and rejection of Western influences.

Key Terms

religion 366	mediums 371	calendric rituals 375	millenarian
religious speech 367	diviners 372	puberty rites 376	movements 387
animism 368	healers 372	funerary rights 376	messianic
animatism 368	shamans 372	spirit possession 379	movements 387
polytheism 368	priests 373	imitative magic 382	cargo cults 387
monotheistic religions 369	rituals 373	contagious magic 382	proselytism 389
ancestor worship 369	sacred rituals 373	cosmology 384	fundamentalism 389
mana 370	rites of renewal 374	prophets 387	
totemism 370	prayer 374	nativistic movements 387	
secret societies 370	sacrifice 374	revivalistic movements 387	

Review Questions

1. What questions do all religions answer?

2. How are animism, animatism, and deism different? What are some examples of ways that these belief systems are expressed?

3. How do different religions define and treat spirits of the dead?

4. What are the differences between a shaman and a priest?

5. What are other types of religious practitioners? What roles and functions do they play in their societies?

6. How do people make distinctions between the sacred and the secular? How are concepts such as mana, taboo, and blessing used to bestow sacredness?

7. In what ways is religion expressed through symbolic culture and religious speech?

8. In what ways is religion expressed through behavior? What religious concepts do people use to explain human behavior?

9. What types of secular and sacred rituals do people everywhere perform?

10. What are the different types of magic? Why do people everywhere sometimes use magical thinking?

11. What are some social and cultural functions of sorcery or witchcraft?

12. What are some examples of the relationship between religion and other social systems in a society, such as the political and economic system, system of social control, and system of social stratification?

13. What five basic functions does religion serve for people and their ways of life?

14. How do religions change in response to dynamics of social and culture change?

15. How do syncretisms reveal adaptations to cultural contact and the diffusion of ideas?

16. What are the types and characteristics of revitalization movements?

17. How were the Ghost Dance movement of the North American Plains Indians and the cargo cults of Pacific Islanders similar? How were they different?

18. What is the impact of globalization on world religions?

The Arts

CHAPTER 15

Preview

1. **How do anthropologists define art?**
2. **What can we learn about people by examining their art?**
3. **How is art embedded in culture? How do cultures shape artistic expression and the aesthetic principles on which it is based?**
4. **What are some universal and culturally specific forms of art? How do those forms of art express or create symbolic culture?**
5. **How does art reflect society and social realities?**
6. **What cultural, social, and personal functions does art serve?**

*A*fter a long time Mataora became jealous of his elder brother Tau-toru; he saw that he ardently desired his wife. In consequence he thrashed his wife Niwareka; which caused her to flee away to the underworld to the home of her ancestors and parents. A great sorrow fell on Mataora, and he deeply lamented his beautiful wife.

And now Mataora started off to search for his wife. When Mataora arrived at the guard-house of the underworld, he asked of the guard "Did you not see a woman pass this way?" "Ah, yes! She has gone on long ago; she was crying as she came along." Mataora then said, "Cannot I go to where she is?"

Mataora then descended, and went on until he came to a shed, at the village of Ue-tonga, where were many people. He found Ue-tonga engaged in tattooing; he sat down there to see the operation, and saw the blood descending from the cuts in the face. He called out, "Your system of tattooing the face is all wrong! It is not done in that manner up above." Ue-tonga said, "This is the custom below here; that above is quite wrong. That system is called by us "painted." That kind of moko [or face tattooing] is used in house building." Mataora replied, "That is called carving with us." Then Ue-tonga placed his hand on Mataora's face and rubbed it—and all the moko came off! The people all burst out laughing, and then Ue-tonga called out, "O ye above! O ye people of above! Ye are quite wrong in calling it carving. Behold the face is quite clean from rubbing. That is only painting."

Mataora now said to Ue-tonga, "You have destroyed the moko on my face; you must tattoo me." Ue-tonga replied, "It is well! Lie down!" Then Ue-tonga called on the artists to delineate the pattern on Mataora's face. Then Ue-tonga sat down by the side of Mataora with his chisel and commenced to tattoo him. Great was his pain and his groans. He then sang his song:

Niwareka! that is lost, where art thou?
Show thy self, O Niwareka! O Niwareka!
'Twas love of thee that dragged me down here below,
Niwareka! Niwareka! love eats me up!
Niwareka! Niwareka! thou has bound me tight.
Niwareka! Niwareka! Let us remain in this world,
Niwareka! Niwareka! Leave behind this underworld,
Niwareka! Niwareka, and thus end my pain.

When Ue-kuru, the younger sister of Niwareka, heard this, she ran off to where Niwareka was engaged in weaving a garment Ue-kuru said to her sister, "There is a man over there who is being tattooed; a very handsome man; who, whilst the operation was going on, was crying and singing. The words of the song often repeated your name." The female companions of Niwareka all said, "Let us all go and see!"

So Mataora was led off. Then was heard the welcome of Niwareka and her lady companions, who became enamored with the appearance of Mataora. She said to her friends, "His bearing is that of Mataora" When Mataora had sat down on the mats, Niwareka asked, "Art thou Mataora?" He bowed his head and held out his arms towards Niwareka, asking her to draw near. Niwareka then knew it was indeed Mataora.

Mataora, now said to Niwareka, "Let us both return to the Earth. She replied, "The customs of the upper *world are bad. Rather let us remain below, and gather our thoughts and turn them from the evils of the upper world."* So Niwareka told her father and brothers the reason of Mataora's visit—to take her back to the Earth. Upon hearing this, her father said, *"You go back, O Mataora! Leave Niwareka here. A custom of the upper world is to beat women, is it not?"*

At this, Mataora was consumed with shame. The brother of Niwareka, said to him, "Mataora! Abandon the upper world—the home of evil—altogether, and let us both live down here. Cut off all above and its evil ways, let all below with its better customs be separate."

"Mataora replied, "I will in future adopt your methods in the upper-world." Then the father said to him, *"Mataora! Do not let a repetition of the evil repute of the upper-world, reach here below."* Mataora replied, *"Look on my moko [face-tattoo]; if it had been painted it might be washed off, but as it is a moko cut in the flesh by you it is permanent and cannot be washed out. I will adopt in future the ways of this lower world and its works."*

From S. Percy Smith, *The Lore of the Whare-Wananga* (New Plymouth, N.Z., 1913), http://www.sacred-texts.com/pac/lww/index.

In this story, the Maori of New Zealand tell the origin of one of their prominent arts, tattooing on the face and body. According to tradition, the art was learned in primordial times from sacred beings who inhabited the underworld. This story gives a divine license to an artistic and aesthetic style. By the early twentieth century, few Maori were getting tattoos because of pressure from European colonial authorities who regarded the practice as savage. But by the late twentieth century, the art had become popular again, partly as a sign of ethnic pride and identity.

WHAT IS ART?

Like the word culture, art is a word that we use in everyday speech but have difficulty formulating a precise definition for it. Even anthropologists often describe the arts of the people they study without defining what they mean, taking it for granted that the meanings are understood. In a study of American arts and **aesthetics**—philosophies about what has beauty and value in art—anthropologist Richard Anderson (2000:8) proposed a number of key characteristics of art. According to Anderson, works of **art** are

- artifacts of human creation;
- created through the exercise of exceptional physical, conceptual, or imaginative skill;
- intended to affect the senses; and
- share stylistic conventions with similar works.

Let us explore these characteristics. Art objects are made by human beings. This characteristic seems straightforward enough, despite occasional museum exhibitions of the "artwork" of gorillas, chimpanzees, and even elephants. Although it might be said that some paintings done by our primate relatives look similar to the works of modern artists, most would dismiss these as "not art" because of the lack of intentionality, at least as we attribute intentionality to human beings. That is, a human artist produces work intended to be art, with a preconceived plan of working through a specific medium. We assume that other animals lack this type of volition and intentionality, even though they may delight in the process of producing new objects.

Second, art is work stimulated by an exceptional creative concept and produced with exceptional physical skill. This criterion suggests that paintings produced by some people may be defined as art, while paintings made by others may not. The concept of "skill" is embedded in the word art, which derives from the Latin *artem*, meaning "skill of any kind." The fact that art continues to mean skillful or a skill is reflected in such expressions as "the healing arts" or "the evil arts."

Artistic productions appeal to the human senses, stirring our minds and imaginations as well as our feelings. Some arts appeal primarily to the visual senses (painting, sculpture), whereas others appeal to the senses of hearing (music, song, prayer, oratory, poetry), touch (sculpture, carvings), and the sense of movement (dance). These sensual characteristics differentiate art objects from mundane utilitarian utensils, tools, or clothing.

aesthetics
Philosophies about what has beauty and value in art.

art
Artifacts of human creation created through the exercise of exceptional physical, conceptual, or imaginative skill; produced in a public medium and intended to affect the senses, sharing stylistic conventions with similar works.

How might the definition of art presented in this chapter be applied to this piece of twentieth-century Americana? American cultural conceptions of art distinguish folk art *from* fine art. *Other cultures may apply a variety of other criteria to evaluate what is art. In ethnographic research, it is important to know what those criteria are.*

Finally, artistic work is influenced by aesthetic conventions that are primarily cultural. In all societies, people have cultural assumptions about the media used to make art and the styles of painting, sculpting, decoration, oral traditions, and dance movements that are considered appropriate. These conventions may be more or less rigid or flexible, depending on cultural attitudes. In certain media, strict adherence to formal conventions may be necessary, while in other realms of artistic work, greater flexibility and latitude are given to the artist or performer. In other words, in every society, people have ideas about what they consider to be art based on their interpretation of the criteria in Anderson's definition. Of course, artistic conventions may change. For example, Western musical styles heard today, both in classical and popular music, are vastly different from those appreciated during earlier centuries or even earlier decades.

In addition to cultural variability in what is considered art, there are similarities and differences in the meanings attributed to artistic production and the purposes that they serve. In some societies, artistic production is primarily destined to serve ritual or religious purposes. In other societies, secular functions of artistic production are paramount. And in both cases, artistic work serves emotional or psychological needs, expressing the creativity of the artist and stimulating emotional responses in the viewers or users of art.

REVIEW

All societies have aesthetic values (ideas about what is beautiful). From an anthropological perspective, art is made by the human hand using exceptional skill. It is intended to affect the senses of people who view it, and it refers in some way to culture-based stylistic conventions. Art has meaning and serves important needs of both individuals and their societies.

CULTURAL AESTHETICS

Not only do cultures differ in the ways in which they express artistic impulses, but they also differ in their aesthetics or philosophies of art. In a cross-cultural study of aesthetic principles, Richard Anderson (1990) demonstrates the variety of cultural attitudes toward art and artists. Although cultural attitudes and philosophies of art are not all the same in his sample of nine societies, many of the foragers and horticulturalists share an understanding of art as a means of improving the world and life experiences or of serving primarily spiritual functions. For example, the Yoruba of Nigeria use art mainly to attract and show respect to spirit beings who then bestow prosperity, happiness, and fertility on the people who honor them.

In Western art, according to one analysis, four aesthetic paradigms or models have developed: mimetic, instrumental, emotionalist, and formalist (Anderson, 2000:201–202). The **mimetic** paradigm focuses on the ability of art to portray the world around us. Art may be **representational,** either imitating, idealizing, or symbolizing form and experience. Or it may be **instrumental,** transforming the world, enhancing our experience, or making the world a better place. In the instrumental paradigm, art should have a beneficial effect on society, enriching our lives, teaching us moral

mimetic
Art that portrays the world accurately.

representational
Art that imitates, idealizes, or symbolizes form and experience.

instrumental
Art that attempts to have a beneficial effect on society, enriching people's lives, teaching moral lessons, and providing insights for improving and changing the world.

Case study

Yoruba Art

Much of Yoruba art is concerned with the body, either decorating and adorning the body to make it more beautiful or representing the body in statuary and masks. The people so represented are not ordinary mortals but, rather, are presented as ideal forms of beauty and energy. Yoruba artists specialize in wooden sculptures that are idealized in their beauty, simplicity of line, and mature energy and body form. According to Yoruba aesthetics and art criticism, carved figures should be representational in that they should look like people, but they should be idealized in that they should not show the wrinkles, bulges, or flaws of ordinary mortals. Statues should depict people in full maturity, strength, and energy. These characteristics summarize the values of Yoruba principles of beauty (Anderson, 1990:127–128). And these traits of strength and energy are consistent with Yoruba valuation of youth and the power that comes from youthful vitality and vigor (Thompson, 1974:6–7).

Art for the Yoruba is, therefore, a projection and encapsulation of their beliefs about goodness, beauty, and morality. Yoruba statues are

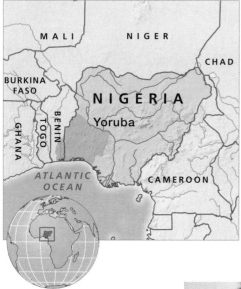

often carved with straight postures but with slightly bent knees, to suggest potential movement. These postures and orientations convey the dual impression of stability and kinetic energy that can lead to movement. The contrasting themes in the statues are consistent with Yoruba philosophies of life, emphasizing both stability and change through the storage and release of strength and energy.

Among the Yoruba, body scarification, as shown on this young girl, traditionally was for both beauty and social status.

In addition to its ritual and representational functions, Yoruba art is used to indicate social status. The traditional leaders of the Yoruba kingdom had personal paraphernalia that included a royal stool, a beaded crown, umbrellas, whisks, scepters, gowns, and slippers. These garments, decorations, and personal gear were richly decorated and carved. No one other than the king was permitted to wear the royal costume. The king's palace was decorated and appointed with beautiful carvings unlike that of any other person. These artworks were displays of the king's wealth, as well as of his closeness to the spirit world, believing that he was chosen and installed with divine blessings.

This kneeling Sango priestess was part of a house post of a Yoruba dwelling. She kneels and holds her breasts as signs of respect, like a young bride. Her hair is dressed in the traditional crested style of a bride, and her strands of waist beads signify virginity. She appears about to rise, perhaps to show hospitality to a guest.

lessons, and providing us with the insights and abilities to improve and change our world. Emotionalist paradigms focus on the role of art to connect to our inner experience and feelings. In this view, art is expressive of the artist's emotions, but it can also serve to release emotions in the viewers of art. In fact, both artists and viewers are linked in the emotional catharsis stimulated by the creative process. And, finally, the **formalist** aesthetic centers on the formal qualities of art—color, composition, sound, words, or movements. Qualities of form and the medium are more important than a true representation of the subject. Thus, art can be abstract.

Is this urban graffiti art? How might an anthropologist study these artistic expressions? In what sense is this an example of political art?

These paradigms may not be foremost in our minds as we view art or as we live our lives in the midst of artworks, but thinking about them can help us understand the different functions of art. Art is part of symbolic culture—that is, art has meaning. Through art, we can learn about the world and be stimulated to make changes in our lives as we understand the messages transmitted through art. Messages may be transmitted through social and political art, for example, which reflects the instrumental potential in artworks. And artistic creations serve as emotional expression for both the artist and the viewer. We are moved when we see paintings and sculptures, when we hear music and song, and when we participate in or watch performances of dance and drama. When we view art, we appreciate that art objects in any medium require skill of execution and conform to principles of style and form that are culturally appropriate in context, time, and place.

REVIEW

Art conveys important messages. Mimetic art attempts to portray the world accurately, whereas representational art portrays the world in an ideal or symbolic way. Instrumental art attempts to change the world or people's experiences of the world or to enrich people's lives. Emotionalist art attempts to express the artist's feelings or to release the feelings of viewers. Formalist art is abstract art that focuses on color, form, texture, medium, or technique rather than on particular subjects, ideas, or feelings.

BODY ART

One of the most common media for the display of art is the human body, as in Maori tattooing and Yoruba **scarification**—piercing the skin to make patterns or designs of healed scars. Although societies differ in the degree to which they employ the human body as a canvas, all peoples take pleasure in the use of body decoration, hairstyles, clothing, and jewelry to enhance one's appearance and to display one's personal and cultural identity. Nomadic peoples are particularly likely to emphasize the use of the body in artistic production. Because they do not have permanent settlements and need to carry with them whatever objects they own, they keep their possessions to a minimum. The human body in this context becomes a sort of movable canvas for painting, tattooing, or decorating with jewelry.

Aboriginal foraging peoples of Australia used elaborate body painting, especially in ritual occasions when people painted themselves with lines, dots, and other designs as they prepared to participate in ceremonies. Nomadic foragers of the Kalahari Desert in Africa decorated their hair and bodies with beads cut from ostrich eggshells. They also fashioned their hair in decorative styles, cutting the hair in rows and patterns to make lines and other designs. And they used facial tattooing. The Inuit of Arctic Alaska and Canada also used **tattooing,** resulting when ink or dyes are injected under the skin at piercing sites, to enhance their appearance. Inuit tattooing was done mainly on the

formalist
Abstract art that focuses on the formal qualities of art—color, composition, sound, words, or movements.

scarification
Artistic and ritualistic scarring of the face or other parts of the body in particular designs, commonly used to mark transitions to adulthood.

tattooing
Injecting inks or dyes under the skin to produce designs.

In Their Own Voices

Artists Talk about Art

In these excerpts some of the major creators of twentieth-century modern art write about the meaning of art, their techniques, and their aesthetic philosophies.

Barnett Newman, from *The Plasmic Image*
The subject matter of creation is chaos. It is now a widespread notion that primitive art is abstract, that the strength in the primitive statement arises from this tendency for abstraction. An examination of primitive cultures, however, shows that many traditions were realistic . . . [and] there always existed . . . a strict division between the geometric abstraction used in the decorative arts and the art of that culture. . . . the practicing artist always employed a symbolic, even a realistic, form of expression. One of the serious mistakes made by artists and art critics has been the confusion over the nature of distortion, the easy assumption that any distortion from the realistic form is an abstraction of that form. . . . In primitive tribes distortion was used as a device whereby the artist could create symbols. It is also very important to try to draw a sharp line between art and the decorative arts. . . . In primitive tribes this separation was well defined.

Mark Rothko, from *I Paint Very Large Pictures*
I paint very large pictures. I realize that historically the function of painting large pictures is painting something very grandiose and pompous. The reason I paint them, however—I think it applies to other painters I know—is precisely because I want to be very intimate and human. To paint a small picture is to place yourself outside your experience, to look upon an experience as a stereopticon view with a reducing glass. However you paint the larger pictures, you are in it. It isn't something you command.

Robert Motherwell, from *Beyond the Aesthetic*
[If] a work is not aesthetic, it is not art by definition. But in this stage of the creative process, the strictly aesthetic—which is the sensuous aspect of the world—ceases to be the chief end in view. The function of the aesthetic instead becomes that of a medium, a means for getting at the infinite background of feeling in order to condense

The abstract expressionist Helen Frankenthaller was influenced by Robert Motherwell, Jackson Pollock, and others of her time. Artists in the same age influence each other in any culture, but at the same time they strive for uniqueness. Frankenthaller noted, "I've explored a variety of directions and themes over the years. But I think in my painting you can see the signature of one artist, the work of one wrist." (Helen Frankenthaller [b. 1928] © Small's Paradise, 1964. Acrylic on canvas, 100 x 93⅜ in. [254 x 237.7 cm]. Smithsonian American Art Museum, Washington, DC/Art Resource, NY)

it into an object of perception. We feel through the senses, and everyone knows that the content of art is feeling.

Feelings must have a medium in order to function at all; in the same way, thought must have symbols. It is the medium, or the specific configuration of the medium that we call a work of art that brings feeling into being, just as do responses to the objects of the external world.

From Kristine Styles, Peter Selz, *Theories and Documents of Contemporary Art: A Sourcebook of Artists' Writings.* Copyright © 1996 The Regents of the University of California. Reprinted by permission.

face, hands, and wrist. In their cold climate, these are the parts of the body that are exposed to the view of other people. Other parts of the body (chest, back, arms, and legs) were nearly always covered with clothing because of the cold temperatures. The fact that the Inuit tattooed those parts of the body exposed to people's view demonstrates one of the uses of personal art, namely, to announce one's identity, embellish one's appearance, and make oneself attractive to others.

These Australian Aborigines (c. 1910) painted traditional symbols and stylized designs on their bodies as part of their religious rituals. These icons and patterns represented features of a sacred landscape or events from the Dreamtime. The differences in body painting among these men represent their different roles in the ceremonies they were performing. Australian Aborigine artists today use the same imagery.

In warm climates, where much of the body is routinely exposed, body tattooing may be much more elaborate, as described for the Maori in the narrative that opened this chapter. In Samoa and other South Pacific societies, young men had much of their bodies, including their face, arms, hands, back, chest, and legs, emblazoned with intricate tattoos as they prepared themselves for marriage. The higher the social status of the individual, the more elaborate the tattooing. Tattooing, therefore, was a signal not only of personal inclination and artistic display but was also a validation of one's social status. Differences in tattooing were correlated with a social system that emphasized rank and distinctions in the social standing of people ordered in a hierarchical system of stratification.

? *Do you practice any body arts? Why?*

Tattooing and other body decoration may be indicators of age and identity. In the United States, tattoos and facial and body piercings have come to be almost necessities for teenagers in some social circles. The practice of multiple piercings may also be a gesture of defiance against parental authority and values. And, while defying adult standards and practices, it also unites teenagers and reinforces their group identity through conformity to youth culture and values.

Throughout the world, people fashion beads, stones, and metals into jewelry that beautifies their appearance. In societies where there are differences in status and wealth, higher ranked and wealthier people are able to accumulate more elaborate and more valuable jewelry for display on their bodies. Thus, they enhance their appearance and attractiveness, advertise their social status and identity, and display their wealth. In addition, jewelry may be a repository of wealth, convertible into other goods through trade or sale. Clothing functions in the same way. While clothes are culturally necessary body coverings, the fineness of their materials and intricacies of design serve to transmit messages about social standing and wealth.

Clothing may be used to differentiate ethnic populations within complex, multi-ethnic societies. Wearing ethnically marked clothing may be a voluntary choice on the part of the wearer. In modern multiethnic states, people may prefer to wear the clothing of their region as a sign of their belonging to an identifiable community. Immigrants may choose to wear clothing typical of their native land to feel comfortable and as a sign of emotional loyalty to their homeland. For example, Indian women living in the United States may continue to wear saris even after otherwise assimilating.

In the past, some state societies used clothing and ornamentation as a means of dramatizing elite power. For example, in the Aztec Empire of Mexico, only high-ranking people were permitted to wear certain kinds of clothing or jewelry (Soustelle, 1961:138–139). Denying access to specific types of clothing and ornaments was not simply a matter of wealth, of being able to afford finery, but was a means of formally differentiating the population. And only the emperor was permitted to wear turquoise nose ornaments. Members of the military had the privilege of wearing particular jewels and feather adornments, depending on their rank. They also had the right to wear distinctive high-back sandals. Any man who was caught wearing an ornament or article of clothing to which he had no right was likely to be punished by death.

Hairstyles, body decoration, clothing, and jewelry are also indications of gender identity in nearly all societies. Women and men may wear their hair at different lengths or arrange it in different styles. They may use body painting or tattooing in different places or employ contrasting patterning and designs. And body adornments such as clothing and jewelry are often styled differently for women and men. Although some

artisans
Specialists in the production of works of art.

of these differences in clothing style may be a response to anatomical or practical differences in work roles, they also highlight and dramatize the social roles of gender and gender identity.

REVIEW

Body art is universal in humans and includes clothing, jewelry, hairstyles, body painting, body piercing, tattooing, and other alterations of the body. Body art primarily communicates individual identity, group affiliation, and social standing.

ORIGINS AND FUNCTIONS OF ART OBJECTS

In many societies, utilitarian objects are sometimes embellished with coloration, designs, carvings, paintings, or other decoration to enhance their beauty or impart magical or spiritual properties. Objects usually referred to as crafts, such as those made of pottery, basketry, wood, or stone, may have ornamental designs that demonstrate people's aesthetic sense and awareness of the ways that human effort and skill can add to the beauty of the object. In many foraging and small farming societies, nearly everyone is a producer of some kind of tool, utensil, or craft necessary for their work. Some individuals may make such objects with only a utilitarian purpose in mind. But other individuals, those more skilled or more imaginative, may add to the basic utilitarian object through the creative use of design and color. Other members of the community may collect their work because of its beauty. These **artisans** may become part-time specialists, exchanging their work either in barter or sale to others, thereby raising their status and increasing their wealth.

Societies differ in the degree to which they stress individuality or conformity to artistic styles. While we value originality and denigrate an artist or craftsperson whose work is derivative and imitative, members of other societies appreciate an artist who adheres to particular artistic conventions. Such artists demonstrate their creativity and inspiration by the level of their skill and variation within specific parameters. Therefore, an archaeologist who unearths a clay pot in Mexico can tell by its style whether a Maya or an Aztec made it.

In the Suriname Maroon society of Saramaka, descendants of slaves who escaped from their masters, women carve and decorate the hard surfaces of calabash gourds as they fashion them into bowls, ladles, and other types of dishes. Men decorate the surfaces of covered calabash containers, but these containers are also considered to be the property of women. There are gender differences in the equipment used to execute the carvings, and there are differences in features of style and design as well (Price, 1984). Men use chisels and compasses that they obtain in the world outside their remote communities, whereas women use pieces of broken glass to etch their designs. Men's work emphasizes symmetry and clear boundaries, but women's designs are more free-flowing and slightly unbalanced, sometimes with marks that disturb a central symmetry. All Saramaka women carve and decorate some of their own calabashes, but some women are known to be experts and others collect their work.

Saramakas have names for various calabash designs. Some styles are traditional, but others are the result of innovation. The people value both conformity to a standard aesthetic and the originality of individual artisans. Regional differences, village by village, are also recognized. These, too, are the result of personal innovations that become popular.

In addition to calabash carvings, women's art includes embroidery and patchwork with which they embellish rectangular cotton capes and cloths. Again, following a traditional aesthetic, both adherence to

This Navajo medicine man is sandpainting as part of a healing ritual. The painting's designs are transformed into the spirits themselves. The sand used in the painting is then no longer just colored grains but contains the spirit powers of the beings that it represents. When the sand is applied to the patient's body, the patient becomes the power itself and is healed.

standard forms and innovation in design are appreciated. Among the compositional principles for these works are bilateral symmetry, sharp contrasts in colors but avoidance of domination by any one color, and avoidance of combining patchwork pieces taken from different grades of cotton (Price, 1984:157).

In most societies, objects used in rituals are embellished with either representational or abstract designs, painting, or beads, feathers, and jewels. These artistic works may add not only to the beauty of the object but also to its effectiveness in ceremonies. Works of art may attract spirit beings, please them, and make them more likely to bestow their blessings on the community. For example, as part of curing rituals performed by Navajo healers, the practitioner may construct a sandpainting to attract spirit beings and gain their beneficial powers. The **sandpaintings** are stylized representations of the Holy People, the Navajos' spirit beings. During the ritual, the practitioner, called a singer, and his or her helpers make a sandpainting on the floor of the ceremonial hogan or house by trickling ground bits of red, yellow, and white sandstone and charcoal through their fingers. The patient sits on one of the figures depicted. The singer then moistens his or her palms with herbal medicines, takes up sand from the painting, and applies it to the corresponding parts of the patient's body. This act identifies the patient with the Holy People and allows the patient to absorb their protective powers and exchange evil for good.

When the ceremonial is completed, the sandpainting is ritually destroyed. The designs are methodically erased, trampled into the dirt by the healer. Once mixed back into the earth, the sand is taken up, removed from the ceremonial house, and disposed of to the north, the direction of power and danger. Although Navajos recognize and appreciate the beauty of the painting, its purpose is not to remain a frozen design but, rather, to create power. It is the act of creation and the use to which it is put that makes the painting powerful and effective. But its power also makes it dangerous. Therefore, it must be destroyed in order to protect human beings from the effects of too much contact with too great a spirit force.

The earliest known works of art date to about 30,000 to 40,000 years ago in Europe and Africa and to about 30,000 to 50,000 years ago in Australia (Peregrine, 2003). Most of these are paintings in caves or on rocks. The most famous European examples come from caves in southern France and northern Spain. There, people used paint to depict animals and hunting gear. Because of the association between the animals and the weapons, anthropologists believe that the paintings were intended to bring about a successful hunt. This is a form of association called imitative magic, discussed in Chapter 14. Perhaps people believed that by drawing pictures of animals being hunted, they were increasing the likelihood of a successful outcome. Although this is a reasonable hypothesis, it is impossible to know what people living so long ago believed or intended by their actions.

Cave paintings and rock paintings of animals have also been discovered in Africa dating to about the same time as those in Europe. Even older examples have been found in Australia. Some of the Australian examples include outline and stick figure drawings of animals and human beings, as well as stenciled outlines of human hands. It is possible that these paintings and etchings, as well as those found in Europe and Africa, may be reflections of images connecting the artists to the spirit world and to experiences of spiritual power obtained through prayer, trance, and shamanic performances. Again, we will never know what these drawings and etchings meant to the people who created them, but we do know that modern Aboriginal Australians intend their paintings and drawings to represent spirit beings alive in the Dreaming, a primordial time when the world was being formed (Hume, 2000). These spirits arose from inside the earth and then crossed the Australian continent, performing works and creating features of the landscape as they went. They also created human beings and taught the people important elements of their culture and beliefs.

Ancient stone sculptures have been discovered in Europe, dating to about 30,000 years ago. These sculptures, known as **Venus figurines,** are thought to represent pregnant women with enlarged breasts and hips. As in the case of cave and rock paintings, several theories attempt to explain the meaning of the carvings (Peregrine, 2003:15). Some researchers suggest that they were fertility objects,

sandpaintings
Paintings made by sprinkling fine, colored sand to make stylized representations of spirit beings, in particular for use in Navajo curing ceremonials.

Venus figurines
Sculptures made in Europe about 30,000 years ago, thought to represent pregnant women.

This 4-inch-high limestone figurine of a woman was found in Willendorf, Austria, and dates to between 26,000 and 24,000 years ago. What hypotheses have been advanced to explain portable Paleolithic art objects like this figurine? What would we need to know to determine which hypothesis offers the best explanation?

Controversies

Interpreting "Art": The Case of Inca Quipus

Looking at the objects produced by ancient peoples, we may have difficulties understanding their intentions. If we consider sculptures or paintings produced by ancient Egyptians, Aztecs, or Greeks, we may infer that they had representational or symbolic meaning. We assume that the designs used to decorate objects or the paints applied to their surfaces had symbolic or expressive meaning to their creators. We may not be sure what that meaning was, but we generally assume that they intended to produce a work of art. But what about objects such as the Inca quipu?

Quipu, a word meaning "knot" and derived from Quechua, an indigenous Andean language, was a device made out of knotted strings that was used for record keeping in the Inca Empire. All complex state societies need some means of keeping track of their population, of their economic output, trade, military service, and tribute or taxes due or collected from citizens. The Inca quipus served to enumerate objects or people and also served as records of events (Urton, 2003).

Looking at quipus today, we are faced with a number of dilemmas. First, archaeologists and historians believe that they understand the counting system used by the Inca in constructing the quipus. However, they do not know what was being counted or recorded. Second, we may find them beautiful, we appreciate the use of color, texture, and design. But what we don't know is whether the people who created them intended them to be works of art as well as utilitarian objects for record keeping. This problem touches on the issues of artistic intentionality and interpretation. Since quipus are no longer used for record keeping, we see them as objects of human creation detached from their utilitarian context. We can value them for their skill and ingenuity of construction and for the beauty created by their textures and colors. But we must reconcile ourselves to the fact that we will never know what was in the minds of their creators. This is a problem that arises in comparing different artistic traditions. If we are studying the aesthetic

Quipus were constructed of strings, thickly spun and interwoven. Main cords contain threads of different colors. The largest known quipu contains more than 1,500 pendant strings. The most complex of the quipus have up to thirteen levels of subsidiary strings attached to the core pendant strings. The great majority of quipus are made from spun cotton, although some are made of wool. A small number also contain human hair. Some archaeologists suggest that the quipus containing human hair may have been used to record kinship groups called ayllus.

principles and artistic traditions of living peoples, we can always ask them what they think about their work. With prehistoric cultures, that is obviously impossible.

CRITICAL THINKING QUESTIONS

Were quipus art? What about utilitarian objects in our own society? Would an anthropologist from the distant future consider an automobile, a stapler, or a light switch as art?

intended through principles of imitative magic to promote human fertility. Others suggest that they were meant as erotic representations of women. And still others analyze them as self-portraits made by women to depict their own bodies (McDermott, 1996). All of these views focus on the disproportionate size of the breasts and hips of the sculpted figurines. By emphasizing secondary sexual characteristics, the figurines could be representations of fertility or of erotic sexual pleasure.

Male figurines with enlarged penises have also been found in Europe and elsewhere. These date from earliest farming communities and may, along with female symbols, be representations of generative impulses and powers (Gimbutas, 1982).

REVIEW

Art is human and ancient, but we cannot know the intentions of prehistoric artists or distinguish utilitarian art (crafts and decorative arts) from high art or fine art. All art may be seen as utilitarian in some way. Quipus and sandpaintings are examples of art with important practical uses, whereas cave art and fertility figurines suggest the importance of art in magic, religion, and ritual.

THE ARTS OF SOUND AND MOVEMENT

Artistic impulses also find expression in the sounds of music and song. In many cultures, music and singing are means of expressing religious themes or making contact with the spirit world. Through the power of song and sound, people attract spirit beings and transmit messages to the spirit realm. In some societies, religious songs must be sung according to prescribed patterns, but in others, people compose their songs spontaneously as they make direct contact with the spirit world.

Among the Gitksan of British Columbia, songs come spontaneously to people when they are called by the spirits to be healers or other religious practitioners. Isaac Tens, a Gitksan healer, had such an experience when he began to receive messages from the spirit world. In the midst of a vision from an Owl spirit, he reported, "My body was quivering. While I remained in this state, I began to sing. A chant was coming out of me without my being able to do anything to stop it. Many things appeared to me presently: huge birds and other animals. They were calling me" (Barbeau, 1975:5).

Secular songs and spontaneous singing often accompany everyday activities. For example, the Navajos of the American Southwest have "riding songs, walking songs, grinding songs, planting songs, growing songs, and harvesting songs" (Witherspoon, 1977). These songs are sung not to entertain the singer but to enhance the beauty and harmony of the activity. According to Gary Witherspoon, Navajos, "count their wealth in songs they know, especially in the songs they have created" (p. 155). It is, therefore, the acts of creation and of artistic expression that make the songs beautiful and meaningful. And, in the words of a Navajo singer quoted by ethnomusicologist David McAllester, "If it's worthwhile, it's beautiful" (1954:71).

Navajo songs are not meant to last and be preserved but, rather, to be created and expressed. The interaction of sound, music, and activity is what makes art meaningful, effective, and powerful. It is what creates *hozho*, or beauty, the goal of every Navajo ritual, daily activity, thought, and speech. In the Navajo language, *hozho* refers to harmony, order, peacefulness, and appropriateness, in addition to its English translation of beauty. *Hozho* resides in the proper functioning of a person's body, mind, and spirit, in people's proper relationship with the holy beings and forces that inhabit the universe, in proper relations with other people, and in the harmony of their environment. Artistic expression is one means of creating and living in beauty and harmony.

The Inuit understand artistic expression in songs as a creative impulse that allows people to convey their inner feelings in ways that ordinary words cannot. As an Inuit man in Arctic Canada explained:

> Songs are thoughts, sung out with the breath when people are moved by great forces and ordinary speech no longer suffices. Man is moved just like the ice floe sailing here and there out in the current. His thoughts are driven by a flowing force when he feels joy, when he feels fear, when he feels sorrow. Thoughts can wash over him like a flood, making his breath come in gasps and his heart throb. And then it will happen that we, who always think we are small, will feel still smaller. And we will fear to use words. But it will happen that the words we need will come of themselves. When the words we want to use shoot up of themselves—we get a new song. (Rasmussen, 1929)

Yoruba musical styles, and West African music generally, are consistent with their aesthetic emphases on strength, energy, and youthful vigor. The rhythmic impulse puts

? *Do you ever find yourself singing spontaneously? What are the occasions? What are the songs?*

Anthropology Applied

Ethnomusicology

Ethnomusicologists point out that music is more than expressive or entertaining in the context of popular culture. It can play a central role in people's religious, political, and economic systems. For example, Javanese gamelan ensembles accompany puppet dramas called *wayang*, which are used to transmit stories from the Hindu epics. Gamelan polyphonal music is made with bronze keyed instruments; gongs; a xylophone, lute, zither, and flute; and choral and solo voices (Knight, 2002). Traditional Mandinka drummers and kora players in Gambia, West Africa, are involved in healing ceremonies; and Tswana boys in Botswana play thumb pianos to calm the family cattle herd. In many societies, music marks rites of passage and is also a medium of social protest and social action (Chernoff, 1981).

Some ethnomusicologists study the globalization of music and the emergence of world music. Zouk, for example, like reggae and calypso before it, is French Creole music of the West Indies. A combination of African, Caribbean, and French colonial influences, zouk has gained global popularity (Guibault et al., 1993). Thus, new and emerging music, such as zouk or benga (Kenyan pop), is as much a legitimate subject of study as ancient, traditional, or folk music, such as cajun (southern Louisiana, United States).

CRITICAL THINKING QUESTIONS

What aspect or type of music might you choose to study as an ethnomusicologist, and why? How would you apply an anthropological perspective?

? *As an ethnomusicologist, how might you design a study of blues, ragtime, country and western, or banjo music?*

---

ethnomusicology
The study of the musical styles and traditions of a people.

---

equal stress on every note, resulting in a steady outpouring of tone and sound (Thompson, 1974:7). By Western standards, music and singing sound equally loud, but this loudness conveys the essence of the Yoruba aesthetic.

Ethnomusicology is the study of music and musical performances, such as dance, in past or present cultural contexts. Ethnomusicologists study music systems, instruments, aesthetic values, symbols (including language), expression (including lyrics and costumes), and communication (including folklore). While ethnomusicology is associated with recording and videotaping traditional or tribal musicians, it is really about studying any music from an anthropological perspective. How do people define, create, and use music in their lives and in the life of their community?

Dance is an art that is truly universal, appearing as a form of individual and group expression in all cultures. As Anya Royce notes, "Dance has been called the oldest of the arts. It is perhaps equally true that it is older than the arts. The human body making patterns in time and space is what makes the dance unique among the arts. Perhaps it explains its antiquity and universality" (1977:3). Furthermore, Royce says, dance shares with other "social dramas" the characteristic of an "intensification or exaggeration of ordinary behavior. These kinds of events allow an outsider to see values stated forcefully" (p. 27).

In most cultures, dance is a central or key aspect of many rituals. Dance styles and movements may express sacred meanings handed down from ancient traditions or believed to indicate the movements of spirit beings. The intricate hand gestures of Balinese and Indian dancers refer specifically to characters or events in sacred narratives and folktales.

Artistic aesthetics influence styles of dance. The Yoruba emphasis on youthful vitality is reflected in dance as well as in sculpture and music. According to this tradition, dancers must be strong and use all parts of their bodies with equal strength and emphasis. The shoulders, the torso, the hips, and the feet—all are driven by a percussive force that parallels the rhythms of the music and singing. And with this force there is flexibility. All movements are linked together, with an emphasis on central balance. Finally, movements have clear boundaries marking beginnings and endings. Many of these elements, linking together movement, sound, and overall aesthetic design, have been carried into African American artistic styles, especially in dance and music (Thompson, 1983).

Dance is everywhere important as a means of using the human body in the process of creating art. It involves movement of the body in ways not typically found in daily mundane activities. Dance is a complex artistic form because it generally combines many other arts as well. It is usually accompanied by the sounds of music, chanting, or singing. Dancers often adorn their bodies with special paint, costumes, and other body decorations. And dance sometimes tells a story or expresses a narrative either in literal or symbolic form. Participation in or observation of a dance performance, therefore, is not only artistically complex but stimulates an appreciation through many realms of the senses. This appeal is a significant factor for an audience even when observing ritual performances. So, for example, Zuni audiences often request encores of public sacred dances that they find beautiful (Bunzel, 1932).

Cultural attitudes vary concerning the kinds of movements and configurations that are properly displayed in dance. And there are cultural norms about the degree of individual innovation permitted to dancers. In some societies, dancers must conform to an already established pattern, contributing very little of their own artistic sense except in some personal aspects of style and performance. In other societies, individual dancers are encouraged to innovate, creating new steps, new movements and new configurations. There are also differences in whether people dance alone, in couples, or in groups. Gender may be a factor influencing the kinds of dancing that people do, or even whether they are permitted to dance in public at all.

As in all aspects of behavior, context is significant. Some dances are reserved for sacred events, others for secular contexts, emphasizing the social element of dance and its entertainment values both for the dancer and the audience. Royce points out that social and recreational dances are usually relatively simple in their steps and movements so that everyone can participate (1977:81). Dances that require greater skill tend to be performed by specialists. These specialized dances are more often restricted to particular contexts and serve other functions. They may celebrate ritual occasions, or they may be performed by specialists for an audience's entertainment. And dance may provide emotional catharsis both for the dancer and onlookers.

Styles of dance, like all other aspects of culture, are subject to change both from innovation and influence. The kinds of social and recreational dance styles popular in the United States today differ vastly from their European, African, and other predecessors. Dances today are far removed in pattern and tempo from the courtly dances popular in Europe in the seventeenth and eighteenth centuries. Today popular dancing may be done in groups rather than pairs, and unique movements may be preferred over the set steps of dance styles of the twentieth century, such as jazz and ballroom dancing, which called for specific steps and patterns of movement. Nevertheless, as in all other aspects of our behavior, as dancers we are influenced by cultural norms that dictate appropriateness in particular contexts. Today's hip-hop dancers conform to contemporary values and expectations just as their parents and grandparents conformed to the practices of their eras.

? *How might you compare and contrast the cultural contexts of a tap dance, a line dance, and a disco dance?*

> **REVIEW**
>
> Music, song, and dance, the subjects of ethnomusicology, are universal in humans and serve critical individual and social functions, such as personal expression, group solidarity, and religious speech. Performances and their meanings must be understood through the cultural contexts in which they occur.

ORAL LITERATURE AND WRITTEN TEXTS

Another universal domain of artistic expression is **oral literature.** All peoples tell stories about their sacred past, their secular histories, and their personal lives. These narratives conform to cultural patterns of content and organization.

Sacred narratives recounting the creation or transformation of the world and the exploits of spirit beings form the central core of oral literature. Sacred stories tell of a primordial world that existed before this one and of the events that led to the formation of our present world. Such narratives present a blueprint for life, giving an

oral literature
Stories that people tell about their sacred past, their secular histories, and their personal lives.

folktales
Secular stories that relate events that teach moral lessons or entertain listeners.

understanding of how things are and how things ought to be. They may set out the roles that men and women ought to have, the relationships that people ought to have with other living creatures, and the responsibilities that people have to other members of their communities. Sacred stories present moral issues, giving guidance as to what is right and what is wrong. And they may be interpreted to validate or justify the prevailing social order, teaching people their place in society.

Folktales of a secular nature relate events that teach moral lessons or simply entertain. Like sacred narratives, folktales also have stylistic features that set them apart. For example, the oral literature of the Zuni begins with the incantation "So'nahchi," a form without a specific translation in English. The stories end with a phrase translated as "lived long ago" (Tedlock, 1972, 1983). The recurrence of these phrasings alerts Zuni listeners that they are hearing a particular type of story.

A traditional Zuni performance style sets the stories off as an artistic event. The performance style includes changes in speaking volume from louder to softer, changes in voice quality, such as raspiness, tightness, and breaks, and pausing both within and between words. The dramatic shifts of pause and voice evoke different emotional states, not only on the part of the speaker but on the part of the listeners as well.

The narratives of the Western Apaches of New Mexico also have distinct stylistic features that convey cues about the type of artistic event being performed. Apache narratives, referred to as "historical tales," recount events occurring at specific, named places involving people a long time ago (Basso, 1990). The stories teach moral lessons by pointing out mistakes that people made in the past and the unfortunate and sometimes humorous consequences that followed. They are morality tales, teaching and transmitting the wisdom of the ancestors and making them relevant to people today. The tales begin and end with the phrase "It happened at (named place)." The place where the event happened is mentioned as the first and last sentences in the tale. This device frames the narrative, signaling to listeners both the beginning and ending.

In many African cultures, proverbs are an important repository of traditional advice and admonitions. They, too, adhere to stylistic patterns. Here are some examples.

The eyes of the wise person see through you. (Haya)
If nothing touches the palm leaves, they do not rustle. (Ashanti)
The house-roof fights with the rain, but he who is sheltered ignores it. (Wolof)
His opinions are like water in the bottom of a canoe, going from side to side. (Efik)
A bird is in the air but its mind is on the ground. (Mandinka)
Between true friends even water drunk together is sweet enough. (Zimbabwe)
Words are spoken with their shells; let the wise man come to shuck them. (Mossi)
A family is like a forest, when you are outside it is dense, when you are inside you see that each tree has its place. (Akan)
The hunter in pursuit of an elephant does not stop to throw stones at birds. (Uganda).
Until lions have their own historians tales of the hunt will always glorify the hunter. (Igbo)
Even the Niger River must flow around an island. (Hausa)
A bird will always use another bird's feathers to feather its own nest. (Southern Sotho)
Where there is no jealousy, a small hare's leather is enough to cover four people. (Burundi)
An egg never sits on a hen (a child is never greater than its parents). (Kiswahili)
If the foot doesn't go (to the place of the quarrel), the mouth won't interfere. (Dagbani)
When they gossip about someone listen as if it were about you. (Ethiopia)
Everybody, even he who has a bad character, can be softened by kind conversation. (Sumbwa)
If a hen crows, kill it. (Northern Sotho)
All bent things, as days go by, will be straightened. (Kaonde)
Wisdom is like termite-hills: each one puts out new earth in its own way. (Luganda)
Where there is no shame, there is no honor. (Congo)
Sticks in a bundle are unbreakable. (Bondei)
He who hates, hates himself. (Zulu)

Proverbs can be used to instruct, amuse, praise, or criticize, their particular meaning depending on the situation. Among the Akan of Ghana, people can use proverbs to indirectly give advice, make requests, or criticize someone's behavior. These are all actions that are considered rude if done directly. For example, a mother can ask her adult son to send money home to contribute to the support of his aged parents by reminding him of his familial responsibilities, quoting proverbs from the "elders." In one recorded conversation, the mother admonished her son (the researcher!) by saying "It is the elders who said, '*If someone looks after you when you're teething, you should also look after him when he loses his teeth.*' You're aware of your father's illness. Now he's incapable of working. Life is hard these days" (Obeng, 1996:532).

Riddles are another way of imparting cultural knowledge and wisdom through an artistic form. Riddles ask questions and provide answers that rely on wordplay, metaphor, and imagery. For example, fifteenth- and sixteenth-century Aztec children and adults tested each other with riddles as a means of both play and instruction. Following are some examples (Carrasco, 1998:168–169).

> What is a little blue-green jar filled with popcorn? Someone is sure to guess our riddle: It is the sky.
> What is that which is a stone offered ochre which goes jumping? The flea.
> What is a mountainside that has a spring of water in it? Our nose.
> What is that which says: You jump so that I shall jump? This is the drum stick.
> What is that which is a small mirror in a house made of fir branches? Our eye.
> What is it that goes along the foothills of the mountain patting [us] with its hands? A butterfly!
> What is it that has a tight shift? The tomato.
> What is that which we enter in three places and leave by only one? It is our shirt.
> What is a tiny colored stone sitting on the road? Dog excrement.
> What is it that bends over us all over the world? The maize tassel.

Although we more readily think of artistic components of sacred and folk narratives, personal stories may also be produced by gifted storytellers with stylistic features that make them art.

For example, in an influential study of the structure of personal narratives told by ordinary people, William Labov collected the following story in response to his question, "Have you ever been in danger of dying? Have you ever said to yourself, 'This is it?'" The storyteller, a man named Harold Shambaugh, told about events that occurred to him when he was in South America. In addition to dialect, his story contains features that produce drama and tension (Labov, 1997:398).

> Oh I w's settin' at a table drinkin'
> And—this Norwegian sailor came over
> an' kep' givin me a bunch o' junk about I was sittin' with his woman
> An' everybody sittin' at the table with me were my shipmates.
> So I jus' turn aroun'
> an' shoved 'im
> an' told 'im, I said, "Go away.
> I don't even wanna fool with ya"
> An' nex' thing I know I'm layin' on the floor, blood all over me,
> An' a guy told me, says, "Don't move your head.
> Your throat's cut."

? *What proverbs and riddles can you recall from your childhood enculturation? Which folktales may have had the greatest impact on your social or moral development?*

Storytellers often have a special role and status in society. West African griots memorized and sang genealogies, local histories, and cultural sagas or myths. Traveling bards and minstrels of medieval Europe recited and sang the news of the day, including what would be known in modern journalism as Op-Ed pieces, commenting on current social and political issues. Fictional storytellers, such as Mother Goose, filled special roles in the socialization of children. Here this storyteller continues this tradition at a Kwanzaa celebration in Chicago.

Shambaugh's story is deceptively short and simple, but it contains all of the basic features of personal narrative. The events are recounted in chronological order with a bare minimum of detail, concentrating on the critical features of context, setting, significant characters, and dramatically relevant moments: the arrival of the Norwegian sailor, Shambaugh's responses (physical and verbal), and the result of the Norwegian's actions. But Shambaugh's skill as a storyteller is in his simplification and streamlining of events, with the effect of heightening the drama. He leaves out important details, not describing the Norwegian's actions directly but leaving it to the listener's imagination to reconstruct what happened. Only the violent consequences are stated. We contribute to the narrative ourselves by using our knowledge and imagination to fill in the empty spaces. This involves the listener as an active participant in the construction of the story.

? *What are some examples of skilled narratives you have read or heard? What literary devices contributed to their effectiveness?*

Notice, too, the use of direct quotation: Shambaugh first quotes himself making what he presumably thought was an appropriate response to the Norwegian's accusations but evidently provoking the latter to retaliate. Then Shambaugh quotes a companion who reported the dramatic conclusion of events with the frightening warning, "Don't move your head" because "your throat's cut." Although the narrative recounts an occurrence of undoubtedly intense emotion for Shambaugh, it is told in objective, dispassionate language. The story is the product of a skilled narrator using the art of verbal construction to create a scene that he and his listeners would not soon forget.

Written texts also have structural principles that reveal cultural norms and allow readers to follow, and, indeed, to anticipate, the content and the plot's development. When reading novels, for example, we expect certain background facts to be made known to us, such as principal characters, physical settings, and motivations. We generally expect the plot to be about some tension or crisis in the main character's life that he or she confronts, deals with, or resolves. We expect some change in the character's circumstances, thoughts, or attitudes. In other words, we want the story to be about "something" where something "happens." Distinct genres of novels have their own structures and expectations. Think about the differences between Gothic romance, detective stories, and science fiction.

Some written texts are made to be visually beautiful in addition to their verbal content. For instance, ancient sacred texts produced in India combine the elegance of Sanskrit writing and the intricate beauty of illustrations embossed in gold and silver. Illustrated texts describe real as well as imagined events. Several decades after the fall of the Inca Empire, for example, Felipe Guaman Pomo de Ayala, a native Peruvian of the Andes, organized a 1,200-page handwritten manuscript around his 400 original drawings of life under the Spanish colonial government. His illustrated manuscript essentially was an account of the Spanish conquest and a letter to King Philip III of Spain asking him to reform the colonial government to save the Andean peoples from destruction (Adorno, 2004).

REVIEW

Oral literature includes folktales, fairy tales, riddles, proverbs, poetry, rhymes, recitations of history and myth, and other skilled narratives. Written texts preserve these forms in various genres that reveal the cultural norms, beliefs, values, and styles on which they are based.

ART AND GLOBALIZATION

Global processes have influenced the kinds of artworks produced, displayed, and performed. In some cases, arts originating in one country have become popular in far distant places. When a particular art form or art product is borrowed, it may keep its identification with its source, functioning as a symbol of the original ethnic or national identity. Sometimes people adopt art forms because they are associated with a dominant group and, therefore, can be interpreted as status symbols. But people also acquire the artwork of small, relatively powerless groups in appreciation of its beauty. In the process of diffusion, art is like any other cultural form, changing both the donor and the receiver. Some indigenous communities have been able to prosper through the sale of pottery, basketry, carvings, and clothing that they formerly made for their own use and currently make for sale as well.

Performers of dance and music travel around the world, disseminating their styles and influencing each other. The current world music movement brings musicians and dancers from Asia, Africa, the Middle East, and Latin America to North American and European audiences. Not only is the music of a different style than Western forms, but the blending of music, dance, and song takes place in both sacred and secular contexts. In contrast, the performance practices of Western styles, where music is played in large concert halls, often removes ethnic musical traditions from their lived contexts (Shannon, 2003). However, audiences can become sensitive to the cultural meanings of the music they hear by being exposed to new sounds and new styles.

Through colonialism and globalization, the arts of Europe and the United States have spread throughout the world. As in all diffusion, art forms carry with them cultural values and practices that contribute to culture change. Western art has also been influenced by the artistic content and styles of other peoples. For example, African music and stylistic features of sound and song for centuries have informed American musical traditions. Gospel singing, jazz, and rock and roll would not be what they are without African melodies and singing styles. African and Asian artistic traditions in music, painting, and sculpture have influenced Western art forms significantly since the nineteenth century.

Contacts between different peoples and cultures have always included introductions to each other's material and performing arts. In the twentieth century, Western art connoisseurs became fascinated with what they referred to as "primitive art," art produced by indigenous or tribal peoples. Such art was unsigned, anonymous to the Western viewer and often stereotyped as expressing a universal unconscious or innocence that modern "civilized" people have lost (Price, 1989). The styles and genres of "primitive art" had a significant influence on the works of many modern painters and sculptors, including Picasso, Gauguin, and Pollock. Together this influence is sometimes referred to as "primitivism" (McEvilley, 1992).

Art and Identity

Art objects and art styles can serve as carriers of cultural identity. This is particularly true in multiethnic states where each group strives to maintain its uniqueness. Language, kinship systems, religion, and ethical values may be used to transmit and maintain cultural identity. But the arts, both art objects and performing arts, can also carry meaning by identifying a particular ethnic group. In modern markets for indigenous "primitive art," the people making the art often come to see themselves through their products as symbols that represent them culturally (Graburn, 1976). This connection between arts and ethnicity led some colonial and national governments to ban certain arts in order to impose control or enforce unity. For example, the Asmat of the part of New Guinea now absorbed by Indonesia as the province of West Irian were forbidden to continue their traditional styles of decorated house building and wood carvings, which incorporated human forms. These were seen as graven images, barred by Islamic principles.

Dance is also a marker of cultural identity. Particular types of dance styles may come to be associated both by in-group members and by outsiders as archetypal or symbolic of that cultural group. For example, we may think of the Mexican hat dance, the Hawaiian hula, and the Plains Indian war dance as representative of their respective cultural groups. This iconic use of a dance style often originates in situations of culture contact, with outsiders looking at "the other" and reinforcing stereotypes. In some situations of culture contact, people may accept others' views of them and associate their art styles with their ethnic identity.

For example, dance style is used to transmit Zapotec ethnic identity in southern Mexico. In the city of Juchitan, Zapotecs are the majority ethnic group (Royce, 1977:166). On social occasions where all the participants are Zapotec, people engage in popular Mexican dances of all types. But when non-Zapotecs are present, especially for celebrations of marriages between Zapotec and non-Zapotec, the Zapotec participants display their own ethnic dance style, emphasizing their Zapotec identity so that "the friends and relatives of the outsider spouse will be impressed with the extravagance

GLOBALIZATION

European classical music is taught and played in every country of the world. While maintaining national musical styles, countries such as Japan, India, and China also play European orchestral compositions. Influences on musical traditions are also evident in pop music, as American and British popular songs are sung throughout the world. All over the world people have translated songs and musical styles into their languages from English and have translated their own songs into English as well.

? *What art do you display in your home? What does it say about who you are and the cultural groups you belong to?*

The dances and costuming associated with the Plains powwow have spread to the northeast, the southeast, and elsewhere in North America. This dancer is performing in Brooklyn, NY. Dances originally associated with particular rituals or social activities are now performed during the summer as the powwows are held on different reservations throughout the season in what has become known as "the powwow trail" (Brewer, 2000:263).

GLOBALIZATION

In the United States and Canada, the Native American powwow has come to symbolize pan-Indian culture and heritage for the participants and for Indian and non-Indian spectators alike. Costumes worn by the dancers and the styles of dancing have spread from reservation to reservation, merging and blending formerly distinctive artistic expressions. Powwows thus symbolize both a local tribal identity and an international native identity.

and richness of the Zapotec heritage, which can more than hold its own in competition with anything else Mexico has to offer" (p. 170).

Art in the Global Economy

In all times and places, incorporation of indigenous peoples into regional, national, and global networks has an impact on artistic production. Local artisans become specialists, creating particular types of work destined for wider markets. These products then become symbols of their ethnic identity. For example, in Panama, women of the indigenous Kuna communities produce embroidered blouses and other items called *molas*, made of cotton appliquéd and embroidered with bright colors and bold designs. Molas were first made as blouses worn by the artisan and female members of her family. Then, in the 1960s, the influx of tourists visiting Kuna communities helped promote and broaden artistic production. Since then, production of molas has rapidly increased and diversified. Now women may sew and embroider privately in their homes or in cooperative workshops where they produce molas as blouses, wall hangings, table coverings, pillows, and numerous other household and personal items. The designs are often adapted according to market demands. Organizers of the cooperatives have contacts with retail outlets in Panama, North America, and elsewhere. These contacts influence styles and motifs by contracting for particular designs.

Through wide dissemination and popularity inside and outside of Panama, molas have become symbols of Kuna uniqueness and autonomy. And the women's incorporation into the global economy helps sustain their families, contributing substantially to their income. An activity that was once part of women's domestic work has now become central to their families' economies. Many Kuna families are able to maintain other aspects of their traditional subsistence patterns and their land base, because the women bring in needed cash to purchase goods that are no longer made at home.

Similarly, in Canada, Inuit sculpture and other artworks are major sources of income in many small communities. Traditional sculptures were made from soapstone and whalebone, carved and etched to represent people, animals, and spirit beings. In the traditional view of artistic creativity, Inuit artists do not create the sculptures from their own imaginations but, rather, release the form hidden but inherent in the medium that they are using. Thus, it is the soapstone that releases its form through the work of the artist rather than the artist who imposes his or her creation on the stone. Market forces have led to a diversification of Inuit artwork since the middle of the twentieth century.

In addition to sculpture, Inuit artisans now make prints and calendars for sale throughout North America and the world. The artworks and styles of carving and stenciled prints have become iconic symbols of Inuit culture.

Art and Tourism

In conjunction with other global processes linking distant places through trade and communication, tourists from North America, Europe, and Asia have traveled throughout the world looking for new experiences. In addition to visiting major cities that house museums, theaters, and stores, people increasingly travel to indigenous communities to learn about other cultures and collect unique arts and crafts. Indigenous peoples have taken advantage of this trend in ecotourism (a subject taken up in more detail in Chapter 17) to earn money and widen the market for their products. Many indigenous groups benefit economically from allowing tourists to explore their territories and even their homes, but others resent this attention or wish to avoid the risk of being viewed as curiosities. Some indigenous peoples use tourism as an opportunity to educate the public and gain support for political causes.

Arts made or performed for tourists often omit traditional intentions and symbolic meanings. In Hawaii, for example, the female hula dancer symbolizes tourist

Culture Change

NAVAJO ART RESPONDS TO MARKET FORCES

The Navajos of the American Southwest are well known for their skill as weavers of blankets and rugs and as makers of silver and turquoise jewelry. Both of these arts were learned from other peoples. When the Navajos' ancestors migrated to the Southwest from western Canada, sometime in the fourteenth century, they settled near Pueblo peoples who had lived in the region for many centuries. Many of the Navajo cultural practices were adopted from the Hopis and Zunis.

Although weaving is a man's job among the Pueblo, Navajo women became the weavers in their families. Pueblo cloth was made from cotton, an art originally diffused from the Aztecs. By the time the Navajos learned to weave, sheep had been introduced into the Southwest by Spanish colonizers and settlers, and Navajo weavers began to work with wool. The earliest fragments of woolen blankets date from the late eighteenth and early nineteenth centuries (Kahlenberg and Berlant, 1972).

There were no artist specialists among the Navajo but, rather, every woman wove blankets for her family's personal use. People draped the blankets over their shoulders as coverings. Women also made dresses, fashioned shirts and leggings for the men in their family, and made saddle blankets, sashes, and cords for their hair. In addition, blankets were thrown on the floor for sitting and sleeping, and were hung in doorways to keep out cold and wind. But they were not used as decorative rugs, a use that became popular later in non-Indian homes.

In the 1870s, shortly after the Navajos returned to their own territory after four years of forced confinement in New Mexico at a U.S. army base called Bosque Redondo, the people gradually became involved in commerce, trading wool and animal skins. Within a decade, Navajo women were supplying regional markets and Anglo communities with woolen blankets. The Anglo purchasers, including the American military, used the blankets mainly as bed coverings, prompting Navajo women to make larger sizes. This was their first adaptation to market demands.

By the 1880s, Navajo blankets were making their way into national trade networks, finally arriving in the homes of eastern buyers. By that time, aniline dyes provided a new range of colors in addition to the traditional white, black, and brown. A further innovation of the 1880s was machine-spun dyed yarn that made a weaver's work much easier, since she no longer had to spin the yarn from wool sheared from her own sheep.

Commercial expansion was facilitated by the establishment of trading posts on the Navajo reservation in the nineteenth century. Traders operated as middlemen in the market, buying rugs woven by independent producers and then selling them to the American domestic market. While commercial dyes and machine-made yarn increased production and lightened workload, these innovations also had the effect of cheapening the product. Soon, wholesale houses sprang up and became the primary suppliers of Navajo blankets to American cities (Weiss, 1984). At the same time, the market for Navajo commodities diversified. Weavers produced blankets, saddle blankets, sash belts, garters, saddle cinches, women's dresses, and knitted socks and leggings.

In addition to the blankets that women wove, men sold silver and turquoise jewelry, an art they learned from Mexican Indians. As the tourist trade grew, national companies became involved in the sale of the jewelry. Several companies sent raw materials (silver, turquoise, and other jewels) to traders on the reservation, who farmed out supplies and gave orders for particular designs. Navajo jewelers were paid by the ounce for the finished product (Weiss, 1984). Silverwork included buttons, bracelets, bridle ornaments, concha belts, tobacco cases, and jewelry with turquoise stones (Bailey and Bailey, 1986). Silversmithing grew in importance when trading posts on the reservation started accepting silver ornaments in exchange for goods. People began to think of their jewelry as a form of savings. Meanwhile, crafts, such as pottery and basketry, declined because these products had little or no commercial value and could be replaced by store-bought items.

People prospered initially through their integration into the national economy with outlets for the sale of wool, woven products, and silverwork. However, that integration proved disastrous at the end of the nineteenth century, because the people were vulnerable to fluctuations in prices for their goods. A further obstacle to Navajo economic prosperity was the fact that as the market for artwork expanded, competing non-Indian establishments were opened off-reservation that produced imitation rugs and jewelry. In response, some companies established workshops on the reservation where they oversaw the production process (Weiss, 1984). Although this practice aided sales against nonauthentic competitors, it undermined the creative and autonomous role of the artists, essentially turning them into wage workers.

By the end of the nineteenth century, traders and other commercial interests had a further impact on Navajo weaving by influencing the choices of color and design. Early Navajo designs were of plain stripes, a style borrowed from their Pueblo neighbors. New motifs were introduced in the 1880s, most popularly diamond-shaped designs and pictorial representations of horses, cows, birds, bows and arrows, knives and forks, shovels, houses, trains, and alphabet letters (Kahlenberg and Berlant, 1972).

Copying from patterns and following instructions conflicted with traditional ways of weaving in which weavers created designs in their own imaginations. Weaving was not just a utilitarian or even artistic act but was seen as a powerful spiritual act as well. Navajo weavers believed that they were expressing their spirituality. The entire process, from building the loom, carding and spinning the yarn, and weaving the pattern, was one of creative enlightenment, reenacting mythic narratives of world creation. According to Navajo sacred narratives

> Spider Woman instructed the Navajo women how to weave on a loom which Spider Man told them how to make. The cross poles were made of sky and earth, the warp sticks of sunrays, the healds of rock crystal and sheet lightening. The batten was a sun halo, white shell made the comb. There were four spindles: one a stick of zigzag lightning with a whorl of cannel coal; one a stick of flash lightning with a whorl of turquoise; a third had a stick of sheet lightning with a whorl of abalone; a rain streamer formed the stick of the fourth, and its whorl was white shell. (Kahlenberg and Berlant, 1972:6)

And then, after Spider Man made the loom, he told the women

> Now you know all that I have made for you. It is yours to work with and to use following your own wishes. But from now on when a baby girl is born you shall go and find a spider web woven at the mouth of some hole; you must take it and rub it on the baby's hand and arm. Thus, when she grows up she will weave, and her fingers and arms will not tire from the weaving. (p. 19)

Navajo weavers and jewelers now sell their work to retail outlets on the reservation and throughout the United States and the world and via the Internet. But jewelry makers in particular have become increasingly concerned about the production and sale of imitation jewelry made in foreign countries that is passed off as American Indian products. Federal and state laws are aimed at preventing fraudulent marketing claims by imitation jewelry, but these statutes are rarely enforced. Fake American Indian jewelry seriously undercuts Navajo (and other Native American) markets. They are made cheaply in mass production factories in foreign countries where wages are very low. In comparison, authentic Navajo and other Native American crafts are expensive.

The Navajos and other southwestern native artisans have appealed to federal and state authorities to crack down on the illegal sale of fake jewelry, forming the Council for Indigenous Arts and Culture. In 1990, the U.S. Congress passed the Indian Arts and Crafts Act (Public Law 101-644). This law makes it illegal to sell any art or craft product "in a manner that falsely suggests it is Indian produced, an Indian product, or the product of a particular Indian or Indian tribe or Indian arts and crafts organization." The act is aimed at protecting Native American artisans and the authenticity of their work.

Case study

Tourists among the Toraja

In Indonesia, the Toraja, a farming people of Sulawesi, have attracted foreign visitors who photograph their elaborate funeral rituals and their intricate carved effigies of the dead. Funeral ceremonies can go on for many days and include water buffalo fights, after which the animals, sometimes more than a dozen of them, are killed as sacrifices to the ancestors. Funerary rites are based on animism and ancestor worship, with influences from Christianity derived from Dutch and British colonial agents. After the animal sacrifices, the deceased person is placed in a coffin and interred in a cave hollowed out of a high cliff side containing the remains of Toraja ancestors. Sometimes the remains are suspended from the cliff wall as a hanging grave. Lifelike statues, called Tau-Tau, house the spirits of the ancestors and guard the grave sites, looking out from balconies high over the living.

The Toraja, who number approximately 350,000, have been inundated in the last decade with foreign and domestic tourists. In 1973, only 422 foreigners came to Toraja territory, but by 1991, more than 215,000 foreign and domestic tourists visited the region annually (Adams, 1995a, 1995b). The explosion of tourism was prompted by efforts of the Indonesian government to promote Toraja culture to attract foreign dollars. The Toraja are marketed through travel brochures, postcards, T-shirts, hotel promotions, and videos. They themselves purchase these commodities, becoming both viewer and viewed, observer and observed.

As tourism increased, conflict and competition among the Toraja intensified. The Toraja live in a ranked society, with status differences based on three ranks (high, middle, and low). High-status people claim descent from ancestral spirit beings who imparted the charter for Torajan society; middle-status Toraja are tradespeople; and lower-status people, the majority, are farmers and laborers.

With the influx of tourism, lower-status Toraja entered into competition with higher-ranking groups. They began to construct elaborate carved decorations and to perform funeral dances for the public, ignor-

The carved buffalo head on this traditional house in Sulawesi is a symbol of well-being and security.

ing or disguising status differences in their society. This trend benefited lower-status Toraja, but it bred dissatisfaction and conflict between elite and nonelite members. The Toraja example demonstrates that outsiders, whether anthropologists or tourists, have an impact on the inner workings of indigenous societies.

entertainment, a projection of tourists' ideas about the South Pacific. With her dark, flowing hair, warm, sunny smile, and alluring gestures and movements, she entices the tourist into a sensual experience. This imagery distorts Hawaiian culture, however, specifically the movements and purposes of Hawaiian dance. As Haunani-Kay Trask observed, "In the hotel version of the hula, the sacredness of the dance has completely evaporated while the athleticism and sexual expression have been packaged like ornaments. The purpose is entertainment for profit rather than a joyful and truly Hawaiian celebration of human and divine nature" (2001:399). Yet the Hawaiian dance form

ethnic art
Art produced by a particular group of people that comes to express and symbolize their ethnic identity.

"hula kahiko" is traditionally dedicated to a celebration of indigenous spirit beings, honoring them for their role in the creation of the Hawaiian Islands and the culture of indigenous peoples. The state of Hawaii has come to rely heavily on income from tourism. By 2000, tourists outnumbered state residents six to one and outnumbered Native Hawaiians by thirty to one (p. 394).

Tourism and the appeal of **ethnic art**—art produced by a particular ethnic group—can make economic changes in people's lives and in village life. An example is the marked increase since the 1980s of interest in wooden carvings called *alebrijes,* produced since the 1950s by villagers in the Oaxacan Valley in Mexico. As tourism has increased, residents of the towns of Arrazola, San Martin, Tilcajete, and Launion Tejalapan have significantly raised their standard of living through sales of the carvings. The *alebrijes* are fanciful representations of lizards, cats, serpents, panthers, and other animals. Most of them are made of a soft wood, called copal, that is easy to carve but also vulnerable to insect infestations. Some artisans work instead with cedar, which is harder and longer lasting but more costly, thus making the carvings more expensive. Many of the *alebrijes* have elaborate detailed decoration and are painted in dazzling colors.

At first, townspeople sold their work to individual buyers, mostly tourists. Then galleries in Mexico and elsewhere began to send in orders for particular designs. In addition, wealthy collectors and their agents descended on the towns to buy the most intricate and skillful of the carvings. Today, an estimated one-fifth of all of the families in the three major art-producing towns are involved in the work (Do, 2004). Men and women, Zapotec Indians and mestizos—all participate. Artwork is often a family affair involving parents and their children. Adults do the carving and decorating, and children help paint the finished product, or different families may cooperate in different phases of the work.

Whatever the level of sophistication of the artist, the appeal of the *alebrijes* in national and international markets has changed the quality of life in the villages. Individual standards of living have improved as people spend their earnings on enlarging their houses and purchasing household goods that make their lives easier. In addition, the towns spend money on paving roads, bringing in electricity, and building and renovating schools. Fewer families are involved in farming, the traditional occupation and subsistence strategy of Oaxacan villagers. Many are now able to devote their time to producing ethnic arts, an occupation that earns them a greater income and is also less arduous. However, the unpredictability of the tourist art market makes the future of the Oaxacan carvers unpredictable as well. One response has been to diversify. Zapotec weavers incorporate motifs and designs from paintings by European masters such as Picasso and Miró as well as from Navajo blankets.

> **REVIEW**
>
> Ethnic arts have become commodities in the global economy, which influences art forms and alters the relationships between artists and their work as well as between artworks and the life of the community. This is because art responds to market forces and tourist interests, as in the examples of the Navajo and the Toraja. Revenues from sales or performances of art have become important sources of income for indigenous peoples and cultural minorities.

Chapter Summary

What Is Art?

- Anthropologists study arts and artistic principles to understand the ways that artworks are produced, by whom, in what context, and for what purposes. They also study cultural aesthetics, or the philosophies of what has beauty and value in art. In some societies, art has primarily representational functions, meant to imitate or represent the natural world. In other societies, art functions in the context of ritual, used to express spirituality, attract spirit beings, and honor the spirit realm.

Cultural Aesthetics

- In Western art, four aesthetic models have developed: mimetic (the ability of art to portray the world around us), representational (imitating, idealizing, or symbolizing form and experience), instrumental (transforming the world, enhancing our experience, or making the world a better place), emotionalist (art connects to our inner experience and feelings), and formalist (focusing on the formal qualities of art, the use of color, composition, sound, words, or movements).

Body Art

- One of the most common media for the display of art is the human body. Body art includes body decoration, hairstyles, clothing, and jewelry. Nomadic peoples are particularly likely to emphasize the use of the body in artistic production because their lifestyle makes it necessary to refrain from accumulating possessions that they would otherwise have to carry with them when they move.

Origins and Functions of Art Objects

- The earliest known works of art date to about 30,000 to 40,000 years ago in Europe and Africa and about 30,000 to 50,000 years ago in Australia. Most of these are paintings found in caves or on rocks. Many have been interpreted as making an association between animals hunted and weapons used, possibly a form of sympathetic magic with the desired result portrayed. In addition, ancient stone sculptures, called Venus figurines, have been discovered in Europe from about 30,000 years ago.

The Arts of Sound and Movement

- Artistic impulses also find expression in the sounds of music and song. In many cultures, music and singing are frequent means of expressing religious themes or making contact with the spirit world through the power of song and sound. Secular songs and spontaneous singing also often accompany everyday activities.
- Dance is a universal art, appearing as a form of individual and group expression in all cultures. In most cultures, dance is a central or key aspect of many rituals. Dance is also important as a means of using the human body in the process of creating art.

Oral Literature and Written Texts

- Another universal domain of artistic expression is oral literature. Oral literature includes sacred narratives told about the spirit world or used in the context of ritual performances and secular folktales that teach moral lessons or entertain. Cultures vary in the ways in which sacred narratives and folktales are structured. They may begin or end with a particular phrase that cues the listener, alerting them to the fact that a particular genre of story is being told. Proverbs, riddles, and other wordplay also function to instruct, amuse, advise, praise, or criticize listeners. Finally, there are cultural styles of personal storytelling, allowing speakers to recount events and experiences in their own lives.

Art and Globalization

- Styles of art, including the production of objects, the use of the voice in song, musical instruments, and dance, are, like all other aspects of culture, subject to change both from innovation and influence. Art can also function as a marker of cultural identity. This is particularly true in multiethnic states where each group strives to maintain and dramatize their uniqueness.
- Incorporation of indigenous peoples into regional, national, and global networks has an impact on artistic production. Local artisans have become specialists creating particular types of work destined for wider markets. These products then become symbols of their ethnic identity. And, like the production of any goods or services, artworks respond to market forces. Preferences of buyers influence styles, materials used, designs, and colors.
- In conjunction with other global processes linking distant places through trade and communication, tourists travel throughout the world looking for new experiences. Indigenous peoples have become tourist attractions, marketing and selling their products, and sometimes their performances, to a national and international audience. Tourism brings in much needed money to remote and marginalized communities. As particular ethnic art objects become popular, people are able to improve their standard of living, as artisans working to benefit their households and the community as a whole.

Key Terms

aesthetics 396	instrumental 397	artisans 402	oral literature 407
art 396	formalist 399	sandpaintings 403	folktales 408
mimetic 397	scarification 399	Venus figurines 403	ethnic art 416
representational 397	tattooing 399	ethnomusicology 406	

Review Questions

1. How do anthropologists distinguish among types or categories of art?
2. On what different aesthetic principles can art be based? What are some examples of the expression of aesthetic principles in African and Native American art?
3. How do Venus figurines and Inca quipu illustrate the problems of defining art from an anthropological perspective?
4. How do individuals and groups use art to signify their identity and status?
5. What is body art? What are other universal categories of art forms?
6. What are some social functions of art forms, such as oral literature?
7. How does art relate to social institutions, such as education and religion?
8. What are some ethnographic examples of the use of art in healing?
9. What do ethnomusicologists contribute to our understanding of being human?
10. What is the role and impact of arts and crafts in people's economies?
11. In what ways is art a part of global culture?
12. What forces encourage people like the Toraja of Indonesia to make funerals into performance art?

Colonialism and Cultural Transformations

North Wind Picture Archives

CHAPTER 16

Preview

1. What is colonialism, and what types of colonies were established?

2. What are the patterns of relationships between colonists and their countries of origin and between colonists and indigenous peoples?

3. How did the European slave trade and traditional forms of African slavery differ?

4. How did the European slave trade change African societies and cultures?

5. How does the history of the North American fur trade illustrate the integrated dynamics of culture change?

6. How did the buffalo trade and the horse change the Lakota way of life?

7. How were patterns of colonization and change different in North and South America?

8. How did plantations, missions, mines, and epidemics change indigenous South American societies?

9. Who were the agents of change, and what were their goals?

10. What were native peoples' patterns of reaction to colonialism?

11. How did native peoples lose their lands, and how did Europeans justify their land-grabbing policies and practices?

12. How did colonialism and the postcolonial era help set the stage for present-day globalization?

*T*he commerce which may be carried on with the people inhabiting the line you will pursue, renders a knowledge of those people important. You will therefore endeavour to make yourself acquainted, as far as a diligent pursuit of your journey shall admit, with the names of the nations and their numbers;

The extent and limits of their possessions;
Their relations with other tribes or nations;
Their language, traditions, monuments;
Their ordinary occupations in agriculture, fishing, hunting, war, arts, and the implements for these;
Their food, clothing, and domestic accommodations;
The diseases prevalent among them, and the remedies they use;
Moral and physical circumstances which distinguish them from the tribes we know;

Peculiarities in their laws, customs, and dispositions;
And articles of commerce they may need or furnish, and to what extent.

And, considering the interest which every nation has in extending and strengthening the authority of reason and justice among the people around them, it will be useful to acquire what knowledge you can of the state of morality, religion, and information among them; as it may better enable those who may endeavour to civilize and instruct them, to adapt their measures to the existing notions and practices on whose on whom they are to operate. . . .

In all your intercourse with the natives, treat them in the most friendly and conciliatory manner which their own conduct will admit; allay all jealousies as to the object of your journey; satisfy them of its innocence; make them acquainted with the position, extent, character, peaceable and commercial dispositions of the United States; of our *wish to be neighbourly, friendly, and useful to them, and of our dispositions to a commercial intercourse with them; confer with them on the points most convenient as mutual emporiums, and the articles of most desirable interchange for them and us. If a few of their influential chiefs, within practicable distance, wish to visit us, arrange such a visit with them, and furnish them with authority to call on our officers on their entering the United States, to have them conveyed to this place at the public expense. If any of*

them should wish to have some of their young people brought up with us, and taught such arts as may be useful to them, we will receive, instruct, and take care of them. Such a mission, whether of influential chiefs, or of young people, would give some security to your own party.

From Thomas Jefferson letter to Meriwether Lewis, 1803, http:www.mt.net/!rojomo/landc.htm.

Thomas Jefferson's 1803 letter to Meriwether Lewis at the start of what came to be called the Lewis and Clark Expedition reveals the thinking behind a common pattern of state expansion. The newly independent United States of America was expanding the territory it perceived itself as rightfully owning in North America. That thinking also helped Europeans and Americans to rationalize colonialism and aggression against native populations on a global scale.

Recall from Chapter 12 that state societies are driven to expand their borders or to expand their spheres of economic and political influence, thus requiring a continuous influx of wealth, either in the form of goods or in the form of laborers to produce more goods. The steady and growing supply of wealth enriches the elites and allows them both to increase their control within their own territories and to exert influence outside. Conquest and colonialism are the results.

The early state societies in the Middle East, North Africa, China, Peru, and Mexico gained their wealth by sending conquering armies into neighboring territories and incorporating the defeated peoples into their empires. Of these, the most long-lasting have been the centralization and strengthening of the Chinese state and Arab expansion and state consolidation in the Middle East and North Africa. Conquerors demanded changes in the cultures of subjugated peoples. The extent to which they forced defeated groups to alter their indigenous cultures varied in different parts of the world and at different times. This chapter focuses on processes of state expansion that originated in Europe in the fifteenth and sixteenth centuries.

EUROPEAN COLONIALISM

European states did what earlier states elsewhere in the world had done before them, but the Europeans were in many ways the most successful. Other states enlarged their borders through expansion into adjacent lands, continuously increasing conquered territory as their borders were extended bit by bit. People who lived at great distances from the center of the state saw the space between them and the state shrink until they were the next group to be engulfed. European expansion eventually achieved worldwide reach not only by expanding the borders of their countries but also by increasing their control over societies hundreds or thousands of miles from their shores. Arab influence also has extensive reach in large regions of the world, especially through the spread of Islam.

Technological advances unique to Europe enabled this expansion and control. The ability to travel long distances was made possible by improvements in sailing vessels, navigation, and mapmaking, enabling European explorers, traders, soldiers, and missionaries to venture to all parts of the world. And technological improvements in armaments allowed Europeans to threaten or kill people who resisted them.

colonies
Settlements of foreign nationals with controlling interests in indigenous territories.

Colonialism Defined

European powers, specifically Great Britain, France, Spain, Portugal, and Holland, endeavored to solidify their control and influence in far-flung regions through the establishment of **colonies**—settlements of foreign nationals with controlling interests in indigenous territories. Colonies were intimately tied to the host country, but colonists remained politically and economically subordinate to their home countries. Residents of the colonies did not have equal legal or social standing with the residents of the home country. Their purpose was to produce wealth that could be extracted from the territories they occupied to enrich the home country as the colonial power. A complex system of trade tied the colonies to the home country. The home country's policies governed the ways that colonial subjects had to behave.

As Jurgen Osterhammel defines it: "A colony is a new political organization created by invasion (conquest and/or settlement colonization) but built on pre-colonial conditions. Its alien rulers are in sustained dependence on a geographically remote (mother country) or imperial center, which claims exclusive rights (possession) of the colony" (1997:10). Colonialism, then, can be defined as

> [a] relationship of domination between an indigenous (or forcibly imported) majority and a minority of foreign invaders. The fundamental decisions affecting the lives of a colonized people are made and implemented by the colonial rulers in pursuit of interests that are often defined in a distant metropolis. Rejecting cultural compromises with the colonized population, colonizers are convinced of their own superiority and of their ordained mandate to rule. (1997:16–17)

This wall painting of the Chinese attacking the Tibetans during the T'ang Dynasty shows that empire building is not strictly a recent European phenomenon. Between A.D. 618 and 907 in Classical Imperial China, emperors of the T'ang Dynasty extended China's borders westward as far as Iran and included Manchuria in the north and the entire Korean Peninsula. Today China's territory and influence on other Asian peoples reflect thousands of years of state expansion and colonization.

Colonialism is often linked with **imperialism,** or empire building—an extension of nation building using other people's lands and resources. Imperialism is

> a concept that comprises all forces and activities contributing to the construction and the maintenance of trans-colonial empires. Imperialism presupposes the will and the ability of an imperial center to define as imperial its own national interests and enforce them worldwide in the anarchy of the international system. Imperialism thus implies not only colonial politics, but international politics for which colonies are not just ends in themselves, but also pawns in global power games. (Osterhammel, 1997:21)

There were both similarities and differences in the tactics and policies of the various European states as they imposed their will and controlled the peoples of distant lands.

Types of Colonies

There are three main types of colonies, depending on the purpose of contact or conquest: exploitation colonies, maritime enclaves, and settlement colonies. **Exploitation colonies** usually result from military conquests in which the colonial power seeks to exploit the economic resources of the region. The power usually sends a relatively small number of its citizens to invade as soldiers. Then it continues to control the colony through government functionaries and traders. In exploitation colonies, the home country exerts complete dominance over the political functioning of the colony and over its soldiers, bureaucrats, and traders.

Maritime enclaves develop from sea trade and coastal exploration. Their purpose is to control trade at the ports of foreign lands and to have an indirect control over internal trade in foreign territories. The colonized country remains formally independent, but through its maritime enclaves the colonizing power has some degree of influence over the political and commercial policies of the supposedly independent state.

Settlement colonies result from military invasions that support permanent settlement by the invader's citizens. By encouraging settlement, the home country aims to acquire abundant cheap land and labor. In establishing a permanent presence, foreign settlers appropriate land from indigenous inhabitants.

imperialism
Empire building through state expansion in both commerce and territory.

exploitation colonies
Colonies established by military conquest for the purpose of exploiting the economic and natural resources of a region.

maritime enclaves
Colonies established as a result of sea trade and coastal exploration for the purpose of controlling trade at foreign ports.

settlement colonies
Permanent colonies established through exploration or conquest for the purpose of occupying land and controlling labor.

Forced resettlement in the former USSR displaced hundreds of thousands of tribal peoples and ethnic minorities. In 1944, the Tatar people, sometimes called Tartars, were deported from Crimea in Ukraine. Nearly half the Tatar population died in the first two years. In the 1990s, the newly independent nation of Ukraine helped 250,000 Tatars return to their homeland and gathered here to honor those who died.

Colonial governments attempt to settle nomadic people in more permanent communities—a common policy in North America in the nineteenth century. In North Africa and the Middle East, where nomadic pastoralists use vast tracts of land for grazing their animals, modern governments institute policies restricting people's access to territory, thus compelling them to abandon their traditional economies and settle in towns and villages. Resettlement policies continue today in other parts of the world, for example among native peoples of the Arctic Circle in the former USSR. As in the past, **resettlement policies** make it easier for central government authorities to control and influence indigenous peoples.

In settlement colonies, colonists have some degree of self-rule, although the home country wields ultimate control. The rights of the indigenous population may be disregarded, and their land taken. Where they resist, they may be killed and, sometimes, whole groups exterminated. Different strategies develop for controlling the labor supply and acquiring land in the colony. In colonial New England and the later United States, indigenous peoples were displaced or killed if they refused to move. After an initial period of coexistence, indigenous peoples were seen as economically unnecessary.

In contrast, colonial settlers in Africa remained economically dependent on the indigenous population. Since their labor was needed on plantations and in mines, colonists could not afford to entirely displace or annihilate them. In the Caribbean and parts of North and South America, slaves were imported from Africa as the indigenous populations began to die off. Slaves performed the vital economic functions of producing crops and manufactures in colonial cities and plantations.

In Africa and elsewhere, Europeans sought to instill their values both directly and indirectly through **missionism**—settlement for the purpose of religious conversion—and education, as well as through social, economic, and political control. For example, a 1919 French reader proclaimed: "It is an advantage for a native to work for a white man, because the whites are better educated, more advanced in civilization than the natives, and because, thanks to them, the natives will make more rapid progress . . . and become one day really useful men. . . . You who are intelligent and industrious, my children, always help the Whites in their tasks. This is a duty" (Buell, 1928:63). And in East African colonies under Italian control, African children read textbooks that contained such sayings as "I am happy to be subject to the Italian government and I love Italy with the affection of a son." Or "Help me, oh God, to become a good Italian!" (DeMarco, 1943:36, 40).

Christian missionaries competed with each other for influence and converts to their particular sect. And missionaries of Islam and Buddhism vied for converts as well. Islam and its cultural influences have spread, especially to North and Central Africa and Asia, from its Middle Eastern origins. More recently, it has spread to Europe and North America. Buddhist missionaries have been primarily successful in Asia. These religions also have aided processes of state consolidation and cultural transformation.

resettlement policies
Efforts of colonial authorities to relocate indigenous people to permanent settlements, usually on less desirable land, to control and influence them.

missionism
Settlement for the purpose of religious conversion.

REVIEW

Imperialism, or empire building, in state societies is achieved through conquest and absorption of neighboring peoples and the establishment of colonies in distant lands. Colonialism involves the domination and exploitation of indigenous peoples. Colonies also were established as military enclaves and settlements. Settlement colonies existed through policies of forced relocation of native peoples. Motivations for colonization included enriching the home country, gaining religious converts through missionism, and extending power and influence.

THE EUROPEAN SLAVE TRADE

The scope of the European **slave trade** in numbers alone is staggering. Between 1451 and 1600, about 275,000 Africans were forcibly sent to Europe and the Americas. During the seventeenth century, about 1,341,000 Africans were enslaved, sent mainly to sugarcane plantations in the Caribbean (Wolf, 1982:195–196). In the eighteenth century more than 6 million people were taken from Africa, two-thirds to the Caribbean and most of the rest to other European colonies in the Americas. Even though Great Britain banned the slave trade in 1807, an additional 2 million Africans were sold into slavery in the nineteenth century. These figures combine to a total of about 10 million people who were stolen from their communities in Africa and sent to labor for the rest of their lives on plantations many thousands of miles away. The wealth produced by slaves in the Americas contributed to the accumulation of capital and resources in Europe, directly and indirectly leading to the Industrial Revolution in the late eighteenth and early nineteenth centuries (Williams, 1944).

The Portuguese initiated the European international slave trade along the western coast of Africa. At first, they were interested in obtaining gold and spices but then shifted to a focus on extracting people to work on the plantations that they were developing in South America, principally in Brazil. Competition soon began as Dutch slave traders were supplying their sugar plantations in the Caribbean. By the late seventeenth century, the British and the French were deeply involved in the slave trade as well. The purchase of slaves was made possible by a rise in production of goods in Europe.

Slavery in Africa

Slavery was practiced in Africa and the Middle East long before European powers arose. Slavery was seen as a source of labor, a means of absorbing conquered peoples, and a solution for people who became destitute for any reason. The growth in the international slave trade depended on preexisting indigenous systems of slavery in West Africa that contributed to the capture and transshipment of other Africans.

GLOBALIZATION

The slave trade was instrumental in developing a globalized system of economic and political networks that Europeans directed and profited from. The slave trade both benefited from and accelerated the growth of manufacturing in Europe, which led to the Industrial Revolution and the worldwide dominance of European commerce for centuries to come.

slave trade
Buying and selling of people into servitude.

This slave family living in Savannah in the 1860s contributed to their master's wealth but did not share his standard of living. In contrast, slaves in Africa lived with their masters and had similar comforts.

Culture Change

IMPACTS OF THE EUROPEAN SLAVE TRADE ON AFRICAN STATES

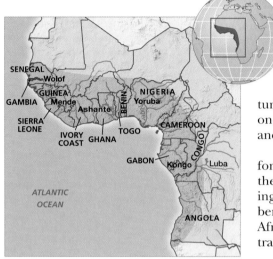

The effects of the European slave trade were borne primarily by its direct victims, but it also affected people who survived in their home communities without family members to aid in their subsistence and welfare. The slave trade tore apart households and disturbed networks of people who shared rights and responsibilities toward one another. At the same time, some Africans benefited economically and politically from the slave trade.

The elites in West African chiefdoms and kingdoms, which existed before European contact, benefited by the wealth and political power that they were able to amass by participating in the European slave trade, acting as intermediaries and distributors of European goods to other members of their communities. The influx of European goods, exchanged for Africans, strengthened the wealth and power of the elites who controlled trade in Africa.

Elite accumulation of wealth and power contributed to the formation of state societies in West Africa whose rulers gained even more control, particularly in Nigeria and in the Congo. The Ashanti in the Gold Coast and Nigeria extended their power both locally and regionally. Ashanti slave traders centralized their wealth and power through access to firearms received from Europeans in exchange for slaves. The proliferation of weapons led to the rise and fall of several small states competing with each other for access to slaves and European goods. The Yoruba in West Africa used military might to subjugate other small states and to demand slaves as tribute from conquered tribes. Through successful campaigns, they extended their trading networks further into Central Africa (Wolf, 1982). In contrast, the precolonial kingdom of the Congo ended in disarray because competing elites had access to the slave trade. Internal competition led to the breakup of the kingdom into rival factions, each vying for control of war captives who could be exchanged for European goods.

The political consequences of the European slave trade for African societies, therefore, depended on the region, access to slaves, and the role of local elites in terms of internal competition or cooperation. Some states were founded, others consolidated their power, and others broke apart during the centuries of upheaval caused by the slave trade. As the trade intensified, people from West Africa moved from their coastal villages toward the east to escape slave-raiding expeditions. Raiders targeted small autonomous societies without strong centralized governments or armed militaries to protect them. As people moved eastward, however, they sometimes came into contact with newly emerging states that took part in or controlled slave trading in their regions. Thus, the trade that began in West Africa had a radiating influence throughout the continent. And in East Africa, European and Arab traders took slaves to supply growing demands for labor in the ivory trade in India and China.

Changes in African cultures as a result of the slave trade included the strengthening of principles of patrilineal descent. In precolonial times, some western and central African societies reckoned descent patrilineally while others were based on matrilineal kinship. However, men gained greater power and authority through involvement in the slave trade and the desire to claim the sons of their slave women to use in raids against other groups, thereby increasing the number of warriors under their direction (Wolf, 1982). This shift may have contributed to the gradual strengthening of patrilineal kinship in previously matrilineal societies.

Many societies in West Africa had extensive networks of long-distance trade that could be used to funnel people forced into slavery or coerced labor. War captives often were taken from enemy communities and forced to work for their captors. Some West African societies also had systems of indenture in which people pawned themselves if they became indebted to another person and were unable to repay a loan. Selling children into slavery or service to prevent their starvation was also an option. In addition, a period of indentured labor often was used as a punishment for wrongdoing in traditional systems of justice.

? *From a cross-cultural perspective, how would you define the social functions of slavery? How would you account for the continuation of an international slave trade in Africa and the Middle East today?*

Slavery in the Americas

Europeans and colonists saw African slaves as racially inferior. In the Americas, slaves were completely cut off from their kin and home communities. Their duration of enslavement was indefinite, with no hope of release and return. They were not seen as economic partners, though they certainly were economic assets. They could be, and were, bought and sold as possessions with no regard to their well-being or family ties or to their personal autonomy and feelings. And they could be subjected to whatever treatment or maltreatment their owners decided to heap upon them.

REVIEW

The European Industrial Revolution was built on the slave trade and on materials and markets created through colonialism. The slave trade was built, in turn, on African slavery. The internationalization of the slave trade had profound human costs as well as impacts on African peoples and cultures. These impacts included the political consolidation of kingdoms, greater competition and conflict between groups (as well as greater cooperation), and changes in families and kinship. The European slave trade contributed to the development of the globalization that we see today.

TRADE AND SETTLEMENT IN NORTH AMERICA

The colonial enterprise in North America took the form of both trading and settler colonies. Europeans first came to North America in the late fifteenth century when Portuguese, Spanish, and French fishermen caught fish in the ocean off the coast of Newfoundland and Québec. But the first European to make an official landfall on the northeastern coast of North America was John Cabot, who arrived in 1497 and promptly declared Newfoundland a possession of England. By 1550, approximately fifty fishing boats from each of the European countries (England, France, Portugal, Spain) were making annual visits to the Atlantic waters. By the end of the sixteenth century, the numbers had tripled (Sauer, 1971).

Intermittent commercial relations in the northeast soon expanded to become the focus of European activities there. Native peoples gradually became enmeshed in trading networks that had far-reaching effects on their cultures and histories. At the same time that French, British, and Dutch traders were establishing commercial ties with indigenous nations in the northeast, Spanish adventurers were invading and plundering Mexico in the south and northward into what later became the southern United States. While the early history of regional contact in the Western Hemisphere reveals different colonial motives, the eventual impact of European contact followed similar patterns throughout the continent. Trade, conquest, and colonization

At first, native peoples were willing and often enthusiastic partners in European trading networks, eager to trade for tools and utensils made of iron, copper, or brass. To obtain these goods, they procured the pelts of fur-bearing animals, especially beaver in the northeast, as depicted here, and otter in the northwest. (North Wind Picture Archives)

fur trade
Exchange of animal pelts or hides between Native Americans and colonists in exchange for European trade goods.

spread everywhere, and in a few centuries all native peoples were engulfed and their cultures transformed.

The Fur Trade

The involvement of Native Americans in the **fur trade,** at first peripheral to their economies, materially transformed their societies, as durable metal goods became mainstays of material culture. Dependence on trade also had unforeseen negative effects. Native trappers could not control the market for furs, which made them vulnerable to changes in demand. When demand was high, people abandoned some traditional practices in an effort to keep pace. They overtrapped nearby territories, leading to a rapid depletion of beaver, otter, and other animals. People had to travel greater distances from their communities to find the desired resource, often entering territories of others who were similarly engaged in trapping and trading. Competition sometimes led to open conflict. When the demands of the fur market declined, people were left without the ability to acquire desired goods. In addition, some desired European products, such as guns and liquor, had negative effects on indigenous communities.

Involvement in the fur trade also led to other changes. As early as the seventeenth century in some eastern nations, trapping and trading became men's central economic activities. Among farming people where farmwork was the responsibility of women, food supplies were maintained, but among foragers, who depended more heavily on the meat and fish brought in by hunters, traditional food resources were not exploited as fully as previously. Many people then traded with Europeans for food as well as for manufactured goods. This process eventually led to increased dependence on traders, further deepening the need to spend even more time trapping animals.

Women, too, were involved in the fur trade, because their labor was necessary to prepare the pelts for market. As the economic roles of both men and women focused more on tasks related to the fur trade, people grew more dependent on trade to supply their needs and wants. Economic systems shifted from subsistence to a focus on trapping and trading. Thus, the shift in gender roles and a new emphasis on acquiring personal wealth and private property also developed.

Through indigenous peoples' contact with Europeans, the concept of personal private property developed, which contrasted fundamentally with most traditional beliefs about ownership of resources either communally or by kinship groups as collective entities. As people lost access to their own territory, competition grew to own or control lands and resources that remained, often leading to warfare. In addition, formerly nomadic communities gradually established temporary and then permanent settlements near trading posts. This change was most marked in Canada and the Arctic. Small groups began to camp near riverbanks and coastal trading posts for access to European goods. Other demographic changes included great losses in population.

Westward Expansion and Depopulation

As trade and European settlement moved steadily westward in the eighteenth and nineteenth centuries, intense wars of survival pitted native groups against one another. Conflicts were often prompted and made worse by Europeans, who forged commercial and military alliances with Indians in opposition to other European nations and their respective indigenous allies. In this new form of warfare, thousands of people were killed, and thousands more were routed from their homes or forced to flee to safety.

The Europeans' desires for settlement intensified competition over land. The British were most successful in establishing growing communities in North America, but French settlements remained comparatively small and isolated along the rivers and ports of their primary dominance in what is now Québec and New Orleans. The Spanish foothold in North America was concentrated in Mexico, and in what is now the southern United States and California. Beginning in the early seventeenth century, English colonists established villages from the Atlantic coast moving steadily westward. In doing so, they expropriated indigenous lands and dispersed, annihilated, or assimilated the original inhabitants.

European expropriation was aided by the spread of diseases of European origin that had never been seen in North America, especially smallpox, measles, and influenza. Native peoples had no natural resistance or immunities to these diseases. In the early 1600s, the Powhatan chief, Wahunsonacock, told John Smith in Virginia: "I have seen two generations of my people die. Not a man of the two generations is alive now but myself" (Hariot, 1972). In Massachusetts, Massasoit, a Wampanoag chief, concluded, "Englishmen, take that land, for none is left to occupy it" (Brasser, 1978:66). And as settlers moved westward, carrying their diseases with them, they caused untold numbers of deaths when they settled in the plains in the early and mid-nineteenth century. As Little Wolf of the Cheyenne noted, "Many have died of diseases we have no name for" (Thornton, 1987:134).

Estimates for the indigenous population of North America vary widely. Today, accepted figures range from more than 2 million (Ubelaker, 1976) to more than 7 million (Thornton, 1987). Whatever the number, rates of decline from the sixteenth through the nineteenth centuries were undoubtedly enormous. By the end of the nineteenth century, only about 250,000 Native Americans survived in the United States. This steep **depopulation** had significant social, economic, and political consequences, in addition to the human tragedy. Whole families, sometimes entire lineages or clans, were wiped out in just a few years. Not only did the most vulnerable, such as young children and elders, die in great numbers, but men and women in their prime also succumbed. Their deaths left survivors without the farmers, gatherers, hunters, artisans, and leaders they needed to sustain themselves and their ways of life.

GLOBALIZATION

Depopulation was a global phenomenon, not limited to European colonies in the Americas. European colonies in Indonesia and the Pacific islands and in Australia also led to depopulation among indigenous peoples.

> **REVIEW**
>
> European trade and settlement in North America began with the fur trade and led to the depopulation of Native Americans across the continent through displacement, warfare, and disease. Participation in European trading networks changed traditional ways of life in ways that made people more dependent on those networks. Native peoples' subsistence activities, settlement patterns, land use, gender relations, political organization, and economic systems were transformed.

SPANISH COLONIZATION IN THE AMERICAS

The Spanish began their invasions and conquests in Mexico and Central and South America in the early sixteenth century. Their goal was originally to find gold and other precious metals. It later shifted to acquiring territory to establish large plantations for growing domestic and imported crops. Spain lost Brazil to Portugal, but the Spanish took land and resources elsewhere on the continent. At first, both groups confiscated indigenous people's land and forced them to work on plantations. Other native people were forced to work in mines, extracting silver and other precious minerals.

An early catastrophic effect of European invasion was loss of life through disease. Reliable figures are not available for the pre-Columbian populations of South America, but estimates for Mexico suggest a native population of approximately 30 million at the time of the Spanish invasions in 1519. The indigenous population of Mexico fell to 3 million in 1568, a loss of 90 percent in barely fifty years (Cowley and Talbot, 2001:281).

In the Andes as well, Spanish invasions took a toll as a result of direct military conflict and the spread of European diseases. Examination of Inca skeletal samples from Ecuador indicates that just prior to contact, the health of native populations was beginning to deteriorate (Ubelaker, 1994). These health deficits resulted from sedentary lifestyles and higher population densities associated with farming as the Inca Empire expanded. Recall from Chapter 7 the benefits and risks of agriculture as a mode of subsistence. These conditions accelerated in the period following the Spanish invasions. Life expectancy dropped further, especially for people under the age of 15, and

depopulation
Reduction in population size as a result of war, conquest, colonization, or disease.

Case study

Lakota Trade and the Consequences of Change in Economic Production

The Lakota were a loose alliance of nations whose original homeland was in what is now central Minnesota. Their economy combined farming and foraging. Women did the planting and gathered wild foods and men were the hunters. In addition, Lakotas had extensive trade networks with nearby settled farming peoples, exchanging meat and animal hides for farm crops.

Although the Lakota were well adapted to their prairie environment, their stay in that region gradually became difficult because of changing conditions caused by the arrival of European settlers and traders. Eastern Indians fled toward the west and inevitably entered territories inhabited by other nations, leading to competition for the remaining land and resources. Sometime in the early years of the eighteenth century, the Lakota crossed west into the Great Plains. In the plains, they became nomadic foragers, eventually extending from central Minnesota into the present-day states of North and South Dakota, Nebraska, and Wyoming.

The most important innovation in eighteenth-century native culture was the incorporation of horses, originally obtained through trading networks in the southwest from Spanish sources. Plains Indians immediately realized the enormous potential for travel and transport afforded by these animals. Men, now on horseback, continued their earlier roles as hunters and traders. They especially hunted the buffalo, which later became important in European and American trade.

Involvement in European trade first increased the people's fortunes. Trade between the Lakota and the French began in the late seventeenth century when the people still inhabited lands in Minnesota. After the people migrated into the plains, they obtained European goods through intermediary nations such as the Mandan, Hidatsa, and Arikara living along the Missouri River. Then, in the early nineteenth century, American traders from St. Louis contacted the Lakota to trade for animal hides and meat. The Lakota soon established themselves as middlemen between American traders and other native peoples living in the plains, thereby increasing their own wealth and asserting economic dominance in the region.

As involvement in trade deepened, both men and women spent more time procuring and preparing animal products for market. Hunters killed numbers of animals far above their subsistence and household requirements. And women spent more time processing buffalo meat into dried pemmican and tanning hides for trade (Klein, 1980).

Economic changes promoted shifts in cultural values and social relations. In contrast to traditional ethics of equality and generosity, greater differences in wealth and rank emerged, counted in the number of horses that an individual or family owned. People accumulated horses either through purchase or, more commonly, through raids of neighboring groups.

Wealthy individuals were able to translate their economic and military success into social prestige. The number of horses people owned became a symbol of their fortunes, as the accumulation of personal property became a desired goal. Wealthy families enhanced their social prestige by being generous to others. However, unlike past practices, when successful people gave away all or most of their surplus abundance, now wealthy families kept more of their personal goods, thereby leading to differences in standards of living.

A complex relationship developed between gender and wealth. To accumulate property and increase status, a man needed women's services to transform raw products into marketable items. One woman working alone could not keep pace, however, with the supply of animals that a man could hunt. Estimates vary but three to ten days of work were probably required to tan one buffalo hide, yielding a seasonal rate of twenty to thirty hides (Klein, 1983:155). Thus, men sought to have more than one wife. Age at marriage rose for men, therefore, as only more experienced hunters and warriors could acquire enough horses through trade and raids to give as obligatory gifts to a woman's parents upon proposal of marriage. At the same time, age at marriage for women declined, as fathers were willing to agree to daughters' unions in exchange for the horses they would receive. The widening gap in age between spouses also strengthened husbands' marital control, since seniority conferred prestige in Lakota society.

Interaction with American traders had a destabilizing effect on power relations within the Lakota nation. Traders and government officials established ties with individuals who they thought could control hunters and warriors, helping to shift the economic balance in favor of hunting and trapping for the market. Although the "chiefs" that Americans contacted did not traditionally have rights to dominate members of their communities, "the more the agents treated them as powerful, the more powerful they became" (Schusky, 1994:263–264). And as native leaders became the conduit for wealth to their nation, they were able to use the situation to their material and social advantage.

Thus, involvement in trade had complex, interconnected consequences for the Lakota, as well as for other indigenous nations of North America (and elsewhere). Changes in subsistence strategies, settlement patterns, gender relations, and the social order were not isolated but were mutually reinforcing in transforming indigenous ways of life.

maximum longevity in years also declined. These health effects were directly caused by trauma and exposure to infectious diseases. As mentioned earlier, one consequence of this die-off of Native Americans was the importation of African slaves to Spanish and Portuguese colonial plantations.

Indigenous depopulation as a direct or indirect consequence of colonialism has been estimated for a number of countries worldwide, such as those shown in Table 16.1.

Table 16.1 ESTIMATED DEPOPULATION IN THE AMERICAS AND THE PACIFIC

	Precontact Population	Population Low Point	Depopulation
United States and Canada	7,000,000	390,000	6,610,000*
South America	8,500,000	450,000	8,050,000
Oceania/Polynesia	1,100,000	180,000	920,000
Micronesia	200,000	83,000	117,000
Melanesia/Fiji	300,000	85,000	215,000
New Caledonia	100,000	27,000	73,000
Australia	300,000	60,500	239,500

* According to the 2000 U.S. Census, Native American and Alaskan native populations have rebounded to nearly 2.5 million people, about a third of the original estimated population. Native Hawaiians, Samoans, Tongans, Tahitians, and other Pacific Islanders numbered 398,000 in 2000.

Source: John Bodley, *Victims of Progress,* 4/e. Copyright © 1999 McGraw-Hill Companies, Inc. Reprinted by permission.

Spanish Landholding in the Colonies

The Spanish crown gave land grants, called **encomiendas,** to soldiers, priests, and settlers. Encomiendas gave the holder rights to use the land and the labor of the Indians residing on that land. The Indians were essentially conscripted laborers, forced to work for others on the very land that they once held themselves. Another landholding system was the estates, or **haciendas,** direct ownership of land by Spanish settlers. Indians on haciendas worked as sharecroppers, owing part of their produce to the owners. A third type of landholding was the mission village, populated by Spanish priests and their forced converts. People in surrounding communities were compelled to relocate to the missions and to provide labor on mission farms. New Spanish settlers promptly confiscated land vacated by the indigenous population.

Mining Quotas

Mining interests were activated by the discovery of silver in Bolivia in 1545. At first, the Spanish obtained indigenous workers for their mines using the model of community service already present in the Inca Empire. In this system, called **mita,** each community was obligated to provide a specified number of workers for state projects. Under Inca control, men worked on public construction projects such as roads and irrigation works and both men and women worked on farms owned by the Inca elite and priesthoods. The Spanish used the same system of labor but for Spanish profit rather than public works. The system became increasingly brutal as people died from disease and the rigors of the work. Burdens on each worker increased as the population shrank and service quotas for each community remained constant. The Spanish also obtained workers for their mines by dispossessing people from their land, turning them into "free" laborers. Unable to earn a living from their land, free laborers found it necessary to take whatever work they could find, essentially consigning themselves to the mines. Later, African slaves were used in the mine industry, especially in the processing of silver with mercury (Wolf, 1982).

Intermarriage

In both South America and Mexico, Spaniards replaced the indigenous social elites but also used some elites to control local populations. Local elites were permitted to continue receiving tribute in produce and labor from members of the common classes. They functioned as supervisors of local populations, helping to keep rebellion in check in their own interests as well as those of Spanish colonists.

Marriage customs reinforced this social system. In Mexico, for example, the Spanish government encouraged intermarriage between Spanish men and Indian women, often through capture and rape. Since most of the Spanish immigrants into Mexico were men, they needed the services, sexual and domestic, of indigenous women. In addition, Spanish authorities believed that intermarriage would create a mixed-race class of people that would stabilize social tensions created by invasion and conquest.

The Mission System

In the southwestern United States and California, the building of missions and military forts more directly destroyed indigenous culture. By the end of the eighteenth century, colonists had enslaved tens of thousands of native people, who were rounded up, removed from their homes, compelled to convert to Roman Catholicism, and forced into labor. Mission Indians typically lived in virtual slavery. Infractions or resistance often were punished by beatings, solitary confinement, mutilation, branding, or execution (Castillo, 1978; Jackson and Castillo, 1995). The brutal treatment, as well as malnutrition, led to a precipitous decline in the native population. As elsewhere in North America, disease was the most significant cause of death, accounting for about one-half of deaths (Cook, 1976; 1978).

encomiendas
Spanish landholding system in the American colonies that granted the use of land and the labor of any indigenous people on that land to soldiers, priests, and settlers.

haciendas
Estates made up of lands directly owned by Spanish settlers.

mita
Traditional Incan system of conscripted labor for public works, adapted by the Spanish for use in obtaining indigenous workers for their mines.

REVIEW

Spanish colonization of Mexico, Central America, and parts of the Caribbean and South America was based on plantation farming and mining using forced native labor and the mita system. Encomiendas, haciendas, and the mission system effectively removed land and resources from indigenous access or control. Intermarriage was encouraged, creating a unique system of social stratification with Native Americans at the bottom of the hierarchy.

AGENTS OF DIRECTED CULTURE CHANGE

Colonial authorities attempted to subdue indigenous populations through military actions and the establishment of law and order in the colonies. But they also applied social, economic, and political pressures on indigenous peoples to persuade them to change their cultural practices to be more consistent with European values and behaviors. Indoctrination was achieved through the work of missionaries, teachers, and enforcers of the rule of law.

Missionaries

Missionaries were a powerful force for cultural transformation in indigenous communities. From the sixteenth century, missionaries preceded, accompanied, and followed military and exploratory campaigns into the Americas. At first, they generally saw their role as compatible with their country's goals, which included converting, civilizing, and, they thought, helping pagan inhabitants, while at the same time exploiting any resources that might benefit their home country and the church. In later periods, though, missionaries sometimes came into conflict with civilian authorities, whose actions and policies toward native people became increasingly brutal at a time when European moral standards had begun to change.

Different groups of missionaries had different approaches to conversion. Many thought that indigenous people were subhuman and should be controlled as one would control animals. As soon as they entered a region and gained control, they forced the people to build churches, destroyed traditional ceremonial structures and paraphernalia, and beat and tortured native religious leaders into submission.

Others assumed that Indians were fully human and capable of intelligent thought and reasoning (Vecsey, 1997). Jesuits, for example, believed that pagan religious and intellectual errors resulted from the powers that the devil had over them or from the control exerted by native people who masqueraded as shamans and religious practitioners. Many missionaries saw their role as enlightening misguided but sincere people. They also made use of economic and political arguments to gain converts. Trading posts gave favorable terms and provided guns to Christian Indians but not to pagans (Bonvillain, 1986).

Later, British missionaries came to convert Indians to Protestantism. They emphasized the spiritual rewards of Christianity along with advantages of protection supposedly bestowed upon converts by the British crown. Christian Indians were favored through trade and military alliances. And missionaries taught people, directly or indirectly, to be ashamed of their culture, their heritage, and themselves. They transferred the Christian notion of sin to people who had no concept of innate sinfulness. In the words of a modern Coast Salish Catholic from the state of Washington, "The priests said, 'You are sinful, vile,' and the Indians wondered, 'What have I done?'" (Hilbert, 1987, quoted in Vecsey, 1997:351).

The missionaries advocated changes in native settlement patterns and systems of leadership and social control. They encouraged people who were previously nomadic to settle permanently, preferably near European ports and trading posts, where they were more easily contacted and controlled. The priests tried to convince their converts to obey laws, their superiors, and colonial government personnel. Many tried to supplant indigenous child-rearing practices that they saw as lenient with more authoritarian

Captive peoples such as these Australian Aborigines were taught to reject their traditional ways by white missionaries.

GLOBALIZATION

Throughout the world, European colonizers banned ceremonial practices they saw as contrary to Christian beliefs and ethics. Also, missionaries, teachers, and government officials distributed clothing to native peoples in the Americas, Africa, and the Pacific. They especially insisted that women wear blouses or dresses to cover their breasts and that men wear shorts or pants instead of traditional clothing styles that revealed all or part of their genitals. Today the same type of native clothing may be found on an Amazonian Indian and a Belgian tourist in New York City or Tokyo.

customary law
Selected aspects of native justice and jurisprudence codified into law by colonial authorities, mainly to secure greater control over indigenous populations.

measures, including corporal punishment as a means of controlling a child's will and compelling obedience. Missionaries also condemned native ethics concerning sexuality, which generally regarded premarital sexual relations as normal and natural. They also criticized marital flexibility and the relative ease of divorce found in most indigenous societies. And they attempted to transform the basically egalitarian gender relations that they observed in most native societies into the system of patriarchal dominance and authority that was typical of Europe.

Schoolteachers

In all countries under colonial control, authorities used education as a means of reorienting indigenous cultures. Forced attendance at boarding schools, for example, separated children from their parents and communities, with the result that children lost touch with traditional ways of interacting, sacred knowledge and rituals, and even their native languages. Values inculcated in schools encouraged children to identify with their teachers while at the same time making them ashamed of their parents and their heritage. They were taught that their people's customs were backward, immoral, and irrational. They were made to believe that civilization, as reflected in European customs, was desirable, if not fully attainable. These lessons were taught subtly in the context of general education, religious instruction, and industrious work. The values of hard work and obedience to authority (whether it be teacher, administrator, or king) were transmitted as necessary attributes of a civilized and educated person.

Missionaries, teachers, and government officials also condemned indigenous religious ceremonies and practitioners. Some practices, especially shamanism, were seen as backward, ignorant, and dangerous. In North America, the U.S. government outlawed the Sun Dance ceremony of the Plains Indians, and the Canadian government outlawed the potlatch ceremonial complex of the Pacific Northwest peoples.

Government Officials

Colonial administrators imposed Eurocentric patterns of law and social control in indigenous and tribal societies, which they saw as essentially disorderly. European jurisprudence, based solely on the facts in a criminal case or civil dispute, was antithetical to native justice, which was based on social context. This social context included common knowledge about the parties in a dispute and the reciprocal obligations that people have toward one another in relatively small, face-to-face communities. To indigenous peoples, the goal of adjudication was conflict resolution—a negotiated settlement that repairs social relations. To colonial administrators, the goal of adjudication was the determination of guilt or fault and its assignment to one of the parties in a dispute.

By imposing European concepts and systems of law, colonial authorities disturbed traditional systems of social relationships and ethical values, creating far-reaching changes in behavior and attitudes. Law has been described as "the cutting edge of colonialism" (Chanock, 1985:4) because of its effect on the fabric of indigenous society. Furthermore, by establishing courts and judicial systems based on European principles, the problems of indigenous people were reinterpreted in a language of law that distorted the indigenous experience. Concepts such as "equality under the law" and "innocent until proven guilty," for instance, were not traditional in native justice.

In some regions, colonial authorities recognized "native courts" that enforced "customary law" (Merry, 1991:893). However, **customary law** was often an inaccurate creation of colonial regimes. For example, in Zambia and Malawi, colonial authorities transformed indigenous systems of adjudication that were flexible and adaptable to different contexts and different social needs into a system of customary law that was based on a rigid written code (Chanock, 1985). Enshrining a particular set of indigenous practices in a written code privileges some practices over others and creates an artificial "tradition" that then becomes identified as part of indigenous culture. Colonial authorities manipulated this process to reflect their interests in the region. When countries in Africa and elsewhere gained their independence, they sometimes used these codes of customary law to establish judicial procedures. These borrowed procedures then became central ingredients in developing statehood, a national culture, and nationalistic pride.

cash economies
Systems of exchange based on the use of currency in modern markets.

A Cash Economy

Colonial law and administrative control benefited elites and their wealth in both the colonies and the home country. Imposed taxes obtained income for the state and compelled changes in indigenous economic systems. In Africa, taxation was used by both British and French administrations. Households were required to pay taxes in cash, but people's access to money was limited, because their economies were based on subsistence farming or cattle herding. Access to manufactured goods, foods, and luxury items also required cash. As a result, some members of the family, usually men, had to obtain work outside of their local communities for which they would be paid in cash. In some areas women sold milk and home-brewed beer for cash.

In Africa, most of the work available was on plantations producing crops for export or in mines extracting valuable mineral resources. Migration from rural areas to plantations, mines, and towns disturbed the social cohesiveness of local communities; and families were splintered by the need for employment to buy the goods that had come to symbolize the good life. Women who remained in the local communities were burdened by additional responsibilities in their households and in subsistence farming that supported their families. Colonial **cash economies** and systems of taxation thus continued the household and community fracturing that had occurred during the slave trade era.

> **REVIEW**
>
> Agents of directed culture change included missionaries, schoolteachers, and government officials. They discouraged or outlawed traditional ways of life, changing the way people ate, dressed, and raised their children. They also imposed European values about governance and justice through so-called customary law. Finally, they introduced a cash economy, which led to labor migration and changes in family relations and replaced traditional systems of reciprocity and redistribution.

JUSTIFICATIONS FOR COLONIAL RULE

Throughout the eighteenth and nineteenth centuries, European control increased in many parts of the world. The colonial presence of the Portuguese, Spanish, and Dutch was gradually replaced by that of Great Britain, France, Germany, Italy, and the United States. As they set up colonial regimes in Africa, Asia, and the Pacific, they developed new justifications for their rule to replace the earlier rationale that Europeans could take lands they conquered simply by self-declared "right of discovery."

The British used the model of European landholding patterns and practices to claim that in order to "own" land, one had to transform it through labor. This agrarian model did not always fit indigenous economies in other parts of the world. Thus, British authorities recognized that indigenous people "used" land but questioned whether they "owned" it. Lack of proof of ownership thus became a rationale for ignoring indigenous claims to land and resources.

The same principle of landownership through farming was used in the United States to justify settler expansion in the plains and the west in the nineteenth century. Many indigenous peoples were nomadic foragers without fixed or permanent settlement sites. American authorities viewed hunting territories as open and unsettled

white man's burden
Paternalistic, racist, colonial attitude that treated colonized peoples as inferiors in need of protection and instruction on how to live.

pacification
Colonial goal of forcing indigenous people to be peaceful and nonresistant so that settlers could safely inhabit their lands.

? *In your opinion should Europeans have refrained from interfering in native practices of cannibalism, infanticide, and domestic abuse? Why, or why not?*

because they did not find permanent villages and plowed fields. In Australia as well, the British and, later, Australian governments ignored the rights of Aborigines to their accustomed territories. They claimed that the land was "unoccupied wasteland" and therefore could be appropriated by the Australian state (Bodley, 1999:88).

White Man's Burden

European colonizers also justified their control of indigenous peoples by claiming cultural and moral superiority. Administering to these people responsibly was the **"white man's burden."** Various versions of the white man's burden were used to justify the eradication of indigenous practices and their replacement with behaviors, values, and attitudes more consistent with those of Europeans. Missionaries working in North and South America in the sixteenth and seventeenth centuries embodied the idea that they were saving the natives and doing God's work by converting them.

In Africa, Asia, and the Pacific, educators and government officials spoke the same Eurocentric and essentially racist attitudes in a language of science and reason. For example, Herman Merivale, a British professor of political economy, wrote in 1861 that the natives deserved protection from the excesses of colonial settlers and also deserved to be civilized by the guidance and superiority of the white men. As Merivale advocated, "Colonial authorities should act upon the assumption that they have the right, in virtue of the relative position of civilized and Christian men to savages, to enforce abstinence from immoral and degrading practices" such as cannibalism, infanticide, and wife abuse (1988:101). Furthermore, "[T]here should be no hesitation in acting on the broad principle that the natives must, for their own protection, be placed in a situation of acknowledged inferiority, and consequently of tutelage" (p. 103).

In 1841, the British House of Commons Select Committee on South Australia issued an official report (*British Parliamentary Papers,* 1841, vol. IV, no. 394) generally deploring the harsh treatment of Aborigines by colonial authorities. It observed that government policy "has thrown impediments in the way of successful colonization; it has engendered wars, and it has vanished from our confines, or exterminated, the native, who might have been profitable workmen, good customers, and good neighbors" (quoted in Bodley, 1988:68). British colonial authorities in the twentieth century elaborated on the white man's burden. In the words of Sir Hubert Murray, lieutenant governor of Papua New Guinea, in the 1930s, colonial governments have a duty "towards subject races"—the duty of "association and collaboration." As he stated, "We are not trying to make the brown man white; we are trying to make him a better brown man than he was before" (Murray, 1933, in Bodley, 1988:43).

A Sacred Trust

The British colonial attitude of "sacred trust" toward indigenous peoples justified their efforts to "civilize" them. Murray advocated a policy of "peaceful pacification" of indigenous peoples through "indirect rule," As he said, a "scientific method of **pacification**" rests on "knowledge of the people whom you propose to pacify, and some idea of what you are going to do with them when they are pacified" (1988:43).

Murray emphasized that "native races are no longer deliberately exterminated" and that colonial governments should refrain from punitive attacks on native villages as a punishment for rebellious acts. Such a policy, he said, was both morally untenable and impractical, because it led to hostility on the part of indigenous peoples and therefore thwarted colonial efforts at "peaceful pacification." Instead, Murray advocated the establishment of a local police force made up of members of the indigenous community. This would foster loyalty to the government and help administer indigenous regions. The police would develop "pride in their uniform." This tactic proved to be divisive in indigenous communities, however, as native police upheld colonial authority and sometimes abused their powers.

Murray also advocated winning over local leaders who would then convince members of their communities to support or at least not oppose colonial authority. This strategy, too, caused divisions within indigenous communities, pitting one faction against another. Colonial administrators were advised

- To establish posts in interior districts in order to deepen their control and create multiple centers of influence;
- To demonstrate benevolence and create goodwill, for example by returning prisoners to their communities as "ambassadors of peace"; to bring gradual rather than abrupt change to the lives of indigenous people;
- And to permit the preservation of indigenous customs so long as they did not contribute to disorder and resistance (1988:49).

The Reservation System

In the United States and Canada, in the nineteenth century, the federal governments obtained land from native peoples through ostensibly legal means, replacing the outright confiscation of territory and annihilation of indigenous peoples. The U.S. government was consistent in its goal of removing native peoples to lands outside areas of American settlement. The philosophy of manifest destiny was at the heart of these efforts, as Americans believed that the land was rightfully theirs. They acquired land through the procedural legality of signing treaties with Indian leaders and establishing reservations (or reserves, as they are called in Canada) for native peoples.

Reservations consisted of land guaranteed by treaty for native residents' ownership and control. Treaty language promised that the government would protect reservations from confiscation or settlement by non-Indians. In exchange, people agreed to cede their territory for protection and the perpetual right to live on their remaining land. Through these treaties, the United States acquired millions of acres of native land and created hundreds of Indian reservations.

However, settlers nevertheless frequently intruded on these protected lands. Once this happened, government officials, claiming they were powerless to stop the settlers, urged the indigenous people to abandon their lands and move farther west, out of the way. Some native groups moved three or four times before finally ending up in "Indian territory," now Oklahoma.

When people resisted giving up their homelands, however, Americans resorted to intimidation and threat of military force, and no justifications were offered. For example, General Edmund Gaines, speaking in 1831 to a delegation of Sauk leaders

reservations
Land guaranteed by treaty for native residents' ownership and control.

These Apache children were photographed before (left) and after (right) they entered a boarding school. Children were subjected to a foreign system of education to teach them new values. Boarding schools physically separated children from the supposedly backward and uncivilized influences of parents and communities. Use of native languages was often forbidden in these schools.

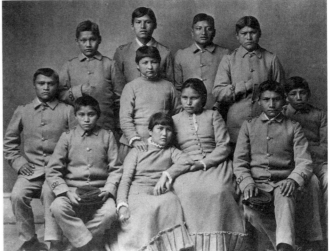

Case study

Captive Societies of Australia and Tasmania

In Australia, Aboriginal ownership of land had been denied from the out-set of British colonization. Because Aborigines were nomadic foragers, their entitlement to the territories they inhabited and where they gath-ered and hunted resources was invisible to the eyes of British farmers, sheep ranchers, and government officials. The people traditionally lived in small, scattered, seasonal encampments. Their presence was barely acknowledged by colonial administrators, who saw them as nuisances to be pushed away from the newly founded and growing towns and cities of colonial Australia. One practice of white settlement in Australia was the taking of young Aboriginal children from their families. The children were placed in institutions or in white foster homes as servants and de-nied further contact with their families. Ironically, this practice was seen at the time as a humane way to assimilate natives into colonial Australian society and culture.

British colonial policies in Tasmania, an island off the southeastern coast of Australia, led to the extinction of the Tasmanian people. When Tasmanians re-sisted the attempts to confiscate their settlement and hunting areas, Australian settlers responded by attacking and killing or capturing whole villages and communities. The native people responded with retaliatory attacks against Anglo ranchers and farmers.

In 1828, Australia Governor Sir Arthur Lawley issued proclamations warning set-tlers to cease their attacks on Tasmanians, but he also ordered Tasmanians to keep clear of Anglo settlements unless they had received official passports allowing them entry. When these proclamations were ignored, Lawley then ordered the clearing of most of Tasmania of its original inhabitants, moving his soldiers from one end of the island to another in an attempt to round up all of the natives within each district and remove them to a place for their own safety. Rewards were offered for natives taken alive, but many more were killed than were captured. In the end, the few hundred native Tasmanians who survived into the 1840s were taken to their final settlement on Flinders Island, off the coast of Tasmania. By 1854, only sixteen Tasmanians were left, and by 1870, there was only one. She died in 1876 (Howells, 2001:263).

Despite the official eradication of the native Tasmanians in 1876, some of the people's descendants continued to elude the settlers and soldiers who attempted to capture them. More than a century later, native Tasmanians, preferring their own name, Palawa, are demanding recognition of their rights to some of their land and sacred sites. In particular, they are reclaiming Eddystone Point, a traditional trading base and ceremonial center. When the Australian government offered the site for pub-lic bidding, the Palawa protested and held public demonstrations. The government then declared a postponement of the bidding process. Meanwhile, Aboriginal peoples from Tasmania and Australia have come to the site, using it as a place to express their solidarity and to perform sacred rituals (*Cultural Survival Quarterly*, 2002:13).

who balked at moving from their Illinois villages, told them: "I came here neither to beg nor hire you to leave your village. My business is to remove you, peaceably if I can, but forcibly if I must" (Jackson, 1964:111–112). And in 1851, Luke Lea, the federal commissioner of Indian Affairs, told Santee delegates in South Dakota, "Suppose your Great Father wanted your land and did not want a treaty for your good, he would come with 100,000 men and drive you off to the Rocky Mountains" (Meyer, 1993:78).

Another land-grabbing strategy, popular through the 1870s, was collusion between government and traders to force native representatives to sign land-cession agreements in exchange for the forgiveness of debts incurred by members of their communities. Traders gave credit to Indian families that amounted to more than they could ever repay. Officials then demanded land in exchange for the debts owed. Bribing and intoxicating Indian delegates to treaty negotiations was another strategy in which leaders signed away their people's land without even knowing what they were doing.

Once Indians were settled on reservations and reserves, the U.S. and Canadian federal governments implemented policies aimed at "civilizing" them. "Civilized" Indians were sedentary farmers who lived in nuclear family households, wore Anglo clothing, spoke English, and attended church. Missionaries often took control of local education and merged religious doctrines with secular training in farming, manual skills, and domestic duties. Participation in traditional religious ceremonies was forbidden.

> ### REVIEW
>
> European justifications for their treatment of indigenous peoples in colonized lands were based on Eurocentric and racist ideas. These ideas, such as the right of discovery, the white man's burden, and the sacred trust, made Europeans the stewards of people they viewed as racially "inferior," culturally "primitive," or simply "wild." "Pacification" was followed by the establishment of the reservation system, designed to "civilize" the natives.

REACTIONS OF INDIGENOUS PEOPLES TO EUROPEAN COLONIZERS

When indigenous peoples first encountered Europeans sailing in the waters off their shores or arriving in their territories, they reacted in different ways. Coastal peoples were amazed at the sight of strange-looking, pale, absurdly dressed men atop huge moving sailing vessels that looked to them like "floating houses" or "hovering clouds" (Bitterli, 1989:21). The open and friendly manner of many indigenous peoples struck European explorers as simple and straightforward. In the journals of Christopher Columbus, writing in October 1492 about his first contact with indigenous people in Hispaniola, now known as Santo Domingo:

> I, in order that they might feel great amity towards us, because I knew they were a people to be delivered and converted to our holy faith rather by love than by force, gave to some among them some red caps and glass beads, which they hung round their neck, and many other things of little value. At this they were greatly pleased and became so entirely our friends that it was a wonder to see. Afterwards they came swimming to the ship's boats, where we were, and brought us parrots and cotton thread in balls, and spears and many other things. (Vigneras, 1960:23)

Columbus also remarked that the residents of the territory would make good slaves.

Slightly more than a century later, Samuel de Champlain described his meeting with Algonkian Indians in Maine in 1604, which began with speeches of friendship. Champlain referred to the desire of the French to visit the country and trade with the inhabitants.

> They signified their great satisfaction, saying that no greater good would come to them than to have our friendship, . . . and we should dwell in their land, in order that they might in future more than ever before engage in hunting beavers, and give us a part of them in return for our providing them with things which they wanted. After he finished his discourse, we presented them with hatchets, caps, knives, and other little knick knacks. (Champlain, 1907:50)

Trade Goods and Gods

Indigenous peoples were usually willing, and often eager, to acquire goods of European manufacture. These were utilitarian objects, especially made of metal, or decorative objects, which Europeans thought of as relatively worthless baubles and trinkets. The eagerness with which natives sought foreign goods confirmed the Europeans' sense of superiority and their view of indigenous peoples as somewhat childish.

Some indigenous peoples had to make compromises between their desire for trade goods and their wariness of the strangers. In some cases, they managed this compromise through indirect or distant exchanges, as in the following example, reported by a French trader exploring the West African coast of Guinea:

> These barbarous people would not venture close to us in order to exchange their fish and water for our tobacco and ship's biscuit. They behaved rather as we behave towards victims of the plague; our people were obliged to take the goods they wanted to exchange for fish some distance from the ship and then turn back. After the natives had observed this, they approached to what had been brought to them, put their fish in the same place, and returned to their huts. (Jannequin, 1643:43–44)

Native North Americans typically saw Europeans as childish, stupid, and cruel. They were shocked at what they perceived as coldness toward human suffering and unwillingness to be generous to people in need. They saw foreigners as stupid for always getting lost in the woods and failing to notice features of the landscape. And they were dismayed by the Europeans' tendency to complain about discomfort, hunger, and pain (Thwaites, 1906).

In other parts of the world, native peoples endowed Europeans with supernatural powers. Their awe may have exaggerated Europeans' feelings of cultural superiority and self-importance. For the Aztecs and Incas, the timing of contact happened to coincide with prophecies of the return of divine beings or strange creatures with supernatural powers. One of these prophecies concerned the Inca creator god Viracocha, who was a bearded white man, just like the Spaniards. When Cortes arrived in Mexico in 1519 and Pizarro came to Peru in 1526, they, with their horses, were greeted and welcomed as returning gods.

People soon realized their mistake, however. In the words of an Inca chronicler, recorded by a Spanish monk in Peru soon after the conquest of the Inca Empire:

> I thought they were kindly beings sent (as they claimed) by Tecsi Viracocha, that is to say, by God; but it seems to me that all has turned out the very opposite from what I believed; so let me tell you, brothers, from proof they have given me since their arrival in our country, they are the sons not of Viracocha, but of the devil." (Wachtel, 1977:22)

These words reveal not only the Inca attitude but also the Spaniards' manipulation of native beliefs. The Spanish claimed to be kindly beings sent by God, giving greater importance to indigenous prophecies as a cause of the conquest than was the case. And native peoples later reinterpreted their histories to fit their circumstances, using concepts from Christianity to explain events.

Guns and Other Technological Wonders

Europeans used their technology to instill awe, confusion, and sometimes fear. For example, Jesuit missionaries working among the Hurons in Ontario in the 1630s used clocks to inspire awe. The Indians were surprised by the "voice" that the clock made when it struck on the hour. They interpreted this "voice" as the sound of the spirit of the clock and were amazed that the missionaries could order the clock to use its voice at will. The Indians did not know that the Jesuits could predict when the clock would strike because they could tell the time. The Hurons interpreted European behavior in their own terms, as all peoples do. As animists, believing that objects may be imbued with spirit power and may have voices and wills, the Indians interpreted the new objects in terms of their prior beliefs.

Guns had more damaging effects. They created fear when fired into the air as a display or directly at animals or people, causing injury and death. The arbitrary, random, and unforeseen manner in which the Europeans used their weapons also instilled fear. In 1606, in the waters off the coast of New Guinea, for example, Luis Baez de Torres had his soldiers shoot at people in their canoes as they were rowing toward him in a friendly greeting. According to de Torres, "On reaching them, we saluted them with our arquebuses and killed some, and when any fell dead they gave

? How is the theme of technologically superior strangers with unknown intentions played out in American popular culture today?

The Aztecs are reported to have recoiled in horror at the display of Spanish artillery: "[I]t was as if one had lost one's breath; it was as if for the time being there was stupefaction, as if one were affected by mushrooms. Fear prevailed. It was as if everyone had swallowed his heart. Even before it had grown dark, there was terror, there was astonishment, there was apprehension, there was a stunning of the people" (Sahagun, 1975:47).

them blows with their clubs to make them get up, thinking that they were not dead" (Hilder, 1980:28).

Native Resistance and Retaliation

Indigenous peoples tended to treat Europeans with generosity and friendliness, until they learned from experience that the strangers were not to be trusted and that they desired their land, resources, and labor. From most reports, attacks on Europeans seem to have been well motivated, as friendliness turned to retaliation, against either a particular offending group or the next party of European intruders. In Spanish colonies in the Americas, for example, residents of marginal regions in Central Mexico resisted foreign control. This resistance was most marked in the north among the Yaqui and Apache in Sonora, the northernmost Mexican state. It was not until the middle and late nineteenth century that these two groups were "pacified" with the help of the U.S. military.

Farther north, the Pueblo peoples (Hopi, Zuni, Cochiti, Tewa, and others), living along the Rio Grande in what is now New Mexico, staged a revolt in 1680. After more than a century of rule by Spanish colonizers and priests, the various communities united to oust the foreigners, killing 21 priests and about 400 settlers, out of a population of 2,500 (Dozier, 1970:59). Then, twelve years later, the Spanish sent another invading force and reestablished control in 1692. Eventually this region became part of the United States after the Mexican-American War ended in 1846 with the signing of the Treaty of Guadalupe-Hidalgo.

In the south of Mexico, Spanish authorities also had a difficult time establishing permanent control, especially in Chiapas. There, members of indigenous Tzotzil and Tzeltal communities put up active resistance through military defense as well as

GLOBALIZATION

Since the 1940s, as dozens of countries have won their independence, much of the world has become free of direct colonial rule. Independence movements spread through forces of globalization are still at work in the world today.

In Their Own Voices

Nelson Mandela on the Struggle against Apartheid in South Africa

In this excerpt, Nelson Mandela discusses the beginnings of the antiapartheid movement in South Africa. This movement was part of the ongoing struggle against colonial rule that grew throughout Africa in the 1950s and 1960s. In South Africa, it took many decades to achieve victory but, finally, in 1992, with all South Africans able to vote, a new government led by the African National Congress was elected. Nelson Mandela was its first president.

Since 1912 and year after year thereafter, in their homes, in provincial and national gatherings, on trains and buses, and in the factories and on the farms, in cities, villages, shanty-towns, schools and prisons, the African people have discussed the shameful misdeeds of those who rule the country.

Year after year they have raised their voices to condemn the grinding poverty of the people, the low wages, the acute shortage of land, the inhuman exploitation, and the whole policy of White domination. But instead of more freedom, repression began to grow in volume and intensity and it seemed that all their sacrifices would end in smoke and dust.

Today the whole country knows that their labours were not in vain, for a new spirit and new ideas have gripped our people. Today the people speak the language of action: there is a mighty awakening among the men and women of our country.

The year 1952 stands out as the year of this upsurge of national consciousness. In June of that year the African National Congress and the South African Indian Congress, bearing in mind their responsibility as the representatives of the downtrodden and oppressed people of South Africa,

took the plunge and launched the campaign for the Defiance of Unjust Laws [especially the pass laws, requiring Black South Africans to carry identity cards that restricted them to certain areas of the cities and countryside as well as curfew regulations]. . . . It spread throughout the country like wildfire. Factory and office workers, doctors, lawyers, teachers, students, and the clergy; African, Coloureds, Indians, and Europeans, old and young, all rallied to the national call. . . . The Campaign called for immediate and heavy sacrifices. Workers lost their jobs, chiefs and teachers were expelled from the service, doctors, lawyers, and businessmen gave up their practices and businesses and elected to go to jail. Defiance was a step of great political significance. It released stronger social forces which affected thousands of our countrymen.

It was an effective way of getting the masses to function politically; a powerful method of voicing our indignation against the reactionary policies of the government. It was one of the best ways of exerting pressure on the government and extremely dangerous to the stability and security of the State. It inspired and aroused our people from a conquered and servile community of "yes-men" to a militant and uncompromising band of comrades-in-arms. . . .

The entire continent is seething with discontent, and already there are powerful revolutionary eruptions in the Gold Coast, Nigeria, Tunisia, Kenya, the Rhodesias, and South Africa. The oppressed people and the oppressors are at loggerheads. The day of reckoning between the forces of freedom and those of reaction is not far off. I have not the slightest doubt that when that day comes truth and justice will prevail.

From *No Easy Walk to Freedom* by Nelson Mandela. Reprinted by permission of Harcourt Education.

passive resistance through retreat to remote mountain areas. Even in later centuries, their resistance simmered, most recently manifested in the Zapatista movement of the 1990s.

REVIEW

Indigenous reactions to European colonizers were diverse, but a common pattern was awe, friendship, interest in trade goods, treaties, acts of resistance or aggression, and ultimate defeat in armed conflict. In some areas resistance movements have persisted to the present day.

Anthropology Applied

Establishing the Xingu National Park

In South America, in the Amazon, national governments have vacillated between policies of recognizing and guaranteeing Indians' rights to land and policies that uproot indigenous peoples to make way for settlement and economic development. In Brazil, several constitutions written between 1891 and 1946 respected Indians' rights to their traditional lands, and some Brazilian states set aside lands under the guardianship of the Indian Protection Service. By 1961, however, the largest of these reserves, originally encompassing 85,000 square kilometers, was reduced to 22,000 square kilometers through incursions of settlers and land speculators. At that time, the reserve, later adding an additional 8,000 square kilometers, became the Xingu National Park (Bodley, 1999:83). This park, along with other Indian reserves, is supposedly protected by the Brazilian National Indian Foundation (FUNAI), but successive Brazilian governments have permitted mining on Indian lands (Gray, 1990).

Anthropologists contributed to establishing the Xingu National Park and work today in both the Brazilian government and with the Indians to protect the people who live in the park from outside interference and economic exploitation. Ethnographies of the Amazonian people date back to the 1880s and 1930s, and in the early 1960s, anthropologists Robert Carneiro and Gertrude Dole supported the efforts of the Brazilian champion of Indians, Claudio Villas-Boas, and his brothers. Their goal was to save the indigenous peoples of the Xingu River valley by creating a preserve. In 1965, it was estimated that only 542 people remained, but today in the Xingu National Park there are more than 6,000 people in thirty villages representing seventeen nations.

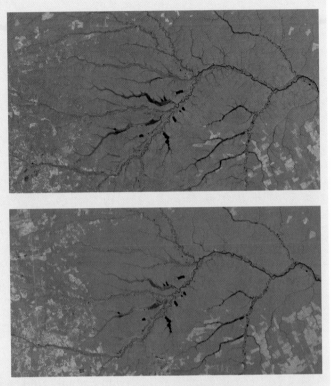

These Landsat photos show the Xingu National Park and Indigenous Peoples Preserve in 1992 (top) and in 2001 (bottom), indicating increases in cleared land, especially in the south. Farming and cattle ranching threaten the future of the park. Additional threats come from gold mining, which has led to mercury contamination of tributaries of the Xingu River, affecting the health of the native peoples.

CRITICAL THINKING QUESTIONS

What factors contribute to the decisions of governments to protect indigenous peoples? What factors contribute to their decisions to exploit protected lands?

GLOBALIZATION IN THE POSTCOLONIAL ERA

India was one of the first large colonized countries to free itself of European control, from Great Britain, in 1947. The independence movement accelerated in the 1950s and 1960s, when many African countries became independent of Great Britain, France, and Belgium. Similar processes occurred in Asia and in the Pacific in the following decades. Indigenous peoples nevertheless seldom obtained equal social, economic, or political rights in their new nations. They often remained marginalized groups under pressure from newly formed central governments to conform to national practices and values. Central authorities justified this pressure in the name of **nationalism,** focusing on the importance of building a common culture to strengthen national unity. In the process of nation building, cultural diversity often was a casualty, as indigenous ways were targeted as backward and obstacles to growth.

nationalism
Movement in independent states to build national identity, pride, and unity.

Table 16.2 AMOUNT OF LAND RESERVED FOR INDIGENOUS POPULATIONS IN DIFFERENT COUNTRIES

	Native Population as Percentage of Total Population	Native Lands as Percentage of Total Area
Bechuanaland	99+	38
Swaziland	98	48
New Guinea	98	97
Zimbabwe	95	33
Botswana/Namibia	87	25
Canada	3	0.2
Chile	2	0.6
United States	0.3	1

Note: These figures are pre-1960. As countries gained independence, native lands as a percentage of total land area rose, by definition, to nearly 100 percent (depending on the amount of foreign-owned land). Most African countries achieved independence with majority rule by 1970. For example, Bechuanaland, a British protectorate, became the Independent Republic of Botswana in 1966. Papua New Guinea achieved independence in 1975, but the western part of the island, Irian Jaya, was annexed by Indonesia in 1968. In Canada, the United States, and South America, both native population as a percentage of total population and native lands as a percentage of total land area generally rose, the latter through recent successful land claims.

Source: John Bodley, *Victims of Progress,* 4/e. Copyright © 1999 McGraw-Hill Companies, Inc. Reprinted by permission.

Land-grabbing did not end with independence. National governments in Peru, Bolivia, Colombia, Venezuela, Brazil, and Chile, for example, changed land policies that had favored Indians' rights and permitted outside interests to exploit Indian lands and resources. And in the United States today, successes in Native American land claims are balanced against the appropriation of resources on those lands, such as oil, uranium, and platinum.

? *Which nations can be characterized as xenophobic today? Why?*

Similar patterns developed in Africa and the Middle East, sometimes contributing tragically to internal competition and intertribal genocide. In **xenophobic** reactions, the governments of newly independent states sought to selectively expel or decimate tribes, ethnic minorities, foreign laborers, merchant elites, or former colonial overlords. Issues over land and resources aggravated these conflicts.

Table 16.2 summarizes data on indigenous populations in selected countries and the land under their control during the height of the colonial period, prior to 1960.

Colonialism began a process of global transformation in all areas of society and culture, affecting economic systems, social life, political organization, and more. In the **postcolonial era,** processes have continued to integrate national societies throughout the world. Migration of peoples from rural to urban areas within their own countries and migration to foreign lands have contributed to the creation of a very different world than existed in 1500. As people have traveled from one place to another, they have brought with them their cultural practices and beliefs, their languages, and their expectations for a new way of life. And they have brought with them some of the plants and animals native to their home regions. This process, begun on a worldwide scale many centuries ago, has had a global impact on environments and economic systems, as well as on an emerging global culture.

xenophobic
Having to do with fear, hatred, and envy of strangers, outsiders, or foreign-born minorities within the society.

postcolonial era
Period (roughly since 1965), following the independence of the last former European colonies as new nations under indigenous leadership and control.

When Christopher Columbus made his second voyage to Hispaniola (now the Dominican Republic) in 1493, he brought seeds and cuttings for planting wheat, chickpeas, melons, onions, radishes, greens, grapevines, sugarcane, and fruit stones (Crosby, 1972:67). Not all of these plants were successfully grown in that region, but many did prosper. Sugar, in particular, came to dominate the economies of Central and South America, and wheat is grown all over North and South America. While many of the European plants and animals that were transplanted to the Americas were brought deliberately, many seeds also came inadvertently, "in the folds of textiles, in clods of mud, in dung, and in a thousand other ways" (p. 73). And many weeds and grasses that are now common in North America are European in origin, including bluegrass, daisies, and dandelions.

Indigenous peoples in the Americas gradually adopted European livestock. Sheep and goats were incorporated into the economies of southwestern peoples, who utilized the animals' wool, milk, and meat. And cattle, chickens, and pigs were kept as sources of food.

In turn, Native American plants have been carried to the other continents as well. Among the most important food crops are maize, beans, peanuts, potatoes, sweet potatoes, manioc (cassava), squashes, pumpkin, papaya, avocado, pineapple, tomato, chili pepper, and cocoa (p. 170). Many of these crops, particularly potatoes, maize, manioc, beans, and peanuts, have contributed to population growth in Europe and Africa, as well as in the Americas. Today, some native foods of the Americas are major export crops of other countries. For example, India is one of the world's largest producers of peanuts, and China produces more sweet potatoes than any other country. Peanuts and cocoa are important export crops for countries in West Africa, while maize and manioc are critical for domestic consumption there. Finally, national cuisines make us realize the impact that worldwide exploration and exchange have made. For instance, the pasta and tomato sauces so common in Italian recipes are the gifts of China and Mexico.

? *In what other ways can present-day globalization be attributed to European colonialism? In what sense, according to some, is colonialism still going on today?*

REVIEW

Since the 1940s, as people gained independence from colonial rulers, forces of nationalism and globalization continued the legacies of colonialism into the postcolonial era. Newly independent nations evicted foreigners in xenophobic reactions and competed internally for power. Ethnic or tribal minorities often were persecuted, marginalized, or pressured to sacrifice their ways of life in the interests of national unity. And the global economy, based on European demand, had irrevocably transformed production and resource use in the new nations.

Chapter Summary

European Colonialism

- Conquest and colonialism have occurred in many parts of the world as state societies expanded their borders or expanded their spheres of economic and political influence. In the process, conquerors and colonizers demanded changes in the cultures of indigenous peoples. In particular, European colonialism affected societies on every continent of the world. Technological advances unique to Europe, especially in sailing vessels, navigation, and mapmaking, enabled this process of expansion and control. Europeans established colonies, that is, settlements of foreign nationals with controlling interests in indigenous territories. These colonies were tied to the home country both politically and economically. The home country governed the ways that colonial subjects had to behave, and it extracted resources through trade with the colonies.

- There were three major types of colonies: exploitation colonies (resulting from military conquests in which the colonial power exploits the economic resources of the region), maritime enclaves (resulting from sea trade and coastal exploration to control trade at the ports of foreign lands and have an indirect control over internal trade in foreign territories), and settlement colonies (resulting from military invasion that supports permanent colonial settlement).

The Slave Trade

- The slave trade in Africa was expanded by the Portuguese in the mid-fifteenth century. Other European nations, especially Great Britain, Holland, and France, also became involved, taking people from Africa to work on plantations in the Caribbean, South America, and the present-day United States. In all, about 10 million people were taken from Africa by the time the slave trade ended in the early nineteenth century.

- The wealth produced by the slaves in the Americas enriched their owners and contributed to the accumulation of capital and resources centered in Europe, directly and indirectly leading to the Industrial Revolution.

- Although slavery as a practice was controlled and profited mainly by Europeans, it elaborated and intensified indigenous West African patterns. Many African societies had systems of slavery or coerced labor in which people were either indentured or enslaved for others. Some enslaved workers were war captives, others were people who pawned themselves if they became indebted to another person and were unable to pay the loan, and still others were indentured for a particular period of time as punishment for wrongdoing.

- Conditions of slavery in the Americas were likely worse than those in traditional African societies. European colonists typically saw African slaves as racially inferior, not deserving the same treatment as Europeans. They were considered the property of the master, who could subject them to whatever treatment he or she decided.

- Involvement in the slave trade caused changes in West African societies. Some people benefited economically and politically from the slave trade, obtaining European manufactures and armaments. These goods enhanced their wealth and status, enabling some individuals and groups to exert dominance over other groups or neighboring communities. The elites of some African societies, such as the Ashanti, were able to centralize their wealth and power, but other African societies, such as the Kingdom of the Congo, fell apart because of internal competition of rival factions for war captives who could be sold into the European slave trade.

Trade and Settlement in North America

- In North America, colonies were established most successfully by Britain, France, and Spain. The British established settler colonies, exporting people in search of cheap farmland and resources. These settler colonies embarked on policies of eradicating indigenous peoples or removing them from their ancestral territories. These policies continued after colonies became independent countries. Eventually, indigenous peoples were relegated to small portions of their ancestral homelands or to unknown lands.

- European and American settlers benefited from the spread of epidemic diseases such as measles and smallpox. The destruction of resources, such as the slaughter of buffalo in the late nineteenth century, and threats of military intervention, persuaded native leaders to sign treaties ceding most of their land to the U.S. government.

- European powers focused their economic interests in North America primarily on the trading of fur-bearing animals, especially beaver. Most native communities welcomed participation in the fur trade because they were able to procure goods of European manufacture, especially those made of metal.

- Native people could not control the market for furs in Europe and Asia, which made them vulnerable to changes in demand. In addition, they overtrapped their territories to obtain as many animals as possible. After their lands were depleted of trade-worthy animals, they competed with other indigenous groups, which led to hostility and open conflict. As settlers pushed farther west, indigenous peoples fled into neighboring territories, increasing competition over resources and warfare.

Spanish Colonies in the Americas

- Spanish colonization in the Americas was focused on exploiting resources, especially silver and other precious metals, and in establishing plantations that would produce marketable crops, principally sugarcane, in the Caribbean and in South America.

- At first, indigenous inhabitants of the regions were compelled to work in mines and on plantations, but due to depopulation they eventually were replaced in some regions by African slaves. Landholding patterns included encomiendas, haciendas, and mission villages. The Spanish appropriated native lands and labor and established missions supported by the forced labor of Native Americans.

- The Spanish generally intermarried with indigenous peoples, creating a social class composed of people with both Spanish and indigenous ancestry. This group functioned as intermediaries and as a growing elite class whose roots were in native culture but whose developing loyalties were with the Spanish elite.

Agents of Directed Culture Change

- Throughout the world, colonial authorities have applied social, economic, and political pressures on indigenous peoples to persuade them to change their cultural practices to be more consistent with European values and behaviors. Missionaries aided in this process by attempting to convert indigenous peoples to Christianity. Schoolteachers inculcated in them European values and norms. Boarding schools separated native children from their parents and communities. Children thus lost touch with their traditional ways, religious beliefs, and even their languages.

- Colonial administrators imposed Eurocentric patterns of law and social control in indigenous societies, disturbing traditional systems of social relationships and ethical values. Economic relationships were changed through the introduction of cash economies based on market principles.

Justifications for Colonial Rule

- Europeans believed that they could take land they conquered simply by their self-declared "right of discovery." Lack of proof of ownership of land also was a rationale for ignoring indigenous claims to land and resources. Nationalism and imperialism helped to justify colonialism as state societies expanded their territories.

- European colonizers also justified their control of indigenous people by claiming a "white man's burden" of cultural, moral, and racial superiority. Europeans believed that they had a "sacred trust" justifying their efforts to pacify and civilize the natives. Many believed that they were doing what was best for the indigenous population, bringing them the gifts of civilized society.

Indigenous Reactions to European Colonizers

- Some indigenous peoples were awed by European technology and manufactures or believed that Europeans were gods, especially as they seemed immune to diseases that brought sickness and death to native communities. In some places the arrival of Europeans seemed to coincide with prophecies of the return of supernatural beings.
- Members of indigenous communities differed in their attitudes toward Europeans. Many were eager trading partners, hoping to acquire European goods. But once people realized the intentions of Europe to control their lands and lives, disagreements often arose. Some people favored accommodation to the demands of the European forces, but others advocated resistance and open rebellion.

Globalization in the Postcolonial Era

- Since the 1940s, much of the world was freed from direct colonial control as countries won their independence. Competition for power and authority among tribes or elites created or favored by colonial governments often led to violence. Indigenous peoples often remain marginalized in the newly established nations, as new governments pressure them to sacrifice more land and resources to "progress" and to conform to national practices and values in the national interest. Nationalism, based on building a common culture for the sake of national unity, is hard to achieve in culturally diverse societies.
- Indigenous foragers and nomadic pastoralists have been encouraged or compelled to settle permanently in one area and to develop farming or wage-working economies. Also, efforts to spread a national language have lessened cultural diversity. Thus the legacies of colonialism live on.

 ## Key Terms

colonies 420	resettlement
imperialism 421	policies 422
exploitation	missionism 422
colonies 421	slave trade 423
maritime enclaves 421	fur trade 426
settlement colonies 421	depopulation 427

encomiendas 430	pacification 434
haciendas 430	reservations 435
mita 430	nationalism 441
customary law 432	xenophobic 442
cash economies 433	postcolonial era 442
white man's burden 434	

Review Questions

1. What were European motivations for colonialism and patterns of colonization?
2. How did the European slave trade help spread colonialism while ultimately undermining African states?
3. How did indigenous peoples of North America become involved in European trading networks, and how did that involvement affect their modes of subsistence?
4. What systems of Spanish landholding and mining labor displaced native peoples from their land and forced them into the colonial system?
5. Why was intermarriage between Spaniards and Indians encouraged? What role did their descendants have in colonial society?
6. What were the three principal agents of directed culture change, and what impacts did they have on indigenous peoples?
7. How did Europeans justify colonial rule? What are some legacies of colonialism in postcolonial nations today?
8. What were some common patterns in indigenous reactions to European colonizers?

Living in a Global World

CHAPTER 17

Preview

1. **How are different types of migration changing national and world demographics today?**

2. **How does migration affect local, national, and global economies?**

3. **How have new nations re-created themselves in the postcolonial era, and how have they adapted to their own cultural diversity?**

4. **In what ways can ethnogenesis reflect both a colonial past and a globalized future?**

5. **What are the characteristics of transnationalism and the emerging "global identity"?**

6. **What is the status of cultural minorities in the world today? How are they threatened, and how can they protect themselves?**

Maran Kai Ra
Female, age 28.
From: Sumprabum, Kachin State.
Occupation: family grocery store and distributing medicine.
Education: BA, Myitkyina University.
Ethnicity: Kachin.
Religion: Baptist.
Left Burma: September 2000.

Q: Why did you leave Burma?

A: Because of the political movement. Since 1988, I started to be involved in the student movement, and after that, when Aung San Suu Kyi came to Myitky-ina, I welcomed her with flowers. After she left, I was asked to come to the MI for interrogation, and after that I had a record. I was also involved with the 1996 student movement and continuously I was involved in the political movements and organizing and distribut-ing political pamphlets. Most recently they suspected me of involvement with Aung San Suu Kyi's party and the underground student movement. My name was on their list.

Q: What was political organizing like as a student?

A: We had to do it as an underground movement, through the religious groups and the Kachin literature and the cultural organizations. We don't have formal organizations like student unions.

Q: How did you get information?

A: News from abroad we get from BBC, VOA and AIR, but within Burma, within the student organization we have a kind of representative or student leader from Myitkyina or Rangoon and they travel and give information to each other.

Q: Were many university students involved in politics?

A: About 60% of the students were interested in politics.

Q: What education was available in Sumprabum?

A: There's only up to 8th grade [standard] in Sumprabum. So mostly they have to go to Myitkyina or Rangoon for higher education.

Q: What were the health conditions in Sumprabum?

A: There's no proper clinic or hospital, there's not a single doctor. And there's plenty of health problems, especially malaria. The local people in Sumprabum are taught by the nurses, not by the doctors, how to avoid the diseases. As far as I know, there's no HIV positive in the area, but some TB. The people who have TB have to go to Myitkyina for treatment, there's no clinic.

Q: Are there traveling doctors in the area?

A: There's a kind of doctor who goes around checking villagers, almost once a year.

Q: What is the food situation in the Sumprabum area?

A: Mostly everything is locally grown. But salt and oil . . . they bring from Myitkyina. There's not enough rice. Because of the hill cultivation we cannot produce enough rice for the local people.

Q: Is there much government army in the area?

A: Yes, they have an army base there.

Q: Do they ever ask people to work for them?

A: Yes, many times. In the past, there's plenty of portering. People were forced to work as porters. But now, there's almost no more portering. But still people are forced to do forced labor to build their army camp or to build roads or such things. There's no payment. Every household has to do it one by one. If this week it's this household, next week it will be the other to help the military.

Q: Is there logging in that area?

A: Yes, the government gives the permit to businessmen, mostly Chinese, to cut the wood, and taking the gold and cane for trading. They hire the local people and people who come from Myitkyina, not just Kachin, everyone. Because of that permission to cut the tree and do the gold mining and other stuff, most of the mountains and the hillsides have been emptied of forests. And the way of the streams, they also changed it to dig the gold. So everything's changed, and also the wildlife. In the past we heard the sound of the wildlife. But no more. They all ran away.

Q: What about fishing?

A: In the past the villagers, the local people only used nets for fishing. But the people from the city, when they arrived, they used the mines [explosives] for the fishing. That's why now there is almost no more fish at all.

Q: How is the water for drinking?

A: The water's very good.

Q: In Sumprabum, in the last two years before you left, was life for the local people getting better?

A: There's not much change, but I would say slightly better because of the cease-fire between the KIA [Kachin Independence Army] and the government, since there is no fighting. So it's a little bit safer than before.

Q: Is the gold mining or logging improving people's economic status?

A: Slightly better, but I believe that for the long term it won't be good.

Q: Are people able to freely practice their religion there?

A: They are allowed to, if they get the permission from the military authorities. In advance they have to ask for permission. How many days the Christian festival or religious festival will take place, how many people will come to the festival.

An Interview with a Kachin Activist Refugee from Burma is reprinted by permission of the author, Edith Mirante.

Maran Kai Ra was interviewed in Guam, where she was seeking political asylum in the United States. In this interview, she discusses some of the conditions in her country, Burma, also called Myanmar, that led her to leave her homeland. Her experiences are fairly typical of political refugees of Asia and other parts of the world. Although refugees account for a large number of people who move from one country to another, many more are voluntary migrants, entering new countries in the hopes of obtaining education or employment. This pattern is not unique to our times, but global processes of change and interaction have accelerated migration.

Processes of transformation and cultural interaction have intensified throughout the twentieth and into the twenty-first century. The present-day global economy, although initiated centuries ago, has accelerated the pace of transferring goods, services, and peoples from one part of the world to others. International migration has brought people far from their homes, some moving voluntarily to seek better employment or educational opportunities, others fleeing oppressive social conditions, political repression, and war. As they settle into their new countries, they adopt many new cultural practices, often adapting them to their own values and perspectives. They contribute their labor and spend their money in their new neighborhoods and countries. And they add cultural diversity and richness to their immigrant communities.

Political processes have also strengthened ties among countries. International organizations such as the United Nations and the World Health Organization and many regional groups strive to coordinate activities; set economic, social, and environmental policies; and resolve conflicts. The success of these organizations varies greatly. Although, in principle, countries come together as equals, in practice, the voices of smaller and poorer nations are typically drowned out by the voices of larger, richer,

GLOBALIZATION

As a result of present-day globalization, international organizations and multinational corporations have tremendous impacts on nations and on cultural minorities living in those nations, as well as on global interrelationships among nations.

The Nenets, Samoyeds of western Siberia, live in an autonomous district as nomadic foragers, fishers, and reindeer herders. Nenets have joined other circumpolar peoples in political action groups to protect themselves and their land from pollution caused by oil drilling, chemical plants, and nuclear plants located in their territories. Nenets inadvertently consume deadly heavy metals from pollution in their meals of mosses and reindeer meat.

and more powerful countries. The rich and powerful countries are able to exert greater influence because they can promise economic rewards, political support, and military aid to those who follow their lead, while they threaten to withdraw aid or retaliate against those who defy their leadership.

All of these factors are part of the process of globalization. Globalization includes the movement of people and the exchange of cultural practices, goods and services, and attitudes worldwide. Through global exchanges, people learn from each other, obtain goods made elsewhere, and share information through media outlets and technological advances such as the Internet. This chapter explores some of the characteristics and consequences of these processes.

The ways of life of **cultural minorities** have come under increasing threat throughout the twentieth century. Their lands and resources are vulnerable to encroachment and exploitation by the governments of the countries in which they live and by multinational corporations that covet their minerals, forests, and other natural products. But in the last quarter of the twentieth century, indigenous peoples began to make important advances in protecting their lands and their cultures.

MIGRATION

Temporary travel and permanent migration have been features of human life for millennia, but the last several centuries have witnessed an acceleration of these processes both in the numbers of people who leave their native countries and in the distances that they travel. In addition to voluntary migrants, some people become refugees because of war and other turmoil. In 2003, for example, 2.1 million Afghan refugees were reported by seventy-two asylum countries, constituting 22 percent of the global refugee population. Pakistan, Iran, and Saudi Arabia were chief among the asylum countries for people fleeing the war in Afghanistan (see Tables 17.1 and 17.2).

Rural-to-Urban Migration

Migration takes place within a country as well. Urban centers attract people from rural areas who seek better employment and income. In Europe and the United States, rural-to-urban migration intensified after the Industrial Revolution of the early nineteenth century, but it, too, accelerated in the last century. Industrial development led to the creation of jobs in manufacturing and service occupations, attracting people from the countryside. In addition, advances in agricultural technology meant that fewer people were needed to grow the food sustaining larger urban populations. The spread of industrial agriculture, particularly in the United States, led to wealthy and efficient corporations buying out small family farmers. And after World War II, many thousands of African Americans left the predominantly rural South, heading north for work and a less overtly racist social and political environment. These are all patterns of **labor migration.**

cultural minorities
Members of ethnic or cultural groups who have become minorities in their native lands due to migrations of other peoples into their territories or due to the historical configuration of a nation-state made up of diverse groups.

labor migration
Migration of people from one area of a country to another or across national borders in search of jobs.

Table 17.1 MAIN ORIGIN OF REFUGEES, 2003

Origin	Begin 2003	End 2003	Annual Change (percent)
Afghanistan	2,510,300	2,136,000	–14.9
Sudan	508,200	606,200	19.3
Burundi	574,700	531,600	–7.5
Democratic Republic of Congo	424,900	453,400	6.7
Palestinians	428,800	427,800	–0.2
Somalia	432,200	402,200	–6.9
Iraq	422,100	368,400	–12.7
Vietnam	373,700	363,200	–2.8
Liberia	275,600	353,300	28.2
Angola	429,400	323,600	–24.6

Source: 2003 Global Refugee Trends, UNHCR, 15 June 2004, p. 3. Reprinted by permission.

Table 17.2 MAIN COUNTRIES OF ASYLUM, 2003

Country of Asylum	Begin 2003	End 2003	Annual Change (percent)
Pakistan	1,227,400	1,124,300	–8.4
Iran	1,306,600	984,900	–24.6
Germany	980,000	960,400	–2.0
Tanzania	689,400	649,800	–5.7
United States	485,200	452,500	–6.7
Serbia and Montenegro	354,400	291,400	–17.8
United Kingdom	260,700	276,500	6.1
Saudi Arabia	245,200	240,800	–1.8
Armenia	247,600	239,300	–3.4

Source: 2003 Global Refugee Trends, UNHCR, 15 June 2004, p. 3. Reprinted by permission.

? *Do you know anyone who has come to this country to work? What circumstances made them come?*

Similar trends in labor migration take place in Asia and Africa. In Malaysia, for example, rural peasant families send some of their children to work in electronics and other factories owned by multinational corporations, especially from Japan and Korea (Ong, 1983). As in Mexico, Malaysian peasants adapt to poverty by sending their daughters to work in factories (see the Case Study).

Industrial work is divided by class and world region. The high-tech skilled jobs in research and development are centered in developed countries, while the low-skilled assembly-line tasks are performed in peripheral areas. The Malaysian government grants tax benefits and reduces tariffs for multinationals because jobs are needed for people who are displaced from their lands, especially in a country experiencing high population growth. Lack of health and safety regulations, no minimum wage, and restrictions on union membership also attract companies. For example, in order to join a union, a worker must be employed in the same job for a minimum of three years, but

Case study

Labor Migration in Mexico

Patterns of labor migration reveal the complex causes of people's reloca-tions and dislocations as a consequence of globalization. A significant trend in many countries of Latin America and Asia is the migration of workers from rural areas to factories owned by multinational corpora-tions set up in development or free trade zones. Companies are attracted to the zones because they receive tax exemptions for capital investment and find a large labor pool predominantly made up of young women with few job skills. Additional features of the zones are low wages, little union activity, and few or absent environmental or workplace health and safety regulations (Fuentes and Ehrenreich, 1983).

The young women who make up the majority of the work force are relatively unskilled. They have enough education to be literate but are rarely graduates of secondary schools and, therefore, are likely to lack higher aspirations. For example, Mexico has seen an enormous growth in manufacturing jobs, generated since the 1960s. At that time, the Mexican government embarked on a policy of industrial development in conjunc-tion with multinational corporations, principally based in the United States, that it hoped would attract investment, create jobs, and alleviate some of its soaring rates of unemployment and poverty.

Through what is called the Border Industrialization Program (BIP), foreign companies established what has come to be known as the maquiladora system. Maquiladoras operate plants that receive electronics parts and precut garment pieces made in the United States or in other foreign factories that are then assembled into finished products that enter the United States under a special agreement at low tariff rates. The companies can lease or acquire land at low prices and pay little or no local taxes. Finally, they have access to a constant supply of workers willing to work for low wages with few, if any, job benefits (Fernandez-Kelly, 1983).

By the 1990s, well over 500 companies were operating through the BIP, employing more than half a million people. The overwhelming majority (about 85 percent) of its workers are young women with some, but low, education. About one-third of the work-ers are single parents and heads of households (Fernandez-Kelly, 1997:526). Women are favored as employees because of their willingness to do monotonous work, accept low wages, and follow orders. Men, in contrast, are not actively recruited as assembly-line workers because, quoting an electronics plant manager, "The man in Mexico is still the man. This kind of job is not doing much for his macho image. It's just a little quirk of a different culture. They'd rather run a factory" (Fuentes and Ehrenreich, 1983:30).

The contemporary Mexican experience is just one example of a familiar pattern in Latin America. Because of the prevailing landholding tradition in Latin America, young men tend to re-main at home to work on and later inherit family lands. But women from peasant communities whose families own little or no land may migrate to urban centers to seek jobs. Population trends in seven Latin American countries indicate that the majority of migrants are young, unmarried women, the daughters of poor peasant families (Jelin, 1977). They move to the cities both in the hope of obtaining jobs and to alleviate their

The establishment of maquiladora plants has affected internal migration patterns in Mexico. Because of widespread poverty throughout the country, young women, like the one shown here, have left their villages to take any kind of employment that will pay them a steady wage. They send part of their wages home to help support family members.

families of the burdens of supporting them. Many of these young women initially find work in domestic service, later leaving to obtain other kinds of jobs or to marry and become housewives. In addition, both male and female migrants often work in the "informal sector," selling food, crafts, and other goods on the streets. While most would prefer factory work, there are not enough jobs for all seekers, therefore creating a marginal population who try to earn a living as best they can.

most of the workers in multinational industries are hired on six-month contracts, resulting in high turnover and little job security. The Malaysian government's goals are both economic (providing jobs) and political (forestalling political unrest) (Ong, 1983).

Transnational Migration

International migration has had a profound effect on people in both the countries of origin and of settlement. Poor countries lose citizens to wealthier countries with better job opportunities. While, in theory, population loss might relieve economic burdens within a poor country, in practice, many of the people who leave are among the better educated and more skilled. Thus the possibilities of economic recovery are undermined in their home countries. However, today's migrants often send a portion of their earnings back to their families, money that makes its way into the local and national economies. Still, the loss of people's skills, experience, and knowledge is more significant and has greater long-term effects than the loss of money alone. Figure 17.1 tallies the foreign-born population in the United States in March 2002 by region of origin.

Until the middle of the twentieth century, the vast majority of migrants were people leaving poor countries that had few jobs, particularly in the industrial sector, when manufacturing and service industries were concentrated in Europe, North America, and Japan. Many initially thought of themselves as temporary residents of their new countries, hoping to save enough money to return home and use their savings to live

better. But this goal was usually unfulfilled. Although the wages that they received were higher than what they could have expected at home, their cost of living was also greater and far exceeded their ability to save. However, although some eventually abandon their desire to return, they may face difficulties adjusting to the countries where they settle.

Some of these difficulties result from the marginalization of migrants within their new countries. They are often segregated in poor neighborhoods, a spatial division that dramatizes and reinforces their separation from the dominant society. Cultural differences of language, religion, and values also set them apart. Eventually, immigrants form "ethnic groups," based on markers of cultural identity, a process called ethnogenesis, first defined in Chapter 2. Ethnic groups are also formed because of rejection from members of the dominant culture, creating "a generalized culture of ethnic inequality in which immigrants are perceived in stereotypical terms by the indigenous population, whatever their actual attributes, as a race apart, as primitives" (Worsley, 1984:239).

Calling the 800 number of your utility company or other service provider, you might reach someone in one of these cubicles in a business office in India or Malaysia. Outsourcing *is another way that multinational corporations take advantage of less expensive foreign labor. Computer and communications technologies make it possible for service workers to be located anywhere in the world.*

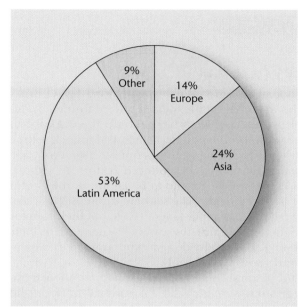

Figure 17.1
U.S. Foreign-Born Population
(in thousands) by World Region,
March 2003
Source: Adapted from U.S.
Bureau of the Census. 2004.
Current Population Survey,
March 2003.

REVIEW

Migration patterns include international or transnational migration to escape persecution, warfare, or poverty; rural-to-urban migration in developing countries; and labor migration to take advantage of new economic opportunities, as in Mexico's maquiladora system. Refugee and immigrant groups affect the communities or countries they leave, as well as the ones they join. Often they become tolerated but isolated ethnic minorities.

ETHNOGENESIS AND ETHNIC IDENTITIES

Ethnic identity is context-bound but changeable, an adaptation to circumstances. Although we may think of an ethnic identity as a single, stable concept, in fact, people can have various identities, depending on the way they see themselves in relation to others. Ethnic groups are formed and transformed in response to interactions with other people. As with other social identities, ethnic labels are applied as conditions arise that favor their use. People may think of themselves as members of groups based on one set of criteria but may find themselves categorized as members of other groups based on different criteria.

Group identity based on a political stance as well as an ethnic or tribal identity complicates social relations, even in comparatively homogeneous societies. An example is Papua New Guinea. Its colonial history began in the nineteenth century, when the British and the Germans divided between themselves the eastern portion of the island of New Guinea. (The western portion was formerly a Dutch colony,

Pakistani Brahmin immigrants to the United Kingdom who may think of themselves as white and as superior to dark-skinned South Indians are shocked to find out that the British may think of them as "black" or "coloured," in the same category as immigrants from the West Indies (Worsley, 1984). Similarly, class distinctions that may be relevant in an immigrant's own country may be overlooked by a system of ethnic or racial categorization in the new country that lumps people together on the basis of socially constructed concepts of race and ethnicity.

Case study

Ethnic Identity in Sudan

In a study of Sudanese agricultural production, Jay O'Brien (1986) details the ways that ethnic identities were formed as different groups of people were incorporated into the work force. Their particular roles in production became linked to their ethnic identity. In the early 1900s, farmers and pastoralists began to work, at least seasonally, on plantations that produced cotton for export. These plantations were located in what came to be known as the Gezira Scheme, a large area of irrigated fields. As elsewhere in the British colonial empire, indigenous people had to pay taxes in cash, but their sources of obtaining money were limited because there were few markets for their subsistence crops, and home craft production was undermined by the importation of manufactured goods sold cheaply.

Sudanese farmers and pastoralists continued to maintain their traditional productive strategies but were available for seasonal work on the plantations when needed during the peak season. They received wages but remained marginal actors in the new economy. Then, as the plantation system expanded, workers from other countries were recruited, especially from Muslim Hausa communities in West Africa. These immigrants were landless and, therefore, readily available to serve as a pool of cheap wage labor. In addition, other groups of West African Muslims settled nearby and provided seasonal labor. They came from several different ethnic groups, with distinct tribal names, and spoke different languages, although many learned Hausa as a second language (O'Brien, 1986:901).

Nearly as soon as the immigrants arrived, distinctions developed between them and the indigenous people with whom they worked. The immigrants came to be known as *Fellata*, a term with negative connotations that obliterated their own, separate tribal distinctions. In response to their new cultural environment, the West Africans adopted some outward traits of their Sudanese neighbors, especially styles of dress and housing. But they also intensified some of their own cultural practices in an attempt to differentiate themselves from the Sudanese, especially emphasizing certain fundamentalist Islamic practices in contrast to the animatistic beliefs in spirit possession and trance found among Arabs in North Africa. They began to apply the word *Takari* to themselves, a respectful term signifying "pilgrims." Although they replaced a negative term (Fellata) with a positive one, they essentially accepted the view of themselves as members of an ethnic group different from their hosts. Thus, they participated in the formation of an ethnic identity, initially imposed on them but then taken up as part of their self-definition.

A third group, the Joama, also were incorporated into plantation production. The Joama, of central Sudan, became known as efficient and hardworking cotton pickers and were actively recruited to help in the harvest. They earned a high reputation and a relatively stable income. Gradually, some migrants from West Africa settled on the outskirts of Joama communities and were hired as seasonal cotton pickers as well. By their own hard work and commitment to the region, they came to refer to themselves and to be referred to as *Joama*. In so doing, they took on an ethnic identity that was theirs only by assertion and by lifestyle. It was an identity that they had to earn.

invaded and annexed by Indonesia in 1975.) At the end of World War I, the two colonial regions were united under Australian administration as Papua New Guinea, becoming an independent country in 1975. Although independence has led to some detribalization as the central government attempts to form a national identity, other factors led to **tribalization,** or the formation of tribal identities. One of the consequences of the competition for access to political power and economic benefits has been a resurgence of "tribal" warfare, especially in the highlands. Such warfare "has defined and redefined groups in such a way as to re-create, in part, an earlier tribal structure—a structure uncomfortably at odds with its own national government" (Strathern, 1992:232).

Even though government agencies have attempted to quell the fighting, people's respect for state authority has declined. Instead, local businessmen vie for economic advantages and political power, very much in the traditional model of the Melanesian big-men. These men attract armed fighters who support them and are in return protected by them. The central government occasionally sends in police and military patrols to keep order, but they are largely unsuccessful in eliminating violence.

Transnationalism

Although migrants adjust to and adapt to their country of settlement, they all do not necessarily focus solely on developing their lives in their new environment. Rather, they also maintain emotional and cultural ties with their homeland. Because of increased ease of communication and travel, a new phenomenon of transnationalism is developing. **Transnationalism** is the constellation of "processes by which immigrants build social fields that link together their country of origin and their country of settlement, connecting them to two or more societies simultaneously" (Schiller et al., 1992:1–2). Transmigrants maintain complex social, economic, religious, and political ties linking them to their immigrant communities and to their communities back home.

tribalization
A process of identification with one's tribal origins.

transnationalism
Processes by which immigrants maintain social, economic, religious, and political ties to both their immigrant communities and their communities back home.

GLOBALIZATION

Transnationalism is a phenomenon in which migrants create new sociocultural networks and identities for themselves that link their country of origin and their country of settlement. Transnationalism, while not new, has redeveloped in the context of the spread of global capitalism, which has shifted populations across borders.

The Internet features many transnational sites like this one, uniting people culturally whatever their citizenship status. This page for Indians abroad embraces all people with roots in India living anywhere in the world, including those who have become citizens of other countries. An estimated 3.2 million Indians live in the United States alone. Transnational groups encourage people to develop social solidarity around a shared cultural identity, which the globalization of Internet technologies encourages.

Transnationalism has developed in the context of the spread of global capitalism that has shifted capital and labor across borders. As capital investments flow from high-wage countries to low-wage regions, labor shifts take place in both developed and developing countries. A transnational identity based on transnational commitments is a sensible and appropriate response to economic vulnerability and possible job displacement. In addition, transmigrants are important players in the creation of ethnic identities in their countries of settlement, forming connections among people who identify as a group on the basis of shared activities, values, beliefs, and goals.

Nationalism and Pluralism

In addition to analyzing the ways that people create themselves as ethnic groups, anthropologists also look at the ways that ethnic groups are formed as structural features that support social, economic, and political systems. Ethnic groupings are especially significant in state societies composed of peoples of disparate origins and traditions. And they are "inherently political, shaped by and shaping the politics of 'us versus them' in political systems" (Ferguson and Whitehead, 1992:15).

At the same time, states also generate nationalistic views of themselves as overriding ethnic differences in the formation of a national identity. Peter Worsley describes nationalism as a form of ethnicity that is the "institutionalization of one particular ethnic identity by attaching it to the State" (1984:247). Nationalism, though, is more than identifying with a state as a political institution. It is also an allegiance to the nation as a symbolic identity, as a people associated with a particular way of life and sets of values. As members of a state develop a national identity, they ignore their differences and concentrate on achieving commonly shared goals and interests. Nationalism also involves the process of selective memory and the construction of a fictive past, as the past is formulated according to contemporary values and goals. And, as Worsley points out, "They project the values of the present onto a past which does not always sustain them" (p. 274).

On May 20, 2002, these East Timorese celebrated their independence after twenty-four years of Indonesian rule and centuries of Portuguese colonization. Their determination to obtain their independence set an example for others, such as the native peoples of Irian Jaya (West Papua New Guinea), which recently won from Indonesia economic benefits due them from the utilization of their timber, minerals, and oil (Ballard, 2002:42).

Culture Change

IMPACTS OF INDONESIAN STATE EXPANSION

Indonesia is an instructive example of a central government's attempts to create a national identity that privileges one ethnic group, the Javanese, as the national norm (Perry, 1996). Javanese cultural traditions are exported to members of other groups through formal education, the media, and public discourse. Following a process of **Islamization,** the religion of Islam is imposed on others, either obliterating or subsuming local beliefs. And a national language called Indonesian (based on a dialect of Malay) is taught throughout the country and used in all public contexts. The Indonesian government has embarked on an aggressive policy of creating and imposing cultural uniformity while giving some recognition to ethnic diversity.

Islamization
The process of imposing the Islamic religion and associated cultural values within a nation to foster cultural uniformity.

But for Indonesia, as Bernard Nietschmann (1988) puts it, "nation-building" sometimes is state expansion by "nation-destroying." Authorities developed a program of forced internal migration, sending Javanese people to outlying regions originally inhabited by various tribal groups who, in turn, were forcibly evicted from their homelands and sent to live elsewhere. It is a program of intense directed culture change in the service of national unity. But it is also an attempt to wrest lands rich in resources from indigenous peoples. The resources can then be exploited by multinational corporations allied with the state government. The Indonesian policy is also aimed at dissipating indigenous resistance movements that were organized for local autonomy and independence. The army is often deployed to indigenous territories, ostensibly to fight terrorism and militant insurgencies.

Just one year after Indonesia gained its independence from the Netherlands (after a war of independence against allied forces following Japanese occupation during World War II), the central government embarked on policies of state expansion by invading and annexing independent islands. In 1950, the army took over South Moluccas, followed in 1962 by the annexation of West Papua (renamed Irian Jaya), and in 1975, the invasion of East Timor. West Papua is a rich prize because it now comprises about 22 percent of the total landmass of Indonesia but has only 1 percent of the country's total population (Ballard, 2002:40). (The eastern half of the island is the independent country of Papua New Guinea.)

In West Papua, the Indonesian government implemented its program of transmigration to "redistribute overpopulation" by importing 5 million people from Java (Nietschmann, 1988). In the process, indigenous peoples were displaced and their lands and resources were appropriated to accelerate economic development and national unity. The region is especially rich in timber, various minerals, and offshore reserves of oil. The Indonesian program was financed in part by the World Bank, the United Nations, the Islamic Development Bank, and several countries, including the United States, Germany, France, and the Netherlands. The government also established "assimilation camps" in which cultural minorities were taught the official national Indonesian language and the Muslim religion. These were also called "centers for social development" with the aim of "cultivating national pride and defending the state." People who resisted the imposition of Indonesian political control and cultural hegemony were branded "terrorists," justifying military action against them.

The eastern half of the island of Timor became a battleground where the struggles of the indigenous East Timorese erupted in violence after decades of clandestine resistance. The Indonesian government had forced many East Timorese from their homes, transporting them to Sumatra and other majority Javanese islands while at the same time importing Javanese to East Timor. An estimated 200,000 East Timorese (about one-third of the population) were killed between 1975 and 1990 (Perry, 1996:204). But in 1991, the East Timorese resistance movement became a more public armed struggle after the Indonesian military attacked a peaceful funeral procession. For more than two decades after 1975, when the Indonesian army invaded and unilaterally annexed East Timor, the international community (including the influential governments of the United States and Australia) ignored the situation. In the 1990s, world public opinion shifted to support independence for East Timor.

States utilize various processes to resolve relationships between a central identity and disparate ethnic groups. A dominant ethnic group may assert itself as the only legitimate identity, equating the national culture with its own. Also, a state may assert a uniformity of culture, subsuming and homogenizing differences. Finally, a state may maintain a pluralistic attitude toward cultural differences, allowing secondary identities to coexist along with a national one (p. 252).

A state's strategies may change over time. A state often chooses a dominant identity as it embarks on consolidation and expansion, exerting control over its constituent populations. An emphasis on uniformity then becomes prominent as states become secure and attempt to eliminate ethnic boundaries. Recognition of cultural pluralism often emerges with the formation of ethnically diverse nation-states as older colonial empires crumble. The rise of ethnic pluralism, therefore, was often a product of decolonization, giving legitimacy to the strivings of disparate groups within a country for recognition and some degree of social and political autonomy. As in the past, however, newly independent states vary in the approaches that they take to ethnic diversity.

Genocide? The Case of Rwanda

Some postcolonial conflicts have centered on internal competition for power rather than independence from expanding new states. Conflicts in many countries in Africa, for example, are often portrayed as ethnic or tribal genocide, but they are more appropriately seen as struggles for power between groups with different interests and loyalties. The civil war in Rwanda in 1994 that took the lives of some 800,000 people at first glance looks like a conflict between the majority Hutus (about four-fifths of the population) and the minority Tutsis (about one-fifth). In addition, about 1 or 2 percent of the population belongs to a tribal group called Twa, who are considered aboriginal and marginal to Rwandan society (Maybury-Lewis, 1997:100).

Although the Tutsis and Hutus are now thought of as ethnic groups, before Belgian colonial rule was established in 1916, they represented political strata. The name Tutsi was applied to lineages that controlled wealth and chiefly power, while Hutu were lineages without wealth whose members formed a majority peasantry. Although the hierarchical system was relatively stable, particular individuals could rise or fall in status. If members of Tutsi lineages lost wealth and prestige, they would be considered Hutus, and Hutus who acquired wealth could become Tutsis. Hutus allied themselves as clients of particular Tutsi chiefs, giving political support and gaining protection.

During the colonial period, lasting until 1962, the Belgian government administered the territory through indirect rule, essentially using Tutsi chiefs as their surrogates. And the chiefs who cooperated enhanced their power. Belgian policies led to an increased rigidity in the system of status and power, fomenting hostility between the Tutsi and Hutu "ethnic groups."

After independence, in 1962, the former Belgian colony split into two countries, Rwanda and Burundi. Civil wars in both countries ensued out of struggles for power. In Burundi, the Tutsi minority persevered and were able to hold on to their positions of power, but Hutu rebels maintained pressure on the Tutsi minority, and in 1972 between 100,000 and 200,000 were killed. In Rwanda, the Hutu majority took control. Many Tutsis fled the country, forming a resistance movement with the aim of returning to Rwanda and regaining power. After many years of conflict, both sides agreed in 1993 to form a coalition government in Rwanda. Then, a few months later, the newly elected Hutu president of Burundi was assassinated by members of the Tutsi-dominated army. As civil war erupted there, about 200,000 Hutus fled into Rwanda, where they joined anti-Tutsi militias that were trying to undermine the peace accords.

In 1994, on their way back from Tanzania to attend a United Nations–sponsored meeting discussing implementation of the agreements, the airplane carrying the presidents of both Rwanda and Burundi was shot down by still unknown assailants. At the news, Hutu militias in Rwanda began genocidal campaigns against Tutsis and moderate Hutus who advocated peace and accommodation, including the moderate Hutu prime minister and many other government officials. Estimates put the number of deaths at about 800,000. The Tutsi-controlled army finally defeated the Hutus, many of whom then fled into neighboring Zaire, where most still remain in refugee camps. These tragic events show the influence of policies that rigidify "collective identities . . . [that are] reactivated, mythologized and manipulated for political advantage" (Lemarchand, 1994:31).

Reactions against Pluralism

In many Western countries, ethnic identities have become significant vehicles for the development, channeling, and recruitment of individuals for social and political action. This rise in cultural identities is coincident with large increases in immigration throughout the twentieth century. Perhaps the worldwide movement toward decolonization since the end of World War II is a contributing factor because it champions political and cultural independence and autonomy.

In addition, large numbers of people immigrating from the same country or region are more likely to maintain ties among themselves. These bonds can create cohesion and solidarity that can be used to achieve social and political goals. They also allow immigrants to resist social and political pressures toward assimilation. For instance, the influx into the United States of people from Central and South America since the 1970s has led to the development of a strong power base wielding political influence both regionally and nationally. In Europe, the rise in immigration from the Caribbean, Africa, and South Asia has brought to the foreground issues of nationality and national identity. For example, the multiracial and multicultural makeup of the populations of the United Kingdom or France must redefine what it means to be "British" or "French."

Cultural pluralism is usually tolerated as long as members of disparate ethnic groups do not attempt to build political power blocs. But at the same time as the complexion (both literally and figuratively) of American and European countries is changing, internal political movements opposing immigration have strengthened. Members of some anti-immigration movements claim that immigrants threaten national unity because they do not share prevailing heritage, values, and attitudes. These claims are based on a view of a nation that has been "mythologized and manipulated" for political purposes. In addition, a rise of xenophobic sentiments—as defined in Chapter 16, the fear and hatred of outgroups—is stimulated by economic shifts and the perceived downward mobility of members of the middle and lower classes who then blame their misfortunes on the newcomers. Thus, xenophobia and anti-immigration movements are two common reactions to cultural pluralism.

Ancestors of these nomadic Rom "Gypsies" originated in northern India in the Punjab and were victims of xenophobia in every country they entered on their long-distance treks. Slated for extermination by the Nazis, the Rom survived their dispersal throughout Europe and the United States, where they continue to face xenophobic reaction and social isolation.

Malaysia, Singapore, and Indonesia are examples of countries with complex histories that in postcolonial times have led to the establishment of multicultural societies (Hefner, 2001). Prior to the European presence in Southeast Asia, these countries had a long history of maritime trade that brought in people from elsewhere, particularly from China and India. Ethnic differences were recognized, but people cooperated in the formation of pluralistic societies. However, the Dutch and the British treated the inhabitants as segregated groups in order to assert control and foster competition for access to influence and rewards. When the countries became independent in the mid-twentieth century, their constituent ethnic groups then vied for control of the newly emerging states. Competition for the benefits of economic development programs contributed to intergroup tensions.

In Malaysia and Indonesia, social and political distinctions were maintained between indigenous peoples and the ethnic Chinese descended from merchants who prospered from trade even before European colonial powers came to dominate the region. But treatment of the Chinese differs in Malaysia and Indonesia. In Malaysia, the Chinese have been permitted to send their children to Chinese-language schools if they wish and maintain their culture. Still, Malaysian political parties are organized along ethnic lines, and although pluralism is part of the social and political fabric of society, ethnic Malays have ascendancy over people of Chinese, Indian, and other origin. Also, while religious differences are protected, Islam is the state religion of Malaysia. In Indonesia, however, the Chinese have faced discrimination despite official statements of ethnic inclusion and pluralism. Cultural and religious distinctions are used to promote Javanese interests and claims to power over those of the Chinese and other groups.

Globalization and Cultural Identities

Globalization is popularly thought of as an economic and cultural process that spreads wealth and investment throughout the world. But, as in the past, wealth and investment are concentrated regionally and in the hands of elites. Today much of the world's wealth comes from Europe and the United States, but investment increasingly goes elsewhere, such as Asia and the Pacific Rim. European companies account for twenty-one of the world's top fifty largest corporations, while the rest are Asian (Friedman, 1999). Since the 1960s, the centers of manufacturing have shifted to Japan and other Asian countries, particularly Hong Kong, Taiwan, Korea, and China. The United States has been a major importer of goods from these and other countries (Friedman, 1999:187–188).

A Global Identity?

These economic shifts have contributed to what some theorists see as the re-creation of an international or **global identity** based on social class. That is, in North America and Europe, regions that Jonathan Friedman (1999) calls "declining hegemonies," members of elite classes have a global identity that links them to elites in other countries on the basis of class. Characteristics include sharing privileges, interests, leisure activities, locations, and tastes. This global identity is different from the global popular culture in which the world's middle classes increasingly participate, in which they eat food from McDonald's, watch the same movies, listen to the same music, discuss the same topics on the Internet, and buy the same books and other consumer goods.

A global identity has developed as middle and lower classes have tended to fragment along ethnic lines, with groups asserting their own interests. In addition, the power of the state to "manufacture consent" (to use the term from Herman and Chomsky [1988]) and to create and transmit a national identity tends to decline as the nation's economic and political elites focus their activities elsewhere. At the same time, immigrants tend to remain identified with their countries of origin or with emigrants residing in other countries. Thus, some theorists see both a rise in ethnic pluralism and an increasing gap between the classes as major factors in the process of globalization and the invention of a global identity.

GLOBALIZATION

Anthropologists and other social scientists have been studying the global marketplace as a kind of borderless society. The shared beliefs, values, expectations, and behaviors of members of this society constitute a global culture. This culture has emerged as a result of rapid changes in technology and the political and economic process known as globalization. Researchers seek to make sense of what may be called a global culture of consumerism.

global identity
An identity of shared interests, practices, and values across international borders, uniting people worldwide.

The mass media contribute to, and reflect, a growing global identity. People throughout the world watch many of the same movies and television programs, listen to much of the same music, and read the same magazines translated into dozens of languages. These sources of information and entertainment disseminate people's activities, attitudes, and tastes, contributing to shared experiences and frames of reference. Although there are, and will continue to be, local variations, the media provide outlets for creating global identities. The Internet also is a powerful and increasingly utilized forum through which people in many countries can communicate, learn from each other, and share ideas. And the global spread of the English language, now the most common second language of the world, helps facilitate this exchange. An estimated 75 percent of all mail and 80 percent of computer data sent worldwide are written in English (Baron, 1990).

> **REVIEW**
>
> Ethnogenesis involves a group's creation of a new ethnic identity through both self-definition and definition by other groups in the society. Proliferating identities can stimulate conflict in new nations, sometimes leading to tribalization rather than national unity. In transnationalism, however, groups identify across nationalities, based on their shared country or culture of origin. Nationalism calls for minimizing differences between groups to achieve national rather than group unity and loyalty. In pluralistic or culturally diverse societies, ethnic minorities may become marginalized or forced to conform to majority culture, as in the Islamization of Indonesia. Ethnic minorities, like immigrant groups, are also often victims of xenophobic reactions against out-groups or outsiders, and conflicts between groups based on their cultural identities can lead to genocide. Some theorists suggest that in this postcolonial era, a global identity is developing, based on social class.

CULTURAL MINORITIES IN A GLOBAL WORLD

The mid- and late twentieth century saw a revitalization of indigenous communities in many countries and a new energy and focus in their struggles for self-determination. An estimated half of the world's conflicts are now fought over lands and resources of foragers, horticulturalists, and pastoralists (Nietschmann, 1988). As defined in Chapter 1, the term *indigenous* refers to comparatively homogeneous peoples or small-scale societies who share the same culture and are "native" to their territory or have occupied it for a long time. Defining who is indigenous is a complex matter, however, and depends also on historical and cultural contexts. In countries with a history as a settler colony (the United States, Canada, Australia, Mexico, and all the countries of modern Central and South America), the term *indigenous* refers to the peoples who lived in these regions prior to the arrival of Europeans, beginning in the late fifteenth century. In these countries, descendants of the original settlers and later immigrants now dominate.

? *Are you or any of your friends members of cultural minorities or indigenous peoples?*

State policies toward indigenous peoples vary considerably in the Western Hemisphere. In the United States and Canada, treaties were negotiated between colonial powers and indigenous peoples, guaranteeing some rights to land and certain rights to limited forms of sovereignty. However, in both countries, federal governments are empowered to override treaty rights in some circumstances, despite the fact that the treaties were legally ratified agreements backed by the force of international law. It should be noted that the U.S. and Canadian governments are "empowered" by their own laws or constitutions. That is, they unilaterally grant themselves the power to break treaties without the consent of the peoples affected. The following sections survey the state of indigenous peoples in the Americas.

United States and Canada

In the United States and Canada, the federal governments recognize the sovereignty of native tribes (or bands, as they are called in Canada), although the people's exercise of sovereignty is limited either by federal law or by judicial rulings. In each country, the specific history of treaty signing and of legislation affecting Indians varies, but the general trends are similar. Since the 1960s, native peoples in both countries have won important advances in their quest for sovereign powers.

The Congress of the United States passed the Indian Self-Determination and Education Act in 1975, establishing principles of self-government for native reservations. Indian tribes have used these principles to broaden their claims of sovereignty and to extend tribal jurisdiction in planning and implementing educational, medical, and social services, as well as to gain control over their territories, economic development plans, and tax immunity.

Tax immunity is a critical issue for native peoples in both Canada and the United States. The concept refers to the fact that Indian lands are immune, not exempt, from all forms of state, provincial, or federal taxation. This means that Indians living on reservations do not pay property taxes, sales taxes on goods purchased on the reservation, or income tax on wages earned on reservations. The tax-immune status of reservations has become especially contentious in New York State since 1997, when the state government first attempted to collect sales taxes on gasoline and cigarettes sold to non-Indians by Indian-run stores on reservations. Because of objections by the native governments, the state delayed its move until 2003, two years after the terrorist attacks of September 11, 2001, in New York City caused a sharp decline in state revenues. Then, New York Governor George Pataki again announced his plan to impose sales taxes on goods purchased by non-Indians from stores on Indian reservations. In 2004, the state legislature passed a bill authorizing collection of those taxes, but in a reversal of position, Governor Pataki vetoed the bill.

The U.S. Congress has dealt several times with the issue of Native American religious practices. In 1978, it passed the American Indian Religious Freedom Act, extending protection for Indians to "believe, express, and exercise" their traditional religions, granting access to sacred sites and sacred objects, and guaranteeing rights to perform ceremonies. Subsequently, the Native American Religious Freedom Restoration Act of 1993 furthered these protections, with an added amendment in 1994 that specifically protects the use of peyote in religious services. The Restoration Act itself has been declared unconstitutional by the U.S. Supreme Court, but the Court has not ruled on the amendments.

While most economic activities of native tribes are not specifically addressed by legislation, Congress has enacted laws dealing with casino gambling on Indian reservations. The Indian Gaming Regulatory Act of 1988 sets standards for gambling on reservations and requires agreements between Indian tribes and their state governments that stipulate the kinds of gaming permitted and the percentage of revenues that the tribes agree to give to the states.

Less than twenty years after the first tribal bingo hall was opened by Florida Seminoles in 1981, there were 273 Indian-owned casinos (Jorgensen, 1998). Other casinos are operated by Indians in Canada. Although Indian casinos account for a mere 5 percent of gambling revenue in the United States, one of the most lucrative is Foxwoods, owned by the Pequots in eastern Connecticut (*American Indian Report*, 1999). With more than 11,000 employees, they are one of the ten largest employers in the state. Their profits, amounting to about $1 billion a year, have been invested in reinvigorating their community and the surrounding area. They have built new housing and roads and provide job training, scholarships, and health services to tribal members. The casino and its accompanying resort generate additional income for nearby hotels, restaurants, and stores (Harvey, 1996).

The presence of a casino can boost income for all residents of an area, but it can also bring changes to the community that all residents do not desire. The work that casinos create tends to be low-wage jobs with little future. And some people do not approve of gambling on moral grounds or because of its historical connection with organized crime.

In the state of Hawaii, some Native Hawaiians are asking for recognition of their claims to ancestral territories and their desire to have a legal status somewhat comparable to that of Native Americans living in the other forty-nine states. In 1978, the state created an Office of Hawaiian Affairs with responsibility for administering 1.8 million acres of royal land held in trust for Native Hawaiians. This land was exempt from

? *Do you think Indians living and working on reservations should not have to pay taxes? Why or why not?*

annexation when Hawaii became a state. The office collects revenues generated by the natural resources, minerals, and use of these lands for the benefit of Native Hawaiians. It also formulates policies regarding social, economic, and health services applicable to native people.

In Canada, the new Constitution Act of 1982 included a short section that affirmed the existing rights of the country's aboriginal peoples. Subsequently, both the federal and provincial governments concluded government-to-government agreements with native reserves covering and expanding indigenous control over health, education, and social services, as well as economic development.

Finally, land claims cases continue to be of paramount importance, enlarging reservation territory and establishing indigenous rights to self-government. Recent settlements in both Canada and the United States usually stipulate some degree of sovereign native control over economic, social, and cultural policies. Hundreds of cases are pending, with outcomes most likely to be decided in the first few decades of the twenty-first century. Some analysts expect large amounts of land and monies to be transferred to native sovereignty, especially in Canada. According to Canadian government estimates, settlements of more than 210 claims may give First Nations (the term currently used in Canada to refer to indigenous people) control over about 10 percent of the country, an increase from the current native land base of 0.3 percent (*New York Times,* December 30, 1999). In the United States, native peoples now control about 2 percent of the country's territory. The increase in their land base is not expected to rise very much because monetary compensation settlements are more the norm in the United States.

Mexico and *Indigenismo*

The Mexican government, like several others in South America, has vacillated in its policies toward indigenous peoples throughout its history since independence from Spain in 1821. At times, some indigenous peoples had recognized rights to land that they held communally, but at other times these rights were ignored and the state appropriated Indian land. The constitution of 1993 acknowledged the rights of indigenous peoples in a policy known as *indigenismo* that guarantees protection of native customs. However, the actual living conditions of native peoples have not improved, particularly in the southernmost state of Chiapas with its majority Maya population. There, some Indians maintain their traditional land-use patterns, holding their land communally in *ejidos*. Others had been forced off their land by intruding settlers and multinational companies. Some retreated farther into the highlands, where they cleared new farmland, many growing coffee for sale and export.

In the early 1990s, the Mexican government embarked on policies to exploit its vast oil deposits. As an adjunct to this strategy, the government abandoned its stated intentions to grant additional Indian groups the right to their communal *ejidos*. The government also eliminated price supports to small farmers, another policy that harmed the Maya farmers of Chiapas. And the government allowed wealthy ranchers to expand their holdings, buying up the land of poor farmers. In addition, public projects to develop and generate electricity from hydropower led to the flooding of Indian lands. Finally, the Mexican government has begun to develop biodiversity projects, concluding agreements with pharmaceutical companies for the exploitation of forests and plants for research into the manufacture of drugs. As a result of these policies, the Maya often become landless wage workers, but their wages are so low that they need to maintain links to strong family networks in traditional communities in order to survive (Barreda and Cecena, 1998).

The Maya suffer discrimination because they have become a cultural minority within their traditional territories. They are outnumbered by Ladino settlers whose incomes and levels of education far exceed those of the Maya. The Ladinos—an ethnic term for Mexicans with an appearance, language, and identity that are more Spanish than Indian—feel justified in their negative attitudes toward the Maya, because the Indians are poor and lack the education or job skills that would suit them for the modern sector. But the Indians' poverty is a result, not a cause, of their marginalization.

The issue of indigenous rights in Mexico became nationally and internationally visible because of the efforts of a group of Mayas in Chiapas to mobilize for their

Controversies

Who "Owns" the Past? NAGPRA and American Anthropology

In the past hundred years, some anthropologists and archaeologists have unwittingly contributed to the "cultural dispossession" of Native Americans. Archaeologists could excavate sites without permission on the grounds of scientific interest alone. Some collected artifacts and human remains for study without much concern for their relationship to present-day native peoples in the region, and a few looted those sites for sales to collectors. Despite successive migrations, it is possible that artifacts and remains found in an area belonged to actual ancestors of living people. This is especially true for finds from recent eras.

Native Americans have spoken out against the desecration of Indian burial grounds. According to Walter and Roger Echohawk, writing in *Battlefields and Burial Grounds—The Indian Struggle to Protect Ancestral Graves in the United States*, Native Americans have had to witness the destruction of their burial grounds and removal of the remains of their ancestors (Echohawk and Echohawk, 1994). In 1989, for example, an "Indian burial pit" was opened in Salina, Kansas, displaying skeletons as a tourist attraction.

In 1979, the U.S. Congress passed the Archeological Resources and Protection Act of 1979, which required archaeologists to obtain the consent of a Native American tribe before they could get a federal permit to excavate on or remove material from tribal lands. And in 1990, Congress passed the Native American Graves Protection and Repatriation Act (NAGPRA). The act does more than protect Native American interests in skeletal and cultural remains found at archaeological sites. Skeletal remains and certain cultural items uncovered on federal or tribal land must be given or returned to the nation concerned upon request. This also includes materials uncovered in the process of demolition and construction of buildings and roadways. In addition, human remains, sacred objects, and other artifacts held in museums receiving federal funds must be returned to the appropriate tribal group, if requested. The items that may be repatriated include human remains and associated grave goods (objects buried with the dead), funerary goods not necessarily found with human remains, sacred objects associated with the practice of indigenous religions, and other articles of "cultural patrimony."

NAGPRA also requires that any group or individual making a claim first satisfy federal officials that they are part of a recognized Native American group. Then they must demonstrate "cultural affiliation" with the people whose objects or remains they are claiming. The law defines cultural affiliation as "a relationship of shared group identity that can be reasonably traced historically or prehistorically between a present-day Indian tribe and an identifiable earlier group." Thus, the older the objects or remains are,

---

collective rights in land and resources. Their organization, called the Zapatista Army for National Liberation (named after the Mexican revolutionary leader Emiliano Zapata), burst upon the world scene on January 1, 1994, when they took up arms against the Mexican military, a move that was timed to coincide with the implementation of the North American Free Trade Agreement, or NAFTA, signed by the United States, Canada, and Mexico.

During the crisis that followed the insurrection of January 1994, the army entered their territory and attempted to arrest their leaders and squelch the resistance. But the government softened its approach because of the media publicity that drew attention to the conflict, generating generally positive support

In March 2001, the Zapatista high command was honored in Mexico City, where they were lobbying to implement the San Andreas peace accords. In April 2004, Mexican militias took action against Zapatistas protesting lack of access to water in Zinacantan, a continuation of decades of conflict. Zapatistas have gained international support for their struggle. Their ultimate goal is to gain autonomy in their region, where they constitute a majority of the population.

the harder it is to establish an unambiguous affiliation between them and a present-day group.

Some of the fiercest controversies generated by the law involve groups claiming the right to repatriate objects many thousands of years old. In 2004, courts upheld the right of scientists to study skeletal remains excavated from a riverbed in Kennewick, Washington. These remains are nearly 10,000 years old, far too early in the history of occupation of North America for any present-day native group to be able to claim them.

The desire of Native American groups to reclaim masks, figurines, and other ritual paraphernalia is an expression of their sense of the sacred. Under NAGPRA's provisions, once a tribe gains possession, it has the right to keep or dispose of the item as it sees fit. Between 1978 and 1992, the Zuni repatriated sixty-nine wooden sculpted sacred figures from public and private museums, art galleries, and private collectors (Merrill, Ladd, and Ferguson, 1993). In one of the most highly publicized repatriations, in 1987, the Zuni got back two of their most sacred wooden sculptures, Twin War Gods, from the Smithsonian Institution in Washington, D.C. The War Gods have subsequently been put to ceremonial use, which exposes them to the elements. As a result, they will eventually decompose, a natural process in keeping with ancient Zuni practices.

The archaeological community has not been uniformly in favor of NAGPRA. Although most archaeological associations support the moral principles underlying the act, many argue about the law's effects on the pursuit of research and on the discovery of knowledge about the past. The clash between the native and archaeological communities reveals underlying tensions and differences in perspectives on science and the past. By letting their War Gods deteriorate

through use and exposure, for example, the Zuni are asserting the precedence of their ethical and religious claims on the sculptures over the scientific and aesthetic claims of scholars who want them preserved as art objects and objects of study. Similarly, groups that rebury remains of their ancestors assert the priority of their beliefs over whatever knowledge might have been gained from further study of those remains. And even when impoverished groups sell repatriated objects for much needed funds, they are asserting their right to dispose of them as they see fit (Killhefer, 1995).

Many archaeologists and anthropologists have begun to confront their own status as privileged experts who, until recently, have been able to frame the discourse about the past and about ownership of cultural artifacts in the terms that suited their needs for research. Many do welcome the opportunity to rethink their assumptions. As archaeologist Tamara Bray noted, " We must acknowledge that archeology, like all other social and natural sciences, is legitimately subject to criticism on the level of "values," not just "facts" (1996:444). According to anthropologist T. J. Ferguson, despite their fears of restrictions and loss of research materials, archeologists may find "new opportunities available . . . if they work in partnership with Native Americans in studying the rich archeological record of the Americas" (1996:64).

CRITICAL THINKING QUESTIONS

Should archaeologists be able to examine cultural, even skeletal, remains from Native American archaeological sites? Why, or why not? What "new opportunities" do you think researchers may find in working with Native Americans on the archaeological record?

from the international community. The government then agreed to enter into negotiations with the Zapatistas to settle some of these issues without further violence. However, the government has not yet agreed to anything other than minor concessions.

The Zapatistas have been particularly effective in utilizing sophisticated communication technologies, especially the Internet, to publicize their movement and to forge alliances with other indigenous and marginalized groups striving for social, economic, and political justice. And they have used these communication channels to gain international support.

Brazil and the "Indian Problem"

Due to the establishment of plantations by the Portuguese in the seventeenth century, the immigration of many Portuguese and Spanish settlers, and the importation of millions of African slaves, the indigenous population of Brazil is relatively small, currently about 300,000 people, only 0.2 percent of the total population. Estimates of the number of inhabitants in 1500 range from 1 million to 6 million. But while enormous population losses occurred in the early centuries of European colonization, about 100 indigenous nations disappeared in the first 70 years of the twentieth century (Ribeiro, 1971). Most remaining Indian communities are located in isolated regions in the Amazon. They are generally small settlements, each consisting of a few hundred residents.

Brazil's "Operation Amazonia" was a direct response to the global economy and the globalization of industries that exploit natural resources. To encourage economic development, this government program granted tax credits to foreign companies and exempted them from paying import or export duties.

Brazil's policies toward its indigenous peoples have wavered between protecting Indian lands and cultures and allowing intrusions into Indian territories by ranchers, settlers, and multinational corporations exploiting their resources. Earlier in the twentieth century, the Brazilian government had established a federal Indian agency to protect Indian rights to maintain their lands and their cultures. The agency was to be guided by the motto of "Die if need be, but never kill" (quoted in Maybury-Lewis, 1997:22). But in the 1960s, the government changed course and instituted aggressive efforts to develop remote regions. Settlers and ranchers took this as permission to go into indigenous territories and either push out or kill the residents. And although the government did not officially condone their actions, it did little to stop them. In fact, it permitted cattle ranchers in particular to invade the region in large numbers and clear the forests for their herds.

Operation Amazonia. In a program called Operation Amazonia, the Brazilian government granted tax credits and exempted companies from paying import or export duties. By 1980, more than $1 billion were invested in cattle ranching in the Brazilian Amazon (Schmink, 1988:168). Forest timber and minerals, especially tin, copper, uranium, iron, gold, and diamonds, are found in rich deposits as well. Finally, Brazil and the other countries that share the Amazon have recently attracted investment in biodiversity projects. Of the estimated 500,000 species of plants currently existing in the world, about 16 percent (35,000 to 50,000 species) are located in the Amazon (Tyler, 1996:7). Brazil in particular is home to about 22 percent of the world's "higher" plant species, as well as about 24 percent of primate species and between 10 million and 15 million species of insects (Elisabetsky, 1996:405).

In order to develop these resources, the Brazilian government has set aside some fourteen "extractive reserves," together containing more than 3 million hectares of land. These reserves are defined as "forest areas inhabited by extractive populations granted long-term usufruct rights to forest resources which they collectively manage" (p. 403). The term *extractive populations* refers to rubber tappers, miners, timber workers, and settlers, but the territories set aside are often also claimed by indigenous peoples, groups whose use of the land is not protected. Instead of protecting Indians' interests in their resources, officials drew up policies aimed at "civilizing" them, attempting to solve the "Indian problem" through assimilation, with the hope of eventually phasing out the government's national Indian Service that oversees Indian land.

However, despite the efforts of the Brazilian government to assimilate Indian nations, from time to time formerly unknown communities of indigenous peoples are "discovered." About five years ago, a group known as the Korubu was found deep in the Amazonian region of northwestern Brazil, near the borders with Colombia and Peru. Brazilian officials have documented at least fifty sites of Indian habitation that were previously unknown (Schemo, 1999). When new groups are found, authorities working for the National Foundation for the Indian (FUNAI) attempt to have further contact by placing tools, utensils, and clothing in forest clearings. This is done with the assumption that the Indians will continue to return to the clearings to obtain more goods and can eventually be convinced to leave the region or settle in supervised communities. Lands claimed by indigenous peoples can then be opened for development of their timber, mineral, and pharmaceutical resources.

Yanomami at Risk. Because of pressure exerted on the Brazilian government by indigenous peoples and their advocates, a number of reservations have been set aside where lands are under indigenous control

Guarani Indians in Paraguay and Brazil today focus on establishing strong communities based on village life. This Guarani Indian family rides a horse-drawn cart on one of the ranches they "repossessed," claiming it as ancestral land.

Anthropology Applied

FUNAI Anthropologists

Anthropologists work both for the Brazilian government and for indigenous communities in efforts to protect or extend Indian rights while at the same time furthering government policies and national goals—a balancing act that often is difficult to maintain. Anthropologists have played crucial roles in mapping aboriginal lands to support Indian claims to ancestral territories; contacting new groups deep in the Amazon to help them prepare for inevitable contact with the outside world; reporting government and civilian abuses of Indians to the world community; representing Indians in disputes with settlers, prospectors, and government agents; educating indigenous communities about their political and economic rights and interests; and spearheading advocacy efforts on behalf of indigenous peoples of the Amazon.

In March 2003, for example, indigenous leaders from across Brazil, politicians, anthropologists, and officials from the National Indigenous Foundation (FUNAI) met in Brasilia to discuss indigenous rights. Topics included proposals to improve the quality of life of indigenous populations and strategies to prevent the invasion of indigenous lands. They also discussed the corruption of some FUNAI officials and the murder of indigenous leaders (Radiobras, 3/18/03, http://forests.org/articles/reader.asp?linkid=21266).

In 2004, anthropologists' interventions helped prevent bloodshed when 3,000 Guarani Indians invaded fourteen ranches on land near the Paraguayan border that they claim as part of their ancestral land. In negotiations through FUNAI, the Guaranis agreed to leave eleven of the farms, but continued to occupy the three largest ranches in an effort to press FUNAI to expand their tribal reserve by incorporating the land on which the ranches are located.

Anthropologists say that under the Brazilian constitution the indigenous community has a legitimate ancestral claim to the property in question. Rubem Almeida, one of the two anthropologists who wrote the report that will serve as the basis for FUNAI's demarcation of the Guarani territory, said the Guaranis are legally entitled to the land. Almeida presented testimony and material evidence that the Guaranis traditionally lived on the property in question, as well as "specific documents from 1927" that confirm their legal claim to the land. Despite the ranchers' protests, under the Brazilian constitution the local indigenous community has a right to that land, which cancels out the land titles held by the ranchers. The anthropologists suggested that the state should pay compensation to the ranchers (Mario Osava, Inter Press Service News Agency, 2/3/04, http://ipsnews.org/interna.asp?idnews=22228).

CRITICAL THINKING QUESTIONS

Why is being a government anthropologist a balancing act in Brazil? How might this compare with being a government anthropologist in the Bureau of Indian Affairs in the United States?

---

and given government protection. The largest of these, and, indeed, the largest indigenous reservation in the world, is an area of 20.5 million square acres inhabited by some 23,000 Yanomami, the largest indigenous nation in the Amazon (Schemo, 1999:72).

Traditional Yanomami territory had been made vulnerable in the early 1980s, when the Brazilian government permitted road construction cutting through their lands. Although the road was never completed, the initial projects brought a number of deadly diseases to the people, including measles, influenza, and malaria. These diseases killed many hundreds of Yanomami, decimating 90 percent of some communities (Gorman, 1991). The government also conducted aerial surveys that revealed valuable deposits of gold, tin, and radioactive materials.

In particular, gold has brought about 50,000 miners to the region. They have illegally built some 120 airstrips hidden in the jungle and dammed dozens of rivers to obtain water pressure to make prospecting easier. In addition, the use of mercury in gold prospecting has polluted many of the rivers, contaminating the fish that the Yanomami eat, in turn leading to birth defects and nerve disorders (Gorman, 1991). New waves of epidemic diseases have stricken the communities. And the miners killed hundreds of people, burned their houses, and destroyed forestland (Wiessner, 1999:77).

? *As an anthropologist, to what extent do you think you would get involved in the political, economic, or medical problems or struggles of the people you were studying? What ethical dilemmas would you face in deciding this question?*

Infringements on their lands, the spread of diseases, and competition over resources had the further effect of creating or exacerbating internal conflicts between neighboring Yanomami settlements and within the communities as well (Ferguson, 1992). Therefore, what might look to an outsider as endemic warfare was actually, at least in part, a response to turmoil caused by external forces.

The plight of the Yanomami came to international public awareness in 1987, when four Indians and one miner were killed in a clash (Gorman, 1991). Brazilian authorities then drew up plans to reduce the size of Yanomami lands, giving the Indians nineteen separate "islands of habitation" and creating state parks and national forests in which gold mining was permitted. But an indigenous advocacy group called Survival International brought a lawsuit to the Brazilian High Court, which ruled the government's plan to be unconstitutional and instead ordered the expulsion of the gold miners. In the following year, the government reached a compromise that would return most of the confiscated land to the Yanomami, keeping about 3,000 square miles for mining operations.

The establishment of reservations grants the Indians their rights to control their own destinies, living according to their own cultural norms and absorbing as much external influences as they choose. However, despite the intentions of FUNAI, ranchers and resource developers continue to encroach on Indian lands. They often operate in remote regions far from contact with government officials. In addition, although reservation lands are formally protected, most have unclear and unmarked boundaries, making it difficult for Indians to assert claims over particular acreage. So far, about 80 percent of the lands in Brazil officially defined as indigenous territory have been mapped, although even their boundaries are vulnerable to encroachment by settlers, miners, and resource companies (Wiessner, 1999:79).

Brazil's "Urban Indians." In addition to the indigenous communities officially recognized by the Brazilian government, there are many more self-identified Indian people who live in small villages, towns, and cities throughout the country, even in the densely settled northeast. Some estimates suggest that urban Indians account for about one-quarter of Brazil's Indian population (Warren, 2001:16). And their numbers are increasing. In Brazil, as in the United States and Canada, the number of people who self-identify as Indian has steadily risen in the last several decades. Part of the increase can be explained on the basis of natural growth, but the numbers far exceed that process. Most of the increase results from the easing of people's reluctance to identify themselves as indigenous because of prevailing racism and social stigma.

Many Indians living in rural or urban settings are oriented to indigenous traditions that have been transformed or destroyed over the past five centuries. Still, they "define indigenous ancestral roots as essential to [their] identity, to make them the anchor of [their] dreams and future, and to work toward their recovery" (Warren, 2001:21). They have an orientation that is "posttraditional" in the sense that they look to traditions but also mold and adapt these traditions in a way that is meaningful today. And many face negative attitudes held in Brazilian society toward Indians and Indianness. Some are denied social recognition as Indians because they are the products of racial mixtures, and their appearance, therefore, does not conform to stereotypical images of Indians. Their behavior similarly combines practices and attitudes of their multiple ancestries. But while they recognize their

Advocates for the Yanomami, including anthropologists from the world community, objected to the Brazilian government's plan to restrict the size of Yanomami territory and to permit gold prospecting by outsiders. They feared that any presence of miners would spread disease, such as mercury poisoning and tuberculosis. Finally, in 1991, a new Brazilian president banned all outsiders from the region and put into motion procedures that established a protected reservation. Here a Brazilian doctor aids the Yanomami.

complex past, they gravitate most toward their Indian identity. They feel most comfortable associating with other Indians, living in Indian communities or neighborhoods, and decorating their homes with symbols of their indigenous heritage (Warren, 2001:254–259).

Brazilian Indians and their supporters are active in forming organizations that advocate for their lands and their rights. Some of these organizations are backed and funded by members of the Catholic clergy, espousing "liberation theology," which looks to the church to ally itself with the struggles of indigenous and other poor people who are fighting for social, economic, and political justice (Ramos, 1997). While they do not represent the dominant or mainstream church, they do constitute a vocal and active faction. In addition, Brazilian Indians forge alliances among themselves, as well as with other indigenous peoples in South, Central, and North America, learning from each other's experiences and working together to accomplish their common goals.

Costs of Economic Development in Ecuador and Bolivia

Indigenous peoples in Ecuador and Bolivia are in the forefront of movements to organize opposition to government policies that encroach on their lands, harm their environments, and destroy their cultures. Both countries have a majority population of indigenous people, the descendants of powerful and complex societies. Today, their territories are the targets of oil exploration and extraction. In Ecuador, for example, the government is focusing on oil as the basis of its projected economic development. Ecuador has the largest petroleum reserves in Latin America, equal to those of Mexico and Nigeria (Forero, 2003). Most of the oil is located in remote areas of the Amazon inhabited primarily by indigenous communities. And many of these communities oppose the oil companies because of the environmental pollution and destruction that follow oil drilling and pipelines, interfering with the people's ability to maintain their traditional economies that rely on horticulture and foraging. In addition, the people do not receive monetary benefits from the resources because profits from the oil are rarely reinvested in their communities. Instead, the resources benefit wealthy investors and consumers elsewhere in Ecuador, as well as in foreign countries.

Indians have organized protests against government policy and have also occasionally sabotaged the drilling equipment and pipelines. The Ecuadorian government responded by sending military patrols to protect oil company gear and personnel. In addition, representatives of the indigenous Kichwa, Achuar, and Shuar have sent delegations to the capital Quito and to meetings of the Organization of American States and of petroleum company shareholders. And they have forged coalitions with environmental groups. Although some indigenous people favor the development, hoping that they will reap economic benefits, the majority oppose petroleum extraction.

In Bolivia, indigenous peoples led protests against government policies in 2003 that eventually led to the resignation of the president, Gonzalo Sanchez de Lozada (Rohter, 2003). And, in 2005, they organized protests calling for nationalizing oil and gas resources. The proportion of indigenous peoples in Bolivia is the highest of all in South America, constituting 55 percent of the total population (Wiessner, 1999:83). Since the 1980s, Indians in Bolivia have gained recognition of their rights to land, obtaining ownership of 1 million hectares of territory in the Andes. In 1994, an addendum to the Bolivian constitution officially designated the country as a "multiethnic, pluricultural society" (p. 84). However, despite favorable political and legal status, indigenous peoples occupy the lowest stratum economically and socially.

Developments in Africa

The situation for indigenous peoples in Africa shares some similarities with, and yet differences from, that of peoples in North and South America. Most European colonial efforts in Africa did not include large numbers of settlers. Therefore, in contemporary Africa, the delineation of who is "indigenous" or "tribal" is more complex than in the settler colonies of the Americas and Australia. After former colonies gained their independence, the new countries developed policies that affected various groups within their borders. In general, members of large and powerful groups came to dominate the

? *Do you think the indigenous people of Ecuador have the right to block oil drilling on their property? How would you resolve the conflict of interest in this situation?*

governments and benefited from political, economic, and social policies, whereas members of small, isolated groups received far fewer advantages. In many cases, they remain marginalized in their own countries and face various forms of discrimination and control. These factors are reflected in various definitions of "indigenous" proposed by scholars of international law. However, a consensus summary states that

> Indigenous communities are best conceived of as peoples traditionally regarded, and self-defined, as descendants of the original inhabitants of lands with which they share a strong, often spiritual bond. These peoples are, and desire to be, culturally, socially and/or economically distinct from the dominant groups in society, at the hands of which they have suffered, in past or present, a pervasive pattern of subjugation, marginalization, dispossession, exclusion and discrimination. (Wiessner, 1999:115)

Central governments in the East African countries of Sudan, Kenya, and Tanzania have continued colonial policies aimed at encouraging or forcing nomadic pastoral societies to become sedentary farmers or wage workers. Colonial and postcolonial governments prefer sedentary citizens because they are more easily supervised and controlled. In addition, nomadic pastoralists rely on large tracts of land to graze their animals. Gaining access to these lands allows national governments to proceed with economic development projects. Also, the governments often phrase their policies in terms of building national unity through cultural uniformity. In some cases, pastoralists are forced to change their economic systems by the unilateral confiscation of their territory. For example, in the 1970s, the Sudanese government undertook the construction of canals on the Nile River that would control flooding but disrupted the traditional economies of the Dinka, cattle pastoralists of southern Sudan (Lako, 1988).

Sudan and the Dinka.   The Dinka rely on floodwaters to irrigate pastureland for their cattle, but the Sudanese authorities claim that such use of water is wasteful. Instead, the government diverts floodwaters for the use of farmers and urban dwellers in the populous northern Sudan. There are political implications of these choices as well since Sudanese society is split between the predominantly Muslim north and the predominantly Christian south. The two regions are frequently at odds, a conflict that periodically erupts in sectarian violence. The government's plan was to build the Jonglei Canal at a part of the Nile that is in the heart of Dinka territory. They claimed that the Dinka would benefit from the changes as the people became incorporated into the modern economy. The authorities tried to convince the Dinka that they would be able to maintain their cattle as sedentary ranchers rather than as nomadic pastoralists. They held out the promise of health care, educational services, and agricultural training as incentives to living in stable villages. In response to the Dinka's complaints that the canal would disrupt animal migration routes, the government established crossing points on the canal. But the crossing points created a further problem because animals would be concentrated in these areas, leading to depletion of resources through heavy use. In addition, the amount of fish available to the Dinka would be diminished, curtailing an important source of food.

Given their awareness of the potential negative effects, most Dinka feared the loss of their traditional way of life. But, although they objected to the presence of the canal in their territory, opposition was relatively weak, and a minority of canal supporters, consisting mainly of traders, businessmen, and civil servants, proved to be more vocal. The Jonglei Canal project uncovered latent class distinctions and contrasts in class interests in Dinka society. Many Dinka were forced to move, although they did receive some financial compensation.

Kenya and Tanzania: The Maasai and the Barabaig.   The Maasai, a group of fourteen independent tribal entities of about 375,000 people, have seen their grazing lands in Kenya and Tanzania decreased, first by actions of British and German colonial authorities and then by postcolonial governments. In the early nineteenth century, European settlers encroached on Maasai lands, taking about half of their acreage (Fratkin and Wu, 1997). Then, in the mid-twentieth century, additional land was taken by the Kenyan and Tanzanian governments to create wildlife parks and reserves. In addition, the Maasai have lost grazing territories to small-scale independent farmers and large-scale corporate estates. Governments and international funding sources claim that the Maasai and other pastoralists are inefficient utilizers of the land, which could be better used for producing cash crops and commercial beef (Fratkin and Wu, 1997). In Tanzania, Maasai grazing lands have been confiscated to make way for commercial rice farms and irrigation projects.

But the Maasai are no longer willing to see their way of life deteriorate. In Kenya, the Loita Maasai have organized the Loita Naimina Enkiyio Conservation Trust to help protect their legal rights to lands in Narok County against a plan to turn some of their acreage into a wildlife reserve that would include the construction of roads and a hotel for tourists.

In Tanzania, the Barabaig, a group of cattle pastoralists numbering about 30,000, are fighting government and private projects that will turn much of their land into commercial wheat farms. In an important decision, the Tanzanian High Court supported the Barabaig suit on the basis of customary use rights. But the decision was overturned in 1986 after the government filed an appeal on the grounds that not all of the plaintiffs in the case were "native" according to official definitions because some were not indigenous Barabaig but instead were descendants of Somali immigrants.

The Kenyan and Tanzanian governments took thousands of square miles of land from the Maasai when they created one of the world's largest and most visited wildlife reserves and national parks. When the British originally established the Serengeti National Park in 1929, the Maasai lost resource-rich grazing and farming territory. In response to protests, the British granted the tribes access to the nearby Ngorongoro Conservation Area (NCA). However, by 1975, the Kenyan government prohibited farming in the NCA, even though the Maasai had come to rely on maize as a necessary supplement to their shrinking herds. Malnutrition is becoming an increasingly serious problem. Restrictions on access to lands now turned into game parks have also created and exacerbated intertribal tensions as various groups compete for scarcer territories and resources.

Nigeria and the Ogoni.   Indigenous lands are confiscated elsewhere in Africa so that economic development can proceed apace. For example, the Nigerian government has granted licenses to the Shell Oil Company for drilling on land claimed by the Ogoni, a group of about 500,000 people (Beveridge, 2003:9). Most of the oil drilled in Nigeria is located in Ogoni territory, land that has been harmed by toxic emissions and oil leakages from ruptured pipelines. A group of eight Ogoni activists and one of their supporters, the internationally known writer Ken Saro-Wiwa, were arrested, charged with murder, and executed in 1995 despite vigorous protests from the United Nations and from many countries in the world.

Biodiversity prospecting is becoming big business in parts of Africa, as in Asia and the Pacific (Reid et al., 1996). But the issue of ownership is a contentious problem in many countries (Iwu, 1996). Africa, for example, is rich in plants and animals containing medicinal properties that could be used to treat many ailments. A research project in Nigeria identified several plants that could be used for the treatment of viral infections, and other agents that have antiparasitic, antiplaque, and antifungal properties, as well as a greaseless body oil (Iwu, 1996:243). Management of these and other resources is complicated by competing needs. Conservation of biodiversity resources is critical to their continuation but at the same time, the intense poverty suffered by many Africans drives the governments to allow rapid harvesting even though future supplies are threatened by this policy.

? *What do you predict for the future of pastoralism as a mode of human subsistence?*

> **REVIEW**
>
> In the United States, issues have centered on indigenous peoples' control of land and resources and gaming, while in Canada, efforts have also focused on achieving sovereignty. In Mexico, the policy of *indigenismo* has granted rights to natives, but cultural minorities such as the Maya continue to struggle for independence. South American governments vacillate between protecting Amazonian Indians and exploiting the natural resources in their homelands. Bolivian and Ecuadoran Indians also protest resource exploitation on their lands. In Africa, pastoralists such as the Dinka and Barabaig struggle to retain grazing land, while people such as the Ogoni of Nigeria take action to keep commercial oil interests at bay.

In Their Own Voices

Viktor Kaisiepo on the International Decade of the World's Indigenous People

In this excerpt, Viktor Kaisiepo, a Papuan activist and member of the Presidium Dewan Papua (an organization of indigenous people in Papua), reflects on some of the goals and accomplishments of indigenous people involved in activities related to the International Decade of the World's Indigenous People (1994–2004), declared by the United Nations. Kaisiepo assesses the gains indigenous peoples made during that decade.

Sometimes I wish I were a carpenter, because if I were a carpenter, at the end of two or three days I could say, "Here's a chair." But in the field of human rights how do you measure success? Some people feel empowered by being part of the U.N. process, and others say, well I've been here 10 years but still nothing has changed. So there has been a huge progress when you look back over the years. Let me put it this way: If I am a member of the liberation movement, 22 years down the road I'm still occupied. Is that success? Is that failure? According to my own objectives it is a failure because I am still occupied, but in terms of building international networks and support I've gained a lot. Like I said, when you throw the stone in the Pacific Ocean, one day down the road the waves will come to the shore. So, I think, the people that are here, they will gain a lot of experience, a lot of knowledge.

I don't think this first International Decade of the World's Indigenous People will be a clear indicator of the success of the indigenous movement, but during this decade we will have accumulated a lot of information, and generated a lot of interaction. The best way to see whether there are big results or not is to wait for the second decade. Whether it's declared a second International Decade by the United Nations or not, the results of the first International Decade will be seen in the next 10 years. Some people become involved in the beginning, some a quarter of the way down the road, some halfway down the road, some three quarters down the road.

You need capacity-building processes for indigenous peoples. Do I understand my rights properly; do I understand the mechanisms made available to me? How do I utilize them, when am I supposed to utilize them, and whom do I have to address? When people come to the United Nations, they think, well, when I address them, that's the end of the story. No, it's the beginning of the story. Things are changing for the better and you must appreciate that. When you meet moments like we did, in 1993, when we asked for the establishment of the Permanent Forum, and in 2002 it was established—within 10 years—then that is a great success. And you have to celebrate it.

The United Nations has declared a Second International Decade of the World's Indigenous People (2005–2015).

From: Viktor Kaisiepo, "We've Gained a Lot," *Cultural Survival Quarterly* 28, 3 (Fall 2004), pp. 19–20. Copyright © 2004. Reprinted by permission.

CRITICAL THINKING QUESTIONS

According to Kaisiepo, what gains have been made by indigenous peoples? What still needs to be done?

LEGAL RIGHTS AND INTERNATIONAL RECOGNITION

To protect themselves and their lands, indigenous peoples have formed coalitions to place their concerns on the agendas of international organizations. In the international forum, the question of who is "indigenous" becomes politically and legally significant. Self-identification and community cohesiveness are some of the relevant factors. But historical changes, migrations of individuals and groups, and intermarriage with members of other communities blur identities and social cohesion. In 1993, a United Nations working group proposed a Draft Declaration on the Rights of Indigenous Peoples that contains forty-five articles outlining international recognition of their rights. Among these are the right to self-determination (to determine their political status and identity), to maintain their cultures, to be protected from genocide, ethnocide (cultural genocide), or forced relocation. In addition, the document

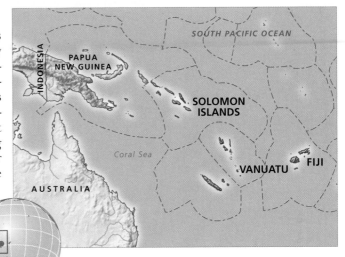

Case study

Papua New Guinea's Customary Law

The history of legal practice in Papua New Guinea has vacillated between formal jurisprudence and customary procedures. Although Papua New Guinea consists of numerous and diverse populations, the traditions of most communities stress the responsibility of kin groups to redress wrongs committed against their members, either by demanding compensation or by physical retaliation against the perpetrators. People resort to personal problem solving with or without the approval of informal councils who hear complaints and attempt reconciliation. These councils have only the force of public opinion; they have no coercive authority. Before taking direct action, kinship groups may try to facilitate agreements through negotiation and compromise with the ultimate aim of resolving problems and reconstituting social harmony.

During most of the colonial period, British and, later, Australian authorities did not recognize customary practices in state legal settings. The adversarial system of due process was imposed through the courts and the laws. But in the villages, away from official view, people continued to seek resolution of disputes through traditional means, either by consulting village councils or by calling on their kinship groups to act as mediators. In the 1960s, colonial jurisprudence began to recognize Papuan customs by accepting defenses or reducing sentences based on customary practices and attitudes.

The courts nevertheless regarded customary law as illegitimate, a product of the "primitive culture and environment of the accused, which made it impossible for the accused to understand and accept Australian values" (Ottley and Zorn, 1983:265). For example, people accused of assault, manslaughter, or murder might offer a defense of provocation, claiming that cultural expectations led them to commit the offense after they had been provoked by a prior act of the victim. The court often accepted such a defense. If the accused were a member of a remote community where traditional practices and attitudes prevailed, she or he might be acquitted or receive a light sentence. But if the accused were, in the court's judgment, sufficiently assimilated, cultural defenses might not be accepted.

In addition, the Australian Supreme Court denied defenses based on retaliation for sorcery, even though beliefs in sorcery are widespread throughout Papua New Guinea. The court did not acknowledge that Papuans consider a belief in sorcery to be "reasonable" but imposed their own cultural and legal standards. The court would allow Australian defendants to plead insanity for killing someone they believed was a sorcerer, but Papuans were not allowed to plead insanity in the same situation. In the court's opinion, "In Papua New Guinea, although most people believe in sorcery, and most sane people do so, no reasonable person would" (Ottley and Zorn, 1983:276).

Following independence, the Papua New Guinea Law Reform Commission formulated a system of law emphasizing customary law consistent with traditional principles of conflict resolution (Ottley and Zorn, 1983). These principles were based on provisions of the new constitution that aimed to legitimate customary practices where possible. However, customary principles and procedures have been only marginally and inconsistently incorporated into the country's legal system. Decisions rendered by the supreme court in cases involving customary practices rely heavily on colonial statutes. For example, the court ruled as unconstitutional a statute called the Inter-Group Fighting Act, passed in 1973 in response to a perceived escalation of fighting in tribal areas. That statute was consistent with customary attitudes that hold each member of a group responsible for the actions of the group as a whole. The act was aimed at limiting fighting by permitting the legal system to punish all members of a group engaged in fighting even though each person may not have been involved in a particular incident. In declaring the act to be unconstitutional, the supreme court referred to the Western tradition of individual responsibility rather than the Papuan tradition of collective responsibility for criminal acts. In addition, the court continues to base its judgments on rulings made prior to independence, again impeding the establishment of customary law.

The actions of the Papua New Guinea courts highlight resistance to custom as a legitimate source of judicial and political processes. This resistance suggests the desire of the state to retain control over competing local interests. Central control and consistency are not possible if communities have the right to develop their own mechanisms of solving disputes and punishing wrongdoers. The postindependence government also is concerned with establishing a national identity distinct from its colonial past and with attracting foreign investment. At the same time, it sees customary law not as an aspect of society that is uniquely Papuan but as a threat to its power.

recognizes indigenous peoples' right to practice, develop, and teach their traditions, histories, languages, and religions. They have the right of access to all forms of media, and they are protected in their rights to fully participate in the development of policies and decisions that affect them through their own chosen representatives. In 2005, the details of this Draft Declaration were still under discussion.

In economic spheres, indigenous peoples have the right to own and control "the total environment of their traditional territories," including the conservation, development, and protection of their lands and resources. In politics, indigenous peoples have the right to autonomy or self-government, to maintain their own systems of justice and conflict resolution, to maintain "traditional relationships with peoples across international borders," and to protect their rights agreed in treaties. Finally, the United Nations is charged with creating a special indigenous body to oversee implementation of the declaration (United Nations, 1993). The Draft Declaration has been introduced in the UN General Assembly for ratification but was postponed in 2004 at the end of the designated International Decade of the World's Indigenous People.

International law supports the claims of indigenous peoples to their lands, resources, and cultural heritage. In North America, treaties signed between representatives of native peoples and European or American colonial powers have the force of international law. Since treaties are documents signed by sovereign countries, they either explicitly or implicitly recognize the basic sovereignty of native nations. The fact that subsequent governments in the United States and Canada have unilaterally abrogated provisions of these treaties does not alter the underlying principles of international law.

However, in most countries, treaties were never signed between governments and native populations. Therefore, the rights of indigenous peoples rest on other principles, especially on the principle of **customary international law.** Customary rights include the right to respect of traditional lands, to maintain languages and cultural practices, to obtain welfare, health, educational, and social services, and the right to self-determination (Wiessner, 1999:98–99). Indigenous peoples, therefore, have both individual rights and collective rights that need to be protected by international organizations as well as by domestic laws. However, as noted in Chapter 12, domestic laws often fail to capture the spirit and intent of native customs.

customary international law
Traditional practices of dispute and conflict resolution, involving mechanisms for mediation and negotiation and principles for punishment or restoration of community relations.

REVIEW

To protect themselves and their lands, indigenous peoples have formed transnational coalitions to place their concerns on the agendas of international agencies and nongovernment organizations. International law supports the claims of indigenous peoples to their lands, resources, and cultural heritage, as well as to basic human rights. The legal systems of newly independent countries, however, tend to be based on colonial rather than customary law.

ECOTOURISM AND INDIGENOUS LANDS

In addition to projects aimed at economic development, increasing numbers of countries in Africa, Asia, and Latin America are infringing on indigenous lands in order to set up national parks and wildlife reserves (Colchester, 2004). **Ecotourism** has created great demand for these areas worldwide. Approximately 12 percent of the earth's landmass currently has been set aside as conservation protected areas. An unlikely coalition has formed between government agencies and conservation organizations that often oppose the people's attempts to secure the resources that they and their ancestors have depended upon for generations.

In an international meeting of the World Parks Congress, held in South Africa in 2003, representatives of indigenous groups issued an appeal protesting their "dispossession and resettlement, the violation of rights, the displacement of peoples, the loss of sacred sites, and the slow but continuous loss of cultures, as well as impoverishment. First we were dispossessed in the name of kings and emperors, later in the name of State development and now in the name of conservation" (quoted in MacKay and Caruso, 2004:14). Their position brings them into conflict with conservation groups who favor preserving "wilderness areas" kept "primitive and natural," that is, uninhabited (Colchester, 2004:18). While firm statistics are unavailable, some estimates suggest that 85 percent of reserved and protected lands in Latin America are actually inhabited by indigenous peoples and some 600,000 "tribal peoples" living in India have been forced to relocate in order to establish protected areas.

This park ranger is an Aborigine working at Ayers Rock (Uluru) in Australia. The rock is sacred to the Aborigines.

However, some countries are attempting to reconcile the needs of indigenous peoples and the desire to conserve natural resources. For example, the Peruvian government has established what it calls "communal reserves" to be managed jointly by indigenous communities and conservation agencies (Newing and Wahl, 2004:38). Indigenous peoples maintain legal title to the land and are guaranteed protection against encroachment by loggers, miners, and settlers. But their activities are also monitored by government agencies to ensure that use of the land does not conflict with the goals of "biodiversity conservation."

In South Africa, government commissions staffed by representatives from indigenous groups and conservation agencies work out equitable management policies that recognize the people's rights to their lands. And the San, an indigenous people whose traditional lands are located in the Kalahari Desert spanning Namibia and Botswana, have concluded agreements with the Namibian government that establishes the Nyae Nyae Conservancy to oversee the people's communal lands with control over management and utilization of natural resources (Hitchcock and Biesele, 2002:9). Other groups of San have won recognition of their rights to land and, importantly, to water, the most critical resource in the desert.

Income from ecotourism potentially supports people, parks, and species, an attractive prospect for developing countries. Some hail this trend as a positive adaptation to irrevocable change, but others argue, at what price? And, it is pointed out, revenues from tourism often go to governments and commercial interests rather than directly benefiting the people.

REVIEW

Ecotourism offers a means of protecting native populations and lands but at the same time encroaches on those lands and the people. The double-edged sword of ecotourism is a metaphor for the complexity of human problems in our postcolonial and increasingly postmodern and globalized world.

ecotourism
Visiting wildlife sanctuaries and national parks in order to enjoy a more pristine environment than found in urban life.

Chapter Summary

Migration

- Processes of transformation and cultural interaction have intensified throughout the twentieth and into the twenty-first century. The global economy accelerates the pace of transferring goods, services, and peoples from one part of the world to others. International migration has brought people far from their homes, contributing their labor, spending money, and adding cultural diversity worldwide. Political processes have also strengthened ties among countries.

- Processes of internal migration have also accelerated, often because people are mobile, seeking job opportunities where they are available. Urban centers attract people from rural areas in particular. The establishment of factories run by multinational corporations in development or free trade zones in many countries in Asia and Latin America has contributed to the increase in internal migration. Young women make up the majority of the work force in labor-intensive factories that produce electronics and garments.

- International migration has shifted populations from poor countries to wealthier countries with better job opportunities. As transnational migrants, people are increasingly maintaining ties with their native countries and communities at the same time that they are establishing themselves in their new countries. A transnational identity is made more likely with the ease of transportation and communication.

- While many international migrants assimilate into their new countries, many others develop an identity based on their origin and ethnicity. But ethnic identities are not immutable. Instead, they are context-bound and adaptable to circumstances. People may think of themselves as members of groups based on one set of criteria but may find themselves categorized as members of other groups based on different criteria. Ethnic groups may develop strong political influence on the basis of their relative numbers and their relative cohesiveness as a social and political community.

Ethnogenesis and Ethnic Identity

- States utilize various processes to develop a national identity. In multiethnic states, various strategies may be employed to resolve relationships between central identities and disparate ethnic groups. One ethnic group may assert itself as dominant and legitimate, equating national culture with its own. A state may assert a uniformity of culture, homogenizing ethnic differences. Or a state may maintain a pluralistic attitude toward cultural differences, allowing secondary identities to coexist along with a national identity. Ethnic strife, resulting from economic and political forces, may lead to tension and conflict internally within a multiethnic country.

And in some cases, cultural pluralism may spawn xenophobic sentiments leading to hostility and even violence against immigrants.

- An international or global identity based on social class has developed. Members of elite classes have a global identity that links them to elites in other countries on the basis of class, sharing privileges, interests, leisure activities, and tastes with other elites. A popular global culture has also developed as people throughout the world eat the same foods, watch the same movies, listen to the same music, and purchase the same types of consumer goods.

Cultural Minorities in a Global World

- Since the middle of the twentieth century, indigenous communities in many countries have gained a new energy and focus for their struggles in self-determination. Policies toward indigenous peoples vary considerably in different countries. In the United States and Canada, native peoples have legally defined rights based on treaties signed between their representatives and the federal governments. These treaties and subsequent court rulings support some limited sovereignty for Indian communities, including some degree of self-government, tax immunity, and rights to control economic, educational, and social programs. In Mexico, federal policies have vacillated between recognizing the land rights of indigenous peoples and ignoring those rights in the interest of national economic development. In other countries of Latin America, governments have followed similar variations in policy. While indigenous communities have gained some recognition to rights to land and resources and their rights to continue cultural practices, their lands have also been the target of resource extraction, especially oil and minerals, and, more recently, biodiversity research.

- The situation for indigenous peoples in Africa differs somewhat from that of peoples in the Western Hemisphere. In Africa, there were relatively few European colonial settlers and, therefore, the delineation of "indigenous" or "tribal" is more complex than in American or Australian settler colonies. In many African states, as in other countries, indigenous peoples remain marginalized and face various forms of discrimination and control. In Sudan, Kenya, and Tanzania, national governments have attempted to force nomadic pastoralists to adopt a sedentary lifestyle, phrased in the interest of a national culture and economic development.

Legal Rights and International Recognition

- To protect themselves and their land, indigenous peoples have formed coalitions to assert their rights under international law. The United Nations is in the process of formulating a Declaration on the Rights of Indigenous Peoples outlining legal, economic, social, and cultural rights.

Ecotourism and Indigenous Lands

- In addition to projects aimed at economic development, many countries are infringing on indigenous lands in order to create national parks and wildlife reserves that have become a trend in ecotourism. However, in some countries, negotiations have resulted in compromises that grant indigenous residents some protections while also monitoring their use of parkland.

 ## Key Terms

cultural minorities 449	transnationalism 455	customary international
labor migration 449	Islamization 457	law 474
tribalization 455	global identity 460	ecotourism 475

Review Questions

1. What are the distinguishing features and effects of forced migration, urban migration, and labor migration?

2. How is Mexico's maquiladora system an example of the role of multinational corporations in labor migration? What might be some other examples?

3. What are the main difficulties that transnational migration can cause for cultural minorities? In what ways might they participate in a culture of transnationalism?

4. What is the process of ethnogenesis? What are some examples of the creation of new ethnic and political identities in newly independent states, such as Sudan and Papua New Guinea?

5. How have postcolonial states treated cultural minorities in the process of nation building, for example, in Indonesia, Rwanda, or Malaysia? How did colonialism influence these outcomes?

6. How has globalization been expressed in both cultural identities and consumerism?

7. What challenges do cultural minorities face in every part of the world? How do situations in Canada, Brazil, Nigeria, and other countries show how those challenges play out in specific cultural contexts?

8. How has the law worked both against and for the interests of cultural minorities?

9. What role does ecotourism play in the future of cultural minorities?

Glossary

acculturation Process by which a group adjusts to living within a dominant culture while at the same time maintaining its original cultural identity.

achieved status A social position attained by a person's own efforts and skills.

aesthetics Philosophies about what has beauty and value in art.

affines People related through marriage.

African-American Vernacular English (AAVE) A dialect of English spoken by some, but not all, Americans of African descent.

age grade (age set) A sociopolitical association of people of more or less similar age who are given specific social functions.

agriculture A subsistence strategy focusing on intensive farming, investing a great deal of time, energy, and technology.

ambilineal descent Principle of descent in which individuals may choose to affiliate with either their mother's or their father's kinship group.

ancestor worship Belief in the importance of ancestors as they affect the lives of their survivors, protecting their descendants in return for rituals of honor performed to show them respect.

animatism Belief that all things are endowed with some spirit form or essence.

animism Belief in the existence of souls.

anthropology The study of humanity, from its evolutionary origins millions of years ago to its current worldwide diversity.

applied anthropology An area of anthropology that applies the techniques and theories of the field to problem solving outside of traditional academic settings.

archaeology The study of past cultures, both historic cultures with written records and prehistoric cultures that predate the invention of writing.

arranged marriages Marriages that are arranged by the parents or other relatives of the bride and groom.

art Artifacts of human creation created through the exercise of exceptional physical, conceptual, or imaginative skill; produced in a public medium and intended to affect the senses, sharing stylistic conventions with similar works.

artisans Specialists in the production of works of art.

ascribed status A social position that a person attains by birth. A person is born into an ascribed status.

assimilation Process by which a less numerous and less powerful cultural group changes its ways and cultural identity to blend in with the dominant culture.

associations Sociopolitical groups that link people in a community on the basis of shared interests and skills.

avoidance relationships Patterns of behavior between certain sets of kin that demonstrate respect and social distance.

avunculocal residence Patterns of residence after marriage in which the couple lives with or near the husband's mother's brother.

balanced reciprocity Exchange of goods and services of a specified value at a specified time and place.

bands Small, loosely organized groups of people held together by informal means.

barter An exchange of products in which one person gives one type of product in exchange for another type of product.

berdaches Male Two-Spirits in some Native American societies who adopted some of the economic and social roles of women.

bilateral descent Principle of descent in which people think of themselves related to both their mother's kin and their father's kin at the same time.

bilocal residence Patterns of residence after marriage in which the couple alternates between living with the wife's kin and the husband's kin.

biological, or physical, anthropology The study of human origins and biological diversity.

blood feud Ongoing conflict between kin groups or communities, based on vengeance.

body language The meanings people communicate through their posture, stance, movements, expressions, gestures, and proximity to other communicants.

brideservice A period of months or years before or after marriage during which the husband performs labor for his wife's parents.

bridewealth Presents given by the husband's family to the wife's kin before, during, or after the wedding ceremony.

calendric rituals Ceremonies performed at specific times during the year, for example, agricultural rituals performed for planting, growing, and harvesting crops.

call systems (signal systems) Animal communication systems that consist of a relatively small number of sounds to express moods and sensations, like fear, delight, contentment, anger, or pain.

capital Land, money, factories, and the like that support and supply the materials needed for production.

capitalism An economic mode of production in which the goal is to amass wealth in the form of money in order to gain control over the means of production and then use this control to accumulate even greater wealth.

cargo cults Revitalization movements arising in Melanesia in the early twentieth century with the aim of obtaining material wealth through magical means.

carrying capacity The number of people who can be sustained by the resources and environment in which they live.

cash economies Systems of exchange based on the use of currency in modern markets.

caste Social grouping whose membership is determined at birth and is generally inflexible.

chiefdoms Stratified societies organized by kinship.

child-rearing practices Methods used to take care of infants and young children, including ways of feeding, playing with, carrying, and sleeping arrangements.

clans Named groups of people who believe that they are relatives even though they may not be able to trace their actual relationships with all members of their group.

class Social grouping usually determined on the basis of a combination of birth and achievement.

cognates Words in different languages that are derived from the same word in their parent language.

colonialism Policies in which countries establish colonies in distant places in order to exploit their resources and labor, and possibly to establish settlements of their own citizens abroad.

colonies   Settlements of foreign nationals with controlling interests in indigenous territories.

commodity   A product that can be sold or traded in return for money or other products.

comparative perspective   An approach in anthropology that uses data about the behaviors and beliefs in many societies to document both cultural universals and cultural diversity.

componential analysis   A technique of analyzing the similarities and contrasts among words in a particular category, such as kinship terms or animal names.

confederacy   A form of political organization in which tribes and bands join together under common leadership to face an external threat.

conflict avoidance   Prosocial behaviors, such as reconciliation, consolation, politeness, or apology, to repair social relationships without aggression.

conflict perspectives   Understanding cultural differences as a consequence of conflict in the interests and goals of various groups within a society and focusing on issues of power and resistance.

consanguines   People related by blood.

consumerism   Culture of consumption of goods and services.

consumption   The use of subsistence resources, including outcomes of production.

contagious magic   Magic that operates on the principle that positive and negative qualities can be transferred through proximity or contact.

contract archaeology   The application of archaeology to assess the potential impact of construction on archaeological sites and to salvage archaeological evidence.

cosmology   Religious worldview of a people, including beliefs about the origin of the world, the pantheon of deities that exist, and their relationships to the spirit realm.

counterculture   An alternative cultural model within a society that expresses different views about the way that society should be organized.

courtship   Period prior to marriage when a couple tests attraction to and compatibility with each other.

creoles   Languages that have historic roots as an amalgamation of vocabulary and grammar derived from two or more independent languages.

cross-cousin   A child of one's mother's brother or of one's father's sister.

cross-cultural comparisons   Means of understanding cultural differences and similarities through data analysis rather than direct observation.

Crow system   Kin terms used by some matrilineal peoples that extend the term for father and father's sister to include cross-cousins on the paternal side.

cult of domesticity   Constellation of beliefs popular in the late nineteenth and early twentieth centuries that promoted the notion that women were, by nature and biology, suited to the domestic tasks of nurturing and caring for their husbands and children.

cultural anthropology   The study of cultural behavior, especially the comparative study of living and recent human cultures.

cultural constructs   Models of behavior and attitudes that a particular culture transmits to its members.

cultural core   Practices by which people organize their work and produce food and other goods necessary for their survival.

cultural ecology   Field that studies cultures as dynamic wholes based on the satisfaction of human needs through cultural behaviors.

cultural evolution   Belief of early anthropologists that cultures evolve through various stages from a simpler and more primitive state to a complex and more culturally advanced state.

cultural integration   Tendency for people's practices and beliefs to form a relatively coherent and consistent system.

cultural knowledge   Information that enables people to function in their society and contributes to the survival of the society as a whole.

cultural materialism   Explanations of cultural differences as the results of cultural adaptations through economic production.

cultural minorities   Members of ethnic or cultural groups who have become minorities in their native lands due to migrations of other peoples into their territories or due to the historical configuration of a nation-state made up of diverse groups.

cultural models   Shared assumptions that people have about the world and about the ideal culture.

cultural pluralism   Condition in a stratified society in which many diverse cultural groups ideally live together equally and harmoniously without losing their cultural identities and diversity.

cultural presuppositions   Shared knowledge and unspoken assumptions that people have as members of their culture.

cultural relativism   An approach in anthropology that stresses the importance of analyzing cultures in their own terms rather than in terms of the culture of the anthropologist. This does not mean, however, that all cultural behavior must be condoned.

cultural resource management   The application of archaeology to preserve and protect historic structures and prehistoric sites.

culture   The learned values, beliefs, and rules of conduct shared to some extent by the members of a society that govern their behavior with one another.

culture change   Changes in peoples' ways of life over time through both internal and external forces.

culture contact   Direct interaction between peoples of different cultures through migration, trade, invasion, or conquest.

culture history   Ongoing culture change in which people respond and adapt to their environment.

culture shock   Feeling an anthropologist may have at the start of fieldwork of being out of place in unfamiliar surroundings.

culture-specific psychological disorders   Psychological disorders that seem to occur with some frequency in certain cultures but are rare or absent in others.

culture wars   Internal disagreements in a society about cultural models or about how society or the world should be organized.

customary international law   Traditional practices of dispute and conflict resolution, involving mechanisms for mediation and negotiation and principles for punishment or restoration of community relations.

customary law   Selected aspects of native justice and jurisprudence codified into law by colonial authorities, mainly to secure greater control over indigenous populations.

deference   Nonthreatening verbal and nonverbal behaviors that convey respect or subordination to others.

depopulation   Reduction in population size as a result of war, conquest, colonization, or disease.

deviance   Behaviors that violate cultural norms and expectations.

dialect   A variety of a language spoken by a particular group of people, based on regional differences or social differences such as gender, class, race, or ethnicity.

diffusion Spread of ideas, material objects, and cultural practices from one society to another through direct and indirect culture contact.

displacement Ability to communicate about something that is not happening at the moment.

diviners Persons with the power to predict the future through messages and omens from the spirit world.

dominance hierarchies In primate groups, social hierarchies established on the basis of sex and age.

double descent Kinship principle in which people belong to kinship groups of both their mother and father.

dowry Gifts given by the wife's family to the married couple or to the husband's kin before, during, or after the wedding ceremony.

duality of patterning Principle that sounds are arbitrarily associated with meaning.

Ebonics Another name for African-American Vernacular English.

economic anthropology Subdiscipline of anthropology that focuses on subsistence strategies and economic systems.

economic system Cultural methods of allocating natural resources, the means of exploiting the resources through technology, the organization of work, and the production, distribution, consumption, and exchange of goods and services.

ecotourism Visiting wildlife sanctuaries and national parks in order to enjoy a more pristine environment than found in urban life.

egalitarian societies Societies in which all members have equal access to valued resources, including land, social prestige, wealth, and power.

elites Members of a social group in a stratified society who have privileges denied to the majority of the population.

emblems Nonverbal actions with specific meanings that substitute for spoken words.

emic Subjective, based on insiders' views, as in explanations people have for their own cultural behavior.

empires States expanded into larger units through conquest and the occupation or annexation of new territories.

empiricism The practice of conducting studies through direct observation and objective description.

encomiendas Spanish landholding system in the American colonies that granted the use of land and the labor of any indigenous people on that land to soldiers, priests, and settlers.

enculturation Process of learning one's culture through informal observation and formal instruction.

endogamy Marriage principle in which people marry members of their own group.

Eskimo system Kin terms making distinctions between the nuclear family and all other types of relatives and on gender.

ethical relativism The belief that all rights and wrongs are relative to time, place, and culture, such that no moral judgments of behavior can be made.

ethnic art Art produced by a particular group of people that comes to express and symbolize their ethnic identity.

ethnicity Social category based on a complex mix of ancestry, culture, and self-identification.

ethnocentrism The widespread human tendency to perceive the ways of doing things in one's own culture as normal and natural and that of others as strange, inferior, and possibly even unnatural or inhuman.

ethnogenesis Ongoing process in which people develop, define, and direct their own cultural and ethnic identities.

ethnography Aspect of cultural anthropology involved with observing and documenting peoples' ways of life.

ethnography of communication Study of communication as it occurs within a particular cultural context, considering such features as settings, participants, and participants' attitudes and goals.

ethnohistory Field of study for reconstructing and interpreting the history of indigenous peoples from their point of view as well as the points of view of ethnohistorians.

ethnology Aspect of cultural anthropology involved with building theories about cultural behaviors and forms.

ethnomusicology The study of the musical styles and traditions of a people.

ethnosemantics Study of culture through people's use of language to categorize and classify people, objects, activities, and experiences.

etic Objective, based on outsiders' views, as in explanations of people's behavior by anthropologists or other observers.

evolutionism View held by early social philosophers that human differences can be accounted for by different rates of progress, leading to different levels of cultural achievement.

exogamy Marriage principle in which people cannot marry members of their own lineage or clan but instead must forge alliances with members of other groups.

exploitation colonies Colonies established by military conquest for the purpose of exploiting the economic and natural resources of a region.

extended family Family formed with three or more generations, for example, parents, children, and grandparents.

external warfare Warfare that takes place at some distance from home communities, requiring warriors' absence from their homes for extended periods of time.

factionalism The tendency for groups to split into opposing parties over political issues, often a cause of violence and a threat to political unity.

family A married couple or other group of adult kinfolk who cooperate economically and in the upbringing of children, and all or most of whom share a common dwelling.

fictive kin Unrelated individuals who are regarded and treated as relatives.

fieldwork In anthropology, living and interacting with the people or group under study.

folklore Texts that relate traditional stories, the exploits of cultural heroes and characters handed down from generation to generation.

folktales Secular stories that relate events that teach moral lessons or entertain listeners.

food producers Users of a subsistence strategy that transforms and manages the environment in order to obtain food.

foragers Early peoples whose subsistence pattern was hunting and gathering.

forensic anthropologists Biological anthropologists who analyze human remains in the service of criminal justice and families of disaster victims.

formalist Abstract art that focuses on the formal qualities of art—color, composition, sound, words, or movements.

formal sanctions Rewards and punishments administered by persons in authority, the state, or the law.

functionalism View that cultural traits have social functions that contribute to the smooth operation of the whole society.

fundamentalism A term coined in the United States in 1920 meaning a commitment to do battle to defend traditional religious beliefs.

funerary rites Rituals performed to mark a person's death and passage to the afterworld.

fur trade Exchange of animal pelts or hides between Native Americans and colonists in exchange for European trade goods.

gender The roles that people perform in their households and communities and the values and attitudes that people have regarding men and women.

gender construct (gender model) The set of cultural assumptions about gender roles and values and the relations between the genders that people learn as members of their societies.

gender equality A constellation of behaviors, attitudes, and rights that support the autonomy of both women and men.

gender gap The difference in wages and income earned by men and women for comparable work.

gender identity The way that people think about themselves in terms of their sex, how they present themselves as men or women.

gender inequality The denial of autonomy and equal rights to one group of people based on their gender.

gender relations Norms of interaction between men and women, which may reflect differences in the relative status, prestige, and power of women and men.

gender roles Constellations of rights, duties, attitudes, and behaviors that are culturally associated with each gender.

generalized reciprocity The exchange of goods and services without keeping track of their exact value, but often with the expectation that their value will balance out over time.

Ghost Dance movement Nineteenth-century revitalization movement of the Plains Indians of North America.

ghost marriage Marriage practice among the Nuer of Sudan in which a widow marries her dead husband's brother and in which the children ensuing from the second marriage are said to be the children of the first, dead husband.

global culture A constellation of technologies, practices, attitudes, values, and symbols that spread internationally from one broad cultural origin, most recently from the Anglo-European-American cultural complex.

global identity An identity of shared interests, practices, and values across international borders, uniting people worldwide.

globalization The rapid transformation of local cultures around the world in response to the economic and other influences of a dominant culture.

haciendas Estates made up of lands directly owned by Spanish settlers.

Hawaiian system Kin terms making distinctions only of generation and gender.

healers Religious practitioners who acquire spirit power to diagnose the spirit cause of illness and effect cures.

historical linguistics The study of changes in language and communication over time and between peoples in contact.

holistic perspective A perspective in anthropology that views culture as an integrated whole no part of which can be completely understood without considering the whole.

horticulture A subsistence strategy that focuses on small-scale farming using a relatively simple technology.

household A group of people occupying a common dwelling.

imitative magic Magic that operates on the principle of "like causes like."

imperialism Empire building through state expansion in both commerce and territory.

incest taboo A ban on sexual relations or marriage between parents and their children and between siblings.

independent self Concepts of individuals as self-contained, independent agents with a focus on their own thoughts, feelings, and achievements.

indigenous societies Peoples who are now minority groups in state societies but who were formerly independent and have occupied their territories for a long time.

industrial agriculture Application of industrial technology and chemicals to farming in order to increase productivity.

industrialism The use of machines to produce products and foods.

informal sanctions Rewards and punishments expressed through praise, ridicule, gossip, and the like.

inheritance rules Rules for the passage of land, wealth, and other property from one generation to the next.

initiation rites Rituals that mark a person's transition from childhood to adulthood.

innovation Process by which new technologies and systems of knowledge are based on or built from previous tools, knowledge, and skills.

instrumental Art that attempts to have a beneficial effect on society, enriching people's lives, teaching moral lessons, and providing insights for improving and changing the world.

intensive agriculture Application of technology and intensive labor to farming, such as the plow and irrigation.

intercultural communication The communication of meanings between people of different languages and cultures.

interdependent self Concepts of individuals as connected to others, related to other people, with a focus on group needs rather than individual inner feelings, opinions, and attitudes.

internal warfare Warfare between closely situated villages or communities.

interpretive anthropology View that cultural differences can be understood as complex webs of meaning rather than through forms.

inventions New technologies and systems of knowledge.

Iroquois system Kin terms that emphasize the difference between one's parents' same-sex siblings and parents' opposite-sex siblings, classifying parallel cousins with one's own siblings.

Islamization The process of imposing the Islamic religion and associated cultural values within a nation to foster cultural uniformity.

jargons Specialized or technical words and expressions spoken by people who share a particular occupation or interest.

joint family Family consisting of siblings with their spouses and children, sharing work and resources.

joking relationships Patterns of behavior between certain sets of kin that involve reciprocal joking, teasing, and playfulness, sometimes taking the form of flirtation and sexual innuendo.

kindred Kinship group consisting of known bilateral relatives with whom people interact, socialize, and rely on for economic and emotional assistance.

kingdom A centralized political organization with the king as the paramount leader.

kinship system System of determining who one's relatives are and what one's relationship is to them.

kinship terminology system System of terms used to address and refer to relatives.

labor migration Migration of people from one area of a country to another or across national borders in search of jobs.

language Any form of communication that involves symbols, displacement, and productivity.

language family A group of languages that are historically related, descendants of a common ancestral form.

length Phonemic characteristic in which the duration of a syllable has meaning.

leveling mechanisms Cultural practices designed to equalize access to food, resources, and social prestige through a community so that no one individual can amass greater wealth or greater prestige than other people.

levirate Marriage preference rule in which a widow marries her deceased husband's brother.

lineage A set of relatives tracing descent from a known common ancestor.

lingua francas Languages used in particular areas by speakers of many different languages in order to communicate with each other.

linguistic anthropology The study of language and communication and the relationship between language and other aspects of culture and society.

loanwords Words borrowed from one language into another.

male dominance A constellation of behaviors and attitudes that grant men access to roles of prestige and reward and deny the same to women.

mana A force, power, or essence that endows people, animals, other living things, and possibly inanimate objects with special qualities or powers.

maritime enclaves Colonies established as a result of sea trade and coastal exploration for the purpose of controlling trade at foreign ports.

market economy Economic system in which products are traded in impersonal exchanges between buyers and sellers using an all-purpose currency.

marriage A socially recognized, stable, and enduring union between two adults that publicly acknowledges their rights and obligations and forms a new alliance between kin groups.

material culture The tools people make and use, the clothing and ornaments they wear, the buildings they live in, and the household utensils they use.

materialist perspectives Explanations of cultural differences that emphasize environmental adaptation, technologies, and methods of acquiring or producing food.

matriclans Clans formed through descent and inheritance from women of their group.

matrilineal Descent system in which kinship group membership and inheritance pass through the female line.

matrilocal residence Pattern for residence after marriage in which the couple lives with or near the wife's family.

medical anthropology A discipline that bridges cultural and biological anthropology, focusing on health and disease in human populations.

mediums Persons having special gifts to make contact with the spirit world, often in a state of trance.

messianic movements Revitalization movements stressing the role of a prophet or messiah as a savior for his or her people.

millinerian movements Revitalization movements incorporating apocalyptic themes, prophesying an abrupt end to the world as we know it, leading to the establishment of a new way of life or form or existence.

mimetic Art that portrays the world accurately.

missionism Settlement for the purpose of religious conversion.

mission system Pattern of Spanish colonization of the Americas in the name of the Roman Catholic Church.

mita Traditional Incan system of conscripted labor for public works, adapted by the Spanish for use in obtaining indigenous workers for their mines.

mobility A principle that people can move from membership in one social group to another.

modernization Complex culture change, both internal and external, based on industrialism and a transnational market economy.

moieties Groups of linked clans that divide a society into two halves, usually exogamous.

monogamy Marriage rule that stipulates a union between two people.

monotheistic religions Belief systems that hold to the existence of one supreme deity who has powers and knowledge that affect all aspects of life.

morpheme A unit of sound and meaning, either a separate word or a meaningful part of a word.

morphology The study of the internal structure of words and the combination of meaningful units within the words.

narratives Stories and myths that dramatize actual memories or events in symbolic form consistent with cultural practices of storytelling.

national character A constellation of behaviors and attitudes thought to be characteristic of a modal personality type prevalent in a particular country.

nationalism Movement in independent states to build national identity, pride, and unity.

nativistic movements Revitalization movements attempting to rid society of foreign elements and return to what is conceived to be a prior state of cultural purity.

naturalization The process of learning and incorporating attitudes, values, and behaviors so that they seem natural or part of one's nature rather than learned cultural behavior.

naturalized concepts Ideas and behaviors so deeply embedded in a culture that they are regarded as universally normal or natural.

negative reciprocity Exchange of goods and services in which each party seeks to benefit at the expense of the other, thus making a profit.

negative sanctions Punishments for offending social norms.

neolocal residence Pattern of residence after marriage in which the couple establishes a new, independent household separate from their relatives.

nomads People who do not have permanent homes but travel to sources of food as the food becomes seasonably available.

nonverbal communication Communication through gestures, facial expressions, body posture, use of space, and touch.

norms Sets of expectations and attitudes that people have about appropriate behavior.

nuclear family Family consisting of parents and their children.

Omaha system Kin terms used by some patrilineal peoples that extend the term for mother and mother's brother to include cross-cousins on the maternal side.

optimal foraging theory Application of animal studies and decision theory to human foraging.

oral literature Stories that people tell about their sacred past, their secular histories, and their personal lives.

oral traditions Cultural narratives that have validity as artifacts of culture and experience.

pacification Colonial goal of forcing indigenous people to be peaceful and nonresistant so that settlers could safely inhabit their lands.

paleoanthropology The study of the fossil record, especially skeletal remains, to understand the process and products of human evolution.

parallel cousin A child of one's mother's sister or of one's father's brother.

parallel descent Kinship principle in which descent and inheritance follow gender-linked lines so that men consider themselves descended from their fathers and women consider themselves descended from their mothers.

pastoralism A subsistence strategy focusing on raising and caring for large herds of domesticated animals.

patriarchy Social system in which men occupy positions of social, economic, and political power from which women are excluded.

patriclans Clans formed through descent and inheritance from men of their group.

patrilineal Descent system in which kinship group membership and inheritance pass through the male line.

patrilocal residence Pattern of residence after marriage in which the couple lives with or near the husband's relatives.

peacemakers Individuals with a specialized social role of preventing conflict from erupting into dangerous combat.

personality A constellation of behavioral traits and dispositions. Some features of personality emerge at birth while others are acquired in the process of enculturation and psychological and cognitive growth.

phoneme A minimal unit of sound that differentiates meaning in a particular language.

phonemics Analysis of the use of sounds to differentiate the meanings of words.

phonetics Study of the articulation and production of human speech sounds.

phonology Study of sound systems in language, including phonetics and phonemics.

phratries Groups of linked clans that are usually exogamous.

pidgins Rudimentary languages that have a simplified grammar and a limited vocabulary.

pitch Phonemic use of rising and falling speech cadences.

politeness strategies Behaviors designed to mute antagonisms and avoid overt hostility by affirming common bonds and recognizing another person's rights and feelings.

political anthropology The study of the ways that communities plan group actions, make decisions affecting the group, select leadership, and resolve conflicts and disputes both within the group and with other groups.

political organization The ways in which societies are organized to plan group activities, make decisions affecting members of the group, select leadership, and settle disputes both within the group and with other groups.

poll taxes Taxes levied on households.

polyandry Marriage between a woman and two or more men.

polygamy Marriage in which the marital unit consists of three or more people.

polygyny Marriage between a man and two or more women.

polyphony The many voices of people from all the different segments and groups that make up a society; a quality of ethnographic writing today that presents multiple views of a culture.

polytheism Belief in the existence of numerous deities that have specific attributes, powers, and functions.

positive sanctions Recognition and rewards for observing social norms.

postcolonial era Period (roughly since 1965), following the independence of the last former European colonies as new nations under indigenous leadership and control.

postconflict reconciliation Patterned behavior that occurs immediately after conflict has erupted and taken its course, to restore some measure of social harmony.

potlatch Ceremonial feast, characteristic of indigenous Pacific Northwest coast societies, during which hosts distributed to guests a great deal of food and goods that had been accumulated over many months or years.

power The ability to exert control over the actions of other people and to make decisions that affect them.

prayer Religious speech or thought through which believers transmit messages to spirit beings.

prestige A social resource reflected in others' good opinions, respect, and willingness to be influenced.

priests Full-time religious practitioners who lead a religious organization and officiate at rituals but are not expected to be able to communicate directly with the spirit world.

primogeniture A system of inheritance of leadership in which the eldest child (usually the eldest son) automatically inherits the position of leadership from his or her parent.

private self One's inner feelings and concepts of oneself.

production System of extracting resources and utilizing labor and technology in order to obtain foods, goods, and services.

productivity Ability to join sounds and words in theoretically infinite meaningful combinations.

prophets Religious leaders who receive divine inspiration, often in a vision or trance.

proselytism The attempt to convert a person or group from one religion to another.

psychological anthropology A subfield of cultural anthropology that studies the psychological motivations of behavior and the personality types prevalent in a society.

puberty rites Rituals performed to mark the passage of an individual from childhood to adulthood; also called initiation rites.

public self The self that one projects in public, in interactions with others.

race A cultural category that groups people according to so-called "racial" distinctions.

ranked societies Societies in which people or, more usually, kinship groups are ordered on a continuum in relation to each other.

reactive adaptation Coping response of captive, conquered, or oppressed peoples to loss and deprivation.

reciprocity Principles of mutual gift giving.

redistribution The gathering together and then reallocation of food and resources to ensure everyone's survival.

redistributive networks Economic systems in which food and other goods are amassed by an organizer and then distributed to community members or guests at large public gatherings.

reflexive anthropology The anthropology of anthropology, which focuses on the labels that anthropologists use, the impacts of anthropologists on the people they study, and professional ethics.

religion Thoughts, actions, and feelings based on belief in the existence of spirit beings and supranormal (or superhuman) forces.

religious speech Invocations, prayers, prophecies, songs of praise, and curses that are powerful means of transmitting messages about the world and also creating the world.

representational Art that imitates, idealizes, or symbolizes form and experience.

republics State societies with elected rather than inherited leadership.

reservations Land guaranteed by treaty for native residents' ownership and control.

resettlement policies Efforts of colonial authorities to relocate indigenous people to permanent settlements, usually on less desirable land, to control and influence them.

residence rules Rules that stipulate where a couple will reside after their marriage.

revitalization movement Type of nonviolent reactive adaptation in which people try to resurrect their culture heroes and restore their traditional way of life.

revivalistic movements Revitalization movements focused on bringing back cultural and religious practices that express core values that have been largely abandoned.

revolution Process by which people try to change their culture or overturn the social order and replace it with a new, ideal society and culture.

rites of passage Rituals that mark culturally significant transitions throughout the life cycle, including birth, puberty, marriage, and death.

rites of renewal Rituals performed with the goal of renewing the bounty of the earth.

rituals Activities, including religious speech, ceremonies, and behaviors, that are demonstrations of belief.

rules of descent Social rules that stipulate the nature of relationships from one generation to another.

sacred rituals Activities, places, or objects that are connected to the spirit realm and are imbued with power.

sacrifice Offerings made to spirit beings in order to show gratitude and honor.

sagamore A leader of a Mi'kmaq band who had some degree of control over a small territory and had some role in economic redistribution.

same-sex marriage Marriage between two men or two women.

sandpaintings Paintings made by sprinkling fine, colored sand to make stylized representations of spirit beings, in particular for use in Navajo curing ceremonials.

Sapir-Whorf hypothesis The assertion that the form and content of language influence speakers' behaviors, thought processes, and worldview.

scarification Artistic and ritualistic scarring of the face or other parts of the body in particular designs, commonly used to mark transitions to adulthood.

secret societies Organizations that control the use of special objects used in religious rituals.

sedentary communities Settlement pattern involving long-term, permanent settlements.

segmentary lineages Lineages organized in a hierarchical structure, ranked according to the number of generations they encompass.

self-concepts Attitudes that people hold about themselves.

semantics Study of systems of meaning in language.

serial monogamy Marriage pattern that stipulates that a person can be married to only one person at a time, although individuals may have two or more spouses during their lifetime.

settlement colonies Permanent colonies established through exploration or conquest for the purpose of occupying land and controlling labor.

settlement pattern The way people distribute themselves in their environment, including where they locate their dwellings, how they group dwellings into settlements, and how permanent or transitory those settlements are.

sex Biological differences between males and females.

shamans Part-time religious practitioners who make contact with the spirit world through prayer, ritual, and trance.

single-parent family Family consisting of one parent (either mother or father) and her or his children.

slash-and-burn (swidden) cultivation A farming technique for preparing new fields by cutting down trees and bushes and then burning them in order to clear the land and enrich the soil with nutrients.

slavery An ascribed status forced on a person upon birth or through involuntary servitude.

slave trade Buying and selling of people into servitude.

social birth Social recognition of the transition to personhood.

social control Informal and formal mechanisms in society through which people's actions are controlled and social norms or laws are enforced.

social Darwinism Early belief that cultures compete for survival of the fittest, as in the process of natural selection in biological evolution.

social fatherhood The status of a man who fulfills the responsibilities of parenting, a role that may or may not be the same as biological paternity.

socialization A similar process to enculturation that emphasizes social rather than cultural factors in learning one's culture.

social reproduction The care and sustenance of people who will be able to contribute productively to society.

social stratification Divison of society into two or more groups, or strata, that are hierarchically ordered.

societies Populations of people living in organized groups with social institutions and expectations of behavior.

sociolinguistics Study of the impacts of socioeconomic and cultural factors, such as gender and class, on language and communication within a society.

song duels Inuit contests in which conflict is expressed and resolved through public response to music.

sororal polygyny Marriage between a man and two or more women who are sisters.

sororate Marriage between a widower and his deceased wife's sister.

specialization of labor System of allocating work in which different people perform different tasks.

spirit possession Belief that spirits can enter a person's body and take over their thoughts and actions.

Standard English Dialect of English chosen as normative, a reflection of the social, economic, and political standing of its speakers.

states Highly organized, centralized political systems with a hierarchical structure of authority.

status The position or rank that one occupies in a group or society that carries certain role expectations.

stratified societies Societies in which people have differential access to valued resources, including land and property, social prestige, wealth, and political power.

stress Phonemic use of accented sounds or syllables.

structuralism View that cultural differences can be explained by differences in forms or conceptual categories rather than in meanings.

subculture A group whose members and others think of their way of life as in some significant way different from that of other people in the larger society.

subsistence patterns Methods of obtaining food using available land and resources, available labor and energy, and technology.

Sudanese system Kin terms that give separate words for all kin relationships.

surplus Food and other goods that are produced at a level greater than that needed for survival.

surplus value The amount of value produced by workers in capitalist production that is greater than the wage paid to them.

survey research Use of formal questionnaires, administered to a random sample of subjects, eliciting social data that can be analyzed statistically.

symbol A word, image, or object that stands for cultural ideas or sentiments.

symbolic culture The ideas people have about themselves, others, and the world, and the ways that people express these ideas.

syncretism Process by which a cultural product is created when people adapt a cultural item selectively borrowed from another culture to fit their existing culture.

syntax The rules that generate the combination of words to form phrases and sentences.

taboos Norms specifying behaviors that are prohibited in a culture.

tattooing Injecting inks or dyes under the skin to produce designs.

terrorism Acts of violence perpetrated by private citizens against groups within their own country or against a foreign country without the cover and sanction of a state-declared war.

theocracies Societies ruled by religious leaders, in which the social order is upheld through beliefs in its divine origin or sanction.

totem An animal or plant believed by a group of people to have been their primordial ancestor or protector.

totemism Belief system in which people believe they are descendants of spirit beings.

trade System of exchange in which goods are exchanged for either other goods or for money.

transhumance The practice among pastoralists of moving to new pastureland on a seasonal basis.

transnationalism Processes by which immigrants maintain social, economic, religious, and political ties to both their immigrant communities and their communities back home.

transvestism Dressing in the clothes usually worn by members of the opposite gender.

tribalization A process of identification with one's tribal origins.

tribes Societies with some degree of formalization of structure and leadership, including village and intervillage councils whose members regularly meet to settle disputes and plan community activities.

Two-Spirits In Native American societies, males who adopted some of the social and economic roles of women, and females who adopted some of the social and economic roles of men.

unilineal descent Principle of descent in which people define themselves in relation to only one side, either their mother's side or their father's side.

universal grammar Abstract rules that underlie the structure of phrases and sentences in all languages, generally thought to be an innate capacity of human thought.

urban anthropology Field that focuses on studying the lives of people living in cities or urban neighborhoods.

uxorilocal Living with or near the wife's parents.

vengeance Aggression against others, based on the principle of revenge.

Venus figurines Sculptures made in Europe about 30,000 years ago, thought to represent pregnant women.

virilocal Living with or near the husband's parents.

warfare Armed aggression and hostilities between groups.

wealth Economic resources, whether in land, goods, or money.

white man's burden Paternalistic, racist, colonial attitude that treated colonized peoples as inferiors in need of protection and instruction on how to live.

witchcraft A belief system that functions as a mechanism of social control by channeling anger toward others.

worldview Culture-based, often ethnocentric, way that people see the world and other peoples.

xenophobic Having to do with fear, hatred, and envy of strangers, outsiders, or foreign-born minorities within the society.

References

Aberle, David. 1961. "Matrilineal Descent in Cross-Cultural Perspective." In *Matrilineal Kinship* (Eds. D. Schneider and K. Gough). Berkeley: University of California Press, pp. 655–727.

Aberle, David. 1983. "Navajo Economic Development." In *Southwest*, Vol. 10, *Handbook of North American Indians*. Washington, DC: Smithsonian Institution Press, pp. 641–658.

Abrahams, Roger. 1983. *African Folktales*. New York: Pantheon.

Abu-Lughod, Lila. 1986. *Veiled Sentiments*. Berkeley: University of California Press.

Abu-Lughod, Lila. 1990. "The Romance of Resistance: Tracing Transformations of Power through Bedouin Women." *American Ethnologist* 17:41–55.

Adams, Kathleen. 1995a. "Cultural Commoditization in Tana Toraja, Indonesia." *Cultural Survival Quarterly* 14:31–36.

Adams, Kathleen. 1995b. "Making Up the Toraja? The Appropriation of Tourism, Anthropology and Museums for Politics in Upland Sulawesi, Indonesia." *Ethnology* 34:143–154.

Adams, Robert. 1982. "Property Rights and Functional Tenure in Mesopotamian Rural Communities." In *Societies and Languages of the Ancient Near East*. Warminster, U.K.: Aris & Phillips, pp. 1–14.

Adorno, Rolena. 2004. *Nueva corónica y buen gabierno* (c. 1615) by Pomo de Ayala, Felipe Gauman. Yale University. http://base.kb.dk/pls/hsk_web. Accessed August 24, 2004.

Ahmadu, Fuambai. 2000. "Female Circumcision." In *Africa: Culture, Controversy, and Change* (Eds. B. Shell-Duncan and Y. Hernlund). London: Lynne Rienner.

Alexander, Alex E. 1975. *Russian Folklore: An Anthology in English Translation*. Belmont, CA: Nordland.

American Anthropological Association. 1998. *Code of Ethics*.

American Anthropological Association. 2001. El Dorado task force papers. http://www.aaanet.org/edtf/.

American Civil Liberties Union. 2005. Briefing Paper No. 6: "English Only." http://www.lectlaw.com/files/con09.htm.

American Indian Report. 1999. "No Dice for Problem Gamblers: Tribes Team Up to Tackle Compulsive Gambling." 2:20–21.

Amott, Teresa, and Julie Matthaei. 1991. *Race, Gender and Work: A Multicultural Economic History of Women in the United States*. Boston: South End Press.

Anderson, Richard. 1990. *Calliope's Sisters: A Comparative Study of Philosophies of Art*. Upper Saddle River, NJ: Prentice Hall.

Anderson, Richard. 2000. *American Muse: Anthropological Excursions into Art and Aesthetics*. Upper Saddle River, NJ: Prentice Hall.

Andrews, George. 1992. "Racial Inequality in Brazil and the United States: A Statistical Comparison." *Journal of Social History* 26 (2):22–63.

Appel, Rene, and Pieter Muysken. 1987. *Language Contact and Bilingualism*. London: Edward Arnold.

Arias, Oscar. 1997. "Esquipulas II: The Management of a Regional Crisis." In *Cultural Variation in Conflict Resolution: Alternatives to Violence* (Eds. D. Fry and K. Bjorkqvist). Mahwah, NJ: Lawrence Erlbaum.

Aries, Phillippe. 1960. *Centuries of Childhood*. Harmondsworth: Penguin.

Armstrong, Sue. 1991. "Female Circumcision: Fighting a Cruel Tradition." *New Scientist* 2:42–47.

Arnold, Fred, and Liu Zhaoxiang. 1986. "Sex Preference, Fertility, and Family Planning in China." *Population and Development Review* 12:221–246.

Bacheller, John. 1997. *A Native American Source Book*. New York: McGraw-Hill.

Bailey, Garrick, and Roberta Bailey. 1986. *A History of the Navajos: The Reservation Years*. Santa Fe, NM: School of American Research Press.

Baker, Lee. 1998. *From Savage to Negro: Anthropology and the Construction of Race, 1896–1954*. Berkeley: University of California Press.

Bakhtin, Mikhail. 1981. *The Dialogic Imagination, Four Essays*. Austin: University of Texas Press.

Balick, M., and P. Cox. 1996. *Plants, People, and Culture: The Science of Ethnobotany*. New York: Scientific American Library.

Ballard, Chris. 2002. "The Denial of Traditional Landrights in West Papua." *Cultural Survival Quarterly* 26 (3):40–43.

Barbeau, Marius. 1975. "The Career of a Medicine Man." In *Teachings from the American Earth* (Eds. D. Tedlock and B. Tedlock). New York: Liveright, pp. 3–12.

Barlett, Peggy. 1989. "Industrial Agriculture." In *Economic Anthropology* (Ed. S. Plattner). Palo Alto, CA: Stanford University Press, pp. 253–291.

Baron, Dennis. 1990. *The English-Only Question*. New Haven, CT: Yale University Press.

Barreda, Andres, and Ana Cecena. 1998. "Chiapas and the Global Restructuring of Capital." In *Zapatista! Reinventing Revolution in Mexico* (Eds. John Holloway and Eloina Pelaez). London: Pluto Press, pp. 39–63.

Barth, Frederick. 1964. *Nomads of South Persia*. Oslo: Universitetsforlaget.

Basso, Keith. 1970. *The Cibecue Apache*. New York: Holt, Rinehart & Winston.

Basso, Keith. 1979. *Portraits of "The Whiteman."* New York: Cambridge University Press.

Basso, Keith. 1989. "Southwest: Apache." In *Witchcraft and Sorcery of the American Native Peoples* (Ed. D. Walker). Moscow: University of Idaho Press, pp. 167–190.

Basso, Keith. 1990. *Western Apache Language and Culture: Essays in Linguistic Anthropology*. Tucson: University of Arizona Press.

Baugh, John. 1984. *Black Street Speech*. Austin: University of Texas Press.

Behzadi, K. G. 1994. "Interpersonal Conflict and Emotions in an Iranian Cultural Practice: Qahr and Ashti." *Journal of Culture, Medicine, and Psychiatry* 18:321–359.

Bender, Barbara. 1978. "Gatherer-Hunter to Farmer: A Social Perspective." *World Archeology* 10:361–392.

Benedict, Ruth. 1934. *Patterns of Culture*. Boston: Houghton Mifflin.

Benedict, Ruth. 1946. *The Chrysanthemum and the Sword*. Boston: Houghton Mifflin.

Beneria, Lourdes, and Gita Sen. 1986. "Accumulation, Reproduction, and Women's Role in Economic Development: Boserup Revisited." In *Women's Work: Development and the Division of Labor by Gender* (Eds. E. Leacock and H. Safa). Cambridge, MA: Bergin & Garvey, 141–157.

Berch, Bettina. 1982. *The Endless Day: The Political Economy of Women and Work*. New York: Harcourt Brace.

Berlitz, Charles. 1982. *Native Tongues*. New York: Grosset & Dunlap.

Berreman, Gerald. 1989. *Social Inequality: Comparative and Developmental Approaches*. New York: Academic Press.

Beveridge, Sydney. 2003. "Human Rights Commission Condemns Mistreatment of Ogoni." *Cultural Survival Quarterly* 26 (3):9.

Bieuyck, Daniel, and Kahombo Mateene. 1970. *Anthologie de la Litterature Orale Nyanga*. Brussels: Academie Royale des Science d'Outre-Mer.

Binford, Lewis. 1971. "Post-Pleistocene Adaptations." In *Prehistoric Agriculture* (Ed. S. Struever). Garden City, NY: Natural History Press.

Bitterli, Urs. 1989. *Cultures in Conflict*. Stanford, CA: Stanford University Press.

Blackman, Margaret. 1982. *During My Time: Florence Edenshaw Davidson, a Haida Woman*. Seattle: University of Washington Press.

Blackman, Margaret. 1989. *Sadie Brower Neakok: An Inupiaq Woman*. Seattle: University of Washington Press.

Boas, Franz. 1896. "The Limitations of the Comparative Method of Anthropology." In *Science* 4 (103).

Boas, Franz. 1897. *The Social Organization and the Secret Societies of the Kwakiutl Indians*. Report of the U.S. National Museum of 1895. Washington, DC, pp. 311–738.

Boas, Franz. 1966. *Kwakiutl Ethnography* (Ed. H. Codere). Chicago: University of Chicago Press.

Boddy, Janice. 2001. "Spirit Possession and Gender Complementarity: Zar in Rural Northern Sudan." In *Gender in Cross-Cultural Perspective*, 3rd ed. (Eds. C. Brettell and C. Sargent). Upper Saddle River, NJ: Prentice Hall, pp. 397–408.

Bodenhorn, Barbara. 1988. "Whales, Souls, Children, and Other Things That Are 'Good to Share': Core Metaphors in a Contemporary Whaling Society." *Cambridge Anthropology* 13 (1):1–19.

Bodenhorn, Barbara. 1993. "Gendered Spaces, Public Places: Public and Private Revisited on the North Slope of Alaska." In *Landscape: Politics and Perspectives* (Ed. B. Bender). Providence, RI: Berg, pp. 169–203.

Bodley, John (Ed.). 1988. *Tribal Peoples and Development Issues: A Global Overview*. Mountain View, CA: Mayfield.

Bodley, John. 1999. *Victims of Progress*, 4th ed. Mountain View, CA: Mayfield.

Bohannan, Laura. 1966. "Shakespeare in the Bush." *Natural History* 75:28–33.

Bones, Jah. 1986. "Language of the Rastafaris." In *Language & the Black Experience* (Eds. D. Sutcliffe and A. Wong). London: Blackwell.

Bonvillain, Nancy. 1978. "Linguistic Change in Akwesasne Mohawk: French and English Influences." *International Journal of American Linguistics* 46:31–39.

Bonvillain, Nancy. 1980. "Iroquoian Women." In *Studies on Iroquoian Culture* (Ed. N. Bonvillain). *Man in the Northeast*. Occasional Publications in Northeastern Anthropology No. 6, pp. 47–58.

Bonvillain, Nancy. 1986. "The Iroquois and the Jesuits: Strategies of Influence and Resistance." *American Indian Culture and Research Journal* 10:29–42.

Bonvillain, Nancy. 2001. *Native Nations: Cultures and Histories of Native North America*. Upper Saddle River, NJ: Prentice Hall.

Bordo, Susan. 2004. *Unbearable Weight: Feminism, Western Culture, and the Body*, rev. ed. Berkeley: University of California Press.

Borg, Marcus. 1994. *Jesus in Contemporary Scholarship*. Valley Forge, PA: Trinity Press International.

Bornstein, Marc, et al. 1998. "A Cross-National Study of Self-Evaluations and Attributions in Parenting: Argentina, Belgium, France, Israel, Italy, Japan, and the United States." *Developmental Psychology* 3 (2):662–676.

Bose, Christine. 1987. "Dual Spheres." In *Analyzing Gender* (Eds. B. Hess and M. Ferree). Newbury Park, CA: Sage, pp. 267–285.

Boserup, Ester. 1970. *Women's Role in Economic Development*. London: Allen & Unwin.

Bourdieu, Pierre. 1991. *Language and Symbolic Power*. Cambridge, MA: Harvard University Press.

Bowers, Alfred. 1992. *Hidatsa Social and Ceremonial Organization*. Lincoln: University of Nebraska Press.

Brasser, T. J. 1978. "Early Indian-European Contacts." In *Northeast* (Ed. B. Trigger), Vol. 15, *Handbook of North American Indians*. Washington, DC: Smithsonian Institution Press, pp. 78–88.

Bray, Tamara. 1966. "Repatriation, Power Relations, and the Politics of the Past." *Antiquity* 70 (268):440–443.

Brazelton, T. B. 1990. *Touch: The Foundation of Experience*. Madison, WI: International Universities Press.

Brewer, Terri. 2000. "Touching the Past, Teaching Ways Forward: The American Indian Powwow." In *Indigenous Religions: A Companion* (Ed. Graham Harvey). New York: Cassell, pp. 255–268.

Briggs, Jean. 1982. "Eskimo Women: Makers of Men." In *Many Sisters* (Ed. C. Matthiason). New York: Free Press, pp. 261–304.

Broadwell, George. 1995. "1990 Census Figures for Speakers of American Indian Languages." *Language in Society* 61:145–149.

Brooke, James. 2003. "Dowry Too High, Lose Bride and Go to Jail." *New York Times*, February 3.

Brown, Judith. 1975. "Economic Organization and the Position of Women among the Iroquois." In *Toward an Anthropology of Women* (Ed. R. Rieter). New York: Monthly Review Press, pp. 235–251.

Brown, Penelope, and Stephen Levinson. 1987. *Politeness: Some Universals in Language Usage*. New York: Cambridge University Press.

Buell, Raymond. 1928. *The Native Problem in Africa*. 2 vols. New York: Macmillan.

Bunzel, Ruth V. 1932. *Introduction to Zuni Ceremonialism*. Bureau of American Ethnology, Annual Report No. 47. Washington, DC, pp. 467–544.

Burger, Richard L. 1992a. *Chavin and the Origins of Andean Civilization*. London: Thames & Hudson.

Burger, Richard L. 1992b. "The Sacred Center of Chavín de Huantar." In *The Ancient Americans, Art from Sacred Landscapes* (Ed. Richard F. Townsend). Art Institute of Chicago/Prestel Verlag, Munich.

Callender, Charles, and Lee Kochems. 1983. "The North American Berdache." *Current Anthropology* 24:443–470.

Carneiro, Robert. 1970. "A Theory of the Origin of the State." *Science*, August, pp. 733–738.

Carrasco, David. 1998. *Daily Life of the Aztecs: People of the Sun and Earth*. Westport, CT: Greenwood Press.

Castillo, Edward. 1978. "The Impact of Euro-American Exploration and Settlement." In *California* (Ed. R. Heizer), Vol. 8, *Handbook of North American Indians*. Washington, DC: Smithsonian Institution Press, pp. 99–127.

Castro, A. 2004. "Anthropologists as Advocates: Power, Suffering and AIDS." *Anthropology News*, October, pp. 9, 11.

Center for Strategic and International Study. 2003. HIV/AIDS Task Force. "Botswana's Strategy to Combat HIV/AIDS, Empowering Women and People Living with HIV/AIDS," November 12.

Chagnon, Napoleon. 1973. "The Culture-Ecology of Shifting Cultivation among the Yanomamo Indians." In *Peoples and Cultures of Native South America* (Ed. D. Gross). New York: Doubleday/Natural History Press, pp. 126–142.

Chagnon, Napoleon. 1997. *Yanomamo: The Fierce People*, 5th ed. New York: Holt, Rinehart & Winston.

Champlain, Samuel de. 1907. *Voyages of Samuel de Champlain, 1604–1618* (Ed. W. L. Grant). New York: Scribner's.

Chance, Norman. 1990. *The Inupiat and Arctic Alaska: An Ethnography of Development*. New York: Holt, Rinehart & Winston.

Chanock, Martin. 1985. *Law, Custom, and Social Order: The Colonial Experience in Malawi and Zambia*. Cambridge: Cambridge University Press.

Chernoff, J. M. 1981. *Aesthetics and Social Action in African Musical Idioms*. Chicago: University of Chicago Press.

Cheshire, Jenny. 1982. "Linguistic Variation and Social Function." In *Sociolinguistic Variation in Speech Communities* (Ed. S. Romaine). London: Edward Arnold, pp. 153–166.

Chitnis, Suma. 1988. "Feminism: Indian Ethos and Indian Convictions." In *Women in Indian Society* (Ed. R. Ghadially). Newbury Park, CA: Sage, pp. 81–95.

Chomsky, Noam. 1968. *Language and Mind*. New York: Harcourt Brace Jovanovich.

Clancy, Patricia. 1986. "The Acquisition of Communicative Style in Japanese." In *Language Socialization across Cultures* (Eds. B. Schieffelin and E. Ochs). Cambridge: Cambridge University Press, pp. 213–250.

Clark, Ella. 1953. *Indian Legends of the Pacific Northwest*. Berkeley: University of California Press.

Clifford, James, and George Marcus (Eds.). 1986. *Writing Culture: The Poetics and Politics of Ethnography*. Berkeley: University of California Press.

Codere, Helen. 1950. *Fighting with Property: A Study of Kwakiutl Potlatching and Warfare, 1872–1930*. Monographs of the American Ethnological Society, No. 18. New York.

Colchester, Marcus. 2004. "Conservation Policy and Indigenous People." *Cultural Survival Quarterly* 28 (1):17–22.

Columbia Encyclopedia. 2003. New York: Columbia University Press.

Cook, Sherburne. 1976. *The Conflict between the California Indian and White Civilization.* Berkeley: University of California Press.

Cook, Sherburne. 1978. "Historical Demography." In *California* (Ed. R. Heizer), Vol. 8, *Handbook of North American Indians.* Washington, DC: Smithsonian Institution Press, pp. 91–98.

Costello, Cynthia, et al. 1998. *The American Woman 1999–2000: A Century of Change—What's Next?* New York: Norton.

Coulmas, Florian. 1981. "Poison to Your Soul: Thanks and Apologies Contrastively Viewed." In *Conversational Routine* (Ed. F. Coulmas). The Hague: Mouton, pp. 69–91.

Cowley, Geoffrey, and Mary Talbot. 2001. "The Great Disease Migration." In *Anthropology: Contemporary Perspectives,* 8th ed. (Ed. P. Whitten). Needham Heights, MA: Allyn & Bacon, pp. 280–283.

Croll, Elizabeth. 1982. "The Sexual Division of Labor in Rural China." In *Women and Development: The Sexual Division of Labor in Rural Societies* (Ed. L. Beneria). New York: Praeger, pp. 223–274.

Croll, Elizabeth. 1986. "Rural Production and Reproduction: Socialist Development Experiences." In *Women's Work: Development and the Division of Labor by Gender* (Eds. E. Leacock and H. Safa). Cambridge, MA: Bergin & Garvey, pp. 224–252.

Crosby, Alfred. 1972. *The Columbian Exchange: Biological and Cultural Consequences of 1492.* Westport, CT: Greenwood.

Crossan, John. 1994. *Jesus: A Revolutionary Biography.* New York: HarperCollins.

Cultural Survival Quarterly. 2002. "The Fight for Tasmania." 26 (2):13.

Cushing, Frank H. 1979. *Zuni: The Selected Writings of Frank Hamilton Cushing.* Lincoln: University of Nebraska Press.

D'Anglure, Bernard Saladin. 1984. "Inuit of Quebec." In *Arctic,* Vol. 5, *Handbook of North American Indians.* Washington, DC: - Smithsonian Institution Press, pp. 476–507.

Dannaeuser, Norbert. 1989. "Marketing in Developing Urban Areas." In *Economic Anthropology* (Ed. S. Plattner). Palo Alto, CA: Stanford University Press, pp. 222–252.

Deloria, Vine, Jr. 1995. *Red Earth, White Lies: Native Americans and the Myth of Scientific Fact.* Golden, CO: Fulcrum.

DeMarco, Roland. 1943. *The Italianization of African Natives: Government Native Education in the Italian Colonies 1890–1937.* Teachers College Contributions to Education No. 880. New York: Columbia University.

Demos, John (Ed.). 1972. *Remarkable Providences 1600–1760.* New York: George Braziller.

Demos, John. 1994. *The Unredeemed Captive: A Family Story from Early America.* New York: Vintage.

Denny, J. P. 1982. "Semantics of the Inuktitut (Eskimo) Spatial Deictics." *International Journal of American Linguistics* 48:359–384.

DeVos, George, and Hiroshi Wagatsuma. 1995. "Cultural Identity and Minority Status in Japan." In *Ethnic Identity: Creation, Conflict, and Accommodation,* 3rd ed. (Eds. L. Romanucci-Ross and G. DeVos). London: Sage, pp. 264–297.

de Waal, Frans. 2000. "The First Kiss: Foundations of Conflict Resolution Research in Animals." In *Natural Conflict Resolution* (Eds. F. Aureli and F. deWaal). Berkeley: University of California Press, pp. 15–20.

Diamond, Jared. 1995. "The Worst Mistake in the History of the Human Race." In *Peoples of the Past and Present* (Ed. J.-L. Chodkiewicz). New York: Harcourt Brace, pp. 114–117.

Diamond, Norma. 1975. "Collectivization, Kinship and the Status of Women in Rural China." In *Toward an Anthropology of Women* (Ed. R. Reiter). New York: Monthly Review Press, pp. 372–395.

Dirks, Nicholas. 2001. *Castes in Mind: Colonialism and the Making of Modern India.* Princeton, NJ: Princeton University Press.

Do, Anh. 2004. "Art Brings Creature Comforts to Villages." http://kicon.com/anhdo/artbrings.html.

Dorson, Richard. 1975. *Folktales Told around the World.* Chicago: University of Chicago Press.

Dozier, Edward. 1970. *The Pueblo Indians of North America.* New York: Holt, Rinehart & Winston.

Draper, Patricia. 1975. "!Kung Women: Contrasts in Sexual Egalitarianism in Foraging and Sedentary Contexts." In *Toward an Anthropology of Women* (Ed. R. Reiter). New York: Monthly Review Press, pp. 77–109.

DuBois, W. E. B. 1903/1995. *The Souls of Black Folk.* New York: Signet Classics.

Dugger, C. W. 1996. "U.S. Grants Asylum to Woman Fleeing Genital Mutilation Rite." *New York Times,* June 14.

Echohawk, Walter, Jr., and Roger C. Echohawk. 1994. *Battlefields and Burial Grounds: The Indian Struggle to Protect Ancestral Graves in the United States.* Minneapolis, MN: Lerner.

Edelstein, Stuart J. 1986. *The Sickled Cell: From Myth to Molecules.* Cambridge, MA: Harvard University Press.

Eggan, Fred. 1966. *The American Indian: Perspectives for the Study of Social Change.* Chicago: Aldine.

Eiselen, W. M. 1934. "Christianity and the Religious Life of the Bantu." In *Western Civilization and the Natives of South Africa* (Ed. I. Schapera). London: Rutledge, pp. 65–82.

Elisabetsky, Elaine. 1996. "Community Ethnobotany: Setting Foundations for an Informed Decision on Training Rain Forest Resources." In *Medicinal Resources of the Tropical Forest: Biodiversity and Its Importance to Human Health* (Ed. M. Balick et al.). New York: Columbia University Press, pp. 402–408.

Ember, Carol. 1981. "A Cross-Cultural Perspective on Sex Differences." In *Handbook of Cross-Cultural Human Development* (Eds. Ruth H. Munroe, Robert L. Munroe, and Beatrice B. Whiting). New York: Garland, pp. 531–580.

Ember, Melvin, and Carol Ember. 1971. "The Conditions Favoring Matrilocal vs. Patrilocal Residence." *American Anthropologist* 73:571–594.

Ember, Melvin, and Carol Ember. 1996. *Comparing Cultures: What Have We Learned from Cross Cultural Research.* Vol. 2, No. 2. Washington, DC: Council for General Anthropology, General Anthropology Division, pp. 1–5.

Ervin-Tripp, S. M., M. C. O'Connor, and J. Rosenberg. 1984. "Language and Power in the Family." In *Language and Power* (Eds. M. Schulz and C. Kramerae). Belmont, CA: Sage, pp. 116–135.

Esposito, Anita. 1979. "Sex Differences in Children's Conversation." *Language and Speech* 22 (3):213–220.

Etienne, Mona, and Eleanor Leacock (Eds.). 1980. *Women and Colonization.* New York: Praeger.

Evans-Pritchard, E. E. 1940. *The Nuer.* Oxford: Oxford University Press.

Evans-Pritchard, E. E. 1955. *Kinship and Marriage among the Nuer.* Oxford: Clarendon.

Fagan, Brian M. 1984. *The Aztecs.* New York: Freeman.

Farnell, Brenda. 1995. *Movement and Gesture.* In *Encyclopedia of Cultural Anthropology* (Eds. D. Levinson and M. Ember). New Haven, CT: Human Relations Area Files.

Fears, Darryl. 2003. "Latinos or Hispanics? A Debate about Identity." *Washington Post,* August 25, p. A1.

Fenton, William (Ed.). 1968. *The Constitution of the Five Nations.* Syracuse, NY: Syracuse University Press.

Ferguson, R. Brian. 1992. "A Savage Encounter: Western Contact and the Yanomami War Complex." In *War in the Tribal Zone: Expanding States and Indigenous Warfare* (Eds. R. Ferguson and N. Whitehead). Santa Fe, NM: School of American Research Press, pp. 199–227.

Ferguson, R. Brian, and Neil Whitehead. 1992. "The Violent Edge of Empire." In *War in the Tribal Zone: Expanding States and Indigenous Warfare* (Eds. R. Ferguson and N. Whitehead). Santa Fe, NM: School of American Research Press, pp. 1–30.

Ferguson, T. J. 1996. "Native Americans and the Practice of Archaeology." In *Annual Review of Anthropology* 25:63–79.

Fernandez-Kelly, Maria. 1983. "Mexican Border Industrialization, Female Labor Force Participation, and Migration." In *Women, Men, and the International Division of Labor* (Eds. J. Nash and M. Fernandez-Kelly). Albany: State University of New York Press, pp. 205–223.

Fernandez-Kelly, Maria. 1997. "Maquiladoras: The View from the Inside." In *Gender in*

Cross-Cultural Perspective, 2nd ed. (Eds. C. Bretell and C. Sargent). Upper Saddle River, NJ: Prentice Hall, pp. 525–537.

Fiorenza, Elisabeth. 1983 In Memory of Her: A Feminist Theological Reconstruction of Christian Origins. New York: Crossroad Press.

Firth, Raymond. 1970. Rank and Religion in Tikopia. London: Allen & Unwin.

Fishman, Joshua. 1981. "Language Policy: Past, Present and Future." In Language in the USA (Eds. C. Ferguson and S. Heath). New York: Cambridge University Press, pp. 516–526.

Flannery, Kent. 1973. "The Origins of Agriculture." Annual Review of Anthropology, No. 2, 274.

Forbes, Jack. 1969. Native Americans of California and Nevada. Healdsburg, CA: Naturegraph Publishers.

Forbes, Jack. 1990. "Undercounting Native Americans: The 1980 Census and the Manipulation of Racial Identity in the United States." Wicazo Sa Review 6:2–26.

Forero, Juan. 2003. "Seeking Balance: Growth vs. Culture in the Amazon." New York Times, December 10.

Foster, George, and Barbara Anderson. 1978. Medical Anthropology. New York: Wiley.

Foucault, Michel. 1976. Madness and Civilization: A History of Insanity in the Age of Reason. New York: Pantheon.

Foulks, Edward. 1972. "The Arctic Hysterias of the North Alaskan Eskimo." Anthropological Studies No. 10. Washington, DC: American Anthropological Association.

Fox, Mary, and Sharlene Hesse-Biber. 1984. Women at Work. Mountain View, CA: Mayfield.

Fox, Robin. 1984. Kinship and Marriage: An Anthropological Perspective. New York: Cambridge University Press.

Fratkin, Elliot, and Tiffany Wu. 1997. "Maasai and Barabaig Herders Struggle for Landrights in Kenya and Tanzania." Cultural Survival Quarterly 21 (3).

Freidenberg, Judith. 2000. Growing Old in El Barrio. New York: New York University Press.

French, Laurence. 2003. Native American Justice. Chicago: Burnham.

Fried, Morton. 1967. The Evolution of Political Society. New York: Random House.

Friedl, Ernestine. 1975. Women and Men. New York: Holt, Rinehart & Winston.

Friedman, Jonathan. 1999. "Class Formation, Hybridity and Ethnification in Declining Global Hegemonies." In Globalisation and the Asia-Pacific (Eds. Kris Olds et al.). London: Routledge, pp. 183–201.

Frisancho, A. R. 1981. "Principles and Definitions in the Study of Human Adaptation." In Human Adaptation: A Functional Interpretation. Ann Arbor: University of Michigan Press, pp. 1–10.

Fry, Douglas. 2000. "Conflict Management in Cross-Cultural Perspective." In Natural Conflict Resolution (Eds. F. Aureli and F. de-Waal). Berkeley: University of California Press, pp. 334–351.

Fuentes, Annette and Barbara Ehrenreich. 1983. "Women in the Global Factory." Cambridge MA: South End Press.

Gailey, Christine. 1980. "Putting Down Sisters and Wives: Tongan Woman and Colonization." In Women and Colonization (Eds. M. Etienne and E. Leacock). New York: Praeger, pp. 294–322.

Gailey, Christine. 1987a. "Evolutionary Perspective on Gender Hierarchy." In Analyzing Gender (Eds. B. Hess and M. Ferree). Newbury Park, CA: Sage, pp. 32–67.

Gailey, Christine. 1987b. Kinship to Kingship: Gender Hierarchy and State Formation in the Tongan Islands. Austin: University of Texas Press.

Galliland, Mary Kay. 1995. "Nationalism and Ethnogenesis in the Former Yugoslavia." In Ethnic Identity: Creation, Conflict, and Accommodation, 3rd ed.(Eds. L. Romanucci-Ross and G. DeVos). London: Sage, pp. 197–221.

Geertz, Clifford. 1973. The Interpretation of Cultures. New York: Basic Books.

Geismar, Joan H. 1982. The Archaeology of Social Disintegration in Skunk Hollow: A 19th Century Rural Black Community. New York: Academic Press.

Ghadially, Rehana, and Pramod Kumar. 1988. "Bride Burning: The Psycho-Social Dynamics of Dowry Deaths." In Women in Indian Society (Ed. R. Ghadially). Newbury Park, CA: Sage, pp. 167–177.

Ghazi, P. 2004. "Unearthing Controversy at the Ok Tedi Mine." In World Resources 2002–2004: Decision for the Earth. World Resources Institute. http://www.ionteraction.org/library/. Accessed November 2, 2004.

Gibbs, James. 1965. "The Kpelle of Liberia." In Peoples of Africa (Ed. J. Gibbs). New York: Holt, Reinhart & Winston, pp. 197–240.

Gill, Sam. 1982. Native American Religions. Belmont, CA: Wadsworth.

Gimbutas, Marija. 1982. Goddesses and Gods of Old Europe: 6500–3500 BC. Berkeley: University of California Press.

Gleason, Jean. 1987. "Sex Differences in Parent-Child Interaction." In Language, Gender and Sex in Comparative Perspective (Eds. Susan Philips et al.). New York: Cambridge University Press, pp. 189–199.

Glick, J. 1975. "Cognitive Development in Cross-Cultural Perspective." In Review of Child Development Research (Ed. F. D. Horowitz). Vol. 4, pp. 595–654. Chicago: University of Chicago Press.

Goffman, Erving. 1971. Relations in Public. New York: Basic Books.

Goldfield, David, et al. 2004. The American Journey, 3rd ed. Upper Saddle River, NJ: Prentice Hall.

Goodale, Jane. 1971. Tiwi Wives: A Study of the Women of Melville Island, North Australia. Seattle: University of Washington Press.

Goodman, Felicitas. 1990. Where the Spirits Ride the Wind: Trance Journeys and Other Ecstatic Experiences. Bloomington: Indiana University Press.

Gordon, Linda. 1982. Woman's Body, Woman's Right: A Social History of Birth Control in America. New York: Grossman, 1976.

Gorman, Peter. 1991. "A People at Risk: The Yanomami of Brazil." Culture-Crossroads, November, pp. 670–681.

Gough, Kathleen. 1968. "Anthropology, Child of Imperialism." In Monthly Review, April.

Gough, Kathleen. 1971. "Nuer Kinship: A Re-Examination." In The Translation of Culture (Ed. T. Beidelman). London: Tavistock, pp. 79–122.

Gough, Kathleen. 1975. "The Origin of the Family." In Toward an Anthropology of Women (Ed. R. Reiter). New York: Monthly Review Press, pp. 51–76.

Graburn, Nelson. 1969. Eskimos without Igloos: Social and Economic Development in Sugluk. Boston: Little, Brown.

Graburn, Nelson (Ed.). 1976. Ethnic and Tourist Arts: Cultural Expressions from the Fourth World. Berkeley: University of California Press.

Gray, Andrew. 1990. "Indigenous Peoples and the Marketing of the Rainforest." The Ecologist 20 (6):223.

Grosjean, Francois. 1982. Life with Two Languages. Cambridge, MA: Harvard University Press.

Grossman, A. 2000. "Napoleon Chagnon's Waterloo: Anthropology on Trial." Dartmouth Review, October 30.

Gruenbaum, Ellen. 1993. "The Movement against Clitoridectomy and Infibulation in Sudan: Public Health Policy and the Women's Movement." In Gender in Cross-Cultural Perspective (Eds. C. Brettell and C. Sargent). Upper Saddle River, NJ: Prentice Hall, pp. 411–422.

Guibault, J., G. Averill, E. Benoit, and G. Rabess. 1993. Zouk: World Music in the West Indies. Chicago: University of Chicago Press.

Guillaume, Alfred. 1986. Islam. New York: Viking/Penguin.

Hafner, Katie. 1999. "Coming of Age in Palo Alto." New York Times, June 10.

Haile, Berard. 1954. "Property Concepts of the Navajo Indians." Anthropological Series No. 17. Washington, DC: Catholic University of America.

Hall, Judith. 1984. Non-Verbal Sex Differences: Communication, Accuracy and Expressive Style. Baltimore: Johns Hopkins University Press.

Halle, Morris, and G. N. Clements. 1983. Problem Book in Phonology. Cambridge, MA: MIT Press.

Halperin, Rhoda. 1990. The Livelihood of Kin: Making Ends Meet (The Kentucky Way). Austin: University of Texas Press.

Hardman, Charlotte. 2000. "Rites of Passage among the Lohorung Rai of East Nepal." In Indigenous Religions (Ed. G. Harvey). London: Cassell, pp. 204–218.

Hariot, Thomas. 1972 (1590). A Briefe and True Report of the New Found Land of Virginia (Ed. P. Hulton). New York: Dover.

Harris, Grace. 1986. *Casting Out Anger: Religion among the Taita of Kenya*. Prospect Heights, IL: Waveland.

Harris, Marvin. 1970. "Referential Ambiguity in the Calculus of Brazilian Racial Identity." *Southwestern Anthropology* 26:1–14.

Harris, Marvin. 1974. *Cows, Pigs, Wars and Witches: The Riddles of Culture*. New York: Random House/Vintage.

Harris, Marvin. 1979. *Cultural Materialism: The Struggle for a Science of Culture*. New York: Random House.

Hart, C. W. M., and Arnold Pilling. 1960. *The Tiwi of Northern Australia*. New York: Holt, Rinehart & Winston.

Hartmann, Heidi. 1979. "Capitalism, Patriarchy, and Job Segregation by Sex." In *Capitalist Patriarchy and the Case for Socialist Feminism* (Ed. Z. Eisenstein). New York: Monthly Review Press, pp. 206–247.

Harvey, Sioux. 1996. "Two Models to Sovereignty: A Comparative History of the Mashantucket Pequot Tribal Nation and the Navajo Nation." *American Indian Culture and Research Journal* 20:147–194.

Harvey, Youngsook Kim. 1979. *Six Korean Women: The Socialization of Shamans*. St. Paul, MN: West.

Hassrick, Royal. 1964. *The Sioux, Life and Customs of a Warrior Society*. Norman: University of Oklahoma Press.

Hays, Sharon. 1996. *The Cultural Contradictions of Motherhood*. New Haven, CT: Yale University Press.

Heath, Shirley. 1977. "Language and Politics in the United States." In *Linguistics and Anthropology* (Ed. M. Saville-Troike). Georgetown University Round Table on Languages and Linguistics. Washington, DC: Georgetown University Press, pp. 267–296.

Hefner, Robert. 2001. "Multiculturalism and Citizenship in Malaysia, Singapore and Indonesia." In *Politics of Multiculturalism: Pluralism and Citizenship in Malaysia, Singapore and Indonesia* (Ed. R. Hefner). Honolulu: University of Hawaii Press, pp. 1–58.

Heine, S. J., et al. 1999. "Is There a Universal Need for Positive Self-Regard?" *Psychological Review* 106 (4):766–794.

Heizer, Robert, and Alan Almquist. 1971. *The Other Californians: Prejudice and Discrimination under Spain, Mexico and the United States to 1920*. Berkeley: University of California Press.

Henley, Nancy. 1977. *Body Politics: Power, Sex and Non-Verbal Communication*. Englewood Cliffs, NJ: Prentice Hall.

Herman, Edward, and Noam Chomsky. 1988. *Manufacturing Consent: The Political Economy of the Mass Media*. New York: Pantheon.

Hilder, B. 1980. *The Voyage of Torres*. St. Lucia: University of Queensland Press.

Hill, A. 2002. Tryptamine Based Entheogens of South America. http://students. whitman.edu/~hillap/tryptamine% 20based%20Entheogens.htm.

Hill, W. W. 1948. "Navajo Trading and Trading Ritual: A Study of Cultural Dynamics." *Southwestern Journal of Anthropology* 4 (4):371–396.

HimRights, International Himalayan Human Rights Monitors (INHURED). www.inhured.org/download/HimRights brochure.pdf. Accessed November 2, 2004.

Hitchcock, Robert, and Megan Biesele. 2002. "Controlling Their Destiny: Ju/'Hoansi of Nyae Nyae." *Cultural Survival Quarterly* 26 (1):13–15.

Hoebel, E. Adamson. 1978. *The Cheyennes: Indians of the Great Plains*. New York: Holt, Rinehart & Winston.

Hollan, Douglas. 1997. "Conflict Avoidance and Resolution among the Toraja of South Sulawesi, Indonesia." In *Cultural Variation in Conflict Resolution: Alternatives to Violence* (Eds. D. Fry and K. Bjorkqvist). Mahwah, NJ: Lawrence Erlbaum, pp. 59–68.

Holmes, Janet. 1990. "Apologies in New Zealand English." *Language in Society* 19:155–200.

Holtzman, J. 2000. *Nuer Journeys, Nuer Lives*. Boston: Allyn & Bacon.

"Honoring Native Languages, Defeating the Shame." 2000. *Tribal College Journal of American Indian Higher Education*. Spring.

Howells, William. 2001. "Requiem for a Lost People." In *Anthropology: Contemporary Perspectives*, 8th ed. (Ed. P. Whitten). Needham Heights, MA: Allyn & Bacon, pp. 268–274.

Hua, Cai. 2001. *A Society without Fathers or Husbands: The Na of China*. Cambridge, MA: Zone Books/MIT Press.

Hulbert, Ann. 2003. *Raising America: Experts, Parents, and a Century of Advice about Children*. New York: Knopf.

Hume, Lynne. 2000. "The Dreaming in Contemporary Aboriginal Australia." In *Indigenous Religion* (Ed. G. Harvey). London: Cassell, pp. 125–138.

Hursey, Charlotte. 2001. Watching the Anthropologists: Reflections on Ethnography as Practice within NGOs. INTRAC (International NGO Training and Research Centre). http://www.intrac.org/. Accessed November 2, 2004.

Hymes, Dell. 1974. *Foundations in Socio-Linguistics: An Ethnographic Approach*. Philadelphia: University of Pennsylvania Press.

Indian Time. 2003. "Minnesota's Indian Bands Bringing Back Banishment." December.

Itoh, Shinji. 1980. "Physiology of Circumpolar People." In *The Human Biology of Circumpolar Populations* (Ed. F. A. Milan). Cambridge: Cambridge University Press.

Iwu, Maurice. 1996. "Resource Utilization and Conservation of Biodiversity in Africa." In *Medicinal Resources of the Tropical Forest: Biodiversity and Its Importance to Human Health* (Eds. M. Balick et al.). New York: Columbia University Press, pp. 233–250.

Jablow, Joseph. 1950. *The Cheyenne in Plains Indian Trade Relations 1795–1840*. Monographs of the American Ethnological Society No. 19. Seattle: University of Washington Press.

Jackson, Donald (Ed.). 1964. *Black Hawk: An Autobiography*. Urbana: University of Illinois Press.

Jackson, Robert, and Edward Castillo. 1995. *Indians, Franciscans, and Spanish Colonization: Impact of the Mission System on California Indians*. Albuquerque: University of New Mexico Press.

Jannequin, C. 1643. *Voyage de Lybie au Royaume de Senegal*. Paris.

Jefferson, Thomas. 1803. Letter to Meriwether Lewis. http://www.mt.net/!rojomo/ landc.htm.

Jelin, Elizabeth. 1977. "Migration and Labor Force Participation of Latin American Women: The Domestic Servants in the City." *Signs: Journal of Women in Culture and Society* 3 (1):129–141.

Johnson, Allen. 1978. "In Search of the Affluent Society." *Human Nature*, September, pp. 50–59.

Johnson, Gregory. 1973. *Local Exchange and Early State Development in Southwestern Iran*. Anthropological Papers No. 51. Ann Arbor: University of Michigan, Museum of Anthropology.

Jolly, Alison. 1985. *The Evolution of Primate Behavior*, 2nd ed. New York: Macmillan.

Jones, Barbara. 1998. "Infighting in San Francisco: Anthropology in Family Court, Or: A Study in Cultural Misunderstanding." *High Plains Applied Anthropologist* 18 (1):37–41.

Jorgensen, Joseph. 1998. "Gaming and Recent American Indian Economic Development." *American Indian Culture and Research Journal* 22 (3):157–172.

Kahlenberg, Mary, and Anthony Berlant. 1972. *The Navajo Blanket*. New York: Praeger/Los Angeles County Museum of Art.

Kaisiepo, Viktor. 2004. "We've Gained a Lot." *Cultural Survival Quarterly* 28 (3):19–20.

Katz, Richard. 1982. *Boiling Energy: Community Healing among the Kalahari !Kung*. Cambridge, MA: Harvard University Press.

Kehoe, Alice. 1989. *The Ghost Dance: Ethnohistory and Revitalization*. New York: Holt, Rinehart & Winston.

Kellman, Shelly. 1982. "The Yanomamis: Their Battle for Survival." *Journal of International Affairs* 36:15–42.

Kelly, Raymond. 1976. "Witchcraft and Sexual Relations: An Exploration in the Social and Semantic Implications of the Structure of Belief." In *Man and Woman in the New Guinea Highlands* (Eds. P. Brown and G. Buchdinder). Special Publication No. 8. Washington, DC: American Anthropological Association, pp. 36–53.

Kendall, Laurel. 1984. "Korean Shamanism: Women's Rites and a Chinese Comparison." In *Religion and the Family in East Asia* (Eds. G. DeVos and T. Sofue). Berkeley: University of California Press, pp. 185–200.

Killhefer, Robert. 1995. "Reburying the Past." *Omni* 17:30–36.

Klein, Alan. 1980. "Plains Economic Analysis: The Marxist Complement." In *Anthropology on the Great Plains* (Eds. W. R. Wood and M. Liberty). Lincoln: University of Nebraska Press, pp. 129–140.

Klein, Alan. 1983. "The Political-Economy of Gender: A 19th-Century Plains Indian Case Study." In *Hidden Half: Studies of Plains Indian Women* (Eds. P. Alvers and B. Medicine). Lanham, MD: University Press of America, 143–173.

Kluckhohn, Clyde, and Dorothea Leighton. 1946. *The Navaho.* Cambridge, MA: Harvard University Press.

Knight, R. 2002. Ethnomusicology, http://www.oberlin.edu/faculty/rknight/. Accessed November 18, 2004.

Koller, John. 1982. *The Indian Way.* New York: Macmillan.

Kopytoff, Igor. 1961. "The Suku of Southwestern Congo." In *Peoples of Africa* (Ed. J. Gibbs). New York: Holt, Rinehart & Winston, pp. 441–478.

Koso-Thomas, Olayinka. 1992. *The Circumcision of Women: A Strategy for Eradication.* London: Zed Books.

Kottak, Conrad. 1999. *Assault on Paradise: Social Change in a Brazilian Village*, 3rd ed. New York: McGraw-Hill.

Krauss, Michael. 1992. "The World's Languages in Crisis." *Language* 68:4–10.

Kroeber, Alfred, and Clyde Kluckhohn. 1952. *Culture: A Critical Review of Concepts and Definitions.* New York: Random House.

Kruks, Sonia, and Ben Wisner. 1989. "Ambiguous Transformations: Women, Politics and Production in Mozambique." In *Promissory Notes: Women in the Transition to Socialism* (Eds. S. Kruks et al.). New York: Monthly Review Press, pp. 148–171.

Kumar, Radha. 1995. "From Chipko to Sati: The Contemporary Indian Women's Movement." In *The Challenge of Local Feminisms: Women's Movement in Global Perspective* (Ed. A. Basu). Boulder, CO: Westview.

Labov, William. 1966. *The Social Stratification of English in New York City.* Washington, DC: Center for Applied Linguistics.

Labov, William. 1972a. *Language in the Inner City.* Philadelphia: University of Pennsylvania Press.

Labov, William. 1972b. *Sociolinguistic Patterns.* Philadelphia: University of Pennsylvania Press.

Labov, William. 1982. "Objectivity and Commitment in Linguistic Science: The Case of the Black English Trial in Ann Arbor." *Language in Society* 11:165–201.

Labov, William. 1997. "Some Further Steps in Narrative Analysis." *Journal of Narrative and Life History* 7:395–415.

Labov, William. 2004. "Can Reading Failure Be Reversed? A Linguistic Approach to the Question." In *Literacy among African American Youth* (Eds. V. Gadsden and D. Wagner). Cresskill, NJ: Hampton Press.

Lacey, Mark. 2004. "Genital Cutting Shows Signs of Losing Favor in Africa." *New York Times*, June 8.

Lafitau, Joseph. 1974 (1724).*Customs of the American Indians.* Toronto: Champlain Society.

Lako, George. 1988. "The Impact of Jonglei Scheme on the Economy of the Dinka." In *Tribal Peoples and Development Issues* (Ed. J. Bodley). Mountain View, CA: Mayfield, pp. 137–150.

Lakoff, George, and Mark Johnson. 1980. *Metaphors We Live By.* Chicago: University of Chicago Press.

Lamphere, Louise. 2001. "The Domestic Sphere of Women and the Public World of Men: The Strengths and Limitations of an Anthropological Dichotomy." In *Gender in Cross-Cultural Perspective*, 3rd ed. (Eds. C. Brettell and C. Sargent). Upper Saddle River, NJ: Prentice Hall, pp. 100–110.

Leacock, Eleanor. 1954. "The Montagnais 'Hunting Territory' and the Fur Trade," Vol. 56, No. 5, Pt. 2, Memoir No. 78. Washington, DC: American Anthropological Association.

Leacock, Eleanor. 1981. *Myths of Male Dominance.* New York: Monthly Review Press.

LeClercq, Chretien. 1968 (1691). *New Relation of Gaspesia.* New York: Greenwood.

Lee, Richard. 1982. "Politics, Sexual and Nonsexual, in an Egalitarian Society." In *Politics and History in Band Societies* (Eds. E. Leacock and R. Lee). New York: Cambridge University Press, pp. 37–60.

Lee, Richard. 2003. *The Dobe Ju/'hoansi*, 3rd ed. New York: Harcourt Brace.

Leibowitz, Lila. 1983. "Origins of the Sexual Division of Labor." In *Women's Nature: Rationalizations of Inequality* (Eds. M. Lowe and R. Hubbard). Elmsford, NY: Pergamon, pp. 123–147.

Lemarchand, Rene. 1994. "The Apocalypse in Rwanda." *Cultural Survival Quarterly* 18 (2/3):29–33.

Levine, Nancy E. 1988. *The Dynamics of Polyandry. Kinship, Domesticity, and Population on the Tibetan Border.* Chicago: University of Chicago Press.

Lévi-Strauss. 1949. *Elementary Structures of Kinship.* Paris: Preses Universitaires de France.

Lewis, I. M. 1989. *Ecstatic Religion: A Study of Shamanism and Spirit Possession*, 2nd ed. London: Routledge.

Lindenbaum, Shirley. 1979. *Kuru Sorcery: Disease and Danger in the New Guinea Highlands.* Palo Alto, CA: Mayfield.

Lindenfeld, Jacqueline. 1969. "The Social Conditioning of Syntactic Variation in French." *American Anthropologist* 71:890–898.

Lindfors, Bernth, and Oyekan Owomoyela. 1973. "Yoruba Proverbs: Translation and Annotation." Papers in International Studies: Africa Series No. 17. Athens: Ohio University Center for International Studies.

Lockwood, Victoria. 1997. "The Impact of Development on Women: The Interplay of Material Conditions and Gender Ideology." In *Gender in Cross-Cultural Perspective*, 2nd ed. (Eds. C. Brettell and C. Sargent). Upper Saddle River, NJ: Prentice Hall, pp. 504–517.

Loeb, Edwin. 1926. "Pomo Folkways." In *American Archeology and Ethnology*, Vol. 19, No. 2, pp. 149–405. Berkeley: University of California.

Lounsbury, Floyd. 1964. "The Structural Analysis of Kinship Semantics." In *Proceedings of the IXth International Congress of Linguistics* (Ed. H. Lunt). The Hague: Mouton, pp. 1073–1093.

MacArthur, R. H., and E. R. Pianka. 1966. "On the Optimal Use of a Patchy Environment." *American Naturalist* 100: 603–609.

Mack, Burton. 1988. *A Myth of Innocence: Mark and Christian Origins.* Philadelphia: Fortress Press.

MacKay, Fergus, and Emily Caruso. 2004. "Indigenous Lands or National Parks." *Cultural Survival Quarterly* 28 (1):14–16.

Malinowski, Bronislaw. 1922. *Argonauts of the Western Pacific.* London: Routledge & Kegan Paul.

Mandela, Nelson (Ed.). 1965. *No Easy Walk to Freedom.* London: Heinemann.

Mann, Barbara, and Jerry Fields. 1997. "A Sign in the Sky: Dating the League of the Haudenosaunee." *American Indian Culture and Research Journal* 21:105–164.

Marable, Manning. 1995. "Beyond Racial Identity Politics: Towards a Liberation Theory for Multicultural Democracy." In *Race, Class, and Gender*, 2nd ed. (Eds. M. Andersen and P. Collins). Belmont, CA: Wadsworth, pp. 363–366.

Marcus, George. 1992. *Lives in Trust: The Fortunes of Dynastic Families in Late Twentieth Century America.* Boulder, CO: Westview.

Markus, Hazel R., and Shinobu Kitayama. 1991. "Culture and the Self: Implications for Cognition, Emotion, and Motivation." *Psychological Review* 98 (2):224–253.

Marwick, M. G. 1967. "The Sociology of Sorcery in a Central African Tribe." In *Magic, Witchcraft, and Curing* (Ed. J. Middleton). New York: Natural History Press, pp. 101–126.

Mataira, Peter. 2000. "Mana and Tapu: Sacred Knowledge, Sacred Boundaries." In *Indigenous Religions* (Ed. G. Harvey). New York: Cassell, pp. 99–112.

Matthaei, Julie. 1982. *An Economic History of Women in America.* New York: Schocken.

Maybury-Lewis, David. 1997. "Indigenous Peoples, Ethnic Groups, and the State." Boston: Allyn & Bacon.

McAllester, David. 1954. *Enemy Way Music.* Cambridge, MA: Peabody Museum.

McDermott, LeRoy. 1996. "Self-Representation in Female Figurines." *Current Anthropology* 37:227–275.

McElroy, Ann and Patricia Townsend. 1989. *Medical Anthropology in Ecological Perspective.* Boulder, CO: Westview.

McEvilley, Thomas. 1992. *Art and Otherness: Crisis in Cultural Identity*. Kingston, NY: McPherson.

McWhorter, John. 1997. "Wasting Energy on an Illusion." *Black Scholar* 27 (1):9–14.

Meggers, Betty. 1971. *Amazonia: Man and Culture in a Counterfeit Paradise*. New York: Free Press.

Meier, John. 1991. *A Marginal Jew: Rethinking the Historical Jesus*. New York: Doubleday.

Mencher, Joan. 1965. "The Nayars of South Malabar." In *Comparative Family Systems* (Ed. M. E. Nimkoff). Boston: Houghton Mifflin, pp. 162–191.

Merivale, Herman. 1988 (1861). "Policy of Colonial Government Towards Native Tribes, as Regards Their Protection and Civilization." In *Tribal Peoples and Development Issues* (Ed. J. Bodley). Mountain View, CA: Mayfield, pp. 95–105.

Merrill, William, Edmund Ladd, and T. J. Ferguson. 1993. "The Return of the Ahayu:da: Lessons for Repatriation from Zuni Pueblo and the Smithsonian Institution." *Current Anthropology* 34 (5):523–566.

Merry, Sally. 1991. "Law and Colonialism." *Law and Society Review* 2:889–918.

Meyer, Roy. 1993. *History of the Santee Sioux: United States Indian Policy on Trial*, rev. ed. Lincoln: University of Nebraska Press.

Michelson, Truman. 1920. *Autobiography of a Fox Woman*. Fortieth Annual Report of the Bureau of American Ethnology for the years 1918–1919, pp. 291–349. Washington, DC.

Mills, C. Wright. 1956. *The Power Elite*. New York: Oxford University Press.

Mina, Hanna. 1993. *Fragments of Memory: A Story of a Syrian Family*. Austin: University of Texas Press, Center for Middle Eastern Studies.

Mintz, Sydney. 1996. *Tasting Food; Tasting Freedom: Excursions into Eating, Culture, and the Past*. Boston: Beacon Press.

Molony, Carol. 1977. "Recent Relexification Processes in Philippine Creole Spanish." In *Sociocultural Dimensions of Language Change* (Eds. B. Blount and M. Sanches). New York: Academic Press, pp. 131–159.

Mooney, James. 1965. *The Ghost Dance Religion and the Sioux Outbreak of 1890*. Chicago: University of Chicago Press.

Moore, Henrietta. 1988. *Feminism and Anthropology*. Minneapolis: University of Minnesota Press.

Morelli, G. A., et al. 1992. "Cultural Variation in Infants' Sleeping Arrangements: Questions of Independence." *Developmental Psychology* 38:604–613.

Morgan, Lewis Henry. 1877. *Ancient Society*. Cambridge, MA: Harvard University Press.

Morioka, Kiyomi. 1984. "Ancestor Worship in Contemporary Japan: Continuity and Change." In *Religion and the Family in East Asia* (Eds. G. DeVos and T. Sofue). Berkeley: University of California Press, pp. 201–216.

Morris, Craig, and Donald Thompson. 1985. *Huanuco Pampa: An Inca City and Its Hinterland*. London: Thames & Hudson.

Munroe R. M., and R. H. Munroe. 1975. "Levels of Obedience among U.S. and East African Children on an Experimental Task." *Journal of Cross-Cultural Psychology* 6:498–503.

Murphy, Jane. 1981. "Abnormal Behavior in Traditional Societies: Labels, Explanations and Social Reactions." *Medical Anthropology*, pp. 809–826.

Murray, Sir Hubert. 1988 (1933). "The Scientific Aspect of the Pacification of Papua." In *Tribal Peoples and Development Issues* (Ed. J. Bodley). Mountain View, CA: Mayfield, pp. 42–52.

Namias, June. 1995. *White Captives: Gender and Ethnicity on the American Frontier*. Chapel Hill: University of North Carolina Press.

Nanda, Serena. 1990. *Neither Man Nor Woman: The Hijras of India*. Belmont, CA: Wadsworth.

Navajo Nation. 1972. *The Navajo Ten Year Plan*. Windowrock, AZ: The Navajo Tribe.

Neihardt, John. 1961. *Black Elk Speaks: Being a Life Story of a Holy Man of the Oglala Sioux*. Lincoln: University of Nebraska Press.

New York Times. 1999. "Indian Affairs Heat Up (Witness the Lobster War)." December 30, pp. A1, A22.

New York Times. 2004. "Plagued by Drugs, Tribes Revive Ancient Penalty." January 18, pp. A1, 25.

Newing, Helen, and Lissie Wahl. 2004. "Benefiting Local Populations? Communal Reserves in Peru." *Cultural Survival Quarterly* 28 (1):38–42.

Newman, Katherine. 1989. *Falling from Grace: Experience of Downward Mobility in the American Middle Class*. New York: Random House.

Nietschmann. 1988. "Third World Colonial Expansion: Indonesia, Disguised Invasion of Indigenous Nations." In *Tribal Peoples and Development Issues* (Ed. J. Bodley). Mountain View, CA: Mayfield, pp. 191–208.

Nongovernmental Organizations Research Guide 2004. http://docs.lib.duke.edu/igo/guides/ngo/, October 10. Accessed November 2, 2004.

Obeng, Samuel Gyasi. 1996. "The Proverb as a Mitigating and Politeness Strategy in Akan Discourse." *Anthropological Linguistics* 38:521–549.

O'Brien, Jay. 1986. "Toward a Reconstitution Ethnicity: Capitalist Expansion and Cultural Dynamics in Sudan." *American Anthropologist* 88 (4):898–907.

Ochs, Elinor, and Caroline Taylor. 1995. "The 'Father Knows Best' Dynamic in Dinnertime Narratives." In *Linguistic Anthropology: A Reader* (Ed. A. Duranti). Malden, MA: Blackwell, pp. 431–449.

Ong, Aihwa. 1983. "Global Industries and Malay Peasants in Peninsula Asia." In *Women, Men, and the International Division of Labor* (Eds. J. Nash and M. Fernandez-Kelly). Albany: State University of New York Press, pp. 426–439.

Osterhammel, Jurgen. 1997. *Colonialism: A Theoretical Overview*. Princeton, NJ: Markus Wiener.

Ottenberg, Phoebe. 1965. "The Afikpo Ibo of Eastern Nigeria." In *Peoples of Africa* (Ed. J. Gibbs). New York: Holt, Rinehart & Winston, pp. 3–39.

Ottenberg, Simon, and Phoebe Ottenberg. 1962. "Afikpo Market 1900–1960." In *Markets in Africa* (Eds. P. Bohannan and G. Dalton). Evanston, IL: Northwestern University Press, pp. 117–169.

Ottley, Bruce, and Jean Zorn. 1983. "Criminal Law in Papua New Guinea: Code, Custom and the Courts in Conflict." In *American Journal of Comparative Law* 31:251–300.

Ozment, Steven. 2001. *Ancestors: The Loving Family in Old Europe*. Cambridge, MA: Harvard University Press.

Peregrine, Peter. 2003. *World Prehistory: Two Million Years of Human Life*. Upper Saddle River, NJ: Prentice Hall.

Perry, Richard. 1996. "From Time in Memorial: Indigenous Peoples and State Systems." Austin: University of Texas Press.

Philips, Susan. 1978. "Participant Structures and Communicative Competence: Warm Springs Children in Community and Classroom." In *A Pluralistic Nation* (Eds. M. Lourie and N. Conklin). Rowley, MA: Newbury House, pp. 390–407.

Platt, John, Heidi Weber, and Ho Minn Lian. 1984. *The New Englishes*. London: Routledge & Kegan Paul.

Price, Sally. 1984. *Co-wives and Calabashes*. Ann Arbor: University of Michigan Press.

Price, Sally. 1989. *Primitive Art in Civilized Places*. Chicago: University of Chicago Press.

Prins, Harald. 1990. *The Mi'kmaq: Resistance, Accommodation, and Cultural Survival*. New York: Harcourt Brace.

Public Information Office. U.S. Bureau of the Census. 2003. Washington, DC.

Pyles, Thomas, and John Algeo. 1982. *The Origins and Development of the English Language*, 3rd ed. New York: Harcourt Brace Jovanovich.

Rabinow, Paul. 1977. *Reflections on Fieldwork in Morocco*. Berkeley: University of California Press.

Raheja, Gloria Goodwin, and Ann Grodzins Gold. 1994. *Listen to the Heron's Words: Reimagining Gender and Kinship in North India*. Berkeley: University of California Press.

Ramos, Alcida. 1997. "The Indigenous Movement in Brazil: A Quarter Century of Ups and Downs." *Cultural Survival Quarterly* 21 (2).

Rappaport, Roy. 1969. "Ritual Regulation of Environmental Relations among a New Guinea People." In *Environment and Cultural Behavior* (Ed. A. Vayda). Garden City, NY: Natural History Press, pp. 181–201.

Rappaport, Roy. 2000. *Pigs for the Ancestors: Ritual in the Ecology of a New Guinea People*, 2nd ed. New Haven, CT: Yale University Press.

Rasmussen, Knud. 1929. *Intellectual Culture of the Iglulik Eskimo*. Vol. 7, No. 1, of the Report of the Fifth Thule Expedition, 1921–1924. Copenhagen: Clydendalske Boghandel.

Rathje W., and Murphy C. 1992. "Five Major Myths about Garbage and Why They're Wrong." *Smithsonian*, July.

Reid, Walter, et al. 1996. "Biodiversity Prospecting." In *Medicinal Resources of the Tropical Forest: Biodiversity and Its Importance to Human Health* (Eds. M. Balick et al.). New York: Columbia University Press, pp. 142–173.

Rensberger, Boyce. 2001. "Racial Odyssey." In *Anthropology: Contemporary Perspectives*, 8th ed. (Ed. P. Whitten). Boston: Allyn & Bacon, pp. 81–89.

Ribeiro, Darcy. 1971. *The Americas and Civilization*. New York: Dutton.

Richeport, Madeleine. 1984. *Macumba Trance and Spirit Healing*. Richeport Films. Written, produced, and directed by Madeleine Richeport.

Richmond, John. 1986. "The Language of Black Children and the Language Debate in the Schools." In *Language and the Black Experience* (Eds. D. Sutcliffe and A. Wong). Oxford: Blackwell, pp. 123–135.

Rickford, John. 1997. "Unequal Partnership: Sociolinguistics and the African American Speech Community." *Language in Society* 26:161–198.

Ries, Paula, and Ann Stone (Eds.). 1992. *The American Woman 1992–1993: A Status Report*. New York: Norton.

Robarchek, Clayton. 1997. "A Community of Interest: Semai Conflict Resolution." *Cultural Variation in Conflict Resolution: Alternatives to Violence* (Eds. D. Fry and K. Bjorkqvist). Mahwah, NJ: Lawrence Erlbaum, pp. 52–58.

Robbins, Jim. 2004. "Ice Age Floodwaters Leave a Walkable Trail across the Northwest." *New York Times*, August 24.

Rodman, Margaret. 1993. "Keeping Options Open: Copra and Fish in Rural Vanuatu." In *Contemporary Pacific Societies: Studies in Development and Change* (Eds. V. Lockwood et al.). Upper Saddle River, NJ: Prentice Hall, pp. 171–184.

Rogoff, Barbara, and Morelli, Gilda. 1989. "Perspectives on Children's Development from Cultural Psychology." *American Psychologist* 44 (2):343–348.

Rohrlich-Leavitt, Ruby, et al. 1975. "Aboriginal Woman: Male and Female Anthropological Perspectives." In *Toward an Anthropology of Women* (Ed. R. Reiter). New York: Monthly Review Press, pp. 110–126.

Rohter, Larry. 2003. "Bolivia's Poor Proclaim Abiding Distrust of Globalization." *New York Times*, October 17.

Romans, Bernard. 1962. *A Concise Natural History of East and West Florida*. Gainesville: University of Florida Press.

Rosaldo, Michelle. 1974. "Women, Culture and Society: A Theoretical Overview." In *Women, Culture and Society* (Eds. M. Rosaldo and L. Lamphere). Stanford, CA: Stanford University Press, pp. 17–42.

Rowe, John. 1950. "The Inca Culture at the Time of the Spanish Conquest." In *Handbook of South American Indians* (Ed. J. Steward). Smithsonian Institution, Bureau of American Ethnology, Bulletin 143, Vol. 2, pp. 183–330. Washington, DC.

Royce, Anya. 1977. *The Anthropology of Dance*. Bloomington: Indiana University Press.

Rubel, Arthur. 1977. "The Epidemiology of a Folk Illness: Susto in Hispanic America." In *Culture, Disease, and Healing: Studies in Medical Anthropology* (Ed. D. Landy). New York: Macmillan, pp. 119–128.

Rumbaugh, Duane, and E. Sue Savage-Rumbaugh. 1994. "Language Research with Animals." In *Animal Learning and Cognition* (Ed. N. J. McIntosh). New York: Academic Press, pp. 307–333.

Ryan, K. 2000. "Edible Wild Plants as Digestive Aids: Ethnoarchaeology in Maasailand. Science and Archaeology." *Expedition* 42 (3):7–8.

Sahagun, Bernardino de. 1975 (1938). *Florentine Codex: General History of the Things of New Spain*. Santa Fe, NM.

Sahlins, Marshall. 1961. "The Segmentary Lineage: An Organization of Predatory Expansion." *American Anthropologist* 63: 332–345.

Sahlins, Marshall. 1970. "Poor Man, Rich Man, Big-Man, Chief: Political Types in Melanesia and Polynesia." In *Cultures of the Pacific* (Eds. T. Harding and B. Wallace). New York: Free Press, pp. 203–215.

Sakajiri, N. 2004. "Japan Cited in Human Trafficking. *Asahi Shimbun*, June 16.

Sanday, Peggy. 1981. *Female Power and Male Dominance*. New York: Cambridge University Press.

Sanders, E. P. 1985. *Jesus and Judaism*. Philadelphia: Fortress Press.

Sanderson, Lilian Passmore, and Neville Sanderson. 1981. *Education, Religion & Politics in Southern Sudan 1899–1964*. London: Ithaca Press.

San Francisco Chronicle. 1996. "EU to Help Pay for Cow Slaughter, Nations Back Plan to Eradicate Disease, Restore Trust." April 3, p. A5.

Sano, Mariko, and Toshiyuki Sano. 2001. *Life in Riverfront: A Middle Western Town Seen through Japanese Eyes*. Fort Worth, TX: Harcourt Brace.

Sapir, Edward. 1949. "Language and Environment." In *Selected Writings of Edward Sapir* (Ed. E. Mandelbaum). Berkeley: University of California Press, pp. 89–103.

Sapiro, Virginia. 1986. *Women in American Society*. Palo Alto, CA: Mayfield.

Sasson, Jack. 1995. *Civilizations of the Ancient Near East, I–IV*. New York: Scribner's.

Sauer, Carl. 1971. *Sixteenth Century North America: The Land and the People as Seen by the Europeans*. Berkeley: University of California Press.

Saussure, Ferdinand de. 1916. *A Course in General Linguistics*. Paris: Editions Payot.

Schemo, Diana. 1999. "The Last Tribal Battle." *New York Times Magazine*, October 31, pp. 70–77.

Scheper-Hughes, Nancy. 1989. "The Human Strategy: Death without Weeping." *Natural History Magazine*, October, pp. 8–16.

Scheper-Hughes, Nancy. 1992. *Death without Weeping: The Violence of Everyday Life in Brazil*. Berkeley: University of California Press.

Scheper-Hughes, Nancy. 2004. *Parts Unknown: Undercover Ethnography of the Organs-Trafficking Underworld*. Thousand Oaks, CA: Sage. http://eth.sagepub.com/cgi/reprint/5/1/29.pdf. Accessed November 2, 2004.

Schiller, Nina Glick, et al. 1992. "Transnationalism: A New Analytic Framework for Understanding Migration." In *Towards a Transnational Perspective on Migration: Race, Class, Ethnicity, and Nationalism Reconsidered* (Eds. N. G. Schiller et al.). Annals of the New York Academy of Sciences, Vol. 645, pp. 1–24. New York: New York Academy of Sciences.

Schmink, Marianne. 1988. "Big Business in the Amazon." In *People of the Tropical Rain Forest* (Eds. Julie Denslow and Christine Padoch). Berkeley: University of California Press, pp. 163–174.

Schmink, Marianne, and Charles Wood. 1992. *Contested Frontiers in Amazonia*. New York: Columbia University Press.

Schneider, David. 1961. "The Distinctive Features of Matrilineal Descent Groups." In *Matrilineal Kinship* (Eds. D. Schneider and K. Gough). Berkeley: University of California Press, pp. 1–32.

Schneller, Raphael. 1988. "The Israeli Experience of Cross-Cultural Misunderstanding: Insights and Lessons." In *Cross-Cultural Perspectives in Non-Verbal Communication* (Ed. F. Poyatos). Lewiston, NY: C. J. Hogrefe, pp. 153–171.

Schusky, Ernest. 1994. "The Roots of Factionalism among the Lower Brule Sioux." In *North American Indian Anthropology: Essays on Society and Culture* (Eds. R. De Mallie and A. Ortiz). Norman: University of Oklahoma Press, pp. 258–277.

Seattle Times. 1996. "British Agree to Destroy Beef in Mad-Cow Scare, Europeans to Help Pay for Industry Losses." April 3, p. A3.

Segall, Marshall. 1979. *Cross-Cultural Psychology: Human Behavior in Global Perspective*. Monterey, CA: Brooks/Cole.

Service, Elman. 1962. *Primitive Social Organization: An Evolutionary Perspective*. New York: Random House.

Shannon, Jonathan. 2003. "Sultans of Spin: Syrian Sacred Music on the World Stage." *American Anthropologist* 105:266–277.

Sharff, Jagna. 1998. *King Kong on 4th Street: Family and the Violence of Poverty on the Lower East Side*. Boulder, CO: Westview.

Shostak, Marjorie. 1983. *Nisa: The Life and Words of a !Kung Woman*. New York: Vintage.

Silverblatt, Irene. 1978. "Andean Women in the Inca Empire." *Feminist Studies* 4:7–61.

Silverblatt, Irene. 1980. "Andean Women under Spanish Rule." In *Women and Colonization* (Eds. M. Etienne and E. Leacock). New York: Praeger, pp. 149–185.

Silverblatt, Irene. 1987. *Moon, Sun, and Witches: Gender Ideologies and Class in Inca and Colonial Peru*. Princeton, NJ: Princeton University Press.

Siskind, Janet. 1973. "Tropical Forest Hunters and the Economy of Sex." In *Peoples and Cultures of Native South America* (Ed. D. Gross). New York: Doubleday/Natural History Press, pp. 226–240.

Skinner, Alanson. 1911. *Notes on the Eastern Cree and Northern Saulteaux*. Anthropological Papers, Vol. 9, Pt. 1. New York: American Museum of Natural History.

Smith, S. Percy. 1913. "The Lore of the Whare-Wananga." New Plymouth, N.Z., http://www.sacredtexts.com/pac/lww/index.

Smitherman, Geneva, and Sylvia Cunningham. 1997. "Moving Beyond Resistance: Ebonics and African American Youth." *Journal of Black Psychology* 28:227–232.

Sofue, Takao. 1984. "Family and Interpersonal Relationships in Early Japan." In *Religion and the Family in East Asia* (Eds. G. DeVos and T. Sofue). Berkeley: University of California Press, pp. 201–216.

Soustelle, Jacques. 1961. *Daily Life of the Aztecs: On the Eve of the Spanish Conquest*. Stanford, CA: Stanford University Press.

Southwold, Martin. 1965. "The Ganda of Uganda." In *Peoples of Africa* (Ed. J. Gibbs). New York: Holt, Rinehart & Winston, pp. 81–118.

Soyinka, Wole. 1981. *Ake, the Years of Childhood*. New York: Vintage.

Spencer, Herbert. 1877. *Principles of Sociology*. Chicago: University of Chicago Press.

Spencer, Paul. 1988. *The Maasai of Matapato: A Study of Rituals of Rebellion*. Bloomington: Indiana University Press.

Spencer, Robert. 1984. "North Alaska Coast Eskimo." In *Arctic*, Vol. 5, pp. 320–337. *Handbook of North American Indians*. Washington, DC: Smithsonian Institution Press.

Spradley, James. 1972. *Guests Never Leave Hungry: The Autobiography of James Sewid, a Kwakiutl Indian*. Montreal: McGill Queens University Press.

Stack, Carol. 1975. *All My Kin: Strategies for Survival in a Black Community*. New York: Harper Torchbooks.

Statistical Abstracts. 2002. Washington, DC.

Stephens, D. W., and J. R. Krebs. 1986. *Foraging Theory*. Princeton, NJ: Princeton University Press.

"Stewards to Shareholders: Eyaks Face Extinction." *Multinational Monitor*. http://multinationalmonitor.org/hyper/issues/1993/03/mm0393_09html. Accessed January 14, 2005.

Stiles, Kristine, and Peter Selz. 1996. *Theories and Documents of Contemporary Art: A Sourcebook of Artists' Writings*. Berkeley: University of California Press.

Strathern, Andrew. 1992. "Let the Bow Go Down." In *War in the Tribal Zone: Expanding States and Indigenous Warfare* (Eds. R. Ferguson and N. Whitehead). Santa Fe, NM: School of American Research Press, pp. 229–250.

Surrette, L. S. Rev. 1942. *Notes on the Life of Abbe Jean Mande Sigogne*. Collections of the Nova Scotia Historical Society, Vol. 25.

Swanton, John. 1946. *The Indians of the Southeastern United States*. Bureau of American Ethnology Bulletin No. 137. Washington, DC.

Tedlock, Dennis. 1972. *Finding the Center: Narrative Poetry of the Zuñi Indians*. Dennis Tedlock, trans.; from performances in the Zuñi by Andrew Peynetsa and Walter Sanchez. Lincoln: University of Nebraska Press.

Tedlock, Dennis. 1983. *The Spoken Word and the Work of Interpretation*. Philadelphia: University of Pennsylvania Press.

Thompson, Robert. 1974. *African Art in Motion*. Berkeley: University of California Press.

Thompson, Robert. 1983. *Flash of the Spirit: African and Afro-American Art and Philosophy*. New York: Random House.

Thornton, Russell. 1987. *American Indian Holocaust and Survival: A Population History since 1492*. Norman: University of Oklahoma Press.

Thwaites, R. G. (Ed.). 1906. *Jesuit Relations and Allied Documents, 1610–1791*. 73 vols. Cleveland, OH: Burrows Brothers.

Titiev, Mischa. 1992. *Old Oraibi: A Study of the Hopi Indians of Third Mesa*. Albuquerque: University of New Mexico Press.

Trask, Haunani-Kay. 2001. "Lovely Hula Hands: Corporate Tourism and the Prostitution of Hawaiian Culture." In *Native American Voices: A Reader*, 2nd ed. (Eds. Susan Lobo and Steve Talbot). Upper Saddle River, NJ: Prentice Hall, pp. 393–401.

Triandis, Harry. 1989. "The Self and Social Behavior in Differing Cultural Contexts." *Psychological Review* 96 (3):506–520.

Tronick, Edward, et al. 1992. "The Efe Forager Infant and Toddler's Pattern of Social Relationships: Multiple and Simultaneous." *Developmental Psychology* 28 (4):568–577.

Trudgill, Peter. 1972. "Sex, Covert Prestige and Linguistic Change in the Urban British English of Norwich." *Language in Society* 1:179–195.

Trudgill, Peter. 1974. *The Social Differentiation of English in Norwich*. New York: Cambridge University Press.

Trudgill, Peter. 1983. *Sociolinguistics*. New York: Penguin.

Tyler, Varro. 1996. "Natural Products and Medicine: An Overview." In *Medicinal Resources of the Tropical Forest: Biodiversity and Its Importance to Human Health* (Eds. M. Balick et al.). New York: Columbia University Press, pp. 3–10.

Tylor, Edward Burnett. 1871. *Primitive Culture*. London: J. Murray.

U.S. Bureau of the Census. 2001, 2003. *Statistical Abstracts*.

U.S. Department of Justice, Federal Bureau of Investigation. 1999. *Thirty Years of Terrorism: A Special Retrospective*, p. ii. http://www.fbi.gov/publications/terror/terror99.pdf. Accessed March 2, 2005.

U.S. Department of Labor. 2002. Bureau of Labor Statistics.

U.S. Department of State. 2004. *2004 Trafficking in Persons Report*. http://www.state.gov/g/tip/rls/tiprpt/2004/. Accessed March 2, 2005.

Ubelaker, Douglas. 1976. "Prehistoric New World Population Size: Historical Review and Current Appraisal of North America." *American Journal of Physical Anthropology* 45:661–666.

Ubelaker, Douglas. 1994. "The Biological Impact of European Contact in Ecuador." In *In the Wake of Contact: Biological Responses to Conquest*. New York: Wiley-Liss, pp. 147–160.

Uchendu, Victor. 1995. "The Dilemma of Ethnicity and Polity Primacy in Black Africa." In *Ethnic Identity: Creation, Conflict, and Accommodation*, 3rd ed. (Eds. L. Romanucci-Ross and G. DeVos). London: Sage, pp. 125–135.

Ukwu, I. U. 1969. "Markets in Iboland." In *Markets in West Africa* (Eds. B. W. Hodder and I. U. Ukwu). Ibadan, Nigeria: Ibadan University Press, pp. 113–250.

United Nations. 1993. *Draft Declaration on the Rights of Indigenous Peoples*. New York.

United Nations. Department of Economic and Social Affairs. 2004. http://www.unstats.un.org/unsd/cdb.

United Nations, Division for the Advancement of Women. 2000. http://www.unstats.un.org/unsd/cdb.

Urton, Gary. 2003. "Quipu Knotting Account in the Inka Empire." Santiago: Chilean Museum of Pre-Columbian Art.

van den Broeck, Jef. 1977. Class Differences in Syntactic Complexity in the Flemish Town of Maaseik. *Language in Society* 6:149–181.

van Gennep, Arnold. 1961. *Rites of Passage*. Chicago: University of Chicago Press.

Vanover, Raymond. 1980. *Sun Songs: Creation Myths from around the World*. New York: New American Library.

Vecsey, Christopher. 1997. *The Paths of Kateri's Kin*. Notre Dame, IN: University of Notre Dame Press.

Vigneras, L. A. 1960. *The Journal of Christopher Columbus*. London: The Hakluyt Society.

Wachtel, Nathan. 1977. *The Vision of the Vanquished: The Spanish Conquest of Peru through Indian Eyes, 1530–1570*. New York: Gordon Willey.

Wallace, Anthony F. C. 1956. "Revitalization Movements." *American Anthropologist* 58:264–281.

Wallace, A.F.C. 1961. *Culture and Personality*. New York: Random House.

Wallace, A.F.C. 1966. *Religion: An Anthropological View.* New York: Random House.

Walraven, B. 1994. *Songs of the Shaman: The Ritual Chants of the Korean Mudang.* New York: Columbia University Press.

Warren, Jonathan. 2001. "Racial Revolutions: Antiracism and Indian Resurgence in Brazil." Durham, NC: Duke University Press.

Waters, Elizabeth, and Anastasia Posadskaya. 1995. "Democracy without Women Is No Democracy: Women's Struggles in Post Communist Russia." In *The Challenge of Local Feminisms: Women's Movement in Global Perspective* (Ed. A. Basu). Boulder, CO: Westview, pp. 351–373.

Watson, Ruby. 1986. "The Named and the Nameless: Gender and Person in Chinese Society." *American Ethnologist* 13 (4): 619–631.

Weber, Max. 1968. *Max Weber on Charisma and Institution Building* (Ed. S. N. Eisenstadt). Chicago: University of Chicago Press.

Weber, Max. 1981. *General Economic History.* New York: Collier Books.

Weiner, Annette. 1976. *Women of Value, Men of Renown: New Perspectives in Trobriand Exchange.* Austin: University of Texas Press.

Weiner, Annette. 1988. *The Trobrianders of Papua New Guinea.* New York: Holt, Rinehart & Winston.

Weiss, Lawrence. 1984. *The Development of Capitalism in the Navajo Nation: A Political-Economic History. Studies in Marxism,* Vol. 15. Minneapolis: MEP Publications.

Wellington, John. 1967. *South West Africa and Its Human Issues.* Oxford: Clarendon/Oxford University Press.

White, Richard. 1983. *The Roots of Dependency: Subsistence, Environment, and Social Change among the Choctaw, Pawnees, and Navajos.* Lincoln: University of Nebraska Press.

Whiting, John W. M., and Irvin L. Child. 1953. *Child Training and Personality.* New Haven, CT: Yale University Press.

Whorf, Benjamin. 1956. "The Relation of Habitual Thought and Behavior to Language." In *Language, Thought and Reality* (Ed. J. B. Carroll). Cambridge, MA: MIT Press, pp. 134–159.

Wiessner, Siegfried. 1999. "Rights and Status of Indigenous Peoples: A Global Comparative and International Legal Analysis." *Harvard Human Rights Journal* 12:57–128.

Williams, Eric. 1944. *Capitalism and Slavery.* Chapel Hill: University of North Carolina Press.

Williams, Robert. 1997. "The Ebonics Controversy." *Journal of Black Psychology* 23: 208–213.

Williams, Walter. 1986. *The Spirit and the Flesh: Sexual Diversity in American Indian Culture.* Boston: Beacon Press.

Wilson, Gilbert. 1981. *Waheenee: An Indian Girl's Story Told by Herself to Gilbert L. Wilson.* Lincoln: University of Nebraska Press.

Witherspoon, Gary. 1972. *Navajo Kinship and Marriage.* New York: Cambridge University Press.

Witherspoon, Gary. 1977. *Language and Art in the Navajo Universe.* Ann Arbor: University of Michigan Press.

Wittfogel, Karl. 1957. *Oriental Despotism: A Study of Total Power.* New Haven, CT: Yale University Press.

Wolf, Eric. 1982. *Europe and the People without History.* Berkeley: University of California Press.

Wolf, Marjorie. 1974. "Chinese Women: Old Skills in a New Context." In *Women, Culture and Society* (Eds. M. Rosaldo and L. Lamphere). Stanford, CA: Stanford University Press, pp. 157–172.

Wong, Aline. 1974. "Women in China: Past and Present." In *Many Sisters* (Ed. C. Matthiasson). New York: Free Press.

Wong, Aline. 1986. "Planned Development, Social Stratification, and the Sexual Division of Labor in Singapore." In *Women's Work: Development and the Division of Labor by Gender* (Eds. E. Leacock and H. Safa). Cambridge, MA: Bergen & Garvey, pp. 207–223.

World Health Organization. Traditional Medicine Fact Sheet. http://www.who.int/mediacentre/factsheets/fs134/en/. Accessed November 18, 2004.

Worseley, Peter. 1967. "Millenarian Movements in Melanesia." In *Gods and Rituals* (Ed. J. Middleton). Garden City, NY: Natural History Press, pp. 337–352.

Worseley, Peter. 1968. *The Trumpet Shall Sound: A Study of Cargo Cults in Melanesia.* New York: Schocken.

Worseley, Peter. 1984. *The Three Worlds: Culture and World Development.* Chicago: University of Chicago Press.

Yap, P. M. 1969. "The Culture-Bound Reactive Syndromes." In *Mental Health Research in Asia and the Pacific* (Eds. W. Caudill and T. Y. Lin). Honolulu: East-West Center Press, pp. 33–53.

Yazzie, R. 1992. *The Navajo Peacemaker Court: Contrasts of Justice.* Windowrock, AZ: Navajo Tribe.

Yeoman, L. (1987). "Universal Primary Education: Factors Affecting the Enrollment and Retention of Girls in Papua New Guinea Community Schools." In *The Ethics of Development: Women as Unequal Partners in Development* (Eds. S. Stratigos and P. J. Hughes). Port Moresby: University of Papua New Guinea, pp. 108–155.

Young, Robert, and William Morgan. 1987. *The Navajo Language,* rev. ed. Albuquerque: University of New Mexico Press.

Zentella, Ana. 1985. "The Fate of Spanish in the U.S.: The Puerto Rican Experience." *Language of Inequality* (Eds. N. Wolfson and J. Manes). The Hague: Mouton, pp. 41–59.

Zolbrod, Paul. 1984. *Dine Bahane: The Navajo Creation Story.* Albuquerque: University of New Mexico.

Credits

CHAPTER 1   PAGE 2: Marilyn "Angel" Wynn/NativeStock.com; p. 5: Everett Collection; p. 6: Donna Wilker/Dr. Thomas Barfield; p. 7: World Music Network, www.worldmusic.net; p. 9: David Waters/CORBIS-NY; p. 12: Natalie Fobes/CORBIS-NY; p. 15: John Reader/Photo Researchers, Inc.; p. 16: London/Topham-HIP/The Image Works; p. 17: Eye of Science/Photo Researchers, Inc.; p. 19: Cultural Survival, Inc.

CHAPTER 2   PAGE 22: Alison Wright/CORBIS-NY; p. 24: Topham/The Image Works; p. 26, top: Imapress/Charreire/The Image Works; p. 26, bottom: Kike Calvo/The Image Works; p. 27: Richard T. Nowitz/CORBIS-NY; p. 29, top: Ariel Skelley/CORBIS-NY; p. 29, bottom: Jack K. Clark/The Image Works; p. 33: Geri Engberg/The Image Works; p. 34, left: Bobby Yip/CORBIS-NY; p. 34, right: Michael Newman/PhotoEdit; p. 37: John Van Hasselt/CORBIS-NY; p. 40, left and right: Everett Collection; p. 42: Topham/The Image Works; p. 44: Z. Bzdak/The Image Works.

CHAPTER 3   PAGE 48: Natalie Fobes/CORBIS-NY; p. 51: Father James Driscoll; p. 52: Bettmann/Corbis/Bettmann; p. 54: © Earl & Nazima Kowall/CORBIS; p. 56: F. C. Sears/LIBRARY AND ARCHIVES CANADA/PA-148589; p. 57: Photolibrary.com; p. 58: Elisha P. Renne; p. 61: Paul Hyman; p. 65: Mark Peterson/CORBIS-NY.

CHAPTER 4   PAGE 75: Terrace/Anthro-Photo File; p. 76: From *Introduction to Linguistics* by R. Wardhaugh, Copyright 1977, Reprinted by permission of McGraw-Hill; p. 79: Topham/The Image Works; p. 80: Karen Huntt/CORBIS-NY; p. 81: AP Wide World Photos; p. 82: Michael Ende/Peter Arnold, Inc.; p. 83: Michael Schwartz/The Image Works; p. 88: Map reprinted by permission of Robert Delaney; p. 89: Jeff Greenberg/The Image Works; p. 94: Markus Dlouhy/Das Fotoarchiv/Peter Arnold, Inc.; p. 96: Margot Granitsas/The Image Works.

CHAPTER 5   PAGE 102: Paul Almasy/CORBIS-NY; p. 106: Jason Laure/The Image Works; p. 110: Steve Winn/Anthro-Photo File; p. 111: Charles Steiner/The Image Works; p. 112: Jose Luis Pelaez, Inc./CORBIS-NY; p. 117: Ariel Skelley/CORBIS-NY; p. 126: Robert Frerck/Odyssey Productions, Inc.; p. 132: Condon/Anthro-Photo File.

CHAPTER 6   PAGE 136: Photo courtesy of Iroquois Indian Museum, Howes Cave, NY; p. 138: Jeff Greenberg/PhotoEdit; p. 140: Michael Freeman/IPNstock.com; p. 141: © Joy May Hilden; p. 144: CORBIS-NY; p. 146: Anthro-Photo File; p. 148: Galen Rowell/CORBIS-NY; p. 150: The Image Works; p. 153: Jon Holtsman; p. 155: Englebert Photography, Inc.; p. 159: Photo Craig Morris, courtesy Division of Anthropology, American Museum of Anthropology.

CHAPTER 7   PAGE 162: Irven DeVore/Anthro-Photo File; p. 164: Jean-Claude Bacle/Peter Arnold, Inc.; p. 165: Photo courtesy Azerbaijan International—AZER.com; p. 166: Bobby Yip/Reuters/CORBIS-NY; p. 168: Jim Wark/Peter Arnold, Inc.; p. 170: Roland Seitre/Peter Arnold, Inc.; p. 173: David Cavagnaro/Peter Arnold, Inc.; p. 175: Owen Franken/CORBIS-NY; p. 177: Englebert Photography, Inc.; p. 178: Fujiphotos/The Image Works; p. 180: Dominick Tyler/Dominick Tyler Photographer; p. 181: Englebert Photography, Inc.; p. 184: Dinodia Picture Agency; p. 187: Deborah Harse/The Image Works.

CHAPTER 8   PAGE 195: Susana Raab/CORBIS-NY; p. 196: Stan Washburn/Anthro-Photo File; p. 199: © Doranne Jacobson/International Images; p. 201, top: Bell/Anthro-Photo File; p. 201, bottom: Jon Burbank/The Image Works; p. 205: Topham/The Image Works; p. 206: John Kahionhes Fadden; p. 214: Brian A. Vikander/CORBIS-NY.

CHAPTER 9   PAGE 220: Benjamin Lowy/CORBIS-NY; p. 222: Sean Cayton/The Image Works; p. 223: Mark Godfrey/The Image Works; p. 225, top: Elizabeth Crews/The Image Works; p. 225, bottom: David Grossman/The Image Works; p. 230: © Doranne Jacobson/International

Images; p. 232: Lauren Goodsmith/The Image Works; p. 234: © Marilyn Humphries/The Image Works; p. 235: Peter Johnson/CORBIS-NY; p. 240: John Van Hasselt/CORBIS-NY; p. 241: Bob Daemmrich/The Image Works; p. 243: Adrian Arbib/Anthro-Photo File; p. 245: Peter Sanders/The Image Works.

CHAPTER 10   PAGE 250: Werner Forman/Art Resource, N.Y.; p. 252: J. Lewis/HAGA/The Image Works; p. 254: Charles Walker/Topfoto/The Image Works; p. 259: Bob Daemmrich/The Image Works; p. 260: David Wells/The Image Works; p. 263: AP Wide World Photos; p. 267: Wendy Stone/CORBIS-NY; p. 268: James Marshall/The Image Works; p. 269: CORBIS-NY; p. 270: CORBIS-NY; p. 279: Maurizio Brambatti/SIPA Press.

CHAPTER 11   PAGE 284: The Bridgeman Art Library International Ltd.; p. 286: Carol Beckwith & Angela Fisher/The Image Works; p. 290: Rachel Epstein/The Image Works; p. 291: Bettmann/Corbis/Corbis/Bettmann; p. 292, top: Andrew Holbrooke/The Image Works; p. 292, bottom: © Doranne Jacobson/International Images; p. 295, top: Abd Rabbo-Niviere/SIPA Press; p. 295, bottom: David Orr/CORBIS-NY; p. 297: J. Patrick Forden/CORBIS-NY; p. 299: Hideo Haga/The Image Works.

CHAPTER 12   PAGE 310: © Marilyn "Angel" Wynn/Nativestock.com; p. 312: Ali Jasim/CORBIS-NY; p. 317: E. R. Faribault, Geological Survey of Canada/LIBRARY AND ARCHIVES OF CANADA/PA-039851; p. 325: K. Hympendahl/Peter Arnold, Inc.; p. 328: Mary Evans Picture Library Ltd.; p. 332: © Doranne Jacobson/International Images; p. 335: Getty Images Inc.—Hulton Archive Photos.

CHAPTER 13   PAGE 338: Lars Smith/Anthro-Photo File; p. 340: Frans de Waal; p. 341: David Young-Wolff/PhotoEdit; p. 347: Stan Washburn/Anthro-Photo File; p. 348: Lynsey Addario/CORBIS-NY; p. 350: JFE Bloss/Anthro-Photo File; p. 356: Greg Wahl-Stephens/AP Wide World Photos; p. 360: AP Wide World Photos.

CHAPTER 14   PAGE 364: Geoffrey Clements/CORBIS-NY; p. 367: Giraudon/The Bridgeman Art Library International Ltd.; p. 368: Getty Images Inc.—Stone Allstock; p. 369: Shimizu Teruyo/Photo Japan; p. 370: Lawrence Migdale/Lawrence Migdale/Pix; p. 372: Cedar Bough Photography; p. 374, top: Christopher D. Roy; p. 374, bottom: Gordon Wiltsie/Peter Arnold, Inc.; p. 376: Edward S. Curtis/CORBIS-NY; p. 378: Raghu Rai/Magnum Photos, Inc.; p. 383: The Bridgeman Art Library International Ltd.

CHAPTER 15   PAGE 394: Topham/The Image Works; p. 397: Kim Grant/Lonely Planet Images/Photo 20-20; p. 398, top: Englebert Photography, Inc.; p. 398, bottom: Used by permission of Lakeview Museum of Arts and Sciences; p. 399: Martha Cooper/Peter Arnold, Inc.; p. 401: Jonathan Hugh Dickson; p. 402: Martha Cooper/Peter Arnold, Inc.; p. 403: © Archivo Iconografico, S.A./CORBIS; p. 404: Werner Forman/Art Resource, N.Y.; p. 409: Lawrence Migdale/Lawrence Migdale/Pix; p. 412: Martha Cooper/Peter Arnold, Inc.; p. 415: Albrecht G. Schaefer/CORBIS-NY.

CHAPTER 16   PAGE 421: The Bridgeman Art Library International Ltd.; p. 422: Gleb Garanich/CORBIS-NY; p. 423: CORBIS-NY; p. 432: Jonathan Hugh Dickson; p. 435, left and right: Getty Images, Inc.; p. 439: Bildarchiv Preussischer Kulturbesitz/Art Resource, NY; p. 441, top and bottom: NASA Earth Observing System.

CHAPTER 17   PAGE 446: AP Wide World Photos; p. 449: Staffan Widstrand/CORBIS-NY; p. 451: Jack Kurtz/The Image Works; p. 452: Sherwin Crasto/CORBIS-NY; p. 453: Michael Nicholson/CORBIS-NY; p. 455: The Image Works; p. 456: Reuters/Lirio da Fonseca/CORBIS-NY; p. 459: The Image Works; p. 464: Josh Reynolds/The Image Works; p. 466: Andrew Hay/Reuters/CORBIS-NY; p. 468: Herve Collart/CORBIS-NY; p. 475: © Richard Nowitz, www.nowitz.com.

Index